Introduction by Geoff Slattery

The Slattery Media Group
140 Harbour Esplanade, Docklands
Victoria, Australia, 3008
visit slatterymedia.com

Copyright © The Slattery Media Group, 2011
First published by The Slattery Media Group, 2011

All rights reserved. No part of this publication may be reproduced, stored in a retrieval system or transmitted in any form by any means without the prior permission of the copyright owner. Inquiries should be made to the publisher.
Images taken from the collection of The Slattery Media Group and the AFL collection

National Library of Australia Cataloguing-in-Publication entry

Title: Grand Finals. Volume I, (1897-1938) / Ashley Browne, editor.
ISBN: 9781921778322 (hbk.)

Subjects: Australian football--Victoria--History.
           Australian football--Competitions.
Other Authors/Contributors:
           Browne, Ashley.
Dewey Number:
           796.33609945

Group Publisher: Geoff Slattery
Editor: Ashley Browne
Deputy Editor: Paul Daffey
Statistics: Cameron Sinclair
Fact checking and research: Geoff Poulter
Art Director: Sam Russell
Photo Production: Natalie Boccassini
Production Manager: Troy Davis
Creative Director: Andrew Hutchison

Images: Slattery Media Group archives, Australian Football League archives

Printed and bound in Australia by McPherson's Printing Group

INTRODUCTION		4
1897	ESSENDON	10
1898	FITZROY	20
1899	FITZROY	30
1900	MELBOURNE	40
1901	ESSENDON	50
1902	COLLINGWOOD	60
1903	COLLINGWOOD	70
1904	FITZROY	80
1905	FITZROY	90
1906	CARLTON	100
1907	CARLTON	110
1908	CARLTON	120
1909	SOUTH MELBOURNE	130
1910	COLLINGWOOD	140
1911	ESSENDON	150
1912	ESSENDON	160
1913	FITZROY	170
1914	CARLTON	180
1915	CARLTON	190
1916	FITZROY	200
1917	COLLINGWOOD	210
1918	SOUTH MELBOURNE	220
1919	COLLINGWOOD	230
1920	RICHMOND	240
1921	RICHMOND	250
1922	FITZROY	260
1923	ESSENDON	270
1924	ESSENDON	280
1925	GEELONG	290
1926	MELBOURNE	300
1927	COLLINGWOOD	310
1928	COLLINGWOOD	320
1929	COLLINGWOOD	330
1930	COLLINGWOOD	340
1931	GEELONG	350
1932	RICHMOND	360
1933	SOUTH MELBOURNE	370
1934	RICHMOND	380
1935	COLLINGWOOD	390
1936	COLLINGWOOD	400
1937	GEELONG	410
1938	CARLTON	420
BIOGRAPHIES		430
BIBLIOGRAPHY		432

INTRODUCTION

AN EVOLVING GAME

The foundation years of Australian Football saw many systems used to define the champion team. By GEOFF SLATTERY

THE Grand Final represents the pinnacle of the season in all team sports. But it has not always been the case in Australian Football. In fact, the path to a Grand Final to decide the season's champion was longer and more varied than one might consider for what is a relatively simple concept.

Much of what has been left us today evolved in the "pre-history" of the game, that period between the game's ultimate foetal period—in Victoria in the 1850s—through to the development of the Page-McIntyre finals series in 1931.

The first forms of management of the game came post-1877, following the formation of the Victorian Football Association. To that point, teams played each other in a form of weekend fun, but as the game developed, and found its way into the DNA of the growing population of Victoria, the newspapers of the day would create tables based on the win-loss record of teams.

It was not until 1888 that the VFA—as visionary a body in that period as is today's AFL Commission—declared that four points be awarded to winning teams and two points for draws, a more regular occurrence in that era. The premier team was generally the team atop the table at season's end, but even then there were complications—some teams played more games, some played significantly lesser opposition. In the end, the declaration of the season's champion was close to arbitrary.

Not surprisingly in such a haphazard competition, there was no crescendo as conclusion to the season, no knockout finals series to decide a true champion.

In a fascinating development, one that was to lead—in part at least—to the fracturing of the VFA, and the introduction of the Victorian Football League, a Grand Final was introduced, controversially, in 1896.

Historian Robin Grow, in an essay in *The Australian Game Of Football*, the official 2008 publication commemorating the 150th anniversary of the game, described events thus: (Before 1896) "There was still no 'final series' to determine the top team. This changed dramatically in 1896, when Collingwood and South Melbourne finished their fixtures locked on an equal amount of points and identical percentage after completing their scheduled matches.

"The VFA decided that it would play a 'Grand Final' but a number of other matches were still to be played, and the VFA made the mistake of deferring the final for two weeks until these matches were completed.

"All of this took place against the backdrop of planning and plotting by the clubs seeking to break away. Collingwood was so incensed at its players having to wait for a fortnight to play the Grand Final that it finally agreed to join the rebel clubs.

"Immediately after the Magpies won their first flag, the new clubs announced their plans and in early October 1896 the Victorian Football League was born."

One can only wonder at a 'sliding doors' model—had things been different in 1896, the fifth season of Collingwood's existence, and Collingwood had stayed in the VFA, would the game in Victoria and its ingrained tribal nature be as it is today?

Perhaps because of the schemozzle of 1896, the first year of the new VFL did not include a designated Grand Final, but a complicated round-robin affair in which each of the top four played each other, with Essendon becoming the League's first premier, having won each of the round-robin matches. Had Melbourne defeated Essendon in the third of the matches, there would have been a Grand Final, but it was not to be with Essendon beating Melbourne 1.8. (14) to 0.8 (8).

That round-robin model was to last just one year, and, no doubt influenced by a rowdy court of public opinion—the fans clearly enjoyed the best teams battling for the premiership at season's end—the concept of a Grand Final to decide the premier team was introduced in 1898, but still there were twists and turns that would last, in various ways, until 1931.

From 1898 to 1900 after 14 rounds, the teams were split into two divisions (split via odds and evens on the table); each of the teams in the divisions played each other, the two leading teams in each division playing off in a Grand Final—with one proviso. If the minor premier failed to lead its section after the last three games, it had the right to challenge, an event that was to take place in 1898 and 1900. But wait, there's more: the minor premier could only challenge if it won at least two of the three round-robin sectional matches.

INTRODUCTION

The messy end to season 1900—when Melbourne, sixth on the table after 14 rounds, and winner of two of its three round-robin matches ended up premiers, the administration came to the realisation that had the season run for an uninterrupted 17 matches—the 14 in the normal season, plus the three added to the round-robin conclusion to the home and away season, Melbourne would not have made the finals!

For one season, 1901, the system changed marginally—there remained sections after round 14, but the results added to the total premiership points won for the season, leading to a final four, graded by points and percentage; for this season only, there was no right of challenge presented to the minor premier, which saw a disgruntled Geelong lose in the semi-final to Collingwood at East Melbourne (one of many suburban grounds that no longer exist, or are not used for League matches [see map page 9]) and be out of the Grand Final. From 1897-1900—and to 1930—Geelong would have had the right of challenge.

This led to yet another change, this time with a little permanence to it: from 1902, the system introduced was called *The Argus* system, named from a suggestion pushed by the leading morning newspaper of the time. This system allowed for a finals series between first and third, and second and fourth. The two winners—subject to another allowance for a challenge—would play off in a Final.

Until 1907, the minor premier could challenge if it lost that Final, *if* it had accumulated more percentage than its competitor for top honours. After 1907, the percentage requirement was dropped, and the minor premier had the right to challenge in all circumstances, should it lose any final.

For example, in 1902, Collingwood, the minor premier, would lose its semi-final to Fitzroy, third after the home and away matches. Essendon, second after the home and away season, beat Melbourne (fourth) in its semi-final, but because of Collingwood's right to challenge, had to front up the following week in what then became the preliminary final against Fitzroy, with Collingwood resting, having the right to challenge the winner of the Essendon-Fitzroy match. The logic was reasonable—particularly given the 1877-95 history of the premier being the minor premier—but the advantage seems extreme with the benefit of hindsight.

Successful challenges were made in 1902 (Collingwood), 1909 (South Melbourne), 1913 (Fitzroy), 1914 (Carlton), 1917 (Collingwood), 1919 (Collingwood), 1920 (Richmond), 1923 (Essendon), 1925 (Geelong), 1929 (Collingwood) and 1930 (Collingwood). Failed challenges were made in 1905, 1910, 1912, 1915, 1916, 1921, 1922, and 1926. In any of the years of challenge, the Grand Final was only the Grand Final in retrospect. Had the challenge not been required, the match labelled as "the Final" was the Grand Final.

If all that's not bizarre enough—admittedly with the benefit of the perspective of a century of hindsight and experience—in 1924 the League re-introduced the round-robin model, this time with the right of challenge available to the minor premier, should it not head the table after the six round-robin matches. In this case, the challenge was not required as although Essendon, the minor premier, was to lose the last of its three round-robin games, it had sufficient percentage break over Richmond which had also won two of three matches.

One can only wonder at the state of mind of the fans of these early years—with multiple versions of challenges, with multiple systems of finals in place, some years with just two weeks of finals, and some years with four. At the very least, the short years cost the central body revenue, which makes the 30 years of the challenge system difficult to comprehend if only for economic reasons. It was also prone to exploitation, and suggestions were made that minor premiers did manipulate early matches to ensure they would have another gate to bank in the challenge to decide the premier team. Perhaps, also, the unscrupulous saw benefit in a loss, in the thriving underworld of sports betting, prevalent even in these medieval times.

Sanity finally prevailed in 1931, when the Richmond delegate to the VFL Percy Page presented a system developed by the rising 21-year-old mathematician Ken McIntyre that was mathematically sound, gave double chances to the top two teams on the table—with first and second on the table having equal chances of progressing, plus a double chance—and gave the League and its fans planning certainty. There would be four weeks of finals for every year, unless a draw would force the season to extend a week.

Page, the chairman of the permit committee, was very frank in his presentation to the League in March, 1931. *The Football Record* of the opening round of 1931 reported: "Mr. Page said that it had been repeatedly suggested that for financial reasons some finals were 'stage managed' in order that a Grand Final would be played. To those who understand the position that is purely 'empty talk'.

"When the cost of putting teams into the field each Saturday is considered, such an assertion is absurd for it costs the teams in the finals very much more than they are allowed by the League for expenses. Mr. Page claimed that under his system clubs could not be accused of finessing for positions towards the close of the home and away matches."

The Football Record noted: "The new proposal has many advantages, the main one being the entire elimination of all suspicion, and though there is

INTRODUCTION

one disadvantage—the placing of the first and second teams on an equal footing—it is claimed the advantages override the one disadvantage."

The editorial listed the main advantages gained by the change, using words and principles that were similar to those used to promote the change to a final eight in 1994:

"1. Increases interest in home and away matches on account of fight for first two places.

"2. Premiership team has to win two matches of final series, as against a possible one under present system."

The Record made no mention of the role of McIntyre in the development of the new system. Remarkably, it was the same Ken McIntyre who was to conceive later iterations of the finals system, including the final five, final six, and the first version of the final eight (1994-99). When the first final eight was introduced, McIntyre was 83. I remember interviewing him in 1996, the Centenary celebrations year, and he was still unhappy that Page, "a mere administrator", had his name attached to "his" finals system, a system that would serve the League so well for more 40 years (The Page-McIntyre system ran from 1931-71. McIntyre died in 2004, aged 93.)

Much of this detail about the game's early years had been locked away from me, despite a lifetime following footy. Unknown, as well, was the detail behind these early premierships, and the culture and societal issues surrounding them.

This book has been developed via that need to know, and a need to commit to permanence an unambiguous history of the beginning years of the game of Australian Football. It came about when two minds (one of a writer, one of a publisher) that understand the value of history as a foundation of what's to come, decided that this book—and its second and third volumes (to come)—needed to be written, to record the earliest years of the game.

The first mind was that of Glenn McFarlane, whose heritage in the game extends to his grandfather Charlie Dibbs, a grand Collingwood defender and member of the legendary Machine—the teams that set the benchmark for premierships in the VFL and now the AFL, winning four in a row from 1927 to 1930 (two of them, I now know, courtesy of the Challenge!). Glenn came to see me in 2008 with a scheme that had been running around his fertile brain for some years—that he would write the complete history of Grand Finals and premierships. In the end, we agreed that such was all but impossible to achieve solo, unless the writer was the beneficiary of the fortune handed down by a long-lost uncle!

We decided that his idea should be spread across an array of writers, adding time and strength and (in some cases) club loyalty and understanding

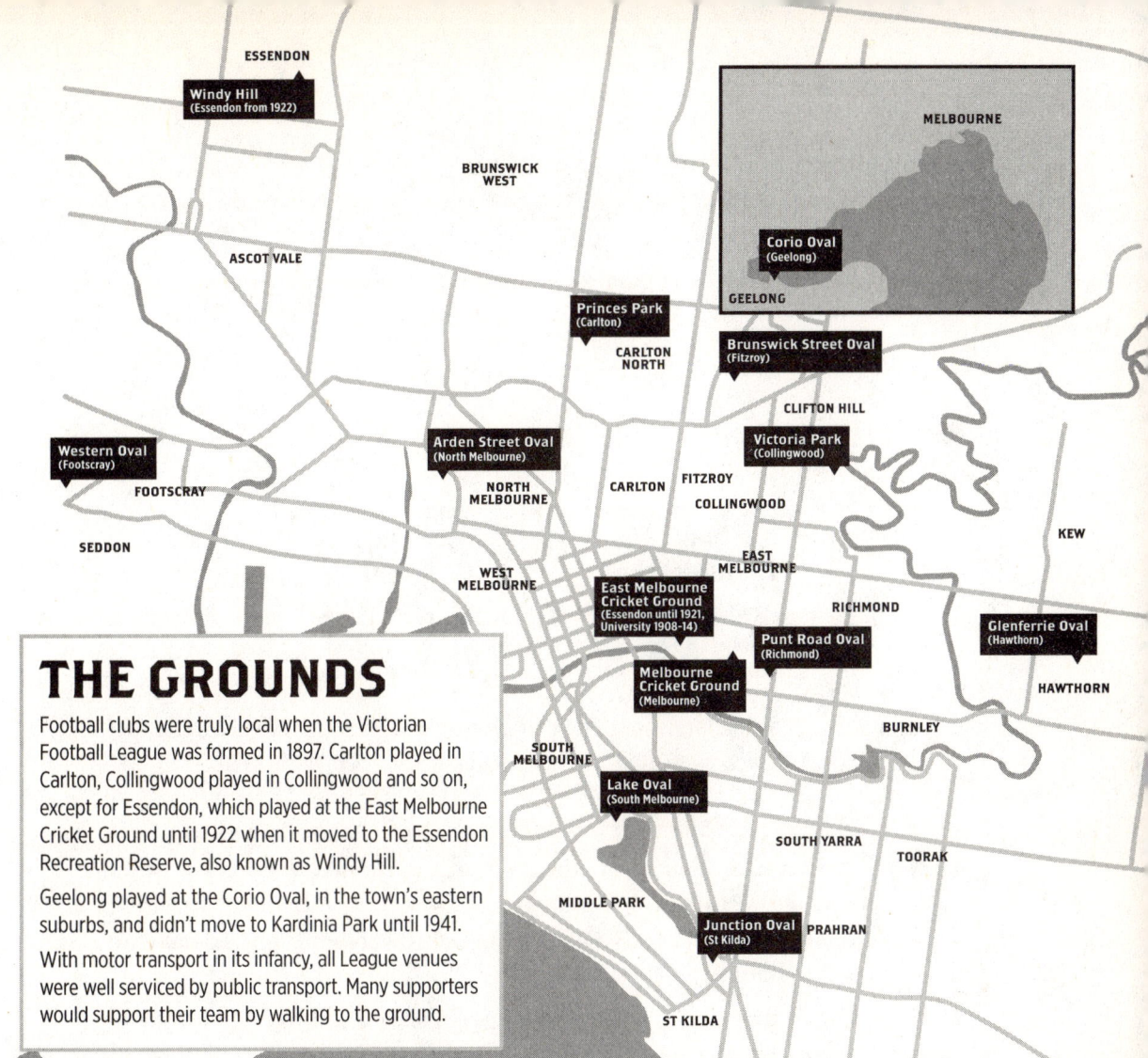

THE GROUNDS

Football clubs were truly local when the Victorian Football League was formed in 1897. Carlton played in Carlton, Collingwood played in Collingwood and so on, except for Essendon, which played at the East Melbourne Cricket Ground until 1922 when it moved to the Essendon Recreation Reserve, also known as Windy Hill.

Geelong played at the Corio Oval, in the town's eastern suburbs, and didn't move to Kardinia Park until 1941.

With motor transport in its infancy, all League venues were well serviced by public transport. Many supporters would support their team by walking to the ground.

to the stories of each season of the game, not just the stories that came at season's end. This book is that idea, formed to paint a picture of an evolving society, an evolving Australian personality, and a rapidly evolving game that had taken deep roots in Victorian life, roots that explain much about its passionate following today.

I hope that *Grand Finals Volume I (1897-1938)* stands the test of time—that it will allow future lovers of the game—into the next century and beyond—to understand the rudimentary nature of our early years as a game and its connection to a similar growing society, both locally and nationally; and that those fans will know that the future will always belong to the past, as long as you understand the reasons why things happened, and why things didn't.

Geoff Slattery, July 2011.

ESSENDON

THE FIRST PREMIER

Essendon was at the forefront of a push for a new Victorian football league and quickly became its first triumphant team. By ROHAN CONNOLLY

THE Essendon Football Club didn't reach the play-off for the 1896 Victorian Football Association premiership. That was the privilege of Collingwood and South Melbourne. But the club had proved only the night before that game where true footballing power resided.

On Friday, October 2, 1896, as Collingwood and South prepared for the biggest game of the year, Essendon was at the forefront of a move that would leave a far bigger imprint on football's future than any mere premiership.

That evening at Buxton's Art Gallery in Collins Street, with Essendon, or the "Same Old" as they were known, leading the charge, six VFA clubs—Essendon, Geelong, Collingwood, South Melbourne, Melbourne and Fitzroy—decided to break ranks to form their own competition, named the Victorian Football League. They would soon invite Carlton and St Kilda to join them.

Agitation for such a revolution had been gathering since the mid-1880s, led by Geelong and Essendon, with Melbourne subsequently also joining the push. The VFA power clubs were frustrated both by the unevenness of the competition and the association's perceived lack of desire to solve the problem.

In a refrain the game would hear several more times over the next century, the strongest clubs had grown tired of being dragged down by the weak. And by the close of the 1800s, disillusionment was rife.

Unchecked closeted professionalism involving secret payments to players was everywhere. The game had turned ugly, a scrappy pack-strewn spectacle that fans were increasingly deserting. And for those who still chose to attend, hooliganism and unruly spectator behaviour was becoming the norm.

The move gathered further momentum midway through 1896 when leading newspaper *The Argus* published a scathing editorial about the state of the game. "It has been painfully apparent for some time that football as now played in Melbourne has altogether lost cause," the editorial said. "The majority of players compare unfavourably indeed with some of the old Melbourne, Carlton, Geelong and Essendon teams who made the game a great one.

"Men of that stamp now prefer cycling, harrier racing and other sports to football, and the game is the loser by it. Attendances have fallen away greatly, and the surviving patrons are unfortunately not the fittest, while not more than a third of the games played excite any general interest."

The historic Grand Final eve meeting resolved sweeping changes to both the game itself and the competitive framework in which it would be played. Rejecting the idea of reforming the VFA into two sections, it preferred a fresh start under the VFL banner.

In the new competition, each of the eight teams would play one other twice during the course of a season, with the top four holding a round-robin finals series to determine the premier. There would be significant changes to the rules to improve the quality of the game and remove some of the clutter. The "little mark", where a player could claim a mark from a ball travelling only two yards, had been part of the game since before the VFA's formation in 1877, but would now be abolished. And a behind would add one point to the score.

The Same Old hadn't been a force early on after the VFA had begun in 1877, but had made up big time during the 1890s for its tardy start, winning four premierships in a row between 1891-94. It effectively revolutionised the game in that period, perhaps the first team to use specialist key position players. It had mobile defenders, smart forwards, clever running players and, perhaps most importantly, the player of the age, Albert Thurgood.

Thurgood arrived at Essendon in 1892 from Brighton Grammar, having been pursued by most clubs in the competition. Tall but extremely agile, Thurgood could play in virtually any position.

He was an instant sensation, heading the VFA goalkicking in his first season with 56, the first man to break the half-century. He kicked more than 60 in each of the following two seasons, in one memorable two-week spell in 1893 booting 12 of his team's 14 goals, then nine out of 10.

Thurgood won the "Champion of the Colony" title, as voted by an annual meeting of VFA club captains, in 1893-94, but caused a sensation when he headed to Western Australia in 1895, eventually donning Essendon colours once more in 1899. It was no coincidence that was when Essendon's premiership run halted. But Thurgood's classic example had at least helped the club groom other would-be stars of the game, and their efforts would be pivotal to the first history-making season of VFL football in 1897.

The captain of Essendon's inaugural VFL side was George Stuckey. He had been part of three of those four straight VFA premierships, and by 1897 was still a force to be reckoned with. Recognised early as an outstanding leader, the half-back and wingman was courageous and versatile, and a true all-round athlete. He played cricket as well as football for Victoria, and what would become a stellar year, also managed to win the Stawell Gift.

Charles 'Tracker' Forbes was Essendon's first great ruckman, a key component of those premiership-winning teams of the early 1890s. Tall and lean, he dominated at the frequent stoppages, and had won the VFA's Champion of the Colony title in 1891. He had a reputation for great strength and courage, and he was a superb mark.

Much of Essendon's goalscoring responsibilities rested with Norman Waugh. While short in stature, Waugh was a star goalsneak, whose career would be cut short prematurely when in 1899 he decided to live in South Africa. But he would be another critical part of the push to win the VFL's first premiership.

The first round in the first season of the new competition arrived on May 8, 1897. Essendon was drawn to play Geelong at that club's Corio Oval home (until the move to Kardinia Park in 1941) an appropriate pairing given the strong legacy both clubs had already built, with 11 VFA premierships between them, and their major roles in helping establish the new football body.

Before a game had even been played, Essendon's prospects of success appeared good. Said *The Argus* on the morning of the first game: "Essendon play their first match at Geelong, and the alterations in their last year's team—confined to about half-a-dozen—should not greatly affect their strength, while Geelong, on the other hand, has made many changes."

The prognosis was spot on. Essendon had its first VFL win as good as inked in by quarter-time, when it had posted 3.2 without a Geelong score in response. It was Waugh who took the honour of kicking his team's first VFL goal, 15 minutes into the match, Essendon soon following it with two more.

The second quarter failed to produce a goal to either team, but Essendon repeated its first-term heroics in the third with another three goals while

Geelong kicked its first. Waugh booted his second of the game before John Graham added two more in what would be his solitary game of league football.

A 29-point three-quarter time lead was, in the context of that time, a huge margin, and while Geelong did improve as the game progressed the final result was a very comfortable 23-point win to the visitors, 7.5 (47) to 3.6 (24).

The Argus's football correspondent, 'Observer', noted that: "Essendon began the game with a fine exhibition of half-distance kicking, and the Geelong novices playing wildly in first-rate company were powerless to check them, so that the Red and Black bagged 20 points to nothing in the first quarter." Essendon's defence was particularly dominant, 'Observer' said, lauding the efforts of Maurie Collins, Jim Darcy and the "plucky and clever" Jim Anderson.

Overall, the reaction to the launch of the new competition was overwhelmingly positive, with good crowds, spectators reportedly delighted by the more open play, and the use of the drop kick expected to increase significantly. The one controversy came with the VFL's decision to abolish the push-in-the-back rule, which sparked strong protests from players concerned about not only fairness, but also safety. Essendon rover and forward George Vautin was so incensed he threatened to retire if the pushing rule was not re-introduced. The league duly complied in time for round two, moving with a haste that would be unimaginable more than a century later.

But if Essendon thought it was going to cruise through this history-making season, it was soon given plenty of food for thought, courtesy of a 20-point loss to Collingwood in its first home VFL game. The Same Old's fast and open game was expected to be too much for the slower, lumbering Collingwood. Instead, it was the 'Woods who made the running and Essendon which looked tardy in comparison.

Essendon skipper Stuckey, said Monday's newspaper reports, had "shouted instructions until he was hoarse" without luck. "The greatest Essendon fault was that when they got the ball they seemed to linger over it, while Collingwood's action in such a case was quick and decisive," said *The Argus*.

Collingwood's cause had also been served by remarkably accurate goalkicking, the Magpies with 6.0 at half-time to Essendon's 1.5. The Same Old lifted after the break, outscoring its opponent in the second half, but the damage had been done.

The wake-up call, though, had plenty of impact. Essendon won its next five games straight, the next week kicking the highest score of the season to date, 12.6 (78) to 6.5 (41), in a 37-point thumping of Carlton. In round four, it more than doubled Fitzroy's score. It beat St Kilda by 37 points, narrowly pipped South Melbourne, and then beat Melbourne by 36 points.

One of the season's most significant games would come on June 26 when Essendon and Geelong squared off, the Same Old looking red-hot, Geelong vastly improved having lost its first three matches of the season.

Close to game time, Essendon appeared unlikely to be able to field a team. Two players, Harry Wright and Baron Salkeld, had taken ill and were too unwell to play, two more players still hadn't turned up, and key ruckman and vice-captain August Kearney, also a champion tennis player, was playing in a tournament at Albert Park.

Rain, though, washed out the tennis, and Kearney arrived at Essendon's home ground, the East Melbourne Cricket Ground, just minutes before game time. Not that it made enough of a difference. Essendon was overrun by Geelong in the final quarter to go under by 25 points.

In a quality game, scores remained close all day, Geelong leading by only two points at the last change, but it slammed on 3.5 in the last stanza while Essendon failed to score. 'Observer' noted the "rapid, upward rush of the Geelong Excelsiors".

"The process of lopping the tall poppies, so fascinating to Roman kings, is being illustrated in football," 'Observer' wrote. "Geelong is the monarch with the cane, and on Saturday a gorgeous red and black poppy was remorselessly shred away at East Melbourne."

What was becoming increasingly clear was that the front-runners for the first VFL flag were Essendon, Geelong, which would put together an 11-game winning streak in the lead-up to the finals series, and Melbourne, which had won its opening six matches.

At the other end of the ladder, Carlton and St Kilda, the last two clubs invited to join the VFL, were patently struggling. Indeed, the Saints failed to win any of their 14 home and away matches, failed to kick a single goal in three of them and their round 12 score of just 0.3 (3) to a rampant Essendon's 13.16 (94) produced the most lopsided scoreline of the season.

Like the earlier loss to Collingwood, however, Essendon's loss to Geelong was a timely reminder of the effort required in a competition very close at the top. The Same Old rebounded effectively the following week against the Magpies at Victoria Park. It then dispensed of Carlton, Fitzroy and St Kilda with ease, before narrowly defeating South Melbourne in a match widely regarded as the best of the season.

'Observer' was full of praise for Essendon's comeback win. "After a struggle, abounding in all the finest points of football, Essendon won a memorable match. They looked to be at their last gasp. They have looked that way before, and yet surprised everyone with a brilliant finish, but in the best periods of their four years of triumph they never rose to a desperate occasion more brilliantly than on Saturday."

Essendon's deadly accurate 8.1 won the day against South's 6.9, four of them from Waugh, who was said to do "more than anyone else to win it for the red-and-black". Fine performances came also from the ruck-rover tandem of Tracker Forbes and Arthur Cleghorn, as well as Kearney, 'Son' Barry, centreman Harry Wright and defender Tod Collins.

Perhaps the effort took some toll on the Dons, because in the final home and away round they registered their third and final loss of the season to Melbourne. It meant that Geelong took top spot on percentage from Essendon, third-placed Melbourne and Collingwood in fourth spot.

Plenty of controversy bubbled about the format of the VFL's first finals system, the round-robin system, which was attracting plenty of criticism before it had even been put to the test. Geelong believed it had negotiated, in the agreement that formed the League, the right to a home final. It was awarded a home final by a reluctant VFL only after it had threatened not to play.

Once that dispute had been settled, there was another obstacle to overcome, provided by nature. So much heavy rain fell in the lead-up to the scheduled first week of the play-offs on August 14 that the league was forced to postpone them until the following weekend.

It was just as well, remarked *The Argus*, as it gave the VFL more time to get its house in order. But the mini-season round-robin that would determine the premiership team continued to cop a critical caning. Four evenly matched finalists, said 'Observer', created the potential for chaos, and further games required to split teams still even after three games against each other.

The finals kicked off on Saturday, August 21, with Essendon taking on Geelong at Corio Oval, while Melbourne met Collingwood in a nail-biter that the Magpies won by four points. Essendon, meanwhile, was doing it very tough.

It was a scrappy and dour game, reported *The Argus*. And even in VFL football's very first finals campaign, the war against time-wasting was on.

"Up to half-time, both sides when defending against the wind showed a desire to get the ball as often as possible into the pavilion reserve, but they were told at half-time that the offence would be punished strictly, and it was significant that the ball rarely went out afterwards," wrote 'Observer'.

The game improved as a spectacle, but for Essendon the situation was desperate by the final change. The Same Old was 13 points down, Geelong having kicked two of just three goals for the entire game. That became 19 points down when almost upon resumption, against the breeze, Geelong booted its third goal. And thus was created the launching pad for the Essendon Football Club's very first VFL finals comeback.

Collins gave his side hope, snapping a clever goal, reported 'Observer'. "Just as it seemed Geelong would hold out successfully, the turning point of the match came. (Arthur) Cleghorn got a fourth goal, and with 12 minutes to play, Geelong had still a six-point lead on behinds. Seven of these minutes precious to Essendon slipped away, and then Colin Campbell earned a shot for goal, a long way out.

"'Further round, Colin,' several of his side shouted eagerly, for it seemed the direction would carry it down the wind, but a magnificent place kick put it high up exactly between the posts, and with five minutes to play the scores were even. Geelong was not long in suspense. Within half-a-minute (Harry) Wright got it, not quite so far out as Campbell, and another fine place kick gave Essendon a goal and the lead.

"It was the last score, and as the bell rang the Essendon fellows and their following cheered wildly in honour of the victory."

Forbes, Collins, Gus Kearney, Son Barry and Edgar Croft all played key roles in the triumph, along with George Vautin, thrown on to the ball in the crisis, and of whom 'Observer' said: "His dazzling rushes and hare-like turns made a wonderful difference."

The following Saturday, at the MCG, Essendon met the other victor in week one, drawing a crowd of 8000 and pulling in a healthy £175 against Collingwood, while Melbourne played Geelong. Again, Essendon struggled to establish a lead, a wasteful 2.8 to the Magpies' 2.2 at half-time not nearly enough reward.

It was two goals apiece in the third quarter, Essendon leading by eight points at the final break, but like the previous week the Dons had a big finish in store. "What occurred was decisive and overwhelming," said 'Observer'. "Essendon scored five goals five behinds without their opponents being able to guard their own goal, let alone making a serious demonstration at the other end."

Key forward Norman Waugh booted four out of Essendon's winning tally of nine in an eventual 40-point thumping, with Forbes again starring in the ruck.

The Dons were now a win and plenty of percentage ahead of all their rivals, and victory against Melbourne in week three would win them the premiership. If they lost, they'd have to front either Geelong or Collingwood to take the title.

Surprisingly, fewer than 4000 turned up to South Melbourne's ground to watch the de facto grand final for Essendon, while only a few hundred less saw Geelong at the same time beat Collingwood. But those who took in the Essendon-Melbourne clash would see a remarkable game, and most remarkable for an amazing scoreline, still to this day the lowest aggregate score recorded in a game of league football.

A crosswind didn't help with accuracy, but simply getting a shot at goal was proving difficult enough, the scores tied at four behinds each at half-time.

Essendon's Waugh seemed to have broken the goal drought right on half-time, but his goal was disallowed when it was ruled to have been kicked a split second after the bell had rung to end the quarter. Melbourne, too, seemed cursed. It would score eight behinds for the afternoon, three of them "posters".

Each side had added another two behinds when, late in the third term, came the defining moment of the match, and, by consequence, the season—and a moment totally in keeping with the bizarre nature of the game.

Forbes, who had once again dominated in the ruck, marked at near to point-blank range. 'Observer' explained what followed: "They were so sure that it would go through that the players flocked to the centre, leaving (Edgar) Croft alone near the fence. Forbes's shot was a miserable one, for the ball spun right round to Croft, who promptly put it through."

The final quarter was another slog, both teams again adding just two behinds each. The final bell of the season rang, confirming Essendon as premier, winning the play-offs by one clear game from Geelong.

Reports said it had been a triumph founded upon Essendon's evenness and experience. "Although Essendon have been fortunate in getting some very capable recruits this last couple of seasons, they owe their satisfactory position largely to the form of old and tried men, who were never so good as in the hardest games," wrote 'Observer'.

"Forbes unquestionably stands out as their champion for the year, with Anderson a good second, and Wright, Stuckey, Barry, Kearney, and Officer in that order next."

The scribe rated Forbes the third best player of the first VFL season, behind Melbourne's Fred McGinis and Geelong's Joe McShane.

So Essendon, one of the key architects of this new competition, had two reasons to smile. The VFL had been an instant success: crowds were good and the game was more entertaining. Essendon had also made off with League football's first piece of silverware, etching in its name as the first in what would become a long, long roll call of the game's greatest teams.

1897 ESSENDON

PREMIER'S SEASON

ESSENDON: 1897

ROUND ONE May 8
ESSENDON	7.5 (47)
GEELONG	3.6 (24)

Best: Essendon – Stuckey, T.Collins, Waugh, Kinnear, Anderson, N.Officer, Graham.
Goals: Essendon – T.Collins 2, Graham 2, Waugh 2, Barry.
Crowd: N/A at Corio Oval

ROUND TWO May 15
ESSENDON	4.6 (30)
COLLINGWOOD	8.2 (50)

Best: Essendon – Croft, T.Collins, Forbes, Gavin, Wright.
Goals: Essendon – Croft 2, T.Collins, Salkeld.
Crowd: N/A at East Melbourne Cricket Ground

ROUND THREE May 24
ESSENDON	12.6 (78)
CARLTON	6.5 (41)

Best: Essendon – Stuckey, G.Officer, Cleghorn, Barry, Ball, Salkeld, Vautin.
Goals: Essendon – Salkeld 2, Cleghorn 2, G.Officer 2, Forbes, Barry, Hastings, Kinnear, Waugh, T.Collins.
Crowd: N/A at East Melbourne Cricket Ground

ROUND FOUR May 29
ESSENDON	6.6 (42)
FITZROY	2.8 (20)

Best: Essendon – Park, Barry, Anderson, Thurgood, T.Collins, Kearny, Ball.
Goals: Essendon – Waugh 2, Thurgood 2, Gavin, Kinnear.
Crowd: N/A at Brunswick St Oval

ROUND FIVE June 5
ESSENDON	9.9 (63)
ST KILDA	3.8 (26)

Best: Essendon – Gavin, Cleghorn, O'Loughlin, M.Collins, Stuckey, White, Vautin.
Goals: Essendon – Cleghorn 2, Gavin 2, Croft, White, Vautin, Anderson, Brown.
Crowd: N/A at Junction Oval

ROUND SIX June 19
ESSENDON	1.13 (19)
SOUTH MELBOURNE	2.3 (15)

Best: Essendon – Martin, T.Collins, M.Collins, Anderson, Park, Forbes.
Goals: Essendon – Croft.
Crowd: N/A at Lake Oval

ROUND SEVEN June 22
ESSENDON	8.15 (63)
MELBOURNE	3.9 (27)

Best: Essendon – Barry, Brown, Stuckey, Vautin, Forbes, Sykes, Waugh.
Goals: Essendon – Gavin 2, Croft 2, Martin, Kearney, Waugh, T.Collins.
Crowd: N/A at East Melbourne Cricket Ground

ROUND EIGHT June 26
ESSENDON	5.2 (32)
GEELONG	8.9 (57)

Best: Essendon – Forbes, Groves, Croft, Waugh, Kinnear, Stuckey.
Goals: Essendon – Waugh 2, Croft, O'Loughlin, Cleghorn.
Crowd: N/A at East Melbourne Cricket Ground

ROUND NINE July 3
ESSENDON	6.10 (46)
COLLINGWOOD	5.7 (37)

Best: Essendon – Gavin, Park, Darcy, Forbes, Moore, Ball, Barry, Leach.
Goals: Essendon – Gavin 2, Cleghorn, Darcy, Waugh, Ball.
Crowd: N/A at Victoria Park

ROUND TEN July 10
ESSENDON	5.12 (42)
CARLTON	2.1 (13)

Best: Essendon – Leach, G.Officer, Moore, N.Officer, Forbes, Stuckey, Thurgood.
Goals: Essendon – Barry, Moore, Kinnear, Waugh, G.Officer.
Crowd: N/A at Princes Park

ROUND ELEVEN July 17
ESSENDON	9.8 (62)
FITZROY	4.6 (30)

Best: Essendon – Gavin, Groves, Kinnear, Stuckey, Forbes, T.Collins.
Goals: Essendon – Gavin 3, Kearney 2, Waugh 2, Forbes, Croft.
Crowd: N/A at East Melbourne Cricket Ground

ROUND TWELVE July 24
ESSENDON	13.16 (94)
ST KILDA	0.3 (3)

Best: Essendon – Forbes, Cleghorn, N.Officer, Anderson, Stuckey, O'Loughlin.
Goals: Essendon – Cleghorn 4, Leach 2, Kearney 2, Waugh 2, Barry, Wright, G.Officer.
Crowd: N/A at East Melbourne Cricket Ground

ROUND THIRTEEN July 31
ESSENDON	8.1 (49)
SOUTH MELBOURNE	6.9 (45)

Best: Essendon – Waugh, Martin, Anderson, Barry, Groves, Forbes, Barry.
Goals: Essendon – Waugh 4, Kearney, Sykes, Moore, T.Collins.
Crowd: N/A at East Melbourne Cricket Ground

ROUND FOURTEEN August 7
ESSENDON	6.3 (39)
MELBOURNE	8.8 (56)

Best: Essendon – Gavin, Wright, Forbes, Brown, Stamp, Moore.
Goals: Essendon – Gavin 2, Hastings, Cleghorn, Waugh, Barry.
Crowd: N/A at the MCG

PREMIER'S FINALS

ROUND ROBIN FINAL August 21
ESSENDON 5.5 (35)
GEELONG 3.11 (29)
Best: Essendon – Forbes, Kearney, Vautin, Barry, Croft, T.Collins.
Goals: Essendon – T.Collins 2, Cleghorn, Wright, Campbell.
Crowd: 5000 at Corio Oval

ROUND ROBIN FINAL August 28
ESSENDON 9.16 (70)
COLLINGWOOD 4.6 (30)
Best: Essendon – Forbes, Cleghorn, Barry, Kearney, O'Loughlin.
Goals: Essendon – Waugh 4, Gavin 2, Cochrane, Croft, Cleghorn.
Crowd: 8000 at the MCG

ROUND ROBIN FINAL September 4
ESSENDON 1.8 (14)
MELBOURNE 0.8 (8)
Best: Essendon – Forbes, Sykes, Cleghorn, Officer, Anderson, Barry, Wright.
Goals: Essendon – Croft.
Crowd: 3800 at Lake Oval

FINALS SQUADS

ESS J. Anderson, S. Barry, C. Campbell, A. Cleghorn, G. Cochrane, T. Collins, E. Croft, D. Ferguson, C. Forbes, H. Gavin, J. Groves, G. Hastings, G. Kearney, T. Kinnear, G. Martin, N. Officer, P. O'Loughlin, G. Stuckey (capt), G. Vautin, N. Waugh, H. Wright

GEEL S. Brockwell, P. Burns, C. Coles, J. Conway (capt), J. Flynn, T. Greeves, T. Holligan, E. James, T. Maguire, F. McCallum, H. McShane, Jim McShane, Joe McShane, J. Parkin, A. Pincott, A. Pontin, J. Quinn, T. Rankin, A. Thompson, F. White, H. Young

Note: There was no Grand Final this season. Geelong had the second best record after the round-robin.

SNAPSHOT

Win-loss record: 14-3

Highest score: 13.16 (94), round 12, v St Kilda.

Greatest winning margin: 91 points, round 12, v St Kilda.

Lowest score: 1.8 (14), round robin final, v Melbourne.

Greatest losing margin: 25 points, round 8, v Geelong.

Most goals by a player in a game: 4, Norm Waugh, round 13, v South Melbourne; round robin final, v Collingwood; Arthur Cleghorn, round 12, v St Kilda.

Most consecutive wins: 5 (twice).

Most consecutive losses: 1 (three times).

Club awards: Leading goalkicker: Norm Waugh (23 goals)

Putting it into perspective:
In winning the 1897—and first—VFL premiership Essendon began a successful early era of the competition; the Same Olds were either a premiership team or runner-up in three of the first five years of the competition.

1897

		P	W	L	D	%	Pts
1	Geelong (2)	14	11	3	0	184.3	44
2	**Essendon (1)**	14	11	3	0	159.0	44
3	Melbourne (4)	14	10	4	0	144.8	40
4	Collingwood (3)	14	9	5	0	113.9	36
5	South Melb	14	8	5	1	138.1	34
6	Fitzroy	14	4	9	1	104.7	18
7	Carlton	14	2	12	0	51.2	8
8	St Kilda	14	0	14	0	29.1	0

(14 home and away rounds)

PLAYERS USED

ESSENDON	GAMES	GOALS
Anderson, Jim	16	1
Ball, Fred	5	1
Barry, Son	17	5
Brown, Harold	6	1
Campbell, Colin	2	1
Cleghorn, Arthur	15	13
Cochrane, George	2	1
Collins, Maurie	12	0
Collins, Tod	14	8
Croft, Edgar	10	10
Darcy, Jim	9	1
Ferguson, Dave	1	0
Forbes, Charlie	16	2
Gavin, Hugh	15	14
Graham, Johnny	1	2
Groves, Joe	16	0
Hastings, George	8	2
Kearney, Gus	11	6
Kinnear, Ted	16	3
Leach, Arthur	4	2
Martin, George	16	1
McCormick, Bob	1	0
Moore, Charlie	4	2
O'Loughlin, Pat	16	1
Officer, Gus	5	4
Officer, Ned	14	0
Park, Jim	6	0
Salkeld, Bert	5	3
Stamp, Alby	2	0
Stuckey, George	15	0
Sykes, Archie	11	1
Thurgood, Jimmy	3	2
Vautin, George	14	1
Waugh, Norm	15	23
White, Jim	1	1
Wright, Harry	16	2

**FITZROY 5.8 (38) d
ESSENDON 3.5 (23)**

ALL POWER TO THEM

The Roys put heart and muscle into their effort to have their community—their suburb—held up as the best in town. By JOHN HARMS

IT MAY seem an historical curiosity now, but Fitzroy was the first real powerhouse of VFL football. In the first decade the Maroons won four premierships and were runners-up three times. Their home ground was the Brunswick Street Oval, where today the original grandstand still stands in all its Victorian glory and elegance. It takes a leap of historical faith to imagine the screaming voices of the thousands of fans who walked to the ground from the streets and lanes of Fitzroy in those days.

Fitzroy was alive with football then.

And so was much of Melbourne. Although sections of the community abhorred the barbaric nature of football and the wild barrackers who were attracted to it, and spoke out against it in letters to newspapers and church bulletins, many people embraced the game with ever-increasing passion. As soccer was in England, football was becoming the game of the industrialised, urbanised metropolis.

Among the respectable class of the genteel, the educated and the comfortable, football fitted in neatly with the 19th-century understandings of sport: that it was a manly pastime which called young men to action, to show their pluck and commitment. Importantly, it prepared them for more important things to come. Football was character-building.

Among workers and battlers, the granting of the 44-hour week (which freed up Saturday afternoons) had given opportunity for football to grow as a sport to be played and, more significantly, as a sport to be watched and followed so enthusiastically that the fortunes of the local footy team became important in the lives of many people.

Such enthusiasm was fuelled by two elements: simple geography, and the ideology of "them" and "us" that prevailed at the time. Football clubs were seen as representative. It was an honour to be selected to play for the club and hence represent the local suburb. Particularly those clubs that ringed the city's centre. Each borough was administered separately— each had its own town hall where the mayor and his aldermen oversaw the development of their proud community. Each had its own identity. The football club was a perfectly formed symbol of that, and contributed to that sense of separateness.

This was an age when people expressed their loyalty to various entities and causes: to the British Empire, the emerging idea of the Australian nation, the school, the parish, and of course—most immediately—the local community, which was usually represented as their suburb.

Fitzroy was regarded as Melbourne's first suburb. It was a microcosm of the broader metropolis in the sense that at the city end it was suburb of the well-heeled who lived in gracious double-storey terraces, yet as it spread out towards the Merri Creek at the northern end, the two-bedroom workers' terraces were crammed together and filled with hungry mouths.

It was something of an embarrassment to the locals that by the early 1880s the suburb still didn't have a football team. Finally, according to *The Mercury and Weekly Courier*, "Fitzroy awoke from its lethargy". At a meeting at the Brunswick Family Hotel a club was formed, with members and a committee, to field a team that would represent the good people of Fitzroy.

Fitzroy, after being admitted to the VFA in 1884, developed a strong side. The Maroons, as they were called because of their colours, won their first premiership in 1895. The people celebrated with what *The Mercury* described as "howling, yelling and singing of *Sweet Marie*". Initially, it was a popular win. Under the presidency of R.W. Best—solicitor, former Fitzroy alderman, and then MLA for the seat of Fitzroy—Fitzroy played fairly, and for the love of the game. Best, who was also a lay preacher at St Mark's Anglican church in Fitzroy, insisted the club embrace the most noble elements of sport.

'Markwell' in *The Australasian* noted that:

> "After twelve years of zealous and honourable effort, Fitzroy have succeeded in acquiring the top place amongst Victorian football teams... [they are] capable, manly and straightforward exponents of the game."

That popularity did not last. In the seasons that followed, the powerful Fitzroy club became the bane of those with their eyes on the same prize, and the Roys were criticised for being a club that was starting to value winning over all else. The purists were not impressed. There were claims and counter claims of bribes, and payments and inducements to players. The debate raged as to whether football should be played for the love of the game, or for 30 pieces of silver.

Tremendous rivalries developed. Just as the powers of Europe were locked in a battle for national superiority—economic, imperial, military, and even cultural—the suburbs of Melbourne were in conflict with each other. And just as some theorists of history were suggesting in Europe that your neighbour was likely to be your fiercest rival, the same antipathies existed across Melbourne.

Fitzroy certainly had developed a keen rivalry with Carlton to its west, and even more so with the new, bold club to the east, Collingwood, which was formed in 1892. Such was the depth of their hatred it was said that the residents of Smith Street (which divides the two suburbs) would abuse each other from across the street on the Friday evening before they met at Brunswick Street or Collingwood's Victoria Park.

At one level, football—noble football—satisfied the romantics and the private school types who played for the glory of the game and the honour of the club and the school. At another level it satisfied the toughs and the larrikins. Both types proved to be fanatical supporters.

Players and supporters were encouraged to be totally committed to their clubs. It was an age of commitment to a higher cause—the age of nationalism and new imperialism, when young men could do no more than offer their service and their lives to king and country. The world had not experienced the horrors of the Somme.

Football held a symbolic role, and a very real role. The nation needed brave young men who would not shirk the issue when called on.

The expectation was high.

The Collingwood doctor, Thomas Heffernan, inspired players to be in tune with their duty. "[They were to] regard themselves as Roman warriors on the [battle] field," wrote historian Richard Stremski in *Kill For Collingwood* "[who] were expected to display the same unflinching loyalty to their captain and club as Roman warriors to Caesar."

Footballers were encouraged to believe, as were those reading *The Mercury's* story, that "the deeds that [win] the premiership are as heroic as the deeds which won the Empire."

Fitzroy had similarly noble men in its ranks: archetypes of the day. Stanley Reid was the son of a doctor from Swan Hill. He was a fine scholar-athlete at Scotch College and then at Ormond College at the University of Melbourne where he studied arts and theology. He played with Fitzroy from 1894, often in the backline, where he was a skilful and reliable defender, and a natural leader. His final season was 1898, after which he was ordained as the Presbyterian minister in Kalgoorlie. A patriot and British Empire man, he felt compelled to join the West Australian Mounted Infantry. He was killed in action in the Boer War.

But Fitzroy also had its knockabouts. The 'Fitzroy Forties' was a collection of local toughs who were an ever-threatening presence on the terraces and in the streets afterwards. They would often get in fights with gangs and members of other clubs. According to Richard Stremski's *Kill for Collingwood*, the Collingwood gangs were more than happy to accommodate the Fitzroy toughs, one saying they loved heading up the road to the Brunswick Street Oval where "if you don't get good football [at least] you're bound to have bloodshed."

It was often rather willing on the field as well.

Fitzroy's opponents had little to fear throughout the first season of the VFL, 1897, when the Maroons struggled. They were nowhere near the standard of Geelong, Melbourne or the eventual premier Essendon.

In 1898 they were determined to win back local pride.

As the teams prepared for the season Fitzroy boasted a strong squad of players, enough to field two teams, even though they had only one. Because it was difficult to win selection the match committee could stipulate strict conditions. Players would only be considered for if they attended both training sessions, and spent time in the gymnasium.

Fitzroy wanted its players to have good wind, that they might stay the match, like a Melbourne Cup thoroughbred. There were many gyms around Melbourne where the sports fraternity would gather to spend time in olde worlde fitness programs involving skipping ropes and medicine balls, boxing bouts, gymnastics and calisthenics.

Through the VFA years, Fitzroy, with an array of nuggetty players, had been noted for its physical strength. It added a belief in athleticism, fitness, and stamina; elements that were to prove a key in many games through the season.

Not that it helped much in the opening round when the Maroons were trounced by Essendon 10.10 (70) to 2.5 (17). On the same afternoon Collingwood beat the strong Geelong side 7.6 (48) to 3.9 (27).

Fitzroy rallied in the second round with a two-goal home win against the rival Magpies, and then showed they would be contenders by surprising Geelong at the Corio Oval when the Pivotonians kicked inaccurately. Geelong came back strongly in the final quarter but the Roys held on 6.3 (39) to 4.10 (34).

The locals were expectant. But the season soured quickly with bad losses to South, 7.9 (51) to 2.10 (22), and Essendon, 8.11 (59) to 2.4 (16). The Same Olds again looked like they were the team to beat.

The burghers of Collingwood, embarrassed by the loss to their arch rivals earlier in the season, offered a prize of £10 to the club if their boys could beat Fitzroy at home. They inflicted the third successive loss to the Maroons.

It didn't make a lot of sense. Fitzroy was not short of talent or leadership, but they weren't winning.

Their skipper was Alec Sloan, another classic 19th-century character. He was earnest and determined in nature, supremely fit, fast and strong. He was happy to earn his living unobtrusively as a postal clerk, preferring to direct his energies at his sporting career. While the captaincy of such a fine club as Fitzroy gave him prominence, he won greater fame as an oarsman. He was for many years the stroke of the Victorian eight. He had won numerous inter-colonial titles and in 1896 he was presented with the Helms Trophy, an international award which celebrated the finest amateur sportsman of the day. In 1898 he was appointed rowing coach at Scotch College, a position he filled (except for a few years) for more than a quarter of a century, taking Scotch to seven Head of the River titles. He was also a prominent cyclist.

Sloan led Fitzroy by example, both on the ball, and in his role across half-back. He was famous for his stubborn defence and dashing runs.

Alongside him at centre half-back was Pat Hickey, a tough man, who knew how to handle himself. He was often the target of abuse from rival fans, but he got on with what he was best at: throwing his weight around and taking strong marks. He was involved in a memorable incident with Melbourne's Vic Cumberland. It was recalled in a reminiscence by 'Spectator' of *The Argus* in 1935. Every time Cumberland got the ball during one match in the late 1890s Hickey lined him up and barrelled him with fair tackles. This happened four times in succession— fair, but robust, and the last one was brutal. Both players continued on.

Fitzroy also had the much-loved Grace brothers. Fans would sing:

> Other clubs may have their stars,
> But Fitzroy have their aces,
> Other clubs put on airs,
> But, Fitzroy have the Graces.

The older brother, Jack, had been the best forward in the VFA in the early 1890s, his bags of goals leading to many a Roys victory. He once kicked 11 (out of 15) against Richmond. By 1898 (he turned 30 three days before the Grand Final) he spent most of his time in the ruck, but, still a fine mark, he posed plenty of problems up forward.

Mick Grace was four years younger. He was fast and strong and was a fine exponent of the high mark. One of the most revered players of the day, Grace thrived on the big occasions. After a fine season, he dominated the finals, after which he was named Champion of the Colony for 1898.

The Fitzroy season, which had been teetering, gained momentum with two come-from-behind wins in the final month of the home and away season. They kicked four goals in the final quarter at Melbourne, and then, having registered just one goal by three-quarter time against Geelong, stormed home to again kick four in the last for a stirring win.

At the conclusion of the home and away season Essendon were on top, with Fitzroy a game behind having lost just four of its 14 matches.

Unhappy with the finals system of 1897, the League implemented an expanded finals competition where the eight teams broke into two sections. Section A was for those who had finished first, third, fifth and seventh on the ladder, and the rest went in to Section B. The venue of each final was decided by lot.

In the first week Fitzroy went to South. The Roys didn't kick a goal in the first half but again finished powerfully to win by 14 points. The next week they slaughtered Carlton who didn't score after quarter-time. In the final sectional match, at home against Essendon, they nearly kicked themselves out of the game again, registering 0.10 in the second quarter. But they were clearly the better side—and the more aggressive side—and thrashed the reigning premier.

Fitzroy led its section and played the winner of Section B, fierce rival Collingwood, in the final, to determine who had the right to play the minor premier Essendon in the Grand Final. The Roys won the draw and a huge crowd of 16,000 gathered at Brunswick Street on a day that the cycling reporter in *The Argus* described as "execrable". A "hurricane" blew from the north and by late afternoon the sky was "dark with debris". Consequently, play was scrappy with the ball caught in the dead pocket. Much of the time it was out of bounds. Collingwood looked the better side in the ungodly scrap, until Pat Hickey slammed the Magpie winger Sime into the ground which "knocked all the go" out of him; this seemed to be a turning point. Mick Grace took control of the match, and in a very low-scoring affair, Bill Potter marked for Fitzroy and sent his place kick through for a goal. The Magpies were too tired to mount a final charge.

So Fitzroy was favourite to beat Essendon in the first true Grand Final. The Maroons nearly won on default, as a dispute over the venue almost prompted the Same Olds to boycott the game. The match was set down for the St Kilda ground but, following a wet winter, it was in poor condition and had already been top dressed in the hope it would recover for the cricket season. The sand was removed and it came up quite well. On the eve of the match, Essendon agreed to play.

In the lead-up to the match Alec Sloan had been in doubt. While rowing his single scull on the Yarra he had bumped in to a corpse, and being a fine, upstanding citizen, had notified the authorities. An inquest was called—to be heard on Grand Final day. It appeared there was no way out. However, the magistrate conducting the inquiry was a passionate Fitzroy fan who found it imperative to adjourn the inquest to a later date.

A crowd of more than 16,000 gathered for the Grand Final. 'Follower' in *The Age* was surprised given that neither team was "local" and the weather was not ideal.

Sloan won the toss and kicked with the wind, which turned out to be very handy, as it dropped off later in the game. Fitzroy started at a frenetic pace, putting considerable physical pressure on its opponent, and the gentler souls in the crowd were concerned for the safety of the players, particularly as some were being barrelled on to the turf, and even on to the asphalt cycling track around the ground. The play for most of the day, reported 'Observer' in *The Argus*, was "vigorous rather than scientific". It was a pretty wild affair.

Billy McSpeerin scored the first major by getting his boot to the leather sphere during a scrimmage in the Fitzroy goal. Soon after Bert Sharpe sent a pass to Mick Grace whose kick was marked by his brother Jim. Jim kicked truly. On one of Essendon's few attacks Tod Collins, who would later captain the club (and play cricket for Victoria), managed to score "a major".

The second quarter was even rougher with Essendon rallying amid "desperate fighting". With the exception of the ball-playing of Mick Grace and Paddy Noonan, Fitzroy countered physically "relying too much on muscle and rush". It came as no surprise that Hickey was in the thick of things. 'Follower' in *The Age* was not amused. "Hickey again disfigured his play by one contemptible attack on Stuckey which was unprovoked and unjustifiable," he wrote. Nor was 'Observer' of *The Argus*, who was critical of a number of the Fitzroy players claiming: "[They] are simply carrying the plan of demoralising and damaging the other sides altogether too far."

George Stuckey, the Same Olds captain, was a target. Another 19th-century all-rounder (he also played cricket for Victoria), he was regarded as an inspirational leader. He was as quick as any player in the League, having won the Stawell Gift the previous year. When he placed a fair bump on Fitzroy's own speedster Kelly Robinson, Stuckey was forced to defend himself as the Fitzroy wingman stood before him with fists raised in the classical boxer's pose.

Essendon countered by trying to open the game up. The Same Olds, according to *The Argus*, "spread out their formation", which brought the quicker players into the game. Fitzroy's Eddie Drohan was influential, setting up a number of forward thrusts, including one that resulted in Jim Grace's second goal. Drohan was being assisted by on-ballers Noonan and Billy McSpeerin, and by Sloan who was "making some grand runs" from the backline.

The game was not characterised by flow. The Roys backs were determined to intimidate the Essendon forwards. It was a problem for Essendon, wrote 'Observer', as not one player had the strength "to stand against the charges of the Fitzroy backs".

Stan Reid was solid in defence, and for a time may well have had as his direct opponent Essendon forward Charles Moore. By remarkable coincidence, Moore was the only other VFL player to be killed in the Boer War.

At the long break Fitzroy led by 10 points but, said 'Follower', Essendon "always gave one the impression they were struggling against a superior force".

The Same Olds rallied after half-time, but their effort was short-lived as, unable to put a score on the board, they watched Mick Grace take a towering mark (the best of the afternoon) and then drop kicked his side's fifth goal. It capped off a brilliant performance. "It would be impossible to overestimate the value of his play to the winning side," wrote 'Follower' who suggested the younger Grace had put on an exhibition of rucking, marking and kicking.

By the final quarter the "tremendous pace [of the game] had cleaned every man on the ground out" and it became a desperate affair with the Roys defending their 16-point lead. Two-thirds of the men created an awful scrum. Exhausted players threw themselves on the football, and it seemed no one would score. A couple of times when Essendon was presented with an opportunity Sloan cleared the football, breaking free of the congestion and racing down the wing.

Again it was the stamina of Fitzroy that served it so well. They did it relatively easily once the Essendon spirit was broken. The final margin was 15 points.

It was a tough match. 'Observer' concluded: "It could have been a better game, but not a harder one."

Fitzroy had won its first VFL flag.

The players were the pride of Fitzroy. They were as fine a body of young men as could be gathered in one place. And the locals walked tall, knowing they lived in the best suburb in Melbourne.

1898 FITZROY

PREMIER'S SEASON

FITZROY: 1898

ROUND ONE May 14
FITZROY 2.5 (17)
ESSENDON 10.10 (70)
Best: Fitzroy – Drohan, Sloane, Grace, Sharpe, B.Dalton, Tulloch.
Goals: Fitzroy – Grace, McSpeerin.
Crowd: N/A at East Melbourne Cricket Ground

ROUND TWO May 21
FITZROY 7.6 (48)
COLLINGWOOD 5.6 (36)
Best: Fitzroy – McSpeerin, Drohan, Hickey, Noonan, Sharpe, Sloan.
Goals: Fitzroy – McSpeerin 3, Kiernan 2, Jenkins, Sharpe.
Crowd: N/A at Brunswick St Oval

ROUND THREE May 24
FITZROY 7.11 (53)
ST KILDA 2.4 (16)
Best: Fitzroy – Kiernan, Cleary, Hickey, McCabe, McSpeerin, Sharpe.
Goals: Fitzroy – Kiernan 2, McSpeerin 2, McCabe, Sharpe, Hickey.
Crowd: N/A at Junction Oval

ROUND FOUR May 28
FITZROY 4.14 (38)
MELBOURNE 2.7 (19)
Best: Fitzroy – B.Dalton, J.Dalton, C.Jenkins, McCabe, Sharpe, Sloan.
Goals: Fitzroy – McCabe 2, Sharpe 2.
Crowd: N/A at Brunswick St Oval

ROUND FIVE June 4
FITZROY 6.3 (39)
GEELONG 4.10 (34)
Best: Fitzroy – Grace, Robinson, Noonan, Jenkins, Reid, Nolan.
Goals: Fitzroy – Grace 2, Kiernan, B.Dalton, Descrimes, McSpeerin.
Crowd: N/A at Corio Oval

ROUND SIX June 11
FITZROY 5.7 (37)
CARLTON 4.9 (33)
Best: Fitzroy – Sloan, J.Grace, M.Grace, Hickey, McDougall, Noonan.
Goals: Fitzroy – McDougall 2, Kiernan, Jenkins, Sharpe.
Crowd: N/A at Brunswick St Oval

ROUND SEVEN June 18
FITZROY 2.10 (22)
SOUTH MELBOURNE 7.9 (51)
Best: Fitzroy – Davidson, Descrimes, McEwen, Noonan, Potter, Sloan.
Goals: Fitzroy – McSpeerin, Sharpe.
Crowd: N/A at Lake Oval

ROUND EIGHT June 25
FITZROY 2.4 (16)
ESSENDON 8.11 (59)
Best: Fitzroy – M.Grace, E.Jenkins, Sloan, Sharpe, J.Grace.
Goals: Fitzroy – M.Grace, Muirhead.
Crowd: N/A at Brunswick St Oval

ROUND NINE July 9
FITZROY 3.5 (23)
COLLINGWOOD 4.11 (35)
Best: Fitzroy – Fontaine, J.Grace, M.Grace, McSpeerin, Potter, Reid.
Goals: Fitzroy – B.Dalton, McDougall.
Crowd: N/A at Victoria Park

ROUND TEN July 16
FITZROY 9.13 (67)
ST KILDA 3.1 (19)
Best: Fitzroy – McCabe, B.Dalton, Drohan, Nolan, J.Grace, M.Grace.
Goals: Fitzroy – J.Grace 2, Kiernan 2, B.Dalton 2, McCabe 2, Shaw.
Crowd: N/A at Brunswick St Oval

ROUND ELEVEN July 23
FITZROY 7.8 (50)
MELBOURNE 5.3 (33)
Best: Fitzroy – McSpeerin, J.Grace, J.Dalton, Sharpe, Clarke, Hickey.
Goals: Fitzroy – McSpeerin 3, McCabe, Kiernan, J.Grace, M.Grace.
Crowd: N/A at the MCG

ROUND TWELVE July 30
FITZROY 5.9 (39)
GEELONG 4.6 (30)
Best: Fitzroy – B.Dalton, Kiernan, Drohan, McCabe, Reid, Sharpe, Sloan.
Goals: Fitzroy – Kiernan 2, B.Dalton 2, Noonan.
Crowd: N/A at Brunswick St Oval

ROUND THIRTEEN August 13
FITZROY 8.6 (54)
CARLTON 3.4 (22)
Best: Fitzroy – Kiernan, Drohan, Fontaine, J.Grace, McSpeerin, Reid, Sloan.
Goals: Fitzroy – Kiernan 4, McCabe 2, M.Grace, McDougall.
Crowd: N/A at Princes Park

ROUND FOURTEEN August 13
FITZROY 9.11 (65)
SOUTH MELBOURNE 1.4 (10)
Best: Fitzroy – J.Grace, M.Grace, Drohan, Noonan, Potter, Sharpe.
Goals: Fitzroy – M.Grace 2, Sharpe 2, McCabe, Kiernan, Potter, McSpeerin, Descrimes.
Crowd: N/A at Brunswick St Oval

SECTIONAL GAMES

ROUND FIFTEEN August 27
FITZROY 6.11 (47)
SOUTH MELBOURNE 5.3 (33)
Best: Fitzroy – Sloan, Potter, Noonan, M.Grace, Drohan, B.Dalton.
Goals: Fitzroy – M.Grace 2, Noonan 2, McDougall, Muirhead.
Crowd: N/A at the Lake Oval

ROUND SIXTEEN September 3
FITZROY 12.18 (90)
CARLTON 1.1 (7)
Best: Fitzroy – M.Grace, J.Dalton, Muirhead, Nolan, Sharpe, Sloan.
Goals: Fitzroy – M.Grace 4, Sharpe 2, McSpeerin 2, Kiernan, J.Grace, Nolan, McDougall.
Crowd: N/A at Brunswick St Oval

ROUND SEVENTEEN September 10
FITZROY 5.15 (45)
ESSENDON 2.4 (16)
Best: Fitzroy – Hickey, Sloan Potter, J.Grace, M.Grace, McSpeerin.
Goals: Fitzroy – J.Grace 2, Kiernan, M.Grace, McSpeerin.
Crowd: N/A at Brunswick St Oval

PREMIER'S FINALS

PRELIMINARY FINAL September 17
FITZROY 2.10 (22)
COLLINGWOOD 1.5 (11)
Best: Fitzroy – M.Grace, Potter, Descrimes, McSpeerin, Noonan, Robinson, Fontaine, Sharpe, J.Dalton.
Goals: Fitzroy – Fontaine, Potter.
Crowd: 13,120 at Brunswick St Oval

GRAND FINAL September 24
FITZROY 2.5 4.5 5.6 5.8 (38)
ESSENDON 1.0 3.1 3.2 3.5 (23)
Best: Fitzroy – Drohan, M.Grace, Hickey, Potter, Reid, Sloan.
Goals: Fitzroy – J.Grace 2, M.Grace, McDougall, McSpeerin.
Crowd: 16,538 at Junction Oval

GRAND FINAL LINE-UPS

FITZ	B:	S.Reid	J.Power	J.Nolan
ESS	F:	C.ten Brink	C.Moore	G.Kearney
FITZ	HB:	A.Sloan (capt)	P.Hickey	J.Dalton
ESS	HF:	T.Collins	C.Campbell	G.Hastings
FITZ	C:	E.Drohan	H.Clarke	K.Robinson
ESS	C:	J.Groves	H.Wright	A.Gray
FITZ	HF:	C.Kiernan	B.Sharpe	B.Dalton
ESS	HB:	G.Stuckey (capt)	J.Anderson	G.Vautin
FITZ	F:	F.Fontaine	J.Grace	A.McDougall
ESS	B:	T.Kinnear	N.Officer	H.Gavin
FITZ	R:	M.Grace	P.Descrimes	B.McSpeerin
ESS	R:	C.Forbes	B.Jackson	S.Barry

SNAPSHOT

Win-loss record: 15-4

Highest score: 12.18 (90), round 16, v Carlton.

Greatest winning margin: 83 points, round 16, v Carlton.

Lowest score: 2.4 (16), round 8, v Essendon.

Greatest losing margin: 83 points, round 16, v Carlton.

Most goals by a player in a game: 4, Mick Grace, round 16, v Carlton; Chris Kiernan, round 13, v Carlton.

Most consecutive wins: 10

Most consecutive losses: 3

Club awards: Best and Fairest: Mick Grace; Leading goalkicker: Chris Kiernan (18 goals).

Putting it into perspective: Fitzroy's first premiership victory and just the second VFL flag to be awarded meant in the first two years of the new competition the minor premier had yet to go through and win the premiership.

1898

		P	W	L	D	%	Pts
1	Essendon	14	11	3	0	202.1	44
2	Collingwood	14	10	4	0	181.0	40
3	**Fitzroy**	14	10	4	0	121.6	40
4	Geelong	14	9	5	0	151.8	36
5	South Melb	14	7	7	0	89.6	28
6	Melbourne	14	5	8	1	97.1	22
7	Carlton	14	3	10	1	60.3	14
8	St Kilda	14	0	14	0	33.5	0

(14 home and away rounds)

Section A Ladder

		P	W	L	D	%	Pts
1	**Fitzroy**	3	3	0	0	325.0	12
2	Essendon	3	2	1	0	171.4	8
3	South Melb	3	1	2	0	94.5	4
4	Carlton	3	0	3	0	17.5	0

Section B Ladder

		P	W	L	D	%	Pts
1	Collingwood	3	3	0	0	207.1	12
2	Geelong	3	2	1	0	238.6	8
3	Melbourne	3	1	2	0	63.3	4
4	St Kilda	3	0	3	0	29.2	0

PLAYERS USED

FITZROY	GAMES	GOALS
Clarke, Harry	10	0
Cleary, Bill	5	0
Dalton, Bill	19	6
Dalton, Jack	19	0
Davidson, Alex	3	0
Descrimes, Pat	19	2
Doherty, Charlie	2	0
Drohan, Eddie	17	0
Fontaine, Fred	9	1
Grace, Jim	17	9
Grace, Mick	16	15
Hickey, Pat	13	1
Jenkins, Charlie	8	0
Jenkins, Ern	8	2
Kiernan, Chris	19	18
Lamley, Roger	2	0
McCabe, Dick	13	9
McDougall, Alf	14	7
McEwen, Hugh	5	0
McSpeerin, Bill	18	17
Muirhead, Arch	4	2
Nolan, Herb	1	0
Nolan, Jerry	18	1
Noonan, Paddy	19	3
Potter, Bill	18	2
Power, Johnny	7	0
Reid, Stan	16	0
Robinson, Kelly	18	0
Sharpe, Bert	18	10
Shaw, George	5	1
Sloan, Alec	19	0
Tulloch, Jim	1	0

**FITZROY 3.9 (27) d
SOUTH MELBOURNE 3.8 (26)**

ROYS EMERGE FROM CLAMOUR

The many diversions in Australian life at this time failed to distract the robust Maroons from clearing a path to triumph. By JOHN HARMS

DURING the winter of 1899, footy fans in the growing city of Melbourne—and there were plenty of them—had a number of things on their minds. They were being hounded by politicians and community leaders who wanted their constituents to be interested in the proposal to bring the six colonies together to form the nation of Australia. They took an interest in the federal cause.

Outside politics, Melburnians took great interest in the plight of their footy side, and the prospects of the Australian Test side that was about to embark on the tour of England. Like football, cricket was enormously popular. During previous tours, crowds of up to 10,000 would brave the freezing night to stand outside *The Age's* office where the Test scores would be posted when each cable arrived—once every 15 minutes!

Cricket had done much to place the idea of the Australian nation in the minds of people. From 1877, the Australian cricket team was just that: the team of the entity that was Australia. Even though the Australian nation didn't exist! And victories over the might of England, the mother country, showed that Australians were as good as their imperial masters.

Football, regarded as the local game, the Australian game (made in the image of Australians), embodied a second type of nationalism; the nationalism of the native born, and of the Flynns, the Flanagans, and the

O'Mearas, and of the radicals and ratbags, who would never genuflect at the imperial altar.

To be at the football in Melbourne was, at one level, to assert that sense of national identity. Just as it was a way of asserting local identity and the feeling of belonging to the suburb which your boys represented.

Politicians understood only too well that the gaze of Australians was more likely to be on Joe Darling and Victor Trumper, Hughie Trumble and the brilliant all-round sportsman Jack Worrall, as they tackled the Englishmen at Lord's. And on the football.

In *The Bulletin* a cartoonist drew a boy (symbolising Australians) watching cricket and not politics, with the caption "They can only watch one game at a time."

So some politicians started using sporting metaphors and terms to make their point.

James Service, briefly premier of Victoria, and for many years a member of the Victorian upper house, in raising a toast to a united Australia, said: "Our very Australian boys drink in federation with mothers' milk, and as soon as their little legs can run and their hands can catch they are ardently devoted to federal football and cricket."

Public figures used sport to their advantage, in any way they could, knowing how meaningful it was to people.

In 1899, the president of the Fitzroy Football Club, the reigning premier, was R.W. Best. He had been an alderman in the Fitzroy council, was the MLA for Fitzroy, and was very much pro-federation. He had aspirations to federal office (he was eventually elected a senator). His popularity had been built on his involvement in the local community particularly through sport. He had been president of the VFA, president of the Victorian Cricket Association, and the Victorian League of Wheelmen.

He knew what the people wanted.

In Fitzroy they wanted another premiership.

But it was going to be a tough year.

In his summation of the 1899 season, published in *The Argus* in the week following the Grand Final, 'Old Boy' lauded the quality of the football throughout the year. It was a happy coincidence, he argued, that a competition of just eight clubs should have six such evenly matched and capable sides.

Fitzroy, despite a terrible run with injuries and illness which saw Alec Sloan, Bill McSpeerin, Bill Potter, Pat Descrimes, Kelly Robinson, Chris Kiernan, the Dalton brothers (Jack and Bill) and Paddy Noonan all miss matches—at one stage, six of them were out—looked like they were every chance of satisfying their fans again. Mick Grace did not have as good a year as 1898 when he was named Champion of the Colony. That honour went to his teammate Pat Hickey (uncle of Reg Hickey, who was to become one of the great characters of the Geelong Football Club). A known hard man, Pat Hickey ruled the roost at centre half-back, and was occasionally sent forward to inflict some pain up there. "Where fighting was the hottest," wrote 'Old Boy' in The Argus, "there was the Fitzroy half-back in the thick of it."

Fitzroy had brawn. The "Fitzroy heavyweights", as they were called, were very physical and intimidating, and sparks would fly when they came across opponents who refused to take a backward step—especially from Collingwood.

But the Roys had their share of quick, talented ball-players as well. Their centre-line of Eddie Drohan, Harry Clarke and Robinson was all class.

McSpeerin was a crowd favourite. A rover, he also spent time in the forward pocket. Fans called him 'The Shark'. He was very skilled, described in some reports as an "artistic" player who handled wet conditions very well.

The idea of "artistry" was alive and well in football. Football "artists" were those whose aesthetic appearance delighted the eye, especially of those middle class reporters whose words filled the dailies. The chaps of the press could not find enough superlatives for the grace and beauty of these types, most of whom were able to set other players up gallantly in what was called "team play".

These same scribes chose a different tone when describing the robust and bullocky play of individuals charging towards goal like rugby players in an effort to win territory. But that did not sway the popularity of the tough men among those who frequented the pubs and gambled in the local laneways. The improvement-of-society men didn't understand these earthy types, or their women.

Essendon and Collingwood had excellent sides. Geelong, said 'Old Boy', was the most brilliant yet most inconsistent side. Melbourne could match it with the best of them on their day. And South Melbourne emerged late in the season as a possible contender. Led by their skilful ruckman, Mick Pleass, with Charlie Colgan, a dangerous goal-scorer, South had also recruited Harry Lampe from Wagga who hit his straps by season's end and was having an impact on games from centre half-forward. They also had in their ranks a 20-year-old beanpole who played in the forward pocket or back pocket and occasionally had a run on the ball. He was Warwick Armstrong who filled out over the years (he was nicknamed 'The Big Ship'), and went on to captain the Australian cricket side.

In the opening round, the Grand Final sides of the previous year met at Brunswick Street. Fitzroy sent a message to the competition by holding the

Same Olds goalless and winning by 38 points, while at Geelong the Pivotonians won 8.6 (54) to 3.11 (29).

The Maroons beat South by four points, in the second round, and the following week trounced Geelong at Corio Oval. Melbourne had a couple of impressive wins at home at the Cricket Ground: against Geelong, and also over Fitzroy. They surprised the premiers, holding them to just 3.6 (24).

The Roys and the Magpies met in round six. It was another willing scrap. Collingwood's wingman Charlie 'Buffer' Sime, who was often at the centre of hostilities (or the cause of them), reacted to the bath he was being given at the hands of the classy Eddie Drohan. The game became more spiteful than usual. Hickey belted champion Collingwood rover Dick Condon in a "disgraceful" incident, which was not reported. 'Old Boy' was not impressed, suggesting the umpire handed out too many warnings and not enough bookings, and that the match was spoiled by both teams who paid "too much attention to the man and too little to the ball". Fitzroy won 5.5 (35) to 1.7 (13) but the local crowd didn't like it. The Collingwood mob smashed the window of one of the cabs which was taking some Fitzroy players away.

The fall-out of the incident reached local government level. In Collingwood, Councillor Cody said: "The Roys had provoked the attack by their gross misconduct on the field."

It was a season where all the sides except Carlton and lowly St Kilda could play good enough football to win on the day and the evenness of the competition and the quality of the football was certainly capturing the attention of the public.

More so than the looming referendum, which was to be held in the week of round eight, on Tuesday, June 20. At the same time the English rugby side, led by the Reverend Mullineaux, played its first-ever Test against Australia in Sydney. The Australians won 13-3, which may have swayed the New South Welsh voters, who weren't so sympathetic to the federal cause, to change their minds.

Also, on that weekend the Australians had beaten England by 10 wickets, at Lord's. Again this could only have helped the vote. As, no doubt, did the reports of the threat of war in South Africa.

The topsy-turvy nature of the VFL season continued into the final month of the home and away season. Fitzroy was thrashed by Geelong at Brunswick Street, beat Melbourne, and then lost at home to Collingwood. The Maroons still finished on top of the ladder, losing just three times for the year. Geelong was second, Collingwood third, Essendon fourth, Melbourne fifth and South sixth.

The sectional system was used again to decide the finalists. In Section B South surprised many by winning all three of its matches: beating Geelong at Geelong in a thriller, thrashing St Kilda, and then dominating Essendon.

In Section A Fitzroy was expected to account for the weak Blues in the first round, but Carlton got away to a good start and it took Fitzroy (which was still nursing a number of injured players, especially Sloan and Descrimes) until late in the third quarter to hit the front. The crowd expected the Roys to storm clear, but Carlton rallied and with just minutes left scores were level, until a scramble in the Fitzroy forward line resulted in a behind. That was the final margin.

The talk around Melbourne was that Fitzroy was faltering, and that its late season form was patchy. Yet the following week at Brunswick Street they held Melbourne to just 0.2 (2). All was set up for a classic encounter against Collingwood, at Collingwood.

A huge crowd gathered at Victoria Park to see the contest between the undefeated teams. Despite the rain, it was quite an occasion. The Collingwood Imperial Military Brass Band played in the reserve. Fitzroy, being the minor premier, enjoyed the insurance that a loss would not be the end of proceedings: the Maroons would still have the right challenge the winner of the final. Early in the game Collingwood's Matthew Fell turned, wrenching his back, and had to be taken off. So the Magpies played with 17 men, which became the key factor in a match which was described as a "battle of giants" involving "grand high-marking, splendid turning and dodging, superb passing with hand and foot, [and] tremendous pace all through".

Not everyone had such a romantic view of the contest. The Magpies went down by 14 points and their fans were seething with the unfortunate loss, at the hands of the Fitzroy thugs, which put an end to the Magpies' season. Pat Hickey was the target of most abuse. A woman clouted him with her umbrella (Collingwood officials promised to discipline her), and about 150 local larrikins jostled the Fitzroy players who had to be escorted by police to the tram-line. Hickey eventually emerged from the dressingroom surrounded by his brother and a few friends. He smiled at the waiting mob, who screamed their anger at him. The body of mythology that helped sustain the Collingwood-Fitzroy rivalry was growing steadily.

On the other side of the Yarra, at South Melbourne, the Bloods had a somewhat surprising victory over Essendon, setting up a clash with Fitzroy in the Grand Final. Much criticism of the sectional system followed. People asked why the team which finished sixth with just five wins from 14 home and away games should have a chance to win the flag. The system was seen as a way of extending the season, keeping all the fans involved, and therefore a money-raiser for the League.

Opinion was divided as people anticipated the outcome of the match. Most tipped Fitzroy, but South was the big improver, and in the eyes of some, a legitimate contender with a real chance to pinch the flag from the Fitzroy powerhouse.

On the morning of the Grand Final heavy rain fell across the city. Only about 5000 spectators braved the elements at the St Kilda Ground, most of them (according to *The South Melbourne Record*) came "armed against the pluvial visitation with overcoats and umbrellas". Conditions were so bad that South wanted the match postponed and called on the League's weather committee. Fitzroy was more keen to play.

Rumours circulating—that the Bloods had a number of injured players—were well-founded. Hence their push to postpone the match. Artie Henley and Harry Purdy were away from town. (Perhaps the presence of their team in the Grand Final had been a surprise to them as well, and they had already made plans!) Mick Pleass had injured his leg, but was still in the side. Bill 'Buns' Fraser's neck was stiff, and Henri Jeanneret's neck was covered in boils.

The Fitzroy camp was in a sombre mood. Bert Sharpe's father had died the day before. Sharpe withdrew from the side, and the Roys players wore black armbands. But they did not want the match postponed. They'd heard the rumours, too, and knew that if they lost, they had the right to challenge South Melbourne again. Given their record over two seasons they had every right to be confident.

A further setback occurred when the maverick Chris Kiernan, one of the more gifted players of the era, failed to show up—one report says because of injury—and the veteran Bill Cleary stripped for the game.

Those persuaded to have a bet on the game were keen to back Fitzroy, but the weather proved something of a leveller. The match was a desperate slog, in the rain and the mud.

"From the first bounce till the very last tinkle of the bell," wrote 'Old Boy' in his *Argus* report, "it was a battle between two earnest, strong teams, and the crowd entered into the excitement, and what it lacked in numbers it made up for in enthusiasm."

The southerly blew towards the city goals of the St Kilda Ground ('Follower' in *The Age* praised the curator McShane for turning out the ground in such good condition given the circumstances). South's skipper, Dave Adamson, won the toss and kicked with the wind. The lightweight Herbie Howson (also described as an "artistic" player) began brilliantly on the wing beating Eddie Drohan for pace, and to the surprise of the most, in the air. The Bloods moved the ball forward where Harold Lampe was awarded a free kick by respected umpire Ivo Crapp (who had a good game, as usual). Lampe's well-timed punt sailed through on the breeze and South led. Two men braving the elements behind the goal waved their umbrellas—one red, one white—for "a long time".

They had opportunity again when South attacked and Lampe kicked a fine running goal to give the Bloods the jump. Fitzroy was uncharacteristically tentative and unsteady, and, wrote 'Old Boy', were "fumbling a lot". The Roys could make little progress into the bluster and were visibly disappointed when Jim Grace's snap from the pocket hit the post. It was one of only four behinds that were kicked for the entire match at that end.

South led 2.3 to 0.1 at quarter-time. Some thought, with rain still falling, that the Bloods had posted a winning score already. Adamson thought so. He moved Charlie James, a fine kick of the football, from half-forward to the backline in the hope to hold back the tide. Other players drifted back as well, and the ensuing scrum pushed the ball around in the mud.

At one point a kick off the ground during a goalmouth scrimmage went through and was initially awarded a goal, but the full-back Adamson pointed to the muddy mark on the arm of his jersey, and Crapp, who had noticed the touch, changed the score to a behind.

South, trying so hard to contain the forceful charges of the Roys, played a tactical game. It drew on the influence of rugby, wrote 'Old Boy', forever kicking the football in to touch. When it wasn't out of bounds, the leather was caught in a rolling pack, which produced "signs of temper" and some rather unsavoury moments. Fitzroy's Robinson, Cleary and Dalton all had their names put in to the book for "roughness".

Hickey was playing an "irresistible" game and was instrumental in driving the Roys forward. Like the skipper Sloan, Hickey was not always drawn to the ball often "skirmishing behind the ruck like a rugby half-back". At the moments the ball came clear both Hickey and Sloan made strong runs. But the game lacked any rhythm and Crapp was forced to pay many free kicks.

Play was concentrated in the Fitzroy forward line, where Mick Grace registered Fitzroy's first goal with an opportune punt from the ruck. He was involved again soon after when his foot-pass found Fontaine who marked and had the chance to put the Maroons on level terms. His shot was accurate.

South failed to score for the quarter and at half-time the Roys led by a point. It was the fightback of a champion side, but in the wind and the mud, it remained anyone's game.

For much of the third quarter the ball was in South's forward line, where Hickey defended determinedly. South scored a couple of behinds and then, from a free kick, Colgan scored a major. South led by seven points at the final change.

If anything the wind freshened for the last quarter and the crowd wondered whether South would have the will and the energy to hang on against the reigning premier's inevitable onslaught. Famous for their strength and stamina, the Roys were relentless. Hickey led the way, rushing the football out of defence, with explosive runs. At one point, in returning the football he found himself within range of goal, but his flying shot hit the post.

South hung on and hung on. The crowd screamed its support. Lampe led an attack for South but Hickey intercepted and kicked in the direction of McSpeerin who marked near the behind post. It was a difficult shot but the Roys rover ran around and kicked truly. Fitzroy led by a point.

South would not concede, pushing forward into the wind, and Lampe missed a terrific opportunity when he kicked poorly for a behind. Fontaine's behind kept Fitzroy ahead, and in the desperate last moments of the match the Southerners forced the ball to within range and were attacking as the bell rang.

Hickey was the star. Often the subject of debate for his overly zealous approach, his match was celebrated for days after. 'Follower' said Hickey had a "magnificent" match and played "without suspicion of undue roughness".

'Old Boy' was just as complimentary. "I have never seen a man do more for his side," he wrote. "Nominally he was half-back; as a matter of fact he was everywhere."

In *The Australasian* 'Markwell' also sang Hickey's praises. "In this final match, as in many a previous game for the year, Hickey proved himself Fitzroy's mainstay. In defence or in attack his value to the team was incalculable and, notwithstanding the unsuitable conditions of ground and ball, I do not think he has ever shown a finer game.'

He was named Champion of the Colony—by commentators and fans—in what was a unanimous decision, if not a popular one.

The people of Fitzroy celebrated again. They had the best footy side in the land. Soon, they could say, the best side in the nation. The June 20 referendum had been successful.

The Australian cricketers won the five-match series in England 1-0.

But things were deteriorating in South Africa. In the same papers as the Grand Final reports the headlines read 'A Very Grave Situation' and 'War Likely To Be Precipitated'.

Within weeks, on October 10, war was declared.

Not that it mattered much, for a while, to the people of Fitzroy.

PREMIER'S SEASON

FITZROY: 1899

ROUND ONE May 13
FITZROY	6.11 (47)
ESSENDON	0.9 (9)

Best: Fitzroy – Descrimes, Drohan, Hickey, Jenkins, McSpeerin, Sharpe.
Goals: Fitzroy – Sharpe 2, McSpeerin 2, Descrimes, McDougall.
Crowd: N/A at Brunswick St Oval

ROUND TWO May 20
FITZROY	6.6 (42)
SOUTH MELBOURNE	5.8 (38)

Best: Fitzroy – Sharpe, Sloan, Hickey, Drohan, Clarke, B.Dalton, Nolan.
Goals: Fitzroy – Sharpe 3, Kiernan, Jenkins, M.Grace.
Crowd: N/A at the Lake Oval

ROUND THREE May 24
FITZROY	4.8 (32)
GEELONG	0.8 (8)

Best: Fitzroy – McSpeerin, J.Grace, M.Grace, Clarke, Deas, Hickey.
Goals: Fitzroy – McSpeerin 2, Kiernan, J.Grace.
Crowd: N/A at Corio Oval

ROUND FOUR May 27
FITZROY	7.14 (56)
ST KILDA	5.3 (33)

Best: Fitzroy – Kiernan, Sharpe, Hickey, Sloan, Deas, Robinson.
Goals: Fitzroy – Kiernan 2, Sharpe 2, Jenkins, Kerrigan, M.Grace.
Crowd: N/A at Brunswick St Oval

ROUND FIVE June 3
FITZROY	3.6 (24)
MELBOURNE	4.11 (35)

Best: Fitzroy – Sloan, Hickey, Sharpe, M.Grace, Descimes.
Goals: Fitzroy – Descrimes 2, J.Grace.
Crowd: N/A at the MCG

ROUND SIX June 10
FITZROY	5.5 (35)
COLLINGWOOD	1.7 (13)

Best: Fitzroy – McSpeerin, B.Dalton, J.Grace, Potter, Sharpe, Sloan.
Goals: Fitzroy – McSpeerin 3, Sharpe, Fontaine.
Crowd: N/A at Victoria Park

ROUND SEVEN June 17
FITZROY	5.15 (45)
CARLTON	1.7 (13)

Best: Fitzroy – Hickey, Descrimes, McSpeerin, Drohan, Sloan, McDougall.
Goals: Fitzroy – J.Grace, Descrimes, McSpeerin, Kiernan, Hickey.
Crowd: N/A at Brunswick St Oval

ROUND EIGHT June 24
FITZROY	10.3 (63)
ESSENDON	6.15 (51)

Best: Fitzroy – J.Grace, M.Grace, Moriarty, Descrimes, Hickey, B.Dalton.
Goals: Fitzroy – J.Grace 3, M.Grace 2, Kiernan, McSpeerin, Descrimes, Sharpe, McDougall.
Crowd: N/A at East Melbourne Cricket Ground

ROUND NINE July 8
FITZROY	9.8 (62)
SOUTH MELBOURNE	4.5 (29)

Best: Fitzroy – McSpeerin, Potter, M.Grace, Jenkins, Hickey, Deas.
Goals: Fitzroy – McSpeerin 4, Kiernan 2, Sharpe 2, Potter.
Crowd: N/A at Brunswick St Oval

ROUND TEN July 15
FITZROY	3.5 (23)
GEELONG	8.10 (58)

Best: Fitzroy – Hickey, Deas, Descrimes, Nolan, Potter, Sharpe.
Goals: Fitzroy – M.Grace, Kiernan, Thompson.
Crowd: N/A at Brunswick St Oval

ROUND ELEVEN July 22
FITZROY	12.12 (84)
ST KILDA	4.6 (30)

Best: Fitzroy – J.Grace, M.Grace, Potter, Cleary, Hickey, McEwen.
Goals: Fitzroy – J.Grace 6, M.Grace 2, Kiernan 2, Noonan, Cleary.
Crowd: N/A at the Junction Oval

ROUND TWELVE July 29
FITZROY	6.5 (41)
MELBOURNE	4.9 (33)

Best: Fitzroy – Clarke, M.Grace, Hickey, McDougall, Noonan.
Goals: Fitzroy – M.Grace 2, Potter, Kiernan, Cleary, McSpeerin.
Crowd: N/A at Brunswick St Oval

ROUND THIRTEEN August 5
FITZROY	3.7 (25)
COLLINGWOOD	5.7 (37)

Best: Fitzroy – Beauchamp, Deas, Fontaine, J.Grace, Sharpe.
Goals: Fitzroy – Foletta, McDougall, Cleary.
Crowd: N/A at Brunswick St Oval

ROUND FOURTEEN August 12
FITZROY	5.9 (39)
CARLTON	2.4 (16)

Best: Fitzroy – Cleary, McSpeerin, Noonan, Robinson, Clarke.
Goals: Fitzroy – McSpeerin 2, Fontaine, Sharpe, Cleary.
Crowd: N/A at Princes Park

SECTIONAL GAMES

ROUND FIFTEEN August 26
FITZROY	5.11 (41)
CARLTON	6.4 (40)

Best: Fitzroy – Hickey, J.Grace, M.Grace, Fontaine, Sharpe, Sloan.
Goals: Fitzroy – Sharpe 2, M.Grace, Clarke, Drohan.
Crowd: N/A at Brunswick St Oval

ROUND SIXTEEN September 2
FITZROY	5.10 (40)
MELBOURNE	0.2 (2)

Best: Fitzroy – J.Grace, Sharpe, M.Grace, Hickey, Jenkins, Potter.
Goals: Fitzroy – J.Grace 3, Sharpe, M.Grace.
Crowd: N/A at Brunswick St Oval

ROUND SEVENTEEN September 9
FITZROY	6.9 (45)
COLLINGWOOD	4.7 (31)

Best: Fitzroy – Sharpe, Hickey, McEwen, Descrimes, McSpeerin.
Goals: Fitzroy – McSpeerin 2, Sharpe 2, Hickey, M.Grace.
Crowd: N/A at Victoria Park

PREMIER'S FINAL

GRAND FINAL September 16

FITZROY	0.1	2.4	2.6	3.9 (27)
SOUTH MELBOURNE	2.3	2.3	3.7	3.8 (26)

Best: Fitzroy – Clarke, Deas, Drohan, Hickey, Jenkins, McEwen.
Goals: Fitzroy – Fontaine, M.Grace, McSpeerin.
Crowd: 4,823 at the Junction Oval

GRAND FINAL LINE-UPS

FITZ	B:	H.McEwen	G.Moriarty	E.Jenkins
STH M	F:	B.Fraser	C.Colgan	A.Henley
FITZ	HB:	J.Deas	P.Hickey	A.Sloan (capt)
STH M	HF:	C.James	H.Lampe	H.Jeanneret
FITZ	C:	E.Drohan	H.Clarke	K.Robinson
STH M	C:	J.O'Hara	B.Windley	B.Howson
FITZ	HF:	J.Grace	F.Fontaine	B.Dalton
STH M	HB:	A.Trim	C.Goding	G.Davidson
FITZ	F:	A.McDougall	B.Sharpe	B.Cleary
STH M	B:	F.O'Hara	D.Adamson (capt)	W.Armstrong
FITZ	R:	M.Grace	B.Potter	B.McSpeerin
STH M	R:	M.Pleass	J.Garbutt	B.Bryce

SNAPSHOT

Win-loss record: 15-3
Highest score: 12.12 (84), round 11, v St Kilda.
Greatest winning margin: 54 points, round 11, v St Kilda.
Lowest score: 3.5 (23), round 10, v Geelong.
Greatest losing margin: 35 points, round 10, v Geelong.
Most goals by a player in a game: 6, Jim Grace, round 11, v St Kilda.
Most consecutive wins: 5
Most consecutive losses: 1 (three times).
Club awards: Best and Fairest: Pat Hickey; Leading goalkicker: Bill McSpeerin (19 goals)
Putting it into perspective: Despite fierce competition over the first three seasons of the competition, Fitzroy's back-to-back premiership wins left it as the only club so far to win Grand Finals following Essendon's round-robin victory in 1897.

1899

		P	W	L	D	%	Pts
1	Fitzroy	14	11	3	0	153.3	44
2	Geelong	14	10	4	0	177.2	40
3	Collingwood	14	10	4	0	135.5	40
4	Essendon	14	9	5	0	140.2	36
5	Melbourne	14	8	6	0	136.7	32
6	South Melb	14	5	9	0	105.2	20
7	Carlton	14	3	11	0	53.1	12
8	St Kilda	14	0	14	0	28.0	0

(14 home and away rounds)

Section A Ladder

		P	W	L	D	%	Pts
1	Fitzroy	3	3	0	0	172.6	12
2	Collingwood	3	2	1	0	131.0	8
3	Carlton	3	1	2	0	103.2	4
4	Melbourne	3	0	3	0	34.1	0

Section B Ladder

		P	W	L	D	%	Pts
1	South Melb	3	3	0	0	239.7	12
2	Geelong	3	2	1	0	304.9	8
3	Essendon	3	1	2	0	177.3	4
4	St Kilda	3	0	3	0	9.6	0

PLAYERS USED

FITZROY	GAMES	GOALS
Beauchamp, Tammy	2	0
Clarke, Harry	17	1
Cleary, Bill	6	4
Dalton, Bill	12	0
Dalton, Jack	6	0
Deas, Jack	15	0
Descrimes, Pat	12	5
Drohan, Eddie	18	1
Foletta, Charlie	5	1
Fontaine, Fred	10	3
Grace, Jim	18	15
Grace, Mick	18	13
Hay, Bob	1	0
Hickey, Pat	18	2
Jenkins, Ern	17	2
Kerrigan, Joe	1	1
Kiernan, Chris	12	12
McDougall, Alf	17	3
McEwen, Hugh	9	0
McSpeerin, Bill	16	19
Moriarty, Geoff	13	0
Mulcahy, Jack	2	0
Nolan, Jerry	3	0
Nolan, Tom	2	0
Noonan, Paddy	6	1
Potter, Bill	15	2
Power, Johnny	3	0
Robinson, Kelly	15	0
Sharpe, Bert	17	17
Sloan, Alec	12	0
Thompson, Bill	6	1

**MELBOURNE 4.10 (34) d
FITZROY 3.12 (30)**

FUCHSIAS LEAVE BEST UNTIL LAST

Melbourne didn't dominate in 1900, but found some form at the right time of the season to eke out its first premiership. By ROBERT PASCOE

MELBOURNE was one of the founding clubs of the Australian game (1858) but had not won a premiership since the 1870s. The best it could manage after 1877, when the VFA was formed, was to run second on four occasions. This lack of success had a great deal to do with its amateur culture. While other clubs were moving inexorably to professional football, Melbourne (and the University Football Club, for that matter) remained comfortable with players who played merely 'for the love of the game'. The club historian E.C.H Taylor writing in the club's centennial history of 1958 lamented the passing of these amateur days:

> In the good old days every member of the club provided his own uniform, paid his cab hire, railway fare and hotel expenses when his club visited the country. But now [in the 1950s] things are entirely changed. The player has to be provided with his uniform and boots and all expenses when he goes away, let alone providing him with a billet, or supplying him with cash when he is out of one.[1]

This traditional amateur sentiment was genuine, particularly in private-school circles, but it restricted the pool of potential recruits into the club at the very time the code was becoming more professional and more cut-throat. Although professional payments were legal after 1911, and codified

---

1 E. C. H. Taylor, *100 Years of Football: The Story of the Melbourne Football Club, 1858–1958*, Melbourne Football Club, Melbourne, 1958, p. 29.

by the Coulter Law of 1930, payments to players in all VFL clubs were disguised as 'expenses'.

The Melbourne players of the 1900 season were, as had been the case for four decades, drawn from the ranks of the elite. Harry Cumberland was an electrician, but from the affluent suburb of Toorak; Stewie Geddes was a successful Richmond florist; Maurie Herring was a solicitor; Frank Langley was a physician who practised in Dandenong; William McClelland was another doctor, later the president of the VFL in whose name a trophy was struck; Bryan McGuigan ran a boot factory in the city; Richard Pirrie was a produce merchant; while Dick Wardill was a timber broker. None of these men needed a salary from the football club.

Melbourne's supporter base mixed the well-heeled with the inner south-eastern, with barrackers streaming on foot or carriage from nearby Richmond, South Yarra, Prahran, Armadale and Toorak to watch the team play at the Melbourne Cricket Ground at Yarra Park. Although most of the larrikin 'pushes' (gangs) supported blue-collar clubs, some of the rowdies were from upper-crust backgrounds. Larrikinism was a social phenomenon from the 1880s through to the 1920s, and it was not confined to the working class:

> Some chaps I know live out [at] South Yarra and that way—real knock-me-down toffs—swell clerks, and such like. Well, these come into town at night just for the purpose of turning over drunken men. I've done it myself with 'em lots of times....[2]

Football club allegiance was one of the badges of larrikin identity. Some players were themselves members of pushes, and were susceptible to bribery. Melbourne's recruiting network was concentrated on the inner south-eastern suburbs—Brighton, Caulfield and St Kilda—with a smaller group from the inner north, around Carlton and Collingwood.

Richmond, still a gentleman's club, was another fruitful source. Three on the 1900 list were graduates of Cumloden College, a private school in St Kilda that also produced the Test cricketer Warwick Armstrong; another three hailed from Melbourne Grammar, while at least one had come from Caulfield Grammar.

With the formation of the VFL in secret talks led by Essendon's Alex McCracken at the end of 1896, Melbourne was a natural candidate for admission, given its political prominence in the game, and it indeed had performed well in the mid-1890s. But the opening seasons of the VFL competition saw the Fuchsias fall back. Its win in 1900 was a fluke, and

---

2 'What a larrikin himself thinks', *Daily Telegraph* (Melbourne) Saturday 7 May 1887, p.6d.

hastened the creation of a finals system that was better than the sectional round-robin scheme that the VFL had begun in 1898. No one doubted that Melbourne was the better team on the final day of the season, but whether it had done enough during the course of the 1900 season itself was a moot point.

This was a well-trained team, with (for Melbourne in that period) an unusually small number of first-year players—only 11 of the 31 used in the 19 games of the season—making this a relatively experienced side. Turnover at Melbourne was often caused by players leaving for professional or business opportunities. Frank Langley played every game, while 14 others played more than 15 of the year's matches. Eddie Sholl, the previous club captain, played 12 games at full-back, including the final match.

The 1900 season was bookended by controversies, with Melbourne featuring in both. In the opening round, having lost its first 48 matches straight, St Kilda finally notched a win, having protested successfully that a Melbourne behind had been scored illegally—as Arthur Sowden passed the ball to Dick Wardill the third-quarter bell sounded—and yet play had gone on. Both clubs were agreed on the facts, and the League subsequently agreed to amend the result in St Kilda's favour. And, although Fitzroy dominated the season with 13 out of 17 possible wins, running out minor premiers, Melbourne defeated the Maroons in the last match of the season, the Grand Final.

Between these two matches involving Melbourne, the season was dominated by the heroics of the great teams of the period, notably Fitzroy (11 wins out of 14), Geelong (nine wins), and Essendon, Collingwood and South Melbourne (eight apiece, separated only by percentage). Lowly Melbourne finished the regular season with only six wins, in sixth place, while Carlton with five wins and St Kilda with just that one win (and a minuscule percentage of 39.1) rounded out the table.

Melbourne's grounds were too muddy for football in round three on May 19, and so the round was postponed to the weekend after round 14. On May 23, Essendon played Collingwood at the East Melbourne Cricket Ground. During the course of this match Albert Thurgood, Essendon's favourite son freshly returned from Kalgoorlie, executed a place kick measuring an impressive 102 yards, 2 feet (94 metres). Essendon triumphed, 13.7 (85) to 2.4 (16).

The other six clubs competed on the Queen's Birthday, May 24. The football crowds carried patriotic flags and streamers in red, white and blue. The Collingwood players appeared with a Union Jack stitched onto the back of their guernseys, while the next day, at the Brunswick Street Oval, Fitzroy's players emerged from their dressing room wearing tricolour sashes and rosettes that they removed before the match started. At each ground the crowd gave three rousing cheers and sang *God Save the Queen*. This was prescient of what would happen during the recruitment drives of World War I, when once again football matches became patriotic venues.

The Carlton-Collingwood rivalry was intensified by a round 6 match at Princes Park on June 2, which saw the Navy Blues win 4.1 (25) to 0.9 (9). Wild scenes broke out at the end of this contest. These two clubs were entering a period of fierce rivalry with both appearing in the finals consistently for the next decade or two.

Later in the season Collingwood lost its star player, Dick Condon, when he was suspended for life on account of his constant complaining about the umpiring. Condon was a gifted player but loose-lipped when dealing with the man in white. Matters came to a head in the finals during a match against Geelong, with Condon demanding that the players withdraw from the contest. In Collingwood's finals match against Melbourne, Condon abused the well-respected, if unfortunately named, umpire 'Ivo' Crapp with the infamous line, 'Your girl's a bloody whore.' For this indiscretion he was expelled from football, initially for life, although he was back playing again within two years.

Women had always been a significant fraction of the barrackers, all through the colonial era, but by the turn of the century women and men tended to sit in separate sections of the grounds. Women and children often sat closer to the fence, or were allocated a separate pavilion. In 1900 Collingwood opened its ladies' pavilion for the one-third of its 2000 members who were female. The building was really just a cheap shed, costing only £80, but it served to keep the women dry in the winter months and it was also indicative of Collingwood's entrepreneurial spirit in building a large membership base. At Albert Park in round 5, the visiting Geelong women spectators were denied free admittance for the match against South Melbourne, sparking a controversy that persisted for much of the season. Geelong reciprocated by refusing all visiting members free admission to Corio Oval, prompting the League to demand that Geelong pay South Melbourne £6/1/- by way of recompense. Geelong called their bluff and caused the League to fine them £20.

Controversy dogged South Melbourne again in 1900. When Fitzroy defeated South Melbourne at Albert Park in round 11 on 14 July, 5.9 (39) to 4.9 (33), the players were jostled by barrackers at the end of the match.

And so the controversial 1900 season reached its conclusion, with a sectional finals system that saw lowly Melbourne take on the minor premiers. This finals system, introduced in 1898, featured two round-robins of three matches—one with the odd-numbered teams on the ladder after the 14 home-and-away matches (Section A), the other with the even-numbered teams (Section B).

Essendon had finished third, so belonged to the Section A grouping and went on to win all three round-robin matches, including against ladder-leaders Fitzroy. Melbourne, from lowly sixth, won only two of the three Section B round-robin matches, but led Collingwood and Geelong on percentage with their trashing of lowly St Kilda, 12.14 (86) to 2.3 (15). So by the skin of their teeth the Fuchsias earned the right to play Essendon.

In the so-called Play Off (Final) at the South Melbourne Cricket Ground Essendon were very unlucky. 'Newhaven' Jackson went down with a crook knee in the first quarter. Fred Hiskins kicked what looked like a goal but was awarded only a behind. Captain George Stuckey ran into an open goal and calmly slotted the ball into the wrong space to earn only a behind. Melbourne squeaked home, 7.3 (45) to 5.13 (43).

All of a sudden the momentum was with Melbourne, and as underdogs they had earned the adulation of the football fraternity. The Grand Final was eagerly anticipated, and the League suddenly found it had the biggest crowd imaginable. Essendon's sudden demise, if unfair, certainly got the turnstiles clicking. Could the upstart Fuchsias go all the way?

The Grand Final between Fitzroy and Melbourne was a closely fought affair. 'Old Boy' (R.W.E. Wilmot) reported on the match in *The Argus* on the following Monday. "Twenty thousand people, who contributed nearly £500 at the gates, assembled on the East Melbourne Cricket Ground to witness the final contest for the premiership of the season 1900, and for well-nigh two hours the large crowd was stirred to enthusiasm by magnificent play, the earnestness of the players, and by the fact that to the ringing of the final bell the issue was in doubt.

"Fitzroy got the first goal, several minutes into the first quarter: A beautiful mark, the forerunner of many more of the same nature, by [Mick] Grace resulted in [Lou] Barker putting up a behind, and a moment later he raised the two flags and a tremendous cheer with another running shot."

Melbourne's first goal came a bit later, with the newspaper reporting, "Then came Melbourne's turn, Leith, with a wonderful mark, putting up [posting] their first goal, and high marking by Grace and [captain Alec] Sloan were prominent features."

One of the features of the match that pleased 'Old Boy' was the close-in work of some of the players. "Parkin was clearing the Melbourne goal well, and three clean half-distance marks between Herring, Wardill, and McGinis took the ball up the centre. McGinis had his shot, and [Geoff] Moriarty stopped it right in goal. Ryan pounced for the ball, and as it dropped, working and turning cleverly, he got between Moriarty and [Bert] Sharpe, and tipped it between the posts. It was a clever bit of work, and Melbourne people cheered Ryan for his cleverness as well as for their second goal."

At quarter-time, Melbourne led by five points. Continued 'Old Boy': "As soon as the teams changed ends Beacham [Tammy Beauchamp] forwarded, and Grace again marked grandly, and dropped [kicked] a goal. The play was all over the ground, and every man was doing his utmost. [Hugh] McEwan and [John Henry Kelly] Robinson relieved their goal, only to find two rushes by Purse bringing the ball back to them again. Fitzroy were having if anything the best of it at this stage, and there was no sparing of friend or foe. The defenders on both sides were very much in evidence…

At half time, Fitzroy had edged to a two-point lead. "Melbourne began very strongly after the interval, Leith and McGinis interchanging unselfishly, and Wardill, with a clever turn, just missed a goal. A few minutes later he repeated the turn, but made no mistake in direction this time, and the two flags waved again. Jenkins's relief saved Fitzroy, and Grace and Kiernan working cleverly Melbourne were hard put to it, but the backs, headed by Langley, beat them off again and again. There was a great struggle down in the right-hand corner of Melbourne's defence for a while, until McGinis kicked right across his goal, hoping for Sholl to get the ball on a clear run. Sholl was slow in starting though, and the ball went out."

'Old Boy' then wrote that Melbourne's fortunes improved when play was switched to the opposite wing. "Geddes was pushed, and a fine drop-kick put up fourth goal and Melbourne, with the premiership—which had been denied to them for 24 long years—well within their reach, were delighted. Langley again relieved the pressure and Wardill and Hay gave Ryan a chance, which Moriarty just saved. It was a wonderfully fast game. Then for nearly a quarter of an hour Melbourne had to fight for dear life down in the corner on the Jolimont wing. Fitzroy were playing magnificent football, but they could not break through. The Melbourne backs, Purse and Langley in particular, together with the ruck, defied all opposition, and time and again drove the maroons back. Up and down the wing the battle raced, neither side flinching, though the knocks were hard and the falls numerous. Fitzroy were fighting for a goal, and a premiership was in the balance, but the quarter ended with no alteration."

By three-quarter time, Melbourne had regained the lead by 13 points, having kept Fitzroy scoreless in the third term.

"When they changed ends, and the last 25 minutes of the 1900 season had begun, Melbourne led by 13 points, and the Fitzroy people thought that Melbourne's efforts in the third quarter would have told a tale, but Wardill began by attacking and at no time during the quarter did they look like breaking up. For a long while Melbourne held the maroons back, and Rippon and Gardner with nice runs, put Fitzroy on the defensive. Beecham lashed forward, and Sholl relieved, but [Chris] Kiernan and Grace added behinds."

Sholl's afternoon was not improving—Fitzroy's Kiernan picked off an errant kick-out—luckily his resulting kick missed the goal. But Melbourne switched its full-back, as 'Old Boy' wrote. "Geddes took Sholl's place and from his kick Young, Hay, Leith and Ryan worked it down to Cumberland who got Melbourne's 9th behind. Fitzroy were pressing hard forward, [Henry] Clarke and Robinson in the lead, but Langley, Herring, and Wardill were full of go and Moodie and McGinis were working like tigers. [William] McSpeerin added another behind. A fine mark to McClelland turned the tide once more, and magnificent play by McGinis sent the ball to Leith. In the excitement Sloan threw McGinis heavily, and the crowd cried "Oh!" but in such a finish one cannot be carping and Fitzroy were taking their gruel like men. They were defending their goal fiercely, but Wardill scored another behind before [Pat] Hickey with fine dash sent the ball to Grace, and with only four minutes to play the third goal appeared for Fitzroy."

The closing minutes were tense: "Then came a desperate four minutes. Hickey was working as if his life depended on the issue, and every man on the side threw his weight into the scale, but Gardner, Rippon, Herring, Parkin, and Sholl, in turn, forced back the rushes, until Barker with a running shot put on a behind. Almost immediately the bell rang, and Melbourne were the winners of the match and the premiership…" concluded 'Old Boy'.

Melbourne had held off a faster finishing Fitzroy to win by four points, earning the club its first premiership and denying the Maroons their third consecutive pennant.

Such was Fitzroy's confidence the club had prepared special carriages, festooned in maroon and blue with banners that read, 'Fitzroy—Premiers 1900', to be waiting outside the East Melbourne Cricket Ground to ferry the players off to a triumphant premiership dance. Melbourne's expectations were, on the other hand, so low that its players had no social event awaiting them. In their rooms after the match they were thronged by well-wishers, including the one of the founders of the Melbourne Football Club, H. C. A. Harrison. (In one of life's happy results, Harrison was also there to celebrate in the rooms after the 1926 grand final.)

The League responded quickly to the upset of 1900 by abandoning the sectional finals system in favour of the Final Four, the so-called '*Argus* system' that to this day enshrines the principle that the minor premiers should have a second chance if knocked out in the first week of the finals.

By 1905 Melbourne had won the wooden spoon, a dubious prize it would win again in 1906. This confirmed that the triumph of 1900 was a great fluke. The club would not return to finals football until 1915, 1925, and (significantly) 1926.

In terms of their later careers, this team can be divided neatly in two between those who went on to win fame and fortune in Australia and those who fell from the limelight. Among the former group, at least four of the players from the 1900 side met untimely deaths. Dan Moriarty died in a railway accident in 1903. Eric Gardner died in Sweden in 1905. William Bowe retired from senior football in 1906 and died at Corowa in 1920. Cumberland was killed in a motorcycle accident at Brighton in 1927. Several tried their luck overseas. Two of the men—Corrie Gardner and Ced Hay—travelled to Canada, the latter settling there. The Tasmanian, Fred McGinis, disappeared from view, but his name appears as a migratory worker in New Jersey in 1930. Austin Lewis went to Wales, dying in Cardiff at the age of 81.

In the second group, there were other players who continued to do well. Stewie Geddes got married in Adelaide in 1910, lived for a while in Coburg West, and died at the age of 72 in Traralgon in Victoria's Gippsland region. Harry Graham settled in leafy South Yarra and Harold Hay in equally glamorous Elsternwick. After Maurie Herring moved to Brisbane to manage its main newspaper he lived to the age of 82, passing away in Queensland in 1962. John Leith, originally from Geelong, lived in Malvern, while McClelland (who never married) continued to run his Brighton medical practice while presiding over the League. McGuigan's boot factory must have prospered, as he ended up in Williams Road, Toorak, and Pirrie, the produce merchant, finished up in Kinkora Road, Hawthorn. Dick Wardill and Charles Young lived respectively in South Yarra and Brighton.

For these men the 1900 premiership win was but one of several personal achievements registered in busy and productive lives. But their pedigree was commercial rather than athletic, for very few of them belonged to football families.

1900 will be remembered in football annals as a fluke year, when chance played a major part. If Condon had been better behaved, Collingwood stood a chance. If Essendon had not dropped some easy mid-season matches with key players absent, it might have challenged Fitzroy for the minor premiership. And, most brutally, if Fitzroy's right as minor premiers to have a second chance of defending its title already existed in the VFL rulebook its name rather than Melbourne's would have been inscribed against the year '1900'.

1900 MELBOURNE

PREMIER'S SEASON

MELBOURNE: 1900

ROUND ONE May 5
MELBOURNE	9.13 (67)
ST KILDA	10.8 (68)

Best: Melbourne – Cumberland, McClelland, Purse, Rippon, Wardill.
Goals: Melbourne – Pirrie 2, Ryan 2, Cumberland 2, McGinis, Langley, Sowden.
Crowd: N/A at the Junction Oval

ROUND TWO May 12
MELBOURNE	5.4 (34)
ESSENDON	2.6 (18)

Best: Melbourne – Geddes, Leith, Moodie, Parkin, Young.
Goals: Melbourne – Adams 2, Langley, Young, Wardill.
Crowd: N/A at the MCG

ROUND THREE August 18
MELBOURNE	3.4 (22)
CARLTON	6.6 (42)

Best: Melbourne – E.Gardner, Leith, Purse, Rippon, Wardill.
Goals: Melbourne – Ryan 2, Riggall.
Crowd: N/A at Princes Park

ROUND FOUR May 24
MELBOURNE	2.3 (15)
GEELONG	11.15 (81)

Best: Melbourne – Langley, Cumberland, McClelland, Sholl.
Goals: Melbourne – Langley 2.
Crowd: N/A at Corio Oval

ROUND FIVE May 26
MELBOURNE	3.9 (27)
FITZROY	10.6 (66)

Best: Melbourne – Cumberland, Lewis, Moodie, Wardill.
Goals: Melbourne – Sowden, Ryan, Wardill.
Crowd: N/A at the MCG

ROUND SIX June 2
MELBOURNE	6.5 (41)
SOUTH MELBOURNE	6.8 (44)

Best: Melbourne – Ryan, Geddes, Langley, Wardill, Young.
Goals: Melbourne – Ryan 3, Langley 2, Wardill.
Crowd: N/A at the Lake Oval

ROUND SEVEN June 9
MELBOURNE	8.18 (66)
COLLINGWOOD	5.7 (37)

Best: Melbourne – Ryan, Leith, Cumberland, McClelland, Rippon.
Goals: Melbourne – Ryan 2, Lewis, Langley, McGinis, Leith, Cumberland, Wardill.
Crowd: N/A at the MCG

ROUND EIGHT June 23
MELBOURNE	15.18 (108)
ST KILDA	4.5 (29)

Best: Melbourne – Wardill, Ryan, Leith, Cumberland, Geddes.
Goals: Melbourne – Wardill 5, Ryan 4, Leith 3, Adams 2, Sowden.
Crowd: N/A at the MCG

ROUND NINE June 23
MELBOURNE	6.8 (44)
ESSENDON	2.6 (18)

Best: Melbourne – Ryan, Cumberland, Graham, McGinis, Sowden, Wardill.
Goals: Melbourne – Ryan 4, Moodie Graham.
Crowd: N/A at East Melbourne Cricket Ground.

ROUND TEN July 7
MELBOURNE	9.14 (68)
CARLTON	5.3 (33)

Best: Melbourne – E.Gardner, C.Gardner, McGinis, Ryan, Wardill.
Goals: Melbourne – Graham 2, McGinis 2, Moodie, Wardill, Ryan, Leith, E.Gardner.
Crowd: N/A at the MCG.

ROUND ELEVEN July 14
MELBOURNE	4.16 (40)
GEELONG	4.5 (29)

Best: Melbourne – Cumberland, E.Gardner, McGinis, Strahan, Sholl.
Goals: Melbourne – Cumberland 2, E.Gardner 2.
Crowd: N/A at the MCG

ROUND TWELVE July 28
MELBOURNE	4.8 (32)
FITZROY	8.9 (57)

Best: Melbourne – Leith, McGinis, Moriarty, Sowden, Wardill.
Goals: Melbourne – Leith 3, Wardill.
Crowd: N/A at Brunswick St Oval

ROUND THIRTEEN August 4
MELBOURNE	6.8 (44)
SOUTH MELBOURNE	7.6 (48)

Best: Melbourne – Leith, Hay, Young, Byers, Cumberland, Wardill.
Goals: Melbourne – Leith 4, Wardill, E.Gardner.
Crowd: N/A at the MCG

ROUND FOURTEEN August 11
MELBOURNE	7.4 (46)
COLLINGWOOD	10.13 (73)

Best: Melbourne – Langley, Moodie, Leith, Cumberland, McClelland.
Goals: Melbourne – Leith, Moodie, Langley, Wardill.
Crowd: N/A at the MCG

SECTIONAL GAMES

ROUND FIFTEEN August 25
MELBOURNE	5.15 (45)
GEELONG	3.10 (28)

Best: Melbourne – Leith, Cumberland, McGinis, Ryan, Wardill.
Goals: Melbourne – Leith 2, Ryan, Hay, Wardill.
Crowd: N/A at East Melbourne Cricket Ground

ROUND SIXTEEN September 1
MELBOURNE	12.14 (86)
ST KILDA	2.3 (15)

Best: Melbourne – McGinis, Ryan, Cumberland, Lewis, McClelland, Sowden.
Goals: Melbourne – Ryan 3, McGinis 3, Rippon 2, Cumberland, Lewis, Leith, E.Gardner.
Crowd: N/A at the Junction Oval

ROUND SEVENTEEN September 8
MELBOURNE	3.6 (24)
COLLINGWOOD	4.6 (30)

Best: Melbourne – Wardill, Cumberland, McGinis, Purse, Sowden.
Goals: Melbourne – McGinis, Wardill, Hay.
Crowd: N/A at the Lake Oval

PREMIER'S FINALS

PRELIMINARY FINAL September 15
MELBOURNE 7.3 (45)
ESSENDON 5.13 (43)
Best: Melbourne – Wardill, Sowden, Young, Cumberland, Moodie, McGinis.
Goals: Melbourne – Wardill 3, McGinis 2, Cumberland, Leith.
Crowd: 16,000 at the Lake Oval

GRAND FINAL September 22
MELBOURNE 2.3 2.5 4.8 4.10 (34)
FITZROY 1.4 2.7 2.7 3.12 (30)
Best: Melbourne – Cumberland, Langley, McGinis, Moodie, Purse, Wardill.
Goals: Melbourne – Geddes, Leith, Ryan, Wardill.
Crowd: 20,181 at East Melbourne Cricket Ground

GRAND FINAL LINE-UPS

MELB	B:	M.Herring	E.Sholl	L.Rippon
FITZ	F:	P.Descrimes	G.Brosnan	C.Kiernan
MELB	HB:	H.Parkin	J.Purse	B.McClelland
FITZ	HF:	T.Beauchamp	A.McDougall	L.Barker
MELB	C:	C.Gardner	C.Young	H.Hay
FITZ	C:	E.Drohan	H.Clarke	K.Robinson
MELB	HF:	A.Lewis	J.Leith	F.Langley
FITZ	HB:	B.Sharpe	A.Sloan (capt)	P.Hickey
MELB	F:	D.Wardill (capt)	S.Geddes	T.Ryan
FITZ	B:	H.McEwen	G.Moriarty	E.Jenkins
MELB	R:	G.Moodie	V.Cumberland	F.McGinis
FITZ	R:	M.Grace	B.Potter	B.McSpeerin

SNAPSHOT

Win-loss record: 10-9
Highest score: 15.18 (108), round 8, v St Kilda.
Greatest winning margin: 79 points, round 8, v St Kilda.
Lowest score: 2.3 (15), round 4, v Geelong.
Greatest losing margin: 66 points, round 4, v Geelong.
Most goals by a player in a game: 5, Dick Wardill, round 8, v St Kilda.
Most consecutive wins: 5
Most consecutive losses: 4
Club awards: Leading goalkicker: Tommy Ryan (24 goals).
Putting it into perspective: In winning its first flag, Melbourne ended Fitzroy's early domination of the competition and thwarted the Maroons' hopes of three consecutive Grand Final victories. Melbourne also won the first and only Grand Final at the East Melbourne Cricket Ground.

1900

	P	W	L	D	%	Pts
1 Fitzroy	14	11	3	0	168.0	44
2 Geelong	14	9	5	0	150.9	36
3 Essendon	14	8	6	0	137.3	32
4 Collingwood	14	8	6	0	116.1	32
5 South Melb	14	8	6	0	90.4	32
6 Melbourne	14	6	8	0	101.7	24
7 Carlton	14	5	9	0	70.6	20
8 St Kilda	14	1	13	0	39.1	4

(14 home and away rounds)

Section A Ladder

	P	W	L	D	%	Pts
1 Essendon	3	3	0	0	296.9	12
2 Fitzroy	3	2	1	0	158.8	8
3 Carlton	3	1	2	0	41.1	4
4 South Melb	3	0	3	0	48.9	0

Section B Ladder

	P	W	L	D	%	Pts
1 Melbourne	3	2	1	0	212.3	8
2 Collingwood	3	2	1	0	167.5	8
3 Geelong	3	2	1	0	112.2	8
4 St Kilda	3	0	3	0	29.9	0

PLAYERS USED

MELBOURNE	GAMES	GOALS
Adams, Ernie	6	4
Bowe, Bill	1	0
Byers, Eddie	7	0
Cumberland, Vic	18	7
Gardner, Corrie	16	0
Gardner, Eric	8	5
Geddes, Stewart	18	1
Graham, Harry	2	3
Hay, Ced	1	0
Hay, Harold	7	2
Herring, Maurie	2	0
Langley, Frank	18	9
Leith, Jack	17	19
Lewis, Austin	16	2
McClelland, Bill	13	0
McCulloch, Bill	1	0
McGinis, Fred	18	10
McGuigan, Bryan	2	0
Moodie, George	18	4
Moriarty, Dan	13	0
Parkin, Harry	16	0
Pirrie, Dick	4	2
Purse, Jack	18	0
Riggall, Harold	1	1
Rippon, Les	17	2
Ryan, Tommy	17	24
Sholl, Eddie	12	0
Sowden, Arthur	17	3
Strahan, Dave	5	0
Wardill, Dick	17	19
Young, Charlie H.	16	1

ESSENDON 6.7 (43) d
COLLINGWOOD 2.4 (16)

HE COULD DO ANYTHING

Albert Thurgood was the first true superstar of League football. All that was missing was his name on a premiership honour roll. By EMMA QUAYLE

ALBERT Thurgood had a simple nickname. People used to call him 'The Great'. Reports of the day suggest he could place kick the ball more than 100 yards, and thump his drop punts just as far. After he played, people would run onto the ground to measure exactly how far his kicks had gone. He was tall for the day—about six feet, or 182 centimetres—but graceful, strong and too quick for most opponents to catch. Aged just 18, he kicked 56 goals for Essendon in his first VFA season in 1892 and he kicked multiple goals at a time when whole teams couldn't muster many. He could also play at centre half-back, in the ruck or on a wing—wherever his Essendon team most needed him.

Thurgood was aggressive and assured. He would set himself apart from the players on his side while simultaneously dragging his teammates along with him, and he was a player who people loved to watch. "He was of gigantic proportions," explained *The Sporting Globe*. "A lovely high mark, he leapt like a kangaroo. He was constructed for pre-eminence in football."

Thurgood had done everything. Almost. Yes, he had led Essendon to four straight VFA premierships in the early 1890s. Yes, he was the club's first champion player, and possibly Australian football's first true star. He had shocked Essendon by moving to the Kalgoorlie goldfields at the end of 1894, straight after that fourth VFA flag, but he only enhanced his reputation in

Western Australia, topping the West Australian league's goalkicking for three years in a row while playing for Fremantle, a long-defunct club that was an inspiration, but nothing more, for the AFL club founded in 1995.

The one place he hadn't really starred, though, was in the new, eight-team Victorian Football League. Returning to Melbourne in 1898, Thurgood wasn't able to slot straight back into a red and black guernsey; for residential reasons, the VFL insisted he sit out the year. He played just one game in 1899 and only 11 the next year, kicking 25 goals to top the League's goalkicking but he never quite looked his old self. He was, noted his former captain Alick Dick, heavier than he had been before heading west. He had lost a little pace, and was perhaps not playing with the energy and eagerness he had started out with. He had just turned 27. Thurgood still had things to prove and as the 1901 season began Essendon needed him to start proving them.

Since winning the 1897 premiership—the VFL's first—the Same Olds hadn't quite been good enough to do it again. They hadn't actually even won a Grand Final, with that first title decided through a round-robin style finals series at the end of a 14-week season, rather than in a final play-off to settle matters. Essendon made the 1898 Grand Final, as a new finals system kicked in, but lost by 15 points to a Fitzroy side filled with small, quick runners, and then followed up with a poor 1899. Vice-captain George Kearney moved to Scotland to continue his medical studies, while goalsneak Norman Waugh shifted to South Africa, where two other teammates were fighting in the Boer War.

Thurgood in 1899 played just the one match and Essendon struggled to score without him. Opposition defenders, not preoccupied by his presence, began to run free. The only real positives were the emergence of Billy Griffith, a skilful wingman who, at just 16, looked like he would be around for a while, and the brighter start to 1900 that followed.[1] Essendon notched some strong early wins, dropped five games during a long mid-season slump, but recovered and finished third after four late victories. They did it despite a badly timed run of injuries: in one late-season game, with his side one man down, club secretary Bill Crebbin, a former player, joined in midway through the first quarter. Funnily enough, after four years on the sidelines the small, nuggety centreman with the mop of curly hair and an odd reputation for being ticklish, played well.

The eight teams were split into two divisions in the first phase of the 1900 finals. Essendon beat South Melbourne and Carlton to win its section and then faced Melbourne—which had finished the home and away season in sixth

---

1 He did stick around, playing 187 games before retiring in 1913. He played in five Grand Finals for three premierships.

spot but found some late form—in one of two semi-finals. The Same Olds were widely tipped to win through to the Grand Final, but lost their way when Bill 'Newhaven' Jackson hurt his knee, leaving the team with just 17 fit players. Melbourne kicked three quick goals before Essendon settled down, and the Same Olds then wasted several second term chances to get back into the game. They did the same thing in a brilliant, attacking final quarter, but one goal from eight scoring shots was not enough to rein in the Melbourne lead. The Redlegs held on by two points, continuing on to beat Fitzroy in a close grand final. Having finished on top of the home-and-away ladder, the Maroons had held the right to challenge them to a decider.

So close, so far, yet Essendon was well placed heading into 1901. Jackson's injury had forced the bulky, aggressive 28-year-old into retirement, and several other players had also moved on. Full-back Gus 'Ned' Officer, a member of the successful 1897 team, had already moved to Perth to pursue his work as a doctor, while Joe Groves, a clever, crafty wingman, had left the club to play with VFA club Footscray and rover Alex Hall had moved on as well. He would become better known as Hawthorn's first League coach in 1925.

In their place were a few new, local youngsters. Bill Robinson was 20, a naturally gifted ruckman destined to take Jackson's place. Another arrival, Jack McKenzie, was considered tall for a rover at 178 centimetres, and soon showed his teammates that he was as hardworking and determined as he was creative and artistic. In 1901, he and his pinpoint skills slipped straight into the Same Olds' forward set-up, where he made a quick impression. "He was an extremely brilliant and consistent performer, for his marking and passing were perfect," noted an *The Australasian*. "His shooting for goal was so accurate that he scarcely missed one possible scoring chance."

Entering his third season, Griffith was still a teenager, hitting his straps as the team's feisty, strong-willed rover. Hercules Vollugi—Herc—was also 19, a quick, tough wingman, who would later play out a game with 16 stitches in a head wound. Also a talented baseballer, he would often play a baseball game as a curtain-raiser to his VFL duties, racing inside afterwards to get changed into his football gear. Officials were also optimistic that Fred Hiskins, who had made a promising four-game debut at the end of the 1900 season, his nine goals including a four-goal haul against Carlton, would be better again, and that the youngsters would complement the remaining members of the successful 1897 side still young enough to do it again.

At 30, George Stuckey, skipper in 1897, was still playing well enough to fill a forward pocket role. He had handed the captaincy to George 'Tod' Collins, who turned 25 just before the season started and, entering his fourth season, was known to bewilder opposition sides with his high marking in defence. Collins' brother Maurie, who was injured during the '97 finals but had missed just two games since, filled another spot in the backline, alongside rover Edward 'Son' Barry. Belfast-born wingman George Hastings, was still just 24, as was Leopold recruit Fred Mann, who hadn't yet made his debut but looked capable of playing as a small defender, to a team that also contained a number of reliable veterans. One, Stuckey, was entering his second-last season. Another, Jim Anderson, was a cool, dependable backman and a third, Herbert 'Harry' Wright, was also entering the last few years of his 89-game career. A midfielder who played in the '97 side and had kept wicket for Victoria in three first-class cricket matches, Wright was turning 31 entering the '01 season.

Then there were the stars. One, Thurgood, was training well. At 27, he was now in great physical shape, while the emergence of the other, 22-year-old defender Hugh Gavin, had officials feeling hopeful Albert the Great would be able to spend most, if not every week, at the other end of the ground. Gavin was determined and resilient, another baby-faced member of the 1897 side who had developed quickly since. One of 13 children—five siblings born before him died in infancy, while another ran away from home—he had an inherent toughness, too. He had started out as a forward, making his debut two rounds into '97, but Officer's move to Perth had seen him switched to defence, where it was correctly hoped his marking, judgment and edgy attitude would be better suited. He was the man who kept things together, the "trusty sentinel," as one observer wrote.

It took a while, though, for Essendon to piece together its best line-up. Injury and patchy form saw the Same Olds make an inconsistent start to the 14-game season. With Geelong and Collingwood leading the way early, Essendon began with a 43-point loss to the Magpies and dropped three of the first four matches. Thurgood was still reaching for his best form and others were struggling as much, although there were some encouraging signs. Although Geelong held firm at the top of the ladder, Essendon's defence was the toughest to penetrate, conceding fewer points than any other side. With Carlton and St Kilda never in contention, South Melbourne mixing some unexpected wins with disappointing losses, Melbourne's side wracked by injury from day one and Collingwood enduring a tough late run despite the impressive form of centreman Fred Leach, a run of six wins from seven games had Essendon back near the top of the ladder by the middle of the year, and another six-win run saw the Same Olds finish the home and away season third, two games behind Geelong, one behind the Magpies and in what many considered the most imposing form.

That was how the finals played out, much to Geelong's unhappiness. After comfortable wins over Carlton, South Melbourne and Essendon in the three-round "sectional finals," the Pivotonians were then beaten by three goals in their semi-final clash with Collingwood, a loss that saw them fall straight out of the finals race. Ordinarily, Geelong would have then been able to challenge the last team standing out of Collingwood, Essendon and Fitzroy to a 'grand final,' as Fitzroy had done to Melbourne one year earlier, but that opportunity had been removed, prompting much debate in the press. "The system under which the premiership was decided has been the subject of much comment, and though the Geelong Club, which won the greatest number of games in the preliminary matches, was put out of the competition before the final, it must be said that interest was maintained right to the very end, and no club could afford to lose a match," wrote *The Argus*, of a season it considered the closest and most competitive it had seen. *The Age* was far less satisfied. "As to the method under which the premiership has been decided," it declared, "although not so bad as last year, it is inequitable and therefore unsatisfactory."

Essendon faced Fitzroy in its semi-final, in front of more than 10,000 people at Victoria Park, and despite having lost the brave, pacy Vollugi to injury the Same Olds were widely tipped to win. Gavin had put together a brilliant season at centre half-back, marshalling the miserly defence, and Thurgood had found some threatening form, forming an excellent combination with Ted Kinnear who, after kicking a combined five goals in his first four seasons, scored 16 in 1901. Veteran half-forward flanker Jimmy Larkin's 17 goals had included a bag of five against Carlton, and the rapidly improving Hiskins had proved another dangerous prong in the forward set-up. The 22-year-old had picked up where he had finished 1900, kicking 34 goals to win the League's goalkicking award in just his second season. He and Thurgood combined for 55 goals, a tally that could have been much higher had Hiskins' two goals against South Melbourne in an early game not been accompanied by 10 behinds.

Fitzroy also took a strong side in and with three quick first-quarter goals were playing what *The Argus* considered the smarter game. They took a 15-point lead into the first break and looked sharp again at the start of the second term. But then along came Thurgood, who took a "grand high mark" at centre half-forward, booted the ball long towards goal, raced forward to follow up his own kick and, as *The Argus* put it, "put his foot to the ball again as up went the two flags, even tough it is by no means certain that the ball did not hit the post." In fact, Fitzroy players were so sure the ball had grazed the post that the full-back was standing in the goalsquare, ready to kick back in, when the ball was called back to the centre square. Even Thurgood's teammates were surprised at the goal umpire's call. "When the two flags went up we stood transfixed with astonishment," wrote Ted Kinnear years later. "Then caps went into the air."

It was the most controversial goal of Thurgood's illustrious career, but his form was not fleeting. In a very fast game, Essendon whittled the Fitzroy lead down by half-time, then held on for a four-point win, with Thurgood kicking five of the team's six goals before shepherding a Larkin shot through for the final goal of the afternoon. He even played alternate quarters in defence, to help his side out as it kicked against the wind, and also spent some time in the ruck. Stuckey, Griffith, Gavin, Kinnear, Wright and Hiskins were among Essendon's best but Thurgood's game was, many agreed, one of the most brilliant individual performances in the League's brief history. "On the whole, honours were fairly divided, but Thurgood's goalkicking, which quite equalled his best form of a few seasons back, was superb," reported *The Age*, of Essendon's 6.10 (46) to 6.9 (45) win. "In force and accuracy, it was well nigh perfect, and while he was, of course, well 'fed', he must be credited with obtaining most of his opportunities by grand high marking, as well as using them to the best advantage, for it need not be said that the other side made every legitimate attempt to stop him."

The Grand Final was played the following Saturday against Collingwood, on a fine but windy afternoon at the South Melbourne ground. Vollugi had overcome his injury problems and was rushed back into the side along with back pocket Fred Mann, the pair's inclusion meaning that Michael Pepperd and James Kennedy, who had played in 16 of the 18 games, missed out. Kennedy retired from the VFL and joined Brighton the following year, his Essendon career confined to that one, nine-goal season.

Again, Essendon was favoured to win. Vollugi's return was a major factor, although, in Fred Leach, Collingwood boasted one of the game's biggest, most in-form names. The game began at 3pm, but long before then the terraces were filled with people, the crowd of around 25,000 thought to be the biggest yet seen at a VFL game. There were so many there that parts of the fence collapsed early in the day, people instead taking seats along the boundary line. The Essendon players were out on the ground first, and spent more than 15 minutes warming up by kicking two balls around. One of the balls weighed 15 ounces; the other weighed 14. Both were prepared by well-known local saddler Tom W. Sherrin and, at the end of their short kick-around, the Same Olds decided, due to wind, that they would use the heavier version. "The balls were made of the best cowhide," began *The Argus's* match report, "double-tanned and cut from the heart of the skin. Although Mr Sherrin is a member of the Collingwood committee, the Essendon men were quite prepared to play with the ball, which gave every satisfaction."

This time, the Same Olds made the stronger start. Kicking against the strong south-westerly, they peppered their goals but struggled to score. With Collingwood defender Lawrence 'Lardie' Tulloch keeping Thurgood under reasonable control—and despite losing veteran Bill Proudfoot to a foot injury early—the persistent Magpies took control of the play and began to attack, peppering their forward line. In doing so, though, they inadvertently brought the brilliant Gavin into the game, a high, pressured mark in defence the first of many for the afternoon, and his ability to impose himself helping bring such teammates as Mann, Vollugi and Stuckey into the play. Kinnear got busy, so did Thurgood, and by the end of the first quarter Essendon had kicked three goals to Collingwood's one behind, a commanding lead at the end of a tough, competitive and, as *The Argus* report put it, "not too gentle" opening term.

The Same Olds didn't relent. Scoring two more goals at the start of the second term they stretched their lead, but Collingwood was not completely done with. After Essendon missed two shots for goal shortly after half-time, quick, consecutive goals to Bob Bryce narrowed the gap. Collins left the ground injured and, forced to send Thurgood down back to cover for him, the Same Olds looked wobbly for the first time all afternoon. By three-quarter-time the Magpies were back to within three goals, but that wasn't quite close enough. As *The Argus* explained: "In the final term it was plain both sides had had enough. They had battled with each other and the breeze, and they had taken all the bumps inseparable from such a contest and now the work was telling its tale." Thurgood kicked his third goal, Gavin took another spectacular mark and Essendon secured its second premiership in four years with a 27-point win, 6.7 (43) to Collingwood's 2.4 (16). "There was little more in it," wrote *The Argus*, but for two dashes down the wing: one by Vollugi and the second by Collingwood half-back flanker Oscar Hyman. "After the game Hyman was proud of that run," reported the newspaper, "and, as he asked if it were not the best of the day, he added 'Oh, give us something. You've won the premiership, let us have the run of the day.'" The teams finished the day together: in the local skittles alley.

Without Gavin's "wonderful high marking, his vigour and his dash," concluded *The Argus*, Essendon would have struggled to hold on. Without Kinnear, Barry, McKenzie, Larkin, Griffith and centreman Wright, whose brilliant effort on Leach saw the Collingwood star play "far below his usual state of usefulness," they might not have won. Without defenders Hyman and George Dow hanging so tough for Collingwood, the Same Olds would not have had to work so hard. It was a tough match, fought until all players were exhausted, and even the umpire, Ivo Crapp, was praised in the press for his performance. "There is little in the game that one would wish to forget, and every man be proud of having played in it," concluded *The Argus*, in no doubt that, on this day, Thurgood had cemented his champion status.

Essendon fell into shock early in 1902 when, despite the vehement objections of Thurgood, he was found guilty of striking two St Kilda players in the same game, and suspended for three games. He was the first Essendon player to miss matches through suspension. Aggrieved, his teammates at first refused to play without him, and in the rooms before the first match he was due to miss they still didn't want to run out. Eventually they did, but only after gathering to give their "disqualified comrade," as *The Australasian* described Thurgood, "three rousing cheers".

It was Thurgood's performance much later in the year, though, that brought his brilliant career to what seemed like a screeching end. He had pieced together yet another good season, topping the Essendon goalkicking tally for the eighth time, and he was again at the heart of the club's hopes leading into September. In the Grand Final, though, he was double teamed, and subdued from start to finish. The crowd was stunned and so was the press. "The Grand Final involved the toppling of Albert Thurgood from his pedestal," declared the *Essendon Gazette*, and the club was confused.

Wondering how their champion could possibly have been so bad, some at Essendon concluded that he must, surely, have been paid by Collingwood to play with minimal energy. Although Thurgood's bank accounts were investigated, and he was cleared, neither party was happy with each other. Essendon cut Thurgood from its list ahead of the 1903 season and refused to clear him to Collingwood, forcing him to sit out of the game once again. Eventually he came back; three years later, beset by injury, the Same Olds welcomed Thurgood into their round seven side and the forward donated his £50 fee to the Melbourne Hospital as a gesture of his willingness to do his best for the club once again. By then, though, he was 32, with just one last season left in him.

At the time, Thurgood seemed to personify how quickly a talented, determined team fractured and fell. Almost 100 years later—75 years after his death in 1927 in a car accident aged only 53—Essendon celebrated its 25 greatest ever players. He was No. 9 on the list.

1901 ESSENDON

PREMIER'S SEASON

ESSENDON: 1901

ROUND ONE May 4
ESSENDON	1.15 (21)
COLLINGWOOD	9.10 (64)

Best: Essendon – Scott, Barry, Hiskins, Kinnear, Ward.
Goals: Essendon – Scott.
Crowd: N/A at East Melbourne Cricket Ground

ROUND TWO May 9
ESSENDON	9.14 (68)
ST KILDA	3.1 (19)

Best: Essendon – T.Collins, M.Collins, Larkin, Scott, Stuckey.
Goals: Essendon – Larkin 2, Scott, Kennedy, Cleghorn, Martin, Hiskins, O'Loughlin, Griffith.
Crowd: N/A at the Junction Oval

ROUND THREE May 11
ESSENDON	6.8 (44)
FITZROY	7.5 (47)

Best: Essendon – Hiskins, Martin, O'Loughlin, Stuckey, Vollugi.
Goals: Essendon – Hiskins 5, White.
Crowd: N/A at East Melbourne Cricket Ground

ROUND FOUR May 18
ESSENDON	4.6 (30)
GEELONG	4.10 (34)

Best: Essendon – Forbes, Hastings, Larkin, White, Wright.
Goals: Essendon – Kinnear, Hastings, Larkin, White.
Crowd: N/A at Corio Oval

ROUND FIVE May 25
ESSENDON	7.8 (50)
MELBOURNE	3.6 (24)

Best: Essendon – Hiskins, Larkin, Anderson, T.Collins, Thurgood, Wright.
Goals: Essendon – Larkin 2, Hiskins 2, Martin, Hastings, Robinson.
Crowd: N/A at East Melbourne Cricket Ground

ROUND SIX June 1
ESSENDON	3.23 (41)
SOUTH MELBOURNE	5.5 (35)

Best: Essendon – Hiskins, M.Collins, T.Collins, Robinson, Thurgood, Wright.
Goals: Essendon – Hiskins 2, Robinson.
Crowd: N/A at the Lake Oval

ROUND SEVEN June 3
ESSENDON	15.15 (105)
CARLTON	3.7 (25)

Best: Essendon – Larkin, Hiskins, Kinnear, Forbes, Stuckey, Anderson.
Goals: Essendon – Larkin 5, Hiskins 4, McKenzie 2, Kinnear 2, Robinson, White.
Crowd: N/A at East Melbourne Cricket Ground

ROUND EIGHT June 8
ESSENDON	7.6 (48)
COLLINGWOOD	7.7 (49)

Best: Essendon – Barry, T.Collins, Kinnear, Larkin, Stuckey, Thurgood.
Goals: Essendon – Kinnear 2, Larkin 2, Barry, Hiskins, McKenzie.
Crowd: N/A at Victoria Park

ROUND NINE June 22
ESSENDON	19.22 (136)
ST KILDA	4.5 (29)

Best: Essendon – Hiskins, Hastings, Kinnea, Thurgood, Griffith, Vollugi.
Goals: Essendon – Hiskins 4, Hastings 3, Kinnear 3, Anderson 2, Thurgood 2, M.Collins 2, Robinson, Gavin, Scott.
Crowd: N/A at East Melbourne Cricket Ground

ROUND TEN June 29
ESSENDON	14.8 (92)
FITZROY	6.8 (44)

Best: Essendon – Anderson, Gavin, Hiskins, McKenzie, Scott, Stuckey, Wright.
Goals: Essendon – Hiskins 4, McKenzie 4, Scott 4, Larkin, Griffth.
Crowd: N/A at Brunswick St Oval

ROUND ELEVEN July 6
ESSENDON	6.13 (49)
GEELONG	2.12 (24)

Best: Essendon – T.Collins, Forbes, Hiskins, McKenzie, Wright.
Goals: Essendon – McKenzie 2, Hiskins 2, Larkin, Scott.
Crowd: N/A at East Melbourne Cricket Ground

ROUND TWELVE July 13
ESSENDON	4.9 (33)
MELBOURNE	6.6 (42)

Best: Essendon – Anderson, Hastings, Forbes, Kinear, McKenzie.
Goals: Essendon – Kinnear 2, McKenzie, Griffith.
Crowd: N/A at the MCG

ROUND THIRTEEN July 20
ESSENDON	6.16 (52)
SOUTH MELBOURNE	8.3 (51)

Best: Essendon – M.Collins, Gavin, J.Kennedy, Mann, Vollugi, Wright.
Goals: Essendon – Larkin 2, J.Kennedy, Robinson, Hiskins, Hastings.
Crowd: N/A at East Melbourne Cricket Ground

ROUND FOURTEEN July 27
ESSENDON	11.13 (79)
CARLTON	3.2 (20)

Best: Essendon – J.Kennedy, T.Collins, Mann, Robinson, Vollugi, Wright.
Goals: Essendon – J.Kennedy 4, Peppard 2, T.Collins 2, Robinson, M.Collins, McKenzie.
Crowd: N/A at Princes Park

ROUND FIFTEEN August 10
ESSENDON	10.9 (69)
SOUTH MELBOURNE	1.3 (9)

Best: Essendon – Thurgood, Hiskins, Anderson, M.Collins, Man, Martin.
Goals: Essendon – Thurgood 5, Hiskins 2, McKenzie 2, Barry.
Crowd: N/A at the Lake Oval

ROUND SIXTEEN August 17
ESSENDON	14.18 (102)
CARLTON	5.3 (33)

Best: Essendon – Kinnear, Hiskins, J.Kennedy, Man, Robinson Thurgood.
Goals: Essendon – Kinnear 5, Hiskins 4, J.Kennedy 4, Thurgood.
Crowd: N/A at East Melbourne Cricket Ground

ROUND SEVENTEEN August 24
ESSENDON	9.12 (66)
GEELONG	5.3 (33)

Best: Essendon – Thurgood, Hiskins, Larkin, Mann, Stuckey, Wright.
Goals: Essendon – Thurgood 5, Hiskins 2, Martin, Robinson.
Crowd: N/A at Corio Oval

PREMIER'S FINALS

SEMI-FINAL August 31

ESSENDON	6.10 (46)
FITZROY	6.9 (45)

Best: Essendon – Thurgood, Stuckey, Griffith, Gavin, Kinnear, Wright, Hiskins.
Goals: Essendon – Thurgood 5, Larkin.
Crowd: 15,000 at Victoria Park

GRAND FINAL September 7

ESSENDON	3.0	5.2	5.4	6.7 (43)
COLLINGWOOD	0.1	0.3	2.3	2.4 (16)

Best: Essendon – Gavin, Griffith, Kinnear, McKenzie, Thurgood, Wright.
Goals: Essendon – Stuckey 3, Kinnear, Martin, McKenzie.
Crowd: 30,031 at the Lake Oval

GRAND FINAL LINE-UPS

ESS	B:	F.Mann	J.Anderson	M.Collins
COLL	F:	J.Farrell	A.Smith	L.Morgan
ESS	HB:	S.Barry	H.Gavin	T.Collins (capt)
COLL	HF:	B.Bryce	T.Rowell	A.Leach
ESS	C:	G.Hastings	H.Wright	H.Vollugi
COLL	C:	C.Pannam	F.Leach	P.Martin
ESS	HF:	F.Hiskins	A.Thurgood	J.Larkin
COLL	HB:	O.Hyman	L.Tulloch	B.McCulloch
ESS	F:	G.Martin	T.Kinnear	G.Stuckey
COLL	B:	C.Dow	B.Proudfoot (capt)	A.Dummett
ESS	R:	B.Robinson	J.McKenzie	B.Griffith
COLL	R:	M.Fell	F.Hailwood	A.Boyack

SNAPSHOT

Win-loss record: 14-5

Highest score: 19.22 (136), round 9, v St Kilda.

Greatest winning margin: 107 points, round 9, v St Kilda.

Lowest score: 1.15 (21), round 1, v Collingwood.

Greatest losing margin: 43 points, round 1, v Collingwood.

Most goals by a player in a game: 5, Albert Thurgood, round 15, v South Melbourne; round 17, v Geelong; semi-final, v Fitzroy; Fred Hiskins, round 3, v Fitzroy; Jimmy Larkin, round 7, v Carlton; Ted Kinnear, round 16, v Carlton.

Most consecutive wins: 7

Most consecutive losses: 2

Club awards: Leading goalkicker: Fred Hiskins (34 goals)

Putting it into perspective:
Essendon's second premiership victory following its 1897 win was its first Grand Final win following its loss in 1898;. Essendon joined Fitzroy with two premiership flags to its name.

1901

		P	W	L	D	%	Pts
1	Geelong (3)	17	14	3		142.9	56
2	**Essendon (1)**	17	12	5		186.4	48
3	Collingwood (2)	17	12	5		158.4	48
4	Fitzroy (4)	17	9	7	1	131.7	38
5	Melbourne	17	9	7	1	117.4	38
6	South Melb	17	8	9		99.6	32
7	Carlton	17	2	15		47.0	8
8	St Kilda	17	1	16		32.1	4

(17 home and away rounds)

PLAYERS USED

ESSENDON	GAMES	GOALS
Anderson, Jim	15	2
Barry, Son	16	2
Beasley, Jim	2	0
Byers, Bobby	1	0
Cleghorn, Arthur	1	1
Cochrane, George	1	0
Collins, Maurie	18	3
Collins, Tod	18	2
Evans, Mark	1	0
Forbes, Charlie	5	0
Gavin, Hugh	15	1
Griffith, Billy	17	3
Hastings, George	15	6
Hiskins, Fred	19	34
Kennedy, Jim	3	9
Kennedy, Ted	18	1
Kinnear, Ted	19	16
Larkin, Jimmy	16	17
Mann, Fred	9	0
Martin, George	10	4
McKenzie, Jack	12	14
Morris, Mick	1	0
O'Loughlin, Pat	3	1
Peppard, Mick	17	2
Robinson, Bill	18	7
Scott, Fred	13	8
Stuckey, George	9	0
Thurgood, Albert	10	21
Vollugi, Herc	15	0
Ward, George	1	0
White, Artie	6	3
Wright, Harry	18	0

**COLLINGWOOD 9.6 (60) d
ESSENDON 3.9 (27)**

STAB KICK CUTS THROUGH

A mid-season jaunt to Tasmania proved to be the unlikely inspiration for the first of Collingwood's League premierships. By GLENN McFARLANE

SOME people thought the only thing that Collingwood brought back from its "business holiday" to Tasmania in July 1902 was a collective case of sea-sickness and a few good memories. The reality was that the Magpies returned home with something much more profound. Still, that much was hardly apparent as the players stepped uneasily off the steamer, Coogee, at lunchtime and prepared for the rail journey to Geelong, where the side was scheduled to play later that afternoon. The "Sea-sick Magpies", as *The Argus* called them, had endured a Bass Strait crossing with little respite from the pounding waves. "Most of them had been seasick on the voyage… and the men did not feel much like going straight from the boat to their special train en route to Geelong." After arriving on the dock late, the Collingwood team finally made their way to Corio Oval, more than a little dishevelled, yet ready—inadvertently, at least—to set about changing the way the game was played.

What Collingwood brought back was a system that would help to revolutionise football. It would also prove the catalyst for the club's first VFL premiership achieved two and a half months on from the docking. It would come from the stab kick; a new style of passing that would soon speed up the game and drag it out of the stop-start congestion that had long defined Australian football. It would also give the Magpies a significant advantage over their rivals before other clubs sought to replicate what they were doing. The genesis for this change came in two exhibition matches the club played in Tasmania. So uneven were the teams, and so one-sided were the results, that one of Collingwood's most controversial characters, Dick Condon, began to experiment with short-kicks. A few of this teammates, most notably Charlie Pannam and Ted Rowell, joined in on the fun and tried out a few of Condon's trick passes. That soon transpired into a tactic that the Magpies would make their own.

Condon was a gifted but erratic enigma. He wasn't meant to be the catalyst for a revolution that season. He wasn't even meant to be playing. Condon had been suspended for "life" two years earlier for abusing one of the most respected umpires in the game, H. "Ivo" Crapp, during a game. When a decision went against him, Condon struck back with words that would cost him dearly. He yelled, "Your girl's a bloody whore". It attracted a massive penalty that stood for 18 months before Collingwood convinced the VFL that it was too harsh. He was given a reprieve and returned to football in time for the second match of the 1902 season. Within two months, Condon joined the team for their Tasmanian excursion and set about having some fun, particularly in the Launceston contest. According to Richard Stremski's *Kill for Collingwood,* the opposition was "so weak that Condon toyed with them, kicking low, sharp passes 20 to 25 yards, just beyond their reach, to his teammates." The stab kick had come to life. Football would never be the same again.

The trip to Tasmania was a stunning success. Not only would Condon first use the system that would become a weapon for his team, it also brought about greater camaraderie among the team. *The Herald's* correspondent in Launceston remarked, "The Collingwood players experienced a good time in Tasmania, and thoroughly enjoyed their trip. They have given fine examples of the game, being in every respect far ahead of the best young locals." They were well received in Hobart, being driven to the "beauty spots of the district, and were taken by steamer to Norfolk." But as tranquil as the trip had been on Tasmanian soil, the journey back was a difficult one. *The Herald* summed it up, "As the Coogee was steaming merrily away towards port, (Collingwood) secretary (E.W) Copeland induced Captain Carr to signal for Queenscliff a request that the railway officials should delay the departure of the Geelong train from Melbourne for them. The Coogee thundered up the bay gallantly and on arriving in town, the Woodsmen found that their request had been granted. The train had been kept at the station until 27 minutes to two and arrived in Geelong at eight minutes to three. The team stripped on the journey down, had their rubdown on the train, and were the first team on the field." It was a close call, as they had arrived with just a few minutes to spare for the three-o'clock game. But officials worried that the team that had locked down second spot on the ladder was not ready for action.

One of the team's most important players, tough defender Bill Proudfoot, was considered too ill to take his part. The other players found it hard to get motivated by the game, and owing to their condition, some of them decided to experiment more with Condon's unique pass that had provided amusement down south. It seemed to work, too. Four goals to one in the first term set the standard. It was said in *The Argus* that, "Collingwood, feeling that their condition after a night's buffeting in the Straits might not see them through a hard game, went away with a rush, and soon had a good lead." Geelong fought back hard in the second term and for a period "looked as if they would overhaul the Magpies." But the "travellers" prevailed and ended up winning this game by 40 points. It was an extraordinary effort, given their delicate state, but the use of their new system had played a very important role in the victory.

So, it would, for the remainder of the season. Football had changed, and Collingwood was about to make the most of their cutting-edge advantage. The win over Geelong was the club's fourth in succession. In all, the Magpies would win 11 VFL games in a row heading into the semi-final clash with Fitzroy. This included an 11-point win over Essendon—the team that had beat Collingwood in the previous year's Grand Final—at East Melbourne in round 13, and a 53-point round 16 thrashing of another serious contender, Fitzroy. This Magpies' team was very different to the one that had lost to the 'Same Old' in 1901. Five new players made a mark that season, and would play in the Grand Final—John Allan, George Angus (back from the Boer War), Jack Incoll, Con McCormack and Harry Pears. Condon was almost like a brilliant new recruit himself, back to his best after a year-and-a-half out of the game. And Lawrence 'Lardie' Tulloch was revelling in his new role as captain of the club. Collectively, the Magpies were determined to make amends for their loss of the previous year.

But just as the premiership pennant appeared to be headed to Victoria Park for the first time since joining the new VFL competition in 1897, there was a sudden and sensational shock. The club's most feared rival, Fitzroy, stunned Collingwood in the semi-final by playing, and beating it, at its own game. Clubs were already trying to mirror the Magpies' free-flowing new style and the Maroons did it to perfection that afternoon to win by 16 points. *The Argus* headlined a story with "Checkmating a system". It said, "Collingwood have this year played with such admirable system that they seemed invincible. With a blackboard and a piece of chalk in the dressingroom at Victoria Park they sketched out imaginary moves, as if in a game of chess, and so the men have been working together like machinery... (but) Fitzroy set themselves to break down that system, and 12,000 people can testify to the fact... that they succeeded." Collingwood barrackers hoped this was a once-off. Others were less convinced and wondered if the stab-pass advantage had been wiped out in the space of only two months. Those of that belief were then swayed by Essendon's powerful win over Fitzroy in the next match, by the Same Olds' experienced campaigners, especially brilliant forward Albert Thurgood, and by the previous year's Grand Final win of 27 points.

The anticipation ahead of the 1902 Grand Final—the first time two teams had backed up in successive Grand Finals—was such that 35,202 people crammed through the MCG gates for the match. It was the first Grand Final at the venue, and the success of it meant it would not be the last. At that time, it was the fourth highest crowd in Australian football, just 2000 fewer than the record of 37,200 who watched Essendon-South Melbourne at East Melbourne back in the old VFA days of 1891. *The Herald* described the frenzy of interest that the game held for the city: "All roads led to this lovely enclosure and were moving masses of humanity from about half past two until three o'clock." The only other social event rivalling the Grand Final that afternoon was the arrival of the renowned opera singer Nellie Melba back from Sydney, with "a splendid public reception" coming out to meet her train, and then following her every step of the way on a carriage through the heart of Melbourne.

The Herald tells the story of a football reporter took his young son into the press box shortly before the start of the Grand Final, with a gentle reminder to keep quiet through the game. As they entered, the young child turned his father and said: "Pa, I'm sure Collingwood will win." His father offered a quick reply: "My son, did your mother tell you to barrack for Collingwood today?" The young boy answered: "Yes, Pa." His father chastised him for listening to his mother, and added: "My son, your mother knows nothing about footy." Everyone, it seemed, had an opinion on who would win the clash. Although the public was divided on the outcome, the general consensus of the press was that the more seasoned, more experienced Essendon would prevail. After the semi-final loss to Fitzroy, Collingwood's season remained alive, thanks to the new *Argus* finals system, something that guaranteed the minor premier a challenge game. The year before, such a loss would have seen the club eliminated.

Everything was seemingly in readiness for the season-decider. Football-maker T.W. Sherrin had "manufactured two balls specifically for the game and if the long kicking shown during the day was any indication, then no fault can be made of the balls", according to *The Argus*. But the one thing that wasn't ready was the sore knee that had been plaguing Collingwood's Jack Monohan since the finals clash with Fitzroy. When the Magpies entered the ground first, *The Herald* observed that "their supporters were disappointed at the non-appearance of Monohan; the committee did not care to risk his injured knee." The man who had played in Collingwood's 1896 VFA flag would have to watch this contest from the grandstand. But he would at least play a role. Earlier in the game, Essendon's champion forward Albert Thurgood was causing predictable problems for the Magpie defenders. It was said that, "Monohan's advice was invaluable to Thurgood's watcher." Incoll was Monohan's replacement in the team, but it was 22-year-old McCormack who took his role on the ever-dangerous Thurgood—the most important player on the field—before the Magpies chose to make a switch at half-time.

Collingwood made first use of the wind from the opening, attacking almost from the first bounce. But after only 10 minutes, most of which was spent attacking, Collingwood had managed only two behinds. Then, Rowell "very smartly dashed up, and for the lack of anything better to do, drove the ball between the posts and this raised the first six-pointer for the Magpies, to the infinite joy of the huge flock of Magpie supporters." *The Herald* summed it up, saying: "They (the fans) whooped and whooped and whooped, and in the exuberance of their joy, they even applauded the umpire." This was an interesting point in itself. The man in charge happened to be the man whom Condon had abused two years earlier, Crapp. But that didn't worry the Magpie fans. They seemed happy with the way the game was panning out in the opening term.

Some stout defence from Bill Proudfoot in the last line of defence saved two likely goals. One of those saves was remarkable, according to *The Herald*. It came as "the ball spun straight to the goal, but to the horror of Collingwood supporters, their goal defender Proudfoot had fallen. On went the ball, straight for the posts. Would Proudfoot rise? Essendon thought not, and were cheering. But they ceased and were drowned in applause of the Collingwood party, who yelled out and rejoiced in a sensational piece of work by the prostrate policeman (Proudfoot's vocation), and he punched the ball and saved the situation." *The Argus* called it, "a dramatic incident—the first of many on the day." Thurgood was getting plenty of the ball, but his accuracy in front of goal left a lot to be desired. "The big man was playing finely, but shooting wildly." The previous year's VFL leading goalkicker, Fred Hiskens, kicked the first goal for Essendon "from a free kick (awarded against Bob Rush)… with a beautifully placed kick." It gave them a one-point quarter-time lead.

Collingwood answered with a goal as soon as play resumed. 'Old Boy', from *The Argus,* said it was attained from "a clever run from (Matthew) Fell (who) got the ball to Condon to (Ted) Lockwood to Pears, who, with a nice shot, scored the goal. This was an instance of that clever passing with which the Magpies have been so dangerous." The crowd at this stage "was in an ecstasy of delight and raged like the ocean in a time of storm". But Essendon was not about to be undone. Thurgood made amends for his poor early kicking with a goal after "marking in the crowd, and with a mighty punt made the scores level again". Yet each time the Same Old responded, the Magpies had the answers. Allan, who had been "invincible on the wing" along with Pannam, made the most of some good work from Incoll and Condon further up the field to give Collingwood the lead back. It was acknowledged that, "the game was being played at a tremendous pace." So much so that when Alf 'Rosie' Dummett "slipped down as he kicked, he had not time to get up off his knees before the ball was back to him, and he marked it kneeling." Collingwood held on gamely to a one-point lead at the half-time break.

In the rooms at half-time, Monohan called for a change on Thurgood, nominating Fred Leach as a potential shadow for him. But there was still plenty of action on the field during the long interval. The crowd was so large that hundreds of people spilled onto the arena at the break, squatting at the fence so that they could watch the action and gain some extra room to breathe. The players "began at the same tremendous pace", according to *The Argus*, "and a peanut man was glad to scamper for the boundary" as the play headed rapidly in his direction. "He had been crossing the ground, but there was no room for anyone but the players and the umpire in that oval when such running and tearing was going on." A collision was narrowly avoided.

Rowell scored a second goal in much the same manner as his first, to give the Magpies some breathing space, despite the best intentions of Essendon defender Jack Geggie, who crashed into the post trying to stop it. Then, *The Argus* said: "Essendon's hopes were shattered as Archie Leach and Rowell, after a great mark, passed to (George) Angus, who ran on and scored (a goal)." Collingwood appeared to be the fresher team, though Essendon would not give in. Just before the three-quarter-time bell, the Same Old scored for the first time in the quarter, with a goal to Pat O'Loughlin. The difference was 10 points at the last change.

Essendon had the advantage of the wind in the deciding quarter, but wasted the first seven minutes with some inexplicable inaccuracy. Then "came the turning point", according to *The Argus*. "(Ted) Kennedy, who had been having the worst of his bout with Allan on the wing, beat his man badly by very clever play. He turned and ran like a hare, but, alas for Essendon's hopes, he kicked straight into Fell, who passed to (Fred 'Charger') Hailwood to (Arthur) Leach in front. He quickly passed to (Ted) Lockwood, and Collingwood's sixth goal came easily." It was one of those dramatic moments that had been mentioned earlier.

Then Rowell received a free kick soon after and his third goal would effectively put the issue—and the premiership—beyond doubt. It was said: "He placed the ball, and as it soared in mid-air it looked as though it was going to fail to bridge the distance against the wind. It was a moment of suspense, and as the ball flew towards the goal the Collingwood supporter in the press box yelled, 'It's there. It's there. By heaven, it's there,' and as the Collingwood team rushed to Rowell to grasp his hand, the excited barracker sank back in his seat. 'That settles it,' he gasped. 'They can't catch us now.'" The gap between the teams could not be bridged.

Rowell's performance in this game was outstanding, and ended a season for him that had been extremely tough. His performance against Fitzroy in round four that season had been uncharacteristically poor for such a good player. *The Argus* had described it as "too bad to be true", which gave rise to speculation that he had not tried in the game. Responding to the rumours, the club initially suspended Rowell as it sought reasons for his display. The player wrote a letter of resignation to the committee in which he pleaded his innocence, and wished the club all the best for the future. Then, after speaking to the committee in person, Rowell explained that his performance had been due to two heavy knocks he had received. In Michael Roberts' *A Century of the Best,* it was said the committee agreed to "unanimously accept his explanation and exonerate him from any suspicion of not having used his best endeavours to cause the Collingwood club to win the match." Rowell would return in round nine and would play a major role in the club's premiership success.

Two more goals followed for Collingwood as it put a full stop on the premiership with a strong finish. Both came from Ted Lockwood, "standing out by himself, getting the ball, first from Angus, and then from Condon." As the bell rang for the last time, it saw the scoreboard locked on Collingwood 9.6 (60) to Essendon 3.9 (27) in what was a comprehensive conclusion to the first MCG Grand Final. There were jubilant scenes in the Collingwood camp and among the throng of black and white barrackers in the crowd. 'Old Boy' noted: "The Collingwood men rushed to one another and to their dressingroom, and were met at the gate by their hon. Secretary (Mr E.W. Copeland) with open arms." Amid the celebrations, Essendon's captain Hugh Gavin appeared in the Collingwood rooms "dripping with perspiration... and with all the evidence of the fray still on him" to congratulate the premiers. It was a fine sporting gesture as he acknowledged that the better team had won.

Special praise internally came to Fred Leach, who had quelled Thurgood in the second half. As Rowell recalled in *The Sporting Globe* four decades later: "Leach did great service, keeping Albert from doing much damage... Fred played shoulder to shoulder with Thurgood all day, going for the ball fairly with him, and had by far the better of the duel." Leach would only have six games left in a career—and a life—far too brief. Within six years, he would die from typhoid fever, just a month beyond his 30th birthday.

'Charger' Hailwood was considered one of the best players that afternoon and was suitably carried from the field. Pannam and Allan dominated their wings. Rowell's three goals took his season tally to 33, the most in the VFL that season. But it was hardly about individuals. 'Old Boy' labelled the victory as "a game in which individuality had to give way to combination, and it is safe to say that every man on the winning team did his share." The Magpies had also believed that their fitness had carried them in great stead, thanks to the fine-tuning and early pre-season training sessions arranged by head trainer Wal Lee.

But as much as it was a team effort, and it truly was, one individual came heavily into focus. It wasn't that Dick Condon performed so well in the Grand Final. He was solid more than spectacular. But he had had an outstanding season, and had been the catalyst behind the system and the stab pass that had set Collingwood apart from the rest. He was a key focus of the celebrations. And, presumably, that unnamed pressman who had chastised his young son for selecting the Magpies earlier in the day, left silently amid the Collingwood cacophony.

1902 COLLINGWOOD

PREMIER'S SEASON

COLLINGWOOD: 1902

ROUND ONE May 3
COLLINGWOOD	5.13 (43)
SOUTH MELBOURNE	3.7 (25)

Best: Collingwood – A.Leach, Pears, C.Pannam, Rusch, Tulloch.
Goals: Collingwood – Pears 2, Rowell, Tulloch, Morgan.
Crowd: N/A at the Lake Oval

ROUND TWO May 10
COLLINGWOOD	8.3 (51)
MELBOURNE	4.10 (34)

Best: Collingwood – Rowell, Condon, T.Leach, Lockwood, Tulloch.
Goals: Collingwood – Rowell 3, Lockwood 2, Condon 2, Hailwood.
Crowd: N/A at the MCG

ROUND THREE May 17
COLLINGWOOD	11.15 (81)
GEELONG	3.2 (20)

Best: Collingwood – Rowell, Tulloch, Hailwood, A.Leach, T.Leach.
Goals: Collingwood – Tulloch 3, Rowell 3, C.Pannam, A.Leach, Hailwood, Lockwood, Incoll.
Crowd: N/A at Victoria Park

ROUND FOUR May 24
COLLINGWOOD	3.4 (22)
FITZROY	7.13 (55)

Best: Collingwood – Dummett, Fell, T.Leach, A.Leach, G.Lockwood, Pears.
Goals: Collingwood – G.Lockwood, McCulloch, Pears.
Crowd: N/A at Victoria Park

ROUND FIVE May 31
COLLINGWOOD	5.12 (42)
ST KILDA	5.5 (35)

Best: Collingwood – Condon, Dow, Incoll, Monohan, Tulloch.
Goals: Collingwood – Incoll, T.Lockwood, Monohan, Pears, Tulloch.
Crowd: N/A at the Junction Oval

ROUND SIX June 7
COLLINGWOOD	6.15 (51)
ESSENDON	11.10 (76)

Best: Collingwood – Condon, A.Leach, T.Leach, C.Pannam, Proudfoot.
Goals: Collingwood – T.Lockwood 2, Condon 2, Pears, Smith.
Crowd: N/A at Victoria Park

ROUND SEVEN June 9
COLLINGWOOD	8.11 (59)
CARLTON	3.3 (21)

Best: Collingwood – T.Lockwood, Smith, C.Pannam, Rush, Tulloch.
Goals: Collingwood – T.Lockwood 3, Smith 2, Tullock, Pears, A.Leach.
Crowd: N/A at Victoria Park

ROUND EIGHT June 14
COLLINGWOOD	4.26 (50)
SOUTH MELBOURNE	1.8 (14)

Best: Collingwood – Condon, Fell, G.Lockwood, C.Pannam, Rush, Tame.
Goals: Collingwood – Condon, Fell, T.Lockwood, Smith.
Crowd: N/A at Victoria Park

ROUND NINE June 21
COLLINGWOOD	7.19 (61)
MELBOURNE	4.7 (31)

Best: Collingwood – Rowell, T.Lockwood, C.Pannam, Pears, Smith, Tulloch.
Goals: Collingwood – Rowell 2, T.Lockwood, Smith, Allan, Condon, A.Leach.
Crowd: N/A at Victoria Park

ROUND TEN July 5
COLLINGWOOD	12.12 (84)
GEELONG	6.8 (44)

Best: Collingwood – Condon, Rowell, T.Lockwood, C.Pannam, Rush, Tulloch.
Goals: Collingwood – Condon 2, Rowell 2, T.Lockwood 2, Fell, Incoll, Tulloch, Allan, Hailwood, Pears.
Crowd: N/A at Corio Oval

ROUND ELEVEN July 12
COLLINGWOOD	9.14 (68)
FITZROY	6.9 (45)

Best: Collingwood – Condon, Rowell, A.Leach, C.Pannam, Proudfoot, Tulloch.
Goals: Collingwood – Condon 3, Rowell 2, Hailwood, Incoll, Tulloch, A.Leach.
Crowd: N/A at Brunswick St Oval

ROUND TWELVE July 19
COLLINGWOOD	19.13 (127)
ST KILDA	1.4 (10)

Best: Collingwood – Allan, Pears, Rowell, Angus, F.Leach, T.Leach, Proudfoot.
Goals: Collingwood – Allan 4, Rowell 3, Condon 3, Pears 3, T.Lockwood 2, A.Leach 2, G.Lockwood, Incoll.
Crowd: N/A at Victoria Park

ROUND THIRTEEN July 26
COLLINGWOOD	7.5 (47)
ESSENDON	5.6 (36)

Best: Collingwood – Dummett, Hailwood, Incoll, T.Lockwood, C.Pannam, Rowell.
Goals: Collingwood – Incoll 2, T.Lockwood 2, Rowell, Tulloch, Condon.
Crowd: N/A at East Melbourne Cricket Ground

ROUND FOURTEEN August 2
COLLINGWOOD	7.10 (52)
CARLTON	2.3 (15)

Best: Collingwood – Boyack, Farrell, F.Leach, T.Leach, Pears, Rush.
Goals: Collingwood – Farrell 2, Pears 2, T.Leach, A.Leach, C.Pannam.
Crowd: N/A at Princes Park

ROUND FIFTEEN August 16
COLLINGWOOD	12.12 (84)
SOUTH MELBOURNE	5.14 (44)

Best: Collingwood – T.Lockwood, Angus, Fell, C.Pannam, Rowell, Rush.
Goals: Collingwood – T.Lockwood 4, Pears 2, Rowell 2, Hailwood, Allan, Condon, Fell.
Crowd: N/A at Victoria Park

ROUND SIXTEEN August 23
COLLINGWOOD	13.9 (87)
FITZROY	5.4 (34)

Best: Collingwood – Rowell, Dummett, A.Leach, Monohan, Tulloch.
Goals: Collingwood – Rowell 6, A.Leach 2, T.Lockwood 2, C.Pannam, Angus, Tulloch.
Crowd: N/A at Brunswick St Oval

ROUND SEVENTEEN August 30
COLLINGWOOD	16.16 (112)
GEELONG	2.11 (23)

Best: Collingwood – Pears, Rowell, Angus, Dummett, T.Lockwood, Rush, McCormack.
Goals: Collingwood – Pears 7, Rowell 3, Incoll 2, Hailwood 2, Condon, C.Pannam.
Crowd: N/A at Victoria Park

PREMIER'S FINALS

SEMI-FINAL September 6
COLLINGWOOD	6.12 (48)
FITZROY	9.10 (64)

Best: Collingwood – Tulloch, Rush, T.Lockwood, F.Leach, Hailwood, Fell, Condon.
Goals: Collingwood – T.Lockwood 3, Rowell 2, Monohan.
Crowd: 13,000 at the MCG

GRAND FINAL September 20
COLLINGWOOD	1.2 3.2 5.5 9.6 (60)
ESSENDON	1.3 2.7 3.7 3.9 (27)

Best: Collingwood – Allan, Hailwood, T.Leach, McCormack, C.Pannam, Rush.
Goals: Collingwood – Rowell 3, T.Lockwood 3, Angus, Allan, Pears.
Crowd: 35,202 at the MCG

GRAND FINAL LINE-UPS

COLL	B:	A.Dummett	B.Proudfoot	G.Lockwood
ESS	F:	P.O'Loughlin	T.Kinnear	J.Larkin
COLL	HB:	B.Rush	M.Fell	C.McCormack
ESS	HF:	V.Hutchins	A.Thurgood	F.Hiskins
COLL	C:	C.Pannam	F.Leach	J.Allan
ESS	C:	T.Kennedy	H.Wright	H.Vollugi
COLL	HF:	J.Incoll	T.Rowell	H.Pears
ESS	HB:	G.Hastings	H.Gavin	J.Anderson
COLL	F:	T.Lockwood	A.Leach	L.Tulloch (capt)
ESS	B:	F.Mann	J.Geggie	B.Robinson
COLL	R:	F.Hailwood	G.Angus	D.Condon
ESS	R:	G.Martin	J.McKenzie	B.Griffith

SNAPSHOT

Win-loss record: 16-3

Highest score: 19.13 (127), round 12, v St Kilda.

Greatest winning margin: 117 points, round 12, v St Kilda.

Lowest score: 3.4 (22), round 4, v Fitzroy.

Greatest losing margin: 33 points, round 4, v Fitzroy.

Most goals by a player in a game: 7, Harry Pears, round 17, v Geelong.

Most consecutive wins: 11

Most consecutive losses: 1 (three times).

Club awards: Leading goalkicker: Ted Rowell (33 goals)

Putting it into perspective:
Collingwood's first premiership victory reversed its 1901 loss to Essendon in the Grand Final. The Magpies became the fourth team to be the VFL premier, and they kicked the highest score in a Grand Final, 9.6 (60).

1902

		P	W	L	D	%	Pts
1	Collingwood (1)	17	15	2		199.5	60
2	Essendon (2)	17	13	4		141.6	52
3	Fitzroy (3)	17	10	7		125.9	40
4	Melbourne (4)	17	9	8		108.8	36
5	South Melb	17	7	10		99.4	28
6	Carlton	17	7	10		77.1	28
7	Geelong	17	7	10		76.8	28
8	St Kilda	17	0	17		41.9	0

(17 home and away rounds)

PLAYERS USED

COLLINGWOOD	GAMES	GOALS
Allan, John	17	8
Angus, George	12	2
Boyack, Alf	5	0
Bryce, Bob	1	0
Condon, Dick	16	17
Dow, Charlie	4	0
Dummett, Alf	18	0
Farrell, Jack	6	2
Fell, Matthew	16	3
Hailwood, Frank	19	7
Incoll, Jack	10	9
Leach, Arthur	17	9
Leach, Fred	10	0
Leach, Ted	8	1
Lockwood, George	15	2
Lockwood, Teddy	17	29
Martin, Peter	1	0
McCormack, Con	18	0
McCulloch, Bill	1	1
Monohan, Jack	17	2
Morgan, Leo	3	1
Newbound, Harry	1	0
Pannam, Charlie	18	4
Pears, Harry	16	22
Proudfoot, Bill	17	0
Rowell, Ted	15	33
Rush, Bob	16	0
Smith, Archie	4	5
Tame, Alby	5	0
Tulloch, Lardie	19	10

**COLLINGWOOD 4.7 (31) d
FITZROY 3.11 (29)**

THE BATTLE OF SMITH STREET

The bitter rivalry between the first two power clubs of the VFL played itself out until the final few moments of the 1903 season. By GLENN McFARLANE

FOOTBALL'S most intense pre-war rivalry froze for a few seconds in the dying moments of the 1903 Grand Final between Collingwood and Fitzroy at the Melbourne Cricket Ground. The Magpie defenders, including one familiar face playing under an unfamiliar name, watched with a sinking feeling of despair when Fitzroy captain and sharpshooter Gerald Brosnan marked as the final seconds of the season ticked away. Many pundits had described Brosnan as the most accurate left-foot kick in the land and it seemed certain that he would land the goal and the premiership for his team. The minor premier, Collingwood, led Fitzroy by only three points, but those manning the MCG scoreboard were readying themselves to add another goal to the tally for Brosnan's team. The crowd of 32,363 fell into a hush as the Fitzroy player carefully studied the shot, commenced his path in towards goals, and faded in finals folklore.

One kick would decide the outcome of 20 weekends of football. One kick would decide another chapter to the short but tempestuous relationship between Melbourne inner northern-suburban rivals Collingwood and Fitzroy. One kick would prove the ultimate conclusion to a season that was tightly contested, particularly between the two Grand Final protagonists, on a stifling spring afternoon.

The struggle was said to be one of "the most desperate yet seen on a Victorian football ground and the issue remained in doubt until the last kick."

Stoushes between these two clubs were only a dozen seasons old, but that infancy belied the rivalry's passionate and sometimes bitter nature. Resentment between the adjoining suburbs, split by Smith Street, went a long way beyond football rivalries. For some, it had more to do with socio-economic reasons. For others, the Smith Street divide was a tribal borderline. Football was often an outlet for those emotions, and that much was certain on the day one man had the destiny of a season in his hands. But the relationship between Collingwood and Fitzroy was already tenuous long before Brosnan got his hands on the ball that day. From its embryonic stages, Collingwood's greatest rival was Fitzroy. And since Collingwood's birth in 1892, it was undoubtedly the same story the other way. This stretched back to their earliest clashes through the 1890s. In the first year of the VFL competition in 1897, *The Argus* summed up the interest that prevailed in contests between the two teams by suggesting: "If you don't get good football (at least) you're bound to have bloodshed."

Indeed, Fitzroy had proven the bulwark against Collingwood's quest for success in those early years. The Maroons were the only club with an equal win-loss ratio against the Magpies; no other team had come close. Matches between the two sides seemed to bring out the best and worst in supporters and players alike. Fitzroy and Collingwood had won three of the first six VFL premierships contested, with the Maroons saluting in 1898 and 1899, and the Magpies producing a revolutionary style of play with the stab kick to win the 1902 pennant. Both were favoured to be the teams to beat in 1903, and this was highlighted when the VFL approached Collingwood in February 1903 to ask them if they would be interested in playing a match in Sydney during the season. The Magpies wanted to play the first game outside of Victoria for premiership points, and they wanted their opponent to be the Maroons.

The move enraged many supporters, particularly Collingwood ones, because no one wanted to give up a home game and miss the contest. It sparked some wild protests at the Magpies' annual meeting on the eve of the 1903 season. A motion at the meeting overwhelmingly opposed a match for premiership points, preferring an exhibition clash. But after a push from the newly formed New South Wales Football Association, it was restored as a home and away game, much to the chagrin of some barrackers. And so, on May 23, the two teams took to the Sydney Cricket Ground for their historic encounter. Various reports put the crowd at the SCG game at between 15,000 and 20,000 fans, but it did not necessarily follow that it would win rave reviews from supporters and scribes alike. The gate receipts totalled £650 for the NSW Football Association, but the trip would cost Collingwood £308 (minus a VFL concessional grant of £50). The match was historic for several reasons. There was the location, for starters.

It was also the first time an ambulance had waited at a ground in anticipation of an injury. And it was the first time players wore numbers - to help the foreign audience identify them. Other games would be played as one-offs in Sydney over the years, but it would be another 79 years before a team from the same competition would be based out of the Harbour City. Ambulances would not become a fixture at Victorian clubs for some time to come. And numbers on the back of the players would not become a permanent part of the game in the VFL until the 1912 season.

One of the leading football journalists, 'Kickero', of the Melbourne *Herald*, said of the Sydney experiment: "The rugby people did not view it with any great favour, and there was a rallying effort to whip up the interest in a rugby game being played at the Showground, next to the Sydney Cricket Ground." And even those attending the "Fitz-Woods game" were keen to gain a vantage point on the SCG hill, so that they could watch the football in front of them, but still keep an eye on the rugby game "at the one and same time". The crowd took a keen interest in what was happening, even if not all of them were totally familiar with the rules. According to *The Argus*: "The buzz of excitement on the ground was such as is heard only when New South Wales and New Zealand are meeting at football (rugby) or England and Australia at cricket, and that was all the more gratifying because the great majority of the spectators had no personal interest in the players."

Collingwood held the early ascendancy, kicking three goals to one in the opening stanza. But Fitzroy fought back doggedly in the second term, booting two goals to claim the lead before their opponents stole it back in the last minutes when Jack Incoll place-kicked a goal just before half-time. But the advantages secured by the inaccurate Maroons in the second quarter carried over to the third, as they booted three goals to one, to open up a 13-point lead at the last change. Collingwood fought bravely, but could not catch Fitzroy. The final margin was 17 points. Local supporters cheered off players from both teams. The Collingwood fans who had protested against the move to switch a home game against an arch-rival were still indignant. Surely, they protested, the Magpies would have beaten the Maroons at home, instead of taking a loss in Sydney. As a team, though, Collingwood regrouped and even managed to knock off Fitzroy on their own dunghill later in the season, which was one of 13 consecutive wins the club had managed leading into the finals. As it worked out, too, the Magpies secured the minor premiership. They took over top spot when the Maroons inexplicably fell to St Kilda in round 12 and did not relinquish it.

Collingwood's performance was considerable, given it had lost its premier defender Bill Proudfoot early in the season. A policeman, Proudfoot played the opening two games of the season and also another in round 4. He also managed a game in round 11. But Victoria's Police Commissioner had deemed it wrong to have men in his force playing football at the highest level, given the game often degenerated into violence on and off the field. He didn't want men from his force playing in the VFL. It was hardly fair on a person of Proudfoot's experience and exemplary record. Seven years earlier, in the midst of a few mad moments on the field, he had come to the assistance of an umpire who had been threatened by a number of spectators who were intent on causing damage. Proudfoot missed the game that he loved playing; and Collingwood missed one of its most important players.

Then, in a semi-final against Carlton, played at Fitzroy's Brunswick Street Oval (of all places), Collingwood unveiled a "recruit" who went by the name of 'Bill Wilson'. He looked and played in the same manner as the thick-set Proudfoot. Fans and opponents knew it was one and the same. The full-back played an important role in the Magpies' thrilling four-point win over the Blues, which came only after Joe Sullivan missed a shot just before the bell sounded. Most newspapers referred to the full-back as "Wilson" in inverted commas, but there were a few slip-ups from those in the know (which seemed to be everyone). In the lead-up to the much-anticipated Grand Final pairing of Collingwood and Fitzroy, *The Argus* had named Proudfoot as part of the Magpies' line-up. Wilson or Proudfoot—whatever his name—the Magpies were happy to have their defender back. But, for the Grand Final, the club would have to do without one of the best recruits of the year, Jim McHale, who would miss out with injury, but who would later carve out a legendary career as a player and coach. He would come to be known as "Jock" and would be at the club in one capacity or another for 50 years.

Grand Final day dawned bright and sunny, and the afternoon of September 12 blossomed into a humid spring day. In the warm conditions, fitness and conditioning would be of great importance. Both teams had past reputations of being on their game when it came to the details of preparation. That much was obvious to anyone who happened to see the two sides preparing themselves before the game. *The Herald* observed: "A glimpse into the dressing rooms revealed men bubbling over with life and health and trained to the hour." In the chase for the premiership, Collingwood and Fitzroy would need every ounce of strength. As the two teams moved out onto the ground, the cheers came from the 32,263 supporters expecting to see—if past games were any consideration—a tight, tough and tense encounter. How right they would be!

Nerves from both sides marred the opening term of the Grand Final, giving some credence to 'Observer', of *The Argus,* and his declaration that: "As a rule, the games from which most is expected in good football are a disappointment, owing to over-anxiety, and for the first few minutes it looked as though this game would be no exception... for players were scrambling, fumbling and falling over each other in an uninteresting way." But after 10 minutes of mistakes, the play became "worthy of the occasion". Collingwood scored first with a behind to Ted Rowell from a "quick and lively snapshot", but it was their opponents who grasped hold of the early ascendancy in the match. Fitzroy's Herbert Milne broke the deadlock with the first goal of the game, with *The Herald* saying: "(Percy) Trotter, being pushed, got a free kick which was marked beautifully by Milne, who went high into the air above the struggling bunch of players and reached the ball down, as it were, from the sky. The long lad (he was 183cm) had a shot at goal and sent the ball spinning through the space between the sticks." Milne's place-kick goal sent a roar through the Fitzroy fans and brought an early despair to those in the Collingwood camp.

Still, those black and white fans who felt down were soon on their feet again. Collingwood's first goal was hardly as spectacular as the Milne goal, but Dick Condon scored it after receiving a free kick after being "flung" by his opponent. It was a contentious decision, with *The Argus* suggesting it was a "very unfortunate affair... Condon got it from a free kick, close up, but a great many were of the opinion that the free kick could have gone to the other side." No one in the Collingwood camp cared. All they worried about was the fact they were on the board with a goal. Yet the Maroons kept coming. Bill McSpeerin, "getting it neatly out of a crush, scored Fitzroy's second goal." But that goal was followed by "some dashing football" from Collingwood, courtesy of "some neat interchanges between (George) Angus, (Charlie) Pannam and (Ted) Lockwood that the latter wound up with a clever goal, while (Ted) Rowell, also helped by Angus, missed one soon afterwards." 'Wilson'—or should we say Proudfoot—went to great lengths to save a goal just before the first bell sounded, leaving Collingwood clinging to a one-point lead.

In keeping with nature of their relationship, Collingwood and Fitzroy were turning on a physical clash, with *The Argus* saying: "The game was being played in a nasty spirit. If the players were not striking each other, they struck out their fists at times, when someone on the other side was most likely run against them, and more than one player was cautioned." Aside from that, the heat was extracting precious energy from the players and there was rising anxiety among the crowd. Players used the brief interlude of the quarter-time change of ends to "gain the refreshment derived from juicy oranges". They needed it as the tempo was about to be raised to another level in the second term. The pressure was about to be elevated.

The Argus deduced: "At the start of the game, Fitzroy was the more fancied—but Collingwood played such good football all through the second quarter that popular opinion swung in their favour... Collingwood were unmistakably playing with a better system." Fitzroy had three scoring shots for the term, but could produce only behinds. Collingwood added 1.1 to narrowly stretch their lead to five points as the players wearily walked from the field. The Magpies' second-term goal came from first-year player Jim Addison. It was said that the "game had improved greatly on the first rough scramble and brilliant football was seen at times."

Through the third term, *The Argus* said Fitzroy's "dashes were strong". "Occasionally slightly frantic and their forwards seemed to be overmatched at any rate," it said. "They could not work the ball into a good position and missed from different angles. In that third quarter, it was a grand game, with all the excitement onlookers could possibly desire." The excitement was there, but the scoring of goals was not. Neither side kicked a major score for the third term, but it was Fitzroy which had the most of the play. That they didn't make a better account of it kept Collingwood in the contest, and only increased the anxiety in both camps. The Magpies could manage only two behinds in the term to the Maroons' three, but they still held a slender four-point lead. Half an hour would decide not only a football match, but also who would be premiers in the seventh VFL season.

Both teams threw themselves into the contest when play resumed, with Collingwood appearing to be the stronger of the two sides. At one stage the Magpies took it almost the full length of the ground with (Alf) Dummett, (Jack) Monohan, Pannam, Condon and Lockwood keeping the ball off their Fitzroy opponents. Soon after, as 'Observer' described: "(Arthur) Leach passed it down to Addison, who scored the fourth goal for Collingwood. They (Fitzroy) appeared for a moment to abandon all hope... Collingwood faces beamed on and off the ground." Both teams were almost at the point of exhaustion, many of the players were "distressed as the day was hot, the ground hard and the pace terrific." 'Kickero', summed up the situation in the crowd when he wrote: "They watched and cheered right on to the middle of the final quarter. Then, there was a cessation of the noise, for it seemed as if the pace had been cracked up and Collingwood would win. (But) Fitzroy forgot their fagged condition, flung it away from them, and with set teeth and desperation characterising their features, they launched themselves in to battle." The Maroons were about to have one final, determined crack at getting the lead back.

Les Millis scored a goal for Fitzroy to bring the Roys within range of a comeback win. The pressure was on, as the last minutes ticked down.

The Argus highlighted the plight of those tired Collingwood defenders—Proudfoot among them—as Fitzroy made a late move. "With unmistakable dismay in their faces, the Collingwood backs saw this beaten team coming at them again." But accuracy once more cost the Maroons. McSpeerin missed. Millis came close once more, but not close enough. "Point by point, the Collingwood lead shrank, but only a few minutes were left to play, and for Fitzroy a goal meant everything."

Then Brosnan stepped forward for his brush with history, after marking from a kick down field from Percy Trotter. Fitzroy's game comeback had seemingly been worth the effort. As *The Argus* suggested: "It seemed that the reward for their rare gameness had come when Brosnan got a mark right in front and within range." The suspense was unbelievable for those who could barely look as the normally accurate and normally unflappable Brosnan lined up for goal. *The Herald* summed up "the hush among the crowd… he took a deliberate shot, straight towards goal from his foot flew the ball, and just when it appeared certain that a winning goal would be obtained, the wind deflected it from its course. Then, in a wild tumult, the final bell rang." Collingwood had won.

Collingwood, *The Argus* recorded, had "won a magnificent game by two points, but beyond the two points there was nothing in it either way. Fitzroy had the melancholy satisfaction of knowing that, after all the hard battling of the season, its captain had the chance to win all the honours with one straight kick—and upon that miss the four months' issue turned. It was a game of which one might well say, 'the victor is vanquished; the vanquished is victorious.'" The Magpie players danced a celebratory jig as a shattered Brosnan came to terms with his stunning miss. His Fitzroy teammates tried to console him. One of them was in no position to do so. Jim Sharp, a defender for the Maroons, had collapsed from exhaustion and did not regain consciousness for half an hour. Ironically, Sharp would end up becoming a Collingwood player and later, president. The Fitzroy captain told reporters after the match: "I have never felt so sure of anything in my life as I did that goal. But the wind got to an almost spent ball and puffed it aside."

Matthew Fell was one of Collingwood's best players. Con McCormack was strong in the centre; Monohan, Pannam and Proudfoot were also important players. Addison ended his first season with two of the four Collingwood goals. Lockwood's goal took his season tally to a competition-best 35, while his teammate Rowell ended up with 30. In the victorious Collingwood rooms, Proudfoot received plenty of backslaps. He had defied the chief commissioner to keep his football career alive. The 35-year-old was the oldest player afield, yet he was more than up to the task on such a stifling afternoon, ending up as one of his team's best players. He was also one of the few to realise just how close Brosnan's kick had come to winning the premiership for Fitzroy. For years, he would tell friends of how the lace of the ball had actually grazed the post and how a puff of wind had been the difference between winning and losing back-to-back premierships for Collingwood. The Magpies had achieved their aim of consecutive flags, mirroring the Maroons' 1898 and 1899 pennants, but they dared to dream of more flags in the future.

1903 COLLINGWOOD

PREMIER'S SEASON

COLLINGWOOD: 1903

ROUND ONE May 2
COLLINGWOOD	5.7 (37)
CARLTON	9.4 (58)

Best: Collingwood – Condon, Dummett, A.Leach, McHale, Rowell, Spears.
Goals: Collingwood – Rowell 2, T.Lockwood, Condon, Spears.
Crowd: N/A at Princes Park

ROUND TWO May 9
COLLINGWOOD	13.14 (92)
SOUTH MELBOURNE	3.6 (24)

Best: Collingwood – Condon, T.Leach, T.Lockwood, McHale, C.Pannam, Tulloch.
Goals: Collingwood – T.Lockwood 2, Rowell 2, Condon 2, Tulloch 2, C.Pannam, T.Leach, Spears, Green, Pears.
Crowd: N/A at Victoria Park

ROUND THREE May 16
COLLINGWOOD	16.17 (113)
ST KILDA	5.3 (33)

Best: Collingwood – Rowell, T.Lockwood, Drohan, F.Leach, C.Pannam, Wilmot.
Goals: Collingwood – Rowell 5, T.Lockwood 4, A.Leach 3, Green 2, Condon, Wilmot.
Crowd: N/A at Victoria Park

ROUND FOUR May 23
COLLINGWOOD	6.9 (45)
FITZROY	7.20 (62)

Best: Collingwood – Angus, Dummett, Incoll, C.Pannam, Rowell.
Goals: Collingwood – Rowell 2, T.Lockwood, Condon, Incoll, Tulloch.
Crowd: N/A at the SCG

ROUND FIVE May 30
COLLINGWOOD	10.17 (77)
MELBOURNE	7.4 (46)

Best: Collingwood – Rowell, T.Lockwood, Drohan, McCormack, Rush, Tulloch.
Goals: Collingwood – Rowell 5, T.Lockwood 3, T.Leach, Tulloch.
Crowd: N/A at Victoria Park

ROUND SIX June 6
COLLINGWOOD	12.12 (84)
GEELONG	8.3 (51)

Best: Collingwood – Dunn, Green, A.Leach, G.Lockwood, C.Pannam, Rowell.
Goals: Collingwood – Green 3, Rowell 2, Condon 2, A.Leach, Pears, Incoll, Allan, Drohan.
Crowd: N/A at Corio Oval

ROUND SEVEN June 8
COLLINGWOOD	4.9 (33)
ESSENDON	2.13 (25)

Best: Collingwood – Condon, Dunn, Fell, Incoll, McHale, C.Pannam.
Goals: Collingwood – Incoll 2, Rowell, T.Lockwood.
Crowd: N/A at Victoria Park

ROUND EIGHT June 13
COLLINGWOOD	12.9 (81)
CARLTON	10.7 (67)

Best: Collingwood – T.Lockwood, Green, F.Leach, Monohan, C.Pannam, Tulloch.
Goals: Collingwood – T.Lockwood 5, Rowell 2, Pears, T.Leach, Green, Condon, Incoll.
Crowd: N/A at Victoria Park

ROUND NINE June 20
COLLINGWOOD	6.6 (42)
SOUTH MELBOURNE	4.11 (35)

Best: Collingwood – Pears, Condon, A.Leach, Angus, Drohan, Tulloch.
Goals: Collingwood – Pears 3, A.Leach, Condon, Green.
Crowd: N/A at the Lake Oval

ROUND TEN July 4
COLLINGWOOD	5.11 (41)
ST KILDA	2.4 (16)

Best: Collingwood – Ayling, Drohan, Fell, A.Leach, T.Lockwood, C.Pannam.
Goals: Collingwood – T.Lockwood 2, A.Leach, Condon, Incoll.
Crowd: N/A at the Junction Oval

ROUND ELEVEN July 11
COLLINGWOOD	8.8 (56)
FITZROY	5.6 (36)

Best: Collingwood – Angus, Green, T.Leach, T.Lockwood, Rowell.
Goals: Collingwood – Rowell 3, Green 2, T.Leach, Tulloch, T.Lockwood.
Crowd: N/A at Victoria Park

ROUND TWELVE July 18
COLLINGWOOD	11.8 (74)
MELBOURNE	4.8 (32)

Best: Collingwood – T.Lockwood, Condon, McCormack, McHale, C.Pannam.
Goals: Collingwood – T.Lockwood 4, Condon 3, Pears 2, T.Leach, Tulloch.
Crowd: N/A at the MCG

ROUND THIRTEEN July 25
COLLINGWOOD	6.15 (51)
GEELONG	5.7 (37)

Best: Collingwood – T.Leach, T.Lockwood, Condon, C.Pannam, McHale.
Goals: Collingwood – Pears, T.Lockwood, Angus, Drohan, T.Leach, Condon.
Crowd: N/A at Victoria Park

ROUND FOURTEEN August 8
COLLINGWOOD	11.7 (73)
ESSENDON	7.4 (46)

Best: Collingwood – Pears, Rowell, Tulloch, McHale, Rush, McCormack.
Goals: Collingwood – T.Lockwood 2, Pears 2, Rowell 2, C.Pannam, T.Leach, A.Leach, Tulloch, Condon.
Crowd: N/A at East Melbourne Cricket Ground

ROUND FIFTEEN August 15
COLLINGWOOD	3.12 (30)
ST KILDA	2.6 (18)

Best: Collingwood – Rush, C.Pannam, Incoll, McHale, Tulloch, Drohan.
Goals: Collingwood – T.Lockwood, Incoll, Rowell.
Crowd: N/A at Victoria Park

ROUND SIXTEEN August 22
COLLINGWOOD	6.7 (43)
CARLTON	5.11 (41)

Best: Collingwood – McCormack, Dummett, Condon, C.Pannam, T.Lockwood.
Goals: Collingwood – T.Lockwood 3, T.Leach, Incoll, Tulloch.
Crowd: N/A at Princes Park

ROUND SEVENTEEN August 29
COLLINGWOOD	13.13 (91)
MELBOURNE	5.10 (40)

Best: Collingwood – A.Leach, Pears, Drohan, Spears, Addison, Angus.
Goals: Collingwood – Rowell 3, A.Leach 3, Condon 2, T.Lockwood 2, Pears, Drohan, Fell.
Crowd: N/A at Victoria Park

PREMIER'S FINALS

SEMI-FINAL September 5

COLLINGWOOD	4.3 (27)
CARLTON	3.5 (23)

Best: Collingwood – Angus, Incoll, A.Leach, McCormack, Drohan, Fell.
Goals: Collingwood – Incoll 2, T.Lockwood, Angus.
Crowd: 16,600 at Brunswick St Oval

GRAND FINAL September 12

COLLINGWOOD	2.3	3.4	3.6	4.7 (31)
FITZROY	2.2	2.5	2.8	3.11 (29)

Best: Collingwood – Fell, McCormack, Monohan, Pannam, Proudfoot, Rowell.
Goals: Collingwood – Addison 2, T.Lockwood, Condon.
Crowd: 32,263 at the MCG

GRAND FINAL LINE-UPS

COLL	B:	G.Lockwood	B.Proudfoot	A.Dummett
FITZ	F:	P.Trotter	L.Millis	B.Sharpe
COLL	HB:	M.Fell	J.Monohan	B.Rush
FITZ	HF:	A.Wilkinson	G.Brosnan (capt)	C.Kiernan
COLL	C:	C.Pannam	C.McCormack	E.Drohan
FITZ	C:	T.Beauchamp	H.Clarke	F.Brophy
COLL	HF:	T.Lockwood	T.Rowell	L.Tulloch (capt)
FITZ	HB:	W.Naismith	J.Sharp	F.Fontaine
COLL	F:	A.Leach	J.Addison	H.Pears
FITZ	B:	A.Sharp	E.Jenkins	L.Barker
COLL	R:	J.Incoll	G.Angus	D.Condon
FITZ	R:	B.Walker	H.Milne	B.McSpeerin

SNAPSHOT

Win-loss record: 17-2

Highest score: 16.17 (113), round 3, v St Kilda.

Greatest winning margin: 80 points, round 3, v St Kilda.

Lowest score: 4.3 (27), semi-final, v Carlton.

Greatest losing margin: 21 points, round 1, v Carlton.

Most goals by a player in a game: 5, Ted Rowell, round 3, v St Kilda; round 5, v Melbourne; Teddy Lockwood, round 8, v Carlton.

Most consecutive wins: 15

Most consecutive losses: 1 (twice).

Club awards: Leading goalkicker: Teddy Lockwood (35 goals)

Putting it into perspective:
Collingwood's second successive Grand Final victory capped an amazing two seasons for the Magpies; over 1902-1903 they won 33 of 38 matches, and in 1903 they finished with a VFL record of 15 consecutive wins.

1903

	P	W	L	D	%	Pts
1 Collingwood (1)	17	15	2		159.4	60
2 Fitzroy (2)	17	14	3		171.6	56
3 Carlton (3)	17	11	6		136.0	44
4 Geelong (4)	17	9	8		120.7	36
5 St Kilda	17	7	9	1	76.4	30
6 Essendon	17	6	10	1	78.6	26
7 Melbourne	17	3	14		64.1	12
8 South Melb	17	2	15		54.9	8

(17 home and away rounds)

PLAYERS USED

COLLINGWOOD	GAMES	GOALS
Addison, Jim	3	2
Allan, John	2	1
Angus, George	18	2
Ayling, Bill	2	0
Blair, Jim	1	0
Carmody, Tom	1	0
Condon, Dick	19	18
Drohan, Eddie	17	3
Dummett, Alf	15	0
Dunn, Johnny	3	0
Fell, Matthew	19	1
Green, George	13	10
Incoll, Jack	16	10
Leach, Arthur	18	10
Leach, Fred	6	0
Leach, Ted	10	8
Lockwood, George	11	0
Lockwood, Teddy	19	35
McCormack, Con	13	0
McHale, Jock	14	0
McKean, Jim	1	0
Monohan, Jack	19	0
Pannam, Charlie	19	2
Pears, Harry	18	12
Proudfoot, Bill	6	0
Rowell, Ted	17	30
Rush, Bob	18	0
Spears, Billy	6	2
Tulloch, Lardie	17	8
Wilmot, Percy	1	

**FITZROY 9.7 (61) d
CARLTON 5.7 (37)**

MAROONS ON A MISSION

Three years without a premiership was enough for Fitzroy, which asserted itself again with some dominant football. By ADAM McNICOL

O N WHAT proved to be the last day of the 1904 VFL season, much of the pre-game chatter centred around whether the hot favourite actually wanted to win. That team, Fitzroy, had finished six points clear on top of the ladder after the home and away rounds. It had then defeated its neighbour and rival Collingwood to reach the game known as 'the Final'.

Under the finals system used at the time, the Maroons were subsequently given two chances to claim the premiership. If they won the Final, the flag was theirs. But if they lost, they could invoke the Challenge rule, forcing the issue to be decided by a further contest—a Grand Final—a week later.

It was this situation that aroused much suspicion among the 32,688 men, women and children who filed into the MCG on September 17 to see Fitzroy take on Carlton, the team that had finished second on the ladder. The mood of the crowd was summed up in a post-match report by 'Observer', published in *The Argus* the following Monday.

"One met of course a great many people firm in the conviction that Carlton would be permitted to win, so that there should be another game and another gate. Those who follow suburban racing and cycling are so accustomed to being swindled that they cannot conceive such a possibility as a straight game when the other sort of match means the chance of eight clubs dividing another

£300 between them. One can only hope that 'sportsmen' of this type, on the strength of their dishonest connections, backed Carlton to win on Saturday."

The people doubting whether Fitzroy would try to win the Final had probably underplayed two key factors: the Maroons were regarded as being the fittest (they had pioneered a number of new physical training regimens), most talented and professional team in Victoria; and they were keen to atone for their two-point loss to Collingwood in the 1903 premiership decider. On that day, their captain and key forward Gerald Brosnan, who was renowned as being a very straight left-foot kick, had missed a shot at goal from 30 yards out after the final bell.

Boasting a team containing a large number of players who had grown up in the streets surrounding its home ground on Brunswick Street, Fitzroy had rollicked its way through the 1904 season. Again under the guidance of Brosnan (Fitzroy would not appoint its first coach until 1911), the Maroons began their campaign on May 7, when they took on local rival Carlton at Princes Park. The game had some added spice because former Fitzroy captain John Worrall coached the Blues. Worrall had played 11 Test cricket matches for Australia from 1885 to 1899. In 1902, he became the first man to hold the position of coach at a VFL club when he was appointed to oversee Carlton. In 1903, he had lured three-time Fitzroy premiership forward Mick Grace over to the Blues. Grace, nicknamed the 'Flying Angel' for his marking ability, was in the Carlton line-up when his current and former teams clashed on the opening weekend of the '04 season.

As it turned out, Grace and Worrall's men were taught a footballing lesson as Fitzroy, which took to the field wearing a lace-up guernsey that was mostly maroon with a gold yoke and stripe down the middle, dominated from start to finish. Brosnan was among the best players as his side completed a 94-point rout by booting nine unanswered goals in the last quarter. *The Argus* correspondent later wrote that: "It would be farcical to attempt any detailed account of the play, since Fitzroy's superiority was so manifest".

The final score, 16.8 (104) to 1.8 (13), signalled to the rest of the competition that Brosnan's team been strengthened a great deal over the summer.

The addition of 21-year-old half-back flanker Joe Johnson was among the reasons for Fitzroy's improvement. Credited as the being the first Aboriginal player to play in the VFL, Johnson, who was born in the New South Wales city of Newcastle, joined Fitzroy after stints with Northcote and Brunswick in the VFA. (Many years later, his grandson Percy Cummings played for Hawthorn and great-grandsons Robert [Fitzroy] and Trent Cummings [Fitzroy and West Coast] also played League football). An often-smiling young man, Johnson boasted a muscular build and was referred to in a number of newspaper reports as being "a very smart player". He was an impressive contributor during the early rounds as Fitzroy continued its barnstorming run, defeating St Kilda by 50 points at the Brunswick Street Oval and Melbourne by 76 points at the MCG. "Fitzroy on present form are invincible—fast, fit and clever—and nothing else in the League can apparently touch them," said 'Observer' in *The Argus*.

The newly introduced boundary umpires dashing along the white line often amused spectators at these early-season games. When the ball went out of bounds, even when kicked over the line on the full, the boundary umpires were ordered to turn their back to the field then throw it over their head towards a contest involving the opposing ruckmen. Previously, the field umpire had retrieved the ball and thrown it in while facing the players, in a similar style to a rugby union line-out.

Fitzroy's first loss of the season came in round four against Collingwood, in what was considered a meeting of the VFL's best teams. On that afternoon at Brunswick Street, the Maroons started well, booting three majors to one in the opening quarter. But they managed only one more goal during the remainder of the game, as Collingwood kicked five. However, some wild weather helped Fitzroy get back on the winners' list a week later when it proved far too good for Essendon. The Dons had played their round-four match against Melbourne in Sydney, as part of the VFL's efforts to increase the popularity of what was then known as Victorian Rules football. Not only was Essendon soundly beaten at the SCG, but dangerous conditions on the ocean meant the team was unable to travel home by steamship until the following Thursday, only two days before it had to front up for its round five fixture against Fitzroy. Remarkably, scores were level at the long break. But Essendon's lack of preparation saw them manage only two behinds in the second half, while the Maroons piled on six goals to win by 42 points.

The rest of the season proved to be one of the most even in the VFL's short history. The early evidence of this came when Collingwood suffered its first ever loss to St Kilda in round seven. Fitzroy's players probably smirked at the ignominy that had befallen their neighbour, yet the Maroons suffered an embarrassing 47-point defeat at the hands of the Saints just two weeks later. Despite also losing to the League's other struggling team, Geelong, towards the end of the season, Fitzroy was still two points clear on top of the ladder once all the sides had played each other twice. Thanks to their players' tremendous ability to pass the ball accurately by foot, a skill that enabled them to move it quickly into attack, the Maroons had scored many big wins, meaning they had a far better percentage than second-placed Carlton.

As the League leader, Fitzroy was placed in Section A for the final three rounds of the regular season. Also in Section A were third-placed South Melbourne, fifth-placed Essendon and seventh-placed Geelong. Carlton, Collingwood, Melbourne and St Kilda were in Section B. Fitzroy began its quest to consolidate top spot by edging out South Melbourne in a game that was marred by bad kicking—4.14 (38) to 3.15 (33). A week later, the Maroons did wrap up the minor premiership when they easily accounted for Geelong at the Corio Oval. Veteran small-man Billy McSpeerin, known as 'The Shark' for his ability to kick freakish goals, was the star of that afternoon. The 29-year-old, who had been playing for Fitzroy since the VFA days of 1894, drew high praise from a journalist covering the game for *The Australasian*. "First performer in the match forms the most fitting phrase to describe Fitzroy's talented and experienced rover McSpeerin who did exceptionally more than anyone else did, or could do, to make his side's win a certainty."

While Fitzroy was sitting pretty, a couple of other clubs still had plenty to play for in the last round to make the sectional spread. To make a rare appearance in the finals, South Melbourne needed to beat Geelong and hope the Maroons' meeting with Essendon was close. South fulfilled its end of the bargain by scoring a 22-point win, but the Maroons, with nothing to play for, let the Dons do as they pleased at the East Melbourne Cricket Ground. Essendon's 10-goal victory boosted its percentage enough for it to leapfrog South into fourth place.

A slightly different finals system for 1904 meant first took on third and second played fourth on the opening weekend. If Fitzroy's rivals were hoping the Maroons' loss to Essendon was a sign of things to come, they were sorely disappointed when Brosnan and highly skilled rover Percy Trotter led them to an 11-point victory over Collingwood in the second semi-final, which drew a crowd of 26,000 to the MCG. The post-match reports credited Collingwood with producing the more eye-catching performance, but the men in black and white had no luck, with Teddy Lockwood hitting the post three times during the afternoon, including once late in the final quarter. Playing as the rover in the first quarter, then up forward for long periods during the rest of the match, McSpeerin was again a star performer for Fitzroy. Trotter (a born and bred Fitzroy local) was considered another influential member of the winning team, his dazzling play in the first term, when Fitzroy was kicking into the wind, having set his side on its path to victory. "Trotter put in two of those incomparable dashes in which he swerves his way so wonderfully among his opponents, and Fitzroy yells were long and loud when each dash ended with a goal," wrote *The Argus*. "There was barely a minute between the two efforts, and each was a bit of the best that Trotter had shown us this season."

Trotter finished with three goals, taking his season's tally to 35 and placing him third on the goalkicking table. For a player who was only 168cm, it was a remarkable effort. In fact, he had booted six more goals than Brosnan—the taller man whom the Maroons' forward line was built around. At the same time as Fitzroy was doing battle with Collingwood, Carlton and Essendon met before a much smaller crowd at Victoria Park. In a tight and tough contest, in which neither side booted a major in the last quarter, Essendon's Jack McKenzie missed a late shot at goal and the Blues hung on to win by three points. With Collingwood and the Dons eliminated from the premiership race, it was left to Fitzroy and Carlton to fight it out for the flag.

The last match of the 1904 VFL season was played on a fine, warm and sunny day, although a strong north-westerly breeze had picked up by the time the players jogged onto the MCG. Under the rules of the time, Fitzroy and Carlton members were admitted free, as were the members of Geelong, who attended the game in large numbers because the club had chartered a special train. The other people in the 32,000-strong crowd paid a shilling for the privilege, which was double the cost of attending a regular season match, and the amount of money taken on the gate totalled £1100. While plenty of these folk were suspicious about Fitzroy's intentions, most agreed that if both teams performed to their potential (Fitzroy's bullocking forward Alf Wilkinson was the only first-choice player missing from either side), the Maroons would be too good. After all, Carlton was yet to win a VFL premiership and boasted far less finals experience than its opponent, which had already won two flags.

The gusty wind, which favoured the Punt Road end, resulted in a mistake-ridden start to the game. The following Monday's match report in *The Age*, written by 'Follower', stated that: "The play from start to finish was hard, fast and full of life, but it would not be correct to describe it as a great game worthy of the occasion. As a matter of fact, it was distinctly otherwise." Nerves also afflicted many players during the early stages, as 'Observer' from *The Argus* witnessed: "For some time after the ball was bounced there was a continual roar sufficient of itself to make the players lose their heads. In the opening dashes Flynn, of Carlton, was prominent, and twice the old Geelong player, whose face, like that of the other men in the game, was white with excitement, stopped a rush on the Carlton goal."

By quarter-time, however, the doubts over Fitzroy's thirst for victory were erased. Despite having kicked into the stiff breeze, the Maroons led three goals to one and many in the crowd were declaring the game all but over. While Brosnan—noted by *The Argus* for his "neat, clean style"—had been dominant up forward, booting a goal after a brilliant mark, centre half-back Jim Sharp was Fitzroy's most influential player. Sharp had set up his team's first major when he cut off a Carlton attack by taking a courageous mark. The ball had then been rushed down to Herbert 'Boxer' Milne, who used a rugby-style place kick to shoot at goal. The shot fell short but was marked and put through the big sticks by Bill Walker. In the ensuing minutes, Sharp stood tall as the Blues' followers tried to batter him at every opportunity.

Carlton's play during the opening term might have lacked skill, but it contained plenty of aggression and Joe Johnson was on the receiving end when he was knocked out by a crude shirt-front from full-forward George Topping. As 'Follower' later wrote in *The Age*: "Topping deserved severe censure for a most unwarrantable attack on Johnson, whose only offence was playing too well. It was one of those contemptible displays of ill-temper for which no excuse can be made." Yet Fitzroy was not a team that simply accepted such targeting of its best players. "One could see by the grim faces and threatening forefingers of some of the sturdy Fitzroy backs that Topping was being warned as to what would happen, and for a long time he was more watchful than useful," noted *The Argus's* correspondent.

Against all expectations, Carlton seized the initiative early in the second quarter. Eddie Prescott moved the Blues to within sight of the lead when he kicked a goal, and if not for the gallantry of Sharp and Fred Fontaine in the backline, along with Les Millis on the wing, Fitzroy would have fallen behind far sooner than it did. In a sign of panic, Brosnan was forced to send fellow forward Milne up the field, but the Maroons soon lost their advantage anyway. George Bruce put the Blues in front when he dashed clear of his opponent to boot a brilliant major, and at half-time Carlton led by a point, 3.3 (21) to 3.2 (20).

It was during the early years of the VFL that the third term became known as the premiership quarter, and this game is one reason why. With centreman Bob Boyle, second ruckman Fred Elliott, rover Archie Snell and wingman Ted Kennedy marshalling the troops, Carlton dominated the half-hour following the long break. However, the Blues wasted chance after chance. "Grace marked beautifully, generally letting his opponents get in front of him, then coming with a soar over their heads, but he always got it in a bad position," was the description of events in *The Argus*. Grace and his teammates managed only five behinds for the quarter. They were made to pay when Fitzroy, which was being kept in the game by the desperate work of Johnson, Sharp and fellow defender Wally Naismith, kicked goals with both its scoring shots late in the quarter. Edgar Kneen booted the first and Trotter slotted the second after he was set up by Fontaine's tremendous dash from full-back to the middle of the ground. At the final change, the Maroons led by seven points, 5.2 (32) to 3.7 (25).

Only a few minutes into the final term, it became clear that the Blues had little run left in their legs, and the late Fitzroy goals had left them dispirited. Carlton's task was made even tougher when Trotter, who had been quiet for much of the afternoon, came to life and his teammates began passing to him at every opportunity. Thanks to the "cool precision" of McSpeerin's play, Trotter booted the Maroons' sixth and eighth goals. In between those straight kicks, Percy Sheehan also split the middle, adding some polish to his many displays of physicality during the contest. At one stage, Sheehan had crudely flattened Carlton half-back flanker Billy Leeds on the boundary line, an action that resulted in umpire Ivo Crapp turning to him and tersely saying: "That's the second time, lad." When Kneen further extended Fitzroy's lead to 36 points, it was clear the Maroons would be the premier team of 1904. They had got the job done without needing to invoke the Challenge rule.

The breeze continued to play havoc with the players' skills, as the game reached a scrappy conclusion. Indeed, the match report in *The Argus* illustrates that congestion around the ball—something the VFL's successor, the AFL, was still struggling to eliminate from the game a century later—was a problem from the code's earliest years. "The ball was so constantly at the Fitzroy end that the field edged up with it, all organisation was destroyed, the players made just a jumbled crowd, where ruckmen could not be distinguished from placemen. There was a period when if one had drawn a line from goal to goal and another across the centre he would have found 33 players jostling, smashing, bumping in one quarter of the ground and only three men outside it." In *The Age,* 'Follower' agreed. "There was too much scrambling and vacating of places, especially by Carlton," he wrote, bemoaning the fact the players refused to stay in their positions.

To its credit, Carlton never gave up. Elliott kept giving his all in the middle of the ground, and he drove the ball forward for Topping to score a consolation goal with a couple of minutes remaining. Elliott was again in the thick of the action when another Blues attack enabled Snell to take a mark, within range, just seconds before the final bell sounded. According to *The Age*: "As Snell took his shot and kicked the last goal of the season, half the Fitzroy players were walking off the ground, and apparently half the crowd swarming onto it to catch a last glimpse of the premiers before losing sight of them for seven months". The newspaper reports listed Topping as Carlton's best player, along with Elliott, Snell, Leeds, Kennedy and Boyle.

The end of the match was certainly a relief for the scribe from *The Argus*. "It is always the case that in these final games the play is disappointing, and Saturday was no exception," he wrote, although he did reserve praise for the controlling official. "The fact that there was little or no howling at the umpire shows that Crapp handled the game with sound judgement."

However, none of the criticism about the mistake-ridden play mattered to Fitzroy, which had won the game by 24 points. Brosnan's men collected their third flag in eight seasons, entrenching their reputation as the VFL's dominant club and leading *The Age* reporter to declare that: "I think it will be generally admitted that the Maroons at the head of the premiership list are decidedly in their proper place." Sharp was named best on ground after a tremendous battle with Grace. "Their defence has been not only powerful but also brilliant," led a summary of his feats in *The Australasian*. "First among their men in this division stood J. Sharp, who has certainly proved himself the star defender of the year. No other half-back has equalled him in the air, in brilliant and determined dashes, or in telling, long drop kicks." The 22-year-old later won the club's best-and-fairest award. Johnson was listed as the winners' second-best performer. Feted along with the other premiership players, his exploits on the football field enabled him to be accepted into 'white' society. Yet he and his fellow indigenous people would not be classed as Australian citizens, or allowed to vote, for another 63 years.

When Fitzroy's celebrations concluded, McSpeerin retired, despite having shown during the 1904 campaign that he was still a force to be reckoned with it at the highest level. He ended his career with the distinction of having played in all of Fitzroy's four premierships since the club was founded in 1883. This included the Maroons' VFA flag in 1895. At that stage McSpeerin was also Fitzroy's VFL games record-holder, having made 127 appearances since the competition was founded in 1897.

1904 FITZROY

PREMIER'S SEASON

FITZROY: 1904

ROUND ONE May 7
FITZROY   16.12 (108)
CARLTON   1.8 (14)
Best: Fitzroy – Brosnan, Milne, Johnson, A.Sharp, Trotter, Wilkinson.
Goals: Fitzroy – Milne 4, Brosnan 4, Trotter 2, Millis 2, Barker, Naismith, Fontaine, Wilkinson.
Crowd: N/A at Princes Park

ROUND TWO May 14
FITZROY   11.17 (83)
ST KILDA   5.3 (33)
Best: Fitzroy – Trotter, Brosnan, Fontaine, Millis, J.Sharp, Walker, McSpeerin.
Goals: Fitzroy – Trotter 4, McSpeerin 2, Brosnan 2, Millis, Wilkinson, Barker.
Crowd: N/A at Brunswick St Oval

ROUND THREE May 21
FITZROY   14.15 (99)
MELBOURNE   3.5 (23)
Best: Fitzroy –Barker, Brosnan, Lethbridge, Naismith, Milne, Sheehan, Trotter.
Goals: Fitzroy – Brosnan 4, Trotter 3, Milne 2, Barker 2, Millis, Kneen, McSpeerin.
Crowd: N/A at the MCG

ROUND FOUR May 28
FITZROY   4.9 (33)
COLLINGWOOD   6.6 (42)
Best: Fitzroy – Brosnan, Lethbridge, Johnson, J.Sharp, Bartlett, A.Sharp.
Goals: Fitzroy – Brosnan 3, Wilkinson.
Crowd: N/A at Brunswick St Oval

ROUND FIVE June 4
FITZROY   11.17 (83)
ESSENDON   6.5 (41)
Best: Fitzroy –Trotter, J.Sharp, L.Barker, Johnson, Clarke, Brosnan.
Goals: Fitzroy – Trotter 5, Brosnan 2, Bartlett 2, L.Barker, Wilkinson.
Crowd: N/A at East Melbourne Cricket Ground

ROUND SIX June 6
FITZROY   12.6 (78)
GEELONG   6.18 (54)
Best: Fitzroy – J.Sharp, Trotter, Millis, Johnson, L.Barker, Kneen.
Goals: Fitzroy – Trotter 3, Shea 3, Millis 3, Brosnan, Wilkinson, Milne.
Crowd: N/A at Brunswick St Oval

ROUND SEVEN June 11
FITZROY   6.9 (45)
SOUTH MELBOURNE   5.14 (44)
Best: Fitzroy – Naismith, Jenkins, Kelly, Johnson, Fontaine, L.Barker.
Goals: Fitzroy – Millis 2, McDonough, Kneen, Trotter, Brosnan.
Crowd: N/A at Brunswick St Oval

ROUND EIGHT June 25
FITZROY   8.8 (56)
CARLTON   7.10 (52)
Best: Fitzroy – Trotter, J.Sharp, Johnson, Wilkinson, L.Barker, G.Barker.
Goals: Fitzroy – Trotter 3, Sheehan 2, Wilkinson 2, McSpeerin.
Crowd: N/A at Brunswick St Oval

ROUND NINE July 2
FITZROY   4.7 (31)
ST KILDA   11.12 (78)
Best: Fitzroy – Brosnan, Jenkins, Johnson, McSpeerin, Sheehan.
Goals: Fitzroy – Brosnan, Kneen, L.Barker, Trotter.
Crowd: N/A at Junction Oval

ROUND TEN July 9
FITZROY   8.10 (58)
MELBOURNE   5.13 (43)
Best: Fitzroy – J.Sharp, Millis, Clarke, Wilkinson, McSpeerin, Trotter.
Goals: Fitzroy – Trotter 2, Shea, McSpeerin, Millis, Brosnan, Milne, G.Barker.
Crowd: N/A at Brunswick St Oval

ROUND ELEVEN July 16
FITZROY   3.6 (24)
COLLINGWOOD   7.13 (55)
Best: Fitzroy – Trotter, Fontaine, Naismith, Brosnan, J.Sharp.
Goals: Fitzroy – Trotter 2, Milne.
Crowd: N/A at Victoria Park

ROUND TWELVE July 23
FITZROY   6.8 (44)
ESSENDON   3.9 (27)
Best: Fitzroy – J.Sharp, Milne, Jenkins, Kneen, A.Sharp, Trotter, Brosnan.
Goals: Fitzroy – Brosnan 2, Trotter 2, Bartlett, Millis.
Crowd: N/A at Brunswick St Oval

ROUND THIRTEEN July 30
FITZROY   4.13 (37)
GEELONG   5.12 (42)
Best: Fitzroy – Milne, Lethbridge, Johnson, Fontaine, McSpeerin, P.Shea.
Goals: Fitzroy – Lethbridge, Brosnan, Milne, Clarke.
Crowd: N/A at Corio Oval

ROUND FOURTEEN August 13
FITZROY   8.10 (58)
SOUTH MELBOURNE   5.16 (46)
Best: Fitzroy – P.Shea, Brosnan, Naismith, Clarke, J.Sharp, L.Barker.
Goals: Fitzroy – P.Shea 2, McSpeerin, Kneen, Trotter, Sheehan, Brosnan, Milne.
Crowd: N/A at the Lake Oval

ROUND FIFTEEN August 20
FITZROY   4.14 (38)
SOUTH MELBOURNE   3.15 (33)
Best: Fitzroy – Brosnan, A.Sharp, J.Sharp, Johnson, Kneen, Naismith.
Goals: Fitzroy – Brosnan 2, L.Sharp, P.Shea.
Crowd: N/A at Brunswick St Oval

ROUND SIXTEEN August 27
FITZROY   8.5 (53)
GEELONG   4.6 (30)
Best: Fitzroy – P.Shea, J.Sharp, L.Barker, Millis, Trotter, McSpeerin.
Goals: Fitzroy – Kneen 2, P.Shea, L.Sharp, Johnson, Sheehan, Brosnan, Trotter.
Crowd: N/A at Corio Oval

ROUND SEVENTEEN September 3
FITZROY   4.2 (26)
ESSENDON   13.9 (87)
Best: Fitzroy – Trotter, McSpeerin, J.Sharp, G.Barker, Brosnan.
Goals: Fitzroy – Trotter 2, Milne, Kneen.
Crowd: N/A at East Melbourne Cricket Ground

PREMIER'S FINALS

SEMI-FINAL September 10
FITZROY 9.7 (61)
COLLINGWOOD 7.8 (50)
Best: Fitzroy – McSpeerin, Brosnan, Trotter, Milne, Walker, J.Sharp.
Goals: Fitzroy – Brosnan 3, Trotter 3, McDonough, Walker, Milne.
Crowd: 25,000 at the MCG

GRAND FINAL September 17
FITZROY 3.1 3.2 5.2 9.7 (61)
CARLTON 1.1 3.3 3.7 5.7 (37)
Best: Fitzroy – Brosnan, Clarke, Fontaine, Johnson, Millis, J.Sharp.
Goals: Fitzroy – Brosnan 2, Kneen 2, McDonough, Millis, Sheehan, Trotter, Walker.
Crowd: 32,688 at the MCG

GRAND FINAL LINE-UPS

FITZ	B:	A.Sharp	F.Fontaine	W.Naismith
CARL	F:	J.Marchbank	G.Topping	E.Prescott
FITZ	HB:	E.Jenkins	J.Sharp	J.Johnson
CARL	HF:	H.McShane	M.Grace	J.McShane (capt)
FITZ	C:	A.Bartlett	H.Clarke	L.Millis
CARL	C:	G.Bruce	B.Boyle	T.Kennedy
FITZ	HF:	E.Kneen	G.Brosnan (capt)	G.Barker
CARL	HB:	B.Leeds	A.Trim	C.Roland
FITZ	F:	J.McDonough	P.Sheehan	P.Trotter
CARL	B:	B.Payne	F.Hince	E.Walton
FITZ	R:	H.Milne	B.Walker	B.McSpeerin
CARL	R:	J.Flynn	F.Elliott	A.Snell
FITZ	Coach:			
CARL	Coach: Jack Worrall			

SNAPSHOT

Win-loss record: 14-5

Highest score: 16.12 (108), round 1, v Carlton.

Greatest winning margin: 94 points, round 1, v Carlton.

Lowest score: 3.6 (24), round 11, v Collingwood.

Greatest losing margin: 61 points, round 17, v Essendon.

Most goals by a player in a game: 5, Percy Trotter, round 5, v Essendon.

Most consecutive wins: 4

Most consecutive losses: 1 (five times).

Club awards: Best & Fairest: Jim Sharp; Leading goalkicker: Percy Trotter (36 goals)

Putting it into perspective:
In winning the 1904 Grand Final, Fitzroy joined fierce rival Essendon in having won the most finals of any club in the competition's still brief history, with seven wins from 11 finals appearances, including four wins at the MCG.

1904

		P	W	L	D	%	Pts
1	Fitzroy (1)	17	12	5		128.2	48
2	Carlton (2)	17	10	6	1	105.5	42
3	Collingwood (3)	17	10	7		117.0	40
4	Essendon (4)	17	10	7		113.1	40
5	South Melb	17	10	7		108.5	40
6	Melbourne	17	8	9		112.7	32
7	Geelong	17	4	12	1	77.2	18
8	St Kilda	17	3	14		62.1	12

(17 home and away rounds)

PLAYERS USED

FITZROY	GAMES	GOALS
Barker, Gilbert	9	1
Barker, Lou	15	6
Bartlett, Alf	16	3
Brosnan, Gerald	18	31
Clarke, Harry	11	1
Fontaine, Fred	14	1
Jenkins, Ern	18	0
Johnson, Joe	19	1
Kelly, Bill G.	7	0
Kneen, Edgar	16	9
Lethbridge, Fred	3	1
McDonough, Jack	14	3
McSpeerin, Bill	15	6
Millis, Les	19	12
Milne, Herbert	16	13
Moriarty, Geoff	1	0
Naismith, Wally	19	1
Sharp, Alf	14	0
Sharp, Jim	18	0
Sharp, Les	5	2
Shea, Mark	2	0
Shea, Paddy	13	8
Sheehan, Percy	12	5
Tomkins, Hedley	4	0
Trotter, Percy	19	36
Walker, Bill	14	2
Wilkinson, Alf	11	7

**FITZROY 4.6 (30) d
COLLINGWOOD 2.5 (17)**

ROYS SNARE MORE GLORY

Fitzroy banished Collingwood to earn its second successive premiership and confirm its status as the best club in the colony. By ADAM McNICOL

DARK clouds hung over Melbourne, rain fell constantly and a strong south-westerly wind lashed the city as Collingwood and Fitzroy prepared to do battle in the 1905 VFL Grand Final at the MCG. The reigning champion, Fitzroy, was aiming to cement its place as the pre-eminent football club in Victoria by winning its fourth VFL premiership in the competition's ninth season. Collingwood, the Maroons' neighbour and fierce enemy, which had finished the regular season in first place, was confident it could take home its third pennant.

The two clubs had filled the top positions on the ladder for most of the year. In fact, little had separated them since the first bounce of the season at Brunswick Street Oval. The cloudless sky on that afternoon—Saturday, May 6—was in stark contrast to the dreary conditions they would face on Grand Final day. It was so warm on the opening day of the season that 'Observer', *The Argus's* football correspondent, was moved to describe it as cricket weather. (It was 27°.) "I never remember seeing the grounds so hard and fast at the start of the season," he wrote. "It needed men at the top of their training to last through the game, especially where the game was open, for this always means pace. There were large crowds at all the League matches, showing that football has lost nothing of the popularity it enjoyed last winter. On such a day, however, it was a privilege to be in the open air, apart altogether from the attractions of football."

Fitzroy began proceedings by unfurling its 1904 flag in front of an impressive new grandstand, which meant at least some of the 20,000 spectators on hand were able to view the contest in relative comfort. Beneath its wooden bench-style seating, the stand contained a new changeroom and a state-of-the-art gymnasium that was the envy of Fitzroy's rivals. (It burned down in 1977.) When the formalities were done, the Maroons, under the captaincy of 26-year-old Gerald Brosnan for the third consecutive season, won a tough and rugged contest by three points, 4.10 (34) to 3.13 (31). The victory was an illustration of the depth on Fitzroy's list, as it had gone into the match without ruckman Herbert 'Boxer' Milne and defender Fred Fontaine, who had broken his leg during a Tuesday evening training session in mid-April. "Fontaine has been a most unfortunate athlete," read a report on the incident in *The Argus*. "This is the third time he has broken his leg, and as a cyclist he was frequently the victim of more or less serious accidents." As the article suggested, there was no doubting Fontaine's toughness, and true to form he was back on the field by the second half of the season.

The Maroons had recruited well, replacing the retired Billy McSpeerin with a dashing, young wingman by the name of Barclay Bailes. Known as 'Titch' because he stood only 157cm, Bailes hailed from Bendigo but joined Fitzroy after spending two years in Western Australia. The club's running power was further boosted by the return of tough centreman Tammy Beauchamp, who had spent the 1904 season with Norwood in South Australia. Beauchamp and Bailes, along with champion rover and goalsneak Percy Trotter, were the driving forces as the Maroons started their campaign with seven straight wins. The seventh came at the expense of South Melbourne at Brunswick Street, and a few days later the two sides travelled to Sydney for an exhibition match at the SCG. Unhappy with the Victorian code's incursion into their territory, the rugby authorities reacted by scheduling a game in the vicinity of the cricket ground. In the following week, *The Argus* lambasted the VFL's efforts to win over the people of New South Wales, describing the initiative of playing games north of the border as "the hopeless crusade against rugby. They have as much chance of supplanting it… as they have of superseding cricket with croquet".

The game in Sydney did throw up one innovation that eventually stuck. In the second half, the Fitzroy boys wore numbers on their backs to help the New South Welshmen in the crowd ascertain who the better players were. The move towards the combatants wearing numbers came in response to a persistent campaign from footy fans in Melbourne, many of whom had written letters to the editors of various newspapers. The rule compelling all VFL teams to have numbers on their players' backs was not introduced until 1912, corresponding with the launch of the game's official organ, the *Football Record*.

Fitzroy's trip to Sydney, which involved many hours in the cramped confines of a rocking and rolling steamship, seemed to upset the team's rhythm. In their first game after returning to Melbourne, the Maroons suffered a 22-point loss to Collingwood at Victoria Park. If not for the Magpies' inaccurate kicking—the final score was 5.11 (41) to 3.1 (19)—the margin would have been far greater. Collingwood, which had not been beaten since round one, was inspired by the combativeness of its 30-year-old leading goalscorer Charlie Pannam (whose grandsons Lou and Ron Richards were later star players at the club). Yet a few days after the game, Pannam was forced to explain himself after the League investigated an incident involving him and Brosnan, the opposition skipper. The hearing took place on a Wednesday evening at the Port Phillip Club Hotel in Flinders Street, and Brosnan stated that Pannam had struck him in the face. His Collingwood adversary replied that Brosnan had provoked him by striking him "behind the ear". After some further exchanges of evidence, during which umpire Ivo Crapp supported Brosnan's version of events, the tribunal banned Pannam for one match.

Two weeks later, however, Collingwood's players and supporters were smiling when Fitzroy suffered a shock thrashing from Geelong at the Corio Oval. The Magpies' 70-point victory over St Kilda on the same day enabled the Pies to replace the Maroons at the top of the ladder. It was not until round 14 that the Black and Whites suffered their second loss of the season, the defeat at the hands of Essendon at Victoria Park snapping a 12-game winning run. Each team had by then played the others twice, and thanks to finishing on top Collingwood was included in Section A for the final three rounds. In the same section were third-placed Carlton, fifth-placed South Melbourne and seventh-placed Melbourne, for the last three rounds before the finals. A narrow triumph over the Blues was followed by a 33-point victory over Melbourne and a 78-point thumping of South. The impressive performances saw the Magpies finish the home and away matches two and a half wins clear of Fitzroy.

Heading into the most important games of the year, Collingwood was widely tipped to win the flag. The club's first-year playing-coach, Dick Condon, a supremely skilful yet often feisty centreman, was considered the finest tactician in the game, having developed what was known as the Collingwood System—essentially a high-possession style of play, in which the players moved the ball into the forward line using a series of short stab-passes rather than the traditional long kicks. Condon, himself, had earlier been credited with inventing the stab-pass in response to the introduction of a more rounded football. To make their system work, the Magpies needed to have loose men in their forward half, and for this to happen the team's midfield players were urged to run forward of the centre at every opportunity. The system regularly confounded opposition defences, enabling Collingwood to become the highest-scoring team in the competition.

The Maroons were inconsistent during the second half of the home and away campaign. Although rover and regular goal-scorer Percy Trotter was certainly in the best half-dozen players in the VFL, plenty of football watchers doubted Fitzroy could repeat its heroics of 1904. A week after the poor showing against Geelong in round 10, the Maroons had gone down to Carlton by two points, the consecutive defeats all but ending their chances of winning the minor premiership (this was particularly important because in those days the minor premier claimed the ability to invoke the Challenge rule if the early finals didn't go its way). In round 14, the Fitzroy faithful sat through another heart-stopper when their team drew with South Melbourne at the Lake Oval. The Maroons were 18 points down early in the last quarter, before they staged a dramatic fightback.

"Fitzroy's hope seemed gone, but the visiting skipper urged his men on, and by combined play they enabled (Edgar) Kneen to snap two goals in quick succession, which roused the spectators to the highest pitch of excitement," wrote *The Age's* correspondent, who estimated the crowd at 15,000. In the frantic final minutes, Trotter kicked a point then Beauchamp put through a goal and suddenly the Maroons were in front. South's Charles Clements had a chance to snatch back the lead when he had a shot from 30 yards out, yet it sailed wide. With the scores now level, Fitzroy had one final chance to snatch victory when Brosnan gathered the ball within range, but he elected to pass rather than shoot at goal. To Brosnan's dismay, the bell rang soon after the ball left his boot.

Fitzroy won its first sectional match against bottom side St Kilda, but it was beaten again by Geelong a week later. Brosnan's players finally rediscovered their best form when they rounded out the regular season by thrashing Essendon at the East Melbourne ground. Fitzroy had finished second on the ladder, with 12 wins and a draw, but its ability to kick winning scores in the finals was in question. Top team Collingwood had scored 1111 points in its 17 games, and third-placed Carlton had tallied 1005, yet Fitzroy's combined scores added up to only 884 points. The media experts of the time were adamant the Maroons relied too heavily on their defenders—players such as Joe Johnson, Wally Naismith, Geoff Moriarty and James Sharp. The common belief was that if they could not strangle the life out of their opposition, they could not win.

The finals series began at Princes Park in Carlton on Saturday, September 16, with the Maroons taking on fourth-placed Essendon for the second time in eight days. "The previous week's play was generally thought by the Essendon supporters not to be their true form, and with a slightly altered team they expected it to do much better," stated *The Age* in its post-game report. However, Fitzroy proved their doubters wrong by kicking eight goals in the opening half on the way to a 43-point victory. Trotter was the hero of the rough-and-ready contest, the little marvel bobbing up with six of his team's 12 majors, his effort setting a record for goal-kicking in a VFL final. Brosnan, who was stationed at centre half-forward, was another outstanding contributor, while Bill Walker was the dominant ruckman on the field. Lou Barker, Beauchamp, Bailes, Les Millis and Johnson were others named among the best players.

On the same day, an even more remarkable result played out when Carlton demolished flag-favourite Collingwood at the MCG. The Blues had played the Magpies three times during the season and each time Carlton had been soundly beaten. Yet the Blues dominated the semi-final to such an extent that their opponent's famous "system" was never sighted. In fact, the ball was so rarely in the Collingwood forward line that Condon's team, which was at full-strength, failed to kick a goal in the opening half. The Blues went on with the job, winning 11.10 (76) to 4.6 (30).

Under the finals system of the time, Collingwood (thanks to finishing the home and away season on top of the ladder) was able to immediately invoke the Challenge rule, meaning the Grand Final would be played between it and the winner of a knock-out match between Carlton and Fitzroy. These days such a game is titled the preliminary final (and is counted as a preliminary final in the AFL's official statistics). In 1905, however, it was simply referred to as being another semi-final. In the lead-up to the clash between the Maroons and the Blues, rumours surfaced that Collingwood had thrown its semi in the hope that Carlton would knock Fitzroy out of the premiership race. The Blues' players and supporters branded these suggestions as an insult.

Around 30,000 people packed into the MCG to see the Maroons and Carlton go at it. The gate totalled £938, making it the second largest in League history, behind the 1904 Grand Final. Thanks to their big win over Collingwood, the Blues went in as favourites and they started the game full of running, but their initial forays into attack yielded only three behinds. Nevertheless, two straight kicks from Mick Grace had them two points up at the opening change. The second quarter was another even and entertaining affair, although, as *The Argus*, reported it was also "a little bit on the rough side, not because the players wished to make it so, but because both sides were eager and anxious". The efforts of Trotter, Brosnan and Millis handed Fitzroy a narrow advantage at the long break. Johnson was also in outstanding touch for the Maroons. Usually a defender, he had begun in Fitzroy's forward line and kicked the opening goal with a snap shot. With Johnson in attack, Percy Sheehan, Sharp and Ernest Jenkins held the backline together in impressive fashion. In particular, Sheehan's dashing play often brought the crowd to life.

The game changed in the third quarter when Fitzroy began to take control. By the final change, the Maroons were 11 points up thanks to a pair of goals from their full-forward Alf Wilkinson, one of which was executed with a place kick. Fitzroy pulled further away in the last term, kicking three unanswered majors to win by 27 points. Johnson was declared best on ground, with Sheehan, Trotter, Millis, Sharp and Jenkins others to rate a mention. The better contributors for Carlton, whose season was now over, were ruckman Jim Flynn, defenders Bert Parke and Hammond, forward Grace and Archie Snell.

So the premiership came down to a battle between Collingwood and Fitzroy. Despite the constant rain that fell on the morning of the game, which was played on Saturday, September 30, a crowd of more than 28,000 headed to the MCG. People came from all over Victoria for the match, many of the rural folk in attendance having travelled aboard the special footy trains that ran on the Bendigo and Ballarat lines. The majority of fans had written off Collingwood's performance against Carlton a fortnight earlier, so for the third week in a row the Maroons (despite having 13 members of their 1904 premiership team in their line-up) went in as underdogs. The wet weather—it had been raining for most of the week—caused the Magpies to field quite a different team from the one that had been thrashed by the Blues. Lighter-bodied players Percy Ogden, George Marsh and Fred Stancliffe were omitted. Big forward Matthew Fell was one of the replacements, with *The Argus* noting that the Collingwood selectors, when choosing the other two, "wanted weight, and places were found for two of their stoutest in [Bill] Proudfoot and [Jack] Incoll, who have only played occasionally during the season".

As the spectators sheltered under their umbrellas, Brosnan won the toss for Fitzroy and elected to kick with the wind, which was blowing towards the left forward pocket at the Punt Road end (today this area is filled by the Olympic Stand). While *The Age* later reported the ground was in "capital order" despite the rain, the conditions made the going tough for players, and 10 minutes of play elapsed before the Maroons opened the scoring with a behind. During the remainder of the first stanza, Fitzroy, inspired by the skill and tenacity of Bailes, tried desperately to register a goal. But its attacks were repelled time and time again, most of them by Collingwood defender Alf Dummett. An experienced campaigner, Dummett booted the ball towards the boundary line in front of the MCC members' stand at every opportunity, as the wind had made that the dead side of the ground. As *The Argus* reporter noted, "from that wing it was a difficult thing to get into a good scoring position". At the opening change, Fitzroy led three behinds to one.

The game opened up in the second quarter, allowing Collingwood, which now had the breeze at its back, to get its system going. Led by rover Harry Pears, the Magpie players thrilled the crowd by stringing together some classy exchanges of stab passes, although they wasted a couple of early chances to take the lead. Fitzroy's full-back, Moriarty, knew only one way to try to get his team out of trouble, and that was by kicking the ball long down the middle of the ground, a tactic that often played into Collingwood's hands. With his team struggling to turn its domination into a handy advantage on the scoreboard, Condon moved Bob Nash from the backline into attack and he responded by kicking the first goal of the game. However, Fitzroy then rallied. Just before the half-time bell rang, Millis capped off a great passage of play by slotting a goal and levelling the scores at 1.3 apiece.

Given these were the days before substitute or interchange players, injuries often decided the outcome of games. But on this score, both sides were just about even after the first hour. As was detailed in *The Argus*: "Towards the end of the [second] quarter, Condon, who had been playing brilliantly for Collingwood, was so seriously hurt that he was of no further use to them. This would have been a severe handicap but that misfortune balanced matters, J. Sharp, the stoutest of Fitzroy's defenders, getting a knock which practically made him useless, though he was able to stay on the field."

As it had a year earlier, when Fitzroy beat Carlton in the Grand Final, the third quarter decided the outcome of the premiership race. Trotter snapped a brilliant goal only a couple of minutes into the second half, and Fitzroy might have put a second on the board soon after when Fontaine received the ball within range. In a remarkable passage of play, Fontaine kicked the ball into the man on the mark, but ran forward to gather possession before having another shot, which was touched on the line. Fitzroy went further ahead when Brosnan slotted a brilliant 50-yard goal from the boundary line, and his team stretched its advantage to 20 points when Lou Barker booted another major. Pears finally bagged a goal for Collingwood only a minute before three-quarter time, which narrowed the gap to 14 points at the final change. Yet the game appeared as good as over. Without Condon, whose serious injury meant his side had only 17 men on the park, Collingwood's famed "system" had broken down. The Magpies' predicament was made worse by the selectors' decision to pick so many stocky players, as the decision robbed the team of the pace needed to keep up with Fitzroy's centreline stars.

Fitzroy's professionalism shone out in the last quarter, as the Maroons bottled up the play at every opportunity. "They did not repeat their plan of kicking straight up the field, but depending on strategy rather than strength, went for the pavilion wing at every opportunity," read the summary in *The Argus*. "The ball was frequently out of bounds there, and Fitzroy were penalised for putting it out a bit too obviously, though in this they were only bettering the example set by Collingwood in the opening quarter." A behind from Eddie Drohan, registered after getting a free kick, proved to be the only score of the final term. "The last half of it was poor football, and I have rarely known a great crowd on a great occasion to be so quiet towards the end of a match," 'Observer' continued in his summary for *The Argus*.

None of this mattered to everyone involved with Fitzroy when the bell rang to signal the end of the 1905 season. As the players shook hands, with the scoreboard showing the Maroons had won by 13 points, thousands of their supporters streamed on to the oval. Fitzroy had won another premiership. Not only that, the club had won consecutive flags for the second time in the VFL's nine-year history. The newspaper reporters all agreed that Bailes was the best player on the ground. Beauchamp, another member of the Fitzroy centreline, was listed as second best, while defenders Jenkins, Moriarty, Sheehan and Naismith were also mentioned. Sheehan's performance, which came after he suffered a leg injury early in the match, was particularly meritorious. Dummett and Pears were named as Collingwood's best players. The Magpies, who had seemed by far the best side in the competition for much of the season, were bitterly disappointed as they trudged from the field.

The Maroons, on the other hand, were given even more cause for celebration when the leading football writers named Trotter, who had only recently turned 22, Champion of the Colony. However, he didn't win his club's best and fairest, which was taken out by Millis. Fitzroy's success confirmed its reputation as the leading Australian Rules football club. It had won five premierships (including the 1895 VFA premiership) since its formation in 1883, and had more than 2500 members, which put it well clear of its rivals. It also boasted the best facilities, the best players and the most professional administration.

The Maroons seemed destined to sit atop the pile for years to come.

1905 FITZROY

PREMIER'S SEASON

FITZROY: 1905

ROUND ONE May 6
FITZROY 4.10 (34)
COLLINGWOOD 3.13 (14)
Best: Fitzroy –Millis, Trotter, Holt, Brosnan, Bartlett, J.Sharp.
Goals: Fitzroy – Millis 2, Sheehan, Wilkinson.
Crowd: N/A at Brunswick St Oval

ROUND TWO May 13
FITZROY 9.10 (64)
ST KILDA 4.9 (33)
Best: Fitzroy –Wilkinson, Trotter, Elliott, Millis, Walker, Moriarty.
Goals: Fitzroy – Wilkinson 3, Kneen 2, Trotter 2, Sheehan, Douglas.
Crowd: N/A at the Junction Oval

ROUND THREE May 20
FITZROY 10.16 (76)
GEELONG 4.11 (35)
Best: Fitzroy – Wilkinson, Bailes, Johnson, Walker, J.Sharp, Jenkins.
Goals: Fitzroy – Wilkinson 4, Trotter 3, Kneen, Bailes, McDonough.
Crowd: N/A at Brunswick St Oval

ROUND FOUR May 27
FITZROY 10.13 (73)
CARLTON 5.7 (37)
Best: Fitzroy – Brosnan, Millis, Johnson, Beauchamp, L.Sharp, G.Barker.
Goals: Fitzroy – Trotter 3, Bailes 2, Brosnan 2, Kneen, Wilkinson, Millis.
Crowd: N/A at Princes Park

ROUND FIVE June 5
FITZROY 5.8 (38)
MELBOURNE 3.12 (30)
Best: Fitzroy – Kneen, Millis, J.Sharp, L.Barker, Naismith, Johnson.
Goals: Fitzroy – Kneen 4, Wilkinson.
Crowd: N/A at the MCG

ROUND SIX June 10
FITZROY 5.5 (35)
ESSENDON 3.10 (28)
Best: Fitzroy – Millis, Holt, Beauchamp, Johnson, Kneen, Jenkins.
Goals: Fitzroy – Wilkinson 2, L.Barker, McDonough, G.Barker.
Crowd: N/A at Brunswick St Oval

ROUND SEVEN June 17
FITZROY 9.14 (68)
SOUTH MELBOURNE 6.6 (42)
Best: Fitzroy – Johnson, Millis, Sheehan, Brosnan, Wilkinson.
Goals: Fitzroy – Sheehan 3, Brosnan 2, Wilkinson 2, Bailes, Millis.
Crowd: N/A at Brunswick St Oval

ROUND EIGHT July 1
FITZROY 3.1 (19)
COLLINGWOOD 5.11 (41)
Best: Fitzroy – J.Sharp, Bailes, Wilkinson, Brosnan, Milne.
Goals: Fitzroy – Walker, Bailes, Wilkinson.
Crowd: N/A at Victoria Park

ROUND NINE July 8
FITZROY 14.7 (91)
ST KILDA 6.4 (40)
Best: Fitzroy – Wilkinson, Kneen, Naismith, Johnson, Millis.
Goals: Fitzroy – Wilkinson 5, Kneen 3, Trotter 2, Walker, Bailes, Sheehan, Milne.
Crowd: N/A at Brunswick St Oval

ROUND TEN July 15
FITZROY 2.15 (27)
GEELONG 9.8 (62)
Best: Fitzroy – Millis, Brosnan, Milne, L.Barker, Bailes.
Goals: Fitzroy – Brosnan, Milne.
Crowd: N/A at Corio Oval

ROUND ELEVEN July 22
FITZROY 5.9 (39)
CARLTON 6.5 (41)
Best: Fitzroy – Millis, Johnson, Holt, Naismith, J.Sharp, Bartlett.
Goals: Fitzroy – Wilkinson 2, Millis 2, McDonough.
Crowd: N/A at Brunswick St Oval

ROUND TWELVE July 29
FITZROY 5.7 (37)
MELBOURNE 2.6 (18)
Best: Fitzroy – J.Sharp, L.Barker, Millis, Kneen, Johnson, Brosnan.
Goals: Fitzroy – Kneen 2, Trotter, Millis, Wilkinson.
Crowd: N/A at Brunswick St Oval

ROUND THIRTEEN August 5
FITZROY 5.12 (42)
ESSENDON 3.11 (29)
Best: Fitzroy – Johnson, Beauchamp, Trotter, Billings, Sheehan.
Goals: Fitzroy – Johnson, Brosnan, Milne, Beauchamp, Trotter.
Crowd: N/A at East Melbourne Cricket Ground

ROUND FOURTEEN August 19
FITZROY 7.8 (50)
SOUTH MELBOURNE 7.8 (50)
Best: Fitzroy – Beauchamp, L.Barker, Fontaine, G.Barker, McDonough.
Goals: Fitzroy – Kneen 2, Beauchamp, Johnson, L.Barker, Trotter, Wilkinson.
Crowd: N/A at the Lake Oval

ROUND FIFTEEN August 26
FITZROY 6.9 (45)
ST KILDA 4.7 (31)
Best: Fitzroy – Brosnan, Millis, Fontaine, Naismith, J.Sharp, Walker.
Goals: Fitzroy – Brosnan 4, Trotter, Wilkinson.
Crowd: N/A at Brunswick St Oval

ROUND SIXTEEN September 2
FITZROY 9.12 (66)
GEELONG 10.8 (68)
Best: Fitzroy – Kneen, Millis, Naismith, Brosnan, L.Barker, Beauchamp.
Goals: Fitzroy – Brosnan 3, Trotter 2, Wilkinson 2, Kneen, Bailes.
Crowd: N/A at Corio Oval

ROUND SEVENTEEN September 9
FITZROY 11.14 (80)
ESSENDON 4.13 (37)
Best: Fitzroy – L.Barker, Bilings, Brosnan, Milne, L.Sharp.
Goals: Fitzroy – Fontaine 2, Millis 2, Milne 2, Kneen, Brosnan, Sharp, Wilkinson, Trotter.
Crowd: N/A at East Melbourne Cricket Ground

PREMIER'S FINALS

SEMI-FINAL September 16
FITZROY 12.7 (79)
ESSENDON 4.12 (36)
Best: Fitzroy – Trotter, G.Barker, J.Sharp, Walker, Beauchamp, Bailes, Millis.
Goals: Fitzroy – Trotter 6, Brosnan 2, Johnson, Sharp, Fontaine, Millis.
Crowd: 14,000 at Princes Park

PRELIMINARY FINAL September 23
FITZROY 11.6 (72)
CARLTON 6.9 (45)
Best: Fitzroy – Johnson, Sheehan, Trotter, Milne, J.Sharp, Jenkins, Naismith.
Goals: Fitzroy – Trotter 2, Milne 2, Wilkinson 2, Johnson 2, Brosnan, Millis, Walker.
Crowd: 30,000 at the MCG

GRAND FINAL September 30
FITZROY 0.3 1.3 4.6 4.6 (30)
COLLINGWOOD 0.1 1.3 2.4 2.5 (17)
Best: Fitzroy – Bailes, Beauchamp, Jenkins, Moriarty, Naismith, Sheehan.
Goals: Fitzroy – L.Barker, Brosnan, Millis, Trotter.
Crowd: 30,000 at the MCG

GRAND FINAL LINE-UPS

FITZ	B:	W.Naismith	G.Moriarty	L.Barker
COLL	F:	G.Angus	E.Drohan	J.Incoll
FITZ	HB:	E.Jenkins	J.Sharp	P.Sheehan
COLL	HF:	C.Pannam (capt)	B.Nash	H.Pears
FITZ	C:	G.Barker	T.Beauchamp	B.Bailes
COLL	C:	G.Green	J.McHale	P.Gibb
FITZ	HF:	G.Brosnan (capt)	F.Fontaine	J.Johnson
COLL	HB:	B.Rush	J.Monohan	D.Fraser
FITZ	F:	A.Wilkinson	J.McDonough	P.Trotter
COLL	B:	M.Fell	B.Proudfoot	A.Dummett
FITZ	R:	H.Milne	B.Walker	L.Millis
COLL	R:	A.Leach	B.Strachan	D.Condon

SNAPSHOT

Win-loss record: 15-4-1

Highest score: 14.7 (91), round 9, v St Kilda.

Greatest winning margin: 51 points, round 9, v St Kilda.

Lowest score: 3.1 (19), round 8, v Collingwood.

Greatest losing margin: 35 points, round 10, v Geelong.

Most goals by a player in a game: 6, Percy Trotter, semi-final, v Essendon.

Most consecutive wins: 7

Most consecutive losses: 2

Club awards: Best & Fairest: Les Millis; Leading goalkicker: Alf Wilkinson (30 goals)

Putting it into perspective:
For the second time Fitzroy achieved back-to-back premiership success and crowned itself the most successful club in the VFL. The club had four wins from six Grand Final appearances and all four wins had been against different teams.

1905

		P	W	L	D	%	Pts
1	Collingwood (2)	17	15	2		175.0	60
2	Fitzroy (1)	17	12	4	1	135.4	50
3	Carlton (3)	17	11	6		127.4	44
4	Essendon (4)	17	9	8		114.4	36
5	South Melb	17	7	9	1	83.7	30
6	Geelong	17	6	11		79.0	24
7	St Kilda	17	4	13		64.1	16
8	Melbourne	17	3	14		70.9	12

(17 home and away rounds)

PLAYERS USED

FITZROY	GAMES	GOALS
Bailes, Barclay	15	7
Barker, Gilbert	18	1
Barker, Lou	19	3
Bartlett, Alf	7	0
Beauchamp, Tammy	15	2
Billings, Syd	13	0
Brosnan, Gerald	18	18
Davison, Sam	2	0
Douglas, Sonny	2	1
Elliott, George	1	0
Fontaine, Fred	7	3
Holt, Jack	12	0
Jenkins, Ern	18	0
Johnson, Joe	19	5
Kneen, Edgar	16	17
McDonough, Jack	15	3
Millis, Les	20	12
Milne, Herbert	13	7
Moriarty, Geoff	13	0
Naismith, Wally	20	0
Plaisted, Ridley	1	0
Sharp, Jim	19	0
Sharp, Les	5	2
Sheehan, Percy	17	6
Trotter, Percy	17	26
Walker, Bill J.	18	3
Wilkinson, Alf	20	30

**CARLTON 15.4 (94) d
FITZROY 6.9 (45)**

A MAN CALLED WORRALL

Carlton's appointment of John Worrall, a former Fitzroy star and Test cricketer, as the first coach in League football proved to be an inspired move. By HOWARD KOTTON and TONY DE BOLFO

IN 1902, not long after his landmark appointment as honorary secretary and delegate, John 'Jack' Worrall put it to the gents of the Carlton Football Club committee that the Latin quotation *Mens sana in corpore sano* be adopted as the club's official motto.

Worrall was long familiar with the quote, whose origins can be sourced to the Roman poet Decimus Junius Juvenalis. It was Juvenalis who around the time of the second century AD was inspired to write: "Our prayers should be for *a sound mind in a sound body.*"

For many years, the inscription *Mens sana in corpore sano* flanked the clock atop the Carlton pavilion at the the northern end of what was known as "The Triangle"—a parcel of land bound by Royal Parade, Cemetery Road and College Crescent—at which Carlton players chased the leather in the pre-Princes Park years of the early 1880s.

The motto had been taken on as the tenet of the Carlton Cricket Club, which Worrall had served so very ably; it was a natural that he would carry those values to the football club and so it came to pass.

Flick the pages of the 1902 Annual Report and you'll find *Mens sana in corpore sano* beneath the Carlton Football Club emblem for the first time—a time when Worrall embarked upon what would be a successful, if tempestuous, football journey with the old dark Navy Blues.

That was more than 100 years ago, and today the words of Juvenalis—the core of Worrall's edict through the history-making premiership years of 1906, '07 and '08—still ring true at Carlton.

To appreciate the spectacular, if turbulent, happenings of the Carlton Football Club in the Edwardian years of the early 20th century, one must first have knowledge of the man at the helm.

John Worrall, footballer, cricketer, journalist and inaugural Carlton coach, was born at Chinamans Flat in Maryborough on the northern slopes of the Great Dividing Range, on June 21, 1861. He was the seventh child of the Irish-born immigrants Joseph Worrall, a miner, and his wife Ann, née Gaynor.

After moving south to the city of Ballarat, where he played football for South Ballarat, young Worrall's football prowess caught the roving eye of Fitzroy recruiters. Worrall was induced to move to Melbourne and join the Maroons in 1884.

Worrall excelled at Fitzroy, serving as captain of the club for seven of his nine seasons, until 1892. He represented Victoria in intercolonial matches and he was named Champion of the Colony in 1887 and 1890. Early scribes regarded him as "a nuggety and determined rover who could soar for marks and kick accurately with either foot". He was commonly regarded as among the best Australian Rules footballers in the country.

In summer, Worrall donned the creams and similarly excelled. In a career of 140 first-class matches between 1883 and 1902, he scored 4660 runs (including seven centuries) at an average of 20.99, took 105 wickets at 23.10 (best figures five for 20) and held 101 catches. While representing Carlton in a club match in 1896, he posted a staggering Australian record of 417 not out.

Worrall represented Victoria on 65 occasions through 121 innings, during which time he accumulated 2407 runs at 20.93 (highest score 109), captured 74 wickets at 22.09 and captained the colony in sixteen games. He also represented Australia in 11 Test matches against England (1885-99), for figures of 478 runs at 25.15, one wicket for 127 runs, and 13 catches.

A right-handed opening bat whose belligerent drives, it was reported, could tear apart any attack, Worrall displayed a real tenacity on sticky wickets, as was the case in the 1899 Test at Headingley when he grafted 76 of Australia's first innings total of 172.

While on tour in England in July 1902 the Australian captain, Joe Darling, formally complained to the Victorian Cricketers' Association that Worrall had informed an English umpire that two Australian Test bowlers, John Victor

Saunders and Montague 'Monty' Noble, were "chuckers" who should be "no-balled out of every game".

The VCA delegates summarily banned Worrall from playing first-class cricket. He accepted the decision without protest and so channeled his energies towards the Carlton Football Club.

Having assumed control at a club whose teams had finished seventh of the eight teams in each of its previous five seasons since the League's formation, Worrall sought to implement a direct, long-kicking game involving young, fast-moving, high-marking, big men. As coach, he was known to don togs at training sessions, organise strict schedules, demand unflinching courage and impose stern discipline.

Worrall's words of 1902 were indeed prophetic. "There is a grand spirit of camaraderie amongst the team, which augurs well for our future prospects, and we trust, by assiduous attention to training, that no stone will be left unturned to achieve the goal of our ambition," he declared.

But by 1904, the lofty aims of all at Carlton, not the least Worrall himself, were torn asunder with the man's sudden dismissal.

In the Carlton Football Club's Annual Report of season 1904, availed to Members at the annual meeting at the Orderly Rooms in Grattan Street, the matter of Worrall was outlined as follows:

"A serious difference having arisen between your Committee and the late Secretary, Mr J. Worrall, a Sub-Committee was appointed by your Committee to inquire into the said differences.

"The report of the Sub-Committee is as follows:-

> That after hearing the evidence of the Treasurer and President, this Committee has come to the following conclusion: That Mr Worrall made a grave error in paying the South Melbourne, Melbourne and Collingwood cheques into his own account, and then paying his own cheques to the Carlton Football Club in exchange.

"The following resolution was passed by your Committee, after full consideration of the report of the sub-Committee:-

> That in the opinion of this Committee, it would be detrimental to the best interest of the Club for Mr Worrall to hold the position of Secretary." [Carried by 16 for and 7 against.]
>
> Signed on behalf of the Committee,
>
> R. HEATLEY, (President), March 1904"

The report also carried the club's statement of receipts and expenditure for that year, listing the proceeds for Carlton's home matches involving Collingwood

(£30 0 2), South Melbourne (£27 8 1) and Melbourne (£12 9 11) and the honorarium for the honorary coach (£25) and late honorary secretary (£25).

Was Worrall dishonest in his dealings? Not according to the authors of *The Carlton Story* (published in 1958), Harry Bell and Hugh Buggy, who in the chapter entitled *The Golden Years* wrote of the dissension among the ranks that threatened to lead to the defection of senior Carlton players, all because of Worrall's sacking.

"There was never any suggestion that Mr Worrall had been in any way dishonest, but his book-keeping methods may have been a little unorthodox," Bell and Buggy wrote.

"Yet the committee not only dispensed with his services but refused his nomination for re-election. A requisition by members for a special general meeting followed immediately. Those who signed the requisition sought to submit a motion that the secretary of the club 'should be a paid servant, with no vote or voice in the management of the club'."

Crucially, the Carlton players rallied behind Worrall in 1904, and it was they, together with the members rather than the committee, who helped heal the rift.

A notice carrying the name of the club captain, J.J. McShane, and 18 senior Carlton players was circulated. The notice carried an emphatic denial to suggestions that they would refuse to play if Worrall was re-elected to the position, and added that Worrall enjoyed their total support in the lead-up to the annual election.

At the election of March 28, 1904, the 19 Carlton players ran a ticket that supported Worrall and opposed the president, vice-president and all members of the committee except the seven who had voted against the proposal to sack Worrall: the then captain Joe McShane, his brother Henry, and Messrs McIntyre, McNamara. Lewis, Coulson, Loan and Ross.

The ticket was successful and Worrall continued in office—thankfully, as this was the beginning of the first golden era of the Carlton Football Club.

Worrall's original accusers—Heatley, vice-president F. Lanyon and treasurer M.B. Hearne—all resigned when their positions became untenable. Heatley was succeeded by Henry Bournes Higgins, the then Federal Attorney-General; Lanyon by Alderman W. Strong; and Hearne, who had served his club as treasurer for 24 years, by John Urquhart.

For Heatley, the sorry affair brought his personal and professional relationship with Worrall to a truly sad conclusion. As late as the end of the 1902 season, just 18 months previously, Heatley had written of Worrall in an addendum to the club's Annual Report of that year:

> "The Committee cannot conclude their report without expressing the high appreciation of your Secretary's indefatigable labors during his first year of office with the Dark Blues. Mr Worrall's regular attendance during the practice and training of the team—giving the benefit of his vast knowledge and experience as a past prominent player—contributed so materially to the Club's improved position in the season's contests that he undoubtedly merits your very best thanks."

By the time the tumultuous events of 1904 had run their course, Worrall's men had advanced to the Grand Final, only to finish four goals adrift of Fitzroy. But Worrall knew that Carlton was on the cusp of greatness. He noted in the Annual Report of 1904:

> "The prominent position occupied by the Club last season must have been a source of extreme satisfaction to all Carltonians, for by sheer merit they gained the proud title of runners-up, occupying the highest position in the annals of the Club for the past 13 years. There has been a progressive increase on the premiership ladder since 1902, but there is still a rung to climb.

> "The grand position occupied by your Club, especially after such a disastrous commencement (in the VFL), speaks volumes for the splendid grit and determination of the players, who never lost heart. They stuck to their task manfully and success rewarded their efforts in a marked and pronounced degree. The playing members of the team deserve the members' warmest and best thanks."

With the recruitment of players like George 'Mallee' Johnson, Frank 'Silver' Caine, Charlie Hammond, Rod 'Wee' McGregor and back pocket player Norman 'Hackenschmidt' Clark—so named because his glorious physique drew comparisons with the famed Estonian-born bodybuilder and wrestler of the day, Georges Karl Julius Hackenschmidt—the 1905 season promised plenty but ended in disappointment. The Carlton team won 11 games through the winter to emerge third after the home and away season, but faltered in the preliminary final against eventual premier Fitzroy.

It was said of the 1905 season that Carlton's cause was lost with Worrall's dismissal the previous year, and while the great man was reinstated amid overwhelming player support, the off-field tumult surely contributed to the team's underperformance.

But, as has often been said, the darkest hour is before the dawn.

Worrall's men gave a tremendous account of themselves in the opening rounds of the 1906 season, posting comfortable victories over Melbourne, St Kilda and Geelong. A 20-point victory over an inaccurate Collingwood in the fourth round at Victoria Park preceded hard-fought wins against South Melbourne at home and Fitzroy at Brunswick Street. The run of victories was ended at six when Essendon's Albert Thurgood quelled the influence of Clark in their match at Princes Park.

Worrall's men rebounded to take the next four matches, but poor conversion was dogging them. The Blues booted a tally of 34.58 in the four matches from round eight to round 11 before experiencing successive defeats at the hands of South Melbourne at the Lake Oval and Fitzroy at Princes Park.

The five-point loss to the Maroons would be Carlton's last defeat for the landmark season, as the team prevailed in the remaining six matches to win the premiership cup.

As *The Argus* noted: "Carlton began to score in a way that made their part of the northern suburbs roar with ever-increasing ardour… goal after goal from all spots and angles".

Carlton's round 17 victory over South Melbourne at the Lake Oval afforded the team the minor premiership and set up its semi-final contest with Collingwood at Brunswick Street. A hard-fought 12-point win over the Black and Whites, with Blues' captain Jim Flynn outstanding in a best-afield showing, set up a rematch of the 1904 decider with Fitzroy.

Carlton suffered a big loss before the Grand Final when Martin Gotz, who had featured in the Collingwood semi-final triumph, withdrew because of injury. To complicate matters, Gotz's intended replacement, Bert Parke, was injured at training. The hapless Parke had represented his team in every match in 1905 and had represented Victoria, yet did not manage a senior appearance for the Blues in 1906. Les Beck filled Gotz's position in defence.

Carlton's inaugural Grand Final victory of Saturday, September 22, 1906, came appropriately enough against Fitzroy—the team Worrall had once served. The Maroons, in their fourth successive Grand Final, proved no match.

The Carlton players established what proved an unassailable 33-point lead by the main change, and although Fitzroy hit back in the third quarter with 5.1 to the Blues' two goals, Worrall's men finished full of running as the team banged on six straight goals in the last term.

Among the heroes were best afield Les Beck and Mick Grace, a dual Fitzroy premiership ruckman who gave the game away in 1900 only to be lured back into the game by Worrall. That day, Grace booted three goals to take his season's tally to 50—the first VFL player to achieve the milestone—together with Frank 'Silver' Caine and George Topping, who also kicked three.

The Blues' final scoreline of 15.4 (94) was to remain the highest Grand Final tally for the next 20 years when surpassed by Collingwood's 17.17 (119) in 1926. Their sequence of 11 goals straight from 4.4 through to 15.4 set another Grand Final record, as did the winning margin of 49 points.

Plaudits for the Carlton team and its coach came from all quarters. *The Age* correspondent wrote:

> "Jack Worrall was the special recipient of congratulations, and deservedly so, as the success achieved may fairly be attributed to his coaching. In his playing Worrall was one of the finest footballers in Victoria, and his aptitude for imparting knowledge of the game to others has been attended by phenomenal success."

A more colourful description was offered by *Center* in the satirical *Melbourne Punch*:

> "Carlton... ain' they blithrers', 'Would have won if it had snowed', 'On Saturday's dewy eve such scraps of dialogue were heard all over this great, great city. No matter where you turned even in the pub, your eardrums were tickled with 'Grace', Great game', Should 'ave 'ad his shot', 'Jack Worrall', 'Bongo' (Alex Lang) and other classic sounds that pattered like a rain of Grand Italian Opera.

> "Everybody was decorated with blue and white ribbons. Their talk was blue. Everybody wanted to get into the blue tram and have a ride. At the finish they were drinking blue beer... it tasted blue anyhow. The pubs dispensed free beer. Free beer. Think of it, free beer in Carlton.

> "After a grand Fitzroy fight-back in the third quarter they had little left in the last. Carlton put on six sixers accompanied by wild war cries and chants of triumph, and waving of hats, scarves, brollies, other people's tall hats, bits of fence, husks of grandstand and anything else lying handy.

> "After 19 dormant years the Old Blues were sailing gaily up the happy harbour, for home and beauty. The globule had been sent through the sticks so often that it seemed to know the way.

> "By the end they were actually handballing, handing the orb round like it was a cheese sandwich, passing like passengers through turnstiles, all in turn, and shoving it right through the gaudy uprights without frightening the children.

> "Carlton broke all the records, attendance, goalkicking, artistic finish, Maroon superiority, most of the fence and heaps of other things. The Blues put up one of the finest exhibitions this wondering world has ever seen. It was a greater and finer exhibition than the Pyramids or the Crystal Palace or the Taj Mahal or the Melbourne Waxworks. The Brewers played team-ball like a well-oiled clock, shining in clusters rather than as bright particular stars."

Jack Worrall's influence extended well beyond the boundaries of the playing arena, as the club's 42nd Annual Report—presented to members at

Russell Street's Temperance Hall on the evening of Wednesday, March 20, 1907—reported:

> "Owing to the dashing play of the team, and to the successful management, the membership has, as a natural corollary, increased greatly, numbering, all told, the satisfactory total of 2811, an increase of 316 from the previous season. The list is as follows: Members 2447, Ladies and Boys, 364. The membership is an easy record so far as the Club is concerned, the increase during the last five years being simply extraordinary, amounting to no less a number than 2339. There's nothing succeeds like success.
>
> "The finances of the Club are in a highly satisfactory condition, especially when it is taken into consideration that the Ground Committee received the large amount of £729, and the players were given a trip to Sydney, besides numerous social entertainments. There is a credit balance of £34 7s. 8d."

And the club's pride was expressed clearly in the Annual Report:

> "After a lapse of nineteen years (since its last premiership in the VFA), the Club has once again attained the highest possible honours in the football world, by winning the League Premiership in the most strenuous and brilliant season in the annals of the game. Nineteen matches were played, sixteen of which were won and three lost. The record is an excellent one, especially considering the great sustained pace of modern football—for 'it's the pace that kills'—and the unavoidable accidents incidental to the game. It is almost an impossibility for a side under existing conditions to go through a season without sustaining a defeat.
>
> "Carlton's win was an extremely popular one, congratulatory messages being received from all parts of Victoria, from every State in the Commonwealth, and from New Zealand and South Africa. There was a record attendance at the final match, the enormous attendance of 44,437 being the greatest concourse of people at any football match in Australasia. And the play was worthy of the occasion, the salient and intricate points of the game being up to the highest standard, the accurate kicking of your representatives being quite the feature of the play."

Worrall's place in football lore is assured, but perhaps his legacy was best articulated in *The Carlton Story* a quarter of a century after his passing. "When Jack Worrall became Carlton's secretary and demanded sole power in putting players on and off the training list, (it) marked the turning point in the club's fortunes. He did not promise miracles. Instead, he decided that the main energies of the club in 1902 should be directed towards finding a group of young players who could be moulded gradually into top-line footballers."

1906 CARLTON

PREMIER'S SEASON

CARLTON: 1906

ROUND ONE May 5
CARLTON	12.11 (83)
MELBOURNE	8.8 (56)

Best: Carlton – M.Grace, Clark, Hammond, T.Kennedy, Lang, Caine.
Goals: Carlton – Grace 4, Caine 4, Johnson, Lang, Elliott, Topping.
Crowd: N/A at Princes Park

ROUND TWO May 12
CARLTON	15.10 (100)
ST KILDA	5.5 (35)

Best: Carlton – Caine, Grace, Elliott, Flynn, Lang, McGregor.
Goals: Carlton – Caine 5, Grace 3, Topping 2, Johnson 2, Lang, Bruce, Snell.
Crowd: N/A at Junction Oval

ROUND THREE May 19
CARLTON	16.10 (106)
GEELONG	6.7 (43)

Best: Carlton – Caine, Grace, Topping, Flynn, Hammond, Clark, Snell.
Goals: Carlton – Caine 4, Grace 3, Topping 3, McGregor 2, Johnson 2, Hince, Hammond.
Crowd: N/A at Princes Park

ROUND FOUR May 26
CARLTON	8.9 (57)
COLLINGWOOD	4.13 (37)

Best: Carlton – Grace, Elliott, Caine, Lang, Bruce, Flynn, Topping, McGregor.
Goals: Carlton – Caine 3, Elliott 2, Grace, Snell, Harris.
Crowd: N/A at Victoria Park

ROUND FIVE June 4
CARLTON	10.9 (69)
SOUTH MELBOURNE	10.5 (65)

Best: Carlton – Grace, Lang, Doug Gillespie, McGregor, Johnston, Hammond.
Goals: Carlton – Grace 4, Lang 2, Bruce, Caine, Elliott, Topping.
Crowd: N/A at Princes Park

ROUND SIX June 9
CARLTON	7.14 (56)
FITZROY	6.8 (44)

Best: Carlton – Caine, Gotz, Hammond, Elliott, Flynn, Johnson.
Goals: Carlton – Caine 4, Lang, Topping, Snell.
Crowd: N/A at Brunswick St Oval

ROUND SEVEN June 16
CARLTON	4.15 (39)
ESSENDON	10.14 (74)

Best: Carlton – Clark, Elliott, C.Hammond, J.Kennedy, Snell.
Goals: Carlton – J.Hammond, Grace, Grant, Caine.
Crowd: N/A at Princes Park

ROUND EIGHT June 30
CARLTON	9.16 (70)
MELBOURNE	3.7 (25)

Best: Carlton – Grace, Flynn, A.Kennedy, Elliott, Topping, Harris.
Goals: Carlton – Grace 4, Johnson 2, Caine 2, Beck.
Crowd: N/A at the MCG

ROUND NINE July 7
CARLTON	6.13 (49)
ST KILDA	3.7 (25)

Best: Carlton – Grace, Hammond, Gibson, McGregor, Lang, Clark.
Goals: Carlton – Grace 3, Elliott 2, Harris.
Crowd: N/A at Princes Park

ROUND TEN July 14
CARLTON	8.15 (63)
GEELONG	5.6 (36)

Best: Carlton – T.Kennedy, Flynn, Grace, Hammond, A.Kennedy, Topping.
Goals: Carlton – Grace 3, Lang 2, Topping 2, Caine.
Crowd: N/A at Corio Oval

ROUND ELEVEN July 21
CARLTON	11.14 (80)
COLLINGWOOD	6.7 (43)

Best: Carlton – Johnson, Caine, Bruce, Harris, Elliott, Flynn, Doug Gillespie.
Goals: Carlton – Caine 2, Johnson 2, T.Kennedy, Grace, Little, Bruce, Harris, Elliott, Lang.
Crowd: N/A at Princes Park

ROUND TWELVE July 28
CARLTON	7.3 (45)
SOUTH MELBOURNE	12.12 (84)

Best: Carlton – Flynn, Johnson, Elliott, Grace, Caine, Payne, McGregor.
Goals: Carlton – Caine 2, Grace 2, Hammond, Jinks, Lang.
Crowd: N/A at the Lake Oval

ROUND THIRTEEN August 11
CARLTON	5.3 (33)
FITZROY	4.14 (38)

Best: Carlton – Grace, Caine, Gotz, Flynn, Clark, Lang, Johnson.
Goals: Carlton – Grace 2, Caine 2, Harris.
Crowd: N/A at Princes Park

ROUND FOURTEEN August 18
CARLTON	10.12 (72)
ESSENDON	4.12 (36)

Best: Carlton – Topping, Flynn, Johnson, Elliott, Marchbank, Lang.
Goals: Carlton – Topping 5, Lang 2, McGregor, Grace, Little.
Crowd: N/A at East Melbourne Cricket Ground

ROUND FIFTEEN August 25
CARLTON	10.12 (72)
ESSENDON	8.6 (54)

Best: Carlton – Grace, Hammond, Doug Gillespie, Flynn, Marchbank, McGregor.
Goals: Carlton – Grace 5, Jinks, Little, Elliott, Topping, Lang.
Crowd: N/A at Princes Park

ROUND SIXTEEN September 1
CARLTON	13.13 (91)
GEELONG	4.5 (29)

Best: Carlton – Grace, Elliott, Flynn, Ingleman, McGregor, Harris.
Goals: Carlton – Grace 6, Caine 2, Topping 2, Hammond, Elliott, Flynn.
Crowd: N/A at Corio Oval

ROUND SEVENTEEN September 8
CARLTON	12.14 (86)
SOUTH MELBOURNE	4.15 (39)

Best: Carlton – Flynn, Topping, Elliott, T.Kennedy, Clark, Doug Gillespie.
Goals: Carlton – Flynn 2, Grace 2, Topping 2, Elliott 2, Hammond, Little, Jinks, Caine.
Crowd: N/A at the Lake Oval

PREMIER'S FINALS

SEMI-FINAL September 15

CARLTON	9.10 (64)
COLLINGWOOD	8.6 (54)

Best: Carlton – Flynn, Jinks, Elliott, Johnson, Hammond, Gotz, McGregor, Bruce.
Goals: Carlton – Grace 2, Jinks 2, Topping 2, Marchbank, Bruce, McGregor.
Crowd: 15,000 at Brunswick St Oval

GRAND FINAL September 22

CARLTON	3.2	7.4	9.4	15.4 (94)
FITZROY	1.6	1.7	6.8	6.9 (45)

Best: Carlton – Beck, Bruce, Clark, Doug Gillespie, McGregor, Payne.
Goals: Carlton – Caine 3, Grace 3, Elliott 2, Little 2, Topping 2, Hammond, Jinks, Marchbank.
Crowd: 44,437 at the MCG

GRAND FINAL LINE-UPS

CARL	B:	N.Clark	D.Gillespie	L.Beck
FITZ	F:	L.Millis	C.Naismith	E.Jenkins (capt)
CARL	HB:	B.Payne	G.Johnson	C.Hammond
FITZ	HF:	F.Fontaine	G.Brosnan	B.Smith
CARL	C:	G.Bruce	R.McGregor	T.Kennedy
FITZ	C:	B.Bailes	T.Beauchamp	E.Kneen
CARL	HF:	F.Caine	J.Marchbank	M.Grace
FITZ	HB:	L.Barker	J.Sharp	P.Sheehan
CARL	F:	A.Lang	G.Topping	I.Little
FITZ	B:	F.Abbott	G.Moriarty	J.Johnson
CARL	R:	J.Flynn (capt)	F.Jinks	F.Elliott
FITZ	R:	B.Walker	H.Milne	P.Trotter
CARL	Coach: Jack Worrall			
FITZ	Coach:			

SNAPSHOT

Win-loss record: 16-3
Highest score: 16.10 (106), round 3, v Geelong.
Greatest winning margin: 65 points, round 2, v St Kilda.
Lowest score: 5.3 (33), round 13, v Fitzroy.
Greatest losing margin: 39 points, round 12, v South Melbourne.
Most goals by a player in a game: 6, Mick Grace, round 16, v Geelong.
Most consecutive wins: 6 (twice).
Most consecutive losses: 2
Club awards: Leading goalkicker: Mick Grace (50 goals).

Putting it into perspective:
The Blues won their first Grand Final defeating Fitzroy; it was only their second Grand Final appearance—compared with the Roys, who were playing in their seventh Grand Final. The Blues became the League's fifth premiership winner.

1906

		P	W	L	D	%	Pts
1	Carlton (1)	17	14	3		153.5	56
2	Fitzroy (2)	17	13	4		153.3	52
3	Collingwood (3)	17	11	6		140.3	44
4	Essendon (4)	17	10	7		115.1	40
5	South Melb	17	8	9		99.9	32
6	St Kilda	17	6	11		88.1	24
7	Geelong	17	5	12		64.3	20
8	Melbourne	17	1	16		48.7	4

(17 home and away rounds)

PLAYERS USED

CARLTON	GAMES	GOALS
Beck, Les	6	2
Bickford, Albert	1	0
Boyle, Bob	1	0
Bruce, George	17	4
Caine, Frank	19	37
Clark, Norman	17	0
Elliott, Fred	19	12
Flynn, Jim	18	3
Gibson, Harvey	1	0
Gillespie, Doug	17	0
Gotz, Martin	14	0
Grace, Mick	19	50
Grant, Jack A.	1	1
Grant, Wal	2	0
Hammond, Charlie	18	5
Hammond, Jack	2	1
Harris, Dick L.	8	4
Harry, William	1	0
Hince, Frank	1	1
Ingleman, Alby	4	0
Jinks, Fred	12	6
Johnson, George	18	9
Johnston, Alex	6	0
Kennedy, Andy	2	0
Kennedy, Jim A.	3	0
Kennedy, Ted	19	1
Lang, Alex	18	12
Little, Ike	8	5
Marchbank, Jim	6	2
McGregor, Rod	19	4
Meadway, Barney	1	0
Payne, Billy	15	0
Snell, Archie	12	3
Topping, George	17	25

**CARLTON 6.14 (50) d
SOUTH MELBOURNE 6.9 (45)**

BLUES TRUMP ON PAIR OF ACES

John Worrall leaned heavily on a couple of his favourite veteran players and they delivered, in doing so helping the Blues to land their second consecutive flag. By HOWARD KOTTON and TONY DE BOLFO

THE *Australasian* perhaps put it best in its report of Grand Final day 1907:

"It was in keeping with the eternal fitness of things that the representatives of the ancient dark Blues and their old time rivals of 'The Hill' should play off for the Premiership... but it may be unhesitatingly affirmed that their encounter last Saturday furnished the best match of the year, and the finest final contest that has been played since the League was established."

And yet even that florid critique of the ultimate contest between Carlton and South Melbourne could barely do justice to the events of Saturday, September 21, 1907, at the old East Melbourne ground—which again vindicated the coaching methods of Jack Worrall and the man's unswerving loyalty to his Blueboys and theirs to him.

Worrall had close associations with two of the great Carltonites of the early period, Jim Flynn and Frank 'Silver' Caine.

James Edward Flynn, forever remembered as Carlton's first premiership captain in League competition, was born on March 21, 1871. The son of John and Ellen Flynn (nee Moloney), Flynn's place of birth has often been listed as Benalla, although registry records suggest Geelong.

Flynn's durability as a ruckman was more than matched by his renowned dynamism as an on-field leader—traits not lost on Worrall. History records

Flynn as having chased the leather for Benalla District, Collingwood's then VFA team and Canterbury in Melbourne's east. A League career with Geelong then ensued from 1897-1902, during which time Flynn played 72 games and kicked 22 goals.

Burdened by Geelong's failure to feature in finals, and promised a real shot at September glory by the unyielding Worrall, Flynn arrived at Princes Park in early 1903. Though not a big man, Flynn proved a canny competitor at ruck contests and always found a way to counter larger opponents.

It was said of Flynn that he was a natural athlete with a good spring and sure hands, who often sharked the taps of his opponents by feigning to jump for the ball and then intercepting.

Flynn's impact at Carlton was immediate. In his first season, he helped his team rise from sixth on the League ladder in 1902 to a creditable third behind Collingwood and Fitzroy in '03. It was the first time that the Dark Blues had made the final four since the League began in 1897.

Flynn was made vice-captain in 1904, lending his support to the fellow ex-Geelong follower and now Carlton captain, Joe McShane. When McShane stood down from the post the end of the 1904 season, Flynn was anointed Carlton captain.

Remarkably, Flynn was 36 when he led his men on to the field for the 1907 Grand Final, having completed his debut for Carlton in the opening round of 1903 against Collingwood at the tender age of 32 years and 42 days. To this day he remains the oldest player to achieve the 50-game milestone for the Blues.

Francis Henry Caine, the second of eight children of the Tasmanian-born James Caine and Luisa Margaret Caine (nee Perdrisat), was born in Horsham in the Wimmera region on July 28, 1881.

Like Flynn, Caine was recruited by Carlton on the strength of Worrall's say-so. Acclaimed as an extravagant, long-kicking forward, Caine was to the fore of Carlton's history-making 1906 Grand Final victory, booting three goals from a flank, including a monster measured at 75 yards.

Carlton earned 1907 line honours in no small part due to Caine's on-field deeds. Nicknamed 'Silver' as a consequence of his greying hair, Caine kicked a record eight goals in Carlton's 78-point demolition of Fitzroy at the old Brunswick Street Oval in July of that year, and topped his club's goalkicking tally with 32.

Carlton's '07 campaign began somewhat tardily; its players lost their opening-round match to St Kilda at Princes Park by 26 points. Prominent among the visitors were Vic Cumberland and Charlie Clymo, who both kicked three goals.

Worrall's men then steadied, posting meritorious victories over Geelong, Melbourne and Fitzroy, before dropping the home match to South Melbourne. Dave Gillespie's first-quarter withdrawal that day with a broken collarbone had a large impact on the team.

Carlton's sixth-round match against Collingwood at Victoria Park was marred by atrocious kicking—4.17. Fortunately, the Black and Whites could manage only 4.6 on an afternoon in which a crosswind forced play on to one side of the arena. As a none-too-pleased observer for *The Age* was prompted to write: "This is a feature of the game as it is now played, which has become much too common, and unless it be checked it may jeopardise the popularity of football, which as a display of skill is undeniably less attractive than it was twenty years ago".

Having clobbered Essendon by 54 points in the seventh round match at Princes Park, the Carlton team reversed its opening round loss to St Kilda with a 29-point victory in the eighth round fixture at the Junction Oval. The match would serve as the final hurrah for Mick Grace, who crossed town to turn out for VFA team Brighton. The following week, Flynn announced his retirement and canvassed his plan to run a pub at St James, by the Albury-Wodonga railway line, about 240 kilometres north of Melbourne.

According to a report in *The Argus*, Flynn was loudly cheered when he offered his services to return to the Blues if required for the finals. As fate would have it, both he and Grace would be coaxed back to contribute significantly to the September cause.

The Carlton players exacted some revenge for their round-five loss to South with a gritty nine-point win at the Lake Oval in the 12th round, and, as was the case with Collingwood at Victoria Park, the South match proved difficult viewing.

"The ball was almost continuously at the South Melbourne end, yet for all their predominance Carlton got very little of it. Their forwards were over-eager, rushed for possession in the independent spirit, tried hurried shots that only a great slice of luck could have helped them to achieve, and so wasted many good opportunities," *The Argus* correspondent reported.

By now, bad blood had developed between these two combatants, so much so that when Carlton and South met again at the Lake Oval just three weeks later, the then captain Fred 'Pompey' Elliott and his Blues teammate Jim Marchbank each incurred substantial penalties for misdemeanours arising from the contest won by South.

And yet, as *The Argus* journalist duly noted: "While hard knocks were necessarily a common occurrence in such a vigorously played match, each side gave and took their share in a manly fashion."

The enforced absences of both Elliott and Marchbank forced Worrall's hand. The master coach implored Grace to once again hunt the leather for Carlton—and so he did with immediate impact, booting three goals to orchestrate his team's 31-point victory over Essendon at Princes Park in the penultimate round of the home and away season.

Carlton's round–17 victory over Melbourne afforded the Dark Blues the minor premiership with a two-match buffer over South Melbourne. The win also meant that Worrall's heroes would be fronting up to St Kilda in the semi-final, on a rock-hard track that made it difficult for all players to keep their feet.

True to his word, Flynn returned to the fray, and did so with distinction, and Grace's trusty boot found the big sticks four times as Carlton won by 56 points. As *The Argus* correspondent noted of the team that had just earned the right to again play off for the pennant: "It is a great gain to them to have Flynn leading and playing for them in the finals".

Carlton ruckman George 'Mallee' Johnson earned the plaudits for his robust showing that afternoon in September 1907. "What a model footballer he is," *The Argus* scribe suggested. "He is ever playing the game for his side with unflailing pluck and judgment. If popularity and play count in combination, Johnson is the footballer of the season because apart from his persistency his merit is he makes so few mistakes."

Carlton's comprehensive semi-final victory came at significant cost when in the dying minutes Rod McGregor, the prodigiously skilled centreman and the first Carlton footballer to achieve the 200-game milestone, incurred a severely broken nose.

A replacement had to be found before the Grand Final against South Melbourne. Worrall pitched for Alby Ingleman, also known as 'The Badger', a tough, no-nonsense midfielder who, since his arrival in 1905, had walked in McGregor's shadow.

The Carlton team boasted 14 premiership players from the previous year. Martin Gotz, deprived a place in the 1906 premiership team because of injury, would make up for his disappointment by taking the field, while Dick Harris, Harvey Kelly and Ingleman were the new boys, replacing McGregor, Marchbank, Elliott and Ike Little.

The scene was set for a supreme contest and as *The Herald* reported: "It was an inspiring moment when the huge crowd greeted the teams with a shout of welcome. Carlton were the first out. In fact, they were so anxious to start that they came out before the schoolboys had finished their game."

The Grand Final proved an enthralling contest—the finest final to be played in the 10-year of the VFL, according to a report in *The Australasian*. The match was notable for its fast pace, physical aggression and uncompromising play which suited Worrall's men.

The Blues emerged with a five-point victory, having retained a slender lead throughout. Ingleman and Caine featured among Carlton's best over a spirited opponent before a crowd of 45,477.

The match, which proved the sweetest of swansongs for Mick Grace, was played on what one unsourced report of the time termed "a softer MCG than might have been expected".

The report read as follows:

> "The League had decided, after representations from the two clubs, that the MCG should be watered if no rain fell before the Grand Final. The semi-finals were plagued by a rock-hard surface and raised dust.
>
> "A committee of three old players last night consulted the oracular groundsman Mr Baracchi as to the prospect of precipitation. On his advice they decided, correctly, to water the ground.
>
> "Carlton were overall taller and heavier than South Melbourne and this told on the 'Lagoonites' in the end. Carlton withstood a Southern fightback in the last quarter to win by five points.
>
> "Appropriately, 'The Silver King' Frank Caine was shooting for goal as the bell rang, and thousands of spectators swarmed on to the field. Jim Flynn modestly gave the laurel to coach Jack Worrall, but his own role was substantial, as he had returned for the finals after a mid-season retirement. And George Johnson named by *The Australasian* as the player of the season, was the biggest and best big man on the ground."

George Topping featured among the leading goalkickers for Carlton with three match-winning majors. Flynn was imperious at centre half-back, Johnson was honest in the ruck and George Bruce was a will o' the wisp on a wing.

The Australasian report perhaps best reflected the quality of the contest. "It was in keeping with the eternal fitness of things that the representatives of the ancient dark Blues and their old time rivals of 'The Hill' should play off for the premiership but it may be unhesitatingly affirmed that their encounter last Saturday furnished the best match of the year, and the finest final contest that has been played since the League was established.

"From start to finish it was a fast, determined and extremely skilful game and it was so evenly fought out that right up to the final bell the outcome was in doubt."

Flynn was justifiably proud of his team's efforts and equally gracious in tribute to his foes. In an extended interview with *The Argus* two days after the 1907 Grand Final, the victorious captain was quoted as follows:

> "Yes, we won, but there was not much in it. They kept us going right to the end, didn't they? It must have been a grand game to watch. I know it was splendid to play in.
>
> "When it was all over, I felt I'd have liked to have had to congratulate South — they played such a fine spirited game. It was a hard struggle with plenty of bumps, but there was very little to complain about. South were out for keeps all right and they kept their heads well. The only mistake they made, I think, was they tried too much low-passing. They rather overdid it. It confused our chaps for a while, but when it failed to come off it cost South a lot.
>
> "South Melbourne surprised me on the form they showed. We expected to beat them easily, but they had us all out. We were tested to our utmost, all right. There was not much in it. Of course, I think our team was the best. I thought we had them settled at half-time, but they came at us again as fresh as ever. I think our weight had a good deal to do with our win. We average about 11½ stone and that's pretty solid for 18 men.
>
> "The real secret of our success is our manager Jack Worrall. There is no doubt most of it is due to him. He's a grand judge of the game, and the youngsters that come up the ground worship him; they'd do anything for him. They take no notice of anyone else. Besides that, we have a grand lot of fellows. There is no jealousy, no cliques, and they pulled together like clockwork... The crowd gave us a grand reception, didn't they? I could not get away from a bunch of barrackers and they carried in as many of us as they could lay hands on."

The Carlton Football Club's 43rd Annual Report, presented to members at the Melbourne Town Hall on the evening of Friday, March 20, 1908, revelled in the events of the season:

> "For the second year in succession your Club has succeeded in obtaining the blue ribbon of the football world, after the grandest contest ever witnessed in a final game. Of the 19 matches played, 15 were won and four lost. The season's record — considering the playing strength of the opposing clubs — is an excellent one. Carlton's success was extremely popular, congratulatory messages being received from all over Australia.
>
> "We offer our old friends and rivals of the South Melbourne Football Club our heartiest congratulations upon the gallant manner in which their chosen representatives fought for premiership honours on that fateful

21st of September. In conjunction with your players, they deserve well of all lovers of football for the magnificent exposition given of the national game.

"The players are to be warmly congratulated for their fine consistent play throughout the season. They attended to their training regularly, and played with great heart and dash. Two of our older players in Messrs A. Ford and C. Roland have returned to the fold, and there is no apparent reason why your representatives should not make another great effort for the leading position in the coming season. The members can rest assured that no legitimate effort will be spared towards attaining the laudable object.

"The Club, however, will suffer a great loss in the retirement from the game of Mr J. Flynn. He has led the team twice to premiership honours, and his position will be most difficult to fill. In the semi-final and final matches, the team was handled perfectly, and it is not too much to say that his exceptional skill as a leader, combined with his rare ability as a footballer, was a great factor in the success of the side.

"Great credit is due to Mr F. Elliott for his leadership during the temporary retirement of the captain. He set the team a fine example, and was the personification of strength and determination.

"The membership of the Club has beaten all records—a distinct compliment to the management. Ever since the Club has emerged from its obscurity, the advance all round—in playing ability, management and increase of membership—has been simply phenomenal. The list is as follows: Members, 2991; Ladies, 443; the total being 3,523—an increase of 712 members from last year. The above is an easy record so far as the Club is concerned, and conclusively proves that the popularity of the Club is increasing every year.

"The finances of the Club are eminently satisfactory, especially when it is taken into consideration that the Ground Committee received the large amount of £428/6/1, and that the players were given a trip as well as numerous social entertainments. There is a credit balance of £188/14/11."

But the story of Carlton's season of 1907 was perhaps best told by its former vice-president and resident club rhymester Cr George Hawkins Ievers, who remarkably penned the following verse on the very day of the Grand Final:

> This great year of Football is ended,
> And old Carlton is still to the fore;
> For our champions have nobly defended
> Their title as Premiers once more.
> Flynn and Elliott are both grand commanders,
> They played for old Carlton rare game;
> Both Elliott and Marchbank 'spite slanders,
> Bear still to all sportsmen fair names.
> "Mallee" Johnson played football the fairest,

The champion this year he has been;
For his play all round was the rarest,
His marking the greatest e'er seen.
Bruce and Kennedy's smart play will ever
Round football memories cling,
For their dash through the season so clever
Made them champions this year on the wing.
"Wee" McGregor was "great" all the season,
In the centre no one could oppose;
But Renfrey's sad rush was the reason
Why he lost the last match by a "nose".
"Hacken" Clark, Payne and Beck are terrors,
They played back with great heart and soul;
With Gillespie right back made no errors,
But nobly defended their goal.
Mick Grace, our goal star last year,
Retired ere the season was o'er;
When the League hit old Carlton severe,
Mick returned and kicked goals as of yore.
Silver Caine's great punt took some stopping,
And Kelly, the star of the West,
With Harris and game little Topping,
Make a quartette that rank with the best.
Jinks and Lang on the ball were splendid,
And both snapped smart goals as well;
Gotz and Hammond most ably defended,
And their dash in the ruck did tell.
Little Ingleman we greet with pleasure
For his roving, his pluck and pace;
He proved to old Carlton a treasure,
For he took "Wee" McGregor's great place.
When misfortune o'ertook so gravely
Eli Elliott, and Marchbank as well,
The great breach was filled so bravely
By Jim Kennedy, young Williams and Snell.
When Vin Gardiner plays like his father,
Who oft captained the old Blues in the past,
In those days of great players—rather,
His fame, like Jack Gardiner's, will last.
Three cheers for our champions to-night, boys,
The old Carlton team so dear;
Three cheers for their flag blue and white, boys,
Which waves for our Premiers this year.

1907 CARLTON

PREMIER'S SEASON

CARLTON: 1907

ROUND ONE April 27
CARLTON   4.6 (30)
ST KILDA   8.8 (56)
Best: Carlton – Grace, Flynn, Williams, Beck, Snell, Lang, Hammond.
Goals: Carlton – Grace 2, Caine, Jinks.
Crowd: N/A at Princes Park

ROUND TWO May 4
CARLTON   8.14 (62)
GEELONG   3.9 (27)
Best: Carlton – Topping, Lang, Caine, Flynn, Bruce, Snell, McGregor.
Goals: Carlton – Topping 4, Grace, Jinks, Lang, Caine.
Crowd: N/A at Corio Oval

ROUND THREE May 11
CARLTON   12.14 (86)
MELBOURNE   7.5 (47)
Best: Carlton – Caine, Bruce, Flynn, T.Kennedy, Clark, Gardiner, Beck.
Goals: Carlton – Caine 6, Grace, Snell, Elliott, Bruce, Marchbank, Hammond.
Crowd: N/A at the MCG

ROUND FOUR May 18
CARLTON   10.17 (77)
FITZROY   3.7 (25)
Best: Carlton – Hammond, McGregor, Grace, Bruce, Flynn, T.Kennedy.
Goals: Carlton – Topping 3, Caine 2, Lang, Gardiner, Elliott, Grace, T.Kennedy.
Crowd: N/A at Princes Park

ROUND FIVE May 25
CARLTON   5.16 (46)
SOUTH MELBOURNE 9.7 (61)
Best: Carlton – Clark, Beck, Flynn, Johnson, McGregor, Lang, Doug Gillespie.
Goals: Carlton – T.Kennedy 2, Lang, Caine, Gardiner.
Crowd: N/A at Princes Park

ROUND SIX June 1
CARLTON   4.17 (41)
COLLINGWOOD   4.6 (30)
Best: Carlton – Hammond, Beck, Snell, Harris, Elliott, Jinks.
Goals: Carlton – Hammond, Grace, Topping, Gardiner.
Crowd: N/A at Victoria Park

ROUND SEVEN June 15
CARLTON   15.14 (104)
ESSENDON   7.8 (50)
Best: Carlton – Gardiner, Topping, Jinks, Grace, Clark, Beck, Lang.
Goals: Carlton – Topping 4, Gardiner 3, Grace 2, Harris 2, Jinks 2, Marchbank, Caine.
Crowd: N/A at Princes Park

ROUND EIGHT June 22
CARLTON   8.14 (62)
ST KILDA   3.15 (33)
Best: Carlton – Lang, Johnson, Topping, Beck, Flynn, McGregor, T.Kennedy.
Goals: Carlton – Topping 2, Caine 2, Harris, Johnson, Lang, Elliott.
Crowd: N/A at Junction Oval

ROUND NINE June 29
CARLTON   5.9 (39)
GEELONG   7.4 (46)
Best: Carlton – Kelly, Topping, Flynn, Bruce, Clark, Williams, Harris.
Goals: Carlton – Topping 2, Kelly 2, Caine.
Crowd: N/A at Princes Park

ROUND TEN July 6
CARLTON   9.16 (70)
MELBOURNE   8.6 (54)
Best: Carlton – Kelly, Lang, Flynn, Payne, Elliott, Bruce, Doug Gillespie.
Goals: Carlton – Kelly 4, Elliott 2, Gardiner, Lang, Topping.
Crowd: N/A at Princes Park

ROUND ELEVEN July 13
CARLTON   15.14 (104)
FITZROY   3.8 (26)
Best: Carlton – Caine, Kelly, Beck, McGregor, Elliott, Gardiner, T.Kennedy.
Goals: Carlton – Caine 8, Kelly 3, Gardiner, Pearce, Elliott, T.Kennedy.
Crowd: N/A at Brunswick St Oval

ROUND TWELVE July 20
CARLTON   4.12 (36)
SOUTH MELBOURNE 3.9 (27)
Best: Carlton – Beck, Clark, Hammond, Topping, McGregor, Pearce.
Goals: Carlton – Topping 2, Elliott, Lang.
Crowd: N/A at the Lake Oval

ROUND THIRTEEN August 3
CARLTON   5.15 (45)
COLLINGWOOD   5.4 (34)
Best: Carlton – Elliott, Hammond, Harris, Kelly, Lang, Payne.
Goals: Carlton – Hammond, Beck, Caine, Elliott, Jinks.
Crowd: N/A at Princes Park

ROUND FOURTEEN August 10
CARLTON   10.18 (78)
ESSENDON   3.7 (25)
Best: Carlton – Caine, Kelly, Jinks, Gotz, Bruce, Hammond.
Goals: Carlton – Caine 4, Marchbank, Jinks, T.Kennedy, Elliott, Kelly, Topping.
Crowd: N/A at East Melbourne Cricket Ground

ROUND FIFTEEN August 17
CARLTON   4.16 (40)
SOUTH MELBOURNE 8.9 (57)
Best: Carlton – Lang, Gardiner, McGregor, Clark, Topping, Harris.
Goals: Carlton – Lang 2, Harris, Marchbank.
Crowd: N/A at the Lake Oval

ROUND SIXTEEN August 24
CARLTON   11.12 (78)
ESSENDON   7.5 (47)
Best: Carlton – Kelly, Grace, Caine, J.Kennedy, Williams, Payne.
Goals: Carlton – Grace 3, Kelly 3, Harris, Johnson, Snell, Bruce, Caine.
Crowd: N/A at Princes Park

ROUND SEVENTEEN August 31
CARLTON   9.8 (62)
MELBOURNE   4.12 (36)
Best: Carlton – Kelly, Johnson, Harris, Lang, McGregor, Grace, Gotz.
Goals: Carlton – Kelly 4, Caine 2, Topping, Grace, Gotz.
Crowd: N/A at Princes Park

PREMIER'S FINALS

SEMI-FINAL September 14

CARLTON	13.13 (91)
ST KILDA	4.11 (35)

Best: Carlton – Johnson, Hammond, Jinks, Bruce, Flynn, Harris, Payne.
Goals: Carlton – Grace 4, Harris 3, Kelly 2, Topping 2, Lang, Caine.
Crowd: 26,100 at the MCG

GRAND FINAL September 21

CARLTON	1.4	4.6	6.10	6.14 (50)
SOUTH MELBOURNE	1.3	3.5	4.7	6.9 (45)

Best: Carlton – Bruce, Flynn, Gotz, Ingleman, Johnson, Kelly.
Goals: Carlton – Topping 3, Jinks, Kelly, Lang.
Crowd: 45,477 at the MCG

GRAND FINAL LINE-UPS

CARL	B:	N.Clark	D.Gillespie	L.Beck
STH M	F:	H.Callan	L.Mortimer	A.Kerr
CARL	HB:	M.Gotz	J.Flynn (capt)	B.Payne
STH M	HF:	D.Casey	B.Strang	B.Kerr
CARL	C:	G.Bruce	A.Ingleman	T.Kennedy
STH M	C:	B.Moxham	T.Wade	H.Drane
CARL	HF:	F.Jinks	H.Kelly	F.Caine
STH M	HB:	P.Wood	B.Atkins	G.Anderson
CARL	F:	M.Grace	G.Topping	D.Harris
STH M	B:	H.Lampe	B.Dolpin (capt)	H.Wilson
CARL	R:	G.Johnson	C.Hammond	A.Lang
STH M	R:	V.Belcher	J.Cameron	C.Ricketts

CARL Coach: Jack Worrall
STH M Coach:

SNAPSHOT

Win-loss record: 15-4

Highest score: 15.14 (104), round 7, v Essendon; round 11, v Fitzroy.

Greatest winning margin: 78 points, round 11, v Fitzroy.

Lowest score: 4.6 (30), round 1, v St Kilda.

Greatest losing margin: 26 points, round 1, v St Kilda.

Most goals by a player in a game: 8, Frank Caine, round 11, v Fitzroy.

Most consecutive wins: 5

Most consecutive losses: 1 (four times).

Club awards: Leading goalkicker: Frank Caine (32 goals).

Putting it into perspective:
Carlton won its second consecutive premiership, becoming the third team in competition history to win back to back flags. It also meant in successive seasons, 1906-1907, the Blues had won 82 per cent of matches played.

1907

	P	W	L	D	%	Pts
1 Carlton (1)	17	13	4		155.7	52
2 South Melb (2)	17	11	6		118.4	44
3 St Kilda (3)	17	9	8		117.5	36
4 Collingwood (4)	17	9	8		110.4	36
5 Fitzroy	17	7	10		85.5	28
6 Geelong	17	7	10		85.3	28
7 Melbourne	17	7	10		81.1	28
8 Essendon	17	5	12		74.0	20

(17 home and away rounds)

PLAYERS USED

CARLTON	GAMES	GOALS
Beck, Les	17	1
Bickford, Albert	1	0
Bruce, George	18	2
Caine, Frank	19	32
Clark, Norman	16	0
Elliott, Fred	15	9
Flynn, Jim	12	0
Gardiner, Vin	8	8
Gillespie, Dave	2	0
Gillespie, Doug	17	0
Gotz, Martin	9	1
Grace, Mick	13	16
Hammond, Charlie	16	3
Harris, Dick	14	8
Hickey, Bill	1	0
Ingleman, Alby	3	0
Jinks, Fred	17	7
Johnson, George	18	2
Kelly, Harvey	11	20
Kennedy, Jim A.	2	0
Kennedy, Ted	19	5
Lang, Alex	19	10
Marchbank, Jim	8	4
McGregor, Rod	17	0
Payne, Billy	18	0
Pearce, Horrie	2	1
Snell, Archie	8	2
Topping, George	17	26
Wheeler, Alf	1	0
Williams, Frank	4	0

**CARLTON 5.5 (35) d
ESSENDON 3.8 (26)**

CARLTON SETS BENCHMARK

By 1908, Jack Worrall had built an outstanding club, on and off the field, and the Blues encountered little opposition on their way to their third straight premiership. By HOWARD KOTTON and TONY DE BOLFO

ON Grand Final night 1908, as the cable car clickety-clacked its way westward from Jolimont to old Melbourne town, an unnamed correspondent from *The Age* eavesdropped on a florid tête-à-tête between fellow commuters.

The correspondent, having just witnessed the Carltonites' history-making third consecutive premiership, pondered what might end the Blues' glorious run, as he reported the following exchange:

> How much longer are they going to hold it, I wonder?' asked one of the occupants of a crowded tram returning to the city, and there was evidence of keen knowledge of what's what in his friend's reply – 'Until Jack Worrall pegs out!'."

History would demonstrate that, within 12 months of Carlton's third premiership, Worrall, dubbed 'The King of football in Victoria' by *The Argus*, would be forced out of his seemingly impregnable rank; and those magnificent men who had followed him on this epic journey would fall just short of a fourth consecutive premiership.

With Worrall at the helm, the famous Old Dark Navy Blues had, through the course of 1908, lowered their colours but once in 20 starts—to an Essendon outfit they ultimately overwhelmed in the much-anticipated rematch on the game's grandest stage.

In the season opener against St Kilda, forward pocket George Topping kicked five. An 18-point defeat of Melbourne at Jolimont followed, with the Kelly brothers, Harvey and Ernie, contributing six to the visitors' nine-goal scoreline... not that *The Argus* correspondent was overly enthused:

> "There were stages in their match of Saturday on the Melbourne Cricket Ground when a stranger might have guessed wrongly on saying which of them was down and which was up. This was particularly noticeable in the first quarter, when a very charitable person might have said that Carlton were taking it too easily, that we know that the modern footballer troubles less about chivalry than about goals and glory, and takes no risks."

In the third round, Carlton met Essendon for what would be the first of three encounters for the 1908 season. In a portent of things to come, both defences were on top but the Carlton attack, ably led by Vin Gardiner with his two goals, just managed to stave off the Same Olds.

Wally Koochew, the game's first player of Chinese origin, completed his senior debut in this game.

Walter John Henry Koochew (sometimes spelled Kou Chow, Kow Chow or Ko Chow) was born in Carlton on July 6, 1887. The son of James Koochew, who migrated to Australia from Whampoa, 13 kilometres south of Guangzhou (Canton), aboard the ship *Frances* from the port of Hong Kong in 1865, Wally was photographed with his arms folded across his chest as the Carlton contingent gathered in the shadows of the Alderman Gardiner Stand just before the first bounce. He was to play only four VFL games.

Victoria Park provided the menacing backdrop for Worrall's men in the fourth round of 1908. The players foundered early, earning the half-time ire of the coaching staff. According to *The Argus*:

> "During the interval... their managers must have had a word with the men, because the alteration in their play upon the resumption of the game was most marked. Carlton put more vim into it. They played the Carlton game, which is distinct from that of other teams, in the drag through the ruck."

The Carlton team emerged with a 28-point victory over the Black and Whites, with Harvey 'Duff' Kelly, recruited from South Fremantle after a stint with South Melbourne in 1902, booting four goals. Kelly followed up his fine form in the following round against Fitzroy. *The Argus* journalist was most impressed:

> "In dealing with individual play, one cannot overlook the marked improvement in H. Kelly's football. It was this form, no doubt, that won him a reputation in Western Australia and a place in the Carlton team."

In the sixth round, against South, Kelly sent three over the goal umpire's hat, including his team's opener and the sealer, in what was a hard-fought two-point win at the Lake Oval. One wordsmith was drawn to write, "If ever Carlton proved their motto to be 'No Surrender', it was in this match. They were a beaten team without a doubt, but in a supreme effort they won the match."

The 11 straight wins took in an 88-point thumping of the fledgling Richmond outfit in the first League contest between the teams, as well as a six-point win in the maiden contest with University. The Blues' only loss, in round 12, was a tight affair in muddy conditions against Essendon at East Melbourne.

A hard-fought 11-point win over Fitzroy in round 14 at the Brunswick Street Oval came at a heavy price when Silver Caine, the long-kicking forward who had featured prominently in the 1906 and 1907 premiership triumphs, buckled with a season-ending leg injury.

On the eve of the final-round match with University, Carlton team members were buoyed by the news that Worrall had coaxed the great Jim Flynn out of retirement. Flynn was imperious across half-back in the ensuing semi-final, which resulted in an emphatic 58-point win at St Kilda's expense. Vin Gardiner banged on four goals in the first quarter.

Gardiner would be kept goalless in the 1908 Grand Final, but he was a key contributor all season. Short for a key forward at 167cm, and 68kg, Gardiner booted 34 goals to take out his club's goalkicking award for the first time.

On the eve of the Grand Final it was reported in *The Argus* that Carlton would take the same 18 into the contest. Essendon, however, was forced to replace its brilliant rover and half-forward Lou Armstrong, who had come down heavily on his heel at match practice the previous Saturday. Astoundingly, the Same Olds called on Harry Prout to make his senior debut in the biggest match of the season.

Of interest were the listed occupations for the Carlton players: Fred Elliott was a slater, Gotz and Kelly were fish-curers, Flynn and Arthur Ford were licensed victuallers (food salesmen), George Johnson a police constable and Jim Marchbank a mill owner.

The Grand Final day edition of *The Argus*—Saturday, September 26, 1908—carried crisp images of the respective Carlton and Essendon captains, Fred Elliott and Billy Griffith. It also carried the prospective line-ups.

> "The final football match, to be played this afternoon on the Melbourne Cricket-ground between Carlton and Essendon, is attracting unusual attention.
>
> "Carlton's bold front all through the season—they have only been beaten once, and that by the team they meet to-day—has won them thousands of admirers, but the dramatic club of the year has been Essendon.

> "To-day's game should, if the weather be fine, be a splendid exhibition of the Australian game. It is remarkable that, whereas Essendon have only one man who has played in a final before, Carlton have only one man who has not so taken part. The men are W. Griffith, the Essendon captain, and V. Gardiner, the Carlton forward, who... are opposed to one another.
>
> "It was feared yesterday that M. Londerigan would not be able to play for Essendon, owing to the death of his father, but he has decided, on account of the importance of the game, and at the request of his family, to place himself in the hands of the committee."

On Grand Final day 1908, Fred 'Pompey' Elliott's men confronted their history-making moment. Could they complete a near-perfect campaign with a third-successive pennant—and become the first team to do so in 12 seasons of the VFL competition?

Worrall was forced to recast his defence because of an ailment suffered by the regular full-back, Doug Gillespie, in the final against St Kilda. Back pocket Les Beck moved across to fill the void, and featured prominently alongside the hardened campaigners Norman 'Hackenschmidt' Clark and Elliott.

The zephyr that greeted the Carlton heroes as they took to the amphitheatre would steadily build to a strong wind by the second half; effectively it ruined the contest as a spectacle.

Carlton started well, with Martin Gotz posting the first goal with a clever snap. As *The Herald* correspondent noted: "With a running punt he bagged (the) first goal of the day. The Carlton flags were fluttered in thousands round the ring and the barrackers from the north roared with delight."

Marchbank, having taken possession of a pass from 'Billy' Payne, followed up with a meticulously executed drop kick for Carlton's second.

The Same Olds struck back with a goal to 'Paddy' Shea, reducing the quarter-time margin to eight points. At the first change Worrall boldly effected changes, replacing his on-ball division of Fred Jinks, Flynn and Alex Lang, with George Johnson, Charlie Hammond and Elliott. The moves paid dividends, with Elliott popping in for a telling goal.

Ted Kennedy put Carlton further ahead with a deftly taken place kick, before Harvey Kelly took advantage of strong play upfield by Kennedy, Gotz and Gardiner to post Carlton's fifth goal.

The old heads took a three-goal lead into the main interval, then committed to what was a dour struggle marred by ugly packs and a succession of boundary thow-ins.

Clearly, Worrall had issued the shutdown edict. As *The Age* reported:

> "In the dressingroom during the interval the Carlton players had evidently been instructed to keep their lead, not by attempted attack, but by playing to the wings. This course they pursued for the whole of the remainder of the game."

'Markwell' of *Football Notes* put his own spin on it:

> "Carlton set themselves determinedly to keep Essendon out of range, and rarely took the ball past half-way in the opposite direction. They made the wind their ally, and they hugged the south-east border for all they were worth."

The Carlton players implemented Worrall's game-plan to the letter—making full use of their experience in Grand Finals.

Carlton's third consecutive premiership was hard won—5.5 (35) to Essendon's 3.8 (26)—and Worrall's legacy was confirmed.

'Markwell' wrote in *Football Notes*:

> "For Carlton's unqualified success in recent years everyone qualified to express an opinion gives predominating credit to the astute and experienced managing director, Mr. J. Worrall, who when he took up the reins... found the club deplorably weak and disorganised, and seemed to have a hopeless task before him.

> "His advert to the old club, however, brought about an immediate improvement. His knowledge of the game, his unerring judgment in the selecting of players fitted for the various positions in his team, his excellent ability as a coach, and, above all, his capacity for infusing into his followers something of his own enthusiasm and devotion to the sport, as well as much of his own pluck and determination, have made his side the most formidable and the most evenly excellent in all departments that has been seen in the field since the establishment of Australasian football."

The Carlton Football Club's 44th Annual Report, the 1908 report, was presented to members at the Melbourne Town Hall on the evening of Friday, March 12, 1909. It reads as follows:

> "For the second time in the history of the Club the premiership has been won three times in succession, the first occasion being the years 1873-4-5. Of the 20 matches played last season, only one was lost—a record unparalleled in the history of the game since the formation of the League, and perhaps the greatest performance ever registered by any club, for in the old days there were no semi-final and final matches. This is also the second time that your Club has achieved Jubilee honors, for in 1887—the late Queen Victoria's Jubilee—the premiership was won by Carlton.

> [The reference to Jubilee related to the 1908 Jubilee of football, celebrating

50 years since its evolution in 1858. The year 1908 saw a Carnival played in Melbourne and a talk fest that saw H.C.A. (Colden) Harrison dubbed 'The Father of Football'.]

"Football reached its zenith last season. The game, as a spectacle, vastly improved, the playing strength of the clubs had levelled up, the spirit of the contestants was admirable, and the attendance at the final match eclipsed in numbers and magnitude all previous efforts—a fitting wind-up to the game's Jubilee year. [50,261 attended the Grand Final, a record.]

"We offer sincere congratulations to our Essendon friends for the gallant manner in which their representatives fought for the honor of their club in that great final match. They played a manly, spirited game, and are deserving of great commendation.

"The players merit unstinted praise for their season's work. All self was eliminated, and every man played for his side. They were the best of comrades on and off the field, and their year's record was a triumph of sustained brilliance and consistency. They were in many tight corners, but with the one exception, against Essendon in the mud, emerged triumphantly.

"When one considers what a football season consists of in the matter of weather, with the ground at times as hard as asphalt, at other times the black mud ankle deep, with the wind roaring a gale, and rain and hail pelting in the faces of the players, then, and only then, can the Club's record and the players' work be thoroughly and properly appreciated. In the opinion of many experts, no finer team ever stepped on to a football field.

"Carlton's wonderful advancement has been a grand thing for football. During the last three years there has been a progressive increase in the attendances at the final matches, each in its turn a record, culminating last season in an attendance of 50,000 spectators. During those three years your Club has played 58 premiership matches, winning 50 and only losing 8, kicking 514 goals 690 behinds (3744 points), and having 308 goals 491 behinds (2333 points) registered against them. The performance is an exceptionally fine one, and eloquently speaks for itself.

"Great credit is due to the veteran commander, Mr F. Elliott, who led the team ably throughout the season. It is his eighth year with the Club as a player, and he has, therefore, earned the distinction of being a life member. Able assistance was rendered by the vice-captain, Mr F. Jinks, who was coolness personified.

"The increase in the membership has been simply phenomenal, and is easily a club record, comprising, all told, 4247, made up as follows: Members, 3483; ladies, 688; donors, 21; life members, 5; players, 30. When it is considered that eight short years ago the membership of the club was only 473, it is clearly seen how extraordinary has been the advancement. It is certainly the greatest compliment that could be paid to the management. When the stand is an accomplished fact, a membership of 5000 is confidently looked forward to.

"The finances are in a most satisfactory condition, showing a credit balance of £510 2s. 10d. Last season the committee set aside a sum of £125 towards the erection of a grandstand, and this year your committee received £549 10s. 7d., and the players were given a trip and suitably entertained during the season. It will thus be seen that your committee recognise the desirability of having stand accommodation for the members, and are safeguarding the Club's funds towards that end."

In the end, 11 young men—Les Beck, George Bruce, Norman Clark, Jim Flynn, Charlie Hammond, Fred Jinks, George Johnson, Ted Kennedy, Alex Lang, 'Billy' Payne and George Topping—played their way into football immortality. For it was they who represented Carlton in each of those three famed Grand Final triumphs.

When 'Pompey' Elliott succeeded Flynn as Carlton captain in 1908, and duly led his men into the finals three wins clear of Essendon, Flynn had already confided in Worrall that his career was all but over.

But the canny mentor would have nothing of it and, on the eve of the finals series, again declared that Flynn would be back playing.

Finding his niche on a half-back flank, Flynn was again sterling in his display, in both the 58-point semi-final rout of St Kilda, and "the Big One"—the nine-point Grand final victory over Essendon to complete the fabulous hat-trick.

'Silver' Caine would doubtless have been amongst the 18 who completed Carlton's premiership hat-trick in '08 had it not injury not intervened that winter. Barely a year after his heroics at Brunswick Street, Caine returned to the scene of his triumph at the top of his craft in a Carlton team sitting pretty atop the table—only to be carried from the field with a leg injury that put paid to what was left of a meritorious season.

In 1910, when Worrall was controversially sacked amid one of the most disorderly periods in Carlton's colorful history, Caine was among four senior players who went out in protest. Carlton's loss would prove North Melbourne's gain, for Caine was part of North's VFA triumph in 1911, a year in which he also emerged as the Association's leading goalkicker.

Some eight years after Caine accepted Worrall's overtures to part company with the Rose of Northcote team and join Carlton, the pair were reunited—this time at Essendon, during which time the Same Olds secured the 1912 Premiership with victory over South Melbourne.

Jinks would part company with Carlton on the cusp of the 1910 season, and hook up with neighbouring VFA club North Melbourne. He would feature in the Shinboners' 1910 Grand Final triumph over Brunswick—but would later give the game away across town in Port Melbourne after famously being found guilty of "charging an opponent with his fists".

Beck would have one year's footy left in him, calling it a day at Carlton after the 1909 preliminary final. Within five years had volunteered for active service.

In October 1917, Beck took a German bullet in his left arm, but refused to vacate his post until there was a lull in hostilities. The following August he was hit again, but completed a full recovery and returned to Australia a few months after the Armistice was signed.

Charlie Hammond would feature in Carlton's next two successful Grand Final campaigns, in 1914 and 1915 and would therefore be consigned to history's page as the club's only five-time premiership player.

Regrettably, Lang's name would be forever tainted from 1910, when the man adjudged by *The Australasian* newspaper as the most "outstanding player in the VFL" became embroiled in what's known in football infamy as the Great Bribery Scandal.

With Doug Fraser, Lang would be found guilty and barred from the game for a total of five years—a suspension Lang would duly serve before remarkably returning to the game in 1916 and completing his 100th senior appearance in the famed Carlton guernsey.

For the captain Elliott, who eight years previously had sauntered in to Princes Park after one forgettable 12-game season with Melbourne, and whose true potential was realised under Worrall's tutelage, the 1908 Grand Final triumph truly atoned for the bitter personal hurt of 12 months earlier when a four-match suspension put paid to his premiership aspirations.

By the time he hung up the boots at the conclusion of 1911, Elliott was already feted as the first League footballer to achieve 200 senior games. More than three quarters of a century later, the name 'Fred Elliott' would be included among those posthumously inducted into the Carlton Football Club's Hall of Fame. A measure of Elliott's prominence in the game and in society was made clear that an Australian World War I Major-General, Harold Elliott, inherited his 'Pompey' nickname.

1908 CARLTON

PREMIER'S SEASON

CARLTON: 1908

ROUND ONE May 2
CARLTON	6.12 (48)
ST KILDA	3.4 (22)

Best: Carlton – Topping, Elliott, T.Kennedy, Clark, Williams, Payne.
Goals: Carlton – Topping 5, Jinks.
Crowd: N/A at Princes Park

ROUND TWO May 9
CARLTON	9.8 (62)
MELBOURNE	6.8 (44)

Best: Carlton – Bruce, Caine, Beck, H.Kelly, E.Kelly, Elliott.
Goals: Carlton – E.Kelly 3, H.Kelly 3, McGregor, Topping, Johnson.
Crowd: N/A at the MCG

ROUND THREE May 16
CARLTON	5.13 (43)
ESSENDON	4.8 (32)

Best: Carlton – Gardiner, H.Kelly, Caine, Bruce, Hammond, Gotz.
Goals: Carlton – Gardiner 2, E.Kelly, Lang, Topping.
Crowd: N/A at Princes Park

ROUND FOUR May 23
CARLTON	10.7 (67)
COLLINGWOOD	5.9 (39)

Best: Carlton – H.Kelly, Jinks, Hammond, Elliott, Bruce, Lang, Payne.
Goals: Carlton – H.Kelly 4, Hammond, Koochew, Jinks, Caine, Gardiner, Topping.
Crowd: N/A at Victoria Park

ROUND FIVE May 30
CARLTON	10.12 (72)
FITZROY	5.10 (40)

Best: Carlton – Caine, Bruce, Elliott, Johnson, H.Kelly, Marchbank, McGregor.
Goals: Carlton – Caine 4, Topping 2, Marchbank, Lang, McGregor, Elliott.
Crowd: N/A at Princes Park

ROUND SIX June 6
CARLTON	8.5 (53)
SOUTH MELBOURNE	7.9 (51)

Best: Carlton – H.Kelly, McGregor, Elliott, Beck, Hammond, Payne.
Goals: Carlton – H.Kelly 3, Lang 2, Caine 2, Roland.
Crowd: N/A at the Lake Oval

ROUND SEVEN June 8
CARLTON	13.14 (92)
GEELONG	2.13 (25)

Best: Carlton – Caine, H.Kelly, Johnson, Hammond, Bruce, McGregor.
Goals: Carlton – Caine 4, H.Kelly 4, Jinks, Koochew, Gotz, Elliott, Johnson.
Crowd: N/A at Princes Park

ROUND EIGHT June 13
CARLTON	17.13 (115)
RICHMOND	2.15 (27)

Best: Carlton – Gardiner, Clark, Johnson, Doug Gillespie, T.Kennedy, Williams.
Goals: Carlton – Gardiner 6, T.Kennedy 2, Johnson 2, Doug Gillespie 2, Hammond 2, Roland, Caine, Elliott.
Crowd: N/A at Princes Park

ROUND NINE June 20
CARLTON	7.15 (57)
UNIVERSITY	6.15 (51)

Best: Carlton – Lang, Ingleman, Elliott, Caine, Bruce, Koochew, McGregor.
Goals: Carlton – Gardiner 2, McGregor 2, Johnson, Jinks, Lang.
Crowd: N/A at East Melbourne Cricket Ground

ROUND TEN June 27
CARLTON	10.12 (72)
ST KILDA	6.5 (41)

Best: Carlton – Gardiner, Lang, E.Kelly, Payne, T.Kennedy, Hammond.
Goals: Carlton – Gardiner 5, Caine 2, Elliott, Bruce, Ingelman.
Crowd: N/A at the Junction Oval

ROUND ELEVEN July 4
CARLTON	8.15 (63)
MELBOURNE	4.7 (31)

Best: Carlton – Beck, Bruce, Doug Gillespie, Hammond, Johnson, Lang.
Goals: Carlton – Caine 3, Gardiner 2, Ingleman, E.Kelly, Lang.
Crowd: N/A at Princes Park

ROUND TWELVE July 11
CARLTON	4.5 (29)
ESSENDON	6.6 (42)

Best: Carlton – Caine, Bruce, E.Kelly, T.Kennedy, McGregor, Elliott.
Goals: Carlton – Caine 2, E.Kelly, Lang.
Crowd: N/A at East Melbourne Cricket Ground

ROUND THIRTEEN July 18
CARLTON	10.17 (77)
COLLINGWOOD	5.7 (37)

Best: Carlton – Gardiner, McGregor, Payne, Elliott, Clark, Beck.
Goals: Carlton – Gardiner 4, Marchbank 2, Johnson, Caine, Elliott, Lang.
Crowd: N/A at Princes Park

ROUND FOURTEEN July 25
CARLTON	6.8 (44)
FITZROY	4.9 (33)

Best: Carlton – Gardiner, H.Kelly, Marchbank, Elliott, Johnson, Bruce.
Goals: Carlton – Gardiner 4, H.Kelly 2.
Crowd: N/A at Brunswick St Oval

ROUND FIFTEEN August 1
CARLTON	8.19 (67)
SOUTH MELBOURNE	6.5 (41)

Best: Carlton – Gotz, Ford, Johnson, Clark, Pattison, Jinks, T.Kennedy.
Goals: Carlton – E.Kelly 3, Johnson, Ford, Gardiner, Gotz, H.Kelly.
Crowd: N/A at Princes Park

ROUND SIXTEEN August 8
CARLTON	6.13 (49)
GEELONG	5.9 (39)

Best: Carlton – H.Kelly, Topping, Gotz, T.Kennedy, Lang, Clark.
Goals: Carlton – H.Kelly 3, Topping 2, E.Kelly.
Crowd: N/A at Corio Oval

ROUND SEVENTEEN August 15
CARLTON	6.12 (48)
RICHMOND	4.17 (41)

Best: Carlton – Ford, Hammond, Beck, E.Kelly, H.Kelly, Marchbank.
Goals: Carlton – Lang 2, H.Kelly, McGregor, Topping, E.Kelly.
Crowd: N/A at Punt Road Oval

ROUND EIGHTEEN September 5
CARLTON	10.7 (67)
UNIVERSITY	4.4 (28)

Best: Carlton – H.Kelly, Ingleman, McGregor, Elliott, Hammond.
Goals: Carlton – H.Kelly 4, Gardiner 3, Topping 2, Ford.
Crowd: N/A at Princes Park

PREMIER'S FINALS

SEMI-FINAL September 19

CARLTON	12.12 (84)
ST KILDA	3.8 (26)

Best: Carlton – Payne, Clark, Beck, McGregor, Bruce, Kennedy, Johnson, Hammond.
Goals: Carlton – Gardiner 4, Elliott 2, Lang, T.Kennedy, H.Kelly, Topping, Gotz, Ford.
Crowd: 25,531 at the MCG

GRAND FINAL September 26

CARLTON	2.3	5.4	5.5	5.5 (35)
ESSENDON	1.1	2.4	3.5	3.8 (26)

Best: Carlton – Clark, Elliott, Hammond, Johnson, Lang, Payne.
Goals: Carlton – Elliott, Gotz, H.Kelly, T.Kennedy, Marchbank.
Crowd: 50,261 at the MCG

GRAND FINAL LINE-UPS

CARL	B:	N.Clark	L.Beck	A.Ford
ESS	F:	B.Heaphy	H.Farnsworth	A.Legge
CARL	HB:	J.Flynn	B.Payne	F.Jinks
ESS	HF:	P.Shea	D.Smith	H.Prout
CARL	C:	G.Bruce	R.McGregor	T.Kennedy
ESS	C:	B.Davies	B.Sewart	L.Minto
CARL	HF:	A.Lang	J.Marchbank	M.Gotz
ESS	HB:	M.Shea	B.Busbridge	B.Johnson
CARL	F:	H.Kelly	V.Gardiner	G.Topping
ESS	B:	L.Bowe	B.Griffth (capt)	B.Daykin
CARL	R:	G.Johnson	C.Hammond	F.Elliott (capt)
ESS	R:	A.Belcher	J.Martin	E.Cameron

CARL	**Coach:**	Jack Worrall
ESS	**Coach:**	Dave Smith

SNAPSHOT

Win-loss record: 19-1

Highest score: 17.13 (115), round 8, v Richmond.

Greatest winning margin: 88 points, round 8, v Richmond.

Lowest score: 4.5 (29), round 12, v Essendon.

Greatest losing margin: 13 points, round 12, v Essendon.

Most goals by a player in a game: 6, Vin Gardiner, round 8, v Richmond.

Most consecutive wins: 11

Most consecutive losses: 1

Club awards: Leading goalkicker: Vin Gardiner (34 goals).

Putting it into perspective:
The Blues became the first team to win three consecutive premierships and joined Fitzroy and Collingwood, with three flags, as the game's most successful team. Over three seasons, 1906-1908, they won 50 of 58 games.

1908

	P	W	L	D	%	Pts
1 Carlton (1)	18	17	1		169.4	68
2 Essendon (2)	18	14	4		142.5	56
3 St Kilda (3)	18	10	8		101.4	40
4 Collingwood (4)	18	10	8		97.0	40
5 South Melb	18	9	9		101.4	36
6 University	18	8	10		96.0	32
7 Fitzroy	18	7	11		109.4	28
8 Melbourne	18	7	11		87.0	28
9 Richmond	18	6	12		73.7	24
10 Geelong	18	2	16		68.6	8

(18 home and away rounds)

PLAYERS USED

CARLTON	GAMES	GOALS
Bruce, George	18	1
Caine, Frank	14	20
Carmody, Bill	1	0
Clark, Norman	19	0
Elliott, Fred	17	8
Flynn, Jim	3	0
Ford, Arthur	6	3
Gardiner, Vin	15	34
Gillespie, Dave	3	2
Gillespie, Doug	16	0
Gotz, Martin	20	4
Hammond, Charlie	19	3
Ingleman, Alby	13	2
Jinks, Fred	19	4
Johnson, George	18	7
Kelly, Ernie	8	11
Kelly, Harvey	14	27
Kennedy, Ted	18	4
Koochew, Wally	4	2
Lang, Alex	20	11
Laver, Bill	1	0
Marchbank, Bill	3	2
Marchbank, Jim	7	2
McGregor, Rod	17	5
Pattison, Andy	4	0
Payne, Billy	20	0
Roland, Charlie	4	2
Topping, George	13	16
Williams, Frank	6	0

**SOUTH MELBOURNE 4.14 (38) d
CARLTON 4.12 (36)**

BLOODS FIGHT FOR FIRST FLAG

South Melbourne captain-coach Charlie Ricketts missed out on some individual honours but had the last laugh in the Grand Final. By JIM MAIN

JUST as Grand Final week celebrations in the modern era open with the Brownlow Medal count, there was a similar event more than a century ago. Although the Brownlow Medal was not inaugurated until 1924, fans 15 years earlier voted for their champion player of the season, with the results of that plebiscite published in *The Argus* of Monday, September 27—five days before the South Melbourne-Carlton Grand Final.

The newspaper reported that more than 105,000 fans cast their votes, with Essendon's Bill Busbridge taking the award with 16,503 votes, 1360 more than South Melbourne's Charlie Ricketts. The poll created enormous public interest and *The Argus* reported that more than 45,000 votes were cast on the final day of the poll, on the Saturday before the Grand Final.

Busbridge, the finest centre half-back of his era, had won Essendon's best and fairest in 1908 and 1909 and was idolised by Dons' fans, with one *Argus* reader penning this verse to accompany his vote for the season's champion player:

> Here's to you, Fuzzy Buzzy,
> You're a champion, and no kid.
> Your orders were to play the game,
> And play the game you did.

Although Ricketts would have been disappointed at missing out on the title referred to as Champion of the Colony, he had far more important matters to worry about as South's captain-coach.

South had yet to win a VFL premiership, but had been runner-up to Fitzroy in 1899 and to Carlton in 1907. It therefore had been 19 years since the Southerners had tasted any flag success, and they were not used to failure. They had won VFA premierships in 1881 and 1885 and had won consecutive premierships from 1888-90.

South, founded in 1874, was strongly supported even from its earliest years and recruited most of its players locally. The club had been formed in an amalgamation with Albert Park and became the most popular club in the area, no mean feat considering it had numerous rivals, including South Melbourne Imperials, South Park, Rising Sun and Emerald Hill Standards.

Whereas the Fitzroy and Collingwood clubs, for example, were based in industrial suburbs, the South Melbourne area had few heavy industries and many of the players worked on the Port Melbourne docks or at iron foundries close to the wharves.

South drew its support from a wide area and, in fact, was instrumental in the birth of a new word in the English language—the barracker. South's Lake Oval ground was relatively close to the St Kilda Road army barracks in the late 19th century and, when soldiers from there started attending South matches, they became known as "the barrackers".

Although most VFA clubs struggled to attract an attendance of 10,000, South regularly drew up to 15,000 fans at the Lake Oval and even saw 12,000 fans there for a match against an English rugby side. The gate was a phenomenal (for that era) £202.

South, in its earliest VFL years, recruited heavily from VFA clubs Williamstown and Port Melbourne, but also drew players from Metropolitan Junior Football Association club Leopold, which was virtually a reserves South side. Leopold, which wore navy blue and white and was based in South Melbourne, was a prolific feeder club for the Southerners over more than half a century.

Ricketts was South's first official coach, the position previously filled by the club captain who, in 1908, was classy defender Bill Dolphin. South was a follower of fashion when it appointed Ricketts, as Carlton had won all three premierships over the 1906-08 seasons under the coaching of Jack Worrall.

South had finished fifth under Dolphin in 1908, and following the appointment of Ricketts as captain-coach Dolphin agreed to become vice-captain. However, he missed the 1909 Grand Final because of injury.

Ricketts, a brilliant rover, had won a reputation as one of the best footballers in Victoria in playing for Richmond in the VFA before he joined South in 1906.

A hard task-master, he trained the South squad harder than it had ever trained, while the club committee did its part in the quest for a first VFL premiership by casting a wide recruiting net.

Recruits for 1909 included brilliant Williamstown (VFA) winger Jim Caldwell, who went on to play 155 games with South and captained the 1918 premiership side. Other newcomers included Dave Barry and Jack Scobie, both from the local Leopold club.

Caldwell was regarded as one of the best footballers in Victoria even before he joined South, and mixed pace and skill with aggression.

Williamstown had been a prolific "feeder" club for South as champion fullforward Len "Mother" Mortimer had been recruited from the VFA Seagulls in 1906. Mortimer won his nickname "Mother" because, after taking a mark, he would hold the ball under his chin "like a mother would hold a baby close to her bosom".

Ricketts and his Southerners had a daunting task in their tilt at the 1909 flag as Carlton appeared to be as strong as ever and hell-bent on a fourth consecutive premiership.

It therefore was ironic that, at the very time Ricketts was emulating Worrall's tough training methods, the Carlton players were in revolt after more than seven years of their coach's iron-fisted discipline.

When University, in just its second VFL season, defeated Carlton by 15 points at Princes Park in the opening round of the 1909 season, the Carlton committee sharpened its axe. Three players had refused to take the field for that match—in part as a protest about match payments, but also because of Worrall's heavy-handed methods.

The dispute gathered momentum when a letter carrying the signatures of several players demanded Worrall's sacking—prompting Worrall to resign on July 26, stating: "For the sake of the club and for peace and quietness, I consider it better to resign."

Worrall remained as club secretary until the end of the year, by which time he had was asked to relinquish that position as well.

Captain Fred 'Pompey' Elliott took over as playing coach for the remainder of the 1909 season and steadied what had been a sinking ship. Incredibly, considering Carlton's internal problems, the Blues finished the home and away season in second position, behind South Melbourne on percentage.

South, on the other hand, had relatively smooth sailing towards the finals, even though it dropped three of four matches mid-season, by 24 points to Carlton at Princes Park in round 11, by 14 points to Fitzroy at the Lake Oval in round 13 and by 11 points to Collingwood at Victoria Park the following week.

South won its final five home and away games to win the minor premiership and, under the final four system operating at that time, had to play third-placed Collingwood in one semi-final; a week later Carlton played the fourth-placed Essendon in the other.

Carlton and Essendon clashed at the MCG on September 11, with the Blues thrashing the Dons by 36 points to put Carlton well on track for a fourth consecutive flag. South's bid for a first VFL flag captured the football public imagination and, when the Southerners played Collingwood at the MCG the following week, *The Herald* reported: "All roads led to the Melbourne Cricket Ground. People on foot swarmed there. Tens of thousands poured down in train and tram, in motor and cab, and, in fact, every kind of wheeled vehicle bore a human burden."

More than 35,000 fans saw South defeat Collingwood by 21 points and all relished the prospect of a Carlton-South Final at the MCG the following week, especially as the Blues had defeated the Southerners by five points in the 1907 Grand Final. If South won this match, it would be the premier, while a Carlton victory would give the Southerners (as minor premiers) the right of challenge in a Grand Final.

Newspapers were divided on which club they saw as the likely premier, but *The Herald* noted following South's defeat of Collingwood: "They (the Southerners) had caught the Collingwood backs napping and their forwards covered themselves with glory. It was a most inspiring series of dashes and roused the spectators to a pitch of great enthusiasm."

South adopted roughhouse tactics in an effort to unsettle Carlton in their Final of September 25 and paid a heavy penalty, losing by 21 points. Even worse for the Southerners, Caldwell was reported for striking Carlton's George Bruce, landing him a nine-match suspension.

'Observer' wrote in *The Argus* the Monday after the final: "It is for 'keeps' next Saturday and public interest in football will be demonstrated by their having paid over £5000 to see the League finals. I find popular desire rather in favour of South Melbourne because of purely sporting reasons as people want to see the Carlton conquerors checked for a season."

'Observer' believed South had been overly physical in the final against Carlton and was particularly critical of Caldwell when he wrote: "Caldwell was conspicuous on the wing for wholly unnecessary roughness and, after the match, (field umpire Jack) Elder reported him for striking Bruce."

The Argus's football writer was correct on one point: South was the sentimental favourite, as most football fans believed Carlton had dipped into the well of success once too often for their liking; they wanted a new champion to hail.

To compound South's worries, Carlton would welcome the return of star defender Norman Clark for the Grand Final after he had missed the first clash because of neuralgia, a nerve condition. Carlton became the warm premiership favourite.

Film of the 1909 Grand Final has long resided in the National Archives of Australia, but was only recently discovered from its dusty vault. The film, of 10 minutes and 30 seconds, pans across the 37,759 crowd pre-match to reveal men in bowlers and boaters, boys in cloth caps and women with large, wide-brimmed hats. There are no banners, no scarves, no real identity of support for either side.

The players are the only ones in team colours, but even then there are discrepancies. South wore white guernseys with a red sash, but the sashes ran in opposite directions from player to player. Carlton wore its traditional navy blue and white, but again with variance. Some wore the newly designed guernsey with the CFC logo, while others wore the old navy blue with a white yoke.

Although *The Argus*'s 'Observer' had hoped it would be a dry, windless day and perfect for football, Grand Final day dawned miserable. There were showers during the morning and rain threatened as the players took the field. However, the rain held off until there was a sprinkling in the final quarter. Despite the threat of rain, 'Observer' noted that one person in 20 living in Melbourne attended either the South Melbourne Grand Final or the VFA Brunswick-Prahran Grand Final (won by Brunswick). Football was king even more than a century ago.

South started brightly, but kicked two behinds that should have been goals. When Mortimer missed a third chance, South fans "groaned in despair". The combatants scored five behinds in a gripping, but mistake-riddled first quarter.

There was no quarter-time break in that era, with sides changing ends at the sound of the bell. There were no interchange, or even substitute, players and, in the usual practice of the time, the ruck group changed each quarter, with South moving Barry, Cameron and Ricketts onto the ball and resting Franks, Belcher and Kerr in pockets or on flanks. Carlton switched Marchbanks, Baquie and Jinks on the ball to "rest" Johnson, Hammond and Lang.

Carlton appeared more settled at the start of the second quarter and, following good play by Johnson, Topping scored the first goal after the resumption. South then bored in ever harder and, following a couple of behinds, goaled through Franks. Minutes later, Ricketts slotted South's second goal.

Carlton was devastated when Baquie badly rolled an ankle and was sent limping to a forward pocket. With no reserve, Baquie was restricted for the rest of the match.

The teams were locked together at the main break, with most fans tipping South to forge ahead because Carlton virtually had been reduced to 17 men. 'Observer' wrote: "South Melbourne were still playing better football than their rivals—the question that interested thousands of people was, 'Can they last it out at the pace?'"

The Southerners, instead of using the brutal tactics they had adopted in the Final, tried to move the ball as quickly as possible to unsettle the heavier-footed Blues, and the tactic appeared to be working, especially as Mortimer kicked a goal early in the third quarter.

However, hopes South might have had of building a solid lead dissipated when the injured Baquie converted from a free kick close to goal to again level scores. 'Observer' wryly noted: "As often happens, the cripple got the goal." *The Argus* man also reported: "With the excitement increasing every instant, everybody was wholly absorbed in the play."

Carlton fans groaned when Gotz fell awkwardly and was forced to leave the ground with a sprained knee. However, Gotz reappeared a few minutes later to a volley of cheers from Blues' fans. The only problem was that Gotz, like Baquie, could only hobble about.

South took advantage of Carlton's injury worries and, through good play by Hiskins and Belcher, moved the ball quickly to Gough for the red and white's fourth goal. But, as 'Observer' noted, Carlton refused to surrender and, in fact, he noted: "The more Carlton suffered, the better they played."

South might have had a seven-point lead at the final break but, as 'Observer' suggested, South fans feared Carlton would "pull the game out of the fire with one of their great-hearted rallies".

He added: "The whole of the last quarter was a period of wild excitement, with trembling South Melbourne hands counting the minutes on their watches and the Carlton thousands roaring their heroes on. It was desperately hard—no player cared for consequences. There was only one thought. Win."

The ball flew from end to end early in the final quarter, with both sides missing chances. Carlton eventually started controlling play and the ball was on the Blues' forward line for 10 minutes.

Finally, the dam wall broke. Johnson forced the ball forward for Carlton and teammate Kelly took a mark tucked on the boundary line. His shot was straight and true and his goal—Carlton's fourth—lifted the Blues' spirits. It now was even money for the premiership.

'Observer' wrote: "There was a roar of delight from their (Carlton) followers. They were going to win after all—South, with all their striving were just two points ahead." He added: "The finish was almost too thrilling for detailed description. People shook with excitement as the play swung from end to end like a pendulum."

Carlton attacked incessantly over the final minutes in efforts to bridge the gap, but South follower Franks heroically took two strong marks to deny them. 'Observer' described him as South's "lion of the side".

Although Franks was not rated the best player on the ground over the entire match (with most football writers nominating Ricketts), he held Carlton at bay when it mattered most and, when the final bell signalled South's two-point victory, the burly West Australian was mobbed by well-wishers.

He and Belcher had controlled the ruck contests over the desperate final quarter and South fans rejoiced in the fact that Franks two years earlier had been suspended following a Carlton complaint.

Carlton, in the lead-up to the 1907 finals series, complained about Franks striking two of its players and he was suspended for a total of 14 matches, putting him out of action until well into the following season.

The suspension forced Franks to miss the 1907 Grand Final, which Carlton won by just five points. South fans wondered for years what might have been if Franks had played, as he was one of the best, and most feared, big men of his era.

Now, two years later, he was chaired from the MCG a hero. South fans stormed onto the MCG at the first peal of the final bell and carried the men in red and white on their shoulders. It was South's first VFL premiership and its first flag since winning the 1890 VFA title.

That long-lost film of the 1909 Grand Final captures the euphoria of the victory, with South fans throwing hats in the air as they parade their champions around the MCG.

'Markwell' from *The Australasian* wrote: "The excitement that prevailed among the 37,000 spectators was indescribable... the playing ground was rushed the moment the first tinkle was heard, and a surging multitude of the madly excited barrackers bore the victors shoulder high from the field. Such a scene of delirious enthusiasm had never before been witnessed at the finish of a football match in Melbourne."

'Markwell' also paid tribute to South captain-coach Ricketts, writing: "Consummate skill in leadership on the field belongs to few men. It would, perhaps, be an exaggeration to say that captain Ricketts is the possessor of such skill... His training and judgement have built up a side largely composed of men who, until recently, were junior players, into a company of artists... To him, therefore, is due chief credit for the team's achievement."

South celebrated its 1909 premiership long and hard and, following a civic reception and dinner at the South Melbourne Town Hall, nursed its collective sore head through a brief tour of country Victoria before playing a "premier of premiers" match against South Australian premier club West Adelaide.

South defeated Hamilton in an exhibition match the week after its Grand Final success and then defeated West Adelaide by 24 points at the Adelaide Oval, with *The Australasian* naming Thomas, Scobie and Pentland as the Southerners' best players.

Each South premiership player, following the tradition of the time, was presented with a premiership medallion and cap but, unfortunately, South rewarded Ricketts with the sack, replacing him with Bill 'Sonna' Thomas for the 1910 season.

Ricketts was reinstated as captain-coach in 1912 but, after Essendon defeated South by 44 points in that season's Grand Final, he was dumped again. The South players elected the rash and often outspoken Ricketts as captain for the following season, but the club committee refused to ratify their decision.

The disillusioned Ricketts walked out on South after 82 games from 1906 and returned to his original club, Richmond, which had been admitted to the VFL in 1908. He played 16 games with the Tigers and was coach from 1914-16. Ricketts was appointed St Kilda coach in 1920, made a five-game comeback as captain-coach in 1921 and continued as non-playing coach in 1922.

Despite being a three-club player, he always will be remembered as South Melbourne's first premiership captain and coach.

PREMIER'S SEASON

SOUTH MELBOURNE: 1909

ROUND ONE May 1
SOUTH MELBOURNE	8.5 (53)
GEELONG	6.8 (44)

Best: South Melbourne – Deas, Ricketts, Caldwell, Wade, Mortimer.
Goals: South Melbourne – Deas 4, Mortimer 3, Casey.
Crowd: N/A at Corio Oval

ROUND TWO May 8
SOUTH MELBOURNE	7.3 (45)
CARLTON	4.4 (28)

Best: South Melbourne – Kerr, Caldwell, Casey, Mortimer, Thomas, Belcher.
Goals: South Melbourne – Casey 3, Mortimer 3, Barry.
Crowd: N/A at the Lake Oval

ROUND THREE May 15
SOUTH MELBOURNE	12.16 (88)
MELBOURNE	3.6 (24)

Best: South Melbourne – Mortimer, Grimshaw, Bower, Belcher, Deas, Ricketts.
Goals: South Melbourne – Mortimer 4, Deas 3, Belcher 3, Casey 2.
Crowd: N/A at the Lake Oval

ROUND FOUR May 22
SOUTH MELBOURNE	11.10 (76)
FITZROY	5.7 (37)

Best: South Melbourne – Ricketts, Franks, Mortimer, Deas, Gough, Kerr.
Goals: South Melbourne – Gough 4, Deas 3, Franks, Mortimer, Cameron, Ricketts.
Crowd: N/A at Brunswick St Oval

ROUND FIVE May 29
SOUTH MELBOURNE	6.10 (46)
COLLINGWOOD	3.8 (26)

Best: South Melbourne – Thomas, Hiskins, Ricketts, Casey, Caldwell, Belcher.
Goals: South Melbourne – Casey 2, Franks, Ricketts, Mortimer, Deas.
Crowd: N/A at the Lake Oval

ROUND SIX June 5
SOUTH MELBOURNE	8.10 (58)
RICHMOND	10.11 (71)

Best: South Melbourne – Ricketts, Mortimer, Barry, Dolphin, Hiskins, Deas.
Goals: South Melbourne – Ricketts 2, Mortimer 2, Kerr, Deas, Franks, Casey.
Crowd: N/A at Punt Road Oval

ROUND SEVEN June 7
SOUTH MELBOURNE	9.9 (63)
ESSENDON	9.8 (62)

Best: South Melbourne – Kerr, Gough, Richardson, Deas, Mortimer, Hiskins, Caldwell.
Goals: South Melbourne – Gough 2, Deas 2, Mortimer 2, Casey 2, Belcher.
Crowd: N/A at East Melbourne Cricket Ground

ROUND EIGHT June 12
SOUTH MELBOURNE	11.15 (81)
UNIVERSITY	2.6 (18)

Best: South Melbourne – Mortimer, Barry, Thomas, Jones, Casey, Gough.
Goals: South Melbourne – Mortimer 5, Gough 2, Jones 2, Casey, Bower.
Crowd: N/A at the Lake Oval

ROUND NINE June 19
SOUTH MELBOURNE	14.13 (97)
ST KILDA	2.8 (20)

Best: South Melbourne – Mortimer, Jones, Ricketts, Scobie, Barry, Moxham.
Goals: South Melbourne – Mortimer 5, Kerr 2, Deas 2, Jones 2, Gough, Caldwell, Casey.
Crowd: N/A at the Lake Oval

ROUND TEN July 3
SOUTH MELBOURNE	17.9 (111)
GEELONG	4.7 (31)

Best: South Melbourne – Deas, Mortimer, Thomas, Grimshaw, Belcher, Callan.
Goals: South Melbourne – Deas 5, Mortimer 4, Gough 2, Franks 2, Belcher 2, Ricketts, Casey.
Crowd: N/A at the Lake Oval

ROUND ELEVEN July 10
SOUTH MELBOURNE	6.8 (44)
CARLTON	9.14 (68)

Best: South Melbourne – Casey, Hiskins, Belcher, Pentland, Mortimer, Ricketts.
Goals: South Melbourne – Casey 3, Mortimer, Ricketts, Kerr.
Crowd: N/A at Princes Park

ROUND TWELVE July 17
SOUTH MELBOURNE	6.9 (45)
MELBOURNE	3.6 (24)

Best: South Melbourne – Thomas, Caldwell, Belcher, Jones, Baird, Franks.
Goals: South Melbourne – Gough, Franks, Mortimer, Casey, Deas, Kerr.
Crowd: 16,270 at the MCG

ROUND THIRTEEN July 24
SOUTH MELBOURNE	4.6 (30)
FITZROY	5.14 (44)

Best: South Melbourne – Kerr, Franks, Thomas, Bower, Hiskins, Pentland.
Goals: South Melbourne – Franks, Deas, Kerr, Caldwell.
Crowd: N/A at the Lake Oval

ROUND FOURTEEN July 31
SOUTH MELBOURNE	6.7 (43)
COLLINGWOOD	8.6 (54)

Best: South Melbourne – Gough, Drane, Deas, Bower, Belcher, Mortimer.
Goals: South Melbourne – Deas 2, Hiskins, Mortimer, Cameron, Jones.
Crowd: N/A at Victoria Park

ROUND FIFTEEN August 14
SOUTH MELBOURNE	18.11 (119)
RICHMOND	3.8 (26)

Best: South Melbourne – Hiskins, Mortimer, Cameron, Caldwell, Kerr, Thomas.
Goals: South Melbourne – Hiskins 6, Mortimer 5, Kerr 2, Thomas 2, Ricketts 2, Franks.
Crowd: N/A at the Lake Oval

ROUND SIXTEEN August 21
SOUTH MELBOURNE	6.5 (41)
ESSENDON	5.7 (37)

Best: South Melbourne – Bower, Caldwell, Belcher, Ricketts, Thomas, Hiskins.
Goals: South Melbourne – Bower 3, Casey, Mortimer, Cameron.
Crowd: N/A at the Lake Oval

ROUND SEVENTEEN August 28
SOUTH MELBOURNE	9.11 (65)
UNIVERSITY	5.9 (39)

Best: South Melbourne – Mortimer, Streckfuss, Cameron, Belcher, Caldwell.
Goals: South Melbourne – Mortimer 5, Franks, Cameron, Deas, Ricketts.
Crowd: N/A at East Melbourne Cricket Ground

ROUND EIGHTEEN September 4
SOUTH MELBOURNE	7.15 (57)
ST KILDA	5.5 (35)

Best: South Melbourne – Thomas, Hiskins, Deas, Gough, Casey, Pentland.
Goals: South Melbourne – Deas 3, Gough 2, Mortimer, Ricketts.
Crowd: N/A at the Junction Oval

PREMIER'S FINALS

SEMI-FINAL September 18
SOUTH MELBOURNE	10.8 (68)
COLLINGWOOD	6.11 (47)

Best: South Melbourne – Kerr, Ricketts, Franks, Belcher, Caldwell, Bower, Thomas.
Goals: South Melbourne – Mortimer 3, Franks 2, Cameron 2, Gough, Casey, Kerr.
Crowd: 35,114 at the MCG

FINAL September 25
SOUTH MELBOURNE	7.5 (47)
CARLTON	10.9 (69)

Best: South Melbourne – Thomas, Bower, Franks, Belcher, Kerr, Barry, Pentland.
Goals: South Melbourne – Gough 3, Franks, Mortimer, Belcher, Bower.
Crowd: 42,418 at the MCG

GRAND FINAL October 2
SOUTH MELBOURNE	0.5	2.9	4.12	4.14 (38)
CARLTON	0.5	2.9	3.11	4.12 (36)

Best: South Melbourne – Cameron, Franks, Kerr, Mortimer, Scobie, Thomas.
Goals: South Melbourne – Franks, Gough, Mortimer, Ricketts.
Crowd: 37,759 at the MCG

GRAND FINAL LINE-UPS

STH M	B:	A.Pentland	J.Scobie	T.Wade
CARL	F:	F.Elliott (capt)	G.Topping	J.Baquie
STH M	HB:	A.Hiskins	B.Thomas	T.Grimshaw
CARL	HF:	F.Caine	H.Kelly	F.Jinks
STH M	C:	H.Drane	G.Bower	B.Moxham
CARL	C:	G.Bruce	R.McGregor	T.Kennedy
STH M	HF:	J.Cameron	B.Deas	D.Barry
CARL	HB:	M.Gotz	B.Payne	A.Ford
STH M	F:	A.Kerr	L.Mortimer	A.Gough
CARL	B:	N.Clark	D.Gillespie	J.Marchbank
STH M	R:	B.Franks	V.Belcher	C.Ricketts (capt)
CARL	R:	G.Johnson	C.Hammond	A.Lang

STH M Coach: Charlie Ricketts
CARL Coach: Fred Elliott

SNAPSHOT

Win-loss record: 16-6

Highest score: 18.11 (119), round 15, v Richmond.

Greatest winning margin: 93 points, round 15, v Richmond.

Lowest score: 4.6 (30), round 13, v Fitzroy.

Greatest losing margin: 24 points, round 11, v Carlton.

Most goals by a player in a game: 6, Arthur Hiskins, round 15, v Richmond.

Most consecutive wins: 5 (twice).

Most consecutive losses: 2

Club awards: Leading goalkicker: Len Mortimer (50 goals).

Putting it into perspective:
The Bloods' first premiership success was at the expense of Carlton, whose quest for a record-breaking four consecutive flag ended in a narrow defeat. South Melbourne's previous finals record prior to 1909 was poor with just a single victory.

1909

		P	W	L	D	%	Pts
1	South Melb (1)	18	14	4		168.9	56
2	Carlton (2)	18	14	4		146.8	56
3	Collingwood (3)	18	12	4	2	130.3	52
4	Essendon (4)	18	11	7		121.7	44
5	Melbourne	18	10	7	1	106.3	42
6	Fitzroy	18	8	9	1	101.6	34
7	University	18	7	9	2	100.1	32
8	Richmond	18	6	12		64.4	24
9	Geelong*	18	3	15		65.5	12
10	St Kilda*	18	2	16		59.3	8

(18 home and away rounds)

PLAYERS USED

SOUTH MELBOURNE	GAMES	GOALS
Baird, Des	5	0
Barry, Dave	10	1
Belcher, Vic	21	7
Bower, George	19	5
Caldwell, Jim	19	2
Callan, Hughie	7	0
Cameron, Jim	15	6
Casey, Dick	20	20
Deas, Bob	20	29
Dolphin, Bill	14	0
Drane, Horrie	2	0
Franks, Bert	21	13
Gough, Alf L.	18	19
Grimshaw, Tom	21	0
Harrison, Ed	1	0
Hiskins, Arthur	19	7
Jones, Jack	6	5
Kerr, Alex	21	9
Moore, Herbert	1	0
Mortimer, Len	21	50
Moxham, Billy	9	0
Pentland, Alan	14	0
Richardson, Jack E.	1	0
Ricketts, Charlie	20	11
Scobie, Jack	19	0
Streckfuss, Bert	2	0
Thomas, Bill D.	21	2
Wade, Ted	11	0

**COLLINGWOOD 9.7 (61) d
CARLTON 6.11 (47)**

SWORN ENEMIES HENCEFORTH

Collingwood's triumph over Carlton in 1910 delivered it a new motto and its fiercest rivalry. By GLENN McFARLANE

A CONCERNED football follower encapsulated the mood of many in the community when he branded the Victorian Football League and its players as avaricious and almost unchristian at a Rechabite meeting on the eve of the 1910 Grand Final between Collingwood and Carlton. Mr S. Mauge preached that "this sort of thing is sucking the blood out of a pure and healthy sport. Do it for the spirit of the thing, and the good that is in it, and not for the money." He was referring to the three constant themes of the season—the brawls, the betting and the clandestine payment of players.

History does not record how many people were in attendance to hear his criticism of football, but there is little doubt that he was not alone in his thoughts as the curtain was about to be drawn on the controversial 1910 season. It had been the VFL's most contentious season to date. Behind-the-play incidents had become more prevalent, three Carlton players were accused of accepting bribes to "play dead" in a match with one exonerated and the other two banned; and the shadow of player payments and under-the-table professionalism shrouded the "amateur" game.

Football's good name had been besmirched and only a return to pure amateurism would stop the game from sliding further into the abyss, according to Mr Mauge. Those closer to the game were hoping (some may even have been praying) for a good, clean conclusion to the season when Collingwood and Carlton qualified for the Grand Final. They had been the best two teams of the season, with the Blues finishing two games clear of the Magpies on the ladder, but the bribery allegations had unsettled their season towards the end. Carlton had beaten Collingwood on two occasions that season, but a close Grand Final was tipped.

For the first decade-and-a-half after Collingwood's birth in 1892, the relationship between the Magpies and the Blues had been relatively harmonious, to the point that the teams were almost charitable to each other. Before 1910, and even for a time after it, Fitzroy was the team that Collingwood supporters hated the most. In some ways, Carlton had been something of an ally. The two teams had met in the Magpies' first game in the VFA in 1892 and the Blues had generously donated their share of the gate to the new team to give them a good kick-start. Collingwood repaid the favour in the VFL five years later when Carlton was struggling financially.

But, on October 1, 1910, things would change utterly, and forever. And a new rivalry would be born out of what occurred on the Melbourne Cricket Ground that afternoon.

Carlton had rallied from its precarious position on entering the VFL competition to become one of the most successful and clinical of football teams. The Blues had become the first team to win three successive VFL pennants (1906-07-08), they had finished runners-up to South Melbourne in 1909, beaten by only two points, and the 1910 Grand Final was the club's fifth Grand Final appearance in a row. Thanks to a tough, disciplined style of football, the Blues had developed a reputation as an outstanding football team, with a decided edge over the Magpies. Before the 1910 premiership play-off, Carlton had won 10 of its past 11 encounters against Collingwood—the most recent Magpies' win had been by a solitary point in 1909. But with so much at stake on Grand Final day, those people hoping for a controversy-free end to a season marred by one event after another were to be disappointed by the game, and its aftermath.

Events leading up to the 1910 Grand Final, the first premiership play-off between the two teams and only the fourth final involving them, hardly suggested signs of harmony. On the morning of Carlton's first final, the semi against South Melbourne, the Blues left three key names—Alex Lang, Douglas Fraser and Doug Gillespie—out of its team list on the advice of a player who had accused them of taking a bribe to "play dead" in the club's inexplicable final-round loss to bottom-of-the-table St Kilda. Gillespie was subsequently exonerated and would take his place at full-back in the Grand Final. But the two others, Lang and Fraser, were later banned for five years for "playing dead" in the game against the Saints. It was hardly the sort of news the VFL needed at the start of the finals series. Carlton battled on through the crisis, but lost to South Melbourne in a semi-final. As minor premiers, though, they were afforded the chance to play off against Collingwood in the Grand Final after the Magpies had disposed of South Melbourne in the semi-final.

There were more ominous signs on the eve of the big game that tensions were running deep. *The Herald's* cartoon depiction of season 1910 had a Collingwood player and a Carlton player brawling, scratching and slinging punches. No one knew just how prophetic this would be. Less than 24 hours after the paper rumbled off the presses and found its way onto the streets of Melbourne, what had been predicted was coming true at the MCG, and with both sides feeling the pressure to perform, this time there would be no holds barred. Before the game, those 42,577 fans clicking through the MCG turnstiles were already predicting trouble. Even the man charged with keeping order, the VFL's premier umpire Jack Elder said later in *The Sporting Globe* that he had felt a "sullen hostility" in the rooms before the game.

Collingwood officials were trying to use past glories to inspire new ones as part of their pre-game inspiration. Magpie heroes from the past such as Fred 'Charger' Hailwood, Jack Monohan, Archie Smith and Charlie Pannam filed into the dressing room. Even Dick Condon, considered *persona non gratis* by many at the club after leaving for Tasmania and then transferring to Richmond, was spotted in the rooms. Bill Strickland, who led Collingwood to its first premiership, in the VFA in 1896, gave a stirring speech before the team ran out to do battle. Strickland said: "Now boys, I hope that in two hours, you will return to this room as premiers. Play the ball, nothing but the ball." The advice would go unheeded.

The Argus highlighted the tensions early in the game as it got under way, saying: "It was clear in the first five minutes that the game was going to be desperately hard." Collingwood made the best of the start and landed the first goal with some brilliant team play. "Collingwood's retaliating charge was more effective (than Carlton's), for ('Jock') McHale, (Tom) Baxter and (George) Angus took the ball the length of the ground and with a fine drop kick, Angus set his side a goal-kicking example by landing the first (goal)." According to *The Argus*, players threw themselves into the early contest as if there were no inhibitions, with one saying: "No one gave a thought about the possible consequences."

Carlton replied with a goal soon after when Ted Rowell slipped over, allowing Carlton forward Jack Baquie to boot the quick reply. It would not be the last time Baquie would feature on the day. Collingwood was, however, playing the superior football. Champion forward 'Dick' Lee, a local lad in his fifth season in black and white, and the son of head trainer Wal Lee, kicked Collingwood's second goal. *The Argus* noted that it came from "another fine Collingwood effort, in which Angus and (Richard) Vernon did most of the battling, and landed the ball well forward where Lee marked and scored with a punt."

Collingwood had a "dazzling rush of success then, and earnt it with some very brilliant football. McHale, (Percy) Gibb, Baxter and (Richard) Vernon dashed in, working well together and Vernon scored their third goal while (Dave) Ryan and McHale were chief helpers in the effort that gave Lee a difficult angle shot and fourth goal." The last goal came just before the quarter-time bell, and it gave Collingwood a 19-point break.

But the Magpies' tactics changed dramatically and inexplicably in the second term after a decision from captain-coach George Angus to go on the defensive. One leading VFL administrator described it as "a winning team playing the game of a losing team." *The Herald* was another critical of the decision to switch from playing attacking football to a more defensive mindset, saying: "Angus massed his men wholly for the defence and, as a consequence, Carlton began to show up, and with anything like the same luck and skill that Collingwood were able to command, the Blues might have recovered their position." Fortunately for the Magpies, they did not. Despite a goal to Vin Gardiner for Carlton, courtesy of an infringement, the Blues squandered many opportunities in attack. They sprayed the ball with their field kicking, and in their path toward goal.

Still, there were more than a few worrying signs for Collingwood. A few serious injuries ruined any rhythm the Magpies had, and put into serious doubt the club's premiership hopes. According to *The Herald*, first-year player Joe Scaddan "soared for a mark and came down heavily, getting a wrench across his loins that kept him out for some time." He was carried from the field in the arms of the trainers and was examined by doctors William Moore and B. Crellin. They "found that he was suffering from a contusion of the kidney." Courageously, Scaddan came back on and did his best for the team. It was his 21st and final game in a brief but successful career, having played every game in his one and only season. Then Ryan, a former Euroa and Geelong ruckman, "had his elbow so severely injured that he was practically of no further use in the match." He had to play in the forward line in the hope that a loose ball might find its way into his hands. At other stages, Angus and Percy Wilson also suffered injuries. But despite these concerns, Collingwood held on gamely to a 15-point half-time lead.

The exhausted players had a few surprise visitors in their rooms at half-time. Collingwood's patron, Justice Sir John Madden, went into the rooms to try and urge the Magpies on. Madden was animated and was heard saying to the players, "it's all right, boys, keep it up." Whether his words had an effect, or whether Angus gave a stirring speech, is unknown, but Collingwood did come out fired up to quell Carlton's challenge in the third term.

The great full-forward Dick Lee was, as always, outstanding. He added his third goal and Collingwood's sixth shortly into the third quarter, giving the Magpies a clear advantage. *The Herald* said: "By clever play, (Lee) scooped up the ball in front, got a fair scoring show, screwed his kick and achieved the sixth goal." It was soon followed by another goal, this time to Richard Daykin. Carlton had trouble scoring once they were in attack, though they did manage to peg one back when Jim Marchbank scored their third major.

But Lee was the stumbling block for Carlton. Each time the Blues looked as if they were about to mount a challenge, the Magpies simply rallied forward and looked for the damaging Collingwood forward. More often than not, he made the Blues pay on the scoreboard. In one passage of play, *The Herald* said "Gillespie and (William) Payne were running the ball out between them when Lee, very cleverly, anticipated the pass, whipped the ball up and kicked the eighth goal." But, just when the Magpies looked to be getting away again, Carlton's Rod McGregor, almost lame from an earlier injury, managed to score a late goal to reduce the margin to 20 points at three-quarter-time.

The crowd tried to read the body language of the respective teams as they rested at the last change. Most of the Carlton players stood in their huddle; many of the Collingwood ones lay on the turf. To some, it highlighted that the Blues were fresh enough to mount one last challenge. Indeed, they did make a number of inroads early in the final term as they threw everything they could at Collingwood to see if the Magpies were going to wilt under the strain. They did not.

Then came the moment that the doomsayers had predicted, the idealists had had nightmares about and the umpire feared was inevitable. It was one of the most infamous moments of Grand Final history, when it was feared the game would degenerate into a riot, with supporters threatening to join in a wild brawl that had erupted between players from both sides, and even some officials. It was described by many observers as the most disgraceful scene witnessed on a Melbourne football field.

The Argus described the incident as follows: "Baquie, standing opposite the Harrison Stand, rose for a mark. Baxter rose a second later. As the two men regained their feet, their arms locked about the ball. Baquie wrenched and twisted. Baxter hung on tenaciously. Baquie fell back and Baxter was still gripping the ball. Baquie released one hand and Baxter freed one of his hands.

Baquie, hot with rage at his possession being so obstinately disputed, raised his hand and in a second the two men fell to the ground fighting." As this happened Collingwood's Jim Shorten "dashed in from the backline and lifted him (Baquie) off the ground with an all mighty punch." This led to an all-in situation where fists and fierce words flew around with dangerous intent.

In all, *The Argus* claimed it lasted about two minutes, "but it was a period fraught with sensational possibilities." Collingwood's Les "Flapper" Hughes was decked and in stepped Daykin to come to the aid of his teammate. "Every one of those players (mentioned above) either struck or were struck," as *The Argus* observed. The fight was rapidly careering out of control. Worse still, attendants from both sides had become involved in the fracas, and spectators were starting to mass and seek to get involved. They "left the grass at their railings and joined in the chase, policemen bolted from the sides and 20 or 30 men from the rival camps jumped over the fence and set out to take part."

Only the cool thinking of the experienced man in white averted a riot. Jack Elder summed up the situation perfectly and sensed some sanity needed to be restored. The only solution he could think of was to bounce the ball, and let the game get running again. That would more than likely stop the trouble as there was still a game to be won and lost. He blew the whistle, threw the ball back to the turf and got on with the match. Years later, in 1935, Elder recalled the seriousness of the situation that was confronting him. He told *The Sporting Globe*: "The whistle and the bounce did the trick. Suddenly players remembered that there was a ball to be chased. The sparring and the grumbling and the swinging rights and lefts stopped like magic. I feel certain that if I had failed to get the game going that day the crowd would have swarmed onto the ground and the rival camps of barrackers would have been at each other's throats." It was a simple act of ingenuity. The fights dissipated, the football resumed and Elder breathed a sigh of relief when the bell finally sounded.

Collingwood had managed only one goal in the last term to Carlton's two, but it was enough for them to win by 14 points. There were celebrations in the Magpie camp, but no such merriment from the VFL or the football writers assigned to cover the match. There was widespread condemnation in *The Herald* and *The Sporting Globe* of the "disgraceful" scenes and calls that "had the League asserted itself years ago, as it should have done, these blots on the reputation of the football world would not have been seen." There was almost as much discussion about the fight as the football played, even if Collingwood had proven itself as the best team in the competition.

Dick Lee had finished the game with four goals, to take his tally to 58 for the season, to equal the record he had set the previous year. He was listed as

Collingwood's best player. 'Jock' McHale was not far behind him, playing an outstanding game in the centre of the ground, taking an advantage of an injury suffered during the game to his counterpart, Rod McGregor. Duncan McIvor, Ted Rowell, Scaddan and Shorten were also key players for the Magpies on the day. Interestingly enough, Baquie was listed as the best of the Carlton players.

After the match Collingwood premiership captain-coach George Angus praised his players for their courage and their willingness to stand up for themselves. Angus said: "I am satisfied that my team is better, and in today's go we were heavily handicapped, for three of us—Wilson, Ryan and I—were crippled after half-time. The boys played magnificent." It was the first time these two teams had meet in a Grand Final. The next five times these two teams would meet in a Grand Final (1915, '38, '70, '79, '81), the Blues would have the last laugh.

But this premiership was Collingwood's. Yet the drama and the headlines arising out of the last-quarter brawl did not finish with the Grand Final. The tribunal case of Magpie Tom Baxter arising out of the game would prove every bit as sensational as the match. By the time of the hearings of the four players reported, it was apparent that the VFL had run out of patience, and that the repercussions would be heavy. Baxter and Bacquie would each receive suspensions of a season, while Jim Shorten and Percy Sheehan each copped a season and a half.

A short time afterwards, however, the VFL received a letter from Collingwood's Richard Daykin, who was conveniently about to retire from the game. He claimed that he—not Baxter—had been the player responsible for starting the melee with Baquie. It was simply a case of mistaken identity, Daykin insisted. The more astonishing thing was that the VFL judiciary took the claims seriously. Two Collingwood figures—playing-coach George Angus and committeeman Jack Joyce—also swore it was Daykin, not Baxter. Umpire Elder, the man who had made the reports, was just as adamant that it had been Baxter and not Daykin.

Incredibly, the ruse worked, despite one key piece of evidence being completely overlooked. Daykin's nickname was 'Ginger' as he had red hair; Baxter had dark hair. Oddly enough, this fact was discounted as the VFL investigations panel overturned Baxter's ban. To make it even more incredible, the panel refrained from imposing a penalty on Daykin for his "confession" because he had been so "manly and courageous" in coming forward with his tale. Collingwood had somehow triumphed on and off the field.

Was it any wonder, then, that shortly after the Grand Final victory, club treasurer Bob Rush came up with a suggestion for the club's new motto? Rush offered up the Latin word *Floreat Pica*. Having struggled to find the Latin for magpie, he settled on *pica*, which scholars assured him meant "part coloured." So Rush's suggestion, as he noted it anyway, stood for "May the Magpies prosper", something which seemed appropriate.

Collingwood had proven that it was prepared to prosper at almost any cost, and any sacrifice. It had prospered, much to the chagrin of Carlton, and almost certainly the rechabite who on the eve of the Grand Final had blasted the VFL and its footballers for their unchristian avarice and aggression. As ugly as the 1910 Grand Final had been, it was responsible for sowing the seeds of one of Australian sport's most intense rivalries.

1910 COLLINGWOOD

PREMIER'S SEASON

COLLINGWOOD: 1910

ROUND ONE April 30
COLLINGWOOD	5.5 (35)
CARLTON	9.9 (63)

Best: Collingwood – Lee, Baxter, Wilson, Angus, McHale, Ryan, Shorten.
Goals: Collingwood – Lee 3, McHale, Ryan.
Crowd: N/A at Princes Park

ROUND TWO May 14
COLLINGWOOD	13.9 (87)
SOUTH MELBOURNE	5.16 (46)

Best: Collingwood – Baxter, Wilson, Lee, Rowell, Vernon, Daykin, Hughes.
Goals: Collingwood – Wilson 4, Lee 3, Baxter 3, Herbert, Ryan, Daykin.
Crowd: N/A at Victoria Park

ROUND THREE May 21
COLLINGWOOD	13.13 (91)
ST KILDA	2.6 (18)

Best: Collingwood – Lee, Jackson, Hackett, Gibb, McHale, Angus, Rowell.
Goals: Collingwood – Lee 6, Ryan 2, Baxter 2, Hughes, Herbert, Vernon.
Crowd: N/A at Victoria Park

ROUND FOUR May 28
COLLINGWOOD	4.17 (41)
ESSENDON	6.7 (43)

Best: Collingwood – Lee, Scaddan, Heatley, Rowell, Baxter, Wilson.
Goals: Collingwood – Lee 2, Baxter, Wilson.
Crowd: N/A at East Melbourne Cricket Ground

ROUND FIVE June 4
COLLINGWOOD	10.16 (76)
MELBOURNE	4.4 (28)

Best: Collingwood – Angus, Gibb, Lee, Ryan, Oliver, Herbert, Wilson.
Goals: Collingwood – Lee 3, Ryan 2, Hughes, Wilson, Heatley, Baxter, Jackson.
Crowd: N/A at Victoria Park

ROUND SIX June 6
COLLINGWOOD	11.14 (80)
FITZROY	7.9 (51)

Best: Collingwood – Ryan, Lee, Angus, Shorten, Sadler, Jones, Gibb.
Goals: Collingwood – Lee 3, Ryan 3, Wilson 2, McHale, Heatley, Baxter.
Crowd: N/A at Brunswick St Oval

ROUND SEVEN June 11
COLLINGWOOD	6.9 (45)
RICHMOND	5.7 (37)

Best: Collingwood – Lee, Harper, McHale, Hughes, Vernon, Shorten.
Goals: Collingwood – Lee 4, Herbert 2.
Crowd: N/A at Punt Road Oval

ROUND EIGHT June 18
COLLINGWOOD	6.10 (46)
UNIVERSITY	6.6 (42)

Best: Collingwood – Scaddan, Gibb, Jones, Lee, McHale, Rowell, Ryan.
Goals: Collingwood – Herbert 3, Hughes, Baxter, Wilson.
Crowd: N/A at Victoria Park

ROUND NINE June 25
COLLINGWOOD	6.11 (47)
GEELONG	10.9 (69)

Best: Collingwood – Lee, Daykin, Hackett, Vernon, McHale, Ryan.
Goals: Collingwood – Lee 3, Herbert, Ryan, Daykin.
Crowd: N/A at Corio Oval

ROUND TEN July 2
COLLINGWOOD	2.10 (22)
CARLTON	6.15 (51)

Best: Collingwood – Heatley, Lee, McHale, Norris, Gibb.
Goals: Collingwood – Lee, Heatley.
Crowd: N/A at Victoria Park

ROUND ELEVEN July 9
COLLINGWOOD	4.9 (33)
SOUTH MELBOURNE	13.17 (95)

Best: Collingwood – Lee, Gibb, Hughes, Sadler, Ryan, Wilson.
Goals: Collingwood – Lee 2, Daykin, Ryan.
Crowd: N/A at the Lake Oval

ROUND TWELVE July 16
COLLINGWOOD	7.12 (54)
ST KILDA	6.8 (44)

Best: Collingwood – Baxter, Angus, Ryan, Lee, Lumsden, Gibb, McHale.
Goals: Collingwood – Lee 2, Ryan 2, Norris, Hughes, Wilson.
Crowd: N/A at the Junction Oval

ROUND THIRTEEN July 23
COLLINGWOOD	5.13 (43)
ESSENDON	2.9 (21)

Best: Collingwood – Hughes, McHale, Shorten, Wilson, Rowell, Lee.
Goals: Collingwood – Lee 2, Ryan, Gilchrist, Hughes.
Crowd: N/A at Victoria Park

ROUND FOURTEEN July 30
COLLINGWOOD	9.12 (66)
MELBOURNE	7.6 (48)

Best: Collingwood – Hughes, Lee, Dummett, Oliver, Rowell, Scaddan, Wilson.
Goals: Collingwood – Hughes 3, Lee 2, Baxter, Heatley, Gilchrist, Norris.
Crowd: 8,784 at the MCG

ROUND FIFTEEN August 6
COLLINGWOOD	7.12 (54)
FITZROY	6.6 (42)

Best: Collingwood – Ryan, Lee, Jones, Shorten, Scaddan, McHale, Rowell.
Goals: Collingwood – Ryan 3, Lee 2, Norris, Vernon.
Crowd: N/A at Victoria Park

ROUND SIXTEEN August 20
COLLINGWOOD	8.13 (61)
RICHMOND	5.4 (34)

Best: Collingwood – Lee, Angus, Gibb, Gilchrist, Jackson, Jones, Vernon.
Goals: Collingwood – Lee 3, Gilchrist 2, Norris, Oliver, Hughes.
Crowd: N/A at Victoria Park

ROUND SEVENTEEN August 27
COLLINGWOOD	10.15 (75)
UNIVERSITY	9.5 (59)

Best: Collingwood – Baxter, Strachan, McHale, Wilson, Norris, Daykin.
Goals: Collingwood – Strachan 3, Baxter 3, Lee 2, Gibb, Daykin.
Crowd: N/A at East Melbourne Cricket Ground

ROUND EIGHTEEN September 3
COLLINGWOOD	4.13 (37)
GEELONG	2.9 (21)

Best: Collingwood – Lee, Strachan, Gibb, Ryan, Vernon, McHale.
Goals: Collingwood – Baxter 2, Lee 2.
Crowd: N/A at Victoria Park

PREMIER'S FINALS

SEMI-FINAL September 10
COLLINGWOOD	14.11 (95)
ESSENDON	5.7 (37)

Best: Collingwood – McHale, Scaddan, Shorten, Lee, Baxter, Ryan, Angus.
Goals: Collingwood – Lee 6, Gilchrist 4, Ryan, McHale, Hughes, Wilson.
Crowd: 23,988 at the MCG

PRELIMINARY FINAL September 24
COLLINGWOOD	8.7 (55)
SOUTH MELBOURNE	6.8 (44)

Best: Collingwood – McHale, McIvor, Wilson, Baxter, Vernon, Shorten, Rowell.
Goals: Collingwood – Lee 3, Angus 3, Gilchrist 2.
Crowd: 44,301 at the MCG

GRAND FINAL October 1
COLLINGWOOD	4.3	5.3	8.5	9.7 (61)
CARLTON	1.2	2.6	4.9	6.11 (47)

Best: Collingwood – Lee, McHale, McIvor, Rowell, Scaddan, Shorten.
Goals: Collingwood – Lee 4, Angus, Daykin, Gibbs, Gilchrist, Vernon.
Crowd: 42,790 at the MCG

GRAND FINAL LINE-UPS

COLL	B:	J.Sadler	T.Rowell	C.Norris
CARL	F:	A.McDonald	V.Gardiner	A.Wilson
COLL	HB:	J.Scaddan	J.Shorten	D.McIvor
CARL	HF:	P.Sheehan	J.Marchbank	J.Bacquie
COLL	C:	P.Gibb	J.McHale	N.Oliver
CARL	C:	E.Jamieson	R.McGregor	T.Clancy
COLL	HF:	G.Angus (capt)	L.Hughes	D.Vernon
CARL	HB:	T.McCluskey	B.Payne	N.Clark
COLL	F:	P.Gilchrist	D.Lee	P.Wilson
CARL	B:	D.Harris	D.Gillespie	B.Goddard
COLL	R:	D.Ryan	R.Daykin	T.Baxter
CARL	R:	J.Wells	M.Gotz	F.Elliott (capt)
COLL	Coach:	George Angus		
CARL	Coach:	Fred Elliott		

SNAPSHOT

Win-loss record: 16-5

Highest score: 14.11 (95), semi-final, v Essendon.

Greatest winning margin: 73 points, round 3, v St Kilda.

Lowest score: 2.10 (22), round 10, v Carlton.

Greatest losing margin: 62 points, round 11, v South Melbourne.

Most goals by a player in a game: 6, Dick Lee, round 3, v St Kilda; semi-final, v Essendon.

Most consecutive wins: 10

Most consecutive losses: 3

Club awards: Leading goalkicker: Dick Lee (58 goals)

Putting it into perspective:
Collingwood's third Grand Final win was their first under captain-coach George Angus; he became only the third premiership coach in VFL history and just the second captain-coach of a premiership team.

1910

		P	W	L	D	%	Pts
1	Carlton (2)	18	15	3		160.1	60
2	Collingwood (1)	18	13	5		122.3	52
3	South Melb (3)	18	12	6		122.2	48
4	Essendon (4)	18	12	6		115.6	48
5	Geelong	18	10	7	1	105.9	42
6	University	18	10	8		101.5	40
7	Richmond	18	7	10	1	102.6	30
8	Fitzroy	18	5	13		90.8	20
9	Melbourne	18	4	14		59.5	16
10	St Kilda	18	1	17		62.3	4

(18 home and away rounds)

PLAYERS USED

COLLINGWOOD	GAMES	GOALS
Baxter, Tom	21	15
Burleigh, Wal	1	0
Campbell, Sam	1	0
Crisp, Roy	1	0
Daykin, Richard	16	5
Duff, Andy	2	0
Dummett, Alf	1	0
Freeman, Artie	1	0
Gibb, Percy	20	2
Gilchrist, Paddy	9	11
Hackett, Charlie	9	0
Harper, Ned	1	0
Heatley, Bill	16	4
Herbert, Marshall	13	8
Hughes, Les	16	10
Jackson, Jim	5	1
Jones, Horrie	10	0
Lee, Dick	21	58
Lumsden, Ernie	2	0
McDougall, Bertie	1	0
McHale, Jock	21	3
McIvor, Duncan	4	0
Norris, Charlie	11	4
O'Donoghue, Dave	8	0
Oliver, Norm M.	18	1
Rowell, Ted	16	0
Ryan, Dave	21	18
Sadler, Jim	16	0
Scaddan, Joe	21	0
Shorten, Jack	21	0
Strachan, Bob	2	3
Vernon, Dick	18	3
Wilson, Percy	20	11

ESSENDON 5.11 (41) d
COLLINGWOOD 4.11 (35)

SAME OLD STORY FOR WORRALL

Having worked his premiership magic at Carlton, John Worrall arrived at Essendon in 1911 with similarly grandiose plans. By EMMA QUAYLE

JACK Worrall had thick shoulders, intense brown eyes, a busy mind and an unblinking focus. As a cricketer, he was a national batsman, called into the 1884-85 Ashes side to replace a teammate who had fallen out with selectors over match fees; as a footballer, he was a brave and skilful rover who spent eight years in the Fitzroy side.

Appointed Carlton secretary in 1902, the 40-year-old had effectively become VFL football's first coach. He had scheduled regular training sessions and stood out on the track, calling orders as the players moved around him. He had made them adhere to stricter tactics than they had ever been taught before, he went out and recruited the players he wanted and he shuffled his side around until he was happy with it. He had turned a team that had lingered around the edge of the top four, without ever being able to take the next step, into a big-bodied, long-kicking side that out-bustled opponents, ran all day long, won three successive premierships, in 1906-08… and then the players got rid of him. They decided they didn't like all this tough training, that they didn't like Worrall looking down on them if they went out for a drink, and that they wanted to be paid more than the equivalent of $3 a week to keep working as hard as they were. Several players signed a letter during the 1909 season saying they wanted Worrall to go. Worrall resigned after round 13 in 1909 and, after seeing out the year as secretary, left the club altogether.

The coach was settled in a new job, as the VFL's umpiring coach, when Essendon called at the end of 1910. The Same Olds hadn't won a flag since 1901, and their supporters were becoming more agitated with each lost opportunity. A quick, skilful, inventive side, they looked capable of success but kept finding new ways to unravel. In 1909, they had won four of their first five matches before injuries and angst set in. Upset that his defenders had kept deserting their posts during a late-season match, captain Bill Griffith argued with half-back Len Bowe, who took offence at how the strong-minded, stubborn skipper had spoken to him. At a meeting of all players and the club's committee, Griffith—a survivor of the successful 1901 side and already a club great—was grilled over his attitude towards training, playing and his teammates. He offered to step down as captain, only for the players to talk him out of it. The next year, in 1910, Essendon had strung nine wins together through the middle part of one of the roughest, toughest seasons ever, only to lose ruckman Bill Busbridge to a two-month knee injury and trail away as the finals neared. For the fifth time in seven years, they were bundled out in a semi-final.

As quick and exciting as they were, the Essendon players lacked one thing: discipline. They needed someone to teach them how to run hard, persist and fight for the ball. Enter Worrall, who had been highly sought after since splitting with Carlton but took up Essendon's offer and became the Same Olds' first non-playing coach, signing for three pounds, 10 shillings per week—a wage that would be raised to four pounds a week should the side make the finals. It was an appointment that made headlines. "Worrall has, in the most practical manner, earned the reputation of being a veritable wizard of the football world," wrote one journalist, 'Follower' of *The Age*. "The Carlton club unwisely dispensed with Worrall's services, and Carlton's subsequent loss has been Essendon's gain."

Worrall inherited a talented group of players, who, like Essendon's supporters, were desperate for the club to do better. Griffith, a teenager in 1901, was nearing 30. He had moved from a wing to full-back but had remained an important member of the side, his combination of competitiveness and cool-headedness suiting the position. Bowe, the half-back flanker he had clashed with, was inconsistent yet seemed to play well every time the team was involved in a big game. Such occasions appealed to him. Centreman Bill Sewart—a state cricketer known as 'Pimp'—was also nearing his 30s, and after initially planning to lead the team, as a sort-of captain-coach, Dave 'Soaker' Smith settled happily for being just the captain when Worrall joined the club. An international cricketer who scored 30 runs in two Tests for Australia, Smith had joined Essendon in 1901 because his home suburb, Richmond, didn't yet have a League side. He had established himself first as a super-quick centre half-forward with safe hands, then gone on to impress in virtually every other position on the ground. So admired was his kicking that he was photographed by *The Argus*, with the pictures sent to international schools and universities, as an example of what this Australian game had going for it.

The Same Olds boasted a strong, steady group of foot soldiers: Lou Armstrong, a 170-centimetre tall marking forward; George McLeod, a 32-year-old back pocket who had crossed from St Kilda via several seasons in Tasmania; and Don Hanley, a 28-year-old defender from South Ballarat. They also had a trio of newcomers they had blooded during 1910 and seen enough of to expect more. One, 20-year-old Fred Baring, was a tall, skinny ruckman who had grown up around West Melbourne and had been playing with a church team before deciding to try out with Essendon. The club hoped to team him more regularly with the bigger, bulkier Alan Belcher. Fred O'Shea had found a place on a wing, and Percy Ogden was a whippet like O'Shea, albeit an older one. Having started out with Collingwood as a 19-year-old in 1905, Ogden had played only four games before returning to the VFA. Known as 'Butch', he was quick and he had endurance, qualities that appealed to the new coach. He had looked cool, calm and clever in his second shot at the big time, and people outside Essendon hoped for big things from him too, noting his "dashing cleverness, quick judgement and resourcefulness" on the field. "He throws himself whole-heartedly into the game," wrote one journalist, "but for all that he keeps his head—and uses it."

Worrall's initial message to the players was simple: compete, and never fall away. He needed the foot soldiers to hang in there and do their bit, but knew their success depended on a handful of others. The new coach introduced Bill 'Johnnie' Walker, a 25-year-old recruit from Carlton, in the first round and he made a quick impression. So did Jack Kirby, who kicked a goal with his first kick early in the year, showed a knack for sneaking away from his opponent and had another much-valued quality: courage. Paddy Shea, recruited to the club from Fitzroy—after a few years on the West Australian goldfields—played alongside him, providing another mature body and just-as-classy foot skills. In fact, he was one of the first players to use the banana kick while shooting for goal. Ernie Cameron, a red-haired rover who had made his debut in 1905, also filled the "small, quick and brave" bill, finding some early form at the feet of Belcher and Baring. And as the wins kept coming—after a first-round draw the Same Olds won seven games in a row—Bill Busbridge became another important part of the new coach's line-up.

'Buzzy' wasn't a new player. He was a child prodigy, who had been thrown into the Essendon VFA side as a 15-year-old in 1902 and made his debut for the

VFL side less than two years later under considerable pressure. Everyone knew who he was, everyone knew how talented he was supposed to be and when the teenager struggled against the bigger, tougher bodies in his first game, and was left out of the team the following week, some wondered if he was going to be good enough. After two weeks on the sidelines, Busbridge was brought back and thrown immediately into the ruck, where he thrived. He played every game for the year, and by the middle of the season was challenging a champion—Hugh Gavin—as the side's best defender. Busbridge was composed, he loved taking on older, more established players and he was gutsy.

Having endured those early doubts, Busbridge then had to deal with some positive hype—people wondering how good he was going to be. By 1911 he had spent nine seasons at centre half-back, becoming everything supporters had hoped for. He was only 25, his place in Essendon's history was already assured and he was widely seen as the best backman in the game. *Punch* magazine called him Essendon's "busy bee," and an annual poll of newspaper writers in 1908 and 1909 had declared him not only the standout defender, but also the best player in the country. He was a powerful runner who worked hard and he had long arms—"wings," was how one reporter described them—and his whole-hearted, honest nature saw him appeal to more than merely Essendon fans. Once, having run down an injured Fitzroy opponent hobbling after the ball, Busbridge "cantered alongside the wounded Maroon," wrote the *Victorian Football Follower*, "refusing, like a true sport, to lay a hand upon him. The Fitzroy barrackers cheered the manly Essendonian." That the Same Olds lost their 1909 semi-final to Carlton was in no way because of their centre half-back. Observed *The Australasian*: "No man rendered more heroic service on Essendon's behalf than did Busbridge, who had his heart, his head and every ounce of his fine physique gallantly employed from end to end of the engagement."

Busbridge performed well every time he played. The trouble was that injury had worn him down. He injured his knee for the first time in 1905—missing the majority of the season when doctors first anticipated he would be out for only six games—and he'd had trouble with it since, also missing a large part of 1908 with a chipped bone in his ankle. When the knee crumbled again, early in 1910, Busbridge returned for a few late-season games and decided he had had enough. He wasn't there as 1911 began, but as the Same Olds started to look more and more like a premiership side, he was happily welcomed back. His persistent knee problems had slowed him down somewhat, but he had not forgotten how to get to where the ball was.

The VFL had 10 teams in 1911, and a home and away season of 18 matches, to be followed with a finals series. By midway through the season, the Same Olds were still well placed. Their first-round draw with Carlton was disappointing, given they kicked 5.15 (45) to the Blues' 6.9 (45), but they strung seven wins together from there and when they did eventually lose—to South Melbourne in round nine, and Carlton the following week—it was by a combined total of only 15 points and after a tumultuous couple of weeks. During their round 8 game against Fitzroy, a 35-point win, Jim 'Bull' Martin had been reported for striking George Holden. Martin, who had crossed from Collingwood in 1907, was big, mean and willing to throw his burly self around. Holden had a feisty streak too. The League ruled Bull out for the rest of the year and he also had to front the district court, having been charged by police over the same incident. Essendon appealed after he was found guilty and fined five pounds and one shilling, convincing the court that the forward hadn't actually been the one to throw the punch. The conviction was quashed, giving the Same Olds hope they could get him back into the side. They couldn't—the VFL refused to re-hear the case—but after dropping those two games straight the Same Olds settled quickly back into form.

As followers, Baring and Belcher were combining just as club officials had hoped they would. Baring was the thin, athletic, high-leaping ruckman—the graceful technician—whereas Belcher barged around the ground. The youngster was bold and enthusiastic—he loved to be where the action was—and he caught eyes when he was out in space too. "He is a wonderful mark in the crush or out of it, on foot or in the air," wrote one reporter. "He is a first-rate kick and is always quick and sure of hand." Belcher was older—he'd made his debut in 1906 and already played in Victorian sides—and he took pride in protecting his smaller teammates and working hard to get around the ground. He wasn't particularly stylish but his teammates adored him. "Belcher's shepherding was all that could be desired, enabling Baring to hit out to the rover with unerring accuracy time after time," wrote the newspaper *Sport* after one game. "Much of Belcher's work was unnoticed by many of the onlookers but his club mates knew his value to the team." He was the battering ram, Baring brought the energy, and together they were considered the dominant ruck combination in the League. The bonus was that Cameron, as rover, was finding easier ways to the ball. After breaking an ankle in 1908, then busting his jaw in 1909, luck had finally turned for "Ginger" and he was piecing together a brilliant season.

As the finals approached, the Same Olds found their most imposing form of the year. They held off an impressive Collingwood, they notched comfortable wins over Geelong, Fitzroy and University and they kicked 23.24 (162) against St Kilda—a staggering tally in such low-scoring times—to finish the home and away season on top of the ladder. People were taking them seriously, yet they were pitted against Carlton—one of only two teams they hadn't managed to beat, and the team Worrall most wanted to knock over—in the first week of the finals.

It was a tough, bruising game. Essendon won by 21 points, but only after reining in Carlton's eight-point lead at the last break. The game marked, incidentally, the first time players wore numbers on the back of their guernseys, as an experiment for the following year, when the *Football Record* was launched. On this day, the Same Olds' numbers were small and red, placed underneath the sash on their black jumper. The recently returned Busbridge, having played well in defence all day, moved into the ruck and became involved in the Same Olds' three last-quarter goals. Bill Sewart was busy, Pat Shea ran hard on a wing, and Percy Ogden and Alan Belcher also got involved as the team sent the ball forward over and over again. Finally—after falling so often in the first week of the finals—the club had a chance to win its second premiership.

Its perfect season had, however, become a little less so. Belcher, as *The Herald* put it, had "met with an accident during the progress of the match between Carlton and Essendon." The ruckman had twisted a knee while turning to grab the ball, and the trainers had rushed to his side. "At first it was thought that he was attacked with cramp, but the affair has proved more serious," continued *The Herald* report. "On Sunday he suffered much pain, and yesterday he went into hospital. Today his condition improved, though it is doubtful whether he will be able to take part in the big match next Saturday against Collingwood."

He wasn't, and the Essendon players were devastated at losing their big-hearted follower. Still, they were confident they could win, even when persistent rain threatened to turn the game into a wet, sloppy slog. Into the side, replacing Belcher, came George McLeod, and the players trusted him. He wasn't brilliant but he had always appreciated his opportunities and done well when called upon. By Saturday, the rain had eased a little, but showers began to float over the MCG shortly before the 2pm game. "There was an instant stir in the crowd," noted 'Observer', in *The Argus's* match report. "Women looked longingly at the grandstands and pavilions, where already every foot of space was taken. Those who had no umbrellas protested against their use. Everyone was angry with that inopportune shower. Nature and the universe had mismanaged things. Public feeling found voice in rotten luck."

The feeling around the ground was that the wet weather would damage Essendon's chances, given the Same Olds relied so heavily on their sharp skills and speed. Those sentiments changed, however, when both sets of players emerged from their changerooms—as *The Argus* noted: "The Collingwood fellows looked smart and athletic with bare muscular arms, the side one would have fancied in a tug of war, but Essendon were wiser in wearing sleeves to their jackets, a fact which Collingwood realised long before half-time." By the start of the game, the rain was heavy. It was so wet, noted another post-match report, that five horses had slipped over while patrolling traffic on the corner of Swanston and Flinders streets in the city.

Almost 44,000 people had crammed into the ground, and they saw Essendon make the more aggressive start, its small, quick runners using the "half-strength wind" at their back to set up a nine-point lead by quarter-time. Baring, without Belcher by his side, took control in the middle. Walker and Ogden both imposed themselves and McLeod again took his chance, kicking the side's first goal. The Same Olds ran and ran, confused their opponents by moving the ball quickly, and played confidently, as though they knew they were the better side. Essendon's defenders were playing "cool and resourceful" football, and Collingwood suffered when its champion forward Dick Lee trod on a fallen Essendon player, "touched his weak knee and walked away". Dan Minogue, the side's other key forward, hurt his shoulder so badly that "although able, when unopposed, to punt a goal, he was quite incapable of earning one," said *The Argus*. "That was Collingwood's luck in the first phase of this vital game, and one almost needs to underline it for the benefit of people who may have lost the sight of one eye, or suffer from defects of memory."

The Same Olds moved further ahead in the second quarter, taking a 16-point lead into the half-time break. Baring got even better, playing what *The Argus* termed "a man's game" in the ruck. Kirby looked dangerous each time they went forward, and the defenders continued to ensure Collingwood's attacks were "short-lived dashes and never sustained," keeping them scoreless. They were not, however, entirely satisfied. Where the Collingwood players had erred by wearing their short-sleeved guernseys, the Essendon players decided during the break that the stops in their boots were too short, and needed replacement. Consequently, they emerged from the rooms in dribs and drabs, at the insistence of the umpire, who, waiting to bounce the ball for the second half with the Collingwood players in position and his whistle poised, had to wander back inside and call them out. Their half-time break wound up lasting for 26 minutes—ironically, the day after the "importance of punctuality" had been discussed at a meeting of the League's powerbrokers.

Collingwood gathered some momentum from there. By the final break they had whittled the lead back down to only three points, and the Same Olds seemed to have tired. The injured Lee made a telling move, shifting to defence and moving Ted Rowell forward in his place. Rowell kicked a goal, hit the post with another shot and although Baring, Cameron and Len Bowe, playing his greatest game for the year in defence, were working as hard as they could, Collingwood kept pressing. Their backmen "became confused," reported *The Argus*, "playing desperately without much method, but struggling anyway to hold their lines. Essendon's lead shrunk; the turning point in the game seemed to have come. Essendon's fear at the moment was "one more river to cross". Had Collingwood not missed three shots in the final few minutes of the term, the Same Olds would have been in huge trouble.

As it was, they still had to reset themselves. "The finish saved the game from being in any sense commonplace," wrote *The Argus*, and it started with Essendon rediscovering its pace, organisation and determination to attack. Ogden was crucial, encouraging his teammates to keep rushing the ball forward, but the Collingwood players refused to relent and levelled up the scores. Mistakes were becoming more costly, though. Collingwood forward Tom Baxter paddled one ball out in front of him and was pushed in the back, but missed the goals with a "shockingly bad kick". He missed another shot minutes later, this time on the run, and then took a mark well within kicking distance. His shot did not end well. "To the dismay of the side," reported *The Argus*, "he kicked the ball into the arms of the man on the mark. He takes the risks always in placing it very close to the mark, and the ball was then very heavy."

It was a terrible error, yet it was one he repeated not long later. Essendon scored another goal to reclaim the lead, but Collingwood responded by forcing the ball forward again. They were six points down, time was almost up and then Baxter earned a free kick, "a bit to one side, but easy distance". Deliberately, noted *The Argus*, he went to place kick the ball. "'Any money if you get it,' roared an excited onlooker, but again from the shot the ball struck the chest of the Essendon man on the mark." With just one minute left, the shot proved to be Collingwood's final chance. Fittingly, the Grand Final finished with the brilliant Cameron dashing downfield towards the goal front.

Essendon had what it wanted—a third premiership, a new reputation as a strongly disciplined side and, according to *The Argus*, a group of "incoherently happy" supporters. The Same Olds won 5.11 (41) to Collingwood's 4.11 (35) and owed much to Baring, Cameron, O'Shea Stewart, Kirby, who "shirked nothing" in the forward line and the cool, clever Armstrong in defence, not to mention the unfortunate Baxter, who soon found himself looking for a new club. The Magpies, suspicious of his final-quarter effort, cleared him to St Kilda. Each player was presented with a commemorative cap, and supporters were assured of several things at the club's annual meeting. Essendon wanted to get better, it wanted to recruit some new players, and it wanted to win another premiership as soon as it possibly could.

1911 ESSENDON

PREMIER'S SEASON

ESSENDON: 1911

ROUND ONE April 29
ESSENDON 5.15 (45)
CARLTON 6.9 (45)
Best: Essendon – B.Armstrong, Martin, Cameron, Sewart, Smith, Belcher.
Goals: Essendon – Baring 2, B.Armstrong 2, Shea.
Crowd: N/A at East Melbourne Cricket Ground

ROUND TWO May 6
ESSENDON 10.16 (76)
RICHMOND 3.11 (29)
Best: Essendon – Martin, Baring, Belcher, Bowe, Cameron, Smith.
Goals: Essendon – Shea 2, L.Armstrong 2, Martin 2, Cameron, Ogden, Baring, B.Armstrong.
Crowd: N/A at Punt Road Oval

ROUND THREE May 13
ESSENDON 6.11 (47)
MELBOURNE 0.9 (9)
Best: Essendon – Cameron, Ogden, Smith, L.Armstrong, Shea, B.Armstrong, White.
Goals: Essendon – Shea 2, B.Armstrong 2, Belcher, L.Armstrong.
Crowd: 11,554 at the MCG

ROUND FOUR May 20
ESSENDON 21.12 (138)
COLLINGWOOD 7.11 (53)
Best: Essendon – B.Armstrong, Ogden, Smith, Anderson, Shea, L.Armstrong.
Goals: Essendon – B.Armstrong 6, Ogden 4, L.Armstrong 3, Shea 3, Cameron 2, Martin 2, Baring.
Crowd: N/A at East Melbourne Cricket Ground

ROUND FIVE May 27
ESSENDON 12.14 (86)
UNIVERSITY 6.6 (42)
Best: Essendon – Cameron, Walker, Belcher, Baring, Griffith, Bowe, Hazel.
Goals: Essendon – Baring 4, L.Armstrong, Walker, Belcher, Shea, Martin, Cameron, B.Armstrong, Ogden.
Crowd: N/A at East Melbourne Cricket Ground

ROUND SIX June 3
ESSENDON 8.11 (59)
GEELONG 6.6 (42)
Best: Essendon – Martin, Bowe, Belcher, Walker, L.Armstrong, Shea, Hazel.
Goals: Essendon – L.Armstrong 2, Shea, Ogden, B.Armstrong, Hazel, O'Connor, Baring.
Crowd: N/A at Corio Oval

ROUND SEVEN June 5
ESSENDON 9.10 (64)
ST KILDA 3.6 (24)
Best: Essendon – L.Armstrong, Smith, O'Connor, Cameron, Ogden, Griffith.
Goals: Essendon – L.Armstrong 3, Shea 2, B.Armstrong 2, Cameron, O'Connor.
Crowd: N/A at East Melbourne Cricket Ground

ROUND EIGHT June 10
ESSENDON 8.7 (55)
FITZROY 3.2 (20)
Best: Essendon – Cameron, Chalmers, Walker, Bowe, Smith, Griffith.
Goals: Essendon – Ogden, Martin, B.Armstrong, Baring, O'Connor, Shea, L.Armstrong, Cameron.
Crowd: N/A at East Melbourne Cricket Ground

ROUND NINE June 17
ESSENDON 5.11 (41)
SOUTH MELBOURNE 6.8 (44)
Best: Essendon – B.Armstrong, Anderson, L.Armstrong, McLeod, White, Bowe, Cameron.
Goals: Essendon – B.Armstrong 3, Baring, Shea.
Crowd: N/A at the Lake Oval

ROUND TEN June 24
ESSENDON 5.10 (40)
CARLTON 6.16 (52)
Best: Essendon – Smith, Hart, Cameron, L.Armstrong, Ogden, Shea.
Goals: Essendon – L.Armstrong 2, Chalmers, Shea, Cameron.
Crowd: N/A at Princes Park

ROUND ELEVEN July 1
ESSENDON 7.15 (57)
RICHMOND 7.5 (47)
Best: Essendon – Cameron, Sewart, Smith, Hay, Belcher, L.Armstrong.
Goals: Essendon – Cameron 2, L.Armstrong 2, Ogden, Shea, Kirby.
Crowd: N/A at East Melbourne Cricket Ground

ROUND TWELVE July 8
ESSENDON 7.15 (57)
MELBOURNE 6.13 (49)
Best: Essendon – Ogden, Smith, Kirby, Sewart, Griffith, Belcher, L.Armstrong.
Goals: Essendon – Smith 2, Belcher, Hazel, L.Armstrong, Ogden, Kirby.
Crowd: N/A at East Melbourne Cricket Ground

ROUND THIRTEEN July 15
ESSENDON 3.11 (29)
COLLINGWOOD 2.11 (23)
Best: Essendon – Kirby, Cameron, Baring, Anderson, Bowe, B.Armstrong.
Goals: Essendon – Cameron, Kirby, B.Armstrong.
Crowd: N/A at Victoria Park

ROUND FOURTEEN July 22
ESSENDON 12.8 (80)
UNIVERSITY 6.6 (42)
Best: Essendon – Smith, B.Armstrong, L.Armstrong, Cameron, Jones, Sewart.
Goals: Essendon – Kirby 2, Hazel 2, Smith 2, B.Armstrong 2, L.Armstrong 2, Baring 2.
Crowd: N/A at the MCG

ROUND FIFTEEN July 29
ESSENDON 9.7 (61)
GEELONG 4.11 (35)
Best: Essendon – L.Armstrong, Busbridge, Shea, Ogden, Cameron, O'Shea.
Goals: Essendon – L.Armstrong 4, Shea 2, Bowe, B.Armstrong, Kirby.
Crowd: N/A at East Melbourne Cricket Ground

ROUND SIXTEEN August 19
ESSENDON 24.19 (163)
ST KILDA 5.8 (38)
Best: Essendon – L.Armstrong, Smith, Walker, Hanley, Anderson, Belcher.
Goals: Essendon – L.Armstrong 8, Smith 6, Walker 3, Shea 2, Belcher, Hanley, Kirby, Ogden, Busbridge.
Crowd: N/A at the Junction Oval

ROUND SEVENTEEN August 26
ESSENDON 6.10 (46)
FITZROY 3.7 (25)
Best: Essendon – Cameron, Ogden, B.Armstrong, Belcher, Bowe, Shea, Chalmers.
Goals: Essendon – B.Armstrong 2, Smith, Shea, Chalmers, L.Armstrong.
Crowd: N/A at Brunswick St Oval

ROUND EIGHTEEN September 2
ESSENDON 9.9 (63)
SOUTH MELBOURNE 8.10 (58)
Best: Essendon – Cameron, Griffith, Ogden, Sewart, Walker, Baring, Belcher.
Goals: Essendon – Ogden 3, L.Armstrong, Walker, Baring, Shea, Cameron, Smith.
Crowd: N/A at East Melbourne Cricket Ground

PREMIER'S FINALS

SEMI-FINAL September 16

ESSENDON	9.15 (69)
CARLTON	6.12 (48)

Best: Essendon – Belcher, L. Armstrong, Chalmers, Baring, Bowe, Sewart, O'Shea.
Goals: Essendon – Kirby 2, Shea 2, Belcher 2, Walker 2, L. Armstrong.
Crowd: 40,669 at the MCG

GRAND FINAL September 23

ESSENDON	2.4	3.9	3.11	5.11 (41)
COLLINGWOOD	1.1	1.5	3.8	4.11 (35)

Best: Essendon – L.Armstrong, Baring, Bowe, Busbridge, Shea, Walker.
Goals: Essendon – Baring, Kirby, McLeod, Shea, Walker.
Crowd: 43,905 at the MCG

GRAND FINAL LINE-UPS

ESS	B:	E.Hazel	B.Griffith	D.Hanley
COLL	F:	P.Gilchrist	D.Lee (capt)	D.Vernon
ESS	HB:	D.Monteith	B.Busbridge	L.Bowe
COLL	HF:	G.Anderson	D.Minogue	P.Wilson
ESS	C:	W.Chalmers	B.Sewart	F.O'Shea
COLL	C:	J.Sadler	J.McHale	P.Gibb
ESS	HF:	P.Shea	L.Armstrong	P.Ogden
COLL	HB:	J.Green	J.Sharp	D.McIvor
ESS	F:	J.Kirby	D.Smith (capt)	B.Walker
COLL	B:	E.Thomas	T.Rowell	P.Rowe
ESS	R:	F.Barin	G.McLeod	E.Cameron
COLL	R:	L.Hughes	D.Ryan	T.Baxter
ESS	Coach:	Jack Worrall		
COLL	Coach:	George Angus		

SNAPSHOT

Win-loss record: 17-2-1

Highest score: 24.19 (163), round 16, v St Kilda.

Greatest winning margin: 125 points, round 16, v St Kilda.

Lowest score: 3.11 (29), round 13, v Collingwood.

Greatest losing margin: 12 points, round 10, v Carlton.

Most goals by a player in a game: 8, Lou Armstrong, round 16, v St Kilda.

Most consecutive wins: 10

Most consecutive losses: 2

Club awards: Best & Fairest: Ernie Cameron; Leading goalkicker: Lou Armstrong (35 goals).

Putting it into perspective:
The Same Old's third premiership was its first under a full-time non-playing coach, Jack Worrall, who became the first man to coach two clubs to premierships. Dave Smith became the club's third premiership captain.

1911

		P	W	L	D	%	Pts
1	Essendon (1)	18	15	2	1	178.3	62
2	South Melb (3)	18	13	4	1	140.4	54
3	Carlton (4)	18	12	4	2	142.0	52
4	Collingwood (2)	18	12	6		124.4	48
5	Fitzroy	18	10	8		113.6	40
6	Geelong	18	8	9	1	99.9	34
7	Melbourne	18	7	10	1	98.6	30
8	Richmond	18	7	11		91.2	28
9	St Kilda	18	2	16		48.1	8
10	University	18	1	17		52.1	4

(18 home and away rounds)

PLAYERS USED

ESSENDON	GUERNSEY	GAMES	GOALS
Anderson, Ramsay		11	0
Armstrong, Bert		15	25
Armstrong, Lou	1	20	35
Baring, Fred	5	18	15
Belcher, Alan	4	17	6
Benstead, Rupe		4	0
Bowe, Len	3	20	1
Busbridge, Bill	2	6	1
Cameron, Ernie	6	19	11
Chalmers, Wally	7	19	2
Freeman, Artie		2	0
Griffith, Billy	8	15	0
Hanley, Dan	9	11	1
Harrison, Billy		1	0
Hart, Johnny		4	0
Hay, Charlie		2	0
Hazel, Ern	21	11	4
Jones, Jimmy		1	0
Kirby, Jack	10	10	10
Martin, Jim		7	6
Masters, Edgar		1	0
McLeod, George	18	18	1
Monteith, Dick	19	11	0
O'Connor, Leo		5	3
O'Shea, Fred	12	16	0
Ogden, Percy	11	20	14
Sewart, Bill	15	14	0
Shea, Paddy	14	17	25
Smith, Dave	13	20	12
Walker, Bill A.	16	16	8
White, Les	17	10	0

ESSENDON 5.17 (47) d
SOUTH MELBOURNE 4.9 (33)

DONS' TRIUMPH OF COURAGE

Of the 16 premierships won by Essendon, its 1912 triumph will be recalled as one of the bravest. By EMMA QUAYLE

BEFORE the 1911 season Essendon had hoped its team of talented yet inconsistent players would toughen up, play with more discipline and win the club's first premiership in a decade. In 1912 they expected them to do the same. With player salaries now out in the open, the Same Olds made sure their Grand Final heroes were well paid, then set about strengthening the team.

One of the additions—Frank 'Silver' Caine—was pitched straight into the side and asked to pick up where he had left off at Carlton two years earlier. A member of the Blues' 1906-07 premiership sides, the grey-haired Silver had fallen out with club officials during 1910 and spent the following year in retirement before being tempted by the Same Olds' offer. Essendon did lose one player—Dave Smith—and his departure was significant. The captain had been an extremely reliable player, playing 71 successive games up until the end of 1911, but there was not much the club could do about his decision to depart—he was touring England with the Australian cricket side.

The Same Olds began the season favoured to win back-to-back titles. The players had fallen in love with Jack Worrall—their strict, demanding coach—after his success with them the previous year, and when the coach stood at the front of the annual meeting, promising supporters they would definitely win another flag, they believed him. With Smith overseas, Alan Belcher was appointed the club's new captain. Back from the badly timed knee injury that cost him his spot in the 1911 Grand Final, the big, bustling ruckman led his side to a 77-point drubbing of University in round one, then five wins from the first seven games, the only blips a six-point loss to South Melbourne, still smarting after its heavy, unexpected loss to the lower-ranked Collingwood in the 1911 semi-finals, and a three-point defeat by Geelong. There was a scandal of sorts in the South game, however, when Fred Baring—Belcher's athletic, agile partner in the ruck—was sent from the ground by one of the VFL's newly appointed game stewards for "playing foully". The stewards were paid by the League to keep an eye out for any rough and unnecessary play that the umpires were not able to notice, given a recent rise in angry clashes and rough play. George Martin, a former Essendon follower, was one of those appointed but the role lasted for only a short time, with the stewards often wandering far too close to the play.

On this day, though, Baring was in trouble, and the steward's decision aggrieved not only the Same Olds, but everyone who had seen the energetic 21-year-old play. "Can impudence and ignorance further go?" wondered one disbelieving reporter in a newspaper the next day. "Everybody knows that Baring is one of the fairest players that ever wore a uniform." In fact, the young man lived by a simple motto—to never "lose prestige"—and had become known for his fair play. Many years later, in 1923, a former Geelong player writing under the pseudonym of 'Cover Point' wrote about one of his battles with the 155-game player. Baring's teammate, Percy Ogden, had swung his boot at a loose ball, missed it, and kicked 'Cover Point' right in the nose instead. The Geelong player was sore, bleeding and his nose was badly out of place, so Baring stopped, turned his back on play and, "exerting considerable force, put it back into its original position," wrote his opponent, still grateful many years on. Not only that, Baring was, in 1912, becoming a very, very good player. He and Belcher were, Ogden often declared, the best ruck combination in the League. Essendon was lucky to have him; as another talented cricketer, it was widely thought that he would make the national Test side before too long.

Despite this setback, the Same Olds were soon back in form. They won five of their next seven matches after that round-four game, losing only to St Kilda and Geelong by narrow margins. The star of their season was Cameron, who had picked up where he left off in the 1911 finals with some brave, brilliant form that relegated his previous three injury-interrupted seasons well into the past. The 24-year-old was quick, which suited Worrall's game plan, and he had thrived since the new coach's arrival. "Nothing could be finer than watching Ernie Cameron's finished display of roving on Saturday," wrote one reporter after a mid-season match, noting how his "lightning streaks from the ruck" had caused the crowd to break into spontaneous applause. "Few footballers use their heads to better purpose than the Essendon rover." Another to take his game to new levels was Ogden, a 26-year-old crumpet manufacturer who had blossomed at Essendon after being cast aside by Collingwood as a youngster. He was small, but possibly the fittest player on the side and smart, too. He ran all day long, knew how to get into space and could snap a sharp goal. And a third big improver was Jack Kirby who, introduced as a small forward midway through the previous season, had played 15 games and in a Grand Final before experiencing his first loss. After a 10-goal season in the premiership year, the flanker had become even more dangerous around the goals.

Several new players, including Caine, had forced their way into the side. Les White, a slight but super-quick midfielder, had missed the 1911 Grand Final with a leg injury but found a new place on the half-back line and continued to play with dash. He was one of Essendon's best players, all season long. Fred Kirkwood, who had crossed from St Kilda, where he'd played 18 games in two years, grabbed a spot on the wing. Jack O'Brien, a 24-year-old debutant, had turned to Essendon after being knocked back by South Melbourne. He was in the side by the middle of the year and although not the most gifted player, he guarded his backline spot with passion. Then there was Jim 'Bull' Martin, who in round seven of the previous season had been found guilty of striking and rubbed out for the rest of the year, even facing court over the incident. Bull was an aggressive player feared by his opponents—interesting, given he was suspended only twice in a seven-year career—but he added much more than that to the Same Olds' side: after overcoming some early awkwardness he was a smart, shrewd forward who made good decisions and could switch into the ruck when his gung-ho style was needed there.

Essendon maintained its strong form as the season reached its end, but this year was not blessed like the previous one and during a mid-year game Bill Busbridge had fallen to ground, clutching his knee. Busbridge had been troubled by knee injuries ever since his debut as a 16-year-old, and had come out of retirement during 1911 to take his place in the premiership side. The centre half-back was only 25, but with three minutes left in the game against Carlton he hurt himself too badly to continue, and retired there and then. Supporters presented him with a gold watch and a wallet filled with 250 pounds, to thank him for his 103 honest, big-hearted games and the sacrifices he had made. He went on to work in Geelong as a train driver, to coach the Geelong Grammar school side and become a committeeman for the Geelong VFL team. His great nephew, Leigh Matthews, would later make something of a name for himself in Hawthorn's teams of the 1970s and '80s. In 2002, 'Buzzy' was announced as Essendon's 14th greatest ever player.

He wasn't the only sore, sorry player at the club, though. When the Same Olds lost a player, they seemed to lose an important one, and Belcher's season was unsettled when he broke a toe mid-season. Off the field, club officials had become exasperated again with Bill Griffith, a temperamental star now in the dying days of his career. Three years earlier Griffith had clashed with teammate Len Bowe and accused his defensive teammates of leaving him exposed in the goalsquare. After offering to resign the captaincy when hauled in front of the group by club officials, he was eventually talked into taking it back. This time around, the veteran asked for a pay rise and stood out of the team when refused the extra money. He was a 160-game player by then, and one of greatest-ever Same Olds, his stubborn nature well suited to the full-back position even though he was only 168cm tall. While his strong-mindedness occasionally worked against him, he was known as a relentless leader and a smart, tactical player. "Griffith guards the bulls-eye with never-failing zeal," wrote *Punch* magazine. "He dashes through the enemies' forwards like a pound of quicksilver and boosts the airbag far into the country." The trouble was, he was soon to turn 32. After sitting out a handful of games and realising the club would not back down, Griffith apologised, and quietly returned to the backline.

There was trouble on the field, too. The Essendon players were not happy with many umpiring decisions made during their mid-year clash with St Kilda, a game they lost by 11 points, and the performance of the field umpire was later assessed by the equally unimpressed *Victorian Football Follower*. Its reporter wrote: "Umpire Norden, whose erratic decisions and dramatic attitudes are difficult to understand, umpired shockingly and Essendonians will be particularly pleased when relieved of his undesirable attentions. Towards the close of the game Frank Caine, dodging an opponent, kicked the ball through, putting Essendon a point in the lead. Whether Norden thought the goal was undeserved or whether it was not even to his liking, one cannot say, but to the unfounded surprise and imagination of all sportsmen, he brought the ball back and gave a free kick to the man who did not touch Caine until the ball had left his boot."

Essendon lost its second last home and away match to St Kilda too, and it was a horrible loss. The Same Olds fell by 58 points to the third worst team in the League, conceding more than 100 points for the first time in five years and all of a sudden they looked a little lifeless. The finals spot that had seemed a given just six months earlier was now in doubt, but this side had not lost its determined streak and, needing to beat Fitzroy to stay above a surging Geelong and keep the Maroons out of the finals, Essendon won by six points at East Melbourne, enjoying the tightly fought game, playing with more enthusiasm and spirit than they had in many weeks and giving their supporters—40,000 came to see the game—fresh hope that they would again be the team to beat in the finals.

The first final was against South Melbourne, the top-placed team of the season and a group of players still determined to make up for their early exit from the previous year's finals series. Back from his toe injury, Belcher was presented with an unusual challenge, and a League first—to not only captain his first final against his younger brother Vic, but to take him on in the ruck. The game was very, very tough, from the start. It was only late in the third quarter that Essendon began to edge away, through a goal to Kirby, who would finish his second season with 43 of them. Forward Paddy Shea, a pioneer of the banana kick, was among the best players, as were veteran centreman Bill Sewart and Les White, perhaps spurred on by South's rejection of him in the early weeks of the season. Kirby kicked three goals, Frank Caine added two and the Same Olds held on for a 12-point win, 7.12 (54) to 6.6 (42), after neither side had scored in the final quarter.

Up next was a more familiar finals foe—Carlton. Ordinarily, this match would have been for the premiership, but under *The Argus* finals system South Melbourne, having topped the home and away ladder, had the right to challenge the last team standing in a grand final. The Same Olds started well, with the wind at their backs, but Carlton soon began to dominate general play, so much so that "there was serious apprehension," reported *The Argus*, "of what would happen when they got the wind. With the change of ends, however, came a surprise—Essendon opened out the game, their players spread into wider formation, played better to each other and were, in this more attractive football, faster to the ball than their opponents and more quick and clever in handling it." The Same Olds extended their lead from three points to nine at the half-time break and somehow managed to hang on, their forward line struggling all day and making "some serious mistakes" but finding three goals through Baring, one of them a jaw-dropping snap, and two more via Kirby.

Essendon won 7.10 (52) to Carlton's 6.12 (48) and was into another Grand Final despite not playing its best football, but this was a bittersweet result. Early in the first quarter Fred O'Shea, a third-year wingman, injured his knee and was carried from the ground. He came back on after half-time but could barely move and was basically forced to stand still in the goalsquare. Then, in the final few minutes, Ernie Cameron collided with another player, collapsed and, as the pack of players around him dispersed, found himself unable to get up. Cameron had been—as he had been every week—brilliant. He had been the most outstanding player on the ground by a long way. Carried off with a broken leg, he made the trainers stop by the boundary line so that he could watch his teammates hold on for the win. It was the injured O'Shea who somehow managed to kick the sealing goal—he had one mark, one kick and one goal for the day—but he got them at the most crucial time imaginable.

It was a brave performance under stressful circumstances and, writing about the match in a 1936 *Argus* article, coach Jack Worrall had not forgotten his players' effort. "I have never been a believer in playing injured men, and set my face against O'Shea's return after half-time," he recalled. "It was for me to decide and I reluctantly agreed upon his re-entry, on the distinct understanding that he was not to move away from the goalmouth. In the dying moments Ernie Cameron went down and it appeared Essendon was doomed. In the stress the Carlton full-back left his post, being sick to death of minding the wounded O'Shea. At the psychological moment the ball was marked by O'Shea on his own a few yards in front. He steadied himself, gave pressure on his wounded leg to see whether it would stand stand the strain, kicked the ball, staggered and fell. The bell won, and Essendon won the day." And another Grand Final day.

Cameron and O'Shea were huge, spirit-sapping losses, and the players were devastated. Busbridge, having been forced into retirement, offered to play should the club need him and remarkably so did Albert Thurgood, the club's first champion player, five years after his retirement and at 38 years of age. However, the club decided to stick with its remaining fit players, and in the feisty Martin and competitive Griffith, was able to bring some experience into the team. It was an emotional week and, to make sure his players minds' were fixed to the job, Worrall took them out for dinner together on the Thursday night before the game, reminding his side that that South Melbourne would be a much more challenging opponent this time around.

They weren't the only ones expecting a fierce game between two attacking, unrelenting sides. The MCG stands were full more than an hour before the 2pm game time, and 54,463 people eventually crammed in to watch. Given Essendon's injury woes, South Melbourne started favourite, but after the Belcher brothers met for the coin toss and the game got under way, the Same Olds started aggressively. They knew their only way to win would be to get the ball out into space and at first were their own worst enemies, rushing the ball forward only to, as *The Argus* observed, "score points where goals were earned, possibly playing themselves out." Fortunately, South Melbourne struggled to convert too, and Essendon's hard work eventually started to count. Ogden kicked a difficult long goal from a wing, Kirby snapped cleverly and at the half-time break the Same Olds were almost two goals clear of their more fancied opponent and looking the more proactive, creative side. "All expectations as to the game were being overturned by the amazing dash and cleverness of the Red and Blacks," noted *The Argus*, "and already nine-tenths of the people on the ground realised that it was only a question of lasting out in order to win."

After the break, South Melbourne lifted, knowing time was running out. But like the Essendon players in the opening quarter, their hard work resulted only in wasted chances and blundered shots at goal. Caine imposed himself in the forward line, kicking an important goal midway through the third quarter, and with Bowe, Lou Armstrong and Martin providing "an exhibition of quick and brilliant passing" the Same Olds moved further ahead of the game South side, if mostly through missed shots, winning 5.17 (47) to South Melbourne's 4.9 (33). Belcher was at the heart of the action all afternoon, with Baring in tow as always, and Dan Hanley, a 28-year-old recruit in 1911, played the best game of his life. With Cameron still in hospital, unable to be depended on for the first time in two years, every player pitched in.

"There was hardly a weak man in their ranks. They were always faster than the South; their passing was better; they beat their rivals both in the crush and in the open," reported *The Argus*. "Not a man in their colours did not have a material share in winning this splendid victory."

Essendon's win was a popular one, but was the last slice of success that the players were able to share. The preliminary final was, as it turned out, the final game Cameron ever played. His injury forced him to retire, as a 113-game champion, and he went on to play district cricket for North Melbourne and manage the Australian air force cricket side's war-time tour. O'Shea never played League football again either, although he managed many more games with the Brunswick VFA side. Baring played until 1924, and in 155 games, although many claimed him as a greater cricketer than footballer when both careers finally ended. Named in Australia's 1914 Test side, he missed out on representing his country in South Africa when the tour was cancelled because of World War I, and was never called up again. Griffith played on but retired only four games into 1913, although he kept his connection with the Red and Black after that, coaching the Essendon VFA side. Martin was cleared to Fitzroy the following year where he became just the second player in history to play in successive premierships for different clubs.

Having lost Cameron, Busbridge and O'Shea all at once, Essendon never captured its form of the past two seasons and slumped to eighth spot on the ladder in 1913. In 1914, with the war looming, injuries hit hard and the club was unable to field the same side from one week to the next all season. Season 1915 was even more miserable—the club lost 12 matches in a row through the middle of the season—and in 1916 the Same Olds, like Melbourne, St Kilda, Geelong and South Melbourne, dropped out of the competition for two years because of the war. Worrall coached until the end of 1918, becoming the first man to lead both a premiership and wooden spoon team, and later become a well-regarded sports writer. Many have credited him with coining the phrase "Bodyline," in reference to England's short-pitch bowling tactics bowling during their tour of Australia in 1932-33. The club was saddened, in 1915, by the loss of former secretary Alex McCracken, the man who had built the club.

His death, after a short illness, was the first of several tragedies the group went on to deal with. Percy Ogden played until 1921, replacing Cameron as the team's rover, thriving with the new responsibility and then becoming captain-coach for the final two years of his career after Worrall's departure. His sons Terry and Gordon followed him into League football; Terry played for Melbourne and Carlton and Gordon played for Melbourne. But the family was plunged into despair when Terry was injured while playing his 15th game for Carlton, and then fell badly ill with pleurisy in both lungs. A blood transfusion from Carlton president Newton Chandler kept him alive, but he sadly died in hospital 10 days after he was hurt. Belcher, Essendon's captain, led the club through to the 1916 break and fittingly passed the job on to Baring three years later. He broke a toe early in 1919, and the injury not only ended his career after 176 games, but saw his life begin to unravel. When the robust, energetic ruckman died, in a Kew psychiatric hospital, he weighed only 57kg and had been declared insane. Belcher had only stopped playing football two years earlier. The champion was only 40.

1912 ESSENDON

PREMIER'S SEASON

ESSENDON: 1912

ROUND ONE April 27
ESSENDON	17.14 (116)
UNIVERSITY	6.6 (42)

Best: Essendon – Cameron, Kirby, L.Armstrong, Martin, McDonald, Bowe.
Goals: Essendon – Kirby 5, Martin 4, L.Armstrong 4, Shea 3, Sewart.
Crowd: N/A at East Melbourne Cricket Ground

ROUND TWO May 4
ESSENDON	10.10 (70)
COLLINGWOOD	6.17 (43)

Best: Essendon – Kirkwood, Belcher, O'Shea, Shea, Busbridge, Cameron.
Goals: Essendon – Cameron 2, Shea 2, Hanley, McLeod, Martin, Ogden, L.Armstrong, Kirby.
Crowd: N/A at Victoria Park

ROUND THREE May 11
ESSENDON	8.11 (59)
CARLTON	6.14 (50)

Best: Essendon – Cameron, Walker, L.Armstrong, Caine, Martin, Kirby.
Goals: Essendon – Cameron 2, Kirby 2, Martin, Caine, Walker, L.Armstrong.
Crowd: N/A at East Melbourne Cricket Ground

ROUND FOUR May 18
ESSENDON	9.8 (62)
SOUTH MELBOURNE	8.8 (56)

Best: Essendon – Kirby, Busbridge, Cameron, B.Armstrong, Baring, Ogden.
Goals: Essendon – Kirby 4, Shea 2, Hanley, L.Armstrong, Cameron.
Crowd: N/A at the Lake Oval

ROUND FIVE May 25
ESSENDON	7.7 (49)
GEELONG	7.10 (52)

Best: Essendon – Baring, Caine, Martin, Monteith, Belcher, Bowe.
Goals: Essendon – Cameron 2, Kirby 2, Baring 2, Harvey.
Crowd: N/A at East Melbourne Cricket Ground

ROUND SIX June 1
ESSENDON	13.14 (92)
RICHMOND	10.10 (70)

Best: Essendon – Walker, Caine, Busbridge, Kirby, Sewart, O'Shea, Baring.
Goals: Essendon – Caine 4, Walker 3, Kirby 2, Ogden, Baring, Martin, Busbridge.
Crowd: N/A at Punt Road Oval

ROUND SEVEN June 3
ESSENDON	16.12 (108)
MELBOURNE	8.6 (54)

Best: Essendon – Kirby, Martin, Cameron, Belcher, Bowe, O'Shea, Busbridge.
Goals: Essendon – Kirby 5, Cameron 3, Martin 3, Hanley, Caine, Ogden, L.Armstrong, Walker.
Crowd: 12,085 at the MCG

ROUND EIGHT June 8
ESSENDON	6.19 (55)
ST KILDA	10.6 (66)

Best: Essendon – Cameron, Hazel, McLeod, Belcher, Martin, Caine, Kirkwood.
Goals: Essendon – Ogden, Kirkwood, Baring, Walker, Chalmers, Caine.
Crowd: N/A at East Melbourne Cricket Ground

ROUND NINE June 15
ESSENDON	8.8 (56)
FITZROY	3.7 (25)

Best: Essendon – Martin, Bowe, Belcher, Hanley, O'Shea, Ogden, Caine.
Goals: Essendon – Caine 3, Walker 2, Kirby, Barin, O'Shea.
Crowd: N/A at Brunswick St Oval

ROUND TEN June 22
ESSENDON	16.24 (120)
UNIVERSITY	7.10 (52)

Best: Essendon – Shea, Ogden, Caine, Cameron, Harvey, Baring, Kirkwood.
Goals: Essendon – Cameron 3, Ogden 3, Caine 3, Kirby 2, Shea 2, Martin, Belcher, L.Armstrong.
Crowd: 8542 at the MCG

ROUND ELEVEN June 29
ESSENDON	6.18 (54)
COLLINGWOOD	6.10 (46)

Best: Essendon – Belcher, Cameron, Bowe, O'Brien, L.Armstrong, Hanley, Shea.
Goals: Essendon – Kirby 2, Ogden 2, O'Brien, Walker.
Crowd: N/A at East Melbourne Cricket Ground

ROUND TWELVE July 13
ESSENDON	4.9 (33)
CARLTON	10.16 (76)

Best: Essendon – Belcher, Kirby, Baring, Shea, Cameron, Bowe, McLeod.
Goals: Essendon – Belcher 2, Kirby 2.
Crowd: N/A at Princes Park

ROUND THIRTEEN July 20
ESSENDON	7.10 (52)
SOUTH MELBOURNE	9.11 (65)

Best: Essendon – Kirby, L.Armstrong, Griffith, Walker, Kirkwood, Cameron.
Goals: Essendon – Kirby 5, Kirkwood.
Crowd: N/A at East Melbourne Cricket Ground

ROUND FOURTEEN July 27
ESSENDON	5.10 (40)
GEELONG	13.14 (92)

Best: Essendon – Martin, Cameron, Ogden, Worle, Sewart, Chalmers.
Goals: Essendon – Kirkwood, Kirby, Martin, Walker, Hanley.
Crowd: N/A at Corio Oval

ROUND FIFTEEN August 3
ESSENDON	10.12 (72)
RICHMOND	5.13 (43)

Best: Essendon – Cameron, Griffith, Belcher, Kyme, Martin, Kirby.
Goals: Essendon – L.Armstrong 2, Kirby 2, Cameron 2, Walker, Martin, Kyme, Baring.
Crowd: N/A at East Melbourne Cricket Ground

ROUND SIXTEEN August 17
ESSENDON	9.8 (62)
MELBOURNE	7.8 (50)

Best: Essendon – Griffith, McLeod, Bowe, White, L.Armstrong, Baring, Sewart.
Goals: Essendon – Walker 2, Shea 2, L.Armstrong 2, Kirby, Kyme, McLeod.
Crowd: N/A at East Melbourne Cricket Ground

ROUND SEVENTEEN August 24
ESSENDON	7.8 (50)
ST KILDA	15.18 (108)

Best: Essendon – Walker, Cameron, McDonald, Bowe, Belcher, L.Armstrong.
Goals: Essendon – Walker 2, Cameron 2, Caine, Shea, Harvey.
Crowd: N/A at the Junction Oval

ROUND EIGHTEEN August 31
ESSENDON	7.13 (55)
FITZROY	6.13 (49)

Best: Essendon – Cameron, L.Armstrong, Martin, O'Brien, Walker, Shea.
Goals: Essendon – Walker 3, Shea, Sewart, Cameron, L.Armstrong.
Crowd: N/A at East Melbourne Cricket Ground

PREMIER'S FINALS

SEMI-FINAL September 14

ESSENDON	7.12 (54)
SOUTH MELBOURNE	6.6 (42)

Best: Essendon – Cameron, Shea, White, O'Brien, Sewart, Bowe, Hanley, Chalmers.
Goals: Essendon – Kirby 3, Caine 2, Cameron, Baring.
Crowd: 34,290 at the MCG

PRELIMINARY FINAL September 21

ESSENDON	7.10 (52)
CARLTON	6.12 (48)

Best: Essendon – Cameron, Baring, Ogden, Bowe, Sewart, White, McLeod.
Goals: Essendon – Baring 3, Kirby 2, Shea, O'Shea.
Crowd: 47,414 at the MCG

GRAND FINAL September 28

ESSENDON	1.4	3.9	4.14	5.17 (47)
SOUTH MELBOURNE	1.3	2.4	2.6	4.9 (33)

Best: Essendon – L.Armstrong, Baring, Bowe, Caine, Ogden, Sewart.
Goals: Essendon – Baring, Caine, Kirby, Ogden, Walker.
Crowd: 54,534 at the MCG

GRAND FINAL LINE-UPS

ESS	B:	J.O'Brien	B.Griffith	G.McLeod
STH M	F:	D.Casey	L.Mortimer	L.Rusich
ESS	HB:	L.White	D.Hanley	L.Bowe
STH M	HF:	V.Belcher	B.Franks	F.Carpenter
ESS	C:	W.Chalmers	B.Sewart	F.Kirkwood
STH M	C:	J.Prince	D.Mullaly	J.Caldwell
ESS	HF:	J.Kirby	F.Caine	P.Shea
STH M	HB:	J.Scobie	B.Thomas	J.Walsh
ESS	F:	J.Martin	L.Armstrong	B.Walker
STH M	B:	H.Saltau	B.Deas	B.Sloss
ESS	R:	A.Belcher (capt)	F.Baring	P.Ogden
STH M	R:	H.Milne	L.Charge	C.Ricketts (capt)
ESS	Coach:	Jack Worrall		
STH M	Coach:	Charlie Ricketts		

SNAPSHOT

Win-loss record: 15-6

Highest score: 16.24 (120), round 10, v University.

Greatest winning margin: 74 points, round 1, v University.

Lowest score: 4.9 (33), round 12, v Carlton.

Greatest losing margin: 58 points, round 17, v St Kilda.

Most goals by a player in a game: 5, Jack Kirby, round 1, v University; round 7, v Melbourne; round 13, v South Melbourne.

Most consecutive wins: 4 (twice).

Most consecutive losses: 3

Club awards: Best & Fairest: Ernie Cameron; Leading goalkicker: Jack Kirby (43 goals)

Putting it into perspective:
Essendon achieved back-to-back premierships for the first time in club history and joined rivals Fitzroy, Collingwood and Carlton as the only teams to win consecutive Grand Finals.

1912

		P	W	L	D	%	Pts
1	South Melb (2)	18	14	4		157.0	56
2	Carlton (3)	18	14	4		131.2	56
3	**Essendon (1)**	18	12	6		114.9	48
4	Geelong (4)	18	11	7		126.7	44
5	Fitzroy	18	10	8		108.5	40
6	Melbourne	18	9	9		98.9	36
7	Collingwood	18	9	9		91.7	36
8	St Kilda	18	7	11		100.4	28
9	Richmond	18	3	15		64.7	12
10	University	18	1	17		57.0	4

(18 home and away rounds)

PLAYERS USED

ESSENDON	GUERNSEY	GAMES	GOALS
Armstrong, Bert	3	7	0
Armstrong, Lou	2	18	14
Baring, Fred	5	19	11
Belcher, Alan	1	19	3
Bickford, Edric	22	1	0
Blencowe, Jack		1	0
Bowe, Len	4	21	0
Busbridge, Bill	21	11	1
Caine, Frank	27	12	17
Cameron, Ernie	6	20	19
Chalmers, Wally	7	16	1
Godfrey, Bruce		1	0
Griffith, Billy	29	6	0
Hanley, Dan	10	21	4
Harvey, Billy	26	9	2
Hazel, Ern	28	1	0
Kirby, Jack	11	21	43
Kirkwood, Fred	9	17	3
Kyme, Bill	30	3	2
Martin, Jim	12	16	13
McDonald, Ted	13	2	0
McLeod, George	14	18	2
Monteith, Dick	24	2	0
O'Brien, Jack	25	11	1
O'Shea, Fred	15	16	2
Ogden, Percy	16	17	11
Sewart, Bill	17	20	2
Shea, Paddy	18	15	14
Walker, Bill A.	20	18	19
White, Les	19	15	0
Worle, Len	8	4	0

**FITZROY 7.14 (56) d
ST KILDA 5.13 (43)**

UNLIKELY DUO IN FINAL TWIST

Fitzroy and St Kilda both recovered from internal ructions to make concerted charges for the premiership cup. By CHRIS DONALD

FITZROY and St Kilda were among the least favoured teams going into the 1913 season. An eventual Grand Final between the pair seemed as likely as the prospect of Collingwood winning the wooden spoon.

The Roys had not played in the finals since 1906. In 1910, after the VFL had approved player payments, the Maroons were beset by a split. The fallout was over the new era of professionalism. The incumbent committee's secretary, Con Hickey, and treasurer, Tom Banks, warned that players could now demand whatever payments they wanted.

During the 1910 season, committee members responded to the gathering feeling against them and stepped aside. President Robert Best resigned after 23 years at the helm. Hickey and Banks also resigned. Captain Jim Sharpe had aligned himself with the incumbent committee, so he resigned as well. Billy Dick (Carlton) and Herbert 'Boxer' Milne (South Melbourne) were also cleared because they had aligned themselves with the incumbent committee.

The division within the club had an unsettling effect on the players. The club won five out of 18 games for the 1910 season and finished eighth of the 10 teams.

A reform group was sworn in during the 1911 annual meeting, and changes were made at all levels. The Maroons appointed their first official coach, former player Geoff Moriarty, a centreman who had played 106 games with the club, including being a member of the 1899 and 1905 premiership teams. Harold 'Lal' McLennan, another centreman, was appointed captain. An enormous tally of 23 new players was introduced into the team during the 1911 season.

The Maroons lost the opening two games of 1911, against Melbourne and Collingwood, before defeating Carlton by two points at Princes Park in round three. The victory fired the club to a surprising finish of 10 wins from 18 games for fifth place. Off the field, the club moved at League level that players should be paid 30 shillings (or £3) a match. The move was defeated but the club continued to show its players that it wanted to establish an equitable payments system.

In 1912, with Jack Cooper replacing McLennan as captain, the Roys again finished with 10 victories and again finished fifth of the 10 teams; a rise into the finals seemed possible the next season. Its inclusions in 1912 included Jimmy Freake, a full-forward from Fitzroy Juniors who made his debut in the opening round against South Melbourne. Freake kicked 53 goals for the season, a tally that broke Percy Trotter's 1904 club record of 36. It also earned him second place on the goalkicking table, behind Melbourne's Harry Brereton, who kicked 56 goals.

In 1913, Moriarty stood down as coach and was replaced by champion forward Percy Parratt, who continued as a player, while rugged ruckman Bill Walker replaced Cooper as captain. The Maroons won the opening game, against University, but disappointed followers by losing the second game to St Kilda. A lacklustre season seemed in prospect, but the Maroons lost only one more game before the finals, to Geelong at the Corio Oval in round 12. At the end of the home and away games they were on top of the ladder.

At the same time as the Roys were sorting out their affairs, St Kilda was rent by a huge row between the committee and the players. The issues were the club's withdrawal of dressingroom tickets for friends and family, as well as queries over management as a whole. The situation came to a head before the match against Melbourne in round 14 in 1911 when players took a vote about whether to take the field. The delay left onlookers wondering whether the match would take place. Eventually the players did straggle into the ground. Melbourne won by the handsome margin of 38 points.

During the subsequent week the St Kilda players confronted the committee, which ordered the players to hand in their uniforms. The club made up the team using players from local clubs in the surrounding district. Carlton thrashed the undermanned Saints by 114 points, 18.21 (129) to 2.3 (15), an extraordinary margin for the time. (The lowly St Kilda had lost to Collingwood by 128 points and 117 points, in 1901 and 1902 respectively.) Carlton's Vin Gardiner scored 10 goals from 22 shots against the Saints.

In the Saints' quest to field a team for the remainder of the season, they dragged in players from wherever they could find them. One who made his debut in this season was Ernie Sellars, a 21-year-old rover from local club Grosvenor. Sellars booted seven goals in his first match, against University. The Saints' tally of 62 players used in the 1911 season remains a record.

The Saints, like Fitzroy, gained energy from upheaval. They finished ninth of the 10 teams in 1911 and eighth in 1912, but a batch of young players was coming through, headed by Wells Eicke. Eicke had made his debut late in the 1909 season as a rover at the age of 15. The club was in a good position if it could remain stable.

In 1913 Fitzroy also introduced several talented players including 22-year-old future captain Chris Lethbridge, a rugged centre half-back from Sydney YMCA; Jim Toohey, 26, a forward from North Fremantle, WA; Charlie Wells, 21, from Richmond; Percy Heron, 20, from Fitzroy Juniors; and Artie Harrison, 20, from VFA club Preston.

Fitzroy included five debutants for its opening match, against University at Brunswick Street on April 26: Lethbridge; Toohey; Roy Millen, 19; Johnny Downs, 23; and George King, 20. The Maroons won 42 by points.

St Kilda opened its season with a hefty loss to South Melbourne, by 33 points, but hit back the next week when it hosted Fitzroy at the Junction Oval.

The Saints scored the first goal against the Roys after former Richmond centreman Bill Schmidt had worked the ball down to Arthur Best, who marked. Big Vic Cumberland kicked the Saints' second goal and the home team held sway from there, winning by 33 points, 10.7 (67) to 3.16 (34).

Fitzroy played strongly and was entitled to think it had some claim to victory had it kicked straight. *The Age* reported: "The kicking was most erratic, for every kick that should have got a goal merely secured a point or went out of bounds."

The Maroons then defeated Geelong and Melbourne before facing South Melbourne, the 1912 runner-up. Freake kicked four goals for the Roys, who had a stunning second half, kicking 9.10 to 2.3, to run out convincing 33-point victors, 11.17 (83) to 7.8 (50).

The Maroons then defeated top team Collingwood by 24 points, 10.15 (75) to 7.9 (51), and third-placed Carlton by 35 points with their highest score of the season, 14.15 (99) to 9.10 (64). Jimmy Freake kicked five goals.

In the return match between Fitzroy and St Kilda, in round 11, Fitzroy captain Jack Cooper won the toss and kicked with the wind at the Brunswick

Street Oval in a move that proved decisive. The Roys kicked six goals to one in the opening quarter to lead by 31 points, 6.3 to 1.2. From then on it was the Saints' game and Fitzroy was forced into what *The Age* described as "strenuous defence" to hold out the Saints and win by 14 points, 7.11 (53) to 5.9 (39). Freake kicked three goals for the Roys in another best-on-ground performance.

The Maroons, with their foot off the pedal following a hard-fought match, surprisingly went down to Geelong by 17 points at Corio Oval, 11.12 (78) to 8.13 (61). They then hit back to defeat Melbourne by 58 points, 12.14 (86) to 3.10 (28), to regain top spot.

The Maroons remained on top but faced hurdles against the other three teams in the top four, South Melbourne, Collingwood and Carlton, in the final three rounds.

Fitzroy scraped in by three points in the match against second-placed South Melbourne at Brunswick Street in round 16. Before hosting the Magpies at Brunswick Street in round 17, the Lions were ahead on the ladder by 18 percentage points, ahead of Collingwood, with South Melbourne, Geelong and St Kilda next.

Tom Heaney kicked three goals for the Maroons as a tight defence kept Collingwood to just four goals. The Maroons won by 27 points, 9.10 (64) to 4.13 (37). The next week they defeated Carlton by 17 points at Princes Park to take the minor premiership with 16 wins from 18 games.

In round 15, St Kilda hosted Carlton in a match between two teams fighting for fourth spot. St Kilda had last been in the top four in round three. Carlton had not missed a finals series since 1902. In this match at the Junction Oval, St Kilda led handsomely at half-time, 6.5 to 3.1, before Carlton fought back with four goals in the third quarter. The difference at the final break was six points. Carlton continued fighting in the last quarter and was five points ahead in time-on. St Kilda made a last fling and got the ball to Schmidt, who kicked a goal with the last kick of the match. Many considered it the Saints' best win in a home and away match. They moved into fourth spot, ahead of Carlton by half a game, and held on to fourth over the final three rounds.

The final four, after such a gripping race, was Fitzroy (16 wins, two losses), South Melbourne (14 wins, three losses, one draw), Collingwood (13 wins, five losses) and St Kilda (11 wins, seven losses).

In the first of the semi-finals, South Melbourne played St Kilda at the MCG. A crowd of 40,180 saw an upset as the Saints won by 33 points. Sellars kicked six goals for the Saints, equal to the VFL's highest tally of the season. Fitzroy and Collingwood played their semi-final before a crowd of 43,630.

The Maroons' defence had been miserly all year, conceding an average of 44 points during the home and away rounds. In the semi-final, defenders Bert Lenne, Wally Johnson, Cooper and Lethbridge played their part to restrict the Magpies, while the Maroons' forwards contributed 11 goals from 25 scoring shots. Freake (three) and George Shaw (two) were the multiple goal-kickers. Fitzroy won by 37 points.

Fitzroy and St Kilda were the combatants in the Final. The Fitzroy team was missing centreman McLennan because his father was seriously ill. A crowd of 54,846 was at the MCG for the match. The match was marred by aggressive incidents and St Kilda shocked the Maroons with a 25-point victory. Roy Cazaly and George Morrissey kicked three goals for the Saints, while Freake kicked three for the Roys.

Fitzroy's Tom Willoughby, who at 180cm and 82kg was one of the Maroons' bigger players, was later found guilty of elbowing and suspended for 16 matches while teammate Tom Heaney was found not guilty of charging. The 1913 season was the first in which an independent tribunal was instituted.

Fitzroy was forced to fall back on its right to challenge in a bid to win the premiership. While smarting from its upset loss and the loss of Willoughby to suspension, they were pleased that McLennan was able to return to the team after tending his sick father. An Australian record attendance of 59,556 filled the MCG with many hoping the Saints could win their first flag. The incentives for the Saints players included a gold medal for each player and £180 to share.

According to the 1983 history of Fitzroy, *The First One Hundred Seasons*, Fitzroy captain Bill Walker told his players that under no circumstances were they to use rough tactics. *The Age* said that Walker's final words to his players were: "Hands off."

The Maroons, heeding the words of their skipper to play the ball, gained a flying start by kicking two goals in four minutes. According to *The Australasian*, "[George] Holden and [George] Shaw, playing brilliantly, passed to [Percy] Parratt, from whose kick Heaney, after shooting in the air like a rocket, kicked the first goal. The opening success whetted the appetites of the Maroons, who, carrying all before them, faced up the ground, and a beautiful pass from Holden to Freake was responsible for the second goal, to great northern rejoicing."

The Argus reported that: "Fitzroy opened with a game that surprised the onlookers. Massing together and trusting to strength chiefly for their progress has been their policy, but they commenced with fine, breezy, open football and for a while seemed to take complete command of the game,.."

The Age reported that: "Fitzroy's policy of open play was adopted right from the commencement, and the fast and tricky men kept clean away from the crushes."

Charlie Norris then snapped a third goal by roving Heaney's spill. St Kilda was goalless, "slightly rattled" and "breaking the rules a good deal", according to *The Argus*, and trailed by 23 points at quarter-time, 3.6 to 0.1.

The Argus, noting the footballers' courage, lauded wounded Fitzroy rover Percy Heron, who was playing well "in spite of the fact that he had lost eight of his teeth in the game of the previous Saturday (it was a marvel how he played so well after that accident)." The newspaper said Heron was "showing up finely for the Maroons".

The only goal for either team for the second quarter came in play from George 'Yorky' Shaw; *The Age* said he "was bumped about a good deal" before kicking a fine goal.

Shaw also managed to attract the attention of the officials in this term, according to *The Argus*. "Little Shaw, the nugget of the Fitzroy team, was spoken to by the steward." (Stewards, appointed for the first time in 1912, had the power to report players.)

Although not as vigorous as the previous week's Final, there were still examples of hard contests. *The Australasian* commented on a rough incident in the second quarter: "As Woodcock was stretched full length with his arms high up, in the act of marking the ball, Walker turned and charged him, bringing him to grass heavily.

"It was certainly unwarranted, and not within the law, and appeared vicious; and, as the man lay stunned on the grass, unable to take his kick, the ball had to be bounced. There was an angry demonstration, and the Fitzroy skipper was hooted freely from all parts of the ground."

The Age regarded the clash as "nothing more than one of the incidents seen at every match".

Fitzroy led by 27 points lead at half-time, 4.8 to 0.5. A victory to the Maroons seemed assured.

Algy Millhouse, who had crossed from Melbourne to St Kilda halfway through the season, broke the Saints' goal drought with a running shot during the third quarter. However, as *The Age* described, Fitzroy's advantage was maintained soon afterwards when brilliant forward Parratt roved a ball that dropped from half a dozen hands and popped through a goal.

The Maroons led by 25 points at the last change, 5.11 to 1.10. There was no indication of a St Kilda fightback.

The opening 10 minutes of the last quarter belonged to Fitzroy. *The Argus* reported that: "Fitzroy commenced it with such power that it seemed they were going to hold their own easily. Then came St. Kilda's splendid effort at recovery."

Sellars took a mark and kicked a goal. Schmidt found Des Baird, who kicked another goal for the Saints. Suddenly they were in contention.

The Age said: "For minutes Fitzroy played like a beaten side and St Kilda, helped on by free kicks, attacked time after time."

Fitzroy's Wally Johnson infringed on George Morrissey, who was given a free kick and booted the Saints' third goal for the quarter and fourth for the game. According to *The Argus*: "There was simply a roar of cheers all round the ground."

Then Schmidt, ever alert to a varied passage to goal, kicked off the ground towards Morrissey, who posted St Kilda's fifth goal.

The Argus described the momentum shift: "St Kilda seemed certain to win. With only five minutes to go they were only one point to the bad. They were still streaming on—Fitzroy a little bit distracted."

Then came the turning point. After St Kilda's Baird had taken a mark within range, he handballed to Morrissey instead of kicking for goal himself. *The Age* said: "Baird had a good opportunity but muddled things up."

Baird told *The Sporting Globe* years later: "As I was expecting the bell to go any tick of the clock, I took more than ordinary time. This momentary delay was responsible for my being surrounded by practically the whole of the Fitzroy backs and incidentally the whole of our forwards surged up to the mark as a sort of protection—momentarily everyone clustered around me.

"As Morrissey saw an open road to goal he called for a handpass. He received the pass OK—it was not intercepted—and instead of running straight into the goal base, as there was no player between him and the goal, he just turned and kicked hurriedly and registered a behind."

All players were weary late in the game. As *The Argus* reported: "Cooper's cool head was invaluable at this stage. More than once he stopped it on the half-back line."

Fitzroy, on the ropes for most of the last quarter, sprang into action. The experienced Jim 'Bull' Martin, who had played in the 1911 and 1912 premierships with Essendon before crossing to Fitzroy halfway through the 1913 season, place kicked a goal to give the Maroons a seven-point lead.

The Argus said: "The last nail in [St Kilda's] coffin was driven home when, as the result of a fine effort by (Jack) Cooper, Shaw got the ball and scored the seventh and last goal just as the bell rang."

Walker said in *The Age*: "I am proud of the team. It is the best eighteen we have had for years, and the most consistent team in the League. I think we thoroughly deserve the premiership. I really thought we were 'gone' towards the end, but our fellows responded grandly."

'Observer' from *The Argus* felt he "could not in justice deny Fitzroy all the credit of a victory, which was a fitting crown to a very fine season of football. They had won through the first phase by sheer merit, and this victory, gained in a game that will be long remembered, was the supreme effort."

The Age noted that the Saints had played only 10 minutes of dominant football, while *The Australasian* praised a trio of Maroons for their performances: "I should say that their three best men [in the Grand Final] were [George] Holden, [Wally] Johnson and [George] Shaw. Holden played beautifully, having much the better of Bowden."

The Australasian described Johnson's influence on the match thus: "The fine marking of Johnson was completely thwarting and baffling the Saints, who were all astray."

'Markwell' in *The Australasian* lauded Walker's leadership: "The veteran Walker displayed fine leadership, his judgment, imperturbability, immense strength, and determination stiffening and encouraging the ranks when danger threatened."

The brains of the team was playing-coach Parratt, who formed a lethal small forward combination with Freake for more than a decade.

Freake said: "Percy made me as a forward, and he would never take the slightest praise. When congratulated on the part he played, he would always say, 'Jimmy has the hard job, he first has to take the pass, then has to kick the goal."

McLennan. on his return after his father's illness, played his part in the premiership victory. Jack Worrall, writing in *The Australasian*, named McLennan as one of "the best half-dozen footballers of the season".

McLennan was awarded the Fitzroy best and fairest award at the end of the season. *The Winner* in 1915 described him thus: "His determination and persistence are wonderful. He never admits defeat, and winning or losing makes no difference to him. He fights it out to the bitter end."

1913 FITZROY

PREMIER'S SEASON

FITZROY: 1913

ROUND ONE   April 26
FITZROY   10.19 (79)
UNIVERSITY   5.7 (37)
Best: Fitzroy – Bamford, Norris, Lenne, Willoughby, Freake, Shaw, Toohey.
Goals: Fitzroy – Willoughby 3, Freake 2, King, Porter, Toohey, Millen, Shaw.
Crowd: N/A at Brunswick St Oval

ROUND TWO   May 3
FITZROY   3.16 (34)
ST KILDA   10.7 (67)
Best: Fitzroy – Freake, Parratt, Lenne, Bamford.
Goals: Fitzroy – Freake 3.
Crowd: N/A at the Junction Oval

ROUND THREE   May 10
FITZROY   8.14 (62)
GEELONG   6.7 (43)
Best: Fitzroy – McLennan, Wells, Parratt, Holden, Walker, Freake.
Goals: Fitzroy – Wells 4, Freake, McLennan, Willougby, Shaw.
Crowd: N/A at Brunswick St Oval

ROUND FOUR   May 17
FITZROY   7.11 (53)
MELBOURNE   4.7 (31)
Best: Fitzroy – Freake, Walker, McLennan, Johnson, Holden, Cooper.
Goals: Fitzroy – Freake 4, Heron, Johnson, Willoughby.
Crowd: 8,770 at the MCG

ROUND FIVE   May 24
FITZROY   7.9 (51)
ESSENDON   5.6 (36)
Best: Fitzroy – Parratt, Bamford, Wilson, Wells, Freake, Heaney.
Goals: Fitzroy – Freake 2, Walker, Heaney, Harrison, Wells, Heron.
Crowd: N/A at Brunswick St Oval

ROUND SIX   May 31
FITZROY   6.7 (43)
RICHMOND   5.6 (36)
Best: Fitzroy – McLennan, Freake, Porter, Parratt, Lenne, Harrison.
Goals: Fitzroy – Freake 3, Parratt 2, Porter.
Crowd: N/A at Brunswick St Oval

ROUND SEVEN   June 7
FITZROY   11.17 (83)
SOUTH MELBOURNE   7.8 (50)
Best: Fitzroy – Freake, Lambert, Shaw, Toohey, Johnson, Lambert, Bamford.
Goals: Fitzroy – Freake 4, Willoughby 2, Lambert, Holden, McLennan, Heaney, Shaw.
Crowd: N/A at the Lake Oval

ROUND EIGHT   June 9
FITZROY   6.11 (47)
COLLINGWOOD   5.7 (37)
Best: Fitzroy – Walker, Heaney, McLennan, Freake, Parratt, Lethbridge, Bamford.
Goals: Fitzroy – Parratt 2, Freake 2, Toohey, Lethbridge.
Crowd: N/A at Victoria Park

ROUND NINE   June 14
FITZROY   14.15 (99)
CARLTON   9.10 (64)
Best: Fitzroy – Freake, Parratt, Wells, Cooper, Walker, Lethbridge, Shaw.
Goals: Fitzroy – Freake 5, Parratt 3, Toohey 2, Heaney, Holden, McLennan, Lethbridge.
Crowd: N/A at Brunswick St Oval

ROUND TEN   June 21
FITZROY   10.15 (75)
UNIVERSITY   5.5 (35)
Best: Fitzroy – Holden, Norris, Walker, Lenne, McLennan, Willoughby, Parratt.
Goals: Fitzroy – Toohey 3, Shaw 2, Heron 2, Lethbridge, Parratt, Willoughby.
Crowd: 9,288 at the MCG

ROUND ELEVEN   June 28
FITZROY   7.11 (53)
ST KILDA   5.9 (39)
Best: Fitzroy – Freake, Bamford, Walker, Shaw, Lambert, Lethbridge, Heron.
Goals: Fitzroy – Freake 3, Heron 2, Toohey, Heaney.
Crowd: N/A at Brunswick St Oval

ROUND TWELVE   July 5
FITZROY   8.13 (61)
GEELONG   11.12 (78)
Best: Fitzroy – McLennan, Holden, Parratt, Willoughby, McArthur, Cooper.
Goals: Fitzroy – Freake 2, Parratt 2, Willougby 2, Toohey, Heaney.
Crowd: N/A at Corio Oval

ROUND THIRTEEN   July 19
FITZROY   12.14 (86)
MELBOURNE   3.10 (28)
Best: Fitzroy – Freake, Heron, Heaney, Bamford, Harrison, Holden, Lenne.
Goals: Fitzroy – Freake 5, Heron 3, Heaney 3, Toohey.
Crowd: N/A at Brunswick St Oval

ROUND FOURTEEN   July 26
FITZROY   7.12 (54)
ESSENDON   4.12 (36)
Best: Fitzroy – Walker, Johnson, Norris, Toohey, Parratt, Freake.
Goals: Fitzroy – Toohey 3, Freake 2, Shaw, Lethbridge.
Crowd: N/A at East Melbourne Cricket Ground

ROUND FIFTEEN   August 2
FITZROY   11.13 (79)
RICHMOND   6.10 (46)
Best: Fitzroy – Toohey, Holden, Walker, Shaw, Lethbridge, Freake, Heaney.
Goals: Fitzroy – Toohey 5, Freake 3, Heaney 2, Martin.
Crowd: N/A at Punt Road Oval

ROUND SIXTEEN   August 9
FITZROY   8.11 (59)
SOUTH MELBOURNE   7.14 (56)
Best: Fitzroy – Freake, McLennan, Bamford, Martin, Parratt, Holden, Toohey.
Goals: Fitzroy – Freake 4, Martin 2, Heaney, Harrison.
Crowd: N/A at Brunswick St Oval

ROUND SEVENTEEN   August 23
FITZROY   9.10 (64)
COLLINGWOOD   4.13 (37)
Best: Fitzroy – McLennan, Martin, Toohey, Holden, Johnson, Heaney.
Goals: Fitzroy – Heaney 3, Toohey 2, Martin, Heron, Freake, Willoughby.
Crowd: N/A at Brunswick St Oval

ROUND EIGHTEEN   August 30
FITZROY   7.13 (55)
CARLTON   4.8 (32)
Best: Fitzroy – Freake, Cooper, Bamford, Buist, Holden, Norris, Toohey.
Goals: Fitzroy – Freake 3, Willoughby 2, Heaney, Martin.
Crowd: N/A at Princes Park

PREMIER'S FINALS

SECOND SEMI-FINAL September 13
FITZROY 11.14 (80)
COLLINGWOOD 6.7 (43)
Best: Fitzroy – Holden, Freake, Parratt, Heron, Heaney, Willoughby, Shaw, Cooper.
Goals: Fitzroy – Freake 3, Shaw 2, Parratt, Norris, Holden, Heaney, Martin, Toohey.
Crowd: 43,631 at the MCG

FINAL September 20
FITZROY 6.9 (45)
ST KILDA 10.10 (70)
Best: Fitzroy – Heron, Shaw, Parratt, Lethbridge, Willoughby, Norris, Johnson, Holden.
Goals: Fitzroy – Freake 3, Toohey, Shaw, Parratt.
Crowd: 54,846 at the MCG

GRAND FINAL September 27
FITZROY 3.6 4.8 5.11 7.14 (56)
ST KILDA 0.1 0.5 1.10 5.13 (43)
Best: Fitzroy – Holden, McLennan, Parratt, Johnson, Cooper, Shaw, Lethbridge.
Goals: Fitzroy – Shaw 2, Norris, Parratt, Heaney, Martin, Freake.
Crowd: 59,556 at the MCG

GRAND FINAL LINE-UPS

FITZ	B:	C.Lethbridge	B.Lenne	A.Harrison
ST K	F:	D.Baird	E.Sellars	G.Morrissey
FITZ	HB:	C.Wells	W.Johnson	J.Cooper
ST K	HF:	R.Cazaly	P.Lynch	P.Jory
FITZ	C:	T.Buist	H.McLennan	G.Holden
ST K	C:	T.Collins	B.Schmidt	B.Bowden
FITZ	HF:	P.Parratt	T.Heaney	J.Toohey
ST K	HB:	W.Eicke	G.Dangerfield	R.Ellis
FITZ	F:	J.Martin	J.Freake	G.Shaw
ST K	B:	H.Hattam	H.Lever (capt)	D.Harris
FITZ	R:	B.Walker (capt)	C.Norris	P.Heron
ST K	R:	V.Cumberland	B.Woodcock	A.Millhouse
FITZ	**Coach**: Percy Parratt			
ST K	**Coach**: George Sparrow			

SNAPSHOT

Win-loss record: 18-3

Highest score: 14.15 (99), round 9, v Carlton.

Greatest winning margin: 58 points, round 13, v Melbourne.

Lowest score: 3.16 (34), round 2, v St Kilda.

Greatest losing margin: 33 points, round 2, v St Kilda.

Most goals by a player in a game: 5, Jimmy Freake, round 9, v Carlton; round 13, v Melbourne; Jim Toohey, round 15, v Carlton.

Most consecutive wins: 9

Most consecutive losses: 1

Club awards: Best & Fairest: Harold McLennan; Leading goalkicker: Jimmy Freake (56 goals)

Putting it into perspective: Fitzroy stamped itself as the most dominant team in the VFL in winning its fifth premiership. After 17 seasons of the new competition, the Maroons sat one flag ahead of Essendon and two flags ahead of Carlton and Collingwood.

1913

	P	W	L	D	%	Pts
1 Fitzroy (1)	18	16	2		144.3	64
2 South Melb (3)	18	14	3	1	128.6	58
3 Collingwood (4)	18	13	5		117.7	52
4 St Kilda (2)	18	11	7		106.3	44
5 Geelong	18	10	8		124.4	40
6 Carlton	18	9	8	1	100.9	38
7 Richmond	18	6	12		94.9	24
8 Essendon	18	6	12		93.4	24
9 Melbourne	18	4	14		71.4	16
10 University	18	0	18		57.6	0

(18 home and away rounds)

PLAYERS USED

FITZROY	GUERNSEY	GAMES	GOALS
Anderson, Henry	12	6	0
Bamford, Fred	1	20	0
Buist, Teddy	1	5	0
Cooper, Jack	5	19	0
Downs, Johnny	0	2	0
Fowler, Orm	13	1	0
Freake, Jimmy	8	21	56
Harrison, Artie	18	10	2
Heaney, Tom	6	18	17
Heron, Percy	11	21	10
Holden, George	30	20	3
Johnson, Wally	14	21	1
King, George	10	2	1
Lambert, George	15	7	1
Lenne, Bert	17	19	0
Lethbridge, Chris	12	13	4
Loughnan, Jack	22	1	0
Lynch, Roland	1	1	0
Martin, Jim	8	15	10
McArthur, Jack	16	8	0
McDonald, Ted	29	3	0
McLennan, Harold	19	16	3
Millen, Roy		1	1
Munro, Don		1	0
Norris, Charlie	20	19	2
Porter, Jim	4	2	2
Shaw, George	23	21	11
Strownix, Tom	26	3	0
Toohey, Jim	7	17	22
Walker, Bill	24	19	1
Wells, Charlie	2	11	5
Willoughby, Tom	25	20	13
Wilson, Billy J.	23	1	0

CARLTON 6.9 (45) d
SOUTH MELBOURNE 4.15 (39)

BLUES BACK IN CHARGE

The coaching feats of Norman 'Hackenschmidt' Clark in 1914 earned him a place in the pantheon of Carlton Football Club greats. By HOWARD KOTTON and TONY DE BOLFO

ON September 26, 1914, a few weeks after the Australian Prime Minister Joseph Cook declared, "If the Old Country is at war, so are we", William John Dick led the Carlton senior XVIII on to the Melbourne Cricket Ground.

This was Grand Final day. The Blues were playing South Melbourne and 'Billy' Dick and his boys were up for infinitely smaller stakes than the tens of thousands of young men—Carlton footballers among them—who would soon enough be called on to serve King and country in World War I.

It had been four years since the Old Dark Navy Blues had contested a Grand Final—and six years since they had completed their premiership hat-trick—and the ensuing seasons had not been without controversy. In September 1912, the team was torn asunder when Rod McGregor, the respected Carlton centreman, was suspended by his club's committee for 12 months after failing to obey a directive from his captain Jack Wells to venture forward during a final.

The suspension sparked a furore but McGregor, to his credit, refused to inflame the situation—and although he did train with North Melbourne, his heart was always with Carlton, and he was back again, at age 30, in 1914.

As a post-script to the crisis, coach Norman 'Hackenschmidt' Clark was granted leave of absence in 1913 and coached VFA club Brighton for a season. Wells the former West Australian, assumed the role of coach.

Not surprisingly, the team's unbroken run of 10 consecutive finals appearances was broken that season, but with the return of Clark in 1914 and, in the fourth round, McGregor—together with the injection of new players—there was cause for optimism that year, the jubilee year of the club's existence. The new players included Kyabram's Charlie Fisher, Morwell's Herb Burleigh and Percy Daykin of South Bendigo.

The years leading up to the 1914 season had not been without controversy. The then president, David Bell, noted in the 1913 Annual Report that "mainly owing to accidents and the illness of many of your most prominent players, your Club was unable to gain a position in the final four, this being the first time during the past eleven seasons that it has not had that proud distinction."

He continued: "Your team, at the beginning of the season, was undoubtedly one of the strongest combinations that ever did battle for the Dark Blues, but misfortune dogged our footsteps, and we were decidedly unlucky to have such a number of your best players idle.

"At one time no less than 11 of your regular players, including the Captain and the Vice-Captain, were unable to take the field. This meant a very severe tax on the old players, and, although the reserves did their share manfully, it was hardly expected under such circumstances to become a premier team."

If ever a man was capable of reversing such fortunes, it was surely the 1914 coach-elect—the great 'Hackenschmidt'.

Norman Childers Clark was born in North Adelaide on December 11, 1878. An outstanding athlete, Clark stood 170cm and weighed in at 86kg.

On the afternoon of Easter Monday 1899, Clark, listed as a resident of Roseberry, South Australia, took out the country's most coveted footrace, the Stawell Gift, in a time of 11.45 seconds off 14½ yards.

Beneath the headline "Clark wins the Gift", *The Stawell News and Pleasant Creek Chronicle* (one newspaper) carried the following account of Clark's epic deed:

> Breathless excitement pervaded the vast assemblage as the above champion athletes made their way to their marks. The six competitors were sent away to a beautiful start, but before half the distance had been traversed it could be seen that there were only three in the race—Clarke (sic), McManus and Murray.
>
> Clarke was apparently running with the strength of a locomotive, but McManus' former heat appeared to have taken a good deal out of him,

> for though his long strides covered as much ground as ever, they did not succeed one another in such rapid succession, while Murray, though slowly overhauling the South Australian, was too slow to actually catch him, with Clarke winning in 11 4/5th of a second, with Murray and McManus close up, placed second and third...
>
> The win proved a very popular one, as Clark had for some time reigned as favourite... The winner of the Gift is a young unassuming man of sturdy build and hails from Roseberry, S.A. He is twenty years of age, and has only been identified with pedestrianism during the past 16 months. He has only won a few minor events in S.A., and was trained for the Stawell Gift by Mr J. Coates of Adelaide...

That victory in the 1899 Stawell Gift would serve as a stunning first achievement in what would be an illustrious sporting career. In 1901 Clark would represent the North Adelaide Football Club in its maiden Grand Final win, and in 1902 he was in North's second premiership team.

He would then form what would be a long and famous association with Carlton, as a stoic backman in 125 senior appearances, including the Grand Final triumphs of 1906, 1907 (as vice-captain) and 1908, and briefly as captain after the suspension of Fred 'Pompey' Elliott.

On the cusp of the 1909 season, Clark was the welcome recipient of an oak-framed hand-painted certificate, featuring a photograph of him resplendent in collar and tie. The certificate carries the signatures of the then Carlton president John Urquhart, treasurer Reginald Blay and secretary Jack Worrall, who was later acknowledged as football's first coach.

The inscription on the certificate reads:

> To Mr N.C. Clark
>
> Dear Sir,
>
> We, the undersigned, on behalf of the Carlton Football Club, wish to place on record our high appreciation of the manner in which you have upheld the honor of the Club by your excellent and manly play during the past four years. Wishing you long life and prosperity. We are, yours sincerely.

Clark is thought to have earned his ostentatious nickname 'Hackenschmidt' because of his resemblance to the famed Estonian-born bodybuilder and wrestler of the day, Georges Karl Julius Hackenschmidt.

He was highly rated by his teammates: "We often wondered how he could lift his bulk so high," McGregor told *The Sporting Globe* years later. "Norman Clark's particular type of play has not been duplicated, chiefly because no one of his pattern has since appeared."

When Clark returned from his 12-month hiatus to coach in 1914, he implemented a series of programs designed to advance the on-field discipline of his young group.

However, the players made a shaky start to the season, sharing the points with Collingwood at Victoria Park. "The many thousands who went there came away satisfied that they had had full value for their money, for the game was magnificently played from the start to the finish," the *Football Record* reported. "There was plenty of ginger in it, but no ill-spirit. Bumps and spills were numerous and hard, and one or two of the players were feeling the effects a day or two after."

The visiting Blues almost paid the price for their inaccuracy in front of goal (6.20) and had the ball in their possession as the final siren sounded. But there were bright spots, particularly the performance of Percy Daykin. Described as "one of the best finds for years", Daykin impressed on debut with his marking, kicking and reading of the play.

The Blues' stuttering start in 1914 continued in the next round with a 13-point defeat at the hands of St Kilda at Princes Park. It was tight for three quarters before the Saints pulled away in the last quarter. The pivotal duel of the match was between Dick and St Kilda star Dave McNamara. Although McNamara finished with two goals, Dick took the honours, battling gamely against the odds. The Blues' contingent in the big crowd did not take too kindly to the defeat, with a group of young men going on to the ground to heckle the field umpire L.C. Whyte.

Billy Dick was born and bred in Stawell, the gateway to the majestic Grampians. He became an admirable footballer who overcame rejection to captain Carlton's 1914 premiership team. Having chased the leather for the inner Melbourne team of East Brunswick, Dick sought a trial with Carlton, only to be turned down, as Worrall's men racked up the Grand Final victories.

Dick was then taken in by rival VFL outfit Fitzroy and soon demonstrated he was a player of renown. A follower and forward who was strong overhead, agile, and dangerous around goals, Dick strung together 53 matches and booted 40 goals for the Roys between 1908 and 1910, including 26 goals in 1909.

Carlton officials, stung by their decision to overlook Dick, launched a concerted effort to get him to Princes Park. He agreed, and ventured into Princes Park on the cusp of the 1911 season.

Dick quickly found his niche at centre half-forward, and personal acknowledgment followed with his appointment as Victorian captain in the third national championships in Sydney.

The following year, in 1912, Dick was appointed vice-captain to Jack Wells, and coach Clark asked him to assume the key defensive post at centre half-back. Billy quickly developed into one of the game's elite defenders.

Carlton's topsy-turvy 1914 season continued with a 70-point win over a struggling University, with Wells and Andy McDonald starring, followed by the Blues' second draw for the season, against South Melbourne. Vin Gardiner and Viv Valentine booted two goals apiece against South in a game in which there was little between the teams all day.

Steve Leehane defied the pain of a broken thumb to put in a superb display in defence against South. McGregor made his return to the field. His influence would become increasingly important in the coming weeks.

The roller-coaster continued with an 18-point loss to Fitzroy at Princes Park before a 58-point win over Melbourne. Bill Cook made an excellent debut against the Demons, booting five goals to equal the record of Melbourne's Tommy Ryan, who kicked five on debut against St Kilda in round one, 1899. He was supported by Gardiner, with four goals, while forward pocket George Topping contributed three.

Although the Blues dropped their third game of the season the following week, against Geelong at Corio Oval, they showed they would be a force to be reckoned with. In round nine, they struggled with a gallant Richmond before triumphing by two points. "Even the most ardent Carlton barracker will tell you that a game with Richmond was poor from a Carltonian's point of view, and that they were lucky to have won," *The Football Record* reported.

Over the next two weeks, the Blues scraped home after tough battles with Collingwood (by seven points at Princes Park) and St Kilda (three points at Junction Oval). Wingman George Challis stood out against the Magpies and Leehane's courage was to the fore again, playing the last three quarters with a broken hand.

McGregor and Dick also starred in these wins. Of Dick, *The Record* reported that he was chaired from the ground after the win over St Kilda. "I wonder how many times Billy Dick's name has been printed as one of the stars of his team in their victories. One always feels the better after seeing him in a match, for his work is always grand and manly and fair," *The Record* said.

The wins continued, against a struggling University and by 20 points over South Melbourne after drawing with the Bloods earlier in the season. The Blues' accuracy helped them triumph narrowly over Fitzroy at a windswept Brunswick Street Oval, 7.4 (46) to 4.13 (37), before crushing Melbourne by 53 points at the MCG.

In round 16, the Blues held off Geelong at Princes Park, but it came at a big cost. Star forward Vin Gardiner injured his hip and the problem was so serious that he did not play for the rest of the season. This forced Clark to reshuffle his attack.

With a revamped forward line, the Blues defeated Essendon at Princes Park and Richmond at Punt Road Oval to finish the home and away season with 13 wins, three losses and two draws, securing the minor premiership by a game and a half ahead of South.

The Blues started the finals series well. After leading Fitzroy by only 11 points at half-time of their semi-final, Carlton kicked five goals to nil in the third quarter, and won by 20 points, setting up the Final against South Melbourne, who had defeated Geelong by six points in the other semi-final. .

"They made the pace a clinker and played splendid football," *The Record* declared of Carlton's semi-final win. "It was a game that served to show Carlton as a team greatly superior in pace and dash and determination to the Maroons, who looked a small and light side as compared with the big, heavy boys of the old brigade.

"The game was fast and clean, full of vigour, and teemed with bright work on both sides; but at the same time it must be said that Fitzroy did not handle the ball with that sureness and skill which they have been displaying up to date. There was not a man on the Carlton side who did not put in telling work."

Cook kicked four of the Blues' nine goals, while Charlie Hammond, Harry Haughton, Ernie Jamieson and Paddy O'Brien also stood out.

Rover Jimmy Morris, defender Alf Baud and Andy McDonald earned high praise in the *Football Record*: "That little rover (Morris) is as gritty as they are made, and battles away in the thick of the strife like a veteran.

"He (McDonald) was dashing and one of the main factors in the Carlton success. He does not know what fear is, and the way he dashes on to the ball as it leaves the other fellow's boot suggests that he is insensible to danger.

"Baud was another whose dashing, clean play was delightful to watch. He was remarkably fast over short distances."

Carlton went down to South Melbourne by 19 points in the Final, but earned the right of challenge because it had won the minor premiership.

Incredibly, the Blues had gone into the match against South with nine first-year players; McGregor and follower Charlie Hammond were the only remaining members of the 1906-08 premiership outfits to take the field.

Clark reacted to the defeat by dropping Stan McKenzie and Frank Triplett for the Grand Final, and recalled Baud and ruckman George Calwell.

After trailing by two points at the first change, the Blues opened up a 21-point lead by half-time. South held the Blues scoreless in the third term, but wasted opportunities. South's men reduced the margin to six points late in the final quarter before a desperate spoil by Carlton full-back Ernie Jamieson proved a match-winning play. The Blues held on to win by a goal.

The Argus's correspondent, 'Observer', commended the heroism of the Southerners: "No side could have died more gallantly. In losing as they did, they won, as far as public esteem goes, something really better than the pennant."

For Carlton, Ted Brown featured prominently on a wing. McGregor and Baud also shone, and Dick was imperious at centre half-back.

'Observer' wrote: "Two men who greatly distinguished themselves for Carlton were Dick and Brown, one being as cool and sure in defence as the other was constantly brilliant in his wing play. Other men who did very valuable work for the winners were Haughton, collected and sure as a defender, and O'Brien, dashing and impulsive, and developing unmistakably into a great footballer. He is very strong and does not use this advantage unfairly.

"McGregor was not quite as good as on the previous Saturday, but still useful, while little Morris held his own against bigger men. Lowe was another Carlton player who greatly improved on the previous week's form. Daykin was plucky and untiring, and made few mistakes; Baud very good in the first half especially; Hammond an undemonstrative worker; and Jamieson a handy man about goal."

The Argus's correspondent noted that as soon as the players had returned to their dressingrooms and the large crowd had dispersed, South Melbourne captain Victor Belcher, accompanied by the president, Mr G. Elmslie, and the vice-president, Mr L.M. Thompson, ventured into the winner's circle.

"The South Melbourne captain congratulated Carlton on their fine victory," the correspondent wrote. "He felt that, though beaten, South Melbourne had shown that they could die fighting. He felt that some of the honours of the game rested with South Melbourne, but, as sportsmen, they congratulated their victors. It had been a grand match and the public had had full value for money."

For Clark's "Baby Blues", this was a famous victory, and the coach's virtues were extolled in Carlton's 1914 Annual Report.

"Your old and popular player, Mr N. C. Clark, was appointed coach for the season. His duties were of an extra heavy nature, on account of the large number of new and inexperienced players in the team. His intimate knowledge of the game and his faculty for imparting that knowledge to others are manifested in the performances of the new players, in the victorious team. His never-say-die spirit had much to do with our success in many of the matches when we were hard pressed. At all times he rendered all the assistance he could to the Captain. His efforts are worthy of the best thanks of the Committee and Members."

All up, Clark served as Carlton coach for nine seasons (1912, 1914-18 and 1920-22) and never missed the finals. He was at the helm in 167 matches for a 67 per cent success rate, ranking him in top four coaches to have coached for 100 games or more. (Those ahead of him were Tom Hafey, 70 per cent at Richmond from 1966-76; Jack Worrall, 70 per cent at Carlton from 1902-09; and John Coleman, 69 per cent at Essendon from 1961-67). Clark's coaching tenure at Princes Park took in 18 finals including four Grand Finals for two premierships.

In 1919, Clark had a one-year stint as coach of Richmond and lifted the Tigers from sixth to second. In 1922, in what was his third stint as Carlton coach, Horrie Clover replaced him after the seventh round. Nine years later he briefly coached North Melbourne before John Pemberton took the reins.

Clark died in Fitzroy at the age of 65 on Boxing Day 1943. His wife survived him by 40 years, while eldest son Norman jnr died in 1998. All three share the family grave at Preston Cemetery.

In 1989, the great 'Hackenschmidt' was inducted into Carlton's Hall of Fame, in the company of Sergio Silvagni and the late Bruce 'Bugsy' Comben.

1914 CARLTON

PREMIER'S SEASON

CARLTON: 1914

ROUND ONE April 25
CARLTON 6.20 (56)
COLLINGWOOD 8.8 (56)
Best: Carlton – Gardiner, Dick, Daykin, Haughton, Baud, Valentine, Brown.
Goals: Carlton – Gardiner 3, Harrison, Daykin, Haughton.
Crowd: N/A at Victoria Park

ROUND TWO May 2
CARLTON 4.11 (35)
ST KILDA 6.12 (48)
Best: Carlton – Hammond, McDonald, Gardiner, Green, Clancy, Calwell.
Goals: Carlton – Gardiner 2, Fisher, Wells.
Crowd: N/A at Princes Park

ROUND THREE May 9
CARLTON 13.24 (102)
UNIVERSITY 4.8 (32)
Best: Carlton – Dick, Leehane, Sharp, Gardiner, Wells, Burleigh, Baud, Hanna.
Goals: Carlton – Gardiner 3, Wells 3, Sharp 2, Burleigh 2, Triplett, McDonald, Fisher.
Crowd: 8,239 at the MCG

ROUND FOUR May 16
CARLTON 7.10 (52)
SOUTH MELBOURNE 8.4 (52)
Best: Carlton – Fisher, Lowe, Dick, Gardiner, Valentine, Hammond, Leehane.
Goals: Carlton – Valentine 2, Gardiner 2, Burleigh, Wells, Sharp.
Crowd: N/A at the Lake Oval

ROUND FIVE May 23
CARLTON 4.4 (28)
FITZROY 6.10 (46)
Best: Carlton – Valentine, Sharp, McDonald, Fisher, Haughton.
Goals: Carlton – Gardiner, Fisher, Leehane, Valentine.
Crowd: N/A at Princes Park

ROUND SIX May 30
CARLTON 13.19 (97)
MELBOURNE 5.9 (39)
Best: Carlton – Cook, Gardiner, Daykin, Andrew, Sharp, Jamieson, Scaddan.
Goals: Carlton – Cook 5, Gardiner 4, Topping 3, Baud.
Crowd: N/A at Princes Park

ROUND SEVEN June 6
CARLTON 3.16 (34)
GEELONG 9.11 (65)
Best: Carlton – Baud, Green, Gardiner, McGregor, Brown, Challis.
Goals: Carlton – Green, Baud, Gardiner.
Crowd: N/A at Corio Oval

ROUND EIGHT June 8
CARLTON 11.10 (76)
ESSENDON 6.3 (39)
Best: Carlton – Clancy, Sharp, Challis, McGregor, Green, Cook, Gardiner.
Goals: Carlton – Green 3, Cook 3, Gardiner 2, Lowe 2, McKenzie.
Crowd: N/A at East Melbourne Cricket Ground

ROUND NINE June 13
CARLTON 5.13 (43)
RICHMOND 5.11 (41)
Best: Carlton – Lowe, Hammond, Scaddan, McKenzie, McGregor, Haughton.
Goals: Carlton – McKenzie, Gardiner, Cook, Scaddan, Leehane.
Crowd: N/A at Princes Park

ROUND TEN June 20
CARLTON 6.16 (52)
COLLINGWOOD 5.15 (45)
Best: Carlton – Cook, McGregor, Dick, Daykin, Fisher, Baud.
Goals: Carlton – Cook 3, Green, Daykin, Fisher.
Crowd: N/A at Princes Park

ROUND ELEVEN June 27
CARLTON 7.11 (53)
ST KILDA 7.8 (50)
Best: Carlton – Dick, Haughton, Burleigh, Cook, McKenzie, Jamieson.
Goals: Carlton – McKenzie 2, Cook 2, Green, Burleigh, Hammond.
Crowd: N/A at the Junction Oval

ROUND TWELVE July 4
CARLTON 11.21 (87)
UNIVERSITY 8.8 (56)
Best: Carlton – Green, McKenzie, Calwell, Dick, Sharp, Lowe, Brown.
Goals: Carlton – Green 4, Sharp 3, Lowe 2, Fisher, Challis.
Crowd: N/A at Princes Park

ROUND THIRTEEN July 11
CARLTON 11.14 (80)
SOUTH MELBOURNE 9.6 (60)
Best: Carlton – Fisher, Dick, Valentine, Daykin, Green, Baud, Jamieson.
Goals: Carlton – Fisher 3, Cook 2, Gardiner, Sharp, Haughton, Hammond, McKenzie, Green.
Crowd: N/A at Princes Park

ROUND FOURTEEN July 18
CARLTON 7.4 (46)
FITZROY 4.13 (37)
Best: Carlton – McDonald, Keily, Daykin, Fisher, Leehane, Brown, McGregor.
Goals: Carlton – Fisher 3, Daykin 2, Green, Cook.
Crowd: N/A at Brunswick St Oval

ROUND FIFTEEN July 25
CARLTON 16.15 (111)
MELBOURNE 8.10 (58)
Best: Carlton – Fisher, Gardiner, Sharp, Daykin, Hammond, Lowe, Cook.
Goals: Carlton – Gardiner 4, Fisher 4, Lowe 2, Cook 2, Daykin, Sharp, Hammond, McKenzie.
Crowd: 8,173 at the MCG

ROUND SIXTEEN August 1
CARLTON 4.12 (36)
GEELONG 5.4 (34)
Best: Carlton – Fisher, Daykin, Sharp, Baud, Dick, Calwell, McKenzie, Dick.
Goals: Carlton – Fisher 2, Cook, Calwell.
Crowd: N/A at Princes Park

ROUND SEVENTEEN August 22
CARLTON 10.11 (71)
ESSENDON 7.8 (50)
Best: Carlton – Dick, Jamieson, Burleigh, Fisher, Challis, Daykin, O'Brien.
Goals: Carlton – Fisher 3, Daykin 3, Lowe 2, Burleigh 2.
Crowd: N/A at Princes Park

ROUND EIGHTEEN August 29
CARLTON 9.9 (63)
RICHMOND 8.9 (57)
Best: Carlton – Jamieson, Brown, McKenzie, O'Brien, Morris, Valentine.
Goals: Carlton – Morris 3, Valentine 2, Dick, Fisher, O'Brien, Baud.
Crowd: N/A at Punt Road Oval

PREMIER'S FINALS

SECOND SEMI-FINAL September 12
CARLTON 9.8 (62)
FITZROY 5.12 (42)
Best: Carlton – Hammond, Lowe, Brown, O'Brien, Morris, McDonald, Jamieson.
Goals: Carlton – Cook 4, Green, Morris, Lowe, Daykin, McGregor.
Crowd: 28,243 at the MCG

FINAL September 19
CARLTON 3.6 (24)
SOUTH MELBOURNE 5.13 (43)
Best: Carlton – Burleigh, Jamieson, O'Brien, McDonald, Leehane, Green, Haughton.
Goals: Carlton – Cook 2, Green.
Crowd: 20,248 at the MCG

GRAND FINAL September 26
CARLTON 2.3 5.8 5.8 6.9 (45)
SOUTH MELB 2.5 2.5 3.11 4.15 (39)
Best: Carlton – Dick, O'Brien, Brown, Lowe, Haughton, Leehane, Jamieson, Daykin.
Goals: Carlton – Green, Burleigh, Cook, Morris, Brown, Fisher.
Crowd: 30,495 at the MCG

GRAND FINAL LINE-UPS

CARL	B:	P.O'Brien	E.Jamieson	A.McDonald
STH M	F:	D.Mullaly	J.Freeman	H.Morgan
CARL	HB:	S.Leehane	B.Dick (capt)	H.Haughton
STH M	HF:	B.Sloss	A.O'Donoghue	L.Rusich
CARL	C:	A.Baud	R.McGregor	T.Brown
STH M	C:	M.Tandy	T.Bollard	J.Price
CARL	HF:	J.Lowe	B.Cook	P.Daykin
STH M	HB:	S.Hiskins	H.Kelly	V.Belcher (capt)
CARL	F:	C.Fisher	G.Green	H.Burleigh
STH M	B:	H.Saltau	B.Deas	A.Rademacher
CARL	R:	G.Calwell	C.Hammond	J.Morris
STH M	R:	L.Charge	B.Hair	J.Caldwell
CARL	**Coach:** Norman Clark			
STH M	**Coach:** Vic Belcher			

SNAPSHOT

Win-loss record: 15-4

Highest score: 16.15 (111), v Melbourne, round 15.

Greatest winning margin: 70 points, round 3, v University.

Lowest score: 3.6 (24), preliminary final, v South Melbourne.

Greatest losing margin: 31 points, round 7, v Geelong.

Most goals by a player in a game: 5, Bill Cook, round 6, v Melbourne.

Most consecutive wins: 12

Most consecutive losses: 1

Club awards: Leading goalkicker: Bill Cook (27 goals).

Putting it into perspective:
Carlton's fourth premiership from seven Grand Final appearances moved it into equal second place, with Essendon, for flags won. The narrow win over South Melbourne in the Grand Final was the club's third win in a decider by less than 10 points.

1914

		P	W	L	D	%	Pts
1	Carlton (1)	18	13	3	2	129.7	56
2	South Melb (2)	18	12	5	1	109.4	50
3	Fitzroy (3)	18	12	6		137.2	48
4	Geelong (4)	18	11	6	1	128.4	46
5	Collingwood	18	10	7	1	120.0	42
6	Essendon	18	9	7	2	120.7	40
7	St Kilda	18	9	8	1	118.2	38
8	Richmond	18	8	10		100.6	32
9	Melbourne	18	2	16		61.3	8
10	University	18	0	18		47.0	0

(18 home and away rounds)

PLAYERS USED

CARLTON	GUERNSEY	GAMES	GOALS
Andrew, Joe	16	2	0
Baud, Alf	25	20	3
Brown, Ted	2	20	1
Burleigh, Herb	28	10	7
Calwell, George	26	11	1
Challis, George	12	16	1
Clancy, Tom	8	6	0
Cook, Bill	22	16	27
Daykin, Percy	3	20	9
Dick, Billy	1	20	1
Fisher, Charlie	21	16	22
Gardiner, Vin	13	13	24
Green, Gordon	17	13	15
Hammond, Charlie	24	17	3
Hanna, Frank	0	1	0
Harrison, Arthur	23	1	1
Haughton, Harry	16	21	2
Jamieson, Ernie	15	20	0
Keily, Dan	11	3	0
Leehane, Steve	7	15	2
Lowe, Jack	30	13	9
McCarthy, Justin	9	2	0
McDonald, Andy	4	18	1
McGregor, Rod	19	18	1
McKenzie, M. Stan	27	14	6
Morris, Jimmy	19	5	5
O'Brien, Paddy	10	7	1
Scaddan, Albert	23	3	1
Sharp, Athol	20	14	8
Topping, George	18	2	3
Triplett, Frank	18	5	1
Valentine, Viv	6	8	5
Wells, Jack	1	5	5
Williamson, Alf	33	9	5
Willis, Jim	9	2	0

CARLTON 11.12 (78) d
COLLINGWOOD 6.9 (45)

MIXED FEELINGS ON WAR GAMES

Carlton defeated Collingwood in the first League title to be decided amid the backdrop of war, but the aftermath for the club was one of sadness. By HOWARD KOTTON and TONY DE BOLFO

IN THE early hours of Sunday, April 25, 1915, to the thunderous echo of relentless Turkish gunfire, the brave young men of the Australian Imperial Force (AIF) converged on that God-forsaken peninsula known as Gallipoli. Among them was Nagambie's Fenley John McDonald, a member of the 7th Battalion and a committed Carlton backman through the winters of 1911 and 1912.

And it was somewhere on that fatal shore that "Fen" was cruelly cut down.

It was about this time, half a world away at Princes Park Oval, that the Carlton committee deliberated over a proposal to curtail the VFL home and away season and proceed at once with the finals.

In keeping with the delegates of most clubs they voted against the proposal, as was noted in Carlton's 1915 Annual Report:

"It was felt that the playing of football on Saturday afternoons had no adverse effect on recruiting, was a relaxation for the public from the serious problems of business and war, and that it would be unwise to deprive thousands of people of that source of recreation".

Further, Carlton's players and staff were twice asked during this difficult year to accept salary reductions, with the result that operational costs of £1100 were reined in when compared with the previous year.

As the report noted:

> All [players and trainers] were called together, and the position placed before them. They cheerfully agreed to the propositions, and are to be complimented on their loyalty to the Club. The reductions had no effect whatever on their training or their zeal to win the Premiership, as the result shows. The action of players and others is worthy of your best thanks".

As the appalling game of life and death was being played out in Europe, and the Germans introduced chlorine gas for the first time at Ypres, the Carlton players set out in the comparatively trivial pursuit of defending their 1914 premiership.

The Carlton campaign opened for coach Norman 'Hackenschmidt' Clark and his lads on the eve of the Gallipoli landing—Saturday, April 24, 1915—with a drawn contest with Fitzroy at Princes Park. "It was Fitzroy's game for three parts of the distance," the *Football Record* reported, "but it was hereabouts when Carlton lived up to their reputation as diehards. They threw themselves into their work with a vim and determination that thrilled the crowd. Within a few minutes they had wiped off much of the deficit, and kept going with grimness and vigour until they were on level terms with the enemy."

Seven days later, at the Lake Oval, the Blues led South Melbourne by 33 points at three-quarter time only to be held goalless in the final term. The Blues staved off a formidable foe to emerge 13-point victors.

The departure from the League of the University Football Club precipitated a third-round bye. Carlton met Essendon in the fourth round in a muddy scrap at Princes Oval. "The wet conditions seemed more to the liking of Essendon, and they handled the heavy, soggy ball better than did the Carltonians," *The Record* reported. "They were leading at the end of each term, and they finished strong and full of power, whereas Carlton were leg-weary."

Carlton's subsequent victories over Melbourne at the MCG and Geelong at Corio Oval ensured an immense build-up for the round-seven match with Collingwood on the King's Birthday long weekend. The punters turned out in their droves and the contest more than lived up to expectations.

"It was a crowd that looked more like a final premiership attendance than one looking on at the home and home series," the *Record* reported.

"You may take this for granted—that you will not see a better exhibition of hard, eager, clean football than the two teams put up on this occasion. The afternoon was one long run of thrilling sights, and never for a moment did the keenness of the players or the onlookers flag."

Dick Lee's nine-goal haul for the Black and Whites was but one of the sterling individual performances. Carlton captain Billy Dick competed with his usual flair and finesse at centre half-back, but he was under some duress because of a severe laceration to the top of his left thumb.

With Lee imperious, the visitors took a well-earned 11-point lead into the main change, during which time Clark adjusted his line-up of followers. Clark's tinkering achieved the desired result and the Blues got up by two points, in a game long regarded as one of the best of the war years.

As 'Observer' in *The Argus* noted: "The marking was quite out of the ordinary, the pace something to marvel at, and the kicking, passing, grit and lasting power a glorious sight to see. It was as even and as brilliant a contest as could possibly be seen."

When the Blues bludgeoned Richmond into submission at Princes Park in round eight, Carlton half-forward George Challis came in for special commendation. "His speed and general skill, combined with his excellent judgment, are A1… against Richmond he was seen at his best," the *Record* reported.

But the 12-point loss to Fitzroy at Brunswick Street just two weeks later was compounded by the disastrous report and subsequent 10-match suspension of Billy Dick for striking Jack Cooper.

So outraged was the Carlton hierarchy that it took legal advice and made a submission to the Victorian Football League. The League representatives ruled that the suspension should stand, costing Dick his date with destiny in the spring.

As a result of Dick's suspension, Alf Baud assumed the captaincy, with the renowned centreman Rod "Wee" McGregor his deputy.

The legendary Roy Cazaly, in an article penned for *The Sporting Globe* of Saturday June 5, 1937, wrote of Baud: "I think that Baud by comparison would have made (Haydn) Bunton look ordinary. Baud would have been a football sensation had it not been for the war."

Through the second half of the 1915 season, Baud formed part of a cohesive defensive unit which, in Dick's absence, comprised the stand-in Billy Robinson, Ernie Jamieson, Andy McDonald, Ted Brown and rugged back pocket Patrick Joseph "Paddy" O'Brien.

O'Brien, who had turned out for his first senior game in 1913, had already excelled at what he said was his preferred sporting pursuit, boxing. At 18, he was crowned Victorian middleweight amateur boxing champion, and he wasn't frightened to mix it with the heavyweights either.

O'Brien was happy to throw his weight around on the football field, and legend has it that when he ran through Collingwood great Gordon Coventry in the 1920s he remarked: "You won't get a toothache where those five teeth were".

O'Brien's niece Mary Martyn, the wife of the late North Melbourne ruckman Bryan "Skinny" Martyn and mother of former North and Carlton full-back Mick Martyn, recently confided that O'Brien once sparred with 'The Manasa Mauler' Jack Dempsey, the American who held the world heavyweight title from 1919-26.

Mary Martin said: "I know he [Paddy] went around the world after he finished his football and that he had a spar with Dempsey. He was a Victorian boxing champion in the railways. I don't know what division he was, but I know he wasn't a lightweight. He was pretty handy with his fists and he always reckoned every footballer should learn to box and defend himself.

"Paddy's father and mother John and Mary came out from Ireland. He was from Limerick and she was from County Clare and neither of them lived very long. He originally ran a hotel, the Great Western Hotel in the city, and when his house was built in Newport he left the pub and joined the railways.

"John and Mary raised eight children—five girls and three boys—and Paddy and his twin brothers followed their father into the railways."

Martyn can recall her uncle making regular visits in later years: "Paddy used to come around and play with the children when my husband went overseas. He liked meeting people, liked going to the football and was the life of the party. He never married.

The old house had a sleep-out at the side, and in his later years he and his younger brother Jim stopped there. Paddy ended up in a boarding house when he died."

Paddy O'Brien, who died in 1964 aged 70, proudly wore the No.10 navy blue guernsey into 167 contests for Carlton between 1913-25, including the Grand Final conquests of 1914 and 1915.

The significance of that number was not lost on Martyn when her son vacated Arden Street for Royal Parade in 2003.

"At the time [North Melbourne coach Dean] Laidley wanted to push the young ones, so Mick followed Denis Pagan to Carlton. It just happened that the person wearing Paddy's old No.10 guernsey [Michael Mansfield] left and Mick was thrown the jumper.

"It was the jumper he wore when he played his 300th game and I tell you what, someone must have been watching."

Paddy O'Brien took his place in the back pocket on the afternoon of Saturday, August 28, 1915, when Carlton confronted Melbourne for the third time that season, this time in a semi-final. On a wet day at Jolimont, the Blues upheld their unbeaten run against the Redlegs that year, prevailing by 11 points, with Vin Gardiner contributing five of Carlton's 11 goals.

A preliminary final against Fitzroy was required after the Roys had surprised Collingwood, the minor premier, in the semi-final at the MCG a week later. In a powerful display, Fitzroy all but doubled Collingwood's score, winning by 34 points. The Magpies' right of challenge would take them through to the Grand Final. The Carlton-Fitzroy preliminary final was labelled a "grand, robust game" by *The Record*. "Right from the bounce, the men went about their work with a will and they had the crowd roaring with appreciation," it reported.

"It was not a place for weaklings, and there was not a weakling among the 36. The pace was great and the play high-class. Carlton worked together with admirable system, and carried all before them at times."

Despite their inaccuracy, the Blues advanced after a 16-point triumph, 6.18 (54) to 5.8 (38), with a long goal by Charlie Fisher late in the game putting the result beyond doubt.

At Victoria Park, Collingwood's build-up to the Grand Final was, to put it mildly, intriguing. The coach, James Francis 'Jock' McHale lured Ted Rowell out of retirement for his one and only game of the season.

Controversy also enveloped Collingwood players Paddy Rowan and Malcolm 'Doc' Seddon. Both men were enlisted in the army. On the morning of the match they had to complete a 16-kilometre march called by the drill sergeant at their Seymour barracks. Collingwood secretary E.W. Copeland chauffeured the pair back to the city for the match, while the rumour mill kicked into action. There was a rumour that the commanding officer was a Carlton fan. Although under duress, Seddon and Rowan took their places in the team.

The 1915 Grand Final proved to be a low-scoring, tight contest. Carlton led by five points at the final change, before Dick Lee marked and goaled to put the Magpies ahead.

Baud and his Carlton contemporaries took up the challenge and finished all over their counterparts, with Herb Burleigh booting three of his goals in the final term as the Blues careered away to a 33-point victory.

Beneath the headline "Fast and furious", and the sub-heading, "Carlton premiers", 'Observer' was glowing in his appraisal in *The Argus*:

After a fast and furious game, in which the fortunes of play varied long enough to work nearly 40,000 people up to the highest pitch of excitement, Carlton won the League premiership against Collingwood on the Melbourne Cricket-ground on Saturday. The scores make it look like an easy victory, but that was not the case. Well into the last quarter there was only a point separating the combatants, and Collingwood, who had looked a beaten side for the greater part of the game, made such a wonderful rally that for a time Carlton seemed to be demoralised. It was just a question of which could last longest, and the survivor was Carlton.

"Once they had got a goal or so in their favour at that critical stage of the match, it was simply a question of getting almost as many goals as they wished, because the other side had shot its bolt. While not always skilful, it was one of the fastest and fiercest games seen for many years, and, though no mercy was shown by either side, the play was, on the whole, fair."

Carlton's 51st Annual Report, tabled to members in late 1915, made for welcome reading:

The proud position of Premiers was once more brilliantly gained by your Club, after a very strenuous season. The committee, on your behalf, wishes to highly compliment and congratulate the players on their splendid efforts.

"The past season was the most successful the club has experienced since 1908, when only one match was lost.

In 1915 we suffered two defeats (Essendon and Fitzroy), and played only one drawn game (first of the season) with the latter club. By the players' careful attention to training, the continuance of the 1914 spirit of comradeship, the efforts of the coach and trainers, the team was kept in good condition during the whole of the season, and was brought out for the semi-final and final matches with every man fit, as was shown in the finish of each of these games.

For the first part of the last quarter of the Grand Final against Collingwood we had some anxious moments, but, by a brilliant and sustained effort—perhaps unequalled in any previous similar game—your team rose to the occasion, and, piling on goal after goal, won the match and the Premiership with five goals to spare.

To be strong enough to play the same 18 men in the three final games was the proud position of the Club, and we think it is unique in the annals of the League.

Your Club also had the distinction of being the only team to defeat every other club in the competition, and this performance, and their consistent play right through, stamped Carlton as being undoubtedly the strongest combination afield. The players are to be highly complimented.

Among Carlton's better performers in the 1915 Grand Final were George

Challis, who featured prominently on a wing, and fellow Tasmanian Viv Valentine. The great Jack Worrall, reporting for *The Australasian*, wrote:

> Challis did many fine things... always making good use of the ball... (and) Valentine, as is his wont against Collingwood, moved capably."

Alf Baud was two days shy of his 23rd birthday and, as such, the youngest footballer in League history to captain his club to a premiership. It would also be his last hurrah in a dark navy Blue guernsey.

By March 1916, Baud was called away to war, and soon was promoted to the rank of sergeant. In September the following year, his battery was in action at ANZAC Ridge, when an enemy shell exploded nearby.

For Baud, the explosion was near fatal, as a shrapnel splinter smashed into his face, fracturing his skull and destroying his left eye. He was rushed to hospital, where his life hung in the balance for days, but eventually he pulled through and was repatriated in March 1918. He was never to play football again.

Baud lived to be 94. Challis wasn't so lucky.

Regarded as one of the finest competitors in the VFL, having built an excellent reputation as a schoolboy footballer, Challis first caught the discerning eye of a Carlton talent scout while representing Tasmania at the 1911 representative carnival in Adelaide.

Challis barely had time to bask in the afterglow of the 1915 Grand Final triumph when armed service beckoned.

Together with his teammates Baud, Burleigh, Frank Triplett, George Calwell, Vic Gordon and George Muir, he was afforded an ardent send-off by members of the Carlton committee. As one observer noted: "Their places were hard to fill, but we feel proud of them, and glad to know that our loss is the Empire's gain."

Less than a month after setting foot on French soil, Challis was blown apart by a German shell.

His old mates at Carlton wore black armbands as they stood with their Fitzroy adversaries while, moments before the 1916 Final, the lone bugler played *The Last Post* in a tribute to Challis's memory.

Challis was one of 83 Carlton footballers who enlisted for active service in World War I, and among 11 to be killed in action.

For many years it was presumed Challis was one of eight Carltonites to have perished, together with Dave Gillespie, Tom Hughes, Tom McCluskey, Fen McDonald, Stan McKenzie, Jim Pender and Alf Williamson.

But not long before the time of writing, three more Carlton footballers were confirmed among those Australian soldiers who died during World War I.

They were 25-year-old Willie Rogers, a three-game player and temporary Sergeant who in September 1918 died of gunshot wounds near Rouen in northern France; 11-game player Harold Daniel, who was awarded a Military Medal and was 39 when he died serving the 5th Battalion in France in August 1918; and the one-gamer Charlie Oliver, a medical practitioner and Captain of the Army Medical Corps in Seymour, who was 43 when, in December 1916, he suffered a fractured skull and brain haemorrhage after accidentally falling from his horse.

1915 CARLTON

PREMIER'S SEASON

CARLTON: 1915

ROUND ONE April 24
CARLTON	5.11 (41)
FITZROY	6.5 (41)

Best: Carlton – Calwell, Baud, Morris, McGregor, Dick, Challis, O'Brien.
Goals: Carlton – O'Brien, Morris, Challis, Daykin, Fisher.
Crowd: N/A at Princes Park

ROUND TWO May 1
CARLTON	8.12 (60)
SOUTH MELBOURNE	6.11 (47)

Best: Carlton – Sharp, Leehane, Dick, Jamieson, Valentine, Morris.
Goals: Carlton – Morris 2, Burleigh 2, Valentine 2, Fisher, Baud.
Crowd: N/A at the Lake Oval

ROUND THREE
BYE

ROUND FOUR May 15
CARLTON	3.13 (31)
ESSENDON	8.8 (56)

Best: Carlton – Leehane, Hammond, Burleigh, Brown, Jamieson, Triplett.
Goals: Carlton – Burleigh, Morris, Valentine.
Crowd: N/A at Princes Park

ROUND FIVE May 22
CARLTON	10.12 (72)
MELBOURNE	8.3 (51)

Best: Carlton – Sharp, Leehane, Dick, Burleigh, Gardiner, Shortill, Daykin.
Goals: Carlton – Sharp 3, Burleigh 3, Gardiner 2, Daykin, Valentine.
Crowd: 9,302 at the MCG

ROUND SIX May 29
CARLTON	9.13 (67)
GEELONG	5.10 (40)

Best: Carlton – Gardiner, Morris, Burleigh, Baud, Calwell, Sharp, Hore.
Goals: Carlton – Gardiner 5, Sharp 2, Burleigh 2.
Crowd: N/A at Corio Oval

ROUND SEVEN June 7
CARLTON	11.9 (75)
COLLINGWOOD	10.13 (73)

Best: Carlton – Valentine, Haughton, Leehane, Robinson, McDonald, Gardiner.
Goals: Carlton – Burleigh 3, Gardiner 2, Hammond, Sharp, Daykin, Haughton, Valentine, Calwell.
Crowd: N/A at Princes Park

ROUND EIGHT June 12
CARLTON	15.17 (107)
RICHMOND	8.5 (53)

Best: Carlton – Gardiner, Sharp, Hammond, Morris, Jamieson, McGregor, Leehane.
Goals: Carlton – Burleigh 3, Sharp 3, Gardiner 3, Daykin 2, Challis, Valentine, Haughton, Morris.
Crowd: N/A at Princes Park

ROUND NINE June 19
CARLTON	5.15 (45)
ST KILDA	1.1 (7)

Best: Carlton – McDonald, Valentine, Gardiner, Dick, Sharp, Robinson, McGregor.
Goals: Carlton – Gardiner 3, Sharp, Haughton.
Crowd: N/A at the Junction Oval

ROUND TEN June 26
CARLTON	5.8 (38)
FITZROY	7.8 (50)

Best: Carlton – Burleigh, Haughton, Challis, McDonald, Robinson, Hammond.
Goals: Carlton – Burleigh 3, Gardiner, Haughton.
Crowd: N/A at Brunswick St Oval

ROUND ELEVEN July 3
CARLTON	7.15 (57)
SOUTH MELBOURNE	7.5 (47)

Best: Carlton – Baud, Jamieson, Sharp, Gardiner, McDonald, Brown, O'Brien.
Goals: Carlton – Burleigh 2, Daykin, Gardiner, Valentine, Sharp, Morris.
Crowd: N/A at Princes Park

ROUND TWELVE
BYE

ROUND THIRTEEN July 17
CARLTON	12.15 (87)
ESSENDON	5.15 (45)

Best: Carlton – Burleigh, Hammond, Valentine, Baud, Jamieson, Leehane.
Goals: Carlton – Burleigh 5, Daykin 2, Hammond 2, Fisher, Gardiner, Valentine.
Crowd: N/A at East Melbourne Cricket Ground

ROUND FOURTEEN July 24
CARLTON	11.8 (74)
MELBOURNE	5.15 (45)

Best: Carlton – Burleigh, Gardiner, Calwell, Baud, Daykin, Sharp, Leehane, McGregor.
Goals: Carlton – Burleigh 4, Gardiner 3, Muir, Sharp, Daykin, Hammond.
Crowd: N/A at Princes Park

ROUND FIFTEEN July 31
CARLTON	9.20 (74)
GEELONG	8.12 (60)

Best: Carlton – Keily, Challis, Baud, McGregor, Gardiner, McDonald.
Goals: Carlton – Gardiner 3, Burleigh 2, Hammond, Green, Sharp, Valentine.
Crowd: N/A at Princes Park

ROUND SIXTEEN August 7
CARLTON	9.9 (63)
COLLINGWOOD	9.8 (62)

Best: Carlton – Valentine, Burleigh, McDonald, Shortill, Haughton, Hammond, Morris.
Goals: Carlton – Valentine 3, Burleigh 3, Calwell, Hammond, Morris.
Crowd: N/A at Victoria Park

ROUND SEVENTEEN August 14
CARLTON	17.15 (117)
RICHMOND	7.7 (49)

Best: Carlton – Jamieson, McGregor, Valentine, Robinson, Burleigh, Green.
Goals: Carlton – Green 4, Burleigh 4, Valentine 2, Morris, Shortill, Sharp, Hammond, Haughton, Daykin, O'Brien.
Crowd: N/A at Punt Road Oval

ROUND EIGHTEEN August 21
CARLTON	14.16 (100)
ST KILDA	6.8 (44)

Best: Carlton – Brown, Green, Hammond, Burleigh, Sharp, Keily, O'Brien.
Goals: Carlton – Burleigh 3, Daykin 2, Fisher 2, Sharp 2, Morris, Gardiner, Hammond, Charllis, Valentine.
Crowd: N/A at Princes Park

PREMIER'S FINALS

FIRST SEMI-FINAL August 28
CARLTON 11.12 (78)
MELBOURNE 10.7 (67)
Best: Carlton – Valentine, McGregor, Baud, Challis, Gardiner, Hammond.
Goals: Carlton – Gardiner 5, Green 3, Burleigh 2, Valentine.
Crowd: 14,446 at the MCG

PRELIMINARY FINAL September 11
CARLTON 6.18 (54)
FITZROY 5.8 (38)
Best: Carlton – Robinson, O'Brien, McDonald, Challis, Gardiner.
Goals: Carlton – Gardiner 2, Green 2, Fisher, Sharp.
Crowd: 30,678 at the MCG

GRAND FINAL September 18
CARLTON 2.5 6.6 6.8 11.12 (78)
COLLINGWOOD 3.0 4.2 5.9 6.9 (45)
Best: Carlton – McDonald, Challis, Brown, Burleigh, Daykin, McGregor, Baud.
Goals: Carlton – Burleigh 4, Gardiner 3, Hammond 2, Green, Daykin.
Crowd: 39,343 at the MCG

GRAND FINAL LINE-UPS

CARL	B:	P.O'Brien	E.Jamieson	A.McDonald
COLL	F:	H.Curtis	D.Lee	G.Dobreigh
CARL	HB:	A.Baud (capt)	B.Robinson	T.Brown
COLL	HF:	P.Rowe	M.Seddon	C.Laxton
CARL	C:	J.Morris	R.McGregor	G.Challis
COLL	C:	T.Clancy	J.McHale	J.Sadler
CARL	HF:	H.Burleigh	P.Daykin	C.Fisher
COLL	HB:	J.Green	D.Minogue (capt)	G.Anderson
CARL	F:	G.Green	V.Gardiner	Athol Sharp
COLL	B:	A.Mutch	T.Rowell	S.Mortimer
CARL	R:	C.Hammond	H.Haughton	V.Valentine
COLL	R:	L.Hughes	P.Reynolds	P.Wilson
CARL	**Coach:** Norman Clark			
COLL	**Coach:** Jock McHale			

SNAPSHOT

Win-loss record: 16-2-1

Highest score: 17.15 (117), round 17, v Richmond.

Greatest winning margin: 68 points, round 17, v Richmond.

Lowest score: 3.13 (31), round 4, v Essendon.

Greatest losing margin: 25 points, round 4, v Essendon.

Most goals by a player in a game: 5, Vin Gardiner, round 6, v Geelong; semi-final, v Melbourne; Herb Burleigh, round 13, v Essendon.

Most consecutive wins: 10

Most consecutive losses: 1 (twice).

Club awards: Leading goalkicker: Herb Burleigh (46 goals).

Putting it into perspective:
The Blues' fifth Grand Final victory saw them join Fitzroy as the competition's most successful club—five premierships from eight Grand Final appearances and for the second time in club history they won back-to-back flags.

1915

	P	W	L	D	%	Pts
1 Collingwood (2)	16	14	2		166.1	56
2 Carlton (1)	16	13	2	1	143.9	54
3 Fitzroy (3)	16	11	4	1	149.4	46
4 Melbourne (4)	16	9	7		99.2	36
5 South Melb	16	8	8		106.2	32
6 Richmond	16	5	11		77.7	20
7 St Kilda	16	5	11		75.9	20
8 Essendon	16	3	13		70.3	12
9 Geelong	16	3	13		68.0	12

(18 home and away rounds)

PLAYERS USED

CARLTON	GUERNSEY	GAMES	GOALS
Barningham, Alex	23	1	0
Baud, Alf	25	19	1
Brown, Ted	9	17	0
Burleigh, Herb	21	19	46
Calwell, George	19	12	2
Challis, George	12	17	3
Daykin, Percy	2	19	13
Dick, Billy	1	9	0
Fisher, Charlie	15	9	6
Gardiner, Vin	13	14	35
Gordon, Vic	26	1	0
Green, Gordon	17	6	11
Hammond, Charlie	16	19	10
Haughton, Harry	5	17	5
Hore, Bill	29	2	0
Jamieson, Ernie	7	16	0
Keily, Dan	8	6	0
Leehane, Steve	6	8	1
McDonald, Andy	3	18	0
McGregor, Rod	11	19	0
Morris, Jimmy	20	19	9
Muir, George	30	1	1
O'Brien, Paddy	10	16	2
Robinson, Billy	24	14	0
Sharp, Athol	14	19	17
Shortill, Joe	23	5	1
Triplett, Frank	25	1	0
Valentine, Viv	4	19	16

**FITZROY 12.13 (85) d
CARLTON 8.8 (56)**

WORST TO FIRST IN A MONTH

Only four teams contested the 1916 season due World War I, leaving Fitzroy to win the flag in remarkable circumstances. By BARRY LEVINSON

THE 1916 VFL season provides the basis for one of football's great trivia questions: which is the only team to win the wooden spoon and premiership in the same season? However, Fitzroy's amazing feat was only achieved because of an extraordinary set of circumstances that almost led to the disintegration of the VFL.

The crippling effects to football club personnel during World War I reduced the number of teams in 1916 to four, with every team qualifying for the finals, regardless of how well they performed during the home and away season. It certainly provides a new perspective to the debates 90 years later about whether a final eight for 16 teams rewarded mediocrity!

It may seem hard to believe in today's football-mad culture, but had many critics had their way, Fitzroy's premiership victory never would have eventuated.

Debate raged throughout the year about the merits of sport during wartime. Fit and able men were encouraged to fulfil their national duty and enlist and footballers were not exempt. Many Melburnians believed that continuing the VFL competition would send the wrong message.

Pressure on the VFL to abandon the competition intensified in mid-January, with news that the South Australian League would be put on hold until the conclusion of the war. Victorian chiefs did not discourage their footballers from enlisting, but they were adamant the sport could provide an important source of relaxation for the mind and body, for those who couldn't go to war. "Personally I can see no objection to carrying on football, unless we are to give up every form of recreation," VFL President O.M. Williams was quoted as saying in *The Argus* in January 1916. "But I think it should only be engaged in by those who, for medical reasons or on account of their responsibilities, cannot enlist."

Although initially the League had intended to continue the competition as normal, it was forced to reconsider in order to quell a public backlash. There was a strong sentiment that players should not be paid, and the League even considered a suggestion to ban all footballers eligible for enlistment.

While the debate continued, a steady stream of footballers enlisted, among them one of Fitzroy's best and most admired players of the era, Jack Cooper. A local boy, recruited from North Fitzroy juniors in 1907, Cooper was a stocky half-back flanker who was a fierce and courageous competitor.

After winning the Maroons' best and fairest in 1911, he was voted captain for the following season and played in the club's 1913 premiership team. Cooper's toughness made him well suited to becoming a soldier. In 1914, for example, he played a starring role in a game despite being treated by a doctor for a broken rib, and he completed the match wearing a substantial bandage.

Cooper's last game for Fitzroy was the 1915 preliminary final loss to Carlton. He was sent off to war by his club mates at a gathering of around 100 people on the eve of the 1916 season. The club presented Cooper with a gold-mounted fountain pen, shaving kit and some money before he left for the battlefields of Europe. He would never return. Cooper was one of 67 VFL footballers who died in World War I, in his case killed at Polygon Wood in Belgium in September 1917. His body was never recovered.

At a meeting at VFL headquarters in the Block Arcade in Collins Street on the evening of February 7, 1916, the League formally decided that the game would go on. It merely "recommended" that clubs should not pay players more than expenses until the war was over. The League also suggested clubs should donate 10 per cent of gate receipts from regular games and 50 per cent from finals matches to patriotic funds.

The decision sparked outrage. *The Argus* columnist 'Old Boy' was seething. "If the nation were not at war, if the country were not calling for the best of her manhood, the attitude adopted by the majority of the delegates of the Victorian Football League… might provide the subject for laughter," he wrote. "When, however, there is a call for every able-bodied man, and for every available shilling, the attitude of the men who control the game of football in Victoria is lamentable.

"Wherever sportsmen congregated yesterday there were expressions of disgust at the action of the League. The general opinion was that the premiership competition should have been abandoned, and that no encouragement should have been offered to either players or spectators to set the pleasures of football before the responsibilities of war."

Letters to the editor of *The Argus* were dominated by debate over whether football should continue while war raged in Europe. But it wasn't just keeping players away from serving their country that aggravated some. Returned soldier R.W. Hornabrook wrote: "It is not the playing of these games that one objects to, but the fact that as long as they continue they prevent thousands of able-bodied men, who are looking on, from realising that their country needs them. It is their duty to help their country when she calls, not to waste time gazing at football matches."

Boxing and racing also continued, but football attracted the most heated argument. The clubs took it upon themselves to devise their own approach as to how they would handle what was becoming a public relations nightmare, with most ignoring the League's recommendation in regard to money.

Fitzroy voted to donate all profits from the 1916 season to patriotic funds, while Essendon players voted to play as amateurs, with their usual match payments going towards the war effort. The VFL later ruled that all players would only receive money for out-of-pocket expenses.

But there was great division between the clubs on the League's overall stance. Melbourne was adamant the competition should be put on hold until the conclusion of the war and led a push for the decision to be overturned. At a meeting on February 18, 1916, Melbourne's position was supported by four other clubs: Essendon, St Kilda, South Melbourne and Geelong. But despite five of the nine clubs wanting to withdraw from the competition, their motion was defeated, as League rules required a three-quarter majority. Fitzroy, Collingwood, Carlton and Richmond sided against the push, creating a bitter divide between the clubs.

More pressure was placed on the VFL when the VFA unanimously voted to abandon its competition, determining "the playing of such matches would be detrimental to the Empire in its present crisis".

The Argus continued to receive angry letters. "I have been a follower of the game for 25 years, but to continue playing the game while this momentous struggle is on seems to me an unpardonable offence," wrote one reader, who described those who chose not to join the service as "eligible shirkers".

The day after its nine-team fixture was published in The Argus, the VFL was rocked by Melbourne's decision to pull out of the 1916 season. The revelation sparked a special meeting of the League, with the expectation that others would now follow. South Melbourne, Essendon and St Kilda were the next clubs to withdraw, while Geelong still intended to field a team, despite originally voting against the season continuing.

The meeting of club delegates on March 6 turned sour when a motion put forward by Fitzroy and Richmond was passed, blocking the four clubs from being able to stand out. The situation descended into a farce. "This is going to drag football through the dirt," South Melbourne president L. Thompson was quoted in The Argus. The four clubs seeking leave from the competition pleaded for common sense, but the clubs wanting to play couldn't see a viable season with only five teams lacing up.

Just days later, with no resolution in sight, five teams became four, when Geelong officially pulled the pin. Although far more serious battles were being fought in Europe, with the British Empire under threat, the VFA was facing the very real prospect of being another war casualty.

It certainly was not the preference of the four remaining clubs to play among themselves and they knew they were facing an uphill battle to force the other five teams to compete. So just 20 years after the formation of the VFL, when Carlton, Collingwood and Fitzroy were among the eight clubs to break away from the VFA and form their own competition, a similar plan was once again on the table.

With Richmond also on board, it was suggested the four clubs retire from the VFL and form a new body, with invitations extended to VFA clubs North Melbourne and Brunswick. But there appeared to be little public sympathy for the predicament of the four remaining clubs and the concept never eventuated..

After a fiery annual general meeting of the VFL on March 10, the nine clubs eventually came to an agreement. Melbourne, Essendon, St Kilda, South Melbourne and Geelong would be allowed to sit out the 1916 season, but still remain part of the League.

Despite several club delegates questioning the validity of a four-team competition, it was determined that Carlton, Collingwood, Fitzroy and Richmond would have to be content to play each other. Approaching the start of the season, all of the remaining clubs had sizeable holes to fill in their playing stocks. Fifteen Fitzroy players alone had already enlisted. But the clubs accepted the challenge of fielding teams each week, made tougher by the League ruling they weren't allowed to poach recruits from the districts of the five non-competing teams.

The clubs had more than a month to prepare for the season, after the League released arguably its most contentious ever fixture.

With the season to start on May 8, 12 rounds were scheduled, with teams to play each other four times during the regular season.

With a final four to commence in August, every team was certain to qualify, regardless of what happened during the home and away season. But it was going to be a tough exercise selling the competition to the wider community, with *The Argus* on March 30 summing up the public sentiment:

> On all sides, one hears expressions of disgust that competition matches should be played at such a time; and with teams meeting each other at least four, and perhaps six, times within three months, the game will be reduced to a farce. After the first couple of matches, the spirit of rivalry will be absent and with little public interest displayed, it will not be surprising if the competition does not fall through before the end of the season.

Less than three years after the team considered to be Fitzroy's greatest of all time won the 1913 premiership, the Maroons were forced to blood a plethora of new players in 1916, with no less than 11 players making their senior debuts during the year. But despite the loss of Cooper to patriotic duties, the inexperienced team still contained some of the club's all-time greats, particularly the forward combination of Percy Parratt and Jimmy Freake.

Parratt was an instant star of the competition after making his debut for Fitzroy in 1909, and was renowned for his great football brain. The playing-coach of the 1913 premiership side and the captain-coach in 1914-15, he did not have any leadership responsibilities in 1916, with George Holden taking over as playing coach and Wally Johnson the captaincy.

Known for his exquisite kicking skills, half-forward flanker Parratt regularly speared the ball onto the chest of the full-forward, Freake. One of only three Fitzroy players to top the League goalkicking table, Freake had wanted to play for Collingwood after growing up near Victoria Park. But with goalkicking great Dick Lee occupying the goalsquare, Freake was told his opportunities with the Magpies would be limited, so he joined the Roys in 1912. Despite his lack of height, Freake booted a club record 53 goals in his debut season and surpassed it with 56 in 1913 to lead the League. In 1915 he equalled Dick Lee's record tally of 66.

Parratt would prove instrumental in Fitzroy claiming the 1916 premiership, but Freake missed the Grand Final because of injury.

Parratt enlisted in the army after the 1917 season and did not return to football until 1920, again taking on coaching responsibilities. He and Freake featured in the 1922 premiership side and Parratt retired in 1923 after playing 196 games, a club record that stood for 22 years.

As the 1916 season approached, the newspapers were far from optimistic about the games attracting decent crowds. And football was hardly dominating the back pages in the way it does now, featuring below horse racing, bowls and billiards for prominence.

About 10,000 people watched Fitzroy defeat Carlton in the opening round at Princes Park, while a crowd of more than 6000 saw Collingwood beat Richmond at Punt Road, with *The Argus* noting an "absence of the enthusiasm usually noted at the beginning of a season". Despite five goals from Blues forward Vin Gardiner, the Maroons scraped home against Carlton by four points, with Freake booting four majors for the winners. At the conclusion of the following round, Fitzroy was sitting on top of the ladder after accounting for Richmond by 29 points, helped by another four goals from Freake.

Then the Roys' wheels fell off. It began with a draw against Collingwood at Brunswick Street after holding a slender lead all day. Heading into the final quarter with a four-point buffer, it was hardly an enthralling finish, with Fitzroy managing only two behinds in the last term and the Magpies sharing the points after a wayward finish of 0.6.

It was after the draw that one of the Maroons' great stalwarts, 28-year-old Harold 'Lal' McLennan decided to hang up the boots after succumbing to a recurring back injury.

For all of his adult life, McLennan was involved with the Fitzroy Football Club in one capacity or another, in a devotion that lasted more than 70 years. After making his debut in 1907, the centreman assumed the captaincy in 1911, during an unstable time at the club that was plagued with infighting and several players wanting to leave.

Throughout his career, McLennan insisted on playing as an amateur, refusing to accept match payments, but he did receive a generous wedding gift from the club of £25 and he missed a couple of games during the middle of 1912 to go on his honeymoon. While it's impossible to imagine a modern-day player getting married during the season, let alone going away on a honeymoon, it didn't hamper McLennan too much, because he still managed to win the club's best-and-fairest that year and back up again in the 1913 premiership year. McLennan later served the club as an administrator and was president in 1944 when the Roys won their last flag.

With the club great now watching on, Fitzroy began a horrible losing streak of nine straight matches, with Carlton beginning the rot; the Blues reversed the round one result with a comfortable 33-point win at Brunswick Street. Holding only a five-point lead at half-time, the Blues piled on eight goals to three after half-time, with Gardiner finishing with four.

Carlton established itself as the team to beat, dropping only two games in the home and away season to finish three and a half games clear of Collingwood on the top of the ladder and earn a second chance. But Fitzroy, with only two wins and a draw, was still in contention, thanks to the extraordinary circumstances.

"The absurdity of the competition was that every team had a chance in the finals," noted 'Observer' in The Argus. "It was possible for a club which never won a game in the first phase to defeat in the finals a side which had not lost a game."

The monotony of four teams playing each other so many times had taken its toll with spectators, with the already low crowd figures dropping by 60 per cent during the season. The Argus reported that less than a thousand people turned up to a Carlton versus Richmond game at Princes Park in round nine.

A record low finals attendance of fewer than 10,000 watched Fitzroy stun Collingwood in their semi-final at the MCG. Few gave the Roys any hope, especially with Jimmy Freake unable to play because of injury.

But with the Maroons able to restrict the Magpies when aided by a strong breeze in the second term, they came out after half-time and kicked 4.2 to just four behinds to set up a 13-point lead at the last change. They were led by some good work at centre half-forward by Tom Heaney and a young Horrie Jenkin, playing in his first final. With Jack Cooper's treasured No.5 on his back, Jenkin booted three pivotal goals and helped Fitzroy hold on to win by six points against a fast-finishing Collingwood. Jenkin later became one of the League's best defenders, in a career spanning 168 games.

With Carlton sneaking home against Richmond by three points in the other semi-final, an unlikely match-up was now in place for the decider. As the top team, the Blues had to win one more game to be declared premiers, but if Fitzroy won this first meeting, Carlton would be given a second chance.

More than 15,000 looked on as Fitzroy surprised yet again in a physical and bruising encounter. While Gardiner kicked three goals, the Blues struggled to find other scoring avenues, booting only five in total for the match, as the Maroons notched an unlikely 23-point win. In front by three points at the last change, the Blues were also unlucky with injuries, reduced to 17 men just before quarter-time and then 16 for the final term. (It was not until 1930 that a 19th man was introduced.) It proved telling in the finish, as Fitzroy ran over the top of the warm favourites.

Injuries forced the Blues to make three changes for the Grand Final and Fitzroy was also dealt a major blow with ruckman Chris Lethbridge, who had gallantly hobbled through the preliminary final after being hurt in an incident with Ted Brown; he was unable to back up.

With Freake still sidelined, Lal McLennan was coaxed out of retirement to take Lethbridge's spot in the side, and it proved an inspired decision.

The Grand Final at the MCG attracted the biggest crowd of the season, with 20,953 in attendance. But it was a long way short of the record 59,556 that had watched Fitzroy beat St Kilda in the 1913 decider.

Aided by the wind in the first quarter, the Maroons caught the Blues on the hop, booting three goals in the first 10 minutes, with youngster Bert O'Dee opening the scoring. The Blues became frustrated, and gave away several free kicks, before ruckman Harry Haughton drifted forward to kick truly and Gardiner slotted another. The Roys wasted several scoring opportunities but Heaney's first major gave them an 18-point buffer at the first break.

Fitzroy's pace and ability to run the ball provided the Blues with major headaches and the margin extended to a match-winning 30 points at half-time. A glorious high mark and goal from Heaney was the highlight of the quarter.

The Blues sent skipper and regular centre half-back Billy Dick forward in the third term and it paid dividends, with Dick booting two goals. But despite the solid efforts of he and Haughton, Carlton still trailed by 27 points at the last change. The Maroons were able to answer every challenge with Heaney and coach George Holden bobbing up with goals when needed and skipper Wally Johnson important at centre half-back with his fine marking skills.

When Charlie Fisher kicked the first goal of the last quarter for Carlton and Dick followed up with his third, Fitzroy's backline was momentarily rattled. The Blues had given themselves enough time to fight their way back into the match, but a crucial miss by Alex Lang in front of goal cost his side dearly and the Maroons steadied. Late goals to Jenkin and Parratt, who finished with three from half-forward, put the result beyond doubt and Fitzroy was celebrating the most remarkable of Grand Final victories.

Winners of the wooden spoon and premiership in the same year; it's unlikely to ever be done again—and one would hope it never is. But it's certainly worth remembering, the next time you're up for some footy trivia at the pub.

1916 FITZROY

PREMIER'S SEASON

FITZROY: 1916

ROUND ONE May 6
FITZROY 9.10 (64)
CARLTON 7.18 (60)
Best: Fitzroy – Freake, Bamford, Abbott, Parratt, Lenne, McLennan.
Goals: Fitzroy – Freake 4, Toohey 2, Lowrie, Parratt, Shaw.
Crowd: N/A at Princes Park

ROUND TWO May 13
FITZROY 9.12 (66)
RICHMOND 5.7 (37)
Best: Fitzroy – Johnson, Freake, Millen, Lowrie, Jenkin, Shaw, Toohey.
Goals: Fitzroy – Freake 4, Toohey 2, Jenkin, Shaw, McLennan.
Crowd: N/A at Brunswick St Oval

ROUND THREE May 20
FITZROY 7.8 (50)
COLLINGWOOD 6.14 (50)
Best: Fitzroy – Lethbridge, Lambert, Heaney, Purcell, Toohey, McLennan.
Goals: Fitzroy – Heaney 3, Toohey 2, Parratt, Freake.
Crowd: N/A at Brunswick St Oval

ROUND FOUR May 27
FITZROY 7.9 (51)
CARLTON 13.6 (84)
Best: Fitzroy – Heaney, Freake, Bamford, Parratt, Smith, Norris.
Goals: Fitzroy – Heaney 2, Freake 2, Purcell, Toohey, Parratt.
Crowd: N/A at Brunswick St Oval

ROUND FIVE June 5
FITZROY 9.14 (68)
RICHMOND 19.13 (127)
Best: Fitzroy – Abbott, Buist, Jenkin, Heaney, Johnson, Lethbridge.
Goals: Fitzroy – Jenkin 3, Heaney 3, Parratt, O'Keefe, Freake.
Crowd: N/A at Punt Road Oval

ROUND SIX June 5
FITZROY 8.17 (65)
COLLINGWOOD 11.13 (79)
Best: Fitzroy – Jenkin, McDonald, Johnson, Lenne, Lowrie, Lethbridge.
Goals: Fitzroy – King 2, Lowrie 2, Toohey 2, Lethbridge, Freake.
Crowd: N/A at Victoria Park

ROUND SEVEN June 17
FITZROY 7.8 (50)
CARLTON 10.19 (79)
Best: Fitzroy – Bamford, Freake, Holden, Parratt, G.King, Ballantyne.
Goals: Fitzroy – Freake 2, O'Dee, Jenkin, Toohey, Heaney, G.King.
Crowd: N/A at Brunswick St Oval

ROUND EIGHT June 24
FITZROY 7.13 (55)
RICHMOND 9.11 (65)
Best: Fitzroy – Holden, Purcell, Freake, Lowrie, Moore, Shaw, Johnson.
Goals: Fitzroy – Lowrie 2, Freake 2, Jenkin, Toohey, Heaney.
Crowd: N/A at Punt Road Oval

ROUND NINE July 8
FITZROY 8.10 (58)
COLLINGWOOD 8.11 (59)
Best: Fitzroy – Heaney, O'Dee, Johnson, Bamford, Lethbridge, Buist.
Goals: Fitzroy – Heaney 3, Parratt, Ballantyne, Toohey, Jenkin, Lowrie.
Crowd: N/A at Victoria Park

ROUND TEN July 15
FITZROY 8.14 (62)
CARLTON 11.15 (81)
Best: Fitzroy – Millen, Holden, Parratt, Lenne, Johnson, Lowrie.
Goals: Fitzroy – Lowrie 3, Freake 2, Heaney, Barrett, Toohey.
Crowd: N/A at Princes Park

ROUND ELEVEN July 22
FITZROY 9.11 (65)
RICHMOND 10.15 (75)
Best: Fitzroy – Holden, Freake, Abbott, Barrett, Bamford, Heaney.
Goals: Fitzroy – Parratt 3, Heaney 2, Lowrie, O'Dee, Holden, Freake.
Crowd: N/A at Brunswick St Oval

ROUND TWELVE July 29
FITZROY 8.9 (57)
COLLINGWOOD 11.9 (75)
Best: Fitzroy – Shaw, Lethbridge, Heaney, B.King, Lenne, Millen.
Goals: Fitzroy – Heaney 2, Lowrie 2, Parratt, Holden, Purcell, Shaw.
Crowd: N/A at Brunswick St Oval

PREMIER'S FINALS

FIRST SEMI-FINAL August 12
FITZROY	9.9 (63)
COLLINGWOOD	8.9 (57)

Best: Fitzroy – Johnson, Lethbridge, Buist, Millen, Heaney.
Goals: Fitzroy – Jenkin 3, Heaney 2, Lethbridge, Lowrie, Moore, Parratt.
Crowd: 9,690 at the MCG

FINAL August 26
FITZROY	9.11 (65)
CARLTON	5.12 (42)

Best: Fitzroy – Shaw, Lenne, Millen, Bamford, Buist, Norris, Holden.
Goals: Fitzroy – Heaney 4, Parratt 2, Lethbridge, Jenkin, Moore.
Crowd: 15,567 at the MCG

GRAND FINAL September 2
FITZROY	4.6 8.8 10.11 12.13 (85)
CARLTON	2.0 4.2 6.8 8.8 (56)

Best: Fitzroy – Millen, Johnson, Shaw, Norris, McLennan, Buist, Heaney.
Goals: Fitzroy – Heaney 3, Parratt 3, O'Dee 2, Lowrie, Moore, Jenkin, Holden.
Crowd: 21,130 at the MCG

GRAND FINAL LINE-UPS

FITZ	B:	B.King	B.Lenne	F.Bamford
CARL	F:	G.Callwell	V.Gardiner	A.Lang
FITZ	HB:	T.McDonald	W.Johnson (capt)	H.McLennan
CARL	HF:	C.Fisher	J.Shortill	P.Daykin
FITZ	C:	T.Buist	G.Holden	R.Millen
CARL	C:	E.Brown	J.Morris	D.Kelly
FITZ	HF:	B.O'Dee	T.Heaney	P.Parratt
CARL	HB:	P.O'Brien	W.Dick (capt)	W.Robinson
FITZ	F:	T.Lowrie	H.Jenkin	E.Purcell
CARL	B:	A.McDonald	S.Leehane	H.Greaves
FITZ	R:	C.Norris	F.Moore	G.Shaw
CARL	R:	H.Haughton	C.Hammond	V.Valentine
FITZ	Coach:	George Holden		
CARL	Coach:	Norman Clark		

SNAPSHOT

Win-loss record: 5-9-1

Highest score: 12.13 (85), Grand Final, v Carlton.

Greatest winning margin: 29 points, round 2, v Richmond; Grand Final, v Carlton.

Lowest score: 7.8 (50), round 3, v Collingwood; round 7, v Carlton.

Greatest losing margin: 59 points, round 5, v Richmond.

Most goals by a player in a game: 4, Jimmy Freake, round 1, v Carlton; round 2, v Richmond; Tom Heaney, preliminary final v Carlton.

Most consecutive wins: 3

Most consecutive losses: 9

Club awards: Leading goalkicker: Tom Heaney (27 goals).

Putting it into perspective:
The Roys' sixth premiership from only nine Grand Final appearances once again stamped them as the competition's most successful club, placing them ahead of the team they defeated in the Grand Final, Carlton.

1916

	P	W	L	D	%	Pts
1 Carlton (2)	12	10	2		137.2	40
2 Collingwood (3)	12	6	5	1	100.0	26
3 Richmond (4)	12	5	7		89.9	20
4 Fitzroy (1)	12	2	9	1	81.6	10

(12 home and away rounds)

PLAYERS USED

FITZROY	GUERNSEY	GAMES	GOALS
Abbott, Paddy	31	6	0
Ballantyne, Frank	32	4	1
Bamford, Fred	8	13	0
Barrett, Maurie	2	2	1
Buist, Teddy	1	10	0
Byrne, Charlie	0	1	0
Fergie, Clive	24	3	0
Freake, Jimmy	9	11	20
Gibaud, Bill	25	1	0
Heaney, Tom	21	15	27
Jenkin, Horrie	5	10	12
Johnson, Wally S.	14	14	0
King, Bob	16	7	0
King, George	15	6	3
Lambert, George	7	3	0
Lenne, Bert	11	12	0
Lethbridge, Chris	12	13	3
Lowrie, Tom	28	14	14
McDonald, Ted	23	11	0
McLennan, Harold	19	4	1
Millen, Roy	26	15	0
Moore, Fred	16	8	3
Norris, Charlie	22	7	0
O'Dee, Bert	29	13	4
O'Keefe, Frank	4	1	1
Parratt, Percy	20	13	15
Purcell, Teddy	6	12	2
Reeves, Bill	2	1	0
Shaw, George	17	14	3
Smith, Jim	18	4	0
Toohey, Jim	3	11	13
Walker, Harold	27	1	0

**COLLINGWOOD 9.20 (74) d
FITZROY 5.9 (39)**

HEAVY-HEARTED PREMIERSHIP

Their mates on the front lines were never far from the thoughts of the Collingwood players throughout a difficult year. By GLENN McFARLANE

A SALIENT reminder of the sacrifice others were making on the other side of the world arrived for Collingwood in September 1917. It came in the form of a horseshoe fashioned from a German shell from the Western Front and was inscribed with a message of "Good Luck". The other words engraved were: "To CFC. From Doc. France 1917." It had been sent by former Collingwood footballer Malcolm "Doc" Seddon, who had played with the club for five seasons before leaving for the war not long after the club's losing 1915 Grand Final. With it came a letter explaining that the horseshoe had been made out of a band of a German shell that Seddon had found at Bapaume, with nails driven into it that had come from pieces of a German plane shot out of the skies by Australian troops over the Somme. The message from Seddon, a Collingwood local from birth, was a simple yet inspirational one for his one-time teammates. His scrawl on the letter said: "I hope that this shoe will bring the boys to the top of the tree this year."

There was an added poignancy to Seddon's horseshoe: it was a gift that many within the Collingwood club considered a good omen. Seddon's best mate, and the man whom he played football with and who had enlisted on the same day as him, had been killed in action after a gunshot wound to the abdomen in December 1916—almost a year to the day since his disembarkation. To the football public, his name was 'Paddy Rowan'. But to his family and friends, he was known by his real name, Percy Rowe. He had taken on the sporting alias so that he could remain eligible to play with Collingwood in 1911, having already played under his given name in a country league match that same season. It was also to conceal from his mother that he had also come to Melbourne to box, as well as play football. Rowan's death had seriously impacted on Seddon, who was still fighting in France, and on his football club, which was chasing a fourth VFL premiership with the added incentive of doing it to honour the footballers who had made the supreme sacrifice.

Sacrifice was the prevailing mood at the time—in Australia and in almost every corner of the globe. And Collingwood coach 'Jock' McHale, a former teammate and coach of 'Rowan' and Seddon, was determined that his team would understand the sacrifice others were making in Europe, and those sacrifices required on a very different note that Collingwood would have to make to turn Seddon's talisman into a triumph. VFL football was not immune to the impact of war. Crowds and memberships were down almost from the moment that news of Australian casualties started filtering in from Gallipoli in 1915, and attendances only continued to plummet once the appalling figures of casualties arrived from France and Belgium in 1916, and beyond. There was a great divide in community sentiment about whether social events such as football and other sports should be curtailed in an attempt to throw everything into the war effort. Debate raged; speakers for and against argued relevant points, and the chasm between the two differing parties grew wider as the war raged on. Some believed the game provided the public with a chance of normality in a world that had seemingly gone mad. Others pointed out that instead of premiership medals, the VFL should hand out Iron Crosses. *The Age* even ran an editorial suggesting that players were either unpatriotic or cowards for not "joining up".

More so than just about any other club, Collingwood insisted that the game must go on. Magpies officials argued that football was the "working man's game" and that it acted as an important divergence and gave the public some respite from the plethora of pitiful news arriving daily with each new cable. The Magpies claimed that the game needed to be retained, but acknowledged—belatedly, it must be said—that costs must be kept to a minimum, that payments to players should be put on hold and that any profits should be redirected to the war effort. Some of this thinking was undoubtedly motivated by self-interest as much as selflessness. The committee knew that the club would be financially disadvantaged if the VFL went into recess. And while it undoubtedly supported Australian soldiers abroad and the war effort that surrounded it, the Magpies wanted the game to go ahead.

1917 COLLINGWOOD

The 1916 season had been a bizarre one. Only four teams competed—Collingwood, Carlton, Fitzroy and Richmond—over 12 rounds. Fitzroy won only two of those games, and drew another, to finish fourth (and last) on the ladder. Collingwood was second at the end of the home and away season. But after securing the 'wooden spoon', the Maroons won all three of their finals to win the most unlikely of premierships. To turn around a season as they had done was remarkable. They ended up beating the Magpies in week one of the finals (by six points) before upsetting minor premier Carlton twice in a fortnight to win the flag.

Early in 1917, the outlook for football was seemingly just as bleak. A few months out from what was meant to be the new football year, only Collingwood and Richmond were confirmed starters. There was much debate and discussion about what would happen, and who would play. As *The Argus* reported in late March: "The question as to whether League football should be played this season is again agitating the minds of the club delegates." In the end, Carlton and Fitzroy decided to play again, and South Melbourne and Geelong agreed to return to the competition, stretching the VFL to a more palatable six-team, 15-round season.

In an attempt to appease critics who claimed that football's continuation was playing a negative role in the war cause, the VFL decided to allow recruiting officers to speak—and spruik—to the crowds for the opening of the season. But these round-one recruiting campaigns were mostly met with a negative reaction. It was not that those attending games were unpatriotic. It was simply that they had paid to go through the turnstiles wanted to enjoy the game, and forget about the war for a few hours. There were enough reminders. They didn't need any more. The weekly dose of football had helped many of them forget about what was happening in Europe.

In early May, before Collingwood's season-opening game against Richmond at Victoria Park, Sergeant W.H. Durand told *The Argus* that he was treated well by the committee, but "the crowd was hostile, and it was hard to get a hearing, and, therefore, we abandoned the attempt." It was worse at the Brunswick Street Oval on the same day for Lieutenant R.H. Maskell, who said: "The majority of the public were adverse to us speaking, and hurled personal interjections at us... when we were coming down the stairs of the grandstand we were attacked by many men and women which necessitated our leaving the ground."

Collingwood had to make its own sacrifices. Payments to players were suspended, the entire team was limited to weekly expenses of five pounds and only one player was allotted "tea money" for the 1917 season ('Gus'

Dobrigh, who had to commute to Victoria Park from Mentone). Five players went further, according to Richard Stremski's *Kill For Collingwood*; Harry Curtis, Charlie Laxton, Matt Cody, 'Pen' Reynolds and Maurie Sheehy refused to take expenses. This attitude in terms of its patriotic efforts was in stark contrast to what existed at the club during the first two years of the war. But if things were tough off the field, they were more prosperous on it. After the win over Richmond (on the day the recruiting officers came to Victoria Park), Collingwood fell to Carlton in week two before steadying with five wins and a draw with Richmond over the next six weeks. South Melbourne accounted for Collingwood in round nine, and Carlton did the same in their return match three weeks later, to put pressure on the Magpies. Collingwood had been on top for all but the second and third weeks of competition, and retained it to the end of the home and away season, winning the minor premiership, despite a last-round loss to Geelong by two points at Corio Oval.

Still, there was nothing to worry about in the semi-final clash with South Melbourne. That performance, and the ease of the win, gave further credit to the club's premiership pretensions. At half-time the Magpies led by only 10 points. *The Argus* reported that: "In spite of bad weather, players kept their footing remarkably well, very few mistakes being made, and up to half-time, it was an interesting and an open match, for although Collingwood had a slight lead, their opponents were attacking just as often, without quite getting home." But after the long interval, and after a trademark half-time rev-up from McHale, a significant change came over the contest in the next half-hour. Collingwood kicked 8.4 to 0.1 in the third term, which was described as "a burst of success which robbed the match of further conviction". The final margin was 60 points, and those believing the Magpies were about to win their first flag in seven years were growing in confidence by the minute.

However, reigning premier Fitzroy had other ideas. The Maroons, who had had their score doubled by the Magpies in their previous encounter, in round 13, threw everything into the final. The clash between the fierce suburban rivals was described as "one of the keenest, closest struggles seen for a long time", according to 'Observer' of *The Argus*. Despite pre-game pleas from McHale that the club should not take the Maroons lightly, the Magpies appeared sluggish and far from the dominant force that they had appeared to be for much of the season. It didn't help that Laxton was injured early in the match. Collingwood narrowly held onto the lead at the first three breaks in the game—by three points at quarter-time; by the same margin at half-time; and by one point at three-quarter-time. But Fitzroy kept on coming, and had the better of the last term—but only just. Star forward Jimmy Freake kicked a goal late in the game to highlight the advantage for the Maroons. A late goal to Reynolds kept Collingwood's hopes alive, but only briefly. The final bell sounded with Fitzroy a goal clear, meaning a Grand Final was needed to settle the issue. As minor premiers, the Magpies had the right of challenge.

The return bout between the Magpies and Maroons was never going to be as aesthetic as the game the week before. Grand Final day, September 22, 1917, dawned with overcast skies after two days of soaking rain that had reduced the Melbourne Cricket Ground to muddy conditions. Still, the rain seemed to stay away through the morning and then for the start of the highly anticipated match. The attendance for the day was a strong 25,512—almost 4000 more than the previous year's play-off—in a sure sign that the mood was shifting in terms of football's popularity at a time when the tide of the war was also swinging—albeit delicately and marginally—in favour of the Allies. But that was cold comfort to the families of loved ones lost at that time. On the day that Collingwood met Fitzroy for the premiership, Casualty List No.330 issued from the defence department was revealed in *The Argus*. It recorded "no fewer than 537 out of a record of 1014 names were of those who had made the supreme sacrifice... in most cases there occurred the phrase 'previously reported missing' and the dates show that they were sustained at Pozieres where the Australians made so brilliant and successful an entrance early in the Somme campaign." As the Collingwood team was preparing for the contest, Seddon was also sick in a hospital unit in France.

Given the solemnity that had been a part of everyday life in Australia through the war years, there was an unusual hint of gaiety on Grand Final day. The crowds jostled for the best vantage points, and adults and children clambered for positions on the rooftops of the various stands. It prompted a rebuke from the correspondent from *The Australasian*, who warned: "If the custom of allowing youths and men to climb out on to the roofs of the various stands is not changed, serious accidents are bound to ensue." Fortunately, there would be no accidents that day, at least not from Collingwood's perspective. McHale was determined not to allow complacency emerge again, as it had the week before. This time he had a plan to use vigour on the wet ground to combat Fitzroy's lighter, leaner combination. The "heavy and holding" ground made for unattractive football, but that was hardly worth worrying about for the Black and White supporters. It was said, in *The Argus*, that Collingwood's performance that day was "more vigorous than scientific", but the McHale plan to physically hold out the Fitzroy team was one that the coach was determined to see through. Body-on-body football was the plan, and McHale believed implacably that it would bring success.

Importantly, the Magpies' most damaging player, Dick Lee, was passed fit to play just prior to the game, brushing off yet another knee injury. Now 28, and in his 12th season, Lee had played the first 14 games of the 1917 season. But his season had been placed in doubt after he aggravated his knee in the round-14 clash with South Melbourne. He missed the last round against Geelong, as well as the semi-final against South Melbourne and the Final against Fitzroy. Harry Curtis had done a sterling job in kicking five of the club's seven goals in the loss to Fitzroy. McHale wanted a dual-pronged attack of Lee and Curtis in the Grand Final. Fortunately, Lee was right to go, and despite some pain, he knew he had an important role to play. He had done so once before to help win a premiership—seven years earlier—when he kicked four goals. Lee would produce the same return on this day, and Curtis would not be far behind him.

From the outset, the 1917 Grand Final was a scrappy encounter, and tight and tense in the first half-hour. *The Australasian* described the opening term "as not a good one… It was evident that the players were overstrung, the play being too bunched and almost from the beginning feeling was shown." Collingwood appeared to be the main cause of this on most occasions, and it didn't take long for Fitzroy to start retaliating, reducing the contest to an aggressive arm-wrestle. The Magpies were the "leaders in the race for the ball", allowing them to take the early ascendancy, but the reward was not what it should have been. *The Argus* insisted that the difference at quarter-time should have been greater than 12 points—given the score of 2.6 to 1.0. "During the whole of the first quarter, Collingwood were playing rather the better game, but their superiority was represented mostly in single points."

Lee had kicked Collingwood's two opening-term goals, proving fitness was never going to be an issue for him. The first came from some canny hitting "out of a crush" from Con McCarthy, and it made for an easy goal. Then Lee received the ball from 'Snowy' Lumsden, and he made no mistake as he registered his—and the club's—second major. But the number of misses that should have been majors had McHale feeling more than a little uneasy about his team's wastefulness.

The Australasian, too, noted just how dominant the Magpies had been in the first term, but acknowledged that it might not necessarily equate to victory unless their accuracy returned. But while the forwards were inefficient, others were not. It was said that Collingwood's "(Percy) Wilson in the centre was very effective. He certainly roams far at times, but he has wonderful depth and dexterity, combined with exceptionally fine kicking. (George) Anderson, in defence, was at his top, with his pace, determination and two-footed kicking." McHale, a former star centreman who was now entrenched in defence in what was his last full-time season (he would play fill-in games in 1918 and 1920), would have been impressed with Wilson's performance. Wilson was on his way to being one of his team's best players.

But while the Magpies again had plenty of the play in the second term, they did not make an impression on the MCG scoreboard. They managed 1.2, the same as the Maroons could mustered. Wasteful play seemed to be the order of the day, though conditions hardly made for spectacular football. Fitzroy's Freake, who had hurt Collingwood the previous week with three goals, scored his first after a "penalty kick" . The free kick was clearly there for the fans to see, with *The Argus* saying it was the result of "too close attention by backs generally given to a capable forward". But the Magpies kept moving forward, with near misses to Curtis and then Lee, followed by an important third goal to Dobrigh. He more than earned his "tea money" when he "kicked a quick and clever goal from a pack", just before the half-time bell. Collingwood had maintained its 12-point lead at the long break, as McHale set about trying to use his half-time speech to produce another big third quarter.

During the interval, a military band marched around the ground, but was met with a lukewarm response. *The Argus* made a point of saying: "Apart from a very large contingent who were already in khaki, there was not a single man amongst the 28,000 who wanted any other game than football." The recruiting would have to wait for another day. There was a Grand Final to win; or lose.

The fans were treated to a better standard of play in the second half, with *The Australasian* saying "in a flash, the play from commonplace approached brilliancy." It was said that Fitzroy, sensing defeat, "assumed the aggressive approach... previously, they had been slow and uncertain, but they seemed to gather pace in an instant, and were a live body again." The change in game style proved beneficial for the Maroons, who slotted the first goal of the term to give their supporters hope. *The Argus* reported: "For 10 minutes there seemed to be every promise of Fitzroy recovering, and then the hope suddenly disappeared." A mix-up between the Fitzroy defenders, who seemed too intent on watching Lee, allowed an unattended Curtis to score for the Magpies. This was followed shortly after by a major from Les 'Flapper' Hughes, who had recovered from a "terrible collision" with Roy Millen. Lee's luck was momentarily out. Twice in the term he hit the goalpost, both of them high up. Then Curtis managed another goal late in the term to secure a comfortable 28-point three-quarter-time lead for Collingwood. McHale's anxiety was not totally extinguished, but he was feeling more comfortable.

The Magpies were only half an hour from a premiership, something that the 34-year-old craved as a coach. Two years earlier, he had coached his team to a loss to Carlton in the Grand Final. This time it was so close he could almost touch it.

The Collingwood camp was confident but not arrogant. The players were primed and ready, urging each other on. It was noted that "in their previous engagement, when refreshments were being distributed, the great majority of players laid full length on the grass, not so on this occasion. With one exception, they were all standing, ready and eager for the fray." While the war raged on across the other side of the world, the Magpies left in Melbourne were intent on winning this sporting battle. Still, Fitzroy was the first side to attack when play resumed in the last quarter. The Maroons knew goals—and quick ones at that—were the only way they were going to get back in the race for the flag. They kicked the opening two for the term, through Gordon Rattray and Jim Toohey, and a brief sense of unease swept through the Collingwood supporters in the crowd. But it was to be short-lived. Within a few minutes, *The Argus* deduced that the Maroons were a beaten side: "It was at once evident that Fitzroy had lost all hope. They played like a beaten side and there was no interest in the finish." Collingwood tightened the screws and went about putting on a number of forward thrusts that would lock in the result.

Curtis kicked his third goal, and Lee, considered a doubtful starter in the lead-up to the game, finished with two more goals—both from trademark high marks—to take his tally to four. *The Australasian* said: "It was fitting their champion forward Lee should, in the greatest match of all, give the side a lead by kicking the first goal and conclude the argument with the last." In the end, it wasn't much of an argument. Collingwood's three goals in the final term had extended the margin to 35 points. It was the highest Grand Final winning margin since 1906, when Carlton had beaten Fitzroy by 49 points. The 9.20 (74) scoreline included the highest number of behinds in a Grand Final to that stage, but not even McHale was worried about that. He had just won his first premiership as a coach, and he dreamed of winning more.

The Magpie players and supporters celebrated their fourth premiership wildly. For a few moments, they forgot about what was happening in another field—a much more deadly one—far away from the MCG. Some of the club's supporters, including leading benefactor John Wren, helped to pay for the premiership medals for the team. McHale was proud of his men. Their sacrifice was nowhere near as important as the one that young Australians were making on the Western Front, but the Magpies were at least "top of the tree" again. That's precisely what Seddon had desired when he sent the horseshoe good luck charm, and it would have been what his mate 'Paddy Rowan' would have wanted.

1917 COLLINGWOOD

PREMIER'S SEASON

COLLINGWOOD: 1917

ROUND ONE May 12
COLLINGWOOD	11.11 (77)
RICHMOND	4.4 (28)

Best: Collingwood – Curtis, D.Lee, Anderson, Drummond, Wilson, Laxton.
Goals: Collingwood – D.Lee 4, Hughes 3, Jose, Wraith, Cody, Curtis.
Crowd: N/A at Victoria Park

ROUND TWO May 19
COLLINGWOOD	8.6 (54)
CARLTON	13.7 (85)

Best: Collingwood – D.Lee, McHale, Sheehy, Wilson, C.Lee, Reynolds, Dobreigh.
Goals: Collingwood – D.Lee 3, Laxton, C.Lee, Wilson, Curtis, Wraith.
Crowd: N/A at Princes Park

ROUND THREE May 26
COLLINGWOOD	11.12 (78)
FITZROY	8.14 (62)

Best: Collingwood – Laxton, Green, Anderson, Sheehy, Hughes, D.Lee.
Goals: Collingwood – D.Lee 4, Saunders 2, Dobreigh 2, C.Lee, Hughes, Wraith.
Crowd: N/A at Brunswick St Oval

ROUND FOUR June 2
COLLINGWOOD	8.18 (66)
SOUTH MELBOURNE	6.9 (45)

Best: Collingwood – C.Pannam, D.Lee, Wraith, Saunders, Laxton, Reynolds, Curtis.
Goals: Collingwood – D.Lee 3, Laxton, Hughes, Reynolds, Dobreigh, Curtis.
Crowd: N/A at Victoria Park

ROUND FIVE June 9
COLLINGWOOD	8.9 (57)
GEELONG	6.7 (43)

Best: Collingwood – D.Lee, McHale, Brown, C.Pannam, Wilson, MacKechnie.
Goals: Collingwood – D.Lee 4, Saunders, Wraith, Curtis, McHale.
Crowd: N/A at Corio Oval

ROUND SIX June 16
COLLINGWOOD	6.14 (50)
RICHMOND	7.8 (50)

Best: Collingwood – McHale, Sadler, Wilson, Green, Colechin, D.Lee, Laxton.
Goals: Collingwood – D.Lee 3, Laxton, Curtis, Dobreigh.
Crowd: N/A at Punt Road Oval

ROUND SEVEN June 23
COLLINGWOOD	13.14 (92)
CARLTON	8.7 (55)

Best: Collingwood – Wilson, McCarthy, Mutch, Lumsden, D.Lee, C.Lee, Hughes.
Goals: Collingwood – Lumsden 5, D.Lee 4, Hughes 2, Saunders, Mutch.
Crowd: N/A at Victoria Park

ROUND EIGHT June 30
COLLINGWOOD	11.11 (77)
FITZROY	10.14 (74)

Best: Collingwood – C.Pannam, Curtis, D.Lee, Anderson, Sadler, Brown, Jose.
Goals: Collingwood – D.Lee 4, Lumsden 2, Reynolds, Wilson, Saunders, Hughes, Sheehy.
Crowd: N/A at Victoria Park

ROUND NINE July 7
COLLINGWOOD	10.13 (73)
SOUTH MELBOURNE	13.12 (90)

Best: Collingwood – Mutch, Wilson, C.Lee, Saunders, Wraith, D.Lee, Anderson.
Goals: Collingwood – D.Lee 3, Curtis 2, Hughes, Reynolds, Wilson, Mutch, Wraith.
Crowd: N/A at the Lake Oval

ROUND TEN July 14
COLLINGWOOD	10.19 (79)
GEELONG	2.11 (23)

Best: Collingwood – Drummond, Curtis, D.Lee, Colechin, McCarthy, Sadler.
Goals: Collingwood – D.Lee 4, Curtis 3, Sheehy, Lumsden, Sadler.
Crowd: N/A at Victoria Park

ROUND ELEVEN July 21
COLLINGWOOD	11.19 (85)
RICHMOND	7.7 (49)

Best: Collingwood – D.Lee, Reynolds, C.Pannam, Dobreigh, Wraith, Laxton, Green.
Goals: Collingwood – D.Lee 6, Wraith 3, Lumsden, Dobreigh.
Crowd: N/A at Victoria Park

ROUND TWELVE July 28
COLLINGWOOD	3.8 (26)
CARLTON	4.13 (37)

Best: Collingwood – Hughes, D.Lee, Wilson, Laxton, Sheehy, Anderson, Saunders.
Goals: Collingwood – C.Lee, D.Lee, Sheehy.
Crowd: N/A at Princes Park

ROUND THIRTEEN August 11
COLLINGWOOD	14.17 (101)
FITZROY	7.3 (45)

Best: Collingwood – D.Lee, Laxton, Sheehy, C.Pannam, Curtis, Mutch, McHale.
Goals: Collingwood – D.Lee 5, Wraith 3, Curtis 2, Reynolds, Laxton, Sheehy, Cross.
Crowd: N/A at Brunswick St Oval

ROUND FOURTEEN August 18
COLLINGWOOD	6.16 (52)
SOUTH MELBOURNE	2.9 (21)

Best: Collingwood – Reynolds, Hughes, C.Lee, Brown, D.Lee, Sadler, Saunders.
Goals: Collingwood – D.Lee 2, Sheehy, Dobreigh, Laxton, C.Pannam.
Crowd: N/A at Victoria Park

ROUND FIFTEEN August 25
COLLINGWOOD	9.9 (63)
GEELONG	8.17 (65)

Best: Collingwood – Dobreigh, Lumsden, McHale, Reynolds, Sharp, Mutch, Lumsden.
Goals: Collingwood – Lumsden 2, Mutch 2, Dobreigh 2, Laxton 2, McHale.
Crowd: N/A at Corio Oval

PREMIER'S FINALS

SECOND SEMI-FINAL September 8

COLLINGWOOD	13.17 (95)
SOUTH MELBOURNE	3.17 (35)

Best: Collingwood – Drummond, Curtis, Wilson, Anderson, Brown, Laxton, McCarthy.
Goals: Collingwood – Laxton 4, Curtis 4, Hughes 2, Wraith, Dobreigh, Lumsden.
Crowd: 16,505 at the MCG

FINAL September 15

COLLINGWOOD	7.10 (52)
FITZROY	8.10 (58)

Best: Collingwood – Curtis, Wilson, Anderson, Green, Mutch, C.Pannam, McCarthy.
Goals: Collingwood – Curtis 5, Reynolds, Wraith.
Crowd: 22,786 at the MCG

GRAND FINAL September 15

COLLINGWOOD	2.6	3.8	6.14	9.20	(74)
FITZROY	1.0	2.2	3.4	5.9	(39)

Best: Collingwood – Wilson, C.Pannam, Anderson, Drummond, Dobreigh, Saunders.
Goals: Collingwood – D.Lee 4, Curtis 3, Hughes, Dobreigh.
Crowd: 25,512 at the MCG

GRAND FINAL LINE-UPS

COLL	B:	J.McHale (capt)	H.Saunders	A.Mutch
FITZ	F:	J.Freake	L.Wigraft	T.Lowrie
COLL	HB:	G.Anderson	C.Brown	J.Green
FITZ	HF:	P.Parratt	T.Heaney	G.Rattray
COLL	C:	T.Drummond	P.Wilson	C.Pannam
FITZ	C:	R.Millen	G.Holden (capt)	C.Keller
COLL	HF:	G.Dobreigh	H.Curtis	C.Lee
FITZ	HB:	C.Lethbridge	J.Toohey	B.King
COLL	F:	C.McCarthy	D.Lee	E.Lumsden
FITZ	B:	B.Byrne	F.Bamford	A.Lenne
COLL	R:	L.Hughes	P.Reynolds	C.Laxton
FITZ	R:	F.Moore	C.Norris	T.McDonald
COLL	Coach:	Jock McHale		
FITZ	Coach:	George Holden		

SNAPSHOT

Win-loss record: 12-5-1

Highest score: 14.17 (101), round 13, v Fitzroy.

Greatest winning margin: 60 points, semi-final, v South Melbourne.

Lowest score: 3.8 (26), round 12, v Carlton.

Greatest losing margin: 31 points, round 2, v Carlton.

Most goals by a player in a game: 6, Dick Lee, round 11, v Richmond.

Most consecutive wins: 3

Most consecutive losses: 1 (five times).

Club awards: Leading goalkicker: Dick Lee (54 goals).

Putting it into perspective:
Collingwood's fourth premiership was its first since 1910; it had suffered Grand Final defeats in 1911 and 1915. It was the club's third Grand Final clash with Fitzroy and its final score of 9.20 (74) was its highest Grand Final score.

1917

	P	W	L	D	%	Pts
1 Collingwood (1)	15	10	4	1	133.4	42
2 Carlton (3)	15	9	5	1	116.4	38
3 South Melb (4)	15	9	6		118.0	36
4 Fitzroy (2)	15	6	8	1	86.4	26
5 Geelong (5)	15	6	9		79.3	24
6 Richmond (6)	15	3	11	1	79.8	14

(15 home and away rounds)

PLAYERS USED

COLLINGWOOD	GUERNSEY	GAMES	GOALS
Anderson, George	1	18	0
Brown, Charlie	2	17	0
Cody, Matt	6	2	1
Colechin, Bert	4	12	0
Cross, Harrie	0	1	1
Curtis, Harry	3	17	24
Dobrigh, Gus	7	14	10
Drummond, Tom	8	14	0
Green, Jack	9	10	0
Hughes, Les	10	16	12
Jose, Horrie	11	3	1
Laxton, Charlie	14	16	11
Lee, Charlie	12	15	3
Lee, Dick	13	15	54
Lumsden, Ernie	26	12	12
MacKechnie, Sam	16	7	0
McCarthy, Con	18	8	0
Mutch, Alec	27	12	4
Pannam, Charlie	19	16	1
Reynolds, Pen	20	18	5
Sadler, Jim	21	7	1
Saunders, Harry	23	15	5
Sharp, Jim	0	1	0
Sheehy, Maurie	23	15	5
Wilson, Percy	24	18	3
Wraith, Tom	25	16	13

**SOUTH MELBOURNE 9.8 (62) d
COLLINGWOOD 7.15 (57)**

FLAG TINGED WITH BLOOD

With World War I nearly over, interest in football reached fever pitch when South Melbourne and Collingwood contested the Grand Final. By JIM MAIN

TO USE an Australian expression in use when South Melbourne and Collingwood played off in the 1918 Grand Final, there was "blood on the wattle".

Almost every Australian household felt the pain and anguish of the Great War. More than 60,000 sons, lovers, brothers and friends were killed. Just as many were maimed and there was mourning in bush shanties and suburban mansions alike.

Far less relevant was that the war reduced the VFL competition to a rump in 1916, with just four teams—Fitzroy (premier), Collingwood, Richmond and Carlton—remaining in the competition.

Geelong and South Melbourne returned to the competition in 1917, making it six teams, and Collingwood defeated Fitzroy in the Grand Final. Essendon and St Kilda rejoined in 1918, bringing the number of clubs to eight and leaving Melbourne the only VFL club in recess.

No one knew it when the VFL season opened in 1918 that the long and exhausting war would be over within months, although news from the Front was encouraging. The Germans had made a massive push for victory in July 1918 but, by the time the Grand Final was played on September 7, optimists could sniff the end of the war.

On the morning of the opening round of the 1918 season, on May 11, the only football coverage in *The Argus* was a listing of the four VFL matches to be played: Richmond v Essendon, South Melbourne v Geelong, Collingwood v Carlton and St Kilda v Fitzroy. The only other sports news *The Argus* published that day was that special trains would operate for the race meeting at Williamstown.

On the other hand, there were several long war reports—all encouraging.

All VFL clubs had been severely affected by the war, with South suffering more than most. The Southerners' "honoured dead" included 1911 Champion of the Colony Bruce Sloss, 1914 club leading goalkicker Jack Freeman, defender Jack Turnbull and the versatile Hugh Callan, a player *The South Melbourne Record* described as "quick, clever and daring".

Several Collingwood players also had made the supreme sacrifice, with Alan Cordner killed in the landings at Gallipoli on April 25, 1915, and champion follower Percy Rowe killed in action 18 months later on the Somme.

Collingwood, the reigning premier, maintained the status quo from 1918, with Jock McHale in his seventh season as coach and Percy Wilson in his second as captain.

Wilson had started with Collingwood in 1909 after being recruited from local club Collingwood Trades. Originally a rover, Wilson moved into the centre when Dan Minogue left for war service and became one of the best players in the competition.

From 1913, Collingwood had the unusual arrangement of McHale coaching the side, but not as Magpie captain. Minogue had captained Collingwood from 1914-16, but with Minogue's departure, the players elected McHale captain for 1917. However, he played just nine games that season because of injury, with Wilson taking over as captain and retaining the position for 1918 when McHale indicated he would play only if required. In fact, McHale played just the one game in 1918, against Essendon. He played another game in 1920, but his playing career was virtually over in 1917.

South, on the other hand, had appointed former player Herb (sometimes known as Bert) Howson as non-playing coach in 1918. It had been assumed for decades that another former player, Henry "Sonny" Elms, had been joint coach and most record books indicate this, but the South Melbourne Annual Report, released in February 1919 states, "Mr H. Howson was appointed with the assistance of Mr H. Elms."

Howson had been a star winger with South in the club's VFA years and then played 152 VFL games with the Southerners from 1897-1910. Elms also had been a star South winger, but had retired well before the formation of the VFL in 1897. He had captained South to consecutive VFA flags from 1888-1890.

Champion ruckman Vic Belcher had been South captain-coach in 1917 but was demoted to vice-captain under classy winger Jim Caldwell in 1918. Caldwell, who had made his South debut in 1909 after being recruited from VFA club Williamstown, missed the 1909 premiership triumph because of suspension.

This meant that the lion-hearted Belcher was South's only premiership player going into the 1918 season, and although the Southerners had other fine ruckmen in Jack Howell and Tom O'Halloran, much of their second-premiership ambitions lied with Belcher.

Collingwood's 1918 recruits included Heidelberg speedster Bill Twomey, who went on to win the 1924 Stawell Gift, and Port Melbourne (VFA) forward Bill Walton.

While Collingwood relied mainly on its 1917 premiership players, South embarked on a massive recruiting drive and blooded no less than 12 new players, including six who went on to play in the 1918 premiership side. Those six were Jack Graham, Samuel "Chip" Turner, Tammy Hynes, Tom O'Halloran, Ernie Barber and Chris Laird.

Both South and Collingwood opened the season well, with the Southerners defeating Geelong and then Fitzroy, while the Magpies disposed of Carlton and then Geelong.

South and Collingwood then clashed at the Lake Oval in round three and when the Red and White triumphed by 18 points the football world hailed a new premiership favourite.

However, the Southerners stumbled to St Kilda the following week—in extraordinary circumstances, with little or nothing known about the cause of South's demise until decades later.

Following the death of 1918 premiership player Mark Tandy in 1965, *The South Melbourne Record* published some interviews with the champion Southerner. Included is Tandy's full account of the five-point loss to St Kilda at the Junction Oval in round four, 1918.

Tandy told the newspaper of how South had been scheduled to play St Kilda on the Monday afternoon of the King's Birthday long weekend and of the team's bizarre lead-up to the match.

He explained: "We were sitting at the top of the League ladder and one of our patrons—a well-known racing man—invited us to spend the weekend at his beautiful home in the Dandenongs, and return to Melbourne on Monday morning for the afternoon match against St Kilda.

"Boy, will I ever forget that wet cupboard—or that weekend! Most of us did not shut eyes for 48 hours, and when they put us on the train at Ferntree Gully near midday, that sleep to Flinders Street was the only shut-eye we had to freshen us up for the game.

"Some of the boys were wobbling at the knees when they walked from the St Kilda train across to the St Kilda Oval. Fair dinkum, when some were dressed to go out on the field, they had to be headed in the direction of the arena gate and given a shove-off. That they ever saw out the game was a miracle."

That long, "wet" weekend cost South what would have been a unique record as the St Kilda defeat was its only loss for the season and, to date, no club has gone through an entire season undefeated.

South's form over the rest of the home and away season was impeccable and it finished on top of the ladder three games clear of Collingwood, which had a slighter better percentage.

One of South's biggest tests was against Carlton at Princes Park in round 12. South had not won there for 11 years, but on this occasion they triumphed by 12 points to underline the Southerners' premiership prospects.

Two weeks earlier, when South defeated Collingwood by seven points at Victoria Park in round 10, the Southerners had become firm premiership favourites, with the Magpies considered their only real threat.

Collingwood had been defeated four times during the home and away season—twice by South Melbourne and also falling to Carlton at Princes Park (by eight points in round eight) and to St Kilda at the Junction Oval (by 13 points in round 12).

The final four consisted of South, Collingwood, Carlton and St Kilda and, under the system operating at that time, Collingwood (second) played St Kilda (fourth) in one semi-final, with South (first) scheduled to clash with Carlton (third) in the other semi-final the following week. Collingwood, as it happened, appeared to be the club under most pressure in the finals as it had been defeated by the other three clubs during the home and away season.

Collingwood reversed its round 12 result against St Kilda by defeating the Saints by nine points at the MCG, but the South-Carlton clash at the same venue had to be postponed a week because of heavy rain. Parts of South Yarra and Richmond were flooded and market gardens along the Yarra were also under water.

When they did play, South scraped home by five points, thanks to late goals by O'Halloran and Jack (sometimes referred to as "Jock") Doherty, and the football public had what it wanted—a South-Collingwood final—with one proviso: if the Magpies defeated the Southerners, the minor premier would have the right of challenge in a Grand Final.

There was very little newspaper publicity in the lead-up to the final and, in fact, *The Argus* on the morning of the match ran just one paragraph at the bottom of page 17: "The match between South Melbourne and Collingwood for the League premiership will be played today at the Melbourne Cricket-ground (sic). Should South Melbourne be defeated, they will have the right, as minor premiers, to another lay-off."

Naturally, the news centred mainly on the war, with numerous reports, including one which read: "The Allies have advanced their whole line so far that there now seems no chance of the Germans being able to make even a temporary rally."

In Melbourne, the weather forecast for the day of the final was for a fine day with mild temperatures. A crowd of 39,262 flocked to the ground.

Although the Yarra was still flooded from the heavy rain from two weeks earlier, the MCG playing surface was in reasonably good condition and fans expected a classic encounter. They were not disappointed.

South had the form, but Collingwood had a vastly more experienced side; 12 of the team had played in its 1917 premiership side. The six newcomers were Twomey, Walton, Maurice Sheehy, Tom Wraith, Albert Colechin and Ernest "Snowy" Lumsden.

South, apart from Belcher, was in new territory as the Red and White had not made a Grand Final since going down to Carlton by six points in 1914. Belcher, Caldwell, Tandy and Aloysius "Alan" O'Donoghue were the only survivors from that side going into the 1918 flag decider.

The VFL would have been delighted with the Grand Final attendance of almost 40,000 as the previous year's Collingwood-Fitzroy Grand Final had attracted just 25,512 fans. One of the MCG stands was reserved for servicemen in uniform, with free admission.

If the less experienced Southerners were nervous, they did not show it in the opening minute; kicking with the aid of a southerly breeze, they attacked relentlessly. South's Harold Robertson kicked the first goal of the match, but Collingwood quickly replied through a snapshot by champion forward Dick Lee.

The Magpies then held sway for most of the quarter only for South to kick a late goal to restrict Collingwood's quarter-time lead to six points.

Collingwood also controlled the second quarter, but could manage just one goal—again from Lee, this time after a one-handed mark. The Magpies twice

NOT THE GRAND FINAL Action from a clash at the MCG between Melbourne and Essendon in 1897. There was no Grand Final played that year. Instead, Essendon emerged with the best record after a round-robin finals series.

BACK TO BACK Fitzroy defeated South Melbourne by one point to win its second successive premiership, in 1899. The team included Mick Grace (second row from bottom, fourth from left), captain Alec Sloan (fifth from left) and Bill McSpeerin (sixth from left).

METEORIC RISE Melbourne took advantage of the system of the day to cut a swathe through the finals to win its first premiership. The team included Vic Cumberland (second row from bottom, far left), Fred McGinis (second from left), captain Dick Wardill (third from left), Eddie Sholl (fourth from left) and George Moodie (fifth from left).

MARKING CONTEST In 1902, Collingwood lost just two matches, and won its first flag by defeating Essendon by 33 points in the Grand Final.

WHAT'S THE SCORE? The scoreboard has robbed Fitzroy of six points, but the Maroons still trailed Collingwood well into the final quarter of the 1903 Grand Final at the MCG. The Magpies won by two points.

FIRST TO THE BALL Carlton rover Arch Snell (left) and Fitzroy's Ernie Jenkins race for the ball in the 1904 Grand Final, which the Maroons won by 24 points.

BIG DAY FOR BLUES Carlton's 1906 premiership flag is unfurled at Princes Park on April 27, 1907, the opening day of the season. Sadly for the Blues, St Kilda spoiled the party, winning by 26 points.

TOP BLUES This picture was taken before Carlton's round-three match against Essendon in 1908. It includes Frank 'Silver' Caine (back row, second from right), George Bruce (middle row, third from left), Fred Elliott (middle row, fifth from left), Alex Lang (front row, second from left) and Norman Clark (front row, second from right). Carlton won the 1906-08 premierships.

PASSIONS INFLAMED Collingwood's defeat of Carlton in the 1910 Grand Final sparked the heated rivalry between the two clubs that exists to this day. The Blues, however, have won the next five Grand Finals between the clubs.

AN EARLY SUPERSTAR Ruckman Fred Baring was a true great of the Essendon Football Club, playing 154 games, including four premierships. He was also a state cricketer for Victoria.

ALL ON THE LINE Things got willing in the 1913 Grand Final between Fitzroy and St Kilda at the MCG, with the Maroons needing to exercise their right of challenge in order to win the premiership.

FLYING HIGH The big men of Carlton and Collingwood fly for the ball in the 1915 Grand Final at the MCG, the first to be played under the serious shadow of a nation at war. The Blues won by 33 points.

NOTHING IN IT South Melbourne claimed its second premiership in 1918 when Chris Laird kicked the winning goal off the ground just seconds before the final bell in the clash against Collingwood. The final margin was five points.

EAT 'EM ALIVE Richmond broke through for its first premiership in 1920, under the coaching of former Collingwood forward Dan Minogue (middle row, fourth from left). Others in the photo include Barney Herbert (back row, fifth from left), Vic Thorp (middle row, sixth from left), Frank Hughes (bottom row, far left) and Clarrie Hall (bottom row, middle).

MOSQUITO FLEET Essendon outlasted Fitzroy in the 1923 Grand Final to win by 17 points. Included here are Fred Baring (back row, second player from left), Syd Barker (captain-coach, middle row, middle), Justin McCarthy (middle row, fifth from left), Rowley Watt (bottom row, far left) and Charlie Hardy (bottom row, middle).

ALL SMILES Geelong is on its way to its way to the 1925 premiership, the first in club history, and so relaxed is the mood at three-quarter time, with the Cats up by 25 points, that Cliff Rankin, Lloyd Hagger and Eric Fleming pose for this photo.

FAIREST AND BEST Edward 'Carji' Greeves (above) was not just the first winner of the Brownlow Medal for the League's fairest and best player, in 1924, he was also a key player in Geelong's maiden premiership win the following season.

CLUB GREAT Sydney-born and Wesley College-educated Ivor Warne-Smith was one of the first great champions of the Melbourne Football Club, playing in the 1926 premiership team and winning the 1926 and 1928 Brownlow Medals.

MUDBATH Collingwood won the 1927 Grand Final, played in the most atrocious conditions at the MCG, despite kicking just two goals for the match. Only 34,551 were in attendance, with many leaving at half-time.

TOUGH MAN Collingwood's Albert Collier was one of the champions of Collingwood's greatest era and played in six Magpie premiership teams, in 1927-30 and 1935-36.

THE MACHINE Collingwood won four consecutive premierships from 1927 to 1930. Its 1929 team, pictured here, included coach Jock McHale (in suit), Gordon Coventry (back row, seventh player from left), Harry Collier (back row, far right), Bruce Andrew (front row, second from left), Syd Coventry (front row, fifth from left) and Albert Collier (sixth from left).

TIGERS OF OLD Perc Bentley (left) and Allan Geddes (right) flank coach Frank 'Checker' Hughes. They were key components in Richmond's 1932 Grand Final win over Carlton. By the next season, Hughes had crossed to Melbourne.

FOREIGN LEGION South Melbourne dominated the second half of the 1933 season to win the premiership. The premiership photo includes president Archie Crofts (middle row, middle), Laurie Nash (second bottom row, third from left) and Bob Pratt (second bottom row, third from right).

ALL ROUNDER Laurie Nash, wearing No.25 and in action here against Richmond in the 1933 Grand Final, was a brilliant key defender and forward for South Melbourne. He also played Test cricket for Australia.

BURSTING AT THE SEAMS A crowd of 74,091 crammed into the MCG to see Collingwood defeat South Melbourne in the 1936 Grand Final. Note the two players still shaking hands and the cricketers in the background.

OFFICIAL BUSINESS Collingwood captain Albert Collier, Victorian Governor Lord Huntingfield and South Melbourne captain Jack Bisset take a moment before the action begins in 1936.

GREAT GAME Geelong's 1937 team won one of the most celebrated Grand Finals. Included here are Reg Hickey (back row, fifth from left), Joe Sellwood (behind Hickey), Tom Arklay (back row, second from right), Peter Hardiman (front row, far left), Tommy Quinn (front row, third from left) and Gordon Abbott (front row, far right).

THE PEOPLE'S GAME The completion of the Southern Stand in 1937 allowed crowds of more than 80,000 to attend Grand Finals at the MCG. With the ground already bursting at the seams for that year's flag decider between Geelong and Collingwood, calls for even more new grandstands at the MCG started afresh.

ENDING THE DROUGHT Carlton's 1938 premiership team, led by former South Melbourne star Brighton Diggins (second bottom row, middle), ended a 23-year run of outs. Also included here are Bob Chitty (back row, far left), Harry 'Soapy' Vallence (second bottom row, third from left) and Jim Francis (second bottom row, fifth from left).

hit the post from hurried shots and, with a little more luck, could have taken control. They led by 16 points at the main break.

The half-time break saw recruiting sergeants spruiking the virtues of signing for war service. However, *The Argus* reported that "no recruits came forward" and added: "The eligible among the crowd evidently thought that only one game counted."

Whereas the first half had been tough and tight, South tried to break into the open as often as possible from the start of the third quarter in an effort to out-speed the bigger Collingwood side. *The Argus* noted: "South Melbourne for the first time showed a glimpse of their true form."

South clawed their way back into the match when Robertson scored following a scramble in the goalsquare, and just minutes later Ernest Barber kicked a goal following a brilliant run through the centre by Artie Woods.

The only problem was that Collingwood replied almost immediately with a goal by Les Hughes. The Magpies appeared to temporarily regain their composure, but misses by Lee and Lumsden proved costly as South whipped the ball forward for Laird to goal.

Collingwood still held a handy lead of 12 points at the final break, but Magpie nerves were fraying. South, realising it had to get its small men into the play, switched Belcher from defence to the ruck—with tremendous success.

Belcher became the South engine-driver and played a huge role in the Southerners attacking in waves. After Collingwood had thwarted several South thrusts, the Southerners grabbed the goal they needed, through Mick Ryan (who won further fame in 1932 when he won the Australian Open golf crown).

When Ryan kicked a second goal minutes later, Collingwood fans shouted in protest, not only at seeing their team's lead dissipate, but because they thought umpire Jack Elder had awarded Ryan a dubious mark.

The scores now were level and Collingwood was on the back foot. But, when Lumdsen scored a behind for Collingwood with just three minutes to play, it appeared the Magpies would hold on for a hard-earned victory.

It was not to be. South refused to surrender and attacked relentlessly. Tandy was brilliant in the final minutes and, along with Ryan, helped move the ball to the forward line where Laird thrust his right foot at the ball—for a goal.

The bell rang less than 30 seconds later. The Southerners had won by five points. They were the 1918 premiers. Happy supporters mobbed the players—particularly Laird—in celebration of the club's second flag, following the 1909 triumph.

The Argus reported: "The game, which was all in favour of Collingwood in the first half, improved considerably in the third and fourth quarters, South Melbourne finishing better than their opponents."

In summary, the report read, "Whether placed or following, O'Halloran was always in the thick of it and easily was South's best man. Howell also rendered invaluable assistance, his high-marking being good.

"Of the back men, Turner, in goal, kicked off well and was ably supported in defence by O'Donoghue and (Arthur) Rademacher. Tandy and Woods shaped well across the centre line, while Laird (three goals) and Ryan (three goals) both proved themselves to be tricky forwards."

On Collingwood, *The Argus* reported: "No one on the Collingwood side worked harder to stave off defeat than Hughes, whose work, whether on the ball or in a place, stamped him as the finest performer of the match and one of the best players of the season.

"He was closely followed by Walton, who played clean and effective football. On the back line (Harry) Saunders in goal was perhaps the pick, while (Charlie) Pannam, Wilson and Twomey were a very effective centre line, Pannam in particular having the best of the duel with his man.

"R. (Dick) Lee (three goals) was as cool as ever forward, while Lumsden and (Charles) Laxton towards the finish were also prominent."

Although *The Argus* nominated South's O'Halloran and Collingwood's Hughes as the best players on the ground, *The Australasian's* John Worrall, who had coached Carlton to the 1906-08 flags, thought otherwise and nominated South's Belcher as best on ground for turning the match when shifted into the ruck for the final quarter.

Worrall wrote: "Caldwell, though not doing much (as South captain-coach), made an extremely clever move in putting Belcher in the ruck... The move won the game, I verily believe, for Belcher played brilliantly in the last term."

Belcher, in helping lift South to the 1918 flag, therefore became the only player in the club's history to date to play in two premiership sides as he also had been a star in the 1909 triumph.

For some unknown reason, Belcher received only one premiership medallion, for his 1918 premiership effort, and this was the only trophy he retained after answering a call from the Australian government during World War II for citizens to donate metal to be melted down for war use.

Belcher went on to play 226 games with South to the end of the 1920 season. *The Herald's* 'Kickero' wrote at that time: "Belcher has been one of the most likeable footballers who have worn the South Melbourne uniform. He has played the game as it should be played—in the manliest spirit, has taken and given bumps in the proper spirit, and has never shown bad temper."

Belcher, who was non-playing coach of Fitzroy's 1922 premiership side and also coached VFA club Brunswick and Launceston City, died in 1977 at 88 years of age.

O'Halloran, one of South's other premiership heroes, had been recruited from VFA club Williamstown and was rated one of the best followers of his era. He played 62 games for South from 1918-21 and represented Victoria three times.

Laird, who kicked South's winning goal in that famous last-minute goal-mouth scramble, had been recruited from NSW club Paddington and played 59 games for the Southerners from 1918-22.

'Flapper' Hughes, rated best on the ground by *The Argus,* like skipper Wilson had joined the Magpies from Collingwood Trades and was enormously popular with Magpie fans.

South's triumph was all the more satisfying because the club learned just before the finals that yet another of its former players had been killed in action.

Private Claude Thomas, who had played 13 games with South from 1914-15 and in 1917, was killed during a push against the Germans at Hamel, France. the *Football Record* of July 27, 1918, paid this tribute: "Claude Thomas, the brilliant wing man of South Melbourne, was killed in action in France on July 5. He is the fifth of the red and white club who have given their lives for their country. The others were Bruce Sloss, Jack Freeman, Norman Bradford and Hughie Callan."

This was slightly incorrect as another former South player, Fred Fielding, had been killed in action at Villers-Bretonneux on August 8, 1918.

Also, the *Football Record* did not refer to Jack Turnbull and another South player who had been killed in action—Jack Fincher (nine games in 1913), who was among those killed at the Gallipoli landings.

The South Melbourne Annual Report for the 1918 season paid tribute to all of the club's fallen footballers and also noted: "In annexing the premiership of 1918, your team have been congratulated from all quarters, and more particularly by their opponents on the field."

South unfurled its 1918 premiership flag at the Lake Oval before its opening round match against Collingwood the following season. However, the Magpies scored a 13-point upset. This was the first "peace time" season since 1913, with Melbourne returning to the competition for a full complement of clubs and Footscray, Hawthorn and North Melbourne joining the VFL in 1925.

1918 SOUTH MELBOURNE

PREMIER'S SEASON

SOUTH MELBOURNE: 1918

ROUND ONE May 11
SOUTH MELBOURNE	7.15 (57)
GEELONG	4.7 (31)

Best: South Melbourne – Caldwell, Brennan, Boyce, Robertson, Howell, Belcher.
Goals: South Melbourne – Howell 2, Robertson 2, Barber, Boyce, Sampson.
Crowd: N/A at the Lake Oval

ROUND TWO May 18
SOUTH MELBOURNE	12.6 (78)
FITZROY	5.8 (38)

Best: South Melbourne – Daly, Hynes, Barber, Graham, Morgan, Howell, Belcher.
Goals: South Melbourne – Barber 3, G.Ryan 2, Howell 2, Robertson, Tandy, Doherty, Boyce, Caldwell.
Crowd: N/A at Brunswick St Oval

ROUND THREE May 25
SOUTH MELBOURNE	12.13 (85)
COLLINGWOOD	9.13 (67)

Best: South Melbourne – G.Ryan, Barber, Caldwell, O'Halloran, Robertson, Belcher, Morgan.
Goals: South Melbourne – Barber 3, G.Ryan 3, Robertson 2, Boyce 2, O'Halloran, Howell.
Crowd: N/A at the Lake Oval

ROUND FOUR June 4
SOUTH MELBOURNE	6.8 (44)
ST KILDA	6.13 (49)

Best: South Melbourne – Howell, Tandy, Graham, Wood, Hynes, Belcher, Robertson.
Goals: South Melbourne – Howell 3, Robertson, Boyce, Doherty.
Crowd: N/A at the Junction Oval

ROUND FIVE June 8
SOUTH MELBOURNE	11.10 (76)
CARLTON	10.12 (72)

Best: South Melbourne – G.Ryan, Wood, Laird, Daly, Tandy, Caldwell, Howell.
Goals: South Melbourne – G.Ryan 5, Barber, Caldwell, Robertson, Howell, Morgan Hair.
Crowd: N/A at the Lake Oval

ROUND SIX June 15
SOUTH MELBOURNE	7.10 (52)
ESSENDON	4.8 (32)

Best: South Melbourne – Graham, Wood, Tandy, Belcher, G.Ryan, Brennan, Barber.
Goals: South Melbourne – G.Ryan 3, Laird, Belcher, Robertson, Tandy.
Crowd: N/A at East Melbourne Cricket Ground

ROUND SEVEN June 22
SOUTH MELBOURNE	12.14 (86)
RICHMOND	4.10 (34)

Best: South Melbourne – Laird, Belcher, Daly, G.Ryan, Rademacher, Wood.
Goals: South Melbourne – Laird 6, G.Ryan 3, Brennan 2, Howell.
Crowd: N/A at the Lake Oval

ROUND EIGHT June 29
SOUTH MELBOURNE	7.13 (55)
GEELONG	7.8 (50)

Best: South Melbourne – Graham, Robertson, Skehan, O'Halloran, Belcher, G.Ryan.
Goals: South Melbourne – G.Ryan 2, Laird, Howell, Robertson, Bulpit, Caldwell.
Crowd: N/A at Corio Oval

ROUND NINE July 6
SOUTH MELBOURNE	12.14 (86)
FITZROY	8.13 (61)

Best: South Melbourne – Brennan, Graham, O'Donoghue, O'Halloran, Laird.
Goals: South Melbourne – Laird 4, O'Halloran 2, G.Ryan 2, Bulpit 2, O'Donoghue, Robertson.
Crowd: N/A at the Lake Oval

ROUND TEN July 13
SOUTH MELBOURNE	7.9 (51)
COLLINGWOOD	6.8 (44)

Best: South Melbourne – Belcher, Robertson, Tandy, Wood, Turner, Morgan, Barber.
Goals: South Melbourne – Barber 2, Laird, Wood, O'Halloran, Tandy, G.Ryan.
Crowd: N/A at Victoria Park

ROUND ELEVEN July 20
SOUTH MELBOURNE	14.17 (101)
ST KILDA	7.9 (51)

Best: South Melbourne – G.Ryan, Caldwell, Prince, Graham, Robertson, Barber, Howell.
Goals: South Melbourne – G.Ryan 5, Barber 4, Laird, Howell, Morgan, Robertson, Doherty.
Crowd: N/A at the Lake Oval

ROUND TWELVE July 27
SOUTH MELBOURNE	8.7 (55)
CARLTON	5.13 (43)

Best: South Melbourne – Rademacher, Wood, Robertson, Laird, Belcher, Tandy, Prince.
Goals: South Melbourne – Laird 4, Barber, G.Ryan, Howell, Robertson.
Crowd: N/A at Princes Park

ROUND THIRTEEN August 3
SOUTH MELBOURNE	12.13 (85)
ESSENDON	7.10 (52)

Best: South Melbourne – Graham Talbot, Daly, Robertson, Howell, Laird, Caldwell.
Goals: South Melbourne – Laird 3, Howell 3, Robertson 2, Caldwell 2, Barber, G.Ryan.
Crowd: N/A at the Lake Oval

ROUND FOURTEEN August 10
SOUTH MELBOURNE	7.17 (59)
RICHMOND	7.12 (54)

Best: South Melbourne – Daly, Tandy, Barber, Belcher, Sampson, Laird, Brennan.
Goals: South Melbourne – Caldwell 2, Laird, Hynes, O'Donoghue, G.Ryan, Barber.
Crowd: N/A at Punt Road Oval

PREMIER'S FINALS

SECOND SEMI-FINAL August 31

SOUTH MELBOURNE	8.10 (58)
CARLTON	7.11 (53)

Best: South Melbourne – Howell, Robertson, Tandy, Wood, Daly, Belcher, Turner, Caldwell.
Goals: South Melbourne – Barber 2, Robertson 2, Doherty 2, Laird, O'Halloran.
Crowd: 36,116 at the MCG

GRAND FINAL September 7

SOUTH MELBOURNE	2.5	2.5	6.6	9.8 (62)
COLLINGWOOD	3.3	4.9	7.12	7.15 (57)

Best: South Melbourne – O'Halloran, Howell, Turner, O'Donoghue, Rademacher, Laird, G.Ryan.
Goals: South Melbourne – Laird 3, G.Ryan 3, Robertson 2, Barber.
Crowd: 39,262 at the MCG

GRAND FINAL LINE-UPS

STH M	B:	J.Graham	C.Turner	V.Belcher
COLL	F:	E.Lumsden	D.Lee	G.Dobreigh
STH M	HB:	A.Rademacher	A.O'Donoghue	B.Daly
COLL	HF:	T.Wraith	W.Walton	J.Green
STH M	C:	M.Tandy	T.Hynes	A.Wood
COLL	C:	C.Pannam	P.Wilson (capt)	B.Twomey
STH M	HF:	J.Caldwell (capt)	T.O'Halloran	H.Robertson
COLL	HB:	B.Colechin	C.McCarthy	C.Brown
STH M	F:	E.Barber	G.Ryan	C.Laird
COLL	B:	M.Sheehy	H.Saunders	A.Mutch
STH M	R:	J.Howell	P.Skehan	J.Doherty
COLL	R:	L.Hughes	P.Reynolds	C.Laxton

STH M	**Coach:**	Bert Howson
COLL	**Coach:**	Jock McHale

SNAPSHOT

Win-loss record: 15-1

Highest score: 14.17 (101), round 11, v St Kilda.

Greatest winning margin: 52 points, round 7, v Richmond.

Lowest score: 6.8 (44), round 4, v St Kilda.

Greatest losing margin: 5 points, round 4, v St Kilda.

Most goals by a player in a game: 6, Chris Laird, round 7, v Richmond.

Most consecutive wins: 12

Most consecutive losses: 1

Club awards: Leading goalkicker: Gerald Ryan (32 goals).

Putting it into perspective:
South Melbourne's second Grand Final success occurred nine years after the club's first premiership in 1909. The final margin of just five points meant five of the Bloods' six Grand Final appearances had been decided by less than a goal.

1918

	P	W	L	D	%	Pts
1 South Melb (1)	14	13	1		143.1	52
2 Collingwood (2)	14	10	4		145.1	40
3 Carlton (3)	14	8	6		116.5	32
4 St Kilda (4)	14	8	6		92.2	32
5 Fitzroy	14	6	8		98.7	24
6 Richmond	14	5	9		87.7	20
7 Geelong	14	3	11		75.8	12
8 Essendon	14	3	11		64.2	12

(14 home and away rounds)

PLAYERS USED

SOUTH MELBOURNE	GUERNSEY	GAMES	GOALS
Barber, Ernie	4	13	20
Belcher, Vic	2	16	1
Boyce, Alf	2	4	5
Brennan, Jack	2	6	2
Bulpit, Harry	5	4	3
Caldwell, Jim	6	14	7
Cummins, Frank	7	1	0
Daly, Bill	9	16	0
Doherty, Jock	8	15	5
Graham, Jim	12	15	0
Hair, Ben	15	1	1
Howell, Jack	14	13	16
Hynes, Tammy	16	12	1
Laird, Chris	17	12	26
Magill, Frank	19	2	0
Morgan, Harry	18	8	2
O'Donoghue, Alan	32	10	2
O'Halloran, Tom	20	16	5
Prince, Joe	21	2	0
Rademacher, Arthur	22	15	0
Robertson, Harold	23	14	18
Ryan, Gerald	24	16	32
Ryan, Mick	24	1	0
Sampson, Reg	27	2	1
Skehan, Phil	26	15	0
Talbot, Bill	31	2	0
Tandy, Mark	27	15	3
Turner, Chip	29	14	0
Wood, Artie	30	14	1

**COLLINGWOOD 11.12 (78) d
RICHMOND 7.11 (53)**

MAGPIES WIN TURF WAR

Collingwood saw off a pesky and ambitious neighbour, and started a ferocious rivalry in the process. By GLENN McFARLANE

SOMETIMES even the best-laid plans of football clubs go astray. Collingwood had planned a brief end-of-season excursion for its players and officials to the picturesque Gippsland Lakes district for October 11, 1919, confident that the premiership would most likely have been secured by that stage. The committee had tentatively booked the retreat, believing that the team would make a clean sweep of the finals after a dominant season. They had every reason for their confidence. The Magpies had finished as minor premiers after winning 13 of their 16 home and away games, then had little trouble pushing their way past Carlton in the semi-final. For some, it seemed, it was almost a foregone conclusion, despite a broken arm suffered in the game by Percy Wilson, which ended his season. Even Jack Joyce, a former player who was the club's resident poet laureate, waxed lyrical during the finals that: "Our team is playing so well together, and is so even, that I do not doubt for one moment that Collingwood will be hailed as the Premiers of the Peace Year." Only Richmond, which had never before won a premiership or even played in a Grand Final in the VFL, stood between the Magpies and a fifth premiership.

But, instead of traipsing their way through the Gippsland Lakes on October 11 and toasting yet another successful season, Collingwood was at the MCG, locked in an immense struggle with a young, fit, hungry Richmond side intent on not letting football's natural order continue without a fight. The reason for this elongated premiership struggle arose a week earlier. In the final between Collingwood and Richmond, one that the Magpies went into as overwhelming favourites, the underdogs somehow dismantled a team that had previously shown few signs of weaknesses. Before that final, on October 4, many were predicting that the premiership was almost a fait accompli for the more experienced, more seasoned Magpies.

There was only one warning, from *The Herald*, which had stated clearly: "There is such a condition as overconfidence." It would prove unheeded advice.

Whether it was overconfidence or simply the result of a stunning performance from Richmond, the fact remained that the Tigers led all afternoon of the first finals encounter between these two teams. At three-quarter-time, the deficit was only 10 points in favour of the Tigers, but a three goals to nil last term pushed the final margin out to 29 points. *The Argus* concluded: "They (Richmond) were the better side in the air, and Collingwood's famous system appeared once only as a flash in the pan… they were beaten on their merits without room for excuse." It was also said that: "The loss upset Collingwood's calculations in more ways than one. Arrangements had been made for a trip to the Gippsland Lakes this week at the end of the season, which Collingwood as premiers had been confidently looked forward to."

For the Magpies, that finals loss to the Tigers meant an extended week of football. But, fortunately, as the minor premier, the club was always going to get a second shot at Richmond under the finals set-up. It set the scene for a highly anticipated Grand Final that seemed fitting for the first season after the armistice had been signed on November 11, 1918.

Eleven months on from the guns falling silent after four years of war, crowds had returned to the game in overwhelming numbers and many of the footballers who had chosen the bigger fight had returned to the game that they loved. More than 50,000 attended the first finals clash between these two sides, and 45,413 would attend the Grand Final. All the signs were that this second clash would be close and tightly contested, with feeling on both sides. Richmond had used a lot of physical pressure on the Collingwood side, with the ploy of having big man Dave Moffatt trying to keep one of the Magpies' best players, Les Hughes, quiet. But could they do it two weeks in a row?

McHale was determined to make a few changes, to freshen up his team and, hopefully, to bring about a different performance. The Collingwood

Annual Report, summing up the 1919 season, highlighted the sense of disappointment: "The result of the final match was certainly a great surprise for everybody connected to Collingwood. However, a respite from training, the complete restoration of health of two or three of our players who had been suffering injuries, the alteration of the team, and the disposition of others on the field brought about the desired result."

Collingwood still went into the Grand Final as slight favourites, given its near perfect balance of young and old players. The Magpies had eight players who were 29 and over, in a team whose average age was 27 years and 91 days. Those veterans included Mal 'Doc' Seddon (31), who had provided some inspiration for his teammates by sending home a "lucky" German horseshoe before the 1917 Grand Final and was back from the war to continue this VFL career.

There was also Les 'Flapper' Hughes (35), Bert Colechin (32), Bill Walton (31), 'Dick' Lee (30), Alec Mutch (30), Charlie Laxton (29) and Ernie Lumsden (29). The only teenager in the team was 18-year-old Ernie Wilson. Incredibly, this Magpie team was as close to a home-grown product as could be expected. While half of the 1910 premiership team had been recruited from the county zones, and two others were from outside of Collingwood municipal boundaries, this 1919 side was very much a local side, with only two players not from the local zone.

Part of the intense feeling between Collingwood and Richmond came from the decision of former Magpie captain Dan Minogue to switch allegiances when he came home from the war in mid-1919. Minogue had been carried off on the shoulders of Black and White fans after a loss to Carlton in 1916 in what was his farewell match before heading abroad. So it had been expected that when he returned to Australia that he would swap his khaki for black and white on weekends, just as Seddon and others had done.

But as Collingwood planned ways to honour him with a special welcome home event, Minogue was about to renounce his football connection and seek a transfer to Richmond—of all clubs. Even today, more than 90 years after the event, the reasons for Minogue's move are unclear, but several reasons have been put up for the switch.

First, he was an excellent leader and had plans to coach, something which would not have happened at Collingwood for some time, given that 'Jock' McHale was entrenched. Given McHale was still at the helm 30 years later, if that had a bearing on his decision, it was a correct assumption. Then, there was the thought that he had developed a close relationship with star

Richmond player Hugh James when both were fighting abroad. Finally, in Michael Roberts' book *A Century of the Best*, it was revealed that Minogue had also been motivated by dissatisfaction over the treatment of his former teammate Jim Sadler. As Minogue said years later in *The Sporting Globe*: "I may have allowed sentiment to sway my feelings in that case—I don't know. But I have never had cause to feel sorry for my action."

Naturally enough, Collingwood was far from impressed with Minogue's plan to play, and coach, Richmond. They refused to allow him a transfer. He would have to wait a year until he was free to head to Punt Road, which cost him the chance to be a part of Richmond's first Grand Final team, in 1919.

Given the Minogue defection, and the close proximity of the suburbs, fans were also a part of the divide. On the eve of the Grand Final, police were called to the neighbouring Collingwood and Richmond areas to break up a few disturbances between supporters. This battle had become quite personal between the two sides. It even came down to the selection of the changerooms for the respective teams.

The Argus documented: "There was a keen desire from both teams to get use of the gymnasium as a dressingroom. Richmond had it a week ago; Collingwood won the toss for it on Saturday, and if Fate had anything to do with football that settled it." The good omens continued for the Magpies as their district side defeated University in the curtain-raiser.

Collingwood's lethargy from the previous week vanished from almost the first bounce, according to *The Argus*. It suggested: "With the best end of the start, Collingwood were attacking in an instant and within a minute or so (Dick) Lee had two shots on goal, the first a well-studied place kick; the second a hurried snap, but neither fully effective."

The early minutes of play showed, at least in part, McHale's plan to bring about a different result to the previous week, particularly in relation to the impact of Hughes. Hughes had been kept very quiet by Moffatt seven days earlier, but the coach was determined to ensure it would not be as easy the next time. This time, McHale had given captain Con McCarthy the task of acting as a foil for his teammate.

'Observer' from *The Argus* noted the ploy's early impact: "McCarthy's mission for Collingwood (was) evidently to block Moffatt and give Hughes a chance." It would prove a match-winning move. Hughes and McCarthy would both be among Collingwood's best players on a day where their strength and talent would be in great need. To highlight the impact of McHale's move, *The Australasian* called it "the most telling of the match".

The first term was "exceptionally hard, fast and bitter" and it was Richmond who brought about the first goal when George Bayliss scored with a "fine, long shot (that) got the goal and some rousing cheers." Neither side took full advantage of their scoring opportunities in the opening term, but the one thing that was not in doubt was the fact that it was a physical start. This was conveyed in the many press reports of the game, with one suggesting it was a clash with "players converging together menacingly" and "fists were shown at various periods".

That force played a part in the Magpies' start, as *The Argus* reported: "Richmond made the fatal mistake of getting Lee by the shoulders, and with only 10 yards to cover in his free shot, he easily got the first goal for Collingwood." There were some more near misses, but no other goals in the term.

While the first half-hour was essentially a battle of the defences, the focus was purely on attack when the resumption of play took place. In the first minute of play, Bayliss missed a sitter for the Tigers after a "bad kick-off" from Harry Saunders. This was followed by a "Collingwood rush, in which ['Snowy'] Lumsden, [Charlie] Pannam and [Harry] Curtis shone, found the goal open and ('Doc') Seddon coolly kicked the ball through." In only his 13th game back from the war, after missing three full seasons, Seddon was doing his best to finally be a part of a premiership. The club had missed out in the 1915 Grand Final—his last game before heading overseas—and he had been in France when the Magpies had won the 1917 flag. This time he desperately wanted to be a part of it as a tribute to his fallen mate Paddy Rowan.

But no sooner had Seddon kicked his goal than the Tigers came again. This time Bayliss did not miss. He slotted one through with his left foot.

Somehow the Magpies clawed their way forward again, a move which resulted in the club's third goal, "a pass from Lumsden to Lee gave them once again an open goal", according to *The Argus*. Collingwood was playing "the better game and their organisation stood all the attention that their rivals could bring to bear", but Richmond continued to stay in touch on the scoreboard. Then Hughes posted Collingwood's fourth goal to stretch the lead out a bit more, which was a fitting reward for his sensational mark. It came when "his long arms shot up out of a pack."

A brilliant goal from Curtis from the boundary line was one of the highlights of the game, with the forward slotting it through "though little of the goal was open to him". Richmond's teenager, Donald Don, reduced the margin back to only four points with a goal just before the end of the second term, allowing the Tigers to go into the long break with renewed confidence.

Collingwood fans had much cause for concern when the teams ran out after the interval and began to assemble in their positions. Lee, one of the club's chief weapons in attack, was "limping when the teams braced for another round, which in the first few minutes might have given Richmond a winning turn".

The Tigers grabbed the lead briefly, before some quick thinking and a fine pass from Lumsden to Lee, who had seemingly recovered from his ailment, resulted in Collingwood's sixth goal. It recovered the lead for the Magpies, and it was the catalyst for more goals for the Magpies.

First, according to *The Argus*: "(Bill) Walton picked it up on the boundary, then snapped through the goal. Immediately, a great dash from (Bill) Twomey's ended with a trip and a free kick, from which he scored the eighth goal." This pushed Collingwood's lead out to 16 points at the last change and, "short of a complete collapse or a Richmond miracle", the Magpies appeared to be home.

Still, Richmond had a wind advantage in the final term and it was here that McHale made another master move that helped to lock in the result. At the last change, as his players gathered around him to hear his last word for the season, the coach implored them to play aggressive, attacking football, and to not fall into the trap of trying to defend their lead. The ploy perplexed the Tigers.

In an era of football where it was commonplace for teams to open a good lead and then settle back to try to defend it, McHale didn't want that to happen. He knew the only way the Magpies would be safe was if they continued to push for scores. Collingwood's slick work, especially with their handballing, had resulted in a strong lead at the last change. It was said that "their handpassing, legitimate or otherwise—and it was principally otherwise—was perfection. Pannam was playing dashingly in the centre, Curtis was marking beautifully, though kicking poorly, and Mutch, heading a grand bunch of defenders, was in wonderful form."

Any chance of a Richmond revival, or perhaps even a miracle, was snuffed out in the opening minutes of the final term when Lumsden helped Seddon to their ninth goal and "it was all over save the formality of playing out time." Lumsden, himself, scored another one soon after, and Walton posted the club's 11th and last, as Collingwood ran out 25-point winners in what was said to be a "triumph of skill over strength".

The Argus said: "The Tigers of the Saturday before were all caged; (and) the Magpies flying high and fast, and staying right out to the finish."

In keeping with the mood of the excited players on the final bell, hundreds of Collingwood supporters "jumped the iron fence into the playing arena, ready to rush to their favourites".

The Argus summed it up, saying: "As decisively as Richmond on their merits won the first game, just as meritoriously Collingwood won this time... Richmond lost power where they were most confident of commanding it—in the ruck. A lot of the jostling and struggling there seemed quite aimless and useless, but there was method in the Collingwood method."

McCarthy, the skipper, had played his role to perfection. He had tried to clear a path for Hughes, by taking Moffatt out of the way. It was said by 'Observer' that "the pushing and butting between McCarthy and Moffatt... seemed to have only the negative effect of keeping both men comparatively idle, until one noticed how Hughes was taking advantage of it... Practically bumped out of the ruck on the previous Saturday, he [Hughes] was again one of the dominating factors."

It was said that "Collingwood had no weak men—everyone did something material to the big result." McCarthy and Hughes played their roles, as previously mentioned. Pannam was outstanding; Lee (three goals to take his season tally to 56), Seddon (two goals) and Curtis (one goal) all performed well in attack; defenders Colechin, Mutch and Walton were key players; and the youngest player on the field, Wilson, played his part in only his 10th game, four days before his 19th birthday.

For Richmond, their best players included Frank Harley, Reg Hede, Barney Herbert and 'Max' Hislop. Bayliss, Hugh James and Don all booted two goals for the Tigers. Vic Thorp did a reasonable job to keep Lee to only three goals.

It was a triumph for McHale, too. It was his first premiership as a non-playing coach, and it had come about in the most trying year of his life to date. Just before the start of the 1919 season, and on the eve of his 10th wedding anniversary, McHale's six-year-old son, also called James Francis, but known to the family as 'Frankie', had died of bronchial pneumonia at the family home in Talbot Street, Brunswick.

It was a bitter personal blow, and one that he would struggle with for much of the season. Yet he had responded when it mattered most, and had played a critical role in getting the Magpies back on track after their initial finals loss to the Tigers.

The 1919 premiership was an important one for Collingwood. Its ageing, experienced list was closing what was a tumultuous decade with a premiership. Some believed that it had taught Minogue a lesson about the club being bigger than the individual, though he would extract his revenge 12 months later when he would lead Richmond to their first VFL premiership at Collingwood's expense. But that was way off in the distance, as Collingwood celebrated its 1919 premiership on the night of October 11. At Victoria Park that night, there were celebrations and backslapping reserved for what was the honeymoon period after "the war to end all wars". And there was even some talk about making an alternative booking for a trip to the Gippsland Lakes in the future.

1919 COLLINGWOOD

PREMIER'S SEASON

COLLINGWOOD: 1919

ROUND ONE May 3
COLLINGWOOD	9.8 (62)
SOUTH MELBOURNE	6.13 (49)

Best: Collingwood – McCarthy, P.Wilson, C.Pannam, Reynolds, Hughes, Brown.
Goals: Collingwood – Walton 2, Wraith 2, Curtis 2, Lumsden, Laxton, P.Wilson.
Crowd: N/A at the Lake Oval

ROUND TWO May 10
COLLINGWOOD	5.15 (45)
ST KILDA	5.18 (48)

Best: Collingwood – Curtis, Twomey, McCarthy, Mutch, Drummond, Dobreigh.
Goals: Collingwood – Curtis 2, Dobreigh, Hughes, Wraith.
Crowd: N/A at Victoria Park

ROUND THREE May 17
COLLINGWOOD	5.19 (49)
GEELONG	5.2 (32)

Best: Collingwood – C.Pannam, Youren, Curtis, Brown, Hughes, Reynolds, Laxton.
Goals: Collingwood – Hughes, Lumsden, Youren, Wraith, Sheehy.
Crowd: N/A at Corio Oval

ROUND FOUR May 24
COLLINGWOOD	11.8 (74)
RICHMOND	8.6 (54)

Best: Collingwood – Utting, Mutch, Twomey, Drummond, C.Lee, Walton.
Goals: Collingwood – Saunders 2, Utting 2, Walton 2, Lumsden, C.Pannam, Dobreigh, Curtis, Hughes.
Crowd: N/A at Punt Road Oval

ROUND FIVE
BYE

ROUND SIX June 7
COLLINGWOOD	16.20 (116)
MELBOURNE	8.7 (55)

Best: Collingwood – Hughes, E.Wilson, P.Wilson, C.Pannam, D.Lee, Walton, Colechin.
Goals: Collingwood – Hughes 6, D.Lee 2, Walton 2, Dobreigh 2, McCarthy, Wraith, Twomey, Sheehy.
Crowd: N/A at Victoria Park

ROUND SEVEN June 14
COLLINGWOOD	8.11 (59)
CARLTON	9.16 (70)

Best: Collingwood – Seddon, Twomey, Hughes, D.Lee, Drummond, P.Wilson.
Goals: Collingwood – D.Lee 3, Seddon, C.Pannam, P.Wilson, C.Lee, Wraith.
Crowd: N/A at Princes Park

ROUND EIGHT June 21
COLLINGWOOD	10.10 (70)
ESSENDON	6.8 (44)

Best: Collingwood – Youren, Saunders, McCarthy, P.Wilson, D.Lee, Mutch, Sheehy.
Goals: Collingwood – D.Lee 4, Wraith 2, Twomey 2, Lumsden, Seddon.
Crowd: N/A at East Melbourne Cricket Ground

ROUND NINE June 28
COLLINGWOOD	9.14 (68)
FITZROY	10.11 (71)

Best: Collingwood – Drummond, McCarthy, Curtis, Mutch, Dobreigh, D.Lee.
Goals: Collingwood – Curtis 4, D.Lee 2, Laxton, Seddon, McCarthy.
Crowd: N/A at Victoria Park

ROUND TEN July 12
COLLINGWOOD	8.11 (59)
SOUTH MELBOURNE	3.18 (36)

Best: Collingwood – Sheehy, McCarthy, E.Wilson, Seddon, Drummond, D.Lee.
Goals: Collingwood – D.Lee 4, Curtis 2, Hughes, E.Wilson.
Crowd: N/A at Victoria Park

ROUND ELEVEN July 19
COLLINGWOOD	13.13 (91)
ST KILDA	5.9 (39)

Best: Collingwood – D.Lee, Haysom, Brown, Twomey, E.Wilson, Curtis.
Goals: Collingwood – D.Lee 6, Curtis 3, Lumsden 2, Wraith, McCarthy.
Crowd: N/A at the Junction Oval

ROUND TWELVE July 26
COLLINGWOOD	12.11 (83)
GEELONG	4.7 (31)

Best: Collingwood – Saunders, Colechin, P.Wilson, C.Lee, Hughes, Lumsden.
Goals: Collingwood – Lumsden 3, Wraith 2, C.Pannam 2, Hughes 2, D.Lee, Seddon, Curtis.
Crowd: N/A at Victoria Park

ROUND THIRTEEN August 9
COLLINGWOOD	11.12 (78)
RICHMOND	9.11 (65)

Best: Collingwood – D.Lee, Saunders, Drummond, Brown, P.Wilson, McCarthy.
Goals: Collingwood – D.Lee 7, Curtis 2, Seddon, Hughes.
Crowd: N/A at Victoria Park

ROUND FOURTEEN
BYE

ROUND FIFTEEN August 23
COLLINGWOOD	20.25 (145)
MELBOURNE	5.6 (36)

Best: Collingwood – D.Lee, Wraith, C.Pannam, Walton, Twomey, Lumsden, E.Wilson.
Goals: Collingwood – D.Lee 7, Wraith 6, Curtis 3, E.Wilson 2, P.Wilson, Seddon.
Crowd: 3,885 at the MCG

ROUND SIXTEEN August 30
COLLINGWOOD	17.11 (113)
CARLTON	5.16 (46)

Best: Collingwood – D.Lee, E.Wilson, McCarthy, Wraith, Colechin, Lumsden.
Goals: Collingwood – D.Lee 6, Curtis 4, Wraith 4, Lumsden 2, Hughes.
Crowd: 3,885 at Victoria Park

ROUND SEVENTEEN September 6
COLLINGWOOD	9.13 (67)
ESSENDON	5.14 (44)

Best: Collingwood – Colechin, Mutch, Haysom, Sheey, C.Pannam, Laxton, P.Wilson.
Goals: Collingwood – Wraith 3, D.Lee 3, Hughes 2, Laxton.
Crowd: N/A at Victoria Park

ROUND EIGHTEEN September 13
COLLINGWOOD	9.10 (64)
FITZROY	6.10 (46)

Best: Collingwood – Twomey, Saunders, Drummond, P.Wilson, D.Lee, Haysom.
Goals: Collingwood – D.Lee 2, P.Wilson 2, Wraith 2, Brown, Lumsden, Hughes.
Crowd: N/A at Brunswick St Oval

PREMIER'S FINALS

SECOND SEMI-FINAL September 27

COLLINGWOOD	9.10 (64)
CARLTON	6.10 (46)

Best: Collingwood – Mutch, Colechin, McCarthy, Twomey, Hughes, Walton, Curtis.
Goals: Collingwood – D.Lee 4, Seddon 2, Wraith 2, Walton.
Crowd: 47,335 at the MCG

FINAL October 4

COLLINGWOOD	6.9 (45)
RICHMOND	10.14 (74)

Best: Collingwood – Twomey, Walton, Mutch, McCarthy, Laxton, C.Pannam, Drummond.
Goals: Collingwood – Wraith 2, D.Lee 2, Lumsden, Laxton.
Crowd: 51,798 at the MCG

GRAND FINAL October 11

COLLINGWOOD	1.5	5.5	8.8	11.12 (78)
RICHMOND	1.2	4.7	5.10	7.11 (53)

Best: Collingwood – McCarthy, Hughes, C.Pannam, Curtis, E.Wilson, Colechin, Seddon.
Goals: Collingwood – D.Lee 3, Seddon 2, Laxton, Walton, Curtis, Hughes, Lumsden, Twomey.
Crowd: 45,413 at the MCG

SNAPSHOT

Win-loss record: 15-4

Highest score: 20.25 (145), round 15, v Melbourne.

Greatest winning margin: 109 points, round 15, v Melbourne.

Lowest score: 5.15 (45), round 2, v St Kilda; 6.9 (45), Final, v Richmond.

Greatest losing margin: 29 points, Final, v Richmond.

Most goals by a player in a game: 7, Dick Lee, round 13, v Richmond; round 15, v Melbourne.

Most consecutive wins: 9

Most consecutive losses: 1 (four times).

Club awards: Leading goalkicker: Dick Lee (56 goals).

GRAND FINAL LINE-UPS

COLL	B:	W.Haysom	H.Saunders	M.Sheehy
RICH	F:	J.Smith	H.James	D.Don
COLL	HB:	A.Mutch	B.Walton	B.Colechin
RICH	HF:	G.Bayliss	P.Maybury (capt)	F.Harley
COLL	C:	T.Drummond	C.Pannam	B.Twomey
RICH	C:	S.Morris	F.Hughes	R.Hede
COLL	HF:	E.Wilson	H.Curtis	M.Seddon
RICH	HB:	F.Huggard	M.Hislop	G.Parkinson
COLL	F:	P.Reynolds	D.Lee	E.Lumsden
RICH	B:	A.Bettles	V.Thorp	P.Abbott
COLL	R:	L.Hughes	C.McCarthy (capt)	C.Laxton
RICH	R:	B.Herbert	D.Moffatt	C.Hall
COLL	Coach:	Jock McHale		
RICH	Coach:	Norman Clark		

Putting it into perspective:
Collingwood's fifth premiership win from 10 Grand Final appearances was its second in three seasons and its third consecutive Grand Final. It was the club's third flag under coach Jock McHale.

1919

		P	W	L	D	%	Pts
1	Collingwood (1)	16	13	3		162.3	52
2	South Melb (3)	16	12	4		158.7	48
3	Carlton (4)	16	10	6		127.6	40
4	Richmond (2)	16	10	6		118.2	40
5	Fitzroy	16	9	6	1	125.3	38
6	Essendon	16	7	9		94.6	28
7	St Kilda	16	7	9		70.6	28
8	Geelong	16	3	12	1	73.4	14
9	Melbourne	16	0	16		43.0	0

(18 home and away rounds)
(Each club had two byes)

PLAYERS USED

COLLINGWOOD	GUERNSEY	GAMES	GOALS
Brown, Charlie	1	15	1
Colechin, Bert	4	16	0
Curtis, Harry	2	16	25
Dobrigh, Gus	4	7	4
Drummond, Tom	5	16	0
Haysom, Wally	7	16	0
Hughes, Les	6	19	18
Jose, Horrie	27	2	0
Laxton, Charlie	11	13	5
Lee, Charlie	9	7	1
Lee, Dick	13	15	56
Lumsden, Ernie	10	18	14
McCarthy, Con	14	16	3
Mutch, Alec	12	16	0
Pannam, Charlie	15	18	4
Reynolds, Pen	16	11	0
Saunders, Harry	18	18	2
Seddon, Mal	26	13	10
Sheehy, Maurie	17	17	2
Twomey, Bill	24	16	4
Utting, Ern	23	1	2
Walton, Bill	21	15	8
Wilson, Ernie	19	10	3
Wilson, Percy	19	14	5
Wraith, Tom	20	14	30
Youren, George	23	3	1

**RICHMOND 7.10 (52) d
COLLINGWOOD 5.5 (35)**

RICHMOND EATS MAGPIES ALIVE

Dan Minogue's defection from Collingwood to the Tigers created a huge stir among the top two contenders for the 1920 premiership. By PAUL DAFFEY

THE Richmond catchcry "Eat 'em alive!" was not long in existence when Richmond began its climb to the top of the VFL ladder after World War I. A *Richmond Guardian* journalist had first coined the nickname the Tigers in 1910. The club first showed that it had adopted the Tigers nickname in its 1916 Annual Report. In 1919, as the Tigers rose towards the top four of the VFL ladder for the first time, *The Richmond Guardian* included cartoons of a Tiger with feathers trailing from its mouth. The Tiger supposedly had eaten the Magpie alive. This led to the "Eat 'em alive" catchcry. Bernie 'Barney' Herbert, a police constable as well as a Richmond ruckman, was the man who implanted the phrase in the consciousness of the football world.

At 190cm, Herbert was an enormous man for the time, and he had a personality to match. He growled out "Eat 'em alive" at training and at social occasions. He especially growled out his favourite phrase after every victory. The most famous, and startling, image of Herbert issuing the catchcry came in the hours after the 1920 Grand Final.

The catchcry suited a club like Richmond, which came to pride itself on a ruthless approach to victory. The suburb of Richmond, like its fellow inner suburbs, was down and out. Unemployment was rife. Crime was high. The condition of the rented houses that comprised most of the accommodation in the suburb was appalling. Such conditions induced a certain aggression among the footballers who wanted to assert themselves in their field of endeavour. "Eat 'em alive," was a perfect catchcry, for Richmond players, officials and supporters alike.

In 1920 Barney Herbert was a member of the most famous following division in the VFL; his fellow followers were burly Dave Moffatt and the diminutive Clarrie Hall. Moffatt was less talented than the other two, but he made up for any shortcomings with a hard edge. In the 1919 Grand Final, he was penalised in the opening minutes for battering Collingwood ruckman Les Hughes. During a match against Essendon in 1920, he incensed Same Old fans by jostling aggressively for position at boundary throw-ins. "To hustle and bustle at such times is not football," wrote a reporter from *The Herald*. Hall was just 160cm, but his courage and goal sense enabled him to be first rover for a decade. His second rover, Frank 'Checker' Hughes, was quick and clever, with a strong competitive edge.

The relief followers included Hughie James, a big, athletic man who took a strong grab. James started in the forward pocket, as an avenue to goal, before relieving Herbert or Moffatt on the ball. Besides his football ability, James had an aura about him because he had earned a Military Cross for bravery during the war, having repaired a bridge while under constant enemy fire. After a newspaper poll in 1920, James was named the best follower in the competition. Richmond full-back Vic Thorp was named the second-best defender.

One of James's greatest contributions to Richmond was suggesting that the club might like to ask his friend Dan Minogue if he would coach the Tigers.

Minogue was born in 1891 in Bendigo and in 1911, after overtures from several VFL clubs, he headed down to Melbourne to join Collingwood, where he established himself as a ruckman and centre half-forward. After three seasons Minogue wanted to leave Collingwood to coach Essendon Town in the VFA, in part because he believed he could never realise his coaching ambitions at the Magpies while Jock McHale was there. Collingwood enticed Minogue to stay by offering the post of captain and he spent three seasons as captain, until 1916, before stepping down to join the war effort. Teammates chaired him off the ground after his last game despite it being a loss.

While at war, Minogue won the heavyweight boxing title for his regiment and he played in the armed services' footy matches. One of his teammates in these matches was Hughie James, the Richmond follower. The pair became close. When they returned after the war, Hughes returned to Richmond but Minogue shied from returning to Collingwood. The Magpies wanted him to lead the club to further greatness but Minogue declined the invitation to a reception for enlisted players. Reports claim that Mingoue fell out with the Magpies over his coaching ambitions and because he was disappointed in the treatment of a teammate called Jim Sadler. Sadler had played more than 100 games for Collingwood before the war but was selected only sporadically during the war. Minogue felt this was unjust.

The Pies, meanwhile, were angry with Minogue. The story, perhaps apocryphal, is told in Richard Stremski's history of the Collingwood club *Kill for Collingwood* and other publications that Magpie officials turned Minogue's portrait around to face the wall. A version in *The Richmond Guardian* has it that the portrait was placed in a cupboard and turned to face the wall.

Minogue agreed to join the Tigers as a player during the 1919 season but Collingwood refused to clear him. As he had not quite fulfilled the three years' absence clause that entitled players to leave one club for another, he was forced to spend the season on the sidelines. When it was over, he gained his clearance to Richmond and was named as playing-coach for the 1920 season, replacing, Norman 'Hackenschmidt' Clark, who returned to coach his original club, Carlton.

At Collingwood Minogue was never a unanimous choice as captain. At Richmond, every player on the senior list—24 of them—came forward to congratulate him after the players had voted him in as skipper as well as coach. As coach, he was not a standover man because, as was reported in *The Richmond Guardian*, he believed Australians could not be bossed. Such a view was no doubt fuelled by his wartime experience. During the week he worked in the postal service.

Minogue was supported strongly by the Richmond committee in terms of recruiting. By 1920 whenever Richmond had a bye or there was a weekend off because of interstate football, club secretary Bill Maybury had clubmen despatched to suburban and country matches. In 1920, however, almost every Richmond player was still from the local area, having gone to school at Yarra Park Primary or St Ignatius' Primary or having played for local clubs such as Beverley, Burnley, Richmond Juniors or Balmain Church of Christ Football Club, better known as Balmain.

Richmond's best defender came to the club by chance. Max Hislop left his home town of Swan Hill to join Collingwood. When the Magpies rejected him, he played one game at Melbourne, where he was also let go. Hislop gave football away for two years. He was living in a boarding house in Richmond in 1917 when a fellow boarder encouraged him to have one last shot at the VFL by heading down to Punt Road. Three years later he was the Victorian centre half-back. The fact that he had been rejected by Collingwood and went on to become a Tigers champion gave Richmond people enormous satisfaction.

Minogue coached his players to move the ball swiftly and he liked tall players who could run. He himself was adept at using handball to bring others into the game and his followers were good at clearing paths to bring others into the game. Minogue rotated Herbert, Moffatt, James, Bob Weatherill and himself as followers. Towards the end of the 1920 season, he added Ernie Taylor as another option. All of the followers were strong at the ball.

The optimism of the post-war period was a boon for football. Richmond's membership in 1919 was 1800. In 1920, as the Tigers challenged for top honours, membership exceeded 5000, and on some training nights there were more spectators at Punt Road on Tuesday and Thursday evenings than there were members the previous season. Watching training was free entertainment, a bonus when the suburb of Richmond was home to some of Melbourne's worst pockets of poverty. It was also a way for fans to remain close to the players. Richmond players truly were idols in their suburb in these years. A great roar was beginning to be heard.

With the suburb behind them, the Tigers were on a roll from the beginning of the 1920 season. They won their opening four games before striking the mighty Collingwood at home in round five. The match was moved forward to 11am so that the Prince of Wales could fit it into his itinerary. A record 30,000 crammed into the Punt Road Oval. There were so many onlookers on top of the verandah of the members' pavilion that, following the excitement of Hughie James taking a big mark in the last quarter, the roof collapsed. Nobody was seriously injured. The Tigers revealed themselves as the great threat to Collingwood by defeating the Magpies by seven points.

The rest of the season featured a series of events that spoke of a club on the rise. In round six, Richmond kept South Melbourne to its lowest score against the Tigers, 5.4 (34). In round seven, officials were shocked when 31,000 went to the MCG to see lowly Melbourne host the Tigers. Barney Herbert, renowned as the club's worst kick for goal, popped one over his head to seal the victory. In round nine, the halfway mark of the season, Essendon led the Tigers by 35 points at three-quarter time of their match at the Punt Road Oval. There was a lull during the opening 10 minutes of the last quarter—then Richmond unleashed a tornado. The Tigers kicked 8.7 to no score to win by 20 points. In doing so, they became only the second team, behind Carlton in 1908, to complete the first round of the home and away round undefeated. According to *The Herald*, the Tigers' slashing comeback against Essendon was "the talk of Melbourne all this week".

The only blip on Richmond's performances was mid-season losses to Fitzroy and Carlton. Then the Tigers faced their greatest rival, their neighbours from Collingwood.

For the return match against Collingwood, in round 13 at Victoria Park, Richmond full-forward George Bayliss was granted a free kick a long way out late in the game. His goal put Richmond two points up on the siren. The Tigers had beaten Collingwood twice during the home and away rounds.

Minogue's work as coach around this time was bringing comment. Mingoue was renowned as a born leader, a talented player and a gifted speaker. *The Richmond Guardian* reported hearing his instructions to his players throughout a game. In the week following a walloping of Geelong, the Tigers scored their first win over South Melbourne at the Lake Oval. Then they defeated Melbourne with a club record score of 20.14 (134), bettering the score of 20.12 (132) they kicked against Prahran in the VFA in 1906. The Tigers were on the march

Richmond unveiled a country recruit, George Ogilvie, in the final game of the home and away season, against Essendon at the East Melbourne Cricket Ground. The strongly built recruit sizzled in the centre. Spectators took to crying "O, O, Ogilvie!" when he soared for a mark. Richmond's cruising victory, by 63 points, gave the club its first minor premiership. The Tigers finished with 14 wins, two losses—to Fitzroy and Carlton—and a percentage of 146. Fitzroy finished with 14 wins, two losses and a percentage of 143. Carlton finished third and Collingwood fourth.

Collingwood upset Fitzroy by 18 points in slushy conditions at the MCG in the first semi-final.

Richmond's lead-up to its semi-final against Carlton was blighted when Minogue picked up a bout of tonsillitis, which confined him to bed. In his absence a pall of gloom hung over Punt Road at Tuesday-night training. Bill 'Son' Thomas, the 1919 captain, whose career had been ended by a broken leg, stood in for Minogue. By the Thursday night Richmond people had overcame their gloom and were excited. Journalists at *The Richmond Guardian* reported that they were barely able to do any work because fans were always calling to ask about team changes and to seek advice on what price they should get for the Tigers with SP bookmakers.

Of the matches between Richmond and Carlton during the home and away rounds, the Tigers had won by 29 points at Punt Road and Carlton had won by 33 points at Princes Park. The round-11 match against Carlton was Richmond's last defeat. For this semi-final, Bob Weatherill was chosen at centre half-forward in place of Minogue. Vice-captain Max Hislop, who had the huge job of trying to quell Carlton's champion forward Horrie Clover, was elevated to captain. George Bayliss, on 62 goals, needed five more to break the record of 66. The crowd was expected to top the attendance record of 59,556, which was recorded during the Grand Final between Fitzroy and St Kilda in 1913.

On the day of the semi-final, torrential rain failed to stop the crowd swelling to a record 62,220. The match, according to *The Richmond Guardian*, was played in "mud and slush as juicy and slippery as the ripest pig sty in the Bungaree district". Bayliss took a mark and kicked a goal in the second quarter but did little else. Jim Smith was typically forthright at half-back. Defender Frank Harley did well when he replaced Don Donald in the forward line in the second half, kicking two goals. Vic Thorp was a tower of strength at full-back, while Ogilvie again soared in the centre. Richmond, according to *The Richmond Guardian*, was the better team during the early stages of the match but the score was only a point the difference in the Tigers' favour at three-quarter time. The last quarter was a stubborn contest until umpire Jack Elder stopped the game for six or seven minutes to enable police to push back those spectators who had encroached on to the field. The Blues better recovered their composure after the break, rattling on four goals to win by 23 points. Richmond's clever forward Gerald Rush ended the match with a ricked knee.

The Tigers' minor premiership meant they would receive another chance in the match that served as the Grand Final. Carlton and Collingwood were to meet in the Final. Minogue was showing no sign of recovering from his illness, while George Bayliss sank into a fever and Rush's knee was revealed to be worse than first thought. A wingman called Bill James, from Kyabram, was lured down to training, while another country star, George Ogilvie, was the subject of outcry because Carlton had lodged a complaint about his availability.

Ogilvie played armed services football in Europe alongside Minogue and Hughie James while he served in the army for almost three years. On his return he lived in Yarraville and played with Footscray Juniors before moving to Echuca to play football. At the time, there was no restriction on country recruits but each VFL club had a suburban recruiting zone. Yarraville, his place of residence during his stay in Melbourne, was in Essendon's zone. (Footscray was not yet in the VFL.) Ogilvie had not been away for three years, which would have earned him exemption for zoning laws. The League rescinded Ogilvie's permit to play. Richmond officials were outraged.

Collingwood, the least favoured of the four teams going into the finals, pulled off a second shock when it defeated Carlton in the preliminary final by four goals. The bad news for Collingwood was that Doc Seddon would miss the

Grand Final after being suspended for striking. Richmond would be missing Gerald Rush, whose knee had failed to come up, and Bayliss, who was barely able to move from his sick bed. His season would end with 63 goals.

Minogue had gone back to Bendigo to convalesce from his illness. During his absence a rumour swept Melbourne that he had died; it even made the newspapers. Minogue returned to Melbourne in time to attend training on the Thursday night before the Grand Final. The mood brightened when he entered the ground, looking seedy but obviously alive. He skipped rope in the clubrooms and declared he would play. An estimated crowd of 5000 watched training, while traffic on Punt Road stood still. At the selection table, Minogue and wingman Bob Carew were reinstated into the team.

Richmond's combative treasurer Jack Archer took the opportunity before the game to point out to the players the calumnies that had been perpetrated on the Tigers during the season. In a passionate speech quoted at length by *The Richmond Guardian*, Archer denigrated the League for denying permits for players who wanted to cross to Richmond and for rubbing out a Richmond player, Norman 'Snowy' McIntosh, for six weeks for an incident in which he broke an opponent's jaw when a player from a rival club had been penalised only three weeks for an incident that almost caused a riot. He berated all those from other clubs who shook their fist at Dave Moffatt, "who is the most maligned player in the game". His greatest vitriol was reserved for Collingwood, "the club we used to hold up as a pattern for sportsmanship".

The Richmond Guardian reported Archer's speech in detail:

> Yes, they (Collingwood) were good sports at social gatherings after when they won, but the scene changed at Collingwood this year when we beat them, and we're going to beat them to-day. At Collingwood I was admiring their beautiful room and its appointments and I noticed a nice souvenir sent by Danny Minogue to the club while away in France fighting for his country. At that time all clubs wanted to boost their representation at the war. While I was admiring the souvenir, the secretary of Collingwood advised me that they had a fine photo of Minogue, which used to adorn their walls, but had been relegated to obscurity, with its face to the wall, on the top shelf of a cupboard. Is that sportsmanship?

His denouement was especially rousing:

> Go in and win, boys. Set your mind on the goal in front, remember the injustices you have been burdened with, grind your teeth and stretch your nostrils wide. All Richmond are expecting great things from you, and let this flag I hold here, 'Defiance', inspire you; and this flag, 'Richmond on top', will be quite in order when you come back into this dressingroom after the match."

The big day was sunny and warm, bringing a crowd of 53,908 to the ground. Collingwood's champion full-forward Dick Lee failed to take his place because of injury. Richmond sprung a big surprise when Bill James jogged out to make his debut in the season's decider. Fellow small men Stan Morris and Bob Carew lined up in bare arms for first time because of the heat.

Richmond won the toss and kicked with the slight breeze. Minogue, playing up forward, was too weak to make much impact but his voice and leadership steadied his team. The first quarter finished with scores even, 1.2 each.

Richmond dominated in the second term but could manage only 1.3, with Hughie James kicking the goal. They did, however, hold the Magpies scoreless. Evidence of the difficulty in kicking goals was shown when a scrimmage involving 12 players just five metres out from the Collingwood goal failed to earn a score. The Tigers led by nine points at half-time, 2.5 to 1.2.

Half-forward Donald Don had two splendid runs in the third quarter that ended in two goals. Collingwood answered on both occasions through goals to crack young full-forward Gordon Coventry. Both teams kicked 2.2 for the quarter. The margin was again nine points at three-quarter time, 4.7 to 3.4.

Both teams attacked ferociously early in the last quarter before Richmond added goals in quick succession through Don and Bob Weatherill. Collingwood, refusing to lie down, kicked two behinds before half-forward Maurie Sheehy made amends with a goal.

Don then missed three consecutive times before James, the debutant, kicked his first goal. It was to be the Tigers' last. Richmond half-back Jim Smith went on an inspiring run in the dying minutes. Coventry kicked a goal for Collingwood just on the final bell, giving him three, but the match was decided. The Tigers had won by 17 points, 7.10 (52) to 5.5 (35), giving them their first premiership flag and bringing great joy to a suburb that loved its football team.

In the Richmond rooms after the match, Barney Herbert could be heard above the throng: "What did we do?"

"Eat 'em alive!"

Late into the evening after the Grand Final, players, officials and supporters from throughout Richmond gathered outside Richmond Town Hall in Bridge Road. Barney Herbert clambered on to the shoulders of a statue of George Bennett, the late mayor of the Richmond council and a president of the football club, and, with a crayfish in each hand, hollering at the night in his joy at winning a cherished premiership, asked the crowd: "What did we do?"

"Eat 'em alive!"

1920 RICHMOND

PREMIER'S SEASON

RICHMOND: 1920

ROUND ONE May 1
RICHMOND	11.13 (79)
FITZROY	8.11 (59)

Best: Richmond – Hall, Hughes, H.James, Rush, Minogue, Bayliss, Hislop.
Goals: Richmond – Bayliss 3, Don 3, Herbert 2, B.Weatherill, Hall, Hughes.
Crowd: N/A at Brunswick St Oval

ROUND TWO May 8
RICHMOND	14.13 (97)
CARLTON	9.14 (68)

Best: Richmond – Bayliss, Thorp, Rush, Hede, Harley, Morris, Bettles, Smith.
Goals: Richmond – Bayliss 5, Herbert 2, H.James 2, Don 2, Hall 2, B.Weatherill.
Crowd: N/A at Punt Road Oval

ROUND THREE
BYE

ROUND FOUR May 22
RICHMOND	9.19 (73)
GEELONG	10.4 (64)

Best: Richmond – H.James, Harley, Morris, Rush, Bayliss, Don, Minogue, Hislop.
Goals: Richmond – Bayliss 3, Hall 2, Moffatt 2, Rush, Herbert.
Crowd: N/A at Corio Oval

ROUND FIVE May 26
RICHMOND	11.12 (78)
COLLINGWOOD	10.11 (71)

Best: Richmond – Minogue, Thorp, Hughes, H.James, Bayliss, Hede, Don.
Goals: Richmond – Bayliss 5, Don 2, Hughes, H.James, Hall, Minogue.
Crowd: N/A at Punt Road Oval

ROUND SIX June 5
RICHMOND	9.7 (61)
SOUTH MELBOURNE	5.4 (34)

Best: Richmond – Thorp, Don, G.Weatherill, H.James, Smith, Bayliss, McIntosh.
Goals: Richmond – Bayliss 4, Hall 3, Hughes, Moffatt.
Crowd: N/A at Punt Road Oval

ROUND SEVEN June 12
RICHMOND	12.16 (88)
MELBOURNE	10.8 (68)

Best: Richmond – Morris, Carew, Minogue, Hebert, Hall, Minogue, H.James, Hughes.
Goals: Richmond – Hughes 2, Bayliss 2, Herbert 2, H.James 2, Don 2, Clarrie 2.
Crowd: 27,712 at the MCG

ROUND EIGHT June 19
RICHMOND	19.15 (129)
ST KILDA	8.6 (54)

Best: Richmond – Rush, Tuck, Minogue, Hislop, Bayliss, B.Weatherill, Abbott.
Goals: Richmond – Rush 5, B.Weatherill 4, Bayliss 4, Hall 3, Hughes, Herbert, Minogue.
Crowd: N/A at Punt Road Oval

ROUND NINE June 26
RICHMOND	13.17 (95)
ESSENDON	11.9 (75)

Best: Richmond – H.James, Thorp, Hede, Hislop, Rush, Hughes, McIntosh, Don.
Goals: Richmond – H.James 5, Rush 3, Don 2, Bayliss, Hall, Carew.
Crowd: N/A at Punt Road Oval

ROUND TEN July 3
RICHMOND	8.12 (60)
FITZROY	12.6 (78)

Best: Richmond – Morris, Minogue, B.Weatherill, Bayliss, Harley, Bettles.
Goals: Richmond – Bayliss 3, Hall 2, H.James, Don, Moffatt.
Crowd: N/A at Punt Road Oval

ROUND ELEVEN July 10
RICHMOND	3.8 (26)
CARLTON	8.11 (59)

Best: Richmond – Moffatt, Harley, Bayliss, Minogue, Thorp, G.Weatherill.
Goals: Richmond – Bayliss, Moffatt, Herbert.
Crowd: N/A at Princes Park

ROUND TWELVE
BYE

ROUND THIRTEEN July 31
RICHMOND	5.8 (38)
COLLINGWOOD	5.6 (36)

Best: Richmond – Bayliss, Minogue, Morris, Rush, Stott, H.James, Hede.
Goals: Richmond – Bayliss 3, Don, Hughes.
Crowd: N/A at Victoria Park

ROUND FOURTEEN August 7
RICHMOND	16.16 (112)
GEELONG	5.14 (44)

Best: Richmond – Bayliss, Hughes, McIntosh, Thorp, Smith, Mahoney.
Goals: Richmond – Bayliss 7, Don 3, Rush 3, H.James, Herbert, McIntosh.
Crowd: N/A at Punt Road Oval

ROUND FIFTEEN August 14
RICHMOND	14.8 (92)
SOUTH MELBOURNE	9.7 (61)

Best: Richmond – Bayliss, Herbert, Minogue, Huggard, Hislop, Rush, H.James.
Goals: Richmond – Bayliss 6, H.James 2, Rush 2, Morris, Moffatt, Don, Hall.
Crowd: N/A at the Lake Oval

ROUND SIXTEEN August 21
RICHMOND	20.14 (134)
MELBOURNE	8.12 (60)

Best: Richmond – Minogue, Mahoney, Don, Bayliss, Hislop, Abbott, Hughes.
Goals: Richmond – Bayliss 4, Don 4, Hughes 3, Mahoney 3, Rush 2, Herbert 2, Moffatt, H.James.
Crowd: N/A at Punt Road Oval

ROUND SEVENTEEN August 28
RICHMOND	12.15 (87)
ST KILDA	7.10 (52)

Best: Richmond – Bayliss, Thorp, Minogue, G.Weatherill, Moffatt, Morris, Rush.
Goals: Richmond – Bayliss 5, H.James 2, Don 2, Herbert, Hughes, Moffatt.
Crowd: N/A at the Junction Oval

ROUND EIGHTEEN September 4
RICHMOND	15.14 (104)
ESSENDON	6.5 (41)

Best: Richmond – Don, Bayliss, Harley, Hall, Taylor, Rush, Smith, Minogue.
Goals: Richmond – Don 6, Bayliss 6, H.James, Herbert, Moffatt.
Crowd: N/A at East Melbourne Cricket Ground

PREMIER'S FINALS

SECOND SEMI-FINAL September 18
RICHMOND 4.6 (30)
CARLTON 7.11 (53)
Best: Richmond – Thorp, Parkinson, Taylor, Smith, Ogilvie, Harley, H.James.
Goals: Richmond – Harley 2, H.James, Bayliss.
Crowd: 62,220 at the MCG

GRAND FINAL October 2
RICHMOND 1.2 2.5 4.7 7.10 (52)
COLLINGWOOD 1.2 1.2 3.4 5.5 (35)
Best: Richmond – Hislop, James, Hall, Moffatt, Herbert, Smith, Hughes, Hede.
Goals: Richmond – Don 2, B.James, Harley, H.James, B.Weatherill, Hall.
Crowd: 53,908 at the MCG

GRAND FINAL LINE-UPS

RICH	B:	R.Hede	V.Thorp	E.Taylor
COLL	F:	E.Lumsden (capt)	H.Curtis	P.Wilson
RICH	HB:	G.Parkinson	M.Hislop	J.Smith
COLL	HF:	E.Wilson	G.Coventry	M.Sheehy
RICH	C:	S.Morris	F.Hughes	B.Carew
COLL	C:	T.Drummond	C.Pannam	B.Twomey
RICH	HF:	D.Don	R.Weatherill	F.Harley
COLL	HB:	C.Brown	P.Rowe	C.Tyson
RICH	F:	H.James	D.Minogue (capt)	B.James
COLL	B:	G.Dobreigh	H.Saunders	B.Colechin
RICH	R:	B.Herbert	D.Moffatt	C.Hall
COLL	R:	L.Hughes	C.McCarthy	C.Laxton
RICH	Coach: Dan Minogue			
COLL	Coach: Jock McHale			

SNAPSHOT

Win-loss record: 15-3

Highest score: 20.14 (134), round 16, v Melbourne.

Greatest winning margin: 75 points, round 8, v St Kilda.

Lowest score: 3.8 (26), round 11, v Carlton.

Greatest losing margin: 33 points, round 11, v Carlton.

Most goals by a player in a game: 7, George Bayliss, round 14, v Geelong.

Most consecutive wins: 8

Most consecutive losses: 2

Club awards: Best & Fairest: Dan Minogue; Leading goalkicker: George Bayliss (63 goals)

Putting it into perspective:
The Tigers' historic first premiership occurred in just their second Grand Final appearance. It was the club's third finals win. They became the seventh of the nine teams to win a flag. Only Geelong and St Kilda had yet to taste premiership success.

1920

	P	W	L	D	%	Pts
1 Richmond (1)	16	14	2		146.4	56
2 Fitzroy (4)	16	14	2		143.2	56
3 Carlton (3)	16	10	6		128.7	40
4 Collingwood (2)	16	10	6		112.3	40
5 South Melb	16	7	9		108.6	28
6 Essendon	16	5	11		87.8	20
7 Geelong	16	5	11		84.4	20
8 Melbourne	16	5	11		74.2	20
9 St Kilda	16	2	14		57.2	8

(18 home and away rounds)
(Each club had two byes)

PLAYERS USED

RICHMOND	GUERNSEY	GAMES	GOALS
Abbott, Paddy	5	3	0
Bayliss, George	2	17	63
Bettles, Artie	16	6	0
Carew, Bobby	8	7	1
Don, Donald	17	18	31
Hall, Clarrie	22	15	19
Harley, Frank	33	17	3
Hede, Reg	6	15	0
Herbert, Barney	1	18	14
Hislop, Max	29	18	0
Huggard, Frank	9	7	0
Hughes, Frank	32	18	11
James, Billy	11	1	1
James, Hughie	4	17	20
Karthaus, Jim	25	5	0
Mahoney, Bill	10	3	3
McIntosh, Norm	4	10	1
Minogue, Dan	1 & 12	17	2
Moffatt, Dave	14	15	9
Morris, Stan	9	16	1
Ogilvie, George	24	2	0
Parkinson, George	23	5	0
Rush, Gerald	19	15	16
Smith, Jimmy	10	18	0
Stott, Wilfred	31	6	0
Taylor, Ernie	7	5	0
Thorp, Vic	5	17	0
Tuck, Charlie	21	1	0
Weatherill, Bob	15	8	7
Weatherill, George	28	8	0

**RICHMOND 5.6 (36) d
CARLTON 4.8 (32)**

LAST MEN STANDING

Richmond and Carlton manned the battle lines in two epic contests before the premier team was decided. By PAUL DAFFEY

THE BEST VFL clubs before the Great War were Collingwood, Carlton, Essendon and Fitzroy, with room for South Melbourne if you're generous. After the Great War, these clubs came up against a contender that strived to usurp them—on the field and off it.

Richmond had come into the competition in 1908. It was an easybeat in its early years but things changed after the Great War. In 1919 the Tigers had 1800 members, but their Grand Final appearance that season generated huge interest. The optimism of the post-War period generated interest in football in general. In 1920 Richmond had 5000 members. In 1921, fresh off their inaugural flag, the Tigers had 7000 members. Carlton had the next highest, with 6000. Richmond, in a few short years after the Great War, had usurped the Pre-War favourites on the field and off it.

Richmond began the 1921 season with the news that rugged follower Dave Moffatt had retired because, he claimed, the media had forced him out of the game. Moffatt had been derided because of what was described in newspapers as "ungentlemanly" tactics. Richmond people loved Moffatt for the way he fought for his club. When he walked into the dressingroom to see old teammates during the 1921 season, ruckman Bernie "Barney" Herbert yelled, "Eat 'em alive!"

Beyond Moffatt, the Tigers had few changes to the squad that won the 1920 premiership. The main recruits were Bill Schmidt (who was the

Richmond captain in 1910 before going to St Kilda), Mel Morris (Elsternwick) and Norman Turnbull (St Kilda). Schmidt and Morris were centremen and Turnbull was a rover.

The Tigers' opponent in the opening round was Carlton. More than 30,000 crammed into the ground. It was a big occasion as the Tigers were unfurling their first VFL premiership flag. Ruckmen Bernie Herbert and Dan Minogue, the captain-coach, were said to be "burly". Fellow follower Hughie James was up from his potato farm in Koo Wee Rup. Full-forward George Bayliss, who had missed the 1920 Grand Final because of illness, was unavailable because a lump of steel had "dinged" one of his toes at work during the week.

The Carlton team had many champions, including Horrie Clover and Bill Boromeo, a high-marking pair who had come down from Maryborough. Clover was a centre half-forward who in 1920 was named in the Victorian team after just three games with the Blues. Boromeo, who later played for Richmond and whose son was instrumental in the career of Richmond and AFL Legend Kevin Bartlett, was a ruckman who was strong as well as being a natural athlete. Centre half-back Paddy O'Brien was considered the best defender in the game, while Alec Duncan was a dangerous forward making his debut. The Blues were too good in the air, and won by nine points.

Another capacity crowd crammed into the Punt Road Oval for the round-five match against the undefeated Collingwood. The match lived up to expectations; in fact *The Richmond Guardian* said it had "one of the most exciting finishes in the history of the game". Collingwood led by 11 points at three-quarter time. Scores were level with three minutes to go. Then, according to *The Richmond Guardian*: "Bob Weatherill brought a gasp from 30,000 people by scoring the winning point with a snap over his head."

The Tigers had defeated their despised northern neighbours by a point. Fans clambered over the fence and carted the players into the dressingroom.

The Tigers' next big game was the return match in round 10 against Carlton at the Princes Park Oval, a ground at which they struggled (winning just twice) because it was the biggest in League, whereas Richmond's Punt Road Oval was the smallest. The Blues were motivated by the loss of rover Lyle Downs, who had collapsed and died after getting a rubdown following Thursday night's training session. They were still undefeated, and some members of the press were describing their team as the best in the history of game; their aerial strength was unmatched and they had champions on every line.

On this day that opinion was strengthened. The Tigers were in with a slight chance at three-quarter time but the Blues kicked 5.7 to one behind in the last quarter to win by 51 points. Two weeks later, the Tigers lost another game, this time to lowly Fitzroy. Their form was hard to pick.

The Tigers then excelled in wet conditions to defeat Geelong by 33 points at the Punt Road Oval. The next week, in round 14, they travelled up Punt Road to play Collingwood at Victoria Park.

As expected, the match was spirited. Headstrong half-back Ernie Taylor, who advertised his wares as a dairyman in *The Richmond Guardian*, wanted to jump the fence to join in a fight, only for Minogue to persuade him against it. Tigers centre half-back Max Hislop was expected to cramp in the legs after being a member of the Victorian team that had returned from Perth by train, but he showed no signs of discomfort. Hislop was best on ground as the Tigers found their best form. Full-forward George Bayliss kicked seven. The Tigers, less daunted than others in the Magpies' fortress, won by 26 points.

In the following three matches, Richmond sharpened up for the finals by cruising to victories over Melbourne, Essendon and St Kilda. Minogue, in his reminiscences in *The Sporting Globe* in 1934, said the Tigers were lacking spark until the last two rounds, when they hit stride with victories over Essendon (35 points) and St Kilda (48 points).

The Tigers' last loss had been against Fitzroy in round 12. Carlton's last loss had also been against Fitzroy, in round 13. At the end of the 1921 home and away season, the Blues finished on top with 13 wins, two draws and one loss from their 16 games. Richmond was second with 12 wins and four losses. Collingwood and Geelong were a further three games back, with nine wins each. Then there was another large gap to Fitzroy and Melbourne, which had six wins and two draws.

The Richmond Guardian said on the eve of the finals: "Richmond supporters apart, few people—and scarcely any critics—rated Richmond a chance, declaring Carlton the top side."

Minogue later revealed in *The Sporting Globe* the plan he had hatched late in the season to beat the so-called 'unbeatables'. "As the season advanced, more and more marked became Carlton's prowess in the air," he said. "To counter it, I developed a swift, low passing game in the speedy Tiger side. Our tactics… were to keep the ball as low and as much out of the air as possible."

According to *The Richmond Guardian*, conversation about the first semi-final between Richmond and Geelong exceeded even talk about the Royal Melbourne Show. Minogue suffered from what was described as lumbago, or lower back pain, early in the week but recovered to take his place. Top wingman Stan Morris was ruled out following a car accident.

About 42,700 fans were at the MCG as the players jogged out in perfect spring sunshine. Richmond players took a series of spectacular marks but their play was disjointed. Geelong led by five points at quarter-time. Richmond edged clear to lead by seven points at half-time—and then took over. "The third and fourth quarters revealed the eclipse of the seasiders," said *The Richmond Guardian*. "The Tigers took complete control of the game and exercised goal-kicking most of the time."

Followers James, Weatherill and Minogue had their finest game of the season as a unit. Bayliss kicked five goals in the second half. But the main feature of Richmond's win was the team's evenness. "There was no stars as there were no drones—every player contributing to the victory," said *The Richmond Guardian*.

Richmond defeated Geelong by 61 points. Its score of 16.19 (115) to 6.18 (54) was the highest score in either a VFL or VFA semi-final, eclipsing Collingwood's score against Essendon, 14.11 (95) to 5.7 (37), in 1910.

Carlton was made to earn its 13-point victory over Collingwood in their semi-final, setting up a highly anticipated Final between the Blues and Richmond.

Since 1908, when Richmond crossed from the VFA to the VFL, the Tigers had played Carlton 33 times. Carlton had won 30 matches and Richmond three. Carlton had also won both matches during the 1921 home and away rounds. The Blues certainly deserved favouritism going into the Final.

Richmond rover Frank "Checker" Hughes told *The Richmond Guardian* the best way to beat the Blues was: "Mix it with them, then add a little for bunce" (bunce being a term meaning profit). Carlton suffered a huge setback when its best player, and arguably the best player in the competition, Clover, was ruled out with an ankle injury.

The first half of the Final was played in fine conditions, with a small breeze blowing towards the eastern goals. Richmond had first use of the breeze and took advantage, with goals to Mel Morris, Donald Don, Don again, and Bayliss. According to *The Age*, Hislop's superb marking at centre half-back against the Carlton aerialists drew huge cheers from the Richmond supporters.

The most significant event in the first quarter was a confrontation between two players, Donald Don of Richmond and Carlton's Jack Greenhill, in the middle of the ground. According to Brian Hansen's *The History of the Carlton Football Club from 1864,* Don was seen walking away from the scene blowing his knuckles. The book says three policemen were soon on the ground. According to *The Herald*, the umpire, a couple of trainers and a policeman were on the scene before the end of the fracas.

What is not in dispute is that Don was punched by a spectator after the game and had stitches inserted in his upper lip. *The Richmond Guardian* reported that Richmond half-back Jim Smith "dropped the assailant with a well-measured stroke on the nose". Don was not reported for the incident during the first quarter but Carlton later sought an investigation. The Richmond half-forward, who was known for his aggression, was suspended for eight matches.

Carlton missed several opportunities to score during the first quarter before forward Percy Daykin kicked a goal with a place kick before the bell. Richmond led by 16 points, 4.2 to 1.4.

The second quarter opened with a free kick at half-forward to Richmond's Weatherill. The big man punted the ball into the teeth of goal, where Herbert took a strong mark. His goal put the Tigers almost four goals ahead. The Blues fought back but could manage only behinds. Neither team, according to *The Herald*, was flinching: "The game was solid, the bumps frequent and hearty."

Minogue received two free kicks and kicked two behinds. Carlton kicked four behinds before, finally, Daykin received a free kick and booted his second goal on the stroke of the bell. Richmond had kicked 1.3 for the quarter to Carlton's 1.6. The half-time score was 5.5 to 2.10, with Richmond leading by 13 points. *The Herald* noted that the Tigers had played with greater teamwork, and were faster. "It had been a most strenuous quarter," it said. There was a sense, according to *The Age*, that the "real Carlton" was yet to emerge.

And then the skies broke. Melbourne, as is its wont, experienced the best of weather and the worst of weather in the space of one afternoon.

According to *The Sporting Globe*:

> The moment the hail hurtled down, spectators scurried for shelter. Bandsmen who had been playing *A Perfect Day* on the turf seized stands and instruments and raced for cover. With terrific force the storm struck the high stands and rattled alarmingly on roofs. In a few minutes the whole arena was white with abnormally large hailstones, mostly of jagged, irregular shape...

> The hail storm, mercifully, lasted only a few minutes. It did vast damage to Melbourne and suburbs. As it passed on, heavy rain came. Seeing badly needed shelter going to waste in the members' enclosure, crowds from the 'outer' surged across the white, storm-swept arena to the sacred reserve, where, in their blind rush, they trampled down Bert Luttrell's prized flower beds and fancy borders...

> Just as the rain had ceased for a while, out came the players—to gaze on a desolate spectacle without parallel in League football. Water was

> everywhere, swirling over the arena. Flood streams from the park outside were pouring into the ground. To make it worse, a water pipe on the ground had burst!
>
> It was a remarkable scene, the more so when above the packed and drenched mass of people rose a cloud of steam.
>
> A tremendous splash in the centre and the game was on again! Into the icy torrent slid the players.

Herbert, not unhappy with the change in weather, described the half-time hailstorm as sounding like a barrage of machine-gun fire.

"I could always manage to turn on a pretty fair game in the slush...," he said. "Pottering around in the ice drifts and slop just suited my cab-horse pace."

The Herald said of conditions in the third quarter:

> Whenever a player fell — and they were falling in a way that had the crowd roaring with laughter — he slid for yards.
>
> Sometimes he fell on his face. That made no difference, for he slid just the same. Water rose in sheets whenever the struggling rucks crowded onto the ball and kicked at the leather as it spun along the ground. And in this method of play, Carlton at last came into their own.

Goals to follower Frank Martin and full-forward Gordon Green enabled the Blues to draw level. Soon afterwards, Richmond full-back Vic Thorp bumped into a post and so soft was the ground supporting it that he knocked it out of the ground. The central umpire took five minutes to get it upright again.

Richmond then rushed the ball into its forward line, where George Bayliss kicked a goal. Edric Bickford then scored to bring Carlton up to Richmond's score and rover Stewart McLatchie seized on a spilt ball from a pack to snap a goal that put the Blues back in front.

The Herald said at this point:

> Rain was falling heavily, lightning tore the heavy clouds apart, and the field became more like a lake than ever. Through it Richmond splashed amphibiously, and to good purpose, for in quick succession two goals were put on by Dan Minogue and Mel Morris.

Carlton regained the lead in peculiar fashion when Charlie Fisher earned a free kick 35 metres out on the three-quarter time bell. The Richmond players were not alert because the bell had gone. Fisher's kick fell 15 metres short but slithered past four Richmond defenders and through for a goal. "The ball floated to its destiny," said *The Age*.

Carlton went into the break with a three-point lead, 7.14 (56) to 8.5 (53). Spectators, though sodden, were enthralled by the tense encounter.

1921 RICHMOND

According to Brian Hansen's *The History of the Carlton Football Club from 1864*, Richmond coach Minogue was an imaginative leader. His response at three-quarter time to the conditions was to order all his heavy players on to the ball. "We'll get the ball forward with strength," he said.

Minogue himself, speaking in reminiscences in *The Sporting Globe* in 1934, gave much of the credit for Richmond's performance to defenders Hislop, Thorp and Smith, who repelled Carlton attacks time and again.

The last quarter began with a heavy downpour to add to the sheets of water already on the ground. Richmond "waded along the left wing", according to *The Herald*, before James kicked the ball to one of his fellow followers, Herbert, who marked and booted the goal that put the Tigers back in front. Both teams traded points before James pounced on a ball in a scrimmage and dribbled it through the goals.

Carlton attacked with fierce determination but Richmond's followers held sway. The Blues were unable to bridge the gap. Richmond won by eight points, 10.7 (67) to 7.17 (59). After the match, Herbert announced that the Grand Final would be his last game while the Richmond Furnishing Company announced that it would donate a Bengal tiger skin worth 50 guineas, more than enough to buy a house, if Richmond won the premiership.

In the saturated second half of the Final, Herbert's sure handling had made him a valuable player. Minogue, James and Weatherill had also played well in the following division. The Blues had missed Clover's considerable talents. At least as the minor premier they had the right of challenge, meaning a re-match with Richmond would ultimately decide the 1921 premiership.

The Grand Final was played in drizzling rain that caused greasy conditions. The crowd was down on previous years, about 43,000—perhaps because of the weather forecast and the fact that the game was held on the same day as the Caulfield Cup. Carlton had the edge in height and weight, Richmond the edge in speed. Carlton won the toss and kicked with the breeze. Clover, back from injury, took several strong marks despite the conditions.

One of Richmond's tactics was to unsettle the Blues. Half-forward Alec Duncan and wingman Jack Stephenson were flattened in the first quarter. Various Tigers hit brilliant Blues follower Boromeo with everything. The Blues, with Boromeo starring, scored two goals in the first quarter. Richmond's James kicked a goal to limit Carlton's lead to six points. Carlton scored one goal while holding Richmond to one behind in the second quarter. The Blues led by 13 points, 3.4 to 1.3, at the main break.

As torrential rain fell in the third quarter, Richmond clawed back into the game. Bayliss kicked two goals for Richmond while Carlton could manage only a behind. The conditions had reduced the game to a scrap much like the previous week. The Blues led by two points at the final change, 3.6 to 3.4.

The finish to the match would develop into a classic as the two teams put their heads down and butted foreheads for the duration. "The last quarter is fresh in everybody's memory—it will remain so for years," said *The Richmond Guardian*.

The Tigers' James kicked a goal straight after the resumption to give the Tigers the lead. Carlton replied with a goal and grabbed the lead. Richmond forward pocket Norman Turnbull took a mark 30 yards out and kicked a goal. The lead had changed hands again. The players, black with mud, settled in for an eight-minute slog to the final bell.

Carlton mounted an onslaught to get the ball forward. Tigers backmen Hislop, Thorp and Smith withstood the charge. Boromeo was felled and given a free kick 40 yards out. His kick fell short. The ball was taken away.

In the final minute, with Richmond leading by four points, the ball flew towards Carlton's Duncan close to goal. It looked certain to be Duncan's mark before Hislop launched himself into the path of the ball and punched it clear. In the final seconds, Richmond's Smith slid into a fence and fractured his kneecap. The siren went. Richmond had won by four points, 5.6 (36) to 4.8 (32). Hislop's desperate lunge had saved the day. Once again the Tigers had gritted their teeth and won.

In 1916, the year when there were only four teams, Fitzroy defeated Carlton in the final and Grand Final to win the premiership. In 1921 Richmond became only the second club under the Challenge system of finals to twice defeat the minor premier and win the premiership.

Umpire Jack Elder later called the two Richmond-Carlton clashes Homeric. Spectators clapped both teams from the ground, satisfied that they might never again see a Grand Final like it. They were certainly unlikely to see two successive finals so tense and taut.

The Richmond Guardian said:

> They cheered till they were hoarse, throwing their hats into the air in ecstasy of joy, while the daring spirits clambered over the fence and surged around the victorious team and shouldered them to their dressing rooms. It was indeed a popular victory which had to be fought for inch by inch against a team which had been thought unbeatable.

1921 RICHMOND

PREMIER'S SEASON

RICHMOND: 1921

ROUND ONE May 7
RICHMOND	7.11 (53)
CARLTON	8.14 (62)

Best: Richmond – Thorp, J.Smith, G.Weatherill, Hughes, Hede, James, Don.
Goals: Richmond – Don 3, James, Hall, Herbert, B.Weatherill.
Crowd: 32,000 at Punt Road Oval

ROUND TWO May 14
RICHMOND	11.16 (82)
SOUTH MELBOURNE	7.9 (51)

Best: Richmond – Harley, Minogue, M.Morris, Smith, James, Don, Bayliss.
Goals: Richmond – H.James 3, M.Morris 3, Bayliss 2, Don 2, Carew.
Crowd: 27,000 at the Lake Oval

ROUND THREE May 21
RICHMOND	5.14 (44)
FITZROY	5.6 (36)

Best: Richmond – Hislop, J.Smith, McIntosh, Hall, H.James, B.Weatherill, M.Morris.
Goals: Richmond – Hall, H.James, Carew, Don, M.Morris.
Crowd: 18,000 at Brunswick St Oval

ROUND FOUR May 28
RICHMOND	9.8 (62)
GEELONG	11.13 (79)

Best: Richmond – S.Morris, H.James, Bayliss, Don, Thorp, M.Morris, Harley.
Goals: Richmond – Bayliss 2, Don 2, H.James 2, Moffatt, Minogue, B.Weatherill.
Crowd: 10,000 at Corio Oval

ROUND FIVE June 4
RICHMOND	7.11 (53)
COLLINGWOOD	6.16 (52)

Best: Richmond – Minogue, J.Smith, Hughes, S.Morris, Don, B.Weatherill, Hede.
Goals: Richmond – Don 2, H.James, Minogue, M.Morris, B.Weatherill, Turnbull.
Crowd: 30,000 at Punt Road Oval

ROUND SIX June 11
RICHMOND	14.11 (95)
MELBOURNE	13.14 (92)

Best: Richmond – Bayliss, S.Morris, Taylor, Don, Schmidt, H.James, Thorp, Nott.
Goals: Richmond – Bayliss 5, Don 3, Minogue 2, M.Morris 2, Schmidt, Herbert.
Crowd: 12,000 at Punt Road Oval

ROUND SEVEN June 18
RICHMOND	12.14 (86)
ESSENDON	10.11 (71)

Best: Richmond – Bayliss, Moffatt, Hughes, H.James, S.Morris, Thorp, G.Weatherill.
Goals: Richmond – Bayliss 6, H.James 2, Hughes 2, Turnbull, M.Morris.
Crowd: 12,000 at Punt Road Oval

ROUND EIGHT June 25
RICHMOND	13.11 (89)
ST KILDA	5.12 (42)

Best: Richmond – H.James, Bayliss, Hall, McIntosh, G.Weatherill, Herbert, Carew.
Goals: Richmond – Bayliss 5, H.James 2, Carew 2, Schmidt, Turnbull, Minogue, Hall.
Crowd: 15,000 at Junction Oval

ROUND NINE
BYE

ROUND TEN July 9
RICHMOND	6.12 (48)
CARLTON	14.15 (99)

Best: Richmond – Hislop, Schmidt, Thorp, Hall, Hughes, Don, G.Weatherill, H.James.
Goals: Richmond – Don 3, Hall 2, Bayliss.
Crowd: 42,000 at Princes Park

ROUND ELEVEN July 16
RICHMOND	9.12 (66)
SOUTH MELBOURNE	8.13 (61)

Best: Richmond – Minogue, Moffatt, Carew, G.Weatherill, M.Morris, Bayliss.
Goals: Richmond – M.Morris 4, Bayliss 3, Nott, Minogue.
Crowd: 15,000 at Punt Road Oval

ROUND TWELVE July 23
RICHMOND	8.12 (60)
FITZROY	14.13 (97)

Best: Richmond – Thorp, M.Morris, Hughes, B.Weatherill, G.Weatherill, Hall, Schmidt.
Goals: Richmond – H.James 2, B.Weatherill 2, Hughes 2, Minogue, M.Morris.
Crowd: 27,000 at Punt Road Oval

ROUND THIRTEEN July 30
RICHMOND	9.15 (69)
GEELONG	5.6 (36)

Best: Richmond – Hislop, Herbert, J.Smith, Harley, Taylor, Minogue, Whitehead.
Goals: Richmond – Don 2, Harley 2, Whitehead 2, H.James, Hall, M.Morris.
Crowd: 10,000 at Punt Road Oval

ROUND FOURTEEN August 20
RICHMOND	10.12 (72)
COLLINGWOOD	6.10 (46)

Best: Richmond – Bayliss, Hughes, Hislop, Parkinson, Carew, Thorp, J.Smith.
Goals: Richmond – Bayliss 7, H.James, Hall, M.Morris.
Crowd: 25,000 at Victoria Park

ROUND FIFTEEN August 27
RICHMOND	12.6 (78)
MELBOURNE	8.11 (59)

Best: Richmond – Bayliss, M.Morris, Don, G.Weatherill, Minogue, H.James, Thorp.
Goals: Richmond – Bayliss 6, H.James, B.Weatherill, Minogue, Turnbull, Herbert, M.Morris.
Crowd: 13,382 at the MCG

ROUND SIXTEEN September 3
RICHMOND	11.14 (80)
ESSENDON	5.15 (45)

Best: Richmond – Harley, M.Morris, Hughes, H.James, G.Weatherill, Don, Turnbull.
Goals: Richmond – Bayliss 4, Turnbull 2, Don 2, Herbert, H.James, B.Weatherill.
Crowd: 14,000 at East Melbourne Cricket Ground

ROUND SEVENTEEN September 10
RICHMOND	14.11 (95)
ST KILDA	7.5 (47)

Best: Richmond – Thorp, Don, Carew, Hislop, S.Morris, Minogue, Bayliss, B.Weatherill.
Goals: Richmond – Bayliss 3, Minogue 3, Turnbull 2, Hall 2, Hughes 2, H.James, B.Weatherill.
Crowd: 15,000 at Punt Road Oval

ROUND EIGHTEEN
BYE

PREMIER'S FINALS

FIRST SEMI-FINAL September 24

RICHMOND	16.19 (115)
GEELONG	6.18 (54)

Best: Richmond – Thorp, Hislop, J.Smith, Hughes, Minogue, M.Morris, Don, B.Weatherill.
Goals: Richmond – Bayliss 5, H.James 2, Hughes 2, B.Weatherill 2, Don 2, M.Morris 2, Minogue.
Crowd: 41,649 at the MCG

FINAL October 8

RICHMOND	10.7 (67)
CARLTON	7.17 (59)

Best: Richmond – Hall, Herbert, H.James, McIntosh, J.Smith, Minogue, Carew, Hughes.
Goals: Richmond – Bayliss 2, M.Morris 2, Herbert 2, H.James, Hall, Minogue, Don.
Crowd: 42,866 at the MCG

GRAND FINAL October 15

RICHMOND	1.2	1.3	3.4	5.6 (36)
CARLTON	2.2	3.4	3.6	4.8 (32)

Best: Richmond – Hislop, J.Smith, Taylor, McIntosh, H.James, Minogue, Hughes, Hall.
Goals: Richmond – Bayliss 2, H.James, Turnbull, M.Morris.
Crowd: 43,122 at the MCG

GRAND FINAL LINE-UPS

RICH	B:	G.Weatherill	V.Thorp	E.Taylor
CARL	F:	P.Daykin	G.Green (capt)	C.Fisher
RICH	HB:	N.McIntosh	M.Hislop	J.Smith
CARL	HF:	A.Duncan	H.Clover	B.Boromeo
RICH	C:	F.Harley	M.Morris	B.Carew
CARL	C:	J.Stephenson	B.Blackman	N.Chandler
RICH	HF:	D.Don	B.Weatherill	N.Turnball
CARL	HB:	W.Raleigh	P.O'Brien	J.Greenhill
RICH	F:	B.Herbert	G.Bayliss	C.Hall
CARL	B:	H.Toole	E.Jamieson	C.McKenzie
RICH	R:	D.Minogue (capt)	H.James	F.Hughes
CARL	R:	F.Martin	R.Hiskins	S.McLatchie
RICH	Coach: Dan Minogue			
CARL	Coach: Norman Clark			

SNAPSHOT

Win-loss record: 15-4

Highest score: 16.19 (115), first semi-final, v Geelong.

Greatest winning margin: 61 points, first semi-final, v Geelong.

Lowest score: 5.6 (36), grand final, v Carlton.

Greatest losing margin: 51 points, round 10, v Carlton.

Most goals by a player in a game: 7, George Bayliss, round 14, v Collingwood.

Most consecutive wins: 8

Most consecutive losses: 1 (four times).

Club awards: Best & Fairest: Hughie James; Leading goalkicker: George Bayliss (53 goals)

Putting it into perspective:
The Tigers went back to back for the first time in club history after playing in their third consecutive Grand Final. The Grand Final date, October 15, was the latest Grand Final in the competition's history to that date.

1921

		P	W	L	D	%	Pts
1	Carlton (2)	16	13	1	2	142.0	56
2	**Richmond (1)**	**16**	**12**	**4**		**116.1**	**48**
3	Collingwood (3)	16	9	7		111.9	36
4	Geelong (4)	16	9	7		106.1	36
5	Fitzroy	16	6	8	2	103.9	28
6	Melbourne	16	6	8	2	95.4	28
7	South Melb	16	5	10	1	84.6	22
8	St Kilda	16	4	11	1	77.1	18
9	Essendon	16	3	11	2	80.8	16

(18 home and away rounds)
(Each club had two byes)

PLAYERS USED

RICHMOND	GUERNSEY	GAMES	GOALS
Bayliss, George	2	15	53
Carew, Bobby	8	14	4
Don, Donald	17	19	23
Hall, Clarrie	22	16	10
Hanley, Eddie	24	1	0
Harley, Frank	33	19	2
Hede, Reg	6	3	0
Herbert, Barney	1	17	6
Hislop, Max	29	18	0
Hughes, Frank	32	15	8
James, Hughie	4	19	23
Karthaus, Jim	33	1	0
McIntosh, Norm	4	19	0
Minogue, Dan	1	19	13
Moffatt, Hugh	14	7	1
Morris, Mel	11	17	21
Morris, Stan	9	15	0
Nott, Cyril	21	4	1
O'Hehir, George	27	1	0
Osmond, Keith	26	1	0
Parkinson, George	23	2	0
Schmidt, Billy	18	4	2
Smith, C. Jimmy	10	17	0
Smith, Charles	22	1	0
Taylor, Ernie	7	12	0
Thorp, Vic	5	19	0
Turnbull, Norm	13	12	9
Weatherill, Bob	15	18	10
Weatherill, George	28	15	0
Whitehead, Reg	16	2	2

**FITZROY 11.13 (79) d
COLLINGWOOD 9.14 (68)**

CANNY TWO FIRE ROYS TO FLAG

Fitzroy played its best football at the business end of the season to win its last peace-time premiership. By CHRIS DONALD

FITZROY went into the 1922 season as the most successful club in the VFL, having won six premierships since the breakaway from the VFA in 1897. Carlton and Collingwood were next with five premierships. Looking back from 1922, Fitzroy had won its most recent flag in 1916, the year that the competition was at its weakest. Only four clubs competed that year; the others were Carlton, Collingwood and Richmond. Fitzroy finished last after the home and away rounds and then won its way through the finals until it had nabbed the premiership. It was a strange season indeed.

By 1922, Fitzroy's most recent "real" flag was in 1913, almost a decade previously. If the Maroons were to hold on their status of being the most successful club, it was about time they won another flag.

Five things had a large impact on the Maroons' fortunes in 1922. The first was the appointment of Vic Belcher as non-playing coach. Belcher to this day, in 2011, is the only South Melbourne or Sydney player to have played in two premierships. In his case, they were in 1909 and 1918. Belcher was a workhorse ruckman in 226 games for South Melbourne from 1907 to 1920. In 1922 he became the first Fitzroy coach to have been appointed from outside the club. He brought with him a sense of discipline and a fresh set of eyes. He saw the Maroons' strengths and weaknesses. His unflappability was important during the ups and downs of the season.

Second, Belcher was smart in enlisting the help of two former Fitzroy captains, Jack Worrall and Alec Sloan during the 1922 finals. Worrall, besides being a Maroons captain in the club's VFA days, was famous as the coach of three VFL premierships at Carlton (1906-08) and two at Essendon (1911-12). Sloan was the captain of Fitzroy's earliest VFL premiership teams, in 1898 and 1899. Together, they attended players meetings and offered advice.

The third plank in the premiership campaign began at 4.30pm on Monday, August 7 in 1922, when a party of 53 Fitzroy players, supporters and officials hopped aboard a train bound for Adelaide. Mid-season trips were relatively common in the early decades of the VFL. Such trips were usually undertaken to Victorian country towns like Numurkah, which is where Richmond went during the 1920 season. Sometimes VFL clubs went to interstate venues like Hobart, which is where Dick Condon invented the stab kick during Collingwood's mid-season trip in 1902. The idea of these trips was to play matches against local combinations, and to enjoy each other's company along the way.

In 1922, Fitzroy became the first VFL team to travel to Perth. The trip by train lasted four nights each way. The Maroons fitted four games into their 18-day sojourn. It's hard to say whether the trip had any tangible effect on morale, but the Maroons did improve appreciably once they had shaken off their exhaustion on their return.

The fourth plank came with the inclusion of Goldsmith "Goldie" Collins, a 21-year-old rugged follower who at the end of the season, his first in the VFL, was named Champion of the Colony. Collins helped to set the tone for a team that was so tough it was called 'the Man's Team'.

The final piece in the five-part jigsaw in 1922 was the return of 35-year-old Percy Parratt, one of the most storied players in the Maroons' history. Parratt was a clever forward with the ability to kick low, skimming passes to his fellow forwards, especially his long-time accomplice Jimmy Freake. Parratt started playing with the Maroons in 1907 and had two stints as captain (1914-15 and 1920-21) and one as coach (1920-21), and he was a member of the 1913 and 1916 premiership teams. After the 1921 season, he retired. Late in the 1922 season, however, the Maroons were struggling with injuries to forwards and they were sluggish after the West Australian trip. Parratt returned to add some spark. In doing so, he revived his canny relationship with Freake.

The Argus captured the pair's understanding during this description from the 1922 finals: "Parratt, with one of his masterly passes—the ball was never more than six feet off the grass—shot it through straight as an arrow to Freake."

Freake played as his name might suggest. At 170cm and 63kg, he was undersized for a leading forward, but he got by with pace, courage, and brains. It was Freake's practice to lead out crouching low, with his chest towards the ground, before unfurling into a form that enabled him to take the ball and weave towards goal. Freake topped the VFL goalkicking with 56 goals in 1913 and 66 in 1915. Some rated him the equal of his contemporary, the Collingwood champion full-forward Dick Lee and, later, Gordon Coventry. In 1922, he was 33 years of age when he created mayhem with his fellow veteran Parratt.

The Fitzroy captain in 1922 was half-back Chris Lethbridge. Lethbridge had played in the Maroons' premiership team in 1913, his debut season. Weekly sports newspaper, *The Winner*, described him thus after a game in 1916: "Lethbridge, whether back or in the ruck, was a hard-working and strenuous fighter, who seemed in his element whenever the play became over-willing."

The Maroons played three debutants in the opening round in 1922: Tommy Corrigan, Steve Donnellan and Norm Cockram. Cockram was a 21-year-old centre half-forward from Northcote in the VFA.

In the final home and away round, against Melbourne, the Maroons showed their desperation to cover for injuries to forwards by bringing down a player from the Wimmera town of Nhill to play his first game. The player, Alwin Dalitz, kicked Fitzroy's first two goals and ended up with three for the match. He showed skill and he made good use of his opportunities. It was his first and last match of League football.

Fitzroy opened the 1922 season with victories over St Kilda and Geelong and a loss to Carlton. For the next match, a crowd of 26,000 crammed into the Brunswick Street Oval to see the match against Essendon. The Dons, after an uncustomary wooden-spoon season in 1921, had risen to be among the finals aspirants. Fitzroy vice-captain Gordon Rattray kicked a late goal to give the home team a one-point lead, but Essendon responded with a behind to seal a draw.

The Age said: "Fitzroy's bulk was looming largely; the team was playing the close game, and needless to say there were falls."

Gordon Rattray played for Victoria in 1922. His long, accurate kicking was notable across the Maroons' half-forward line, where for years he and Parratt were a mighty combination. Sometimes it was a Fitzroy tactic to play a decoy centre half-forward and attack down the flanks through Rattray and Parratt.

A mainstay of the Maroon's backline was James 'Snowy' Atkinson, who ran himself ragged whenever he stepped onto the field. Len Wigraft was a rugged follower who cleared a path for his smaller teammates.

An enormous crowd of 30,000 was shoe-horned into the Brunswick Street Oval for the round-six match against Richmond, the 1921 premiers. In the first sign of the changing of the guard, Fitzroy comfortably beat the Tigers. According to *The Age*, Fitzroy "shattered Richmond's forces completely".

The next week, the Maroons failed against Collingwood at Victoria Park, 15.19 (100) to 10.8 (68). Dick Lee, with four goals, and Gordon Coventry (three) were key contributors for the victors.

The loss signalled a righting of the ship by Fitzroy, who won the next five games. They started with an 11-point home at home over South Melbourne, with Atkinson among the best. Of their win over Melbourne the following week, *The Argus* said: "Fitzroy played a strong, vigorous game all through— their forcing style of play simply overwhelmed the Redlegs."

Full-forward Bob Merrick kicked nine goals to help the Maroons to a 27-point win over St Kilda in round 10.

Fitzroy climbed to the top of the League ladder in round 11 with an outstanding win over fourth-placed Carlton at Brunswick Street. The Blues led by five goals in the third term but the Roys fought back to win by three goals. Merrick and Freake both contributed four goals while Collins, Len Gale (the father of club great Alan 'Butch' Gale) and Atkinson were prominent. "The whole football soul of Fitzroy was stirred by the complete triumph of their men in the last half of the game," declared *The Age*.

Three special trains were put on to enable Fitzroy supporters to travel to Geelong to watch their game at the Corio Oval in round 12. The match was an arm-wrestle. Skipper Lethbridge led the Maroons home with the winning goal.

The bubble of expectation then burst when the Maroons lost their next three matches, to Essendon (round 13), Richmond (round 15; round 14 was a bye) and Collingwood (round 16). The Maroons received terrible news after the Collingwood loss when it emerged that Bob Merrick had injured his knee. *The Age* said he had "come out of a crush limping badly".

Merrick was something of a character in the Fitzroy line-up; it was his practice to talk to the ball, commanding it to "go straight", when he lined up for goal. He had kicked 47 goals, one behind the leader, Carlton's Horrie Clover, when he went down against Collingwood. The injury was revealed as a damaged cartilage. Merrick would miss the rest of the season. Freake moved across from the forward pocket to replace him in the goalsquare.

The loss to Essendon in round 13 was by nine points. On the Monday after the game, a large party of Fitzroy representatives boarded the train for their eventual destination of Perth. On the way over, the players took advantage of the train's wayside stops of 20 minutes to have a kick by the railway line. During one stop, according to Fitzroy's 1922 Annual Report, defender Stan Molan and follower Collins injured themselves while having a kick and had to be ruled out from playing in any of the four matches.

In Perth, the Maroons played West Perth (victory by a point), East Fremantle (victory by 11 points) and a combined WAFL team (loss by 16 points). On their way home they stopped in Kalgoorlie and, drained by exhaustion, suffered a loss by of an undisclosed margin against a combined team from the Goldfields Football Association.

The crowds for these exhibition matches were large. The match against West Perth at the Perth Oval attracted 15,000. The match against East Fremantle at the Subiaco Oval attracted 11,000 despite the fact that it was a work day. More than 18,000 turned up for the match against the WAFL at the Perth Oval. (There was no crowd figure for the Goldfields game.)

The draining aspect of the WA trip was drawn from the constant receptions and smoke nights, coupled with tours of the Swan River or the industrial works in Fremantle or the excellent racecourse in Boulder. The party was ready for a rest when it arrived at Spencer Street Station at 1pm on Friday, July 25. Instead the players had to turn their minds to the match against Richmond at the Punt Road Oval the next day.

The Tigers won by eight points. The Magpies then won by 17 points after an ill-spirited match that prompted headlines such as 'An Unpleasant Game' and 'Is Football Becoming Too Rough?'

Fitzroy's paucity of able-bodied forwards was never more apparent than on the day of the round-17 match against South Melbourne at the Lake Oval. *The Age* noted: "The match was slightly late in starting, owing to Fitzroy having difficulty in raising a strong team."

Gordon Rattray missed through injury and Norm Cockram broke his collarbone during the last quarter, ruling him out for the season. Parratt made his return in this match. He kicked three goals and Freake kicked four as the Maroons overcame their personnel problems to win by 15 points.

The Maroons then finished off the home and away rounds with another victory, by eight points over Melbourne, with Dalitz playing his solitary game in attack. The wins in the final two matches enabled the Maroons to finish third in the ladder. The final four was: Collingwood (12 wins), Essendon (10 wins, one draw and 111 per cent), Fitzroy (10 wins, one draw and 108 per cent) and Carlton (10 wins, 112 per cent).

Under the Challenge system, the semi-finals pitted first against third and second against fourth. Essendon and Carlton attracted a record crowd of 64,148 to the MCG for their semi-final. The Dons got home by five points.

The second semi-final was marred by a pre-game deluge that reduced the crowd to 43,405. Fitzroy's loss of Merrick was offset by Collingwood's loss of star forward Lee to injury.

Collingwood dominated the first half but failed to gain the lead it deserved. The margin at half-time was 12 points. Early in the third quarter, the dark clouds broke, and the Man's Team found another gear. Within minutes Fitzroy had wiped out Collingwood's lead and set up a five-point lead of their own. Jimmy Freake was reading the conditions better than anyone. At three-quarter time the Maroons led by two goals.

Collingwood clawed back into the game in the last quarter, but scored only behinds. Fitzroy's backline saved the game. The Maroons emerged the winner by four points, 6.10 (46) to 5.12 (42). Freake's five goals out of his team's six was the difference.

Under the Challenge system, Collingwood went through to the Grand Final while Essendon and Fitzroy were left to battle out a preliminary final before a crowd of 50,021 at the MCG.

Essendon led by a point at half-time. Within 40 seconds of the restart, the Maroons had kicked their fourth goal. They continued to attack but they were wayward. They kicked 1.8 for the third quarter compared to Essendon's 3.1 The Dons led at three-quarter time by six points.

Ruckman Len Wigraft snapped the Maroons' first goal of the last quarter, putting them a point ahead. Essendon scored a behind. Scores were level. Essendon scored another point. Fitzroy backmen Bert Taylor and Len Wigraft then spirited the ball down to Freake, who booted the goal. In quick succession, Fitzroy's Tom Corrigan, Gordon McCracken and Wigraft all kicked goals. Corrigan and Collins kept turning back the tide. Fitzroy kicked 5.2 to three behinds in the last quarter to won by 23 points, 9.14 (68) to 6.9 (45).

The last-quarter performance was described as Fitzroy's best of the day. "It was a triumph in the science of football adaptability—the faculty of being able to match the style of opponents, break it down or better it in the course of a game," *The Age* said.

The Argus was just as effusive: "It was a game won by dash, valour, unconquerable resolution and 18 fine footballers—the finer, the faster the play, the more evident was the mastery of Fitzroy. One got the impression—it came frequently in the match—that wherever Essendon had one man playing, Fitzroy had two."

1922 FITZROY

Unlike conditions early in the finals, the day was fine and warm for the Grand Final on October 14, 1922, before 50,054 (almost exactly the same as the Final).

In 1980 Wigraft recalled the 1922 decider against Collingwood. The interview is in *Roar of the Lions* by Garrie Hutchinson and John Ross. "Fitzroy were physically big and they were rough. If a man was coming with the ball you had to meet him and knock him down. I don't mean that we were doing the wrong thing, but as I say, we had big, strong players."

Wigraft said the traditional rivalry between the clubs fuelled the tension: "It was an all-in battle when we met. At the end of the game there was no man left standing and that's just about the strength of it. No man was left standing."

Collingwood's legendary Lee, playing in his last game, posted the first goal of the match with a drop kick after a mark. His eventual successor at full forward, Gordon Coventry, added to the lead by snapping a goal from an angle.

Enter Parratt, who kicked the Maroons' first goal from a free kick. For his second, scored soon afterwards, Parratt raced through a pack of players, scooped up the ball and steered the ball through for a goal. Fitzroy finished two points up at quarter-time. Both defences were strong.

Collingwood scored the first goal of the second quarter after diminutive rover Ted Baker had sharked a Fitzroy hit-out. However, at this stage *The Age* commented that: "Fitzroy had now the more versatile team, and were more successful forward." *The Argus* noted that Lee was having trouble with the place kick and was not drop kicking well.

Freake took a mark and kicked a goal. The Maroons continued to play vigorous football but Collingwood applied pressure of its own. Freake added the Maroons' third goal receiving a pass from Gale.

The Argus said Fitzroy "were towering for the ball in the crushes and playing with splendid power". Atkinson and Taylor were prominent.

Fitzroy often had the ball in its forward line but it wasted chances. Coventry took a great mark and kicked a "towering punt" to gave the Magpies a five-point lead at half-time.

The Maroons came out breathing fire after the main break. Freake slammed through Fitzroy's fifth goal within five seconds. Within minutes he struck again. Parratt then had a shot and missed. Follower Gordon McCracken hit out to rover Clive Fergie, who kicked truly. The Roys had stolen the march by kicking three goals in six minutes.

Umpire Jack Elder later commented that Collingwood was briefly bewildered by Fitzroy's onslaught. The ever-alert Parratt added Fitzroy's seventh goal from a ball that bounced of Fergie's shoulder and into his hands.

Collingwood threw everything into a fightback. Finally, Syd Coventry found his brother Gordon, who kicked the Magpies' first goal for the quarter.

Defender Stan Molan kicked to Freake, who booted his fourth goal and Fitzroy's eighth. Then Fergie passed to ruckman McCracken, who kicked the Maroons' ninth goal. Collingwood responded with two late goals but the Maroons were 15 points ahead at the final change, having kicked 6.4 to Collingwood's 3.3.

The last quarter began as a battle of the defences. Fitzroy's Horrie Jenkin kicked clearing punts from full-back. Both teams were desperate. Then a breakthrough. Fitzroy wingman Fred Williams, aided by Freake, kicked the first goal of the quarter. Collingwood replied through Tom Drummond to reduce the margin to 11 points and raise Magpie hopes.

Fitzroy, as *The Argus* noted, began playing the flanks, hoping to save the match. Maroons defenders were playing out of their skin. Atkinson was a hero in this period, according to *The Sun News-Pictorial*: "He got the ball out of danger time after time, battling hard and putting in telling kicks. He was an immense factor in Fitzroy's success and played with such dash that, at the finish, he could hardly raise a trot."

Then came the sealer, as described by *The Age*: "Fitzroy took possession. It was their ball. It passed from Rattray, via Taylor, McCracken, Fergie and Freake, to Wigraft, who kicked the goal. It was all over."

In a fitting end to a magnificent career, Lee kicked the last goal of the game, his second for the match and the last of his career. He had kicked 707 goals from 230 games. But Fitzroy emerged victorious by 11 points.

The heroes of the Grand Final victory were Fitzroy's veteran forwards Freake (four goals) and Parratt (three). *The Argus* said: "In putting in their old pair of forwards, Parratt and Freake, two of the coolest men that ever played the game, Fitzroy really played their winning card."

The Age rated Atkinson the best on the ground, while *The Argus* preferred fellow defender Bert Taylor, in what proved to be his last game in a Maroons jumper. Each premiership player was later presented with a commemorative pipe while Parratt received £50 during a testimonial at the Fitzroy Town Hall "in recognition of his valuable services to the club".

The Maroons had won their last peacetime premiership. The club saluted again in 1944 while World War II was raging and would not win another premiership before its merger with the Brisbane Bears at the end of 1996.

But in 1922, with a seventh premiership in their safekeeping, the Maroons were the most successful club in league history, with seven flags to their name, two more than Collingwood and Carlton.

1922 FITZROY

PREMIER'S SEASON

FITZROY: 1922

ROUND ONE May 6
FITZROY 10.9 (69)
ST KILDA 8.8 (56)
Best: Fitzroy – Merrick, Elliott, McNeil, Gale, Lethbridge, Carter, McCracken.
Goals: Fitzroy – Merrick 5, Carter 2, Gale 2, McCracken.
Crowd: 12,000 at the Junction Oval

ROUND TWO May 13
FITZROY 9.9 (63)
CARLTON 10.13 (73)
Best: Fitzroy – Wigraft, Elliott, Lethbridge, Collins, Merrick, Lenne, Chalmers.
Goals: Fitzroy – Merrick 4, Rattray 2, Carter, Donnellan, Cockram.
Crowd: 25,000 at Princes Park

ROUND THREE May 20
FITZROY 14.13 (97)
GEELONG 10.12 (72)
Best: Fitzroy – Merrick, Atkinson, Wigraft, Gale, Rattray, Millen, Carter, Molan.
Goals: Fitzroy – Merrick 7, Rattray 3, Gale 3, Donnellan.
Crowd: 12,000 at Brunswick St Oval

ROUND FOUR May 27
FITZROY 6.15 (51)
ESSENDON 7.9 (51)
Best: Fitzroy – Atkinson, Gale, Elliott, Lethbridge, Corrigan, Scales, Jenkin, Rattray.
Goals: Fitzroy – McCracken 2, McNeil, Cockram, Gale, Merrick.
Crowd: 26,000 at Brunswick St Oval

ROUND FIVE
BYE

ROUND SIX June 10
FITZROY 9.18 (72)
RICHMOND 7.9 (51)
Best: Fitzroy – Collins, Hicks, Boyne, Atkinson, Merrick, Sherry, Gale, Elliott.
Goals: Fitzroy – Merrick 2, McCracken 2, Gale 2, Rattray, Cockram, Boyne.
Crowd: 30,000 at Brunswick St Oval

ROUND SEVEN June 17
FITZROY 10.8 (68)
COLLINGWOOD 15.10 (100)
Best: Fitzroy – Lethbridge, Atkinson, Fergie, Millen, Merrick, Gale, Taylor.
Goals: Fitzroy – Gale 3, Merrick 3, Cockram 2, McNeil, Donnellan.
Crowd: 30,000 at Victoria Park

ROUND EIGHT June 24
FITZROY 9.13 (67)
SOUTH MELBOURNE 8.8 (56)
Best: Fitzroy – Merrick, Fergie, Scales, McCracken, Williams, Keller, Gale.
Goals: Fitzroy – Merrick 5, Gale 2, Rattray, Cockram.
Crowd: 20,000 at Brunswick St Oval

ROUND NINE July 1
FITZROY 5.19 (49)
MELBOURNE 4.9 (33)
Best: Fitzroy – Gale, Williams, Rattray, Corrigan, Freake, Keller, Cockram.
Goals: Fitzroy – Freake 2, Fergie 2, Hamilton.
Crowd: 12,000 at Brunswick St Oval

ROUND TEN July 15
FITZROY 13.11 (89)
ST KILDA 8.14 (62)
Best: Fitzroy – Merrick, Lethbridge, Collins, Atkinson, Hamilton, Molan, Carter.
Goals: Fitzroy – Merrick 9, Freake, Fergie, Carter, McCracken.
Crowd: 17,000 at Brunswick St Oval

ROUND ELEVEN July 22
FITZROY 11.13 (79)
CARLTON 9.7 (61)
Best: Fitzroy – Corrigan, Cockram, Jenkin, Taylor, Freake, Fergie, Williams.
Goals: Fitzroy – Freake 4, Merrick 4, Gale 2, Rattray.
Crowd: 30,000 at Brunswick St Oval

ROUND TWELVE July 29
FITZROY 5.19 (49)
GEELONG 5.9 (39)
Best: Fitzroy – Taylor, Freake, Atkinson, Lethbridge, Donnellan, Williams, Keller.
Goals: Fitzroy – Donnellan 3, Hamilton, Lethbridge.
Crowd: 15,000 at Corio Oval

ROUND THIRTEEN August 5
FITZROY 12.16 (88)
ESSENDON 15.7 (97)
Best: Fitzroy – McCracken, Gale, Jenkin, Warren, Merrick, Cockram, Atkinson, Fergie.
Goals: Fitzroy – Merrick 3, Cockram 3, Fergie 2, McCracken, Freake, Hamilton, Corrigan.
Crowd: 20,000 at Windy Hill

ROUND FOURTEEN
BYE

ROUND FIFTEEN August 26
FITZROY 3.14 (32)
RICHMOND 5.10 (40)
Best: Fitzroy – Lethbridge, McCracken, Merrick, Elliott, Carter, Wigraft, Fergie.
Goals: Fitzroy – Merrick 2, Fergie.
Crowd: 5,000 at Punt Road Oval

ROUND SIXTEEN September 2
FITZROY 8.14 (62)
COLLINGWOOD 11.13 (79)
Best: Fitzroy – Collins, Lenne, Corrigan, Keller, Molan, Lethbridge, Merrick, Carter.
Goals: Fitzroy – Carter 2, Donnellan 2, Merrick 2, Rattray, Corrigan.
Crowd: 25,000 at Brunswick St Oval

ROUND SEVENTEEN September 9
FITZROY 14.9 (93)
SOUTH MELBOURNE 11.12 (78)
Best: Fitzroy – Gale, Elliott, Sherry, Freake, Lethbridge, Parratt, Collins, Donnellan.
Goals: Fitzroy – Freake 4, Parratt 3, Gale 2, Fergie 2, Wigraft, McCracken, Donnellan.
Crowd: 10,000 at the Lake Oval

ROUND EIGHTEEN September 16
FITZROY 8.15 (63)
MELBOURNE 7.13 (55)
Best: Fitzroy – Taylor, Molan, Atkinson, Collins, Jenkin, Gale, Freake, Jenkin, Parratt.
Goals: Fitzroy – Dalitz 3, Freake 3, Donnellan.
Crowd: 5,000 at Princes Park

GRAND FINALS VOLUME I

PREMIER'S FINALS

SECOND SEMI-FINAL September 30
FITZROY	6.10 (46)
COLLINGWOOD	5.12 (42)

Best: Fitzroy – Corrigan, Freake, Rattray, Atkinson, Lethbridge, Elliott, Collins, Sherry.
Goals: Fitzroy – Freake 5, Collins.
Crowd: 43,045 at the MCG

PRELIMINARY FINAL October 7
FITZROY	9.14 (68)
ESSENDON	6.9 (45)

Best: Fitzroy – Molan, Gale, Rattray, Lethbridge, Elliott, Atkinson.
Goals: Fitzroy – Wigraft 3, Freake 2, McCracken, Corrigan, Fergie, Parratt.
Crowd: 50,021 at the MCG

GRAND FINAL October 14
FITZROY	2.5	3.6	9.10	11.13 (79)
COLLINGWOOD	2.3	4.5	7.7	9.14 (68)

Best: Fitzroy – Taylor, Fergie, Atkinson, Molan, Jenkin, Wigraft, McCracken, Parratt.
Goals: Fitzroy – Freake 4, Parratt 3, McCracken, Wigraft, Fergie, Williams.
Crowd: 50,054 at the MCG

GRAND FINAL LINE-UPS

FITZ	B:	J.Atkinson	H.Jenkin	B.Taylor
COLL	F:	E.Cock	D.Lee	E.Baker
FITZ	HB:	C.Lethbridge (capt)	S.Molan	E.Elliott
COLL	HF:	H.Chesswas	S.Coventry	G.Coventry
FITZ	C:	C.Sherry	T.Corrigan	F.Williams
COLL	C:	T.Drummond (capt)	C.Pannam	L.Wescott
FITZ	HF:	P.Parratt	S.Donnellan	G.Rattray
COLL	HB:	C.Tyson	C.Brown	B.Twomey
FITZ	F:	L.Wigraft	J.Freake	L.Gale
COLL	B:	E.Wilson	H.Saunders	Laurie Murphy
FITZ	R:	G.McCracken	G.Collins	C.Fergie
COLL	R:	P.Rowe	M.Sheehy	R.Webb
FITZ	Coach: Vic Belcher			
COLL	Coach: Jock McHale			

SNAPSHOT

Win-loss record: 13-5-1

Highest score: 14.13 (97), round 3, v Geelong.

Greatest winning margin: 27 points, round 10, v St Kilda.

Lowest score: 3.14 (32), round 15, v Richmond.

Greatest losing margin: 32 points, round 7, v Collingwood.

Most goals by a player in a game: 9, Bob Merrick, round 10, v St Kilda.

Most consecutive wins: 5 (twice).

Most consecutive losses: 3

Club awards: Best & Fairest: Jim Atkinson; Leading goalkicker: Bob Merrick (47 goals).

Putting it into perspective:
Fitzroy's amazing success continued with its seventh flag from 11 Grand Final appearances and it stamped the club as the competition's most successful and powerful team. The Maroons were now two premierships ahead of rivals Carlton and Collingwood.

1922

		P	W	L	D	%	Pts
1	Collingwood (2)	16	12	4		127.8	48
2	Essendon (3)	16	10	5	1	111.6	42
3	Fitzroy (1)	16	10	5	1	108.8	42
4	Carlton (4)	16	10	6		112.8	40
5	Richmond	16	7	9		92.0	28
6	Melbourne	16	7	9		88.9	28
7	St Kilda	16	5	10	1	93.6	22
8	Geelong	16	5	11		84.0	20
9	South Melb	16	4	11	1	91.3	18

(18 home and away rounds)
(Each club had two byes)

PLAYERS USED

FITZROY	GUERNSEY	GAMES	GOALS
Atkinson, Jim	17	14	0
Boyne, Les	32	2	1
Carter, Harold	19	8	6
Chalmers, Percy	7	1	0
Cockram, Norm	4	15	9
Collins, Goldie	29/10	16	1
Corrigan, Tommy	27/33	15	3
Dalitz, Alwin	33	1	3
Donnellan, Steve	28/8	16	11
Elliott, Ern	5/18	19	0
Fergie, Clive	3	15	10
Freake, Jimmy	9	18	26
Gale, Len	6	18	17
Hamilton, John P.	20	5	3
Hicks, Bill	8	2	0
Jenkin, Horrie	4/5	16	0
Keller, Carl	1	15	0
Lenne, Bert	11	3	0
Lethbridge, Chris	12	18	1
McCracken, Gordon	24/22	19	10
McNeil, Hector	23	7	2
Merrick, Bob	24	13	47
Millen, Roy	26	4	0
Molan, Stan	2/28	18	0
Parratt, Percy	30	5	7
Rattray, Gordon	7/27	16	9
Scales, Joe	36	4	0
Sherry, Clarrie	18/14	10	0
Taylor, Bert R.	8/2	12	0
Warren, Les	31	4	0
Wigraft, Len	10/29	10	5
Williams, Fred	16/15	11	1

Note: Several players wore more than one number during the season.

**ESSENDON 8.15 (63) d
FITZROY 6.10 (46)**

PINT-SIZED PREMIERS

Essendon's famed 'mosquito fleet' delivered an overdue pennant to the club's swank new headquarters at Windy Hill. By ROHAN CONNOLLY

BY THE early 1920s, Essendon was both a club and a football team in desperate need of a makeover. Fortunately, it would get both at the same time. And with spectacular results.

Essendon had been an early VFL power, and by 1912 had won its fourth premiership in 16 years of a still newish competition. But hard times had fallen. In seven subsequent seasons over nine years (the club had pulled out for two seasons during World War I) the Dons hadn't even reached the finals, with a best finish of sixth.

And come the end of 1921, it didn't even have a home. Essendon had been at the East Melbourne Cricket Ground, located adjacent to the MCG on the corner of Jolimont Road and Wellington Parade, for 38 years. But at the conclusion of the 1921 season, the ground closed and was demolished to make way for an extension of the Jolimont Yard railway sidings.

At one stage, Essendon looked likely to share Arden Street with the North Melbourne Football Club, still at that stage competing in the VFA. But that shift seemed to many Essendonians a virtual amalgamation. The forces against the Arden Street proposal were led by Essendon councillor Arthur Showers, later to become club president and have a Windy Hill stand named after him.

Showers' persuasiveness won the day, the council eventually agreeing to spend more than £12,000 to bring Windy Hill up to VFL standard, including fencing and a grandstand. The Essendon committee approved the move back to the club's geographic heartland on October 20, 1921.

The groundswell of support that shift generated became apparent at Essendon's annual general meeting on February 16, 1922. The crowd spilled out of the town hall, the atmosphere one of excitement and anticipation at the club's homecoming. The rest of the football world looked on approvingly.

"Essendon's new quarters are like fairyland as compared with the drab, cramped and unattractive East Melbourne ground," reported *The Herald*. "Prettily situated, the grounds are surrounded by four streets and ten acres in area, the park is a delight to the eye with its layout of plantations."

Essendon had no right, however, to expect much good on the field in 1922. It had "won" the previous year's wooden spoon, finishing ninth of nine teams with just three wins in 16 games. But in 1922 it was just pipped for a spot in the Grand Final when Fitzroy kicked five unanswered goals in the last quarter to win the Final.

There was plenty of disappointment about the spoiling of what might have been a last-to-first fairytale. As it turned out, it took just 12 months to make amends. With a team that would revolutionise football.

Ruckman Syd Barker had been part of four premierships with North Melbourne in the VFA, the last two as captain. But when that club unsuccessfully attempted to join the VFL and temporarily disbanded in 1921, Barker joined Essendon. Fellow North players Charlie Hardy and George Rawle also joined Essendon.

By the end of 1922, Barker had taken over as the Dons' captain-coach, and by the time 1923 had arrived Barker had put the finishing touches to a group of players and playing philosophy which would come to be known as the "Mosquito Fleet".

Until then, football had been a game largely dominated by the big men. But Essendon's injection of more than half-a-dozen little men to their team altered the equation dramatically. Pace and ball-handling at ground level became huge advantages for the Dons; their bigger, slower opponents were regularly left in their wake.

The Mosquito Fleet revolved around stars such as Hardy, who at just 157 centimetres was the equal second-shortest man ever to play League football. He was already a star at North with Barker and Rawle, and was a driving force in his old teammate's cunning plan for his new club.

There were the likes of George 'Tich' Shorten, just 163 centimetres and 51 kilograms. Shorten had electrifying pace and smarts, drawing free kicks so regularly by throwing the ball out in front of him before being tackled that he helped prompt a rule change.

There was Jim Sullivan (168 centimetres), a wingman and half-forward. Vince Irwin (169 centimetres), another North Melbourne pick-up, an agile utility who could play both in defence and attack. And Jack Garden and Frank Maher (both 170 centimetres). Garden was a brilliant wingman with sublime foot skills, Maher a durable and clever rover who'd string together a then-record 118 consecutive games over seven seasons. He played 137 in total over eight years.

It was a formidable band. But Essendon coach Barker balanced his stockpile of small speedsters with as many as half-a-dozen players taller than six feet, which was also considered a large number for the time.

Barker was one. Another was champion centre half-back Tom Fitzmaurice, who had represented his state at the age of just 20. Fitzmaurice was a superb high mark and had great athleticism for his size.

An elder statesman of this Essendon team, and another important key-position player, was full-back Fred Baring, who was 32 by the start of the 1923 seasons. Baring made his debut in 1910, and played big roles in the club's most recent premiership triumphs of 1911-12.

At the other end of the ground, the Dons had a big, strong centre half-forward in Justin McCarthy, who would go on to make a telling contribution to the season at the most important time.

At full-forward was Greg Stockdale. He'd been a half-back for almost three seasons before being thrown to full-forward during the 1922 preliminary final against Fitzroy, from where he kicked five of his team's six goals in a losing score.

Stockdale had been a controversial selection in the key post, with leading goalkicker Jack Moriarty dropped to make way. But Stockdale's stellar preliminary-final performance had a big impact on selectors' thinking, and by the start of the 1923 season he was ensconced in the goalsquare. Moriarty was forced to bide his time in the reserves, and eventually he left the club to play for Fitzroy, where he became a leading goalkicker.

At one stage early in 1923 Stockdale seriously considered returning to his Corowa home. Essendon would be eternally grateful he decided against it. The left-footer would end the season with a record VFL goalkicking haul of 68, including bags of seven, eight, nine and 10 goals.

Despite that considerable stockpile of talent, and the significant gains made the year before, there remained plenty of scepticism about Essendon's prospects when the 1923 season kicked off on May 5, with the Dons drawn to play St Kilda at Windy Hill.

The visitors held the narrowest of leads at quarter-time, but Essendon gradually gained the ascendancy. "Essendon were a more even side," wrote 'Observer' in The Argus the following Monday, "and they played with better unison and judgement. It was a strenuously contested game but Essendon lasted better than their opponents who were a tired team towards the finish."

Indeed, the Dons slammed on six goals in the last quarter to win going away by 43 points. And clearly the dominant player on the ground was spearhead Stockdale, who, incredibly, finished with 10 of the winning side's 15 goals, and was carried from the ground. No Essendon player had kicked more in a game, and the record-breaking effort set the scene for big years from both player and team.

A bigger test would come in round two, when Essendon journeyed to Victoria Park to take on the previous year's runner-up, Collingwood.

The Dons held a two-goal lead for most of the day, and increased it to nearly five when it added three goals in the third quarter to the Magpies' solitary behind. The Woods came home strongly but Essendon held on to win by 14 points.

Stockdale followed up his first-game heroics with a haul of five goals against Collingwood, while Tom Jenkins kicked three. But despite remaining undefeated and heading the ladder, the doubts about just how far Essendon could go seemed to linger in the minds of the critics.

"Playing rather the better and more skilful football, Collingwood had still lost the match, and while the winners were very dashing one realised what a great side they might be with just a little of Collingwood's skill blended with their own dashing solidity," wrote 'Observer'. "Their fault was that the execution was never equal to the intention."

Essendon defeated South Melbourne by 10 points the following week in a low-scoring slog, and was a very comfortable 38-point victor over Carlton. Stockdale kicked another four goals against the Blues to take his tally after four games to 21.

After four rounds, Essendon was on top of the ladder, undefeated. It set the scene for the Dons' biggest test, against the reigning premier, Fitzroy, the side that had sent it packing one game short of a Grand Final in 1922.

There was much anticipation in the lead-up, and come game day around 35,000 people crammed into Windy Hill. The redevelopment at the ground included a new scoreboard and a new press box. 'Observer' was impressed enough to laud those responsible in his Monday morning wrap-up of the round.

"For many years, members of the press have had to carry out their duties in primitive press boxes, which, besides being invariably dirty and uncared for, have long since outlived their usefulness," he wrote. "A pleasing feature at Essendon is the new press box and scoring board, erected by the council, which was opened on Saturday. It is a long way ahead of anything at other grounds, and has every convenience, with provision for the timekeepers."

But while the respected correspondent would have a suitably comfortable afternoon, most of the big crowd didn't. The home side lost its first game for the year, the 'Roys leading from quarter-time onwards.

In a low-scoring game, Essendon still trailed by only 12 points at three-quarter time, but the reigning premier added three goals to the Dons' solitary reply to run out winners by 23 points.

Again, Stockdale was a shining light, kicking three of Essendon's four goals. He led the VFL goalkicking by 13 as a result, miles in front of the game's other full-forwards, who happened to include one of the greatest names in football history, Collingwood's Gordon Coventry.

"None of the Essendon team played up to form," reported 'Observer', "and it was evident that Fitzroy's strong rushing tactics were not to their liking. The best work was done in defence, where (Clyde) Donaldson stood out as the best player on the side."

Essendon responded well, though, scoring three comfortable wins in a row over Richmond, Melbourne and Geelong, the last of which saw Stockdale kick eight goals.

Not even he could kick a goal in round nine after the day went horribly awry against St Kilda, the Dons managing only a pitiful 1.12. But it was a setback followed by another string of three victories. Indeed that pattern would recur three times during the season.

Essendon suffered a second loss to Fitzroy in round 13, a comprehensive 21-point defeat that raised questions about the Dons' capacity to cope with the 'Roys when it counted.

Essendon finished off the home and away rounds accounting for Richmond, Melbourne and Geelong a second time. It meant the Dons went into their finals campaign in the best of form, but also, by the numbers, "due" for a loss.

The Dons went into their second semi-final against South Melbourne full of confidence, sitting back for a week while Fitzroy easily dispensed with Geelong in the first semi-final. But the Dons were about to receive a rude awakening.

Essendon had comfortably accounted for South twice already during the home-and-away rounds, but couldn't shake off the Southerners in the semi-final, leading by just four points at three-quarter time. And it got only worse, as South booted four last-quarter goals. Its star forward Ted Johnson finished with seven as the Bloods won by 17 points. Essendon had suffered only its fourth, but by far its costliest, defeat of the season.

Fortunately, under the "Challenge" proviso of the finals system, Essendon could still win the premiership if it could defeat the winner of the Fitzroy-South Melbourne preliminary final, which proved to be the 'Roys.

Having suffered two of its three home and away defeats at the hands of Fitzroy, Essendon, despite going into the finals two games clear on top of the ladder, did not go into the Grand Final as favourite. Most expected the 'Roys greater physical strength to prevail once more.

A considerable spanner was thrown in the works, however, following a torrential and prolonged downpour in Melbourne during the week leading up to Grand Final day.

The conditions were perfect for Fitzroy. But with the MCG waterlogged the match was postponed, although, as it turned out, the weather on what should have been Grand Final day was fine. It was only the second time a finals match had been rescheduled.

The Argus called it the correct decision, though, 'Observer' noted, not one the players would necessarily have taken. "There were pools of water everywhere, and at the best all that could be expected was a mud scramble," he wrote. "Later, when the sun came out, delegates may have repented their decision, for in the circumstances there would have been a tremendous attendance. The players, had they had to decide, would probably have gone on, for they have had many months of training, and are anxious to be done with football for the year."

It meant that the Grand Final would not be played until 20 October, producing a clash with the Caulfield Cup. It also meant that Essendon would go into the game having played just one game of football in five weeks. But the sodden MCG turf had dried out. And when Grand Final day did finally loom, the Dons were ready.

Not, however, before a selection bombshell. With Ken Adams and Harry Hunter ruled out through injury, the Dons selected veteran full-back Baring—and a debutant. Not a youngster, either, but 33-year-old veteran George Rawle, who, like captain-coach Syd Barker, had crossed from North Melbourne after starring with that club for 10 years.

Rawle had carved out a fine career despite having a deformed foot that had to be heavily bandaged and did not enable him to train during the week. He had been coaching the Essendon junior side, but the selectors believed he would help add stability to the line-up.

The weather was fine on Grand Final day. The ground had dried magnificently, and a crowd of 46,566 supporters—mainly Essendon supporters—turned out. And the red-and-black army, even then, was noted for its one-eyed support.

"One looks to the balcony of the Melbourne Cricket Club pavilion as the last place from which unsportsmanlike cries should emanate, but I was surprised to hear men, presumably members, jeering at Fitzroy men, in fact insulting them for no apparent reason but that of partisanship," scalded 'Old Boy' in *The Argus*.

Essendon started the game well with a goal to Stockdale, his 67th for the season, a new League record. But the Dons' wastefulness with their opportunities threatened to cost them dearly.

After three goals each in the opening quarter, Essendon could add only 1.8 in the second quarter to the 'Roys' 2.2. The Roys led by a point at half-time, even if the Dons were on top in general play. Tom Fitzmaurice's high marking was particularly impressive at centre half-back, while the Mosquito Fleet was doing its job. George 'Titch' Shorten was starring and Garden was cutting up the Roys with his run from a wing.

Essendon looked fresher than Fitzroy early in the second half, and its resolve to cope with the Roys' more physical approach saw it stand firm whereas in its two home-and-away defeats to Fitzroy it had crumbled.

"Essendon's watchword for this game was 'stand to them' and when Essendon's big men had 'stood' the bumping, their small men were too sharp and clever," said *The Argus*. "Fitzroy did not seem to have the vim of their previous games, their field kicking was weak, and they tired before their opponents. It was not the same earnest, purposeful side we saw before."

Now the Dons started to take their chances. Shortly after the third quarter began, with Shorten continually pumping the ball into attack, centre half-forward Justin McCarthy cleverly snapped Essendon's fifth goal. McCarthy typified the Dons' determination, earning the ire of the Fitzroy crowd after a heavy clash with the Roys' James 'Snowy' Atkinson.

Shock inclusion Rawle was doing more than his bit. His attention to Fitzroy star follower Goldsmith 'Goldie' Collins greatly reduced the state representative's influence.

Wingman Rowland 'Rowley' Watt wasted another opportunity, neglecting to pass to Stockdale or McCarthy, who were both free, but soon enough the Dons had a second goal for the quarter after Frank Maher snapped truly. Essendon had a 12-point lead. In the context of a hard-fought game it was a handy break.

The last term began at a frantic pace with both Essendon and Fitzroy blowing chances to score. The Roys hit back after six minutes, however, through Harold Carter, to reduce Essendon's lead to just five points. After a behind to Fitzroy, the margin was four points with 10 minutes remaining.

The Dons steadied at the perfect time. Charlie Hardy, busy all day, scouted a pack perfectly to take possession and dish off to Maher, who ran in and snapped his second goal.

Full-back Baring turned back a final, desperate Fitzroy flurry, then, as time-on was being played, the Dons kicked the sealer, Shorten dashing into space to split the goalposts to thunderous cheers from the Essendon faithful.

They would erupt again only a couple of minutes later when the final bell confirmed the Dons' fifth VFL premiership, a triumph for both the club and the tactical innovation of captain-coach Barker. Despite much scepticism, Essendon's Mosquito Fleet had engineered a famous premiership.

"Essendon's football was of the best class, the dashes of the little men leaving the taller and heavier Fitzroy opponents well behind," wrote 'Forward' in *The Argus*. "Essendon finished in grand style, playing beautiful football, and it was then that the crowd realised that last year's premiers, who had been forecasted as winners of the important game, were to be soundly beaten."

'Observer' singled out the efforts of key forward McCarthy, little men Shorten, Watt, Hardy and Jack Garden, along with Barker, first-gamer Rawle, Norm Beckton, and defenders Fitzmaurice, Baring, Joe Harrison and Roy Laing. The next season, Fitzmaurice would walk out on Essendon after a controversy in which some of his Dons teammates were accused of throwing a charity match against VFA premier Footscray.

An elated Barker told *The Age*: "Our pace beat Fitzroy at the finish, and Fitzroy died away. The day suited us, and we had a fine, fast game, and our backmen held them well. They may have been superior to us in the hitting out department in the ruck, but our rovers had been instructed to go for the Fitzroy hit-out if they found the Essendon rucks were being beaten. They did.

"We beat them across the centreline, and our backline played a wonderful game in the last quarter. Our rucks were changed repeatedly, and I never let the men go more than 10 minutes at a stretch."

Barker's Mosquito Fleet had carried all before it, and a different brand of football had reaped the ultimate reward. Indeed, in Barker's post-match explanation of his side's success resides an even more resounding endorsement of his football thinking. They are words that wouldn't sound at all out of place coming from the mouth of an AFL coach some 90 years later.

1923 ESSENDON

PREMIER'S SEASON

ESSENDON: 1923

ROUND ONE May 5
ESSENDON 15.13 (103)
ST KILDA 8.12 (60)
Best: Essendon – Stockdale, Fitzmaurice, Garden, Jenkins, Barker, McCarthy.
Goals: Essendon – Stockdale 10, McCarthy 3, Beckton, Jenkins.
Crowd: 20,000 at Windy Hill

ROUND TWO May 12
ESSENDON 12.7 (79)
COLLINGWOOD 9.11 (65)
Best: Essendon – Stockdale, Beckton, Adam, Jenkins, Fitzmaurice, Barker.
Goals: Essendon – Stockdale 5, Jenkins 3, McCarthy, May, Garden, Barker.
Crowd: 30,000 at Victoria Park

ROUND THREE May 19
ESSENDON 6.13 (49)
SOUTH MELBOURNE 4.15 (39)
Best: Essendon – Donaldson, Hardy, Fitzmaurice, Barker, Garden, Laing, Maher.
Goals: Essendon – Stockdale 2, Jenkins, Beckton, Hardy, Maher.
Crowd: 20,000 at the Lake Oval

ROUND FOUR May 26
ESSENDON 14.19 (103)
CARLTON 9.11 (65)
Best: Essendon – Barker, Garden, Jenkins, Stockdale, Campbell, May, Fitzmaurice.
Goals: Essendon – Stockdale 4, Irwin 2, Sullivan 2, Jenkins 2, Beckton 2, Shorten, Maher.
Crowd: 33,000 at Princes Park

ROUND FIVE June 2
ESSENDON 4.13 (37)
FITZROY 8.12 (60)
Best: Essendon – Stockdale, Shorten, Marchesi, Beckton, Fitzmaurice, Laing, Maher.
Goals: Essendon – Stockdale 3, Barker.
Crowd: 35,000 at Windy Hill

ROUND SIX June 9
ESSENDON 12.15 (87)
RICHMOND 9.11 (65)
Best: Essendon – Laidlaw, Sullivan, Barker, Stockdale, Donaldson, May, McCarthy.
Goals: Essendon – Stockdale 4, McCarthy 3, Jenkins 2, Watt, Barker, Beckton.
Crowd: 16,000 at Punt Road Oval

ROUND SEVEN June 16
ESSENDON 11.8 (74)
MELBOURNE 8.12 (60)
Best: Essendon – Baring, Laing, May, Watt, Jenkins, Garden, Irwin, Callahan.
Goals: Essendon – Jenkins 4, McCarthy 2, Irwin, Garden, Stockdale, Barker, Beckton.
Crowd: 29,979 at the MCG

ROUND EIGHT June 23
ESSENDON 14.13 (97)
GEELONG 8.6 (54)
Best: Essendon – Stockdale, Maher, Harrison, Garden, Hayes, Barker, Watt.
Goals: Essendon – Stockdale 8, Watt 2, Irwin, Beckton, Jenkins, Shorten.
Crowd: 13,000 at Windy Hill

ROUND NINE
BYE

ROUND TEN July 14
ESSENDON 1.12 (18)
ST KILDA 5.5 (35)
Best: Essendon – Beckton, Hunter, Shorten, Laing, Laidlaw.
Goals: Essendon – Shorten.
Crowd: 24,000 at the Junction Oval

ROUND ELEVEN July 21
ESSENDON 13.13 (91)
COLLINGWOOD 7.9 (51)
Best: Essendon – Stockdale, Barker, Fitzmaurice, Harrison, McCarthy, Maher.
Goals: Essendon – Stockdale 7, McCarthy 2, Maher 2, Harrison, Beckton.
Crowd: 15,000 at Windy Hill

ROUND TWELVE July 28
ESSENDON 10.8 (68)
SOUTH MELBOURNE 7.9 (51)
Best: Essendon – Fitzmaurice, Jenkins, Laing, Shorten, Adam, Callahan, Watt.
Goals: Essendon – Stockdale 3, McCarthy 2, Shorten, Maher, Sullivan, Callahan, Watt.
Crowd: 25,000 at Windy Hill

ROUND THIRTEEN August 4
ESSENDON 15.13 (103)
CARLTON 5.7 (37)
Best: Essendon – Stockdale, Adam, Shorten, McCarthy, Hardy, Campbell, Barker.
Goals: Essendon – Stockdale 9, Hardy 2, Hunter 2, McCarthy, Beckton.
Crowd: 25,000 at Windy Hill

ROUND FOURTEEN August 11
ESSENDON 8.9 (57)
FITZROY 10.18 (78)
Best: Essendon – Donaldson, Marchesi, Fitzmaurice, Garden, Campbell, Stockdale.
Goals: Essendon – Stockdale 3, Campbell 2, McCarthy, Shorten, Maher.
Crowd: 34,765 at Brunswick St Oval

ROUND FIFTEEN August 25
ESSENDON 9.8 (62)
RICHMOND 8.6 (54)
Best: Essendon – Watt, Callahan, Maher, Garden, Stockdale, Barker, Fitzmaurice.
Goals: Essendon – Stockdale 3, Jenkins 2, Callahan, McCarthy, Barker, Watt.
Crowd: 18,000 at Windy Hill

ROUND SIXTEEN September 1
ESSENDON 13.20 (98)
MELBOURNE 6.5 (41)
Best: Essendon – Marchesi, Fitzmaurice, Watt, Laing, Farrell, Donaldson.
Goals: Essendon – Barker 3, Beckton 2, Callahan 2, Jenkins 2, Stockdale, Maher, McCarthy, Shorten.
Crowd: 10,000 at Windy Hill

ROUND SEVENTEEN September 8
ESSENDON 8.14 (62)
GEELONG 9.6 (60)
Best: Essendon – Hunter, Garden, Shorten, McCarthy, Irwin, Sullivan, Laing.
Goals: Essendon – Irwin 2, McCarthy 2, Beckton 2, Stockdale, Callahan.
Crowd: 20,000 at Corio Oval

ROUND EIGHTEEN
BYE

PREMIER'S FINALS

SECOND SEMI-FINAL September 29

ESSENDON	8.9 (57)
SOUTH MELBOURNE	10.14 (74)

Best: Essendon – Donaldson, Watt, Shorten, Maher, Farrell, Hunter, Beckton.
Goals: Essendon – Stockdale 2, Maher 2, McCarthy 2, Shorten, Watt.
Crowd: 55,617 at the MCG

GRAND FINAL October 20

ESSENDON	3.2	4.10	6.13	8.15 (63)
FITZROY	3.3	5.5	5.9	6.10 (46)

Best: Essendon – Shorten, McCarthy, Fitzmaurice, Maher, Garden, May, Watt.
Goals: Essendon – Stockdale 2, McCarthy 2, Maher 2, Shorten, Jenkins.
Crowd: 46,566 at the MCG

GRAND FINAL LINE-UPS

ESS	B:	V.Irwin	F.Baring	C.Donaldson
FITZ	F:	L.Bryant	J.Freake	H.Carter
ESS	HB:	J.Harrison	T.Fitzmaurice	R.Laing
FITZ	HF:	P.Parratt	N.Cockram	G.Rattray (capt)
ESS	C:	J.Garden	C.May	R.Watt
FITZ	C:	A.Dickens	T.Corrigan	C.Sherry
ESS	HF:	T.Jenkins	J.McCarthy	G.Shorten
FITZ	HB:	J.Tarbolton	S.Molan	E.Elliott
ESS	F:	S.Barker (capt)	G.Stockdale	C.Hardy
FITZ	B:	J.Atkinson	H.Jenkin	L.Wigraft
ESS	R:	N.Beckton	G.Rawle	F.Maher
FITZ	R:	G.McCracken	G.Collins	C.Fergie
ESS	Coach: Syd Barker			
FITZ	Coach: Vic Belcher			

SNAPSHOT

Win-loss record: 14-4

Highest score: 15.13 (103), round 1, v St Kilda; round 13, v Carlton; 14.19 (103), round 4, v Carlton.

Greatest winning margin: 66 points, round 13, v Carlton.

Lowest score: 1.12 (18), round 10, v St Kilda.

Greatest losing margin: 23 points, round 5, v Fitzroy.

Most goals by a player in a game: 9, Bob Merrick, round 10, v St Kilda.

Most consecutive wins: 4

Most consecutive losses: 1 (four times).

Club awards: Best & Fairest: Tom Fitzmaurice; Leading goalkicker: Greg Stockdale (68 goals).

Putting it into perspective:
Essendon's fourth premiership from seven Grand Final appearances was its first in 11 years and first Grand Final win over Fitzroy. The Dons had now won Grand Finals at two different venues, the Lake Oval and the MCG.

1923

		P	W	L	D	%	Pts
1	Essendon (1)	16	13	3		135.8	52
2	Fitzroy (2)	16	11	5		115.7	44
3	South Melb (3)	16	9	7		107.3	36
4	Geelong (4)	16	9	7		104.0	36
5	Collingwood	16	8	7	1	109.1	34
6	St Kilda	16	8	8		98.7	32
7	Carlton	16	6	9	1	84.0	26
8	Richmond	16	4	12		79.5	16
9	Melbourne	16	3	13		80.4	12

(18 home and away rounds)
(Each club had two byes)

PLAYERS USED

ESSENDON	GUERNSEY	GAMES	GOALS
Adam, Ken	26	10	0
Baring, Fred	5	4	0
Syd Barker	1	18	8
Beckton, Norm	3	18	13
Callahan, Joe	22	14	5
Campbell, Garnet	17	4	2
Donaldson, Clyde	2	17	0
Farrell, Charlie	11	9	0
Fitzmaurice, Tom	6	14	0
Garden, Jack	28	18	2
Hardy, Charlie	33	6	3
Harrison, Harry	9	3	0
Harrison, Joe	13	9	1
Hayes, Bill	4	2	0
Hunter, Harry	7	15	2
Irwin, Vince	18	11	6
Jenkins, Tommy	21	13	19
Laidlaw, Col	12	2	0
Laing, Roy	15	17	0
Maher, Frank	24	18	11
Marchesi, Val	27	7	0
May, Charlie	14	15	1
McCarthy, Justin	16	16	23
Raisbeck, Ralph	20	1	0
Rawle, George	6	1	0
Shorten, George	30	14	8
Stockdale, Greg	25	18	68
Sullivan, Jimmy	8	14	3
Watt, Rowland	10	16	6

**ESSENDON 6.11 (47) d
RICHMOND 9.13 (67)**

A FLAG TAINTED BY SCANDAL

A farcical finals system and claims of match-fixing ensured that Essendon's triumph would be the least celebrated in VFL history. By ROHAN CONNOLLY

ESSENDON broke an 11-year premiership drought with its win over Fitzroy in the 1923 Grand Final, and expectations of another premiership were high when the 1924 season began.

The Dons, after all, had managed to add the 1912 premiership to the one earned in 1911. Why couldn't they double up again? Particularly given the fact the club were heading into the new season with virtually the same playing list as the year before.

The 1924 season, however, proved a difficult exercise not just for Essendon, but for the entire game, which, thanks to some poor administration and other events nobody had counted on, became mired in confusion, controversy, and ultimately, allegations that went to the heart of the game's integrity.

First, there was new finals system to grapple with. The first VFL premiership, Essendon's win in 1897, was determined by a finals round-robin. Now it would have to attempt to win back-to-back premierships by similar means, as the league ditched the formula it had used since 1902.

The round-robin was back. The significant difference with this version was that a percentage advantage on the finals ladder would be enough to win were that edge held by the minor premier. The minor premier also had the right to challenge if it didn't finish the finals play-offs on top.

Essendon started the year slowly, losing the season-opener to Collingwood at home and managing only a draw against Carlton at Princes Park in round two. The Dons were disappointing in the launch of their premiership defence, losing by 16 points to the Magpies. They led by four points at the last change, having kicked a wasteful 6.13 to the Pies' 7.3. But Essendon added only 2.2 to Collingwood's final-term burst of 5.4.

The following week, the reigning premier was lucky to emerge with a tie against the Blues. Inaccuracy again plagued the Dons, but fortunately for them, also their opponents. Essendon had just 2.11 to Carlton's 4.5 at half-time. The Dons hit the front in the third quarter, kicking a much-straighter 4.1 while holding the Blues goalless. Then Carlton got the yips, finishing with a costly 3.7. Both sides were locked on 7.14 (56) at the finish.

The breakthrough finally came against South Melbourne at home in round three. The Dons had a big third quarter, giving them a 40-point lead. They eventually won by 26 points in a victory that kick-started the season.

The win over South would be the first of three straight, and indeed the Dons would win seven of the next eight. The one defeat was a loss to Fitzroy, by seven points, in a re-match of the 1923 grand final.

The run of good form took in a 63-point win over Richmond in which spearhead Greg Stockdale booted six goals. But Stockdale was being overtaken as Essendon's main man near goals by Tom Jenkins, who was on his way to a 50-goal haul for the season.

Jenkins was another former North Melbourne player who'd headed to Essendon. At just 175 centimetres, he was undersized for a key forward, but hardly underweight; his rotund frame nearly tipped the 100-kilogram mark.

But neither Jenkins nor Stockdale kicked the highest tally in a single game for Essendon in 1924. That honour went to Vince Irwin, who booted an amazing 10.9 of Essendon's 16 goals in an 82-point thrashing of St Kilda.

Irwin, however, hadn't even been picked in the original team. "Stockdale, who had injured his knee during the week, stood out of the Essendon team, and Irwin, who was not in the original selection, was allotted the centre-forward position," reported 'Forward' in *The Age*. "He proved to be the hero of the match by registering 10 goals, the last three of which were obtained in a sensational burst a few minutes before the final bell, putting enthusiasm into the game, from which all interested had long since faded.

"Irwin had numerous shots, scoring in all 10 goals and nine behinds, but allowance must be made for the strong wind which blew across the ground."

Irwin, another "mosquito" at just 168 centimetres, was a utility whose tremendous pace and agility made him a valuable back-pocket in the 1923 premiership win. It was only in 1924 that he became a dangerous forward.

Big tallies, both by individuals and teams, were clearly on the rise.

Essendon's Stockdale had headed the VFL goalkicking charts in 1923 with 68 goals. In 1924, it was his former Essendon teammate Jack Moriarty who, with Fitzroy, managed to boot 82. When the Roys had beaten Carlton by two points in the opening round, it was the first time in a VFL game in which both sides had scored more than 100 points.

Essendon lost to South Melbourne in round 11, won its next four games comfortably, then, with top spot on the ladder already sewn up, lost its final home and away game by 14 points to Melbourne. It was the Redlegs' first win at Windy Hill, and only the club's fourth victory of the season.

Essendon shrugged off that hiccup to go into the first of the finals play-offs, against Fitzroy at the MCG, full of confidence. Neither Essendon nor the Roys could manage a goal in the first quarter, but the Dons booted four to one in the second.

The third term was again goalless but the Bombers kicked four goals to one in the last quarter to win by 40 points, Jenkins kicking three goals and Frank Maher two.

In *The Age*, 'Forward' called the game "far from being a good exhibition". "For some unexplainable reason, Fitzroy failed to produce anything like their form and with Essendon playing fine football the Dons soon demonstrated their superiority and won easily," he wrote.

It was a day for defenders; Essendon back-pocket Clyde Donaldson was judged a clear best-on-ground. "His magnificent dashes from the backline were the feature of the game," 'Forward' wrote. Half-back Roy Laing also earned plaudits for his game, and Maher for his "cleverness".

There was at least one unusual story. Field umpire Arthur Wickham's performance was so good that, according to 'Forward', "He was applauded by the crowd when he left the arena."

The controversial finals system was already under the microscope. While 45,000 watched the Dons and Roys play in one final, an underwhelming 22,300 turned out at Windy Hill to watch the other first-round final between Richmond and South Melbourne.

Richmond won by 28 points, but the size of Essendon's victory and the paltry 2.6 (18) Fitzroy had managed to kick already gave the Dons a distinct edge in the race for the premiership. Another decent-sized win over South Melbourne in the second round and Essendon might have the flag as good as won.

The match was at the MCG. After a two-goals-to-one first quarter, Essendon stole a march in the second quarter with four goals to one. The Dons added another four to two in the second half to win with ease, by 33 points. Jenkins booted four for the winners. Maher and George Shorten kicked two goals apiece.

Essendon was never troubled at any stage, and, according to the critics, would prove a very worthy premier, as now seemed inevitable.

"Their form was magnificent, and after a very little while it was evident that they had nothing to fear from the Southerners who, perhaps by contrast, were slow and ineffectual," wrote 'Old Boy' in *The Argus*. Essendon were the faster, the more purposeful, more methodical, and more capable, and only the heroic work of the Southern defenders prevented a debacle.

"It was the all-round excellence which made the performance so impressive. There seemed a purpose, an object, in all they did, and no one failed."

As in 1923, the "Mosquito Fleet" had again caused havoc, with Essendon's best against South including little men Rowley Watt, Maher, Shorten and Jim Sullivan. Norm Beckton starred in the ruck and Tom Fitzmaurice at centre half-back.

For Essendon, the goal of successive premierships was already as good as achieved. At Princes Park the same afternoon, Fitzroy defeated Richmond by 20 points in front of another poor crowd of 26,000.

That left Essendon as the only finalist still undefeated, and with a massive percentage gap to its rivals. Richmond was the only club now that could possibly prevent the Dons taking out the flag. It would require the Tigers to defeat the Dons by 45 points at South Melbourne in the final week of the playoffs. Then, with Essendon having the right to challenge, the Tigers would have to beat the Dons again in what would effectively prove a Grand Final.

As it turned out, the results of the last round of finals pleased nobody. Not Fitzroy or South Melbourne, which were already out of the running. Not Richmond, which managed to beat the hot flag favourite, but not by enough to force the Dons' right to challenge. And particularly not Essendon, which "celebrated" the attaining of its premiership with its worst performance of the season.

If that wasn't bad enough, the premier was about to be torn asunder by acrimony, not just about the loss, but at the unpalatable suggestion that some players had taken bribes to play poorly.

Essendon had been completely jumped at the start by Richmond, conceding four goals to one in the first quarter, and gaining no ground in the second. A comeback of sorts in the third term saw the Dons draw within five points at the final change, but they could manage only two behinds in the last quarter. The final margin in favour of the Tigers was 20 points.

The Essendon defence had stood up. Donaldson, Laing and Fitzmaurice were all impressive, while Beckton rucked tirelessly, and Charlie Hardy, a late replacement for the injured Jack Garden, acquitted himself well. But there cannot have been a more subdued reaction to the winning of a League premiership than Essendon's that day. In *The Argus*, 'Old Boy' felt compelled to underline the credentials of the Dons to carry the mantle of premier.

"Essendon has proved to be the best side of the year, and it is a pity that they have not had the opportunity of proving it in a Grand Final," he wrote. "It was a well-blended team, strong in every department, with able reserves, each worthy of a permanent place in the side."

The lacklustre effort in the final against the Tigers raised eyebrows. But the extent of the angst that enveloped the club came as a huge shock. Whereas most premiership wins are the stuff of champagne, Essendon's celebrations, incredibly, were marked by flailing fists.

The trouble began in the Lake Oval dressingrooms immediately after the game and continued at Carlyon's Hotel in Bourke Street. The dispirited players then journeyed back to Windy Hill, where more fighting ensued. Just hours after it had secured what should have been a famous premiership triumph, Essendon was a rabble.

"It was evident that all was not harmony," 'Old Boy' wrote, in a nice touch of understatement. "In the dressing room at South Melbourne there were blows struck, and after the team had dined at Carlyon's and had resumed to their quarters at Essendon, there was further trouble. There were some arguments, and again fists were flying."

If the gloss had been taken from the significant achievement of successive premierships, it was tarnished entirely the following Saturday when Essendon, as VFL premier, took on VFA premier Footscray in a charity match to raise funds for the Limbless Soldiers Fund.

With Footscray considered a likely starter the following season in an expanded VFL, the Bulldogs' chance to press their credentials further beckoned. Their opponent, meanwhile, was reluctant to play. It was only after a personal appeal from Dame Nellie Melba, who was behind the Limbless Soldiers charity, that the Dons relented.

With the benefit of hindsight, it was a decision that might have cost the club much of its next decade or so. The cracks exposed in that final game against Richmond season were torn wide open. The morality of the team was questioned. An era ended and champions left.

Essendon was widely expected to defeat Footscray, with the VFL seen as clearly a superior competition in standard. It led by one point at half-time. But Footscray kicked six goals to the uninterested Dons' solitary goal in the second half to win by 28 points.

In *The Argus*, 'Old Boy' argued that the result underlined his belief the standard of League football had fallen. He was highly critical of the Dons.

"Essendon by comparison to Footscray were slow and indecisive, and with about four exceptions, the men did not show up. Whether they were beaten by a better team or that they held their opponents too cheaply, or that they had slackened in their training, it would be hard to say. On the form that they displayed it was fortunate that the premiership had been already won, but its lustre has been sadly diminished by the defeats by Richmond and Footscray," he wrote.

It would be diminished further still by the unsavoury allegations that a number of Essendon players had been paid off to enable Footscray to win the game. There were reports of more fighting in the post-match dressingrooms between players who had been trying and those who hadn't.

The fractured team was now very publicly falling apart. Tom Fitzmaurice was so disgusted that when the players returned to the rooms after the Footscray match, he told Essendon officials he would never play for the club again. He crossed to Geelong, where he would play in a third successive VFL premiership, in 1925. Fitzmaurice coached Geelong in 1928, and later played with North Melbourne and coached the club.

Essendon secretary Frank Reid was forced to deny the rumours of match-fixing, which included a tale that one star player had arrived home from the match to find a new car parked in his driveway.

In Fitzmaurice's final year of VFL football, as North coach in 1935, the tainted 1924 premiership again became a sensational story when he and former Essendon rover Charlie Hardy aired their allegations in the pages of *The Sporting Globe* of teammates taking bribes.

Fitzmaurice, while not naming names, bluntly stated that the Footscray game had been a fix. He recalled having words with a teammate, who he alleged said to him, "Why grouch? You could have been in the cut-up, too."

"The game was a frame-up," Fitzmaurice wrote. "A few players sold Essendon and the League without compunction. It was evident to me that some of our players were not doing their best and at three-quarter time some of us had an indignation meeting on the ground. When I came in, I told officials at Essendon that I was disgusted. I said I would not play for them again, and I didn't."

Fitzmaurice's teammate Hardy went even further, claiming the final defeat against Richmond had also been the subject of a fix. According to Hardy, it was "only direct action in the third quarter by a couple of players not to 'stay put' that enabled us to prevent Richmond forcing another game."

Essendon's official club history, Michael Maplestone's 1996 book *Flying Higher*, documents Hardy's claims about the Footscray game in detail:

> An Essendon player broke clear—I had foiled my opponent and made perfect position to receive the pass from him... imagine my surprise to see it go skimming about 15 feet over my head. Before the quarter closed the same player performed the same 'uncanny' feat in the same 'uncanny' way on two more occasions.
>
> After the game things were anything but harmonious in our dressingroom. One player in particular created a scene. He declared openly that he had been offered 20 pounds that morning to 'run a bye'. 'I wouldn't take my pals on,' he said, 'as did some chaps in the side. What did some of them get when I was offered 20 pounds'?

The simmering controversy that refused to die was hardly helped by the lacklustre efforts of the Essendon committee, which was expected to launch an inquiry into the game, but tried to sweep it under the carpet.

Though neither Fitzmaurice nor Hardy had implicated their teammates by name, the slur cast upon an entire premiership team was profound. It moved five members of the side—Frank Maher, Norm Beckton, Greg Stockdale, Charlie May and George Rawle—to publicly protest their innocence.

Nearly 90 years later, the question of whether Essendon "took a dive" is still being debated. In a long paper for the Australian Society of Sports History, Dale James Blair argues in an ASSH periodical a strong case *against* the game having been rigged.

Blair points to Fitzmaurice and Hardy's failure to name those they believed had accepted bribes, match reports that suggested little other than that Essendon had been beaten by a better side, and the fact that it was only in the final quarter that Footscray took charge of the game, and then only after Essendon had registered three straight behinds, including a "poster", as evidence that the result was fair and square.

But while the bribery accusations would never be definitively proven, they left an indelible black mark on a premiership that should have been a glittering triumph. The football year ended in chaos, and not just for Essendon.

The round-robin finals play-off system was an abject failure. Crowds had been uniformly low; the disenchantment of the public at being denied a suitable climax to the season was widespread.

It was a costly error of judgement by the VFL; the gate takings for the six finals were down several thousand pounds on the amount taken in four finals the previous year. The round-robin system was immediately consigned to the dustbin; instead the League reverted back to the method used for the previous 22 years.

Sadly, the finals farce was an appropriate footnote. The football year had been marked by spite and unsavoury incidents. The VFL had put its public off side. And ultimately even the winners were losers, in a fashion.

That's sad for the reputations of those involved with one of Essendon's most successful eras, men like Syd Barker, whose Mosquito Fleet was perhaps the most daring tactical innovation the game had seen to that point.

Barker had already proved himself one of the game's elite players with North Melbourne in the VFA. At Essendon he further enhanced his status. At only 183 centimetres, he was a short but powerful ruckman, with superb skills and endurance that enabled him to ruck all day.

Perhaps Barker's greatest asset had been his natural leadership qualities. His iron discipline and on-field daring lifted the Dons from last to third in his first season as captain-coach, in 1922, then to two straight premierships.

Those controversial final two games of the 1924 season were Barker's last with Essendon. He retired as a player only to make a brief comeback with North Melbourne in 1927. He died only three years later at just 42 years of age. His name is immortalised, however, at North Melbourne, where the club's best-and-fairest award is named the Syd Barker Medal.

For Essendon the glory days were well and truly over after 1924. The Dons made the finals the following two seasons, in 1925 and '26, but would not reach them again until 1940. The 1930s have been the club's least successful decade.

The events that surrounded the conclusion of the 1924 season have made it the least celebrated of Essendon's 16 premierships. What should be remembered also is that the team remains one of just four sides in the club's history to achieve back-to-back triumphs, in 1923 and '24, having headed the home and away ladder both years.

Essendon's Mosquito Fleet was a work of football art. But it's hard to appreciate even the finest of silk when there's the whiff of scandal in the air.

1924 ESSENDON

PREMIER'S SEASON

ESSENDON: 1924

ROUND ONE April 26
ESSENDON 8.15 (63)
COLLINGWOOD 12.7 (79)
Best: Essendon – Laing, Harrison, Barker, Jenkins, Stockdale, Watt, Shorten.
Goals: Essendon – Stockdale 3, McCarthy 2, Jenkins 2, Barker.
Crowd: 25,000 at Windy Hill

ROUND TWO May 3
ESSENDON 7.14 (56)
CARLTON 7.14 (56)
Best: Essendon – Jenkins, Rawle, Beckton, McCarthy, Fitzmaurice, Marchesi.
Goals: Essendon – Jenkins 5, Stockdale, Irwin.
Crowd: 40,000 at Princes Park

ROUND THREE May 10
ESSENDON 12.13 (85)
SOUTH MELBOURNE 8.11 (59)
Best: Essendon – Maher, Jenkins, Campbell, Donaldson, Laing, Stockdale, Hunter.
Goals: Essendon – Jenkins 5, Maher 3, Stockdale 3, Beckton.
Crowd: 25,000 at Windy Hill

ROUND FOUR May 17
ESSENDON 12.8 (80)
GEELONG 8.12 (60)
Best: Essendon – Farrell, May, Garden, Gregory, Fitzmaurice, Rawle, Beckton.
Goals: Essendon – Jenkins 3, Beckton 2, Rawle 2, Stockdale 2, Irwin, Maher, Shorten.
Crowd: 12,000 at Corio Oval

ROUND FIVE May 24
ESSENDON 13.16 (94)
RICHMOND 3.13 (31)
Best: Essendon – Stockdale, May, Barker, Laing, Sullivan, Campbell, Hunter.
Goals: Essendon – Stockdale 6, Callahan 2, Maher 2, Sullivan 2, Beckton.
Crowd: 22,000 at Windy Hill

ROUND SIX May 31
ESSENDON 8.13 (61)
FITZROY 10.8 (68)
Best: Essendon – Hunter, Donaldson, Laing, Stockdale, Sullivan, Callahan.
Goals: Essendon – Stockdale 2, Sullivan 2, Shorten, Beckton, Watt, Callahan.
Crowd: 35,000 at Brunswick St Oval

ROUND SEVEN
BYE

ROUND EIGHT June 14
ESSENDON 16.17 (113)
ST KILDA 3.13 (31)
Best: Essendon – Irwin, Gregory, Laing, Beckton, Adam, May, Fitzmaurice.
Goals: Essendon – Irwin 10, Rawle, Beckton, Maher, Shorten, Watt, Barker.
Crowd: 20,000 at Windy Hill

ROUND NINE June 21
ESSENDON 10.11 (71)
MELBOURNE 5.12 (42)
Best: Essendon – Callahan, Hunter, Donaldson, Barker, Harrison, Laing, Irwin.
Goals: Essendon – Irwin 4, Jenkins 2, Maher, Campbell, Shorten, Callahan.
Crowd: 18,769 at the MCG

ROUND TEN June 28
ESSENDON 8.12 (60)
COLLINGWOOD 4.10 (34)
Best: Essendon – Shorten, Fitzmaurice, Barker, Gregory, Hardy, Watt, Jenkins.
Goals: Essendon – Irwin 2, Jenkins 2, Maher, Stockdale, Shorten, Beckton.
Crowd: 20,000 at Victoria Park

ROUND ELEVEN July 5
ESSENDON 10.19 (79)
CARLTON 8.14 (62)
Best: Essendon – Fitzmaurice, Jenkins, Irwin, Sullivan, Maher, Campbell, Rawle.
Goals: Essendon – Irwin 4, Jenkins 3, Maher, Beckton, Callahan.
Crowd: 28,000 at Windy Hill

ROUND TWELVE July 12
ESSENDON 6.13 (49)
SOUTH MELBOURNE 9.8 (62)
Best: Essendon – Watt, Rawle, Donaldson, Farrell, Maher, Campbell, Gregory.
Goals: Essendon – Irwin 2, Maher 2, May, Jenkins.
Crowd: 33,000 at the Lake Oval

ROUND THIRTEEN July 19
ESSENDON 10.14 (74)
GEELONG 8.14 (62)
Best: Essendon – Jenkins, Fitzmaurice, Maher, Laing, Rawle, Kittle, Hunter.
Goals: Essendon – Jenkins 7, Irwin, Beckton, Sullivan.
Crowd: 20,000 at Windy Hill

ROUND FOURTEEN July 26
ESSENDON 12.13 (85)
RICHMOND 7.14 (56)
Best: Essendon – Maher, McCarthy, Watt, Shorten, Jenkins, Baring, Rawle.
Goals: Essendon – Jenkins 4, Irwin 3, Stockdale 2, McCarthy 2, Maher.
Crowd: 38,000 at Punt Road Oval

ROUND FIFTEEN August 2
ESSENDON 9.19 (73)
FITZROY 9.7 (61)
Best: Essendon – Garden, McCarthy, Stockdale, Laing, Shorten, Fitzmaurice.
Goals: Essendon – Campbell 2, Jenkins, Maher, Shorten, Garden, McCarthy, Beckton, Rawle.
Crowd: 26,000 at Windy Hill

ROUND SIXTEEN
BYE

ROUND SEVENTEEN August 30
ESSENDON 11.17 (83)
ST KILDA 9.5 (59)
Best: Essendon – Laing, May, Farrell, Barker, Jenkins, Shorten, Sullivan, Donaldson.
Goals: Essendon – Jenkins 4, Shorten 2, Cookson 2, Barker 2, Maher.
Crowd: 20,000 at the Junction Oval

ROUND EIGHTEEN September 6
ESSENDON 12.10 (82)
MELBOURNE 14.12 (96)
Best: Essendon – Donaldson, Jenkins, May, Callahan, Fitzmaurice, Garden.
Goals: Essendon – Jenkins 4, Shorten 2, McCarthy 2, Cookson, Barker, Stockdale, Beckton.
Crowd: 10,000 at Windy Hill

PREMIER'S FINALS

ROUND ROBIN FINAL September 13

ESSENDON	8.10 (58)
FITZROY	2.6 (18)

Best: Essendon – Donaldson, Laing, Maher, Hunter, McCarthy, Shorten, Fitzmaurice.
Goals: Essendon – Jenkins 3, Maher 2, McCarthy, Fitzmaurice, Stockdale.
Crowd: 44,522 at the MCG

ROUND ROBIN FINAL September 20

ESSENDON	10.12 (72)
SOUTH MELBOURNE	4.15 (39)

Best: Essendon – Maher, Shorten, Watt, Sullivan, Farrell, Fitzmaurice.
Goals: Essendon – Jenkins 4, Shorten 2, Maher 2, McCarthy, Hunter.
Crowd: 35,407 at the MCG

ROUND ROBIN FINAL September 27

ESSENDON	6.11 (47)
RICHMOND	9.13 (67)

Best: Essendon – Fitzmaurice, Beckton, Laing, Hardy.
Goals: Essendon – Hardy 2, Stockdale 2, Beckton 2.
Crowd: 25,000 at the Lake Oval

FINALS SQUADS

ESS: F.Baring, S.Barker (capt), N.Beckton, C.Donaldson, C.Farrell, T.Fitzmaurice, J.Garden, H.Gregory, C.Hardy, H.Hunter, T.Jenkins, R.Laing, F.Maher, C.May, J.McCarthy, G.Rawle, G.Shorten, G.Stockdale, J.Sullivan, R.Watt

ESS Coach: Syd Barker

RICH: J.Barnett, T.Bourke, R.Empey, C.Hall, J.Harrison, D.Hayes, G.Hislop, M.Hislop, J.Karthaus, A.MacIssac, B.McCaskill, N.McIntosh, K.Miller, D.Minogue (capt), M.Morris, R.Reid, G.Rudolph, J.Smith

RICH Coach: Dan Minogue

Note: There was no Grand Final this season. Richmond had the second best record after the round-robin.

SNAPSHOT

Win-loss record: 13-5-1

Highest score: 16.17 (113), round 8, v St Kilda.

Greatest winning margin: 82 points, round 8, v St Kilda.

Lowest score: 6.11 (47), round robin final, v Richmond.

Greatest losing margin: 20 points, round robin final, v Richmond.

Most goals by a player in a game: 9, Bob Merrick, round 10, v St Kilda.

Most consecutive wins: 4 (twice).

Most consecutive losses: 1 (five times).

Club awards: Best & Fairest: Tom Fitzmaurice; Leading goalkicker: Tommy Jenkins (50 goals).

Putting it into perspective: For the second time in club history the Bombers went back to back, taking home their sixth premiership flag. It now left them behind only Fitzroy as the competition's most successful club, in total they had now played 29 finals.

1924

		P	W	L	D	%	Pts
1	Essendon (1)	16	11	4	1	131.6	46
2	South Melb (4)	16	11	5		116.5	44
3	Fitzroy (3)	16	10	6		112.1	40
4	Richmond (2)	16	10	6		102.5	40
5	Geelong	16	8	8		107.2	32
6	Collingwood	16	8	8		96.0	32
7	Carlton	16	5	10	1	92.3	22
8	Melbourne	16	4	12		83.3	16
9	St Kilda	16	4	12		75.7	16

(18 home and away rounds)
(Each club had two byes)

PLAYERS USED

ESSENDON	GUERNSEY	GAMES	GOALS
Adam, Ken	26	2	0
Baring, Fred	5	5	0
Syd Barker	1	14	5
Beckton, Norm	3	18	13
Callahan, Joe	22	9	5
Campbell, Garnet	17	12	3
Cookson, Bill	19	2	3
Donaldson, Clyde	2	19	0
Farrell, Charlie	11	7	0
Fitzmaurice, Tom	6	18	1
Garden, Jack	28	10	1
Gregory, Harry	12	17	0
Hardy, Charlie	33	2	2
Harrison, Joe	13	5	0
Hayes, Bill	4	2	0
Hunter, Harry	7	19	1
Irwin, Vince	18	15	28
Jenkins, Tommy	21	16	50
Kittle, Les	23	1	0
Laing, Roy	15	19	0
Maher, Frank	24	19	19
Marchesi, Val	27	1	0
May, Charlie	14	19	1
McCarthy, Justin	16	12	9
Rawle, George	6	17	4
Shorten, George	30	18	12
Stockdale, Greg	25	16	24
Sullivan, Jimmy	8	12	5
Watt, Rowley	10	16	2

**GEELONG 10.19 (79) d
COLLINGWOOD 9.15 (69)**

CORIO KINGS FOUND NEW AGE

Geelong was a powerhouse in the VFA, but it took the Cats 28 years to win a flag in the VFL. By MICHAEL LOVETT

LIKE every club that joined the breakaway VFL in 1897, Geelong had its origins in the VFA where it built a blueprint for success, winning seven premierships in nine seasons.

Geelong's entry to the VFL in 1897 was hardly a great surprise. Twice it had won three successive flags in the VFA (1878-80 and 1882-84). It had also claimed another title in 1886 and, in its penultimate season before joining the VFL, it was runner-up to Fitzroy in 1895.

What astonished many good judges of the day was that it took until 1925 before Geelong could win its first VFL premiership, 39 years after its last success in the VFA.

There were the usual hard-luck stories of missed opportunities, particularly in the opening VFL season in 1897 when Geelong finished on top but the premiership was awarded to Essendon under a round-robin finals system that was scrapped the following season. Geelong also finished on top in 1901 but the Challenge system for the minor premier was not introduced until 1902.

Geelong was also one of several sides to be hard hit by the loss of players to military duty in World War I. In 1916, the club joined Melbourne, South Melbourne, Essendon and St Kilda as non-participants, leaving a four-team competition—Carlton, Collingwood, Richmond and Fitzroy.

However, it was only a one-year absence and by 1917 Geelong (which used just 25 players that season), together with South Melbourne, had resumed, and by 1919, when the war had ended, all nine teams were back.

In Melbourne and Geelong, life was gradually returning to normal, albeit the ravages of the Great War were still being felt keenly.

Geelong had nine players killed in action, including Team of the Century half-back flanker Joe Slater, who died on May 3, 1917 in France while fighting on the Western Front. However, by the early 1920s, Australia's economy had improved and so had the fortunes of the Cats, the nickname the club adopted.

For many years, Geelong was known at the Pivotonians as the city had been considered the 'pivot' of rural Victoria. In 1923, *The Herald* cartoonist Sam Wells drew Geelong captain Bert Rankin running into goal carrying a black cat. After losing five of its first seven games in 1923, Geelong finally defeated Carlton at Princes Park, prompting Rankin to suggest the club adopt the black cat mascot. "I believe it was the black cat that did the trick," Rankin said. And so the Cats were born.

The improvement was gradual, with Geelong finishing fourth in 1921 and 1923, its first taste of finals since 1914. Alas, a breakthrough win was not forthcoming. Those semi-final losses in 1921 and 1923 meant the Cats had played nine finals since joining the VFL for just two wins (in the round-robin finals system of 1897).

There was a mini coaching merry-go-round, with former Fitzroy premiership player Bert Taylor appointed non-playing coach for just one season, in 1923. Despite making the finals, Taylor was replaced by star forward Lloyd Hagger, who was made playing-coach in 1924.

However, at the end of the 1924 season, after the Cats had finished just outside the four, the committee moved again, this time deciding to allow Hagger to concentrate on playing. It replaced him with another forward, Cliff Rankin.

It was a bold move because two years earlier, in 1923, Rankin had pulled out of the Cats' semi-final side to play Fitzroy after his brother Bert was dropped. The local newspaper, the *Geelong Advertiser*, reported: "He would not do himself or the team justice in view of the fact that he would be troubled by the thought that his brother Bert had not been selected."

For all that, Rankin was held in high esteem by the club. He'd put his body on the line for his country and his club, starting with Geelong as an 18-year-old in 1915 in four games, before enlisting and serving on the Western Front in Europe the following year.

The small forward—he stood just 175cm and weighed 69kg—returned home in the middle of 1919 and, despite not playing football for four years, he kicked three goals in his comeback game.

Rankin led Geelong's goalkicking from 1920-23 and was the VFL's leading goalkicker in 1921 with 61 goals in 16 home and away games. In 2001 he was named an emergency in Geelong's Team of the Century and when he retired in 1928 after 153 games and 400 goals, he was regarded as one of the club's key figures during its early life in the VFL. Rankin's influence on the Cats in the 1925 season would be profound.

The commercial landscape was also changing for the better in Geelong by 1925. The Ford Motor Company made a momentous decision to base its Australian headquarters in Geelong, opening up greater employment opportunities for locals and starting a partnership that still exists.

Much to the chagrin of the VFA, the VFL turned its attention to the competition that had pre-dated the VFL (the VFA started in 1877) and decided to add three VFA clubs before the 1925 season.

Footscray, which had won the 1924 VFA Grand Final and later defeated Essendon in a highly controversial charity match between the VFA and VFL premiers, was admitted together with Hawthorn. The third place went to North Melbourne, just ahead of Prahran.

That Footscray-Essendon charity match, in which Essendon players were alleged to have been paid to not perform at their best, gave Geelong a leg-up the following season. Essendon champion centre half-back and triple best-and-fairest winner Tom Fitzmaurice was furious that some of his teammates might have played dead and declared he'd never play with Essendon again.

Essendon's loss was Geelong's gain and Fitzmaurice joined a team that was building momentum and strength. In 1924, centreman Edward 'Carji' Greeves won the inaugural Brownlow Medal, an award struck to honour long-serving Geelong administrator Charles Brownlow, who had died earlier that year.

In 1925 Greeves was entering his third season and had quickly become a star alongside players such as full-back George 'Jocka' Todd, rugged defender Dave Ferguson and ruckman Eric Fleming, while Rankin and Hagger were among the VFL's top forwards.

The start to the 1925 season didn't exactly go to script for the Cats—far from it in fact.

Geelong was drawn to play newcomer North Melbourne in the opening round at Corio Oval; on their home ground the Cats were clear-cut favourites. The club had also planned a big celebration to coincide with the opening of a new stand honouring Brownlow and former captain Henry 'Tracker' Young.

But it proved to be the first of two controversial games the Cats would play against North that season, with the Shinboners hauling in Geelong's 16-point lead at quarter-time to win by eight points.

While the elation in the North Melbourne camp was understandable, the Geelong natives were quite restless. "There was great joy amongst the visitors and much disappointment shown by the majority of Geelong people," wrote 'Forward' in *The Age* on May 4.

He might have been understating the discontent. Many Geelong supporters were so incensed by the loss they ripped up their membership tickets—a practice that was to haunt them later when the club declared members would be admitted to finals free of charge upon production of their season ticket. The club apparently received numerous requests stating that membership tickets had been "lost" or "misplaced" and that a replacement was required.

The loss stirred Rankin and his men into action and the Cats hit back in round two with a 33-point victory over Richmond at Punt Road. That win triggered a remarkable run for the Cats, who went on a 12-game winning streak that ended only in round 14 when they lost to St Kilda by 11 points

During that unbeaten period, Geelong held out eventual Grand Final opponents Collingwood by three points at Victoria Park, only the seventh time the Cats had won in 31 contests to that stage at the Magpies' home ground.

Geelong also scored a 93-point win against South Melbourne at Corio Oval in round 10, helped by a club record first-quarter score. The Cats had 11.4 (70) on the board at quarter-time, having held the Bloods scoreless. But it was the return clash with North Melbourne in round 12 that might have defined Geelong's season and certainly caused one of the game's biggest controversies.

After their opening round upset over Geelong, the Shinboners had fallen back to the pack; coming into the game at Arden Street, they had scored just two more wins, over fellow new chums Hawthorn and Footscray. The Cats by now were at the top of their game; on the previous weekend Rankin had starred for Victoria, kicking 10.1 in the Big V's win over Western Australia at the MCG.

Geelong was flexing its muscle in preparation for the finals but things turned nasty despite the fact the Cats were well in command of the game. Under the heading 'A BRUTAL EXHIBITION', *The Age* reported: "One of the roughest and most spiteful games ever played was witnessed at North Melbourne. It was apparent from the outset that certain players were out to play the man, and although a number of charges have been laid against the participants, it is a wonder there were not more men reported by the various umpires.

"Instances of fair, clever football were few and far between, and many lovers of the game left the ground disgusted with the exhibition."

A series of incidents saw six players reported—and some hefty suspensions handed out. North's Fred Rutley was outed for life for attempted kicking (the decision was reversed in 1930, allowing him to make a brief comeback), while Geelong pair Arthur Coghlan and Stan Thomas were suspended for 26 games each, Coghlan for striking and Thomas for elbowing.

Other charges saw North Melbourne's Bill Russ suspended for five games for striking Rankin, North's Harold Johnson was found guilty of attempted kicking but was not suspended and another Shinboner, Tim Trevaskis, received three games for striking. Geelong's Thomas was found guilty of elbowing but escaped punishment on that charge.

The incidents and suspensions angered Geelong officials and supporters, many who believed North Melbourne had instigated most of the trouble. About 500 fans crammed into His Majesty's Theatre in Geelong to attend a rally called by local MHR (Member of the House of Representatives) J.H. Lister to protest the innocence of Coghlan and Thomas.

However, their plea fell on deaf ears and the suspensions stood. The Cats pair missed the remainder of 1925 and the entire 1926 season; Thomas never played again but Coghlan returned in 1927, played six more seasons and was a member of the Cats' 1931 premiership side.

The loss of Coghlan, who had played 48 games to that stage of his career, and Thomas (136 games), gave the Cats added determination and they finished the home and away season on top, two games clear of Essendon. In the run home to the finals, Geelong had again defeated Collingwood narrowly (by nine points) in front of a record crowd of 26,025 at Corio Oval.

The finals system of the day certainly favoured the Cats, who played third-placed Melbourne in the semi-final at the MCG. Despite the fact Geelong lost that final by 15 points, it was able to use its right of challenge and advance to the Grand Final.

The Redlegs went through to the preliminary final, where they played Collingwood, winners of the other semi-final over Essendon. The Magpies enjoyed a comfortable 37-point margin over Melbourne to set up the decider against Geelong—the Cats' first VFL Grand Final and Collingwood's 13th, for five premierships to that stage.

Geelong locals embraced the thought of such an historic day for the club and the city. Most industries allowed workers to stay back an hour each day during Grand Final week so they would not have to work a half-day on Saturday, which was the standard practice at the time. Almost 10,000 Geelong fans crammed on to special trains, others went there by any means they could and the crowd of 64,288 was a then record for a Grand Final.

The Cats had become used to the fact the suspended pair of Coghlan and Thomas would not be playing but they were still able to field a formidable combination. Interestingly, many were playing just their first or second seasons: Jack Chambers, Dave Ferguson and Arthur Rayson were second-year players while Denis Heagney, Ken Leahy, Jim Warren and Jack Williams were in their first seasons. Heagney, 27, was playing just his fourth VFL game.

"There was a fair wind blowing from the west, which favoured the team kicking towards the Richmond goal," reported the *Geelong Advertiser*. It continued: "Rankin then met C. Tyson, captain of Collingwood, and they shook hands and walked towards the members' stand for the right to make first use of the wind. The hush was broken by the applause that seemed to come from all over the ground as the Geelong skipper won the spin of the coin."

Geelong had struck the first blow—the Cats would be kicking with the wind. Just before the coin toss, Dave Hickinbotham, who had captained Geelong's last premiership in the VFA in 1886, shook Rankin's hand on the sidelines and passed on some advice.

The Cats, with Rankin kicking two goals in the first 10 minutes, made the most of the wind early but the Magpies hit back and if not for some inaccurate kicking, might have been in front at the first break. Geelong led 3.2 (20) to Collingwood's 2.5 (17) and, more importantly, the Magpies' champion forward Gordon Coventry had been relatively quiet.

Geelong's second quarter proved to be crucial. The Cats kicked 4.6 into the wind while the Magpies managed just 2.4 with it, allowing Geelong to stretch its lead to 17 points at half-time. The combined pipe bands marched on to the field at the interval as the two sides headed inside and the partisan *Geelong Advertiser* believed the Cats were on track for their first premiership.

Upon resumption, umpire Jack McMurray snr paid a free kick against the Cats for throwing the ball, a call that did not please the *Geelong Advertiser* correspondent. "Geelong were penalised for throwing the ball, but it was not as flagrant as some of the throws by the Magpies that McMurray evidently did not see." It didn't get much better later in the quarter, according to the *Advertiser*: "(Collingwood's) Lawn was awarded a free and Webb forwarded where Baker was allowed a free, but only the umpire seemed to know what it was for. Baker set the two flags in motion."

Both sides had scored a goal each but the Magpies crept closer with another major—this time there were no protests from the *Advertiser*—and the ball was moving freely from end to end. However, Collingwood's back-to-back goals were answered by the brilliant Rankin, who kicked his fifth (from a free kick no less), and late in the quarter Ted Stevenson gave the Cats breathing space with another goal to give Geelong a 25-point lead at three-quarter time.

Rankin, Hagger and Fleming were obviously pleased with the Cats' position at that stage—during the last break, they posed for a photograph for the *Advertiser* with Hagger even raising his cup of cordial.

Their optimism was a little misplaced because Collingwood threw everything at the Cats in the final term. Under the sub-heading 'Strenuous Last Quarter', the *Advertiser* described how the Magpies kicked the opening two goals, conceding: "Collingwood were having the better of the play at this stage."

The Cats were off target and blowing their chances. When Collingwood skipper Charlie Tyson sent through a long punt kick for a goal, suddenly the difference was only eight points. "Players left their places in the excitement that followed and the game was crowded," according to the *Advertiser*.

In the helter-skelter, both sides attacked desperately; shots at goal went agonisingly close but the tension was broken when Geelong's Ferguson fell to the ground and somehow marked the ball while horizontal on the turf. With the Magpies in attack, the bell rang, sounding the Cats' first premiership and igniting scenes of jubilation both at the ground and in Geelong.

"Crowds rushed to meet the players during the cheering and applause that followed… Cliff Rankin was carried shoulder high to the dressingrooms," the *Advertiser* reported. "Scenes of the wildest enthusiasm were witnessed after the match in the big dressingroom occupied by the Geelong team. Everyone in the rooms seemed to be shaking hands; the players embraced each other, supporters danced and sang…"

Federal Senator J.F. Guthrie, well-known Geelong business identity, was the first to publicly congratulate the players. In a voice that "trembled with emotion", he said: "Boys I am so excited I cannot make a decent speech. I have never been so proud of the old city and the boys of old Geelong in my life, as I was today."

Not surprisingly, Hickinbotham, captain of Geelong's last premiership team in 1886, was given "a wonderful reception". "For 39 years, you have let me stand up alone—now I have got a cobber," he said referring to Rankin, the five-goal hero and captain-coach of Geelong's first VFL premiership side.

Rankin, for his part, was spent. "What can I say?" he said. His father Ted, a former Geelong player, was more effusive. "I am the happiest man in Melbourne. I never thought I would live to see the day." He also denied a report that he won a considerable amount of money on the result.

The celebrations then moved to Geelong as the masses returned home. About 4000 people flocked to Geelong Railway Station to greet returning fans and, of course, the players. The crowd was entertained by the St Augustine's Band and at 9pm the train carrying the players finally arrived.

"The fire bells rang almost simultaneously and a number of detonators exploded as the train drew into the station to the tune of *See the Conquering Hero Comes* by the band," the *Advertiser* reported.

"As the players stepped from the train they were rushed by supporters and friends and several of them were carried on the shoulders of enthusiastic supporters. When the crowd broke away from the station they went to the City Hall where the Mayor (Cr Ritchie) made arrangements to entertain the players and committee. Cars were used to convey the players to the hall, but Cliff Rankin was denied a motor ride as he was kept on the shoulders of a number of young men who took him over to the City Hall. Thousands of people followed."

The Mayor stood on the City Hall steps and at one stage grabbed a whistle from a band member to signal for silence. But he had to wait until the crowd gave three cheers for Rankin, the undisputed hero of the day.

After the crowd was addressed—and thanked—by several speakers including club president Dr J.E. Piper, it was Rankin's turn to say a few words. Again, he was carried shoulder high to the steps and after some urging he finally spoke.

"I don't think I can speak. I've got a terrible crook throat," he said. But he pushed on. "Today I captained the finest lot of players one could wish to meet on the football field. I ask you in fairness to them, are you going to give them three cheers? It may never come again, and you have been looking forward to it. Make the most of it. On behalf of the members of the football team I wish to thank you very sincerely. I may be captain, but a player is as good as the captain in his own position. I thank you very much."

The revelry continued into the night and the next day a Geelong premiership "tradition" started when a magpie was buried at Corio Oval. Not having a real magpie to bury, former Collingwood secretary Ern Copeland, who was representing the Magpies at the celebrations, took a gold ring containing the inscription of a magpie from his finger and generously allowed it to be buried (he later retrieved the ring).

More importantly, the Cats had buried the demons of their past. At last they had a VFL premiership to savour.

1925 GEELONG

PREMIER'S SEASON

GEELONG: 1925

ROUND ONE May 2
GEELONG	8.11 (59)
NORTH MELBOURNE	9.13 (67)

Best: Geelong – Rayson, Rankin, Williams, Ferguson, Pink, Stevenson, Hall.
Goals: Geelong – Pink 2, Rayson 2, Hagger 2, Fleming, Sharland.
Crowd: 12,500 at Corio Oval

ROUND TWO May 9
GEELONG	13.14 (92)
RICHMOND	9.5 (59)

Best: Geelong – Fitzmaurice, Todd, Coghlan, Hagger, Greeves, Hudd, Rankin.
Goals: Geelong – Hagger 4, Rankin 3, Stevenson, Smith, Rayson, Paterson, Greeves, Warren.
Crowd: 20,000 at Punt Road Oval

ROUND THREE May 16
GEELONG	9.8 (62)
ST KILDA	3.12 (30)

Best: Geelong – Smith, Todd, Fitzmaurice, Rayson, Warren, Thomas, Rankin, Greeves.
Goals: Geelong – Hagger 3, Rayson 3, Rankin 2, Paterson.
Crowd: 12,500 at Corio Oval

ROUND FOUR May 23
GEELONG	13.12 (90)
COLLINGWOOD	13.9 (87)

Best: Geelong – Greeves, Fitzmaurice, Warren, Hall, Fleming, Hagger, Smith.
Goals: Geelong – Warren 3, Todd 2, Hagger 2, Paterson 2, Stevenson, Rayson, Rankin, Fleming.
Crowd: 16,000 at Victoria Park

ROUND FIVE May 30
GEELONG	22.12 (144)
CARLTON	10.12 (72)

Best: Geelong – Rayson, Hagger, Fleming, Todd, Hudd, Paterson, Greeves, Smith.
Goals: Geelong – Rayson 6, Hagger 5, Smith 3, Warren 3, Rankin 2, Greeves, Hall, Todd.
Crowd: 12,500 at Corio Oval

ROUND SIX June 6
GEELONG	12.11 (83)
FOOTSCRAY	9.8 (62)

Best: Geelong – Todd, Leahy, Greeves, Ferguson, Hagger, Rankin, Smith, Thomas.
Goals: Geelong – Rankin 4, Hagger 4, Rayson, Smith, Warren, Fleming.
Crowd: 14,000 at the Western Oval

ROUND SEVEN June 13
GEELONG	15.11 (101)
HAWTHORN	7.7 (49)

Best: Geelong – Hagger, Fleming, Williams, Thomas, Leahy, Rankin, Warren.
Goals: Geelong – Hagger 7, Rankin 3, Sharland 2, Warren 2, Fleming.
Crowd: 11,000 at Corio Oval

ROUND EIGHT June 20
GEELONG	9.15 (69)
FITZROY	7.15 (57)

Best: Geelong – Hagger, Warren, Hudd, Sharland, Chambers, Todd, Johns.
Goals: Geelong – Hagger 7, Todd, Chambers.
Crowd: 25,000 at Brunswick St Oval

ROUND NINE June 27
GEELONG	15.9 (99)
MELBOURNE	10.15 (75)

Best: Geelong – Fleming, Thomas, Warren, Fitzmaurice, Smith, Todd, Leahy.
Goals: Geelong – Warren 5, Hagger 4, Rankin 2, Stevenson, Brushfield, Fitzmaurice, Smith.
Crowd: 19,500 at Corio Oval

ROUND TEN July 11
GEELONG	18.13 (121)
SOUTH MELBOURNE	3.10 (28)

Best: Geelong – Hagger, Coghlan, Stevenson, Chambers, Rankin, Greeves, Hall.
Goals: Geelong – Hagger 7, Rankin 4, Fleming 2, Warren 2, Smith, Rayson, Todd.
Crowd: 11,000 at Corio Oval

ROUND ELEVEN July 18
GEELONG	11.10 (76)
ESSENDON	9.11 (65)

Best: Geelong – Fitzmaurice, Johns, Greeves, Todd, Fleming, Hagger, Leahy, Rayson.
Goals: Geelong – Hagger 3, Fleming 3, Rayson 2, Rankin, Todd, Chambers.
Crowd: 30,000 at Windy Hill

ROUND TWELVE August 1
GEELONG	22.22 (154)
NORTH MELBOURNE	9.5 (59)

Best: Geelong – Rankin, Thomas, Greeves, Hagger, Johns, Stevenson, Todd, Hall.
Goals: Geelong – Hagger 5, Todd 4, Rayson 3, Leahy 3, Fleming 2, Warren 2, Hall, Chambers, Rankin.
Crowd: 10,000 at Arden St Oval

ROUND THIRTEEN August 8
GEELONG	11.20 (86)
RICHMOND	4.8 (32)

Best: Geelong – Leahy, Williams, Hagger, Ferguson, Fitzmaurice, Rankin, Greeves.
Goals: Geelong – Hagger 3, Warren 2, Rayson 2, Pink, Todd, Rankin, Fleming.
Crowd: 13,500 at Corio Oval

ROUND FOURTEEN August 22
GEELONG	7.9 (51)
ST KILDA	9.8 (62)

Best: Geelong – Greeves, Todd, Chambers, Brushfield, Rankin, Smith, Hall, Mockridge.
Goals: Geelong – Fleming 2, Stevenson, Brushfield, Ferguson, Hagger, Rankin.
Crowd: 15,000 at the Junction Oval

ROUND FIFTEEN August 29
GEELONG	11.8 (74)
COLLINGWOOD	8.17 (65)

Best: Geelong – Fitzmaurice, Leahy, Rayson, Williams, Hagger, Smith, Johns, Greeves.
Goals: Geelong – Rankin 4, Hagger 3, Todd 2, Fleming, Warren.
Crowd: 26,025 at Corio Oval

ROUND SIXTEEN September 5
GEELONG	15.13 (103)
CARLTON	14.10 (94)

Best: Geelong – Hagger, Rayson, Todd, Williams, Ferguson, Rankin, Fitzmaurice.
Goals: Geelong – Hagger 7, Warren 2, Rankin 2, Fleming, Chambers, Todd, Rayson.
Crowd: 10,000 at Princes Park

ROUND SEVENTEEN September 12
GEELONG	14.16 (100)
FOOTSCRAY	9.7 (61)

Best: Geelong – Rayson, Fitzmaurice, Hall, Chambers, Stevenson, Rankin, Hagger.
Goals: Geelong – Hagger 3, Rankin 3, Jones 2, Todd 2, Fleming 2, Murrells, Ferguson.
Crowd: 10,800 at Corio Oval

PREMIER'S FINALS

SECOND SEMI-FINAL September 26

GEELONG	13.8 (86)
MELBOURNE	14.17 (101)

Best: Geelong – Warren, Greeves, Hall, Chambers, Heagner, Hagger, Johns.
Goals: Geelong – Hagger 7, Rankin 4, Jones, Fleming.
Crowd: 51,256 at the MCG

GRAND FINAL October 10

GEELONG	3.2 7.8 10.13 10.19 (79)
COLLINGWOOD	2.5 4.9 6.12 9.15 (69)

Best: Geelong – Chambers, Johns, Rankin, Rayson, Leahy, Warren, Hudd, Greeves.
Goals: Geelong – Rankin 5, Stevenson, Chambers, Hall, Heagney, Hagger.
Crowd: 64,288 at the MCG

GRAND FINAL LINE-UPS

GEEL	B:	L.Smith	K.Johns	D.Ferguson
COLL	F:	L.Stainsby	G.Coventry	R.Baker
GEEL	HB:	B.Hudd	T.Fitzmaurice	K.Leahy
COLL	HF:	J.Harris	F.Murphy	J.Lawn
GEEL	C:	E.Stevenson	E.Greeves	J.Williams
COLL	C:	C.Milburn	H.Chesswas	L.Wescott
GEEL	HF:	A.Rayson	G.Todd	J.Chambers
COLL	HB:	C.Tyson (capt)	B.Makeham	E.Wilson
GEEL	F:	C.Rankin (capt)	L.Hagger	S.Hall
COLL	B:	G.Beasley	C.Dibbs	J.Shanahan
GEEL	R:	E.Fleming	D.Heagney	J.Warren
COLL	R:	S.Coventry	Laurie Murphy	R.Webb
GEEL	**Coach:** Cliff Rankin			
COLL	**Coach:** Jock McHale			

SNAPSHOT

Win-loss record: 16-3

Highest score: 22.22 (154), round 12, v North Melbourne.

Greatest winning margin: 95 points, round 12, v North Melbourne.

Lowest score: 7.9 (51), round 14, v St Kilda.

Greatest losing margin: 15 points, second semi-final, v Melbourne.

Most goals by a player in a game: 9, Bob Merrick, round 10, v St Kilda.

Most consecutive wins: 12

Most consecutive losses: 1 (three times).

Club awards: Leading goalkicker: Lloyd Hagger (78 goals).

Putting it into perspective:
Geelong's first premiership now left St Kilda as the only remaining foundation club yet to capture a flag. While Geelong had played finals in seven previous seasons, this was their first Grand Final appearance.

1925

	P	W	L	D	%	Pts
1 Geelong (1)	17	15	2		152.7	60
2 Essendon (4)	17	13	4		119.3	52
3 Melbourne (3)	17	12	4	1	138.5	50
4 Collingwood (2)	17	12	5		127.1	48
5 Fitzroy	17	12	5		125.7	48
6 St Kilda	17	8	9		99.6	32
7 Richmond	17	6	10	1	86.7	26
8 South Melb	17	6	11		85.7	24
9 Carlton	17	5	12		79.0	20
10 North Melb	17	5	12		75.2	20
11 Footscray	17	4	13		82.7	16
12 Hawthorn	17	3	14		66.1	12

(17 home and away rounds)

PLAYERS USED

GEELONG	GUERNSEY	GAMES	GOALS
Brushfield, Nick	7	16	2
Chambers, Jack	8	13	5
Coghlan, Arthur	13	11	0
Ferguson, Dave	3	18	2
Fitzmaurice, Tom	23	15	1
Fleming, Eric	11	19	19
Greeves, Edward	20	19	2
Hagger, Lloyd	14	19	78
Hall, Syd	4	16	3
Heagney, Denis	29	4	1
Hudd, Bill	31	8	0
Johns, Keith	9	14	0
Jones, Jockie	27	4	3
Leahy, Ken	25	13	3
Mockridge, Frank	18	6	0
Murrells, Frank	26	2	1
Paterson, Jack	5	6	4
Pink, Arthur	1	3	3
Plane, Charlie	10	2	0
Profitt, Vic	2	1	0
Rankin, Cliff	6	19	43
Rayson, Arthur	28	17	23
Sharland, Wallace	22	4	3
Smith, Les	16	19	7
Stevenson, Edward	15	13	5
Thomas, Stan	21	11	0
Todd, George	19	18	16
Warren, Jim	12	18	24
Williams, Jack	24	14	0

**MELBOURNE 17.17 (119) d
COLLINGWOOD 9.8 (62)**

THE SPIRIT OF TWENTY-SIX

Melbourne rebuilt slowly in the aftermath of World War I but eventually boasted a team that was both tough and skilful. By ROBERT PASCOE

AFTER winning the 1900 premiership, another quarter of a century would pass before Melbourne would again enter the winner's circle. This was mainly because other clubs had overtaken it in several aspects, such as acquiring better physical facilities, building a loyal membership, developing a stronger club administration and devising coaching strategies.

Since Melbourne's incorporation in 1889 into the Melbourne Cricket Club, it had become less self-reliant as a football club. Melbourne and the other five VFL clubs that ceased to compete during the Great War were disadvantaged by their absence from the competition. At one extreme, University disappeared; at the other, by staying in the competition, Richmond was catapulted from its lowly role in the pre-war seasons to its back-to-back flags in 1920 and 1921. Essendon recovered from the war quickly, and Melbourne, until 1933 still nicknamed the Fuchsias, had come good by 1926.

The first factor was better recruitment. By 1926, the Melbourne Football Club's catchment had extended into country Victoria—Ballarat, Gippsland and Bendigo—while its metropolitan reach was also wider than it had been in 1900. In this regard Melbourne was not alone—the team lists of the 1920s had more bush lads in their number than those of the Edwardian period.

Second, clubs began to offer employment to these recruits: Essendon at the Fire Brigade, Collingwood at the Collingwood council or the Abbotsford brewery. Melbourne had its own new inducement to prospective players—namely, guaranteed employment at Miller's rope works or at the major oil company, Vacuum. High up in the club hierarchy was Joe Blair, who in 1920 had become the general manager of Vacuum Oil Company after starting with the firm (later known as Mobil) as a clerk in 1905. Blair, nicknamed 'JCB' in business circles, later served as Melbourne club chairman from 1929 until his death in 1946. As many as 13 of the 18 men who ran out for Melbourne in the 1926 Grand Final were employed at Vacuum.

Among these 13 men was Sydney-born Ivor Warne-Smith, a product of Melbourne's Wesley College, who was quietly spoken and the winner of the 1926 and 1928 Brownlow medals. He was also in charge of Vacuum Oil's Yarraville depot. Bert Chadwick was also an oil man, working in the arm of the business that converted low-grade to higher-quality oil. Another Vacuum Oil employee was the tough Bob Corbett, who lived in Yarraville. Jimmy Davidson came down from Gippsland to play for Melbourne and got work at Vacuum. Stan 'Bunny' Wittman ended up with a good job at Vacuum. Wittman's selection followed a chance conversation between the gripman on a cable tram trundling along Bridge Road towards the city and the club secretary, Andrew Manzie, who had been immersed in his morning newspaper: "This fellow's right out of the box," said the gripman. "Name of 'Bunny' Wittman. A real beaut. Plays for Rosedale." (Wittman's nickname derived from his large floppy ears.)

There had been an interesting change in the culture of this team from the one that had fluked the premiership in 1900. The 1926 players owed a debt to their employers at Vacuum and Miller's rope works—and they repaid their bosses in full. They were expected to observe appropriate behaviour both on and off the field. 'If you misbehaved, they'd talk about you', recalled Gordon Ogden, one of the players of this era in a 1997 interview. Like their contemporaries at other clubs, the Melbourne players from whatever geographical location became adopted into their new metropolitan community. They went about their football in a business-like way. And, despite some variations in their background, they liked and respected each other.

A focal point for the teammates was the Bentleigh milk bar owned by the family of Hugh Dunbar, the side's big ruckman. Bob Johnson snr came into the side from a Catholic background. Derek Mollison was a Melbourne Grammar product and the son of the State Coroner. Harold Coy was a tradesman on the Victorian Railways.

The Melbourne coaching also improved, under Chadwick's leadership as captain-coach.

The best sides of 1926 were Collingwood and Geelong, each registering 15 wins out of 18 in the home and away season, but with a narrow percentage advantage to Collingwood. Melbourne finished third, with 14 wins but a better percentage than Geelong. Essendon filled out the final four with 12 wins. The three new clubs—respectively Footscray, Hawthorn and North Melbourne—ended in the three lowest rungs of the ladder. The Northerners did not win a match all season, but lost five games by less than a kick and drew at Glenferrie with Hawthorn in round 13, 10.10 (70) apiece. Hawthorn's three wins were against North Melbourne, Fitzroy and Footscray.

The middling teams were South Melbourne, Carlton, Richmond, Fitzroy and St Kilda. Among these, the unluckiest was clearly South Melbourne. By round 10, the Southerners were 5-5, with some close results. In round 11 at Lake Oval they defeated Geelong, 9.13 (67) to 8.8. (56), continuing a fine winning streak against the Pivotonians at that venue that stretched back to 1905. This should have been the catalyst for a strong second half of the season. The following Saturday, in front of 27,000 people at Punt Road Oval, South was 8.8 (56) to Richmond's 9.14 (68) at lemons (three-quarter time), but slotted eight goals to one in the last stanza, thanks to fine teamwork from playing coach and former Magpie Charlie Pannam, captain Paddy Scanlan and Edward Johnson. South won the next four straight before going down at home to Collingwood in round 17 by one goal and then defeating Essendon at Windy Hill the following Saturday by only three points. The late-season push was not enough to replace Essendon as the fourth team after round 18. Both teams were on 12 wins, but Essendon had the better percentage (124.3 to 118.9).

The same four teams that led the ladder in 1925 were there in 1926, but they had reached there through a combination and luck and skill. Collingwood started emphatically, with seven wins out of the first eight, losing in round 9 to Carlton at Princes Park in front of 30,000 fans on a wet day. Two trams going home collided in Lygon Street and 40 people were rushed to hospital.

Collingwood continued well, defeating Melbourne at the MCG by 50 points in round 15. (Between 1922 and 1937 Melbourne defeated Jock McHale's Collingwood only twice.) Second to Collingwood by four percentage points, Geelong also put in a good season, winning the first four matches, losing to Collingwood in round 5 at Corio Oval (ending Collingwood's six-match Geelong hoodoo), and then winning the next five straight, including Corio Oval matches against Essendon in round 7 and Melbourne in round 10.

Melbourne's run was aided by strong wins against the lower teams (such as a 59-point drubbing of Footscray at the Western Oval in round 6; or the 141-point demolition of Hawthorn at the MCG in round 9, attended by a miserly 7514 people; a 89-point win at the Junction Oval in round 12) and respectable losses against their strong rivals (five points to Collingwood at Victoria Park in round four and 14 points to Geelong at Corio Oval in round 10). By the end of round 18, Melbourne's percentage was only three points behind Collingwood's. Essendon also had a good year, keeping ahead of South Melbourne on percentage and earning its spot in the finals.

In the first week of the finals, Essendon defeated Geelong comfortably after an even first half to produce a record finals score of 17.15 (117) to 10.10 (70). The following Saturday, also at the MCG, Melbourne surprised the football world with a win over Collingwood, 13.17 (95) to 12.12 (84), but the doubting Thomases were convinced that when the Magpies got their second chance (as minor premiers) they would perform predicably well. In the Melbourne camp, the mood was one of ebullience; after all, this was their first win against Collingwood in 11 recent encounters.

September now gave way to October and Melbourne had earned the right to play Essendon in the preliminary final, with Collingwood—with the right to chellenge—having a week off. In dry and windy conditions scores were low and the game was tight. At half-time Melbourne led 3.4 (22) to 2.7 (19). As the players left the field, Essendon's 'Chooka' May belted Bob Corbett from behind and broke his jaw. (For this he was suspended and his senior career came to an end; later he mentored Jack Dyer!) Without the 19th man (introduced in 1930) Corbett's departure reduced the Melbourne side to 17 men. Late in the match Corbett escaped the club doctor and came back onto the field swathed in bandages. Essendon's tough man, Harry Hunter, had a chance to clean Corbett up but as a mark of respect for Corbett's courage he side-stepped him. Corbett did not get a kick in the last quarter but inspired his team mates to hang on for a three-point win, 6.6 (42) to 5.9 (39). Melbourne kicked just one behind in the last term. Essendon was shattered by this unexpected defeat and its next finals appearance would not occur until 1940.

For Melbourne, this was its first Grand Final since 1900, when it won the premiership in most unusual circumstances, coming from sixth before the sectional rounds. A huge crowd of 59,632 took advantage of the fine conditions.

Collingwood, wrote 'Old Boy' (R.W.E Wilmot) in *The Argus*, were "a tailless Magpie":

> The ground after all the rain was in surprisingly good condition. The central patch of black turf, and a square in front of the Richmond goal, were a little

sticky, but all the conditions were in favour of a good exhibition. A slight breeze favoured the Richmond goal, and Chadwick, winning the toss, decided to have first use of the breeze. The bright sunshine and the packed stands made the scene a gay one, and there was a hum of excitement in the crowd of nearly 60,000 spectators as the teams came out, which added to the interest.

'Old Boy' paid close attention to 'Pop' Vine, playing his very first game of senior football, coming in to replace Corbett, writing:

> "As the teams took their places it was interesting to notice the disposition of the players. Vine, the new man in the Melbourne team, was given an encouraging cheer as he took place beside [Joe] Poulter. Vine, standing 6ft 2½in., and weighing 13st. 6lb., was an ½in. taller, but 1lb. lighter than Poulter, and they were two very fine specimens of the Australian athlete."

Melbourne got off to a flying start, with a characteristic attacking move ending with Bob Johnson snr. Continued 'Old Boy':

> "There was no delay, and when the ball was bounced, [Harold] Cheswass and [Charles] Milburn sent it forward, but Dunbar turned them back, and before Collingwood could realise it the Melbourne 'advance by the right wing' system was at work. Warne-Smith punched the ball to Wittman, who forwarded to Moyes, who took a wonderful mark. His shot was straight, but short, and Johnson marked it close in, and, after barely a minute's play, Melbourne had the first goal.

Having established this early lead, Melbourne held on to it:

> "Collingwood were slow in their movements, but they were playing with grim determination, and the game increased in vigour.... Melbourne, realising that they must keep the game open, were playing wide to the wings, and thus they kept Collingwood off till quarter time, when the board showed:--Melbourne, 4.5; Collingwood, 1.1."

The second quarter was won by Collingwood:

> "A dash by [Jack] Beveridge gave Chesswas a chance, but his shot hit the man at his mark; the ball, however, flew to H. Collier, who snapped [their] second goal after four minutes' play... It had been a stirring quarter, and, with Collingwood playing desperately and developing their 'shock' tactics to the full, it looked as if they might wear Melbourne down."

The Melbourne side of 1926 was famous for its third quarter performances, and this day was no different:

> "[T]hey had been playing only three minutes when Wittman passed to Moyes, and a left foot drop kick brought [Melbourne's] eighth goal. Defence

by Tymms at one end, and Beasley at the other were applauded before the Taylor-Wittman-Moyes trap snapped again for [their] ninth goal.... Melbourne were slowly forging ahead and, with Collingwood striving to check the onrush, it was full of sparkle and "ginger," and as one watched it one wondered if it could last. Tyson was throwing himself into it, leading what gradually became a forlorn hope, but nothing came of it. "

Then, late in the term, followed what 'Old Boy' termed the 'Wonderful Six Minutes' that proved the highlight of the match:

"Suddenly Melbourne swept all opposition aside, and in six wonderful minutes they took charge of the game and added four goals. Warne-Smith and Collins led up to the first goal, Wittman, after being twice checked, scoring brilliantly, and after paying the penalty of a heavy "roll" from A. Collier. This was a bad feature of Collingwood play, and it cost them dearly. A long shot by Vine found an unguarded goal, and a clever hit out by Vine to Warne-Smith, and a pass to Duff brought another. Lightning passes— White to Wittman to Moyes to Johnson—ended in [the] 14th goal, and in that bright patch Melbourne obtained such a hold on the premiership that it would have taken a miracle to dislodge them. Collingwood were fighting it out, but they were powerless, and the quarter ended with Melbourne 14 goals 9 behinds, Collingwood 7 goals 6 behinds, or a lead of 7½ goals.

The last quarter was the dénouement, 'A Tame Ending':

"All the fire was out of the game in the final term. Melbourne, keen not to give their opponents a chance, pressed forward, and when Johnson, marking almost in goal, kicked [their] 15th goal, and brought to the total to 101 points there was nothing more in it.

The final scores were 17.17 (119) to 9.8 (62), a big score in that era, just exceeding Essendon's winning total of four weeks earlier.

"MELBOURNE PREMIERS". "Stirring Success". "Enthusiastic Scenes". "The Best Team Premiers." These were headline and sub-heads over the account of the match the following Monday morning in *The Argus*. 'Old Boy' wrote:

The football season for 1926 closed on Saturday in a blaze of triumph for the Melbourne team, which won its first premiership since 1900, by such a brilliant, forceful exhibition of the game as to leave no doubt that it was the best team of the year."

The game was faster now and the players were treated more like matinee idols. A new morning newspaper, *The Sun News-Pictorial*, introduced much more photographic accounts of football than had been the case previously, and other newspapers, even the dowager *Argus*, rushed to compete. Radio broadcasts became common. Films were taken of players and their styles of play.

1926 MELBOURNE

In the film, *Pictures and Personalities of the Melbourne Football Scene in the Late 1920s or Early 1930s*, players from various clubs are shown while training on their home grounds. The Melbourne sample must have been taken in or around 1926, as it includes Warne-Smith, Herbert White, Johnson, William Tymms, Dick Taylor, and Corbett. Part of the coverage is of a match between Melbourne and Essendon around this time.

The play of the era was still kick and mark, but the handballs were slicker and less often done in desperation when a player was cornered. Short passes and handballs were now employed to break the lines or switch the angle of attack. Essendon's 'Mosquito Fleet' of 1923 and '24 had devised a clever strategy for attacking, by leaving spaces in their forward half for their forwards to drop into. In 1926 Melbourne had unpicked this strategy, with their backmen anticipating the Essendon moves and covering for each other.

Following 1922 and 1924, 1926 was the third VFL season during which all the competing clubs kicked annual scores of more than 1000 points. Another five decades would pass before teams reached the 2000 mark for a season, but, conversely, very seldom would teams kick fewer than 1000 points again (North Melbourne in 1930; St Kilda in 1943 and 1955; Hawthorn in 1953; Fitzroy in 1963). This was initially due to the 1922 rule that penalised players who forced the ball out of bounds; from 1924 to 1939 the out-of-bounds penalty applied to the last team that touched the ball, whether the action was deemed to be deliberate or not. (Boundary throw-ins only returned to replace these free kicks in 1939.)

This made the key positions down the spine of the ground all the more important, and team plans turned on building a strong forward line, further pushing up the score tally. Team plays were still less important in the game's thinking than the one-on-one contests that were the order of the day. Defensive players were not as fully recognised as would later be the case. Full-backs were dour in an era with many glamorous full-forwards. By contrast, the centre half-back role was more appreciated in the 1920s, with players in the Melbourne line-up like Chadwick or Dunbar positioned there. Centremen generally remained in the pivot of the ground throughout the play, though Ivor Warne-Smith, listed as the Grand Final centreman, also played in the ruck at times. Rovers like Corbett were critical to the game as it was played in that period, but Melbourne had to make do without him in the Grand Final after he was famously KO'd in the previous week's encounter with Essendon. Centre-half forwards and full-forwards were also key positions. Melbourne relied heavily on Johnson in the centre half-forward role.

The half-forward flank was a graveyard in this period, with 'Bunny' Wittman kicking only 16 goals over the 20 games he played in 1926. The wing roles also went to players of less renown; their job was to rush into the play in bursts and less often to be the truly linking players of later eras. The back pocket's main job was to mind the resting rover, crumb the ball from the high-flying full-back, and swap with the half-back flanker if he was not doing so well. It was a role in which you learnt a great deal. "You saw all the play up the field. You got to understand the team plan better than most. You knew what had to be done to keep the opposing team's score down," Gordon Ogden recalled.

Over the course of the 1926 season, Melbourne's leading goal kickers were Moyes from the forward pocket (55 goals in 19 matches), Johnson (50 from 20 appearances), Harry Davie, from full-forward (50 from just 15 games), and Dave Duff (26 goals from 11 matches), who played full-forward on the big day. Moyes, Johnson and Davie were third, fourth and fifth on the League's goal-kicking list for 1926. (As an omen of what was in store for the next four years, Collingwood's Gordon Coventry kicked 83 in all, 27 more than Geelong's skyscraping Lloyd Hagger.)

After the 1926 win, Melbourne's next finals campaigns were conducted in 1928, 1936, 1937, and 1939. The tendency to recruit far and wide continued at Melbourne: by 1940 only five of the 21 senior Demons were locals. This was to prove beneficial in the decades to follow.

As the heroes of 1926 retired from senior football and took up their regular suburban lives, many lived in the south-eastern suburbs, from South Yarra and Toorak out as far as the farming country of Oakleigh and Carnegie. Their deeds were never forgotten by the club and indeed were immortalised in song. "The spirit of 'Twenty-six'" became a line in the second (but rarely used) verse of the Melbourne theme song.

Hopes of a back-to-back premiership in 1927 were dashed with a rash of injuries and it would be 13 long seasons before Melbourne once more entered the winning annals in Australian football.

On April 17, 2011, during the Gold Coast-Melbourne match, the West Australian football commentator Dennis Cometti—who likes to quote the late Bob Johnson jnr (they crossed paths at East Fremantle)—said that Bob snr told his son that at the 1926 Grand Final they ran out of *Football Records*.

The story is possibly apocryphal, but it serves the purpose, as all good stories do, of linking that distant October afternoon with the present day.

1926 MELBOURNE

PREMIER'S SEASON

MELBOURNE: 1926

ROUND ONE May 1
MELBOURNE   13.14 (92)
ST KILDA   8.15 (63)
Best: Melbourne – Johnson, Davie, Chadwick, Anderson, Thomas, Green, Tulloh.
Goals: Melbourne – Tulloh 4, Davie 4, Warne-Smith 3, Anderson 2.
Crowd: 18,742 at the MCG

ROUND TWO May 8
MELBOURNE   8.10 (58)
CARLTON   9.15 (69)
Best: Melbourne – Green, Davidson, Coy, Warne-Smith, Davie, O'Brien, Johnson.
Goals: Melbourne – Davie 3, Johnson 2, White, Warne-Smith, Cannan.
Crowd: 18,000 at Princes Park

ROUND THREE May 15
MELBOURNE   17.17 (119)
NORTH MELBOURNE   14.5 (99)
Best: Melbourne – Johnson, Davie, White, Corbett, Davidson, Moyes, Collins.
Goals: Melbourne – Johnson 6, Davie 6, Tymms 2, Abernethy, Duff, Moyes.
Crowd: 9,495 at the MCG

ROUND FOUR May 22
MELBOURNE   12.7 (79)
COLLINGWOOD   12.12 (84)
Best: Melbourne – Tymms, White, Wittman, Taylor, Johnson, Moyes, Veal, Corbett.
Goals: Melbourne – Johnson 5, Moyes 3, Davie 2, Abernethy, Taylor.
Crowd: 15,000 at Victoria Park

ROUND FIVE May 29
MELBOURNE   19.8 (122)
RICHMOND   12.17 (89)
Best: Melbourne – Davie, White, Coy, Streeter, Collins, Wittman, Moyes.
Goals: Melbourne – Davie 9, Moyes 3, Abernethy 2, Johnson 2, Taylor, Warne-Smith, White.
Crowd: 28,628 at the MCG

ROUND SIX June 5
MELBOURNE   15.15 (105)
FOOTSCRAY   6.10 (46)
Best: Melbourne – Davie, Collins, Johnson, Abernethy, Warne-Smith, Streeter, Tymms.
Goals: Melbourne – Davie 6, Moyes 2, Warne-Smith 2, Green, Deane, Davidson, Johnson, Collins.
Crowd: 16,000 at the Western Oval

ROUND SEVEN June 7
MELBOURNE   12.16 (88)
SOUTH MELBOURNE   8.17 (65)
Best: Melbourne – Deane, Taylor, Coy, Davidson, Moyes, Johnson, Dunbar, Corbett.
Goals: Melbourne – Moyes 4, Johnson 2, Davie 2, Thomas, Duff, Abernethy, Taylor.
Crowd: 20,974 at the MCG

ROUND EIGHT June 19
MELBOURNE   11.9 (75)
ESSENDON   10.9 (69)
Best: Melbourne – Corbett, Wittman, Veal, White, Deane, Davie, Tymms, Thomas.
Goals: Melbourne – Davie 3, Moyes 2, Johnson, Wittman, Taylor, Veal, Davidson, Warne-Smith.
Crowd: 23,000 at Windy Hill

ROUND NINE June 26
MELBOURNE   21.28 (154)
HAWTHORN   1.7 (13)
Best: Melbourne – White, Warne-Smith, Corbett, Tymms, White, Chadwick, Streeter.
Goals: Melbourne – Moyes 6, Duff 3, Warne-Smith 3, Davie 3, White 2, Tymms 2, Dick, Taylor.
Crowd: 7,514 at the MCG

ROUND TEN July 3
MELBOURNE   8.5 (53)
GEELONG   8.19 (67)
Best: Melbourne – Abernethy, Wittman, Duff, Green, Chadwick, Deane, Thomas, Johnson.
Goals: Melbourne – Johnson 2, Warne-Smith 2, Duff, Wittman, Deane, Moyes.
Crowd: 21,500 at Corio Oval

ROUND ELEVEN July 10
MELBOURNE   14.15 (99)
FITZROY   8.12 (60)
Best: Melbourne – Coy, Streeter, Chadwick, Green, Moyes, Taylor, Davidson, Collins.
Goals: Melbourne – Deane 4, Moyes 3, Davie 2, Johnson 2, Warne-Smith, White, Wittman.
Crowd: 11,651 at the MCG

ROUND TWELVE July 17
MELBOURNE   17.16 (118)
ST KILDA   3.11 (29)
Best: Melbourne – Chadwick, Dick, Streeter, Dunbar, Wittman, Johnson, Moyes, Warne-Smith.
Goals: Melbourne – Johnson 4, Davie 3, Moyes 3, Deane 2, Wittman 2, Dunbar, Davidson, Warne-Smith.
Crowd: 14,000 at the Junction Oval

ROUND THIRTEEN August 7
MELBOURNE   12.18 (90)
CARLTON   8.10 (58)
Best: Melbourne – Abernethy, Thomas, Coy, Davie, Moys, Johnson, Dick, White, Deane.
Goals: Melbourne – Johnson 3, Moyes 3, Davie 3, Mollison, Deane, Warne-Smith.
Crowd: 27,785 at the MCG

ROUND FOURTEEN August 14
MELBOURNE   9.16 (70)
NORTH MELBOURNE   10.7 (67)
Best: Melbourne – Warne-Smith, Chadwick, Deane, Johnson, Moyes, Coy, Mollison.
Goals: Melbourne – Davie 3, Moyes 3, Johnson, Wittman, White.
Crowd: 6,000 at Arden St Oval

ROUND FIFTEEN August 21
MELBOURNE   6.7 (43)
COLLINGWOOD   13.15 (93)
Best: Melbourne – Johnson, Davidson, Thomas, Dunbar, Moye, Deane.
Goals: Melbourne – Johnson 2, Moyes 2, Wittman, Deane.
Crowd: 32,475 at the MCG

ROUND SIXTEEN August 28
MELBOURNE   13.16 (94)
RICHMOND   10.8 (68)
Best: Melbourne – Moyes, Corbett, Collins, Tymms, Wittman, Taylor, Green.
Goals: Melbourne – Moyes 6, Wittman 3, Duff 2, Johnson, Warne-Smith.
Crowd: 15,000 at Punt Road Oval

ROUND SEVENTEEN September 4
MELBOURNE   20.20 (140)
FOOTSCRAY   9.14 (68)
Best: Melbourne – Johnson, Tymms, Corbett, Duff, Green, Abernethy, Moyes, Chadwick.
Goals: Melbourne – Johnson 6, Moyes 4, Duff 3, Jones 2, Wittman 2, Chadwick, Coy, White.
Crowd: 6,684 at the MCG

ROUND EIGHTEEN September 11
MELBOURNE   18.13 (121)
HAWTHORN   11.12 (78)
Best: Melbourne – Duff, Tymms, Abernethy, Jones, Streeter, Deane, Wittman, Warne-Smith.
Goals: Melbourne – Duff 7, Wittman 3, Deane 3, Moyes 2, Johnson 2, Davie.
Crowd: 5,000 at Glenferrie Oval

PREMIER'S FINALS

SECOND SEMI-FINAL September 25
MELBOURNE	13.17 (95)
COLLINGWOOD	12.12 (84)

Best: Melbourne – Deane, Wittman, Corbett, Collins, Streeter, Coy, Thomas, Tymms.
Goals: Melbourne – Moyes 4, Duff 3, Wittman 2, Abernethy, Johnson, Deane, Collins.
Crowd: 44,286 at the MCG

PRELIMINARY FINAL October 2
MELBOURNE	6.6 (42)
ESSENDON	5.9 (39)

Best: Melbourne – Streeter, Abernethy, Tymms, Collins, Corbett, Davidson, Deane.
Goals: Melbourne – Duff 3, Johnson, Davidson, Deane.
Crowd: 50,162 at the MCG

GRAND FINAL October 9
MELBOURNE	4.5 7.7 14.9 17.17 (119)
COLLINGWOOD	1.1 6.4 7.6 9.8 (62)

Best: Melbourne – Abernethy, Johnson, Moyes, Streeter, Warne-Smith, Wittman.
Goals: Melbourne – Johnson 6, Moyes 3, Wittman 3, Duff 2, Deane, Taylor, Vine.
Crowd: 59,632 at the MCG

GRAND FINAL LINE-UPS

MELB	B:	C.Streeter	H.Coy	J.Abernethy
COLL	F:	C.Tyson (capt)	G.Coventry	H.Collier
MELB	HB:	B.Tymms	H.Dunbar	T.Thomas
COLL	HF:	R.Baker	F.Murphy	H.Chesswas
MELB	C:	D.Taylor	I.Warne-Smith	J.Collins
COLL	C:	J.Harris	J.Beveridge	C.Milburn
MELB	HF:	S.Wittman	B.Johnson	J.Davidson
COLL	HB:	E.Wilson	A.Collier	J.Shanahan
MELB	F:	F.Vine	D.Duff	H.Moyes
COLL	B:	L.Wescott	G.Beasley	J.Poulter
MELB	R:	B.Chadwick (capt)	C.Deane	H.White
COLL	R:	S.Coventry	R.Makeham	B.Libbis
MELB	Coach:	Bert Chadwick		
COLL	Coach:	Jock McHale		

SNAPSHOT

Win-loss record: 17-4
Highest score: 21.28 (154), round 9, v Hawthorn.
Greatest winning margin: 141 points, round 9, v Hawthorn.
Lowest score: 6.6 (42), Final, v Essendon.
Greatest losing margin: 50 points, round 15, v Collingwood.
Most goals by a player in a game: 9, Harry Davie, round 5, v Richmond.
Most consecutive wins: 6
Most consecutive losses: 1 (four times).
Club awards: Leading goalkicker: Harry Moyes (55 goals).

Putting it into perspective:
Melbourne's second flag from as many Grand Final appearances broke a 26-year premiership drought and it was the club's first MCG Grand Final victory. The 1900 win occurred at the East Melbourne Cricket Ground.

1926

		P	W	L	D	%	Pts
1	Collingwood (2)	18	15	3		149.3	60
2	Geelong (4)	18	15	3		145.2	60
3	Melbourne (1)	18	14	4		146.4	56
4	Essendon (3)	18	12	6		124.3	48
5	South Melb	18	12	6		118.9	48
6	Carlton	18	11	7		106.5	44
7	Richmond	18	9	9		92.0	36
8	Fitzroy	18	6	12		86.1	24
9	St Kilda	18	6	12		75.8	24
10	Footscray	18	4	14		69.9	16
11	Hawthorn	18	3	14	1	66.4	14
12	North Melb	18	0	17	1	73.7	2

(18 home and away rounds)

PLAYERS USED

MELBOURNE	GUERNSEY	GAMES	GOALS
Abernethy, Jim	4	19	6
Andersen, Eric	32	2	2
Cannan, Jack	25	1	1
Chadwick, Bert	17	13	1
Collins, Jack	10	18	2
Corbett, Bob	12	20	0
Coy, Harry	19	17	1
Davidson, Jim	29	13	4
Davie, Harry	24	15	50
Deane, Col	31	18	16
Dick, Fred	33	4	1
Duff, Dave	34	11	26
Dunbar, Hugh	28	17	1
Green, Ossie	5	20	1
Johnson, Bob	16	20	50
Jones, Tom	11	2	2
Jorgensen, Frank	7	2	0
Lawrence, Bert	30	3	0
Mollison, Derek	11	3	1
Moyes, Harry	22	19	55
O'Brien, Tom	21	4	0
Pie, Bruce	11	1	0
Streeter, Charlie	9	21	0
Taylor, Dick	35	21	6
Thomas, Ted	3	18	1
Tulloh, Percy	18	2	4
Tymms, Bill	26	13	4
Veal, Jim	6	3	1
Vine, Fred	23	1	1
Warne-Smith, Ivor	14	20	17
White, Herbie	8	21	7
Wittman, Stan	1	16	20

**COLLINGWOOD 2.13 (25) d
RICHMOND 1.7 (13)**

MUDDY MAGPIES CLEAN UP TIGERS

Collingwood had gone eight years without a premiership and it prompted some unpopular but necessary changes. By GLENN McFARLANE

"**T**HEY'RE kicking with the tide," one wise-cracking Magpie supporter screamed out moments before the start of the 1927 Grand Final between Collingwood and Richmond. It was the first day of October, but there was nothing spring-like about the weather that afternoon. The fan's humour was not lost on the freezing fans braving the elements in the near vicinity as incessant rain swept across the MCG. In what many observers declared was the worst day they had ever seen for football, the ground presented as a series of "miniature lakes". *The Argus* football correspondent, 'Old Boy', described the conditions as "more suitable for an aquatic carnival than football. Had the ground been frozen, ice skating would have been better to the liking of the crowd... Many hundreds, protected to some extent by Macintosh and umbrella, stood out in the rain all the afternoon, but the seats in the members' reserve were unoccupied, save for 14 hardy women, who, as if to put shame on their men friends, who had sought and secured cover, sat through it all."

The irony was that only a few days earlier fears had been expressed that Victoria's unseasonably dry winter and early spring could herald a crippling drought and severe crop losses. Melbourne had experienced a spate of dry conditions and more than a few people had been praying for some time for the heavens to open. Those prayers were answered on Grand Final eve. Rain moved swiftly over the state with intensity, easing to a drizzle on the morning of the match, before degenerating into another downpour throughout the play-off. This torrential burst of weather was such that it even prompted Victoria's Superintendent of Agriculture, Mr H.A. Mullett to issue a statement, allaying fears of a drought. The rain had arrived, almost on cue. Mr Mullett said it had come "just in time" to save the state. But it would make the Grand Final a messy spectacle.

Collingwood was hoping its drought was going to be over, too. The Magpies were playing off in a third successive Grand Final, but had not tasted the ultimate success since 1919. Worse still, the team that had prided itself on winning premierships had missed the finals in successive years, in 1923 and '24, putting pressure back on everyone associated with the club. It wasn't just the players. It was also coach 'Jock' McHale, who had been in charge since 1912. The committee, made up of so many past players who had been involved in previous successes, was also under pressure. Another flag win was not only required, it was almost demanded. Grand Final appearances in 1925 and '26 had not sated the thirst for success. Collingwood had been beaten narrowly by Geelong in the 1925 play-off, but had suffered an embarrassing 57-point loss to Melbourne a year later. The club had appeared to be travelling nicely halfway through the 1926 regular season, but the efforts of the team on the only afternoon that matters were simply not good enough. When the 1926 premiership flag that the club and its supporters craved failed to eventuate, something had to give… or perhaps someone.

At the annual meeting there were a number of hostile supporters who "tore up their (membership) tickets… in rage". In his season preview of the Magpies' hopes, 'Kickero', from *The Herald*, said: "Knowing the Collingwood club ever since it was formed in 1892… I have never seen such disappointment at the loss of the (1926) Premiership as was shown by their barrackers when Melbourne whipped them in the fight for last year's flag. There were many who had not recovered from the shock."

Nothing happened over the pre-season as Collingwood, and McHale, got on with the job of chasing the 1927 premiership. But there were murmurs about significant changes occurring before the start of the season. That's just how it happened, when on Anzac Day news leaked out about the sacking of the club's captain Charlie Tyson, and a handful of other senior players. This "stir in the football world", as it was referred to, wasn't canvassed as a sacking by officials. It was stated that Tyson had simply not made the Collingwood playing list for the 1927 season.

Tyson had been a loyal, laid-back but key player at Victoria Park since 1920. The native West Australian had been skipper since 1924, and was only a moderate performer in the 1926 Grand Final. He had been criticised at the time for two positional changes at the start of the second half against Melbourne. His own performance in the game had been described as "peculiar", not because it did not look as if he was trying, but because the normally genial and fair footballer had been cautioned for "spiteful and dirty play" on a few occasions. The decision to replace Tyson had been orchestrated by Collingwood president Harry Curtis, who was convinced that Tyson was past his best, and perhaps past his usefulness. The fact that it took the club five months to make their decision indicates there was not universal support for the move. It was said that the club's vice-president Charlie 'Torchy' Laxton had misgivings that Tyson was being used as a scapegoat for the sins of 1926. Clearly, McHale was complicit with the decision. Perhaps that was because he knew he had a more than suitable replacement waiting in the wings.

From the outset, Tyson suspected a conspiracy at committee level. He told the press: "A man is only an individual and it does not pay to have a body of officials against you." It wasn't long before the decision gave rise to rumours that Tyson had "played dead" in the previous year's Grand Final—a strange observation given how he had been cautioned by the umpire for going too hard. Tyson suspected the real reason for his axing was that he had organised a players' meeting the previous December to discuss the prospect of bonus payments to the players. Tyson transferred to North Melbourne, and with him went the cruel talk that a Collingwood captain had not tried his best in a Grand Final. Almost three months after his departure, Tyson had finally had enough of the campaign against him. He wrote a letter to *The Herald* to threaten legal action over the "untrue and ungenerous statements". Tyson added: "My omission from the list of players of the Collingwood club at the beginning of the season has originated conjectures which, owing to much repetition, are now spoken of as facts. Allegations, which it is unnecessary for me to say are quite without foundation, are now being widely circulated that I received sums of money to induce me not to do my best for Collingwood in last year's Final." He threatened to act against "those foolish and credulous people who are responsible for this injury being done". As Richard Stremski would reveal in his club history, *Kill For Collingwood,* almost 60 years later, the allegations were almost certainly without foundation.

The Sporting Globe summed up the bizarre situation, saying: "It appears the Magpies must be very confident of their own strength if they can afford to let him go." Collingwood was confident, no doubt about it. McHale, who could easily have worn some of the blame of that 1926 loss, declared his playing list was steadily improving, some of the club's young players were fast maturing and the experienced players were ready to avenge past defeats. And one man was ready to step from the shadows to become a leader unparalleled in the history of the club, and perhaps even the game. Syd Coventry, the son of a Diamond Creek orchardist, was deemed as the ideal man to take over the captaincy at Victoria Park. He was a tough, hard and uncompromising footballer. He was also a brilliant team player, committed to success, committed to the cause. He was, some said, a born leader, ready to redirect the attentions of the team.

The club was determined to afford Coventry every chance of making a success of his role. To help heal the wounds of the Tyson affair, it was decided that the players should take a mid-season trip to Perth during the representative break in August. By that stage of the season, Collingwood was the flag favourite. That rail journey across the Nullarbor and the sea journey home would help to unite this group of players for several seasons, and play a massive role in the success of the team that would become known as "the Machine". Many players, and officials, would describe the trip as the fire that forged the greatest team in VFL history. While the men are now gone, photographs of the trip are testament to its success, giving a remarkable insight of the togetherness this journey inspired in the players. There they are: young Harry Collier skylarking on a pier in Perth; full-back Charlie Dibbs in front of a war memorial; brilliant recruit Harold Rumney (picked up at the start of that season after being discarded by Carlton for being "too old, too slow and too weak"); a baby-faced Albert Collier and Harry 'Bottles' Chesswas on their arrival; plus most of the team posing on a beach, making pyramids and sitting by a car. There was even a hint of a smile on Jock McHale's face. As a student of club history, he knew mid-season trips had helped to build team morale in the past. Was it any wonder that he said in *The West Australian*: "I had heard it was the golden west and I was not disappointed… it was the best trip I have been on in my long experience."

Part of the vindication for appointing Syd Coventry as captain came when the new skipper won the club's first Brownlow Medal near the end of the 1927 season, proving he was the best footballer in the competition. Not bad for a player whose 1927 pre-season had consisted of just a few serious training sessions owing to the fact that he and his brother Gordon had helped Diamond Creek into the finals of the local cricket competition. It clearly didn't impact on Syd, and neither did it with Gordon, who booted a League record of 95 goals leading into the 1927 Grand Final. The VFL's first century of goals seemed to be in the offing. Surely only bad luck, a bad game or the weather could stop him.

1927 COLLINGWOOD

The indications were good for Collingwood leading into the 1927 Grand Final, having finished minor premiers, having not lost consecutive games all season and having thrashed Geelong by 66 points in the semi-final. In that game, it was said in *The Argus* that the Cats were "not merely beaten—they were annihilated, being eclipsed of every point from start to finish… the Magpies were smarter at the ball than their opponents, and they were the superior side on the ground." Only Richmond and a flooded MCG stood between them and the club's sixth VFL flag. And under the challenge finals rule of the day, the Tigers had to beat Collingwood on successive Saturdays to win the premiership. For some football pundits, the rain further enhanced Collingwood's prospects of winning. 'Kickero', from *The Herald,* said: "They (the Magpies) were favoured all week, but, owing to the heavy rain overnight and the unsettled conditions for this afternoon, their prospects of winning have strengthened." He also knew of the fierce determination at Victoria Park, saying: "Never have the Magpies been as keyed up by the intention to win a premiership as they have been all season." The committee had made an enormous risk-taking decision to get rid of their captain before the start of the season and to anoint his successor. Success was almost essential. If it wasn't achieved, the pressure would be even more intense, and the casualties even more far reaching.

The Grand Final almost didn't proceed that day. The VFA had postponed its preliminary final because of the appalling weather. The VFL met that morning and decided to push on regardless, but the weather did have a big impact on the size of the crowd. Only 34,551 fans attended, most of them cramming for any space under the limited cover on offer. It was the smallest Grand Final attendance since the Magpies won the 1917 Grand Final during war time. Richmond officials tried to conceal the fact that there would be a late change; their star forward, Jack Baggott, would not take his place. He arrived at the game with his gear, trying to spring a ruse. But the Collingwood "spies" knew half an hour before the game that Baggott would not play. There would be no changes in the Collingwood team, despite the weather issues.

When the play started, the Tigers used the new ball to full advantage, as George Rudolph and Perc Bentley delighted the crowd with two towering marks. They were rarities on this waterlogged day hardly designed for aesthetics. After a few minutes of play, the game degenerated into a muddy arm-wrestle of slipping and sliding. With the wind, the Tigers performed better in the early stages of the game, although Collingwood did manage to score first. Rugged big man Percy Rowe made the most of some canny play from Harry Collier and Bob Makeham to gather possession. But Rowe's kick slid through for a behind, on a day when scoring would be incredibly difficult in itself.

Richmond controlled the play for the rest of the quarter, kicking four behinds to open a three-point lead at the first change of ends. No goals came in the first half hour of play. 'Kickero' made the observation in *The Herald* that "on the whole, Richmond had played a better game in this term, though it had not been football of the type that the public appreciates." Public appreciation was never going to be centred on the skills and talent in this game, but the fans who braved the conditions could not have helped but admire the desperation and resourcefulness of both teams, in the atrocious conditions.

The Grand Final, according to *The Herald*, was "spiteful" from the outset and "fists flew surreptitiously" in the opening quarter. Collingwood's defence was holding together well, especially across half-back where Syd Coventry and Ernie Wilson were prominent, even though supporters found it difficult working out which team was which. The players were drenched and covered in mud. *The Sporting Globe* recorded: "Already, it was apparent, that stamina—and not science—would be the deciding factor." Collingwood had the distinct advantage there. McHale had ensured his team was as fit as any other in the competition. They were like a well-oiled machine, capable of performing to the best of their ability in any conditions and any circumstance. But the Magpies were also using science, too, or plain old-fashioned logic. The Collingwood decrees that day included: marking on the chest, not out in front, and kicking the ball off the ground wherever possible. So, against the wind, it seemed that the Magpies had done well to keep the Tigers goalless in the first term.

Richmond actually controlled the early stages of the second quarter, although Dibbs and those around him defended well. There was, according to *The Sporting Globe*, "slipping and sliding everywhere, the players afforded the spectators plenty of amusement. For the participants, it was a particularly grim affair." The rain, which had eased late in the first term, was back in full volume. But, so, too, was Collingwood's determination. They refused to give in, and kept coming at Richmond, with the sort of desire that wins premierships. Gordon Coventry eventually broke the deadlock of behinds, kicking truly from a free kick to give the Magpies a four-point lead. The goal came after 36 minutes of actual play, a welcome relief for the Collingwood fans in the crowd. Goals would be like gold on a day like this. In tune with the eerie atmosphere at the MCG, some Collingwood "enthusiast" started playing bagpipes. Much of Collingwood's success came from the fact that Richmond made the mistake of trying to pick up the ball and Collingwood were down on them "like a load of bricks". Collingwood's grip on the game strengthened when Gordon Coventry scored his second goal with a left foot snap just before half-time. It gave the

Magpies a 14-point lead at the break, a big advantage as the rain was not abating. It was to be Coventry's 97th and last goal of the season. His 100 would have to wait two more years.

The rain was still falling heavily at half-time and hundreds of fans cleared out and went home. Never before had so many barrackers abandoned a Grand Final at half-time when the scores were so closely locked together. For the players, the half-time break provided the opportunity for a hot shower and a rubdown. *The Sporting Globe* reported that "the majority of the players were massaged during the interval. To keep the cold out, they were freely coated with oil. Most of the players changed their togs at half-time, and some appeared wearing highly coloured sweaters under their club colours." It was said that Richmond's "chief failing" had been a tendency to play fine weather football, but their coach Frank "Checker" Hughes laid plans at half-time to "pull the game out of the fire". They hit the Magpies hard in the third quarter, resuming with greater passion and more vigour. Three Collingwood players were thumped in the opening minutes of the second half. *The Sporting Globe* observed that "(Jack) Beveridge and Rumney were winded. Syd Coventry was knocked down." It showed just how intent Richmond was on staging a comeback. They were not a spent force just yet.

However, despite controlling the early part of the third term, the Tigers booted behinds when they needed goals; those wasted opportunities in attack were proving costly. They were followed by several Collingwood moves forward, which also yielded behinds. The Magpies still led by 14 points, the Tigers were still goalless. At last, after three completed quarters and a few minutes of the final term, the Tigers managed to post their first goal of the game. Richmond's hopes were raised by "bungling among the Collingwood backs", and Jack Fincher kicked a goal off the ground. This reduced the deficit to eight points and gave the desperate Tigers fans braving the conditions some false hope. In reality, Collingwood snuffed out Richmond's chances soon after with a series of behinds and a resolve to win the match. The Magpies had prevailed in the shocking conditions to win the 1927 Grand Final by 12 points, 2.13 (25) to 1.7 (13).

Richmond was "defeated, but far from disgraced," according to *The Argus*. "They worked like the 'tigers' after which they were named, but they lacked the concentration of the 'magpies' who, in defiance of all natural history laws, seemed to be amphibious." On hearing the final bell, the Collingwood players were delirious, as "supporters and trainers rushed onto the ground immediately the bell sounded and vainly tried to carry Syd Coventry and others in. There were many handshakes and some even went to the extent of kissing the players." A Scottish band in attendance actually "serenaded" the Magpies to their dressingroom where there was a mad rush to congratulate the players on their wonderful achievement. There were 21 speeches of congratulations in the rooms, which must have been some sort of record. The crush was so great at the dressingroom door that many leading supporters and some officials were unable to get in.

Jock McHale spoke in glowing terms about his team, forecasting that it had the perfect blend of hardened experienced players with young talented stars. The coach considered the team was still a prospect of winning the flag the following year, too, saying that there was still plenty of improvement left in them. He told pressmen: "They are a modest band and most of them are quiet living fellows. In fact some of the players are real silent men." Collingwood had registered its lowest score in a match since 1910. But it mattered little. They had won the premiership, and that was all that anyone worried about. And Syd Coventry was the hero of the season. In the Grand Final he "dominated the situation completely with his wonderful play… and also proved that the arduous duties of leadership did not prevent him from playing well and at the same time exercising a shrewd control over his players. At times (he) rose to phenomenal heights and he was the main factor in winning the Premiership."

The decision to cut Tyson, however ruthless and however harsh, had been justified by the premiership success attained on that wet and wild October afternoon. The club had replaced him with a man who was on the path to becoming the greatest leader the club had ever seen. And McHale knew that he had in his midst a team that was only going to get better. Collingwood's eight-year premiership drought was over. And the reign was only just starting.

1927 COLLINGWOOD

PREMIER'S SEASON

COLLINGWOOD: 1927

ROUND ONE April 30
COLLINGWOOD 16.11 (107)
GEELONG 12.12 (84)
Best: Collingwood – G.Coventry, Murphy, Libbis, S.Coventry, Poulter, Wescott, H.Collier.
Goals: Collingwood – G.Coventry 8, H.Collier 4, Rumney 2, Libbis, Murphy.
Crowd: 20,000 at Victoria Park

ROUND TWO May 7
COLLINGWOOD 11.11 (77)
HAWTHORN 7.9 (51)
Best: Collingwood – Beveridge, A.Collier, G.Coventry, Dibbs, Chesswas, Harris, Makeham.
Goals: Collingwood – G.Coventry 4, Rumney 2, Poulter 2, H.Collier 2, Harris.
Crowd: 9,000 at Glenferrie Oval

ROUND THREE May 14
COLLINGWOOD 6.13 (49)
RICHMOND 7.13 (55)
Best: Collingwood – A.Collier, Makeham, S.Coventry, MacLeod, Murphy, Chesswas.
Goals: Collingwood – G.Coventry 4, Rowe, H.Collier.
Crowd: 20,000 at Victoria Park

ROUND FOUR May 21
COLLINGWOOD 16.10 (106)
SOUTH MELBOURNE 9.13 (67)
Best: Collingwood – S.Coventry, Dibbs, Beveridge, Libbis, Poulter, H.Collier, Murphy.
Goals: Collingwood – G.Coventry 4, H.Collier 3, Rumney 2, Beasley 2, Murphy 2, Libbis, Poulter, Harris.
Crowd: 29,000 at the Lake Oval

ROUND FIVE May 28
COLLINGWOOD 18.15 (123)
FITZROY 9.5 (59)
Best: Collingwood – G.Coventry, A.Collier, Libbis, Murphy, Makeham, Rowe, Rumney.
Goals: Collingwood – G.Coventry 11, Harris 3, Libbis 2, Rowe, Rumney.
Crowd: 16,000 at Victoria Park

ROUND SIX June 4
COLLINGWOOD 7.14 (56)
ESSENDON 7.7 (49)
Best: Collingwood – Wescott, Libbis, Dibbs, Milburn, A.Collier, Beasley, Rumney.
Goals: Collingwood – Rumney 3, G.Coventry 2, H.Collier 2.
Crowd: 25,000 at Windy Hill

ROUND SEVEN June 11
COLLINGWOOD 25.19 (169)
ST KILDA 7.15 (57)
Best: Collingwood – G.Coventry, S.Coventry, Libbis, Dibbs, H.Collier, Rowe, Murphy.
Goals: Collingwood – G.Coventry 11, Rumney 4, Harris 3, H.Collier 3, Murphy 3, Rowe.
Crowd: 16,000 at Victoria Park

ROUND EIGHT June 18
COLLINGWOOD 7.16 (58)
FOOTSCRAY 4.12 (36)
Best: Collingwood – A.Collier, Makeham, Clayden, G.Coventry, Dibbs, Milburn, Harris.
Goals: Collingwood – G.Coventry 4, H.Collier 2, Rumney.
Crowd: 17,000 at the Western Oval

ROUND NINE June 25
COLLINGWOOD 13.5 (93)
CARLTON 14.11 (95)
Best: Collingwood – Libbis, Clayden, S.Coventry, Rowe, Rumney, H.Collier, Wescott.
Goals: Collingwood – G.Coventry 4, H.Collier 3, Murphy 2, Beveridge 2, S.Coventry, Rowe.
Crowd: 33,000 at Victoria Park

ROUND TEN July 2
COLLINGWOOD 8.11 (59)
NORTH MELBOURNE 3.11 (29)
Best: Collingwood – Rowe, Dibbs, Poulter, Murphy, A.Collier, S.Coventry, Makeham.
Goals: Collingwood – G.Coventry 3, Libbis, Morelli, Murphy, A.Collier, H.Collier.
Crowd: 7,000 at Victoria Park

ROUND ELEVEN July 9
COLLINGWOOD 11.13 (79)
MELBOURNE 10.12 (72)
Best: Collingwood – S.Coventry, Harris, Wilson, Ross, Dibbs, G.Coventry, Milburn.
Goals: Collingwood – G.Coventry 5, Libbis 3, Chesswas, H.Collier, Makeham.
Crowd: 27,092 at the MCG

ROUND TWELVE July 16
COLLINGWOOD 9.11 (65)
GEELONG 7.7 (49)
Best: Collingwood – A.Collier, Murphy, Libbis, Milburn, Chesswas, Harris, S.Coventry.
Goals: Collingwood – G.Coventry 4, Milburn, Poulter, H.Collier, Libbis, Murphy.
Crowd: 21,500 at Corio Oval

ROUND THIRTEEN July 23
COLLINGWOOD 18.13 (121)
HAWTHORN 6.11 (47)
Best: Collingwood – G.Coventry, S.Coventry, Beveridge, Harris, Poulter, Wilson, Hughson.
Goals: Collingwood – G.Coventry 8, Murphy 2, Poulter 2, Harris, Rowe, Beveridge, A.Collier, S.Coventry, Hughson.
Crowd: 7,000 at Victoria Park

ROUND FOURTEEN July 30
COLLINGWOOD 12.12 (84)
RICHMOND 9.7 (61)
Best: Collingwood – Wilson, Rowe, Clayden, Rumney, Makeham, Wescott, Chesswas.
Goals: Collingwood – Harris 2, Rumney 2, Clayden 2, Chesswas 2, H.Collier, S.Coventry, Libbis, Murphy.
Crowd: 38,000 at Punt Road Oval

ROUND FIFTEEN August 6
COLLINGWOOD 18.14 (122)
SOUTH MELBOURNE 6.7 (43)
Best: Collingwood – S.Coventry, Dibbs, Rumney, G.Coventry, A.Collier, Beveridge, Libbis.
Goals: Collingwood – G.Coventry 6, Libbis 3, Poulter 3, H.Collier 2, Harris, Chesswas, Rumney, Murphy.
Crowd: 15,000 at Victoria Park

ROUND SIXTEEN August 27
COLLINGWOOD 13.10 (88)
FITZROY 14.11 (95)
Best: Collingwood – Clayden, Libbis, H.Collier, Murphy, Milburn, Wilson, A.Collier.
Goals: Collingwood – G.Coventry 4, Murphy 3, H.Collier 2, Libbis, Poulter, Makeham, Rumney.
Crowd: 25,000 at Brunswick St Oval

ROUND SEVENTEEN September 3
COLLINGWOOD 3.13 (31)
ESSENDON 4.6 (30)
Best: Collingwood – S.Coventry, Clayden, Rumney, Libbis, H.Collier, Murphy.
Goals: Collingwood – G.Coventry, Murphy, H.Collier.
Crowd: 8,000 at Victoria Park

ROUND EIGHTEEN September 10
COLLINGWOOD 11.16 (82)
NORTH MELBOURNE 7.14 (56)
Best: Collingwood – Murphy, Wescott, G.Coventry, Dibbs, Milburn, Poulter, Harris.
Goals: Collingwood – G.Coventry 5, H.Collier 3, Makeham, Chesswas, Poulter.
Crowd: 11,000 at Arden St Oval

GRAND FINALS VOLUME I

PREMIER'S FINALS

SECOND SEMI-FINAL September 24
COLLINGWOOD   16.18 (114)
GEELONG   7.6 (48)
Best: Collingwood – S.Coventry, G.Coventry, H.Collier, Chesswas, Harris, Rumney, Makeham.
Goals: Collingwood – G.Coventry 7, H.Collier 4, Murphy 2, Harris, Rowe, Libbis.
Crowd: 40,595 at the MCG

GRAND FINAL September 24
COLLINGWOOD   0.1   2.6   2.9   2.13 (25)
RICHMOND   0.4   0.4   0.7   1.7 (13)
Best: Collingwood – Beveridge, H.Collier, S.Coventry, Makeham, Murphy, Rowe.
Goals: Collingwood – G.Coventry 2.
Crowd: 34,551 at the MCG

GRAND FINAL LINE-UPS

COLL	B:	L.Wescott	C.Dibbs	J.Poulter
RICH	F:	G.Robinson	J.McCormack	J.Fincher
COLL	HB:	E.Wilson	G.Clayden	A.Collier
RICH	HF:	H.Weidner	G.Ruldolph	S.Jamison
COLL	C:	H.Chesswas	J.Beveridge	C.Milburn
RICH	C:	F.O'Brien	L.Gallagher	A.Geddes (capt)
COLL	HF:	F.Murphy	B.Makeham	J.Harris
RICH	HB:	D.Lilburne	P.Bentley	B.McCormack
COLL	F:	H.Rumney	G.Coventry	H.Collier
RICH	B:	D.Harris	C.Powell	A.MacIsaac
COLL	R:	S.Coventry (capt)	P.Rowe	B.Libbis
RICH	R:	T.O'Halloran	B.O'Neill	D.Hayes
COLL	Coach:	Jock McHale		
RICH	Coach:	Checker' Hughes		

SNAPSHOT

Win-loss record: 17-3
Highest score: 25.19 (169), round 7, v St Kilda.
Greatest winning margin: 112 points, round 7, v St Kilda.
Lowest score: 2.13 (25), Grand Final, v Richmond.
Greatest losing margin: 12 points, round 9, v Carlton.
Most goals by a player in a game: 11, Gordon Coventry, round 5, v Fitzroy; round 7, v St Kilda.
Most consecutive wins: 6
Most consecutive losses: 1 (three times).
Club awards: Best & Fairest: Syd Coventry; Leading goalkicker: Gordon Coventry (97 goals).

Putting it into perspective:
The Magpies' sixth premiership was their fourth under coach Jock McHale and it was also a successful season for the Coventry brothers. Syd captained the Pies for the first time to a winning Grand Final and won a Brownlow Medal, while Gordon topped the league goalkicking with 97 goals.

1927

		P	W	L	D	%	Pts
1	Collingwood (1)	18	15	3		150.6	60
2	Richmond (2)	18	14	4		134.6	56
3	Geelong (3)	18	14	4		132.0	56
4	Carlton (4)	18	13	5		121.7	52
5	Melbourne	18	12	6		132.4	48
6	South Melb	18	9	9		95.9	36
7	St Kilda	18	8	10		75.3	32
8	Essendon	18	6	11	1	96.8	26
9	Fitzroy	18	6	11	1	85.7	26
10	Footscray	18	6	12		85.4	24
11	North Melb	18	3	15		73.5	12
12	Hawthorn	18	1	17		63.1	4

(18 home and away rounds)

PLAYERS USED

COLLINGWOOD	GUERNSEY	GAMES	GOALS
Beasley, George	5	6	2
Beveridge, Jack	2	20	3
Chesswas, Harry	10	16	5
Clayden, George	11	12	2
Collier, Albert	4	19	2
Collier, Harry	5	20	36
Coventry, Gordon	7	20	97
Coventry, Syd	8	20	3
Dibbs, Charlie	12	19	0
Harris, John	11	20	13
Hughson, Les	29	1	1
Lauder, Albert	13	1	0
Libbis, Billy	14	20	15
MacLeod, Norm	16	3	0
Makeham, Bob	15	20	3
Milburn, Charlie	16	16	1
Morelli, Clarrie	18	7	1
Muir, Bob	19	3	0
Murphy, Frank	20	20	20
Poulter, Joe	18	18	11
Ross, Hector	28	2	0
Rowe, Percy	22	17	6
Rowlands, Trevor	23	2	0
Rumney, Harold	24	17	19
Sneazwell, Bill	27	10	0
Wescott, Leo	26	20	0
Wilson, Ernie	24	11	0

**COLLINGWOOD 13.10 (96) d
RICHMOND 9.9 (63)**

BROTHERLY SHOVE

A word from Syd Coventry to his brother Gordon set in motion one of the great Grand Final performances. By GLENN McFARLANE

COLLINGWOOD captain Syd Coventry strode over to his brother Gordon moments before the start of the 1928 Grand Final against Richmond and issued him with a challenge. Syd spoke six simple words, but they would have an impact: "A lot depends on you today." The siblings barely said another word to each other for the next two-and-a-half hours. They didn't have to. Words were secondary to deeds for the Coventrys.

In that span of time, three important things occurred. For a start, the Magpies managed to correct a season that briefly threatened to slide out of control and fragment the spirit engendered only a year earlier on the mid-season trip to Perth, something that sowed the seeds of that 1927 flag. They had also succeeded in adapting an effective game-plan years ahead of its time into a winning formula on the most important day of the year. And, in responding in a most positive manner, the younger and more reserved of the Coventry brothers would turn his sibling's personal challenge into a record-breaking performance.

Just a few weeks earlier, such achievements—team or otherwise—seemed in serious jeopardy. Collingwood had clearly been the best side of the home and away season, finishing as minor premiers, but there had been some divisions over two contentious issues. Also, the form of some of the club's most important players, including the VFL's leading goalkicker Gordon Coventry, had slipped alarmingly. The previous year's runner-up, Richmond, loomed as a real threat, and the Tigers were hell bent on avenging their defeat to the Magpies in the atrocious conditions of the previous year's Grand Final.

The first sign of division came about in July when the Collingwood administration used the worsening economic situation to trim the players' weekly wage from £3 back to 2/10/-. This caused considerable angst amongst the playing group. Some of those players had once claimed they would have "played for nothing", but in the tightening economic circumstances, more than a few had come to rely on their money out of football. As a result, there was a players' meetings and a motion put forward by veteran Ernie Wilson and seconded by Albert Collier (who had turned 19 a day earlier) that the players refuse to play if the club did not back down. For a time, it appeared as if the unthinkable might happen—that Collingwood players might actually go out on strike unless the club reinstated their normal pay packet.

Percy Bowyer, who had the luxury of having a job at Carlton and United Breweries, said years later: "To go back to two pounds 10 didn't worry me, nor most of the young boys." But some of the older players, especially those with families, were not as happy. Bowyer confirmed this, saying: "Yes, they were upset, particularly Ernie (Wilson). Of course, he was a senior player then, and some of the senior players were annoyed."

Almost predictably, the man who averted the near strike was inspirational skipper, Syd Coventry. He refused to accept that Collingwood players would withdraw their services, and he managed to pull the players back from the precipice just in the nick of time. A strike may have crushed the spirit and harmony of the team, and could have been a stain on the players, the team and, most importantly, the club. Coventry halted the dissension in its tracks and remarkably the issue did not cause any lingering resentment for the remainder of the season. Bowyer concluded: "He was our captain, and after all was said and done; you had to be sensible about things." There were no recriminations. The players rallied in an effort to win another flag, even if they felt that they were being short-changed by the powers that be.

The other issue that threatened unity was the wash-up of the final home and away loss to Carlton. Most people had naturally assumed the Magpies would defeat the Blues on their home turf, at Victoria Park, even if the greater incentive was in Carlton's corner. Collingwood had already secured the minor premiership, while Carlton had to win to displace Essendon from the finals. Even before the game, there had been speculation that the home side might not have the urgency as it normally showed. 'Kickero', in *The Herald,* suggested: "No match for years has been the subject of as much rumour and talk... I have not heard it suggested that any inducements have been handed out to anybody not to win. What has been said is that as Collingwood are safe with the two chances of the premiership, there is not the necessity for them to work as hard tomorrow. However, the assurance has been given that Collingwood will go their hardest."

But there were allegations that two unnamed Collingwood players were paid £50 to perform below their expectations that afternoon. It is important to note that the talk was never proven as fact. But Syd Coventry would admit that he had been offered a similar amount and had instantly knocked it back. He joked later that he might as well have taken it, for his performance was not a good one. In *The Sporting Globe*, 'Jumbo' Sharland had said that: "In no other game this season have they (Collingwood) played with such apparent indifference and lack of devil."

What is certain is that the Carlton players *were* offered money by their club to beat Collingwood that afternoon, and that's precisely what they did. The Blues would prove the only club to enjoy a better than 50 per cent winning ratio against Collingwood in the club's 1927-1930 string of success. They led at every change and the result was never in doubt, as the Collingwood side was surprisingly booed as it came off Victoria Park that day.

Whether or not the rumours had foundation the last-round loss to Carlton showed an erosion of confidence within the team. Still, things appeared to have changed for the better when the players went into their three-quarter-time break five goals ahead of Melbourne in the semi-final. A direct path to a fourth successive Grand Final seemed a formality. But the doubts that had emerged about how well the Magpies were playing emerged again in the last half-hour of play, when the Redlegs stormed home. Melbourne kicked 5.0, while Collingwood failed to score in an almost unbelievable end to the game. As the siren sounded on the first finals draw in VFL history, players stood there almost in disbelief, not knowing what to do. Coach Jock McHale, though, was fuming at how the Magpies had let their opponents back into the contest.

Collingwood found the going just as tough in the semi-final replay. Melbourne took the game right up to McHale's men, and looked capable in the final stages of stealing the game. The margin was always a tight one, but somehow the Magpies managed to hold on to win by four points. But something had to change if the Magpies were to get back to their form of earlier in the year.

The Magpies limped into the Grand Final with flagging confidence, while Richmond had been impressive in disposing of Carlton in the earlier semi-final. Some suggested that the Tigers appeared to be the fresher team, though they would have to beat the Magpies—the minor premier—twice to secure the flag. They were well equipped to "run the 'Woodsmen off their feet." Even some of those within the club were concerned that the players had become stale heading into the finals series. One of the chief concerns was in the club's forward line. The Magpies were simply not scoring enough goals. Gordon Coventry had enjoyed a strong season, kicking 80 goals in the home and away season, but he had not kicked more than two goals since the round 15 clash with Hawthorn.

But Coventry was carrying a secret that he had told no one—not even his brother. It would not be revealed for another decade when in a rare, double interview with the siblings in *The Herald*, Gordon finally told Syd about his circumstances near the end of the 1928 season. He revealed that a knock to the head in a state game that season had affected his balance and his football. Asked why he had never told Syd, Gordon said: "He would have dropped me out of the side if I had told him. A man at Collingwood in those days had to be really crook before he reported a crack."

Still, if the pundits said "stamina and not science" had won the 1927 flag, it would almost certainly be reversed in the 1928 Grand Final. While the Magpies were still one of the fittest teams in the VFL, perfectly turned out by McHale and head trainer Wal Lee, science would play a significant role in Collingwood's endeavours in chasing a second successive flag. It was said that never before had a football team put in as much pre-game planning into clinically disposing their opposition.

On the Thursday night before the Grand Final, McHale came to the conclusion that his players were mentally and physically exhausted. As a result, he gave the team a light night on the training track and allowed them to collectively toss around their thoughts on how they could defeat the improving Tigers in a frank team meeting after training.

Syd Coventry revealed some of the details of the club's Thursday night meeting a week after the Grand Final, documenting how the unique think-tank session dissected their opponents—position by position, player by player. As a group, the Magpies realised they were a better and smarter team. It was decided that Richmond could be made vulnerable by some pre-planning. The Tigers' "deficiencies" were openly discussed, as were various plans to expose them. Nothing was left to chance.

It was decided by the Magpies that their opponents were more than a little over-confident in the lead-up to the game. Coventry recalled in *The Sporting Globe*: "There was one thing that helped us a lot. Richmond were brimming with confidence. That is a great thing for a side, but it seemed to us that they were just a little too sure of their own ability to dominate the whole field."

This misplaced confidence would be used against Richmond, and would be one of the weapons in bringing about the downfall of the Tigers.

Coventry also detailed the decision to goad the Richmond players because they were "easily annoyed and thrown out of their natural stride, even by jokes made at their expense". In the Grand Final, Collingwood deliberately tried to elicit a response from their opponents by calling them names, annoying them with words and taunting them with actions. The Tigers would become so frustrated that they had no alternative but to retaliate more often than not. Consequently, several players, including George Clayden and Harry Collier, copped some heavy treatment during the course of the match. But the pain was only momentary.

At the meeting, it was agreed that the Collingwood players would punch the ball unless they were certain they could mark it. This would halt Richmond's supposed supremacy in the air. The Magpies skipper summed it up later: "We followed it (the plan) to the letter… marking only when they felt they had a reasonable chance and on other occasions punching the ball clear from Richmond's big men." Another ploy, constantly referred to in match reports of the game, was to keep the ball as low as possible.

Versatility would be a further key. The plan was to change the followers with monotonous regularity in order to keep some of the key Magpie players fresh for the second half, as well as to try to confuse their Richmond opponents. Coventry said: "We decided to run plenty of men into the ruck. We put them on the ball for two or three minutes, resting our other men and bringing those useful fellows into the fray with extra dash." This move "puzzled" the Richmond followers all day and made for a fresher, more effective four-quarter performance from the team.

This Thursday night gathering was a legitimate team meeting, with several players casting suggestions as how to best bring about the Richmond defeat. However, the presence of the coach still hung over the room, with Coventry saying later: "Jock McHale broke into that discussion with the definite command that every man—at every minute of the game—and regardless of what might occur, should make the ball always his one objective." McHale's decree was as important as any other uttered that famous Thursday night.

And so Collingwood took to the field armed with ambitious plans and renewed enthusiasm, with the knowledge that they had gone through every single line on the Richmond team and believing they were a better side. The execution of those plans was just as swift and as precise as the pre-game planning mechanisms.

In many ways, the 1928 Grand Final was almost the complete antithesis of the previous year's premiership play-off. While the 1927 Grand Final was a miserable afternoon with just over 34,000 hardy souls braving the elements, this one was held on a "glowering" afternoon with 50,026 people in attendance. Collingwood entered the ground before Richmond, and as the Magpies were warming up, Syd Coventry sensed his younger brother needed a lift to regain the form that had made him the competition's leading goalkicker for the past three years. He uttered those six words, and Gordon would accept the challenge, aided by the support and backing of one of the club's toughest and most popular players.

Percy Rowe, recalled for the Grand Final after a month on the sidelines because of injury, came into the team with a purpose. He was there to assist Gordon Coventry in gaining some space in attack. The ploy—another that had been devised and discussed at the team meeting—worked magnificently, and as Syd recalled: "Percy Rowe saved Gordon from any interference in going for marks, he was very important." Rowe's burly frame and toughness created a clear path in the attacking zone for Gordon to unleash his goal-kicking magic. It was to be Rowe's 96th—and final—match for Collingwood. He was determined to make it a memorable one.

The Grand Final opened in "ideal conditions" and the pace was "terrific" from the opening bounce. Collingwood led the way early, being "slightly in favour" of the Tigers with the first two goals of the game. First-year player Len Murphy scored the first goal of the game midway through the opening term with a "55-yard free kick". The Magpies produced some "dazzling football", according to *The Herald*, in the early stages of the game with the Tigers constantly defending. It was a frustrating start for Richmond. Demonstrating this fact, Clayden was decked in an incident which prompted some retaliation before the football once more became the object.

Then, with his brother's words undoubtedly ringing in his ears, and with his favourite boots on, Gordon Coventry commenced his date with destiny. He booted his first goal of the day. The champion full-forward, "marking from Len Murphy", put Collingwood 13 points ahead shortly before the first bell, according to *The Sporting Globe*. There was no sign of "staleness" in Coventry's game this week.

While major scores were hard to come by in the first half-hour, the second term produced a relative string of goals. Richmond, sensing the game was on the verge of slipping away, booted two goals at the start of the term with marks and set shots from Tom O'Halloran and Harry Weidner. But Collingwood, "prevailing by greater dash, more accurate passing and air supremacy", was not willing to be outdone. They stunned the Tigers with 10 minutes of dazzling football, the best form they had shown for over a month. In this period of time, the Magpies kicked four goals. Three of these came from the boot of Gordon Coventry, who was strong in the air and accurate, while John 'Jiggy' Harris managed the other goal, just a few minutes before Richmond got one back.

But Coventry's goal-kicking gluttony in the second term did not abate. Just as Collingwood's timekeeper was ready to pick up the bell and sound half-time, he posted Collingwood's fifth for the quarter, to push the margin out to a comfortable 21 points. As the Magpie players vanished into the rooms to hear McHale's assessment of the first half, and another inspirational speech from the long-time coach, Richmond skipper Donald Don—who also was the poor soul minding Coventry—had a few words with the press as he was leaving the arena. Don said: "The style of game is not suiting us. Too many of our chaps are flying for the ball, allowing Collingwood to mark over them. But the game is not lost."

Richmond kept its hopes alive by kicking the first goal of the second half, but those believing a Tiger revival would follow were sorely disappointed. Soon after, Len Murphy marked a pass from busy centreman Jack Beveridge and converted his second goal. Then Gordon Coventry added another "through unguarded posts", but the margin had been reduced to 17 points at the last break. Tigers fans still gave themselves a chance, but the Magpies were equally buoyant that they would finish the game hard.

Goals to Bob Makeham and Coventry once more in the early stages of the last term saw that "the Tigers were dying hard." The Magpies managed four goals to two in the last term. Coventry slotted through his ninth for the match, far exceeding the goals any other individual had previously kicked in a premiership-deciding match. Collingwood fans savoured the last term as the result was beyond question. And when the final bell rang, declaring the Magpies 33-point winners, they celebrated the first time the club had won back-to-back premierships since 1902-03. The fans were delirious and many of them invaded the ground to reach their heroes.

When the players reached the rooms, they were again greeted by a swarm of well-wishers. *The Herald* described the scenes: "The shouts and gaiety of the victors and their supporters, there seemed to be an unlimited supply of impromptu speakers. Men vied with each other to press congratulations upon the players."

Incredibly, this Collingwood team had three sets of brothers, and all played their part to perfection. Albert and Harry Collier were adjudged among the best players on the field; Frank Murphy was an important player, while his sibling Len had booted two goals in his first final.

But, fittingly, most of the attention fixed in on the Coventry brothers, even though neither of them was altogether comfortable basking in the limelight.

In the rooms after the game, Syd was described as "the quietest speaker and calmest of them all. He might have been discussing the most commonplace subject imaginable; only his smiling eyes and lips told of his delight."

Syd took time out to praise the efforts of Rowe, saying in *The Herald* he "was worth his weight in gold... Percy saved Gordon from any interference in going for marks, and to a man who relies so much on his marking ability, it meant the difference between the nine goals he got, and the two or three he might have got without protection." Some people associated with the club would dub the 1928 win as "Rowe's premiership". Gordon, himself, credited Rowe with the most important role of the game, saying: "No one thought it possible for one man to shoulder such a burden, but Rowe thought lightly of it."

It is not known whether legendary benefactor John Wren slipped a note into Gordon Coventry's large hands that night, as was his usual custom, but the club's secretary, George Connor, did hand over a coin to Gordon. It wasn't just any old coin, mind you. It was a sovereign from 1820 which he had "treasured for many years". As grateful as he was, the only things Coventry cared about was winning a second premiership medallion, and responding positively to his brother's pre-game challenge. Gordon's performance to kick nine goals from Collingwood's tally of 13 was an extraordinary one, and he had matched the number of goals from the opposition team. It would not be for another 61 years—21 years after his death—that Coventry's record of goals in a Grand Final would be equalled, by Gary Ablett who kicked nine in a losing Geelong side in the 1989 Grand Final.

1928 COLLINGWOOD

PREMIER'S SEASON

COLLINGWOOD: 1928

ROUND ONE April 21
COLLINGWOOD 9.12 (66)
GEELONG 8.12 (60)
Best: Collingwood – G.Coventry, Harris, Rowe, S.Coventry, H.Collier, Clayden, F.Murphy.
Goals: Collingwood – G.Coventry 6, Beasley, H.Collier, Rumney.
Crowd: 18,000 at Corio Oval

ROUND TWO April 28
COLLINGWOOD 14.18 (102)
FITZROY 9.13 (67)
Best: Collingwood – G.Coventry, Wilson, Chesswas, Bird, Dibbs, Beveridge, H.Collier.
Goals: Collingwood – G.Coventry 9, Libbis 3, F.Murphy, Harris.
Crowd: 20,000 at Victoria Park

ROUND THREE May 5
COLLINGWOOD 5.12 (42)
RICHMOND 5.14 (44)
Best: Collingwood – Dibbs, Bowyer, F.Murphy, A.Collier, H.Collier, G.Coventry, Makeham.
Goals: Collingwood – G.Coventry 4, Libbis.
Crowd: 36,000 at Punt Road Oval

ROUND FOUR May 12
COLLINGWOOD 15.22 (112)
HAWTHORN 5.9 (39)
Best: Collingwood – Harris, F.Murphy, Dibbs, Rowe, Clayden, Chesswas, Angus, G.Coventry.
Goals: Collingwood – G.Coventry 5, Harris 5, Makeham 2, Angus, H.Collier, F.Murphy.
Crowd: 8,000 at Victoria Park

ROUND FIVE May 19
COLLINGWOOD 15.12 (102)
ST KILDA 11.8 (74)
Best: Collingwood – G.Coventry, Wilson, A.Collier, Makeham, H.Collier, Thomas, Beveridge.
Goals: Collingwood – G.Coventry 9, H.Collier 2, Libbis, Harris, Rumney, S.Coventry.
Crowd: 16,000 at the Junction Oval

ROUND SIX May 26
COLLINGWOOD 12.12 (84)
NORTH MELBOURNE 6.9 (45)
Best: Collingwood – H.Collier, Rumney, Libbis, G.Coventry, F.Murphy, Rowe, Bowyer.
Goals: Collingwood – G.Coventry 6, Clayden 2, F.Murphy 2, Libbis, H.Collier.
Crowd: 25,000 at Victoria Park

ROUND SEVEN June 2
COLLINGWOOD 13.9 (87)
CARLTON 12.12 (84)
Best: Collingwood – Bowyer, Beveridge, A.Collier, Rowe, Dibbs, Wilson, Thomas.
Goals: Collingwood – G.Coventry 4, Bird 3, Harris 2, L.Murphy, H.Collier, Libbis, F.Murphy.
Crowd: 30,000 at Princes Park

ROUND EIGHT June 4
COLLINGWOOD 13.7 (85)
SOUTH MELBOURNE 9.14 (68)
Best: Collingwood – S.Coventry, Clayden, A.Collier, H.Collier, Wilson, Bowyer, G.Coventry.
Goals: Collingwood – G.Coventry 5, F.Murphy 2, Makeham 2, Libbis 2, Chesswas, Harris.
Crowd: 22,000 at the Lake Oval

ROUND NINE June 9
COLLINGWOOD 13.14 (92)
MELBOURNE 11.14 (80)
Best: Collingwood – Beveridge, Chesswas, S.Coventry, Rumney, MacLeod, H.Collier.
Goals: Collingwood – Makeham 5, Libbis 4, H.Collier 3, G.Coventry.
Crowd: 27,000 at Victoria Park

ROUND TEN June 23
COLLINGWOOD 11.12 (78)
FOOTSCRAY 9.10 (64)
Best: Collingwood – S.Coventry, Chesswas, Wilson, Libbis, L.Murphy, Clayden.
Goals: Collingwood – G.Coventry 3, H.Collier 2, Rowe 2, Clayden, Makeham, Libbis, Rumney.
Crowd: 30,000 at the Western Oval

ROUND ELEVEN June 30
COLLINGWOOD 12.13 (85)
ESSENDON 8.9 (57)
Best: Collingwood – G.Coventry, Bowyer, Wilson, Libbis, H.Collier, Makeham, S.Coventry.
Goals: Collingwood – G.Coventry 6, Harris, Beveridge, Libbis, Chesswas, H.Collier, Makeham.
Crowd: 16,000 at Victoria Park

ROUND TWELVE July 7
COLLINGWOOD 9.13 (67)
GEELONG 12.6 (78)
Best: Collingwood – L.Murphy, Muir, Harris, Clayden, F.Murphy, H.Collier, Dibbs, Libbis.
Goals: Collingwood – G.Coventry 3, Clayden 2, F.Murphy 2, Beveridge, A.Collier.
Crowd: 17,000 at Victoria Park

ROUND THIRTEEN July 14
COLLINGWOOD 14.15 (99)
FITZROY 7.12 (54)
Best: Collingwood – Angus, Muir, Libbis, H.Collier, F.Murphy, Sneazwell, Bird, Makeham.
Goals: Collingwood – Libbis 4, G.Coventry 4, F.Murphy 2, Clayden 2, S.Coventry, Beveridge.
Crowd: 18,000 at Brunswick St Oval

ROUND FOURTEEN July 28
COLLINGWOOD 11.15 (81)
RICHMOND 10.13 (73)
Best: Collingwood – A.Collier, H.Collier, Angus, Dibbs, Clayden, Rowe, Harris.
Goals: Collingwood – Clayden 4, G.Coventry 3, F.Murphy 2, Libbis, Rumney.
Crowd: 30,000 at Victoria Park

ROUND FIFTEEN August 4
COLLINGWOOD 17.18 (120)
HAWTHORN 9.9 (63)
Best: Collingwood – G.Coventry, Rowe, Libbis, Angus, Andrew, MacLeod, Rumney.
Goals: Collingwood – G.Coventry 8, Libbis 3, F.Murphy 2, L.Murphy, Harris, Rowe, H.Collier.
Crowd: 5,000 at Glenferrie Oval

ROUND SIXTEEN August 11
COLLINGWOOD 15.16 (106)
ST KILDA 6.14 (50)
Best: Collingwood – H.Collier, Dibbs, Beveridge, MacLeod, Bowyer, Clayden, L.Murphy.
Goals: Collingwood – H.Collier 5, Clayden 3, Bird 2, F.Murphy 2, Rowe 2, Libbis.
Crowd: 25,000 at Victoria Park

ROUND SEVENTEEN August 18
COLLINGWOOD 8.17 (65)
NORTH MELBOURNE 8.9 (57)
Best: Collingwood – Makeham, Bowyer, Dibbs, Muir, Clayden, Andrew, Chesswas.
Goals: Collingwood – Clayden 3, H.Collier 2, F.Murphy, Muir, Harris.
Crowd: 11,000 at Arden St Oval

ROUND EIGHTEEN September 3
COLLINGWOOD 8.19 (67)
CARLTON 12.15 (87)
Best: Collingwood – A.Collier, Beveridge, Libbis, Dibbs, H.Collier, Harris, L.Murphy.
Goals: Collingwood – G.Coventry 2, Harris 2, H.Collier 2, L.Murphy, F.Murphy.
Crowd: 30,000 at Victoria Park

PREMIER'S FINALS

SECOND SEMI-FINAL September 15
COLLINGWOOD	9.8 (62)
MELBOURNE	9.8 (62)

Best: Collingwood – Beveridge, Dibbs, Rumney, S.Coventry, Clayden, Andrew, H.Collier.
Goals: Collingwood – Makeham 3, G.Coventry 2, F.Murphy 2, Libbis, H.Collier.
Crowd: 41,423 at the MCG

SECOND SEMI-FINAL REPLAY September 22
COLLINGWOOD	10.8 (68)
MELBOURNE	9.10 (64)

Best: Collingwood – S.Coventry, Libbis, Makeham, Harris, H.Collier, A.Collier, L.Murphy.
Goals: Collingwood – Libbis 3, Makeham 2, H.Collier 2, Harris, A.Collier, Beveridge.
Crowd: 42,175 at the MCG

GRAND FINAL September 29
COLLINGWOOD	2.4 7.8 9.11 13.18 (96)
RICHMOND	0.3 4.5 7.7 9.9 (63)

Best: Collingwood – A.Collier, H.Collier, G.Coventry, S.Coventry, F.Murphy, Rumney.
Goals: Collingwood – G.Coventry 9, L.Murphy 2, Harris, Makeham.
Crowd: 50,026 at the MCG

GRAND FINAL LINE-UPS

COLL	B:	H.Rumney	C.Dibbs	A.Lauder
RICH	F:	R.Empey	J.Titus	F.Goding
COLL	HB:	A.Collier	G.Clayden	B.Makeham
RICH	HF:	H.Weidner	G.Ruldolph	J.Baggott
COLL	C:	N.McLeod	J.Beveridge	B.Andrew
RICH	C:	S.Judkins	L.Gallagher	C.Watson
COLL	HF:	J.Harris	F.Murphy	H.Chesswas
RICH	HB:	J.Murdoch	B.Foster	B.McCormack
COLL	F:	P.Rowe	G.Coventry	H.Collier
RICH	B:	D.Harris	D.Don (capt)	J.Bisset
COLL	R:	S.Coventry (capt)	Len Murphy	B.Libbis
RICH	R:	T.O'Halloran	D.Lilburne	J.Fincher
COLL	Coach: Jock McHale			
RICH	Coach: 'Checker' Hughes			

SNAPSHOT

Win-loss record: 17-3-1

Highest score: 17.18 (120), round 15, v Hawthorn.

Greatest winning margin: 73 points, round 4, v Hawthorn.

Lowest score: 5.12 (42), round 3, v Richmond.

Greatest losing margin: 20 points, round 18, v Carlton.

Most goals by a player in a game: 9, Gordon Coventry, round 2, v Fitzroy; round 5, v St Kilda; grand final, v Richmond.

Most consecutive wins: 8

Most consecutive losses: 1 (three times).

Club awards: Best & Fairest: Harry Collier; Leading goalkicker: Gordon Coventry (89 goals).

Putting it into perspective:
It was back to back premierships for Collingwood for the second time in its history, following its 1902-03 successes.

1928

		P	W	L	D	%	Pts
1	Collingwood (1)	18	15	3		134.6	60
2	Richmond (2)	18	14	4		133.6	56
3	Melbourne (3)	18	14	4		122.2	56
4	Carlton (4)	18	11	7		121.4	44
5	Essendon	18	11	7		113.0	44
6	St Kilda	18	11	7		102.0	44
7	Footscray	18	9	9		109.3	36
8	Fitzroy	18	7	11		88.4	28
9	Geelong	18	6	12		99.5	24
10	South Melb	18	5	13		85.5	20
11	North Melb	18	5	13		67.7	20
12	Hawthorn	18	0	18		61.6	0

(18 home and away rounds)

PLAYERS USED

COLLINGWOOD	GUERNSEY	GAMES	GOALS
Andrew, Bruce	27	9	0
Angus, Les	26	9	1
Baker, Reg	33	11	7
Beasley, George	2	1	1
Beveridge, Jack	1	18	4
Bird, Tommy	28	7	5
Bowyer, Percy	3	14	0
Chesswas, Harry	9	18	2
Clayden, George	6	19	17
Collier, Albert	4	21	2
Collier, Harry	5	21	26
Coventry, Gordon	7	20	89
Coventry, Syd	8	19	2
Dibbs, Charlie	10	21	0
Harris, John	12	20	16
Kent, Cyril	29	1	0
Lauder, Albert	14	3	0
Libbis, Billy	13	21	28
MacLeod, Norm	16	15	0
Makeham, Bob	19	20	17
Muir, Bob	30	5	1
Murphy, Frank	18	21	19
Murphy, Len	17	19	7
Poulter, Joe	26	15	7
Rowe, Percy	21	14	5
Rumney, Harold	22	17	4
Sneazwell, Bill	23	6	0
Thomas, Les	24	2	0
Wilson, Ernie	25	14	0

**COLLINGWOOD 11.13 (79) d
RICHMOND 7.8 (50)**

DARK HORSES STEP INTO LIGHT

A pair of unlikely heroes provided the spark for the Collingwood 'Machine' as it pushed for three straight flags. By GLENN McFARLANE

VFL hopefuls Charlie Ahern and Horrie Edmonds cast contrasting shadows at Victoria Park as they sought to win a spot on Collingwood's playing list early in 1929.

Ahern was rising 24, stood at 180cm and weighed 79kg as he tried to make an impression. Originally from Northcote, he had tried to win his way into the Magpie team from the Collingwood District side. He was tough and tenacious, could use his fists better than the next man, and was more of a battler than brilliant when it came to football. Edmonds was from Diamond Creek, just a few drop kicks from the Coventry family orchard. He was 20, shorter than Ahern at 175cm and weighed more than him as well, which gave rise to his nickname 'Tubby'.

The ambitions of these two new Magpies were lofty ones, perhaps as onerous as any in Australian Football. Collingwood had won consecutive premierships and had gone a fair way towards changing the face of VFL football. The side operated like a 'machine', with brilliant individuals welding in with a host of consistent footballers to make up one of the most admired and respected teams in the game's history. This was the environment confronting Ahern and Edmonds at the start of their VFL careers. But, as much as their size and shape differed dramatically, both were equally determined to give it their best shot.

Neither was particularly highly rated by those at the club before the start of the 1929 season, but each had done enough to secure a final spot on the list. Ahern and Edmond would start the season in the Collingwood District team under renowned coach Hughie Thomas, but they would eventually find openings in the senior team. Neither could have known, then, that within the space of six months, both would prove unlikely heroes in Collingwood's third successive premiership, performing grand deeds on a day that would change their lives forever.

Having won the 1927 and '28 flags, Collingwood made no secret of the fact that it wanted to equal Carlton's record of three successive premierships from 1906-08. There would be no resting on the laurels of the previous two seasons; no feeling of satisfaction in the fact that they had restored pride to Victoria Park. President Harry Curtis flagged the administration's intentions at the club's annual meeting a month before the start of the 1929 season. The Magpies had won seven premierships—the same tally as suburban rivals Fitzroy—and a hat-trick of flags was the stated goal of all involved.

If there was confidence in the camp, it was only heightened after the first game, against Richmond, the team that had been runner-up the previous two years. On the day Collingwood opened its new grandstand, Jock McHale's extraordinary side turned on a remarkable football display, kicking 13 goals without a blemish to three-quarter time. The Magpies led by 17 points at the last change, despite the fact they had had three fewer scoring shots than their opponents. It was only when Harold 'Bottles' Chesswas missed with a shot early in the last term that the scoreboard attendant had to finally put up a behind to the Collingwood tally. There were cheers to accompany the point, not from black and white fans, but from frustrated Tigers supporters almost incredulous at the accuracy.

Collingwood was clearly the team of the season. Incredibly, it won every match of the home-and-away season, and there were suggestions that Jock McHale's team might just be unbeatable. Only one club, St Kilda, in round nine, came within two goals of the Magpies, and that came on a blustery winter's afternoon at the Junction Oval. Fittingly, just as Collingwood's winning streak looked like coming to an end, Gordon Coventry snatched victory over the Saints with one of the last kicks of the day. The Magpies had won by four points.

The team's average winning margin from its 18 wins of the regular season was a massive 43 points. Those wins from 1929, and the two finals victories from the previous season, took the club to a record of 20 consecutive games, a benchmark that would last until 1953, when Geelong stretched the mark to 23. Collingwood also became the first team to push beyond the 2000-point threshold in a season. Records would fall, and some would last for decades.

Albert Collier, in his fifth season at the ripe age of 20, won the club's second Brownlow Medal after a season that stamped him in the eyes of many as "the greatest footballer in Australia". Gordon Coventry kicked the first century of goals, with his final tally at the end of the 1929 being 124—almost double that of his nearest rival. He also broke the record for the most goals in a match, 16 against Hawthorn in round 13. He would break his own record a year later. But there were few accolades handed out to individuals at the club. It was all about the team. There was little more than a few tempered backslaps.

Amazingly, Coventry's smashing of the 100-goal barrier rated only a few lines in the newspapers. The club also didn't want to make too much of a fuss about it. In an interview in *The Herald,* Gordon Coventry attributed the lack of recognition to the fact that McHale "wasn't the sort of bloke to encourage individual players. His whole idea of coaching was to develop teamwork and discipline, with every man working together." Coventry's compensation came in the form of some special handshakes from club benefactor John Wren.

Collingwood's near perfect season was such that few thought the Magpies would be beaten that season. Even the normally conservative Syd Coventry admitted later that he thought, for a time, that the standard of VFL had dropped. "I thought the game had slipped, as we were beating everybody," he said.

There were "scarcely any changes" to the Collingwood team in 1929. This was partly beacuse of the exceptional form shown by the players in the team, but also because only the most serious of injuries would keep players out of the side. Some members pushed on through pain on many occasions because they were fearful of losing their spot forever, especially as the economic situation started to deteriorate. By luck and by good form in the District side, both Ahern and Edmonds got their chances. The former played two games (round nine against Footscray, and round 12 against Richmond) before returning to the seconds. The latter made his debut in that game against the Tigers, but seized his opportunity almost immediately with three goals from half-forward. He would retain his place in the team for the rest of the season.

Then, just when the premiership seemed a formality, Collingwood "met its Waterloo". In a match that was described as "the most extraordinary upset in the history of football", Richmond put into practice a plan from coach Frank 'Checker' Hughes to attack the ball and the man aggressively in the semi-final. There was, perhaps, a touch of over-confidence in the Collingwood camp, but no one had reckoned on just how unrelenting the Tigers were going to be. It started in the first five minutes of the game when Syd Coventry and George Clayden were flattened, and their impact on the match was dulled.

Richmond had been beaten by Collingwood in the home and away games by 17 points in round one and by 42 points in round 12. No one really saw what happened in the semi-final coming, least of all McHale and his Magpies. The Tigers somehow got the jump on their opponents with a nine goal to two first half to lead by 41 points at the main break. Such was the awe with which the Collingwood team was held that many fans and most of the players still expected the team would come back and win the game. They didn't. Those thoughts evaporated in a sea of goals to Richmond in the second half. The difference at the end of the game was 62 points. *The Herald* summed it up: "Eighteen spanners were thrown into the works, and the Machine was smashed to smithereens."

There seemed to be no plausible explanation for what had happened, other than, in the words of McHale, "we had many players off their form." In reality, the coach had almost certainly been out-thought by his old adversary, who had long been plotting the demise of the Magpies. Frustrated by two Grand Final losses to Collingwood, Hughes was determined to do everything in his power to not make it a third. His team played with unbridled aggression. Its coach said no other club had dared to physically intimidate Collingwood, but he was certain the Magpies would "crack" when the pressure was applied. On that strange day, that is exactly what they did.

But the loss stung Collingwood, with several players, including young Harry Collier, lamenting the fact that they had cost themselves the chance to go through a season undefeated. McHale was shocked by the sudden vulnerability of his team. But as minor premier, Collingwood got the chance to meet the winner of the Richmond-Carlton preliminary final in the Grand Final, and the coach forced the entire team to attend the MCG game as the Tigers overcame the Blues to earn another crack at the Magpies. And this time, for Collingwood, there would no second chances.

McHale remained confident in the ability of his players, but forewarned them against adopting Richmond's strong-arm tactics. In the lead-up to the game McHale said: "We will hold a meeting of our players after training on Thursday evening and my instructions will be for our men to play the ball at all times—Collingwood want to win the premiership by fair means only." It was clearly a slap at Hughes, and the Tigers' tactics a fortnight earlier.

But there would be changes. After the semi-final loss to Richmond, McHale had sought the advice of Hughie Thomas to see which one of his players might provide the best protection for Syd Coventry, who was certain to be targeted again. The answer was instant—Ahern. He would be brought in for his third career game—and, as it turned out, his last game—with the main task to "protect" his captain. Sadly, this meant George Gibbs, who had played 16 games that season, was dropped from the team. Two others were sacrificed in Norm MacLeod and 'Jiggy' Harris, with Len Murphy and Percy Bowyer returning to the side.

At the team meeting on the Thursday night after training, it was revealed that Ahern had been picked to add some size and strength to the team, as well as being a foil for any physical attention that Syd Coventry might receive. McHale also had another plan that was much more unorthodox. He wanted to use the game's best goalkicker, Gordon Coventry, as a decoy in the forward line, in an effort to allow Edmonds the chance to get under the guard of the Tigers, who had only seen him once before. McHale had placed his trust in Ahern and Edmonds, seeing them as key figures in Collingwood's quest for a third successive flag.

The anticipation of a close contest brought out 63,336 fans to the MCG on a day that dawned overcast, but proved clear, despite a blustering breeze. From early in the morning, fans began to gather at the gates of the ground. "Football fans queued up in their thousands," *The Herald* recorded. "Every seat was taken, every vantage point occupied. Children and lunchboxes were hoisted overhead, and after a great deal of struggle and labour, the camel passed through the eye of the needle." There were no more spots around the ground available and a sprinkling of "boys and men" sat perched in the trees outside the ground.

Collingwood was as focused as it had been all season. They Pies were desperate to gain revenge. But, evidently, there were others willing to try and put the Magpies off their game. Before the start of the game a collection of handwritten letters arrived at the Collingwood dressingroom addressed to 11 key players. The names of Ahern and Edmonds were not among them. Fortunately, eagle-eyed officials spotted them first. They turned out to be death threats and those officials kept the existence of the letters a secret until the end of the match, when it was too late to do anything about them. The players carried on in blissful ignorance that their lives had been threatened. Instead, they had been focused on trying to destroy the Tigers on the field.

But Richmond was expecting a big day, as evident by its secretary Percy Page, who spoke to pressmen moments before the team ran out. "Surely, it is our turn this season?" he asked rhetorically. Many Tiger fans were confident, too, that the past two Grand Final losses were about to be consigned to history, and that Hughes' team would finally salute for the club's third premiership. This match was do or die, and the fans knew it. It prompted a few little skirmishes off the field. *The Sporting Globe* said: "The appearance of the team produced a fury of applause and exhortations which never completely died down. Those who came, but could not see, could follow the changing fortunes of the game through the voice of the crowd." The outer was particularly "vociferous and even bloodthirsty".

It was a similar situation on the other side of the fences after a few minutes of play. From the outset, the two teams fought doggedly, without fear or favour. Richmond had the early ascendancy, with Jack Baggott marking and kicking the first goal after only two minutes of play. He had the chance to put another on the board just a few minutes later, but squandered the opportunity with woeful disposal. Richmond "were going very fast" in the opening stanza, hoping to exploit a perceived lack of speed in the legs of some of the Magpies. The Tigers were "moving smartly and early had more dash", but they could not transfer those chances into successful scoring. In hindsight, this would be a costly period of play for them.

Eventually, Collingwood got its systems going, and sought to make Richmond pay for its waste. Harry Collier marked in the forward pocket and threaded the ball neatly through the goals from an acute angle, which "heartened his side". It was the lift they needed. Then 'Tubby' Edmonds stepped forward on the most important day of his football life. While Gordon Coventry led to various parts of the ground, his teammates had no issue in seeking Edmonds as their target. His first goal, according to *The Herald,* came from "wonderful persistence… Collingwood thundered it down quickly, Edmonds cleverly backed out of a crush with the ball, and booted it through."

Charlie Ahern was in the heat of the action from the outset. Twice, early, he was "fouled" by Richmond players. One of his free kicks resulted in a Collingwood goal. Ahern's kick ended up in the arms of a grateful Frank Murphy, who accepted the ball and snapped a goal. Ahern was wounded in the course of the battle in trying to clear a path for Coventry. But he fought on bravely. It would later be revealed that he had suffered a greenstick fracture of the arm. His wife, Evelyn, and his family in the crowd would later blame those incidents with certain Richmond players for the tough road he had ahead of him in the next two years. But Ahern knew what his role was that day, and he played it to great effect. He was there to clear a path for his captain, and nothing was going to get in his way of achieving this goal.

Late in the first term, Gordon Coventry "seized" a loose ball and kicked Collingwood's fourth goal of the day to extend its lead to 15 points. But it was Edmonds who was causing most of the damage in Collingwood's attack. He "popped" through his second goal soon after to push the margin out further, prompting one journalist in the press box to declare "what a find this Diamond Creek lad is!" Edmonds added a third goal, courtesy of some pinpoint accuracy from rover Billy Libbis, to give the Magpies a comfortable 27-point lead at quarter-time.

McHale was delighted with the way in which his plan was unfolding. The only worrying sign was the fact that Bob Makeham had been concussed. He had been knocked out "for a few minutes", but carried on with playing when he finally came to. Ahern, too, was almost incapacitated on several occasions. He was feeling the effects of some very close attention, but shrugged it off as best he could. All he cared about was providing Syd Coventry with some space, and the opportunity to have a bearing on the match.

Richmond kicked the opening goal of the second term, to stay in the hunt. It came from Harry Weidner after he received a free kick for some close attention. But the expected charge from the Tigers did not eventuate. Another goal to Edmonds kept the buffer at a reasonable level. It came from a chain of good play, which started from Syd Coventry.

This was the Collingwood of old, and McHale's men had no intention of taking the foot off the accelerator. Collingwood's freshness was becoming a factor. The Magpies appeared to benefit from the week's break, while the Tigers' bruising encounter with the Blues the previous week had made them more than a little sluggish. The Magpies had maintained that 27-point advantage heading into half-time.

Both coaches worked overtime on their charges at the long break. McHale was demanding more of the same. Hughes wanted a lift from his team. When the two teams squared off for the second half, it was the Tigers who kicked the first score for the third term, albeit a behind. Then Frank Murphy took advantage of some smart play in a pack to kick the Magpies' eighth goal. Richmond scored the next two goals, through Weidner and Baggott, and at one stage had come to within 20 points of the Collingwood side. It was almost game-on again.

One amusing incident came when the umpire warned Jack 'Skinny' Titus for his "rough play" on Collingwood strongman George Clayden, as it was observed "Clayden is nearly four stone heavier." But there was nothing funny for Tigers fans when Edmonds, once more, managed to break free and kick his fifth goal just before three-quarter time, to all but put the issue beyond doubt. The buffer was back out to 25 points.

Richmond did manage the opening goal of the last term, but any hopes of a remarkable comeback were doused by an opportunistic goal to Libbis not long after. And, fittingly, before the end of the match, Gordon Coventry would register his 124th goal of the season, on a rare day in which he was used as a decoy rather than a destructive force. He finished with two goals. Edmonds—also from the Creek—kicked five goals.

Collingwood's hat-trick of premierships was attributed to several factors—its "rock solid" defence, the unusual decoy plan which allowed Edmonds the chance to monopolise the scoreboard, and the courage of several players to see out the contest, despite carrying serious injuries. Makeham played on, concussed and "groggy". Ahern had taken a battering, and dished out a few of his own along the way, yet still kept trying to do the right thing by his team, and his skipper. It was to be the match of Ahern's short life, though no one knew it at the time.

The final margin was 29 points. It had been a stunning reversal from the semi-final a fortnight earlier, one that Syd Coventry attributed to the great planning and hard work of the team. After he was carried off the field by the delighted Magpie trainers, the captain wore the broadest grin. When asked the inevitable question about whether this 1929 side was the best of the three that had won the three-straight premierships, Coventry was typically diplomatic. He declared that it was too difficult to compare sides. But he added: "The young players such as the Collier brothers, Libbis, (Jack) Beveridge and others have been improved all the time, and gained experience." He saved special credit for Ahern, whom he praised as playing one of the most selfless roles on a great day for the club.

The only two first-year players in that 1929 Grand Final side—Ahern and Edmonds—had more than achieved their pre-season goals of breaking into the Collingwood side. They had done that, and more. They had played significant roles in securing the premiership.

Edmonds would play in the club's premiership side the following season before transferring to Richmond, of all clubs, in 1934. Ahern was not so fortunate. He would never take to the football field again; his performance on that day proved his lasting tribute to the club.

Despite the fact that he had a greenstick fracture of his arm, Ahern's wife recalled more than 70 years later that he had managed to play the piano at the premiership celebrations that night. Despite feeling unwell, he went on the end-of-season trip to Tasmania, after some coaxing from Harry Collier. But by the start of the next season, he was seriously ill with bowel cancer. His teammates rallied around him, and tried to raise money for him.

Sadly, in 1931, Ahern succumbed to the disease and to "exhaustion", before his 26th birthday. His brief strut upon the football stage would be almost lost over time, but never forgotten by his grateful teammates.

1929 COLLINGWOOD

PREMIER'S SEASON

COLLINGWOOD: 1929

ROUND ONE April 27
COLLINGWOOD 15.2 (92)
RICHMOND 11.9 (75)
Best: Collingwood – G.Coventry, Clayden, Gibbs, MacLeod, Makeham, A.Collier, Libbis.
Goals: Collingwood – G.Coventry 6, F.Murphy 3, H.Collier 3, Andrew, Bowyer, Harris.
Crowd: 25,000 at Victoria Park

ROUND TWO May 4
COLLINGWOOD 18.18 (126)
HAWTHORN 11.7 (73)
Best: Collingwood – Harris, Chesswas, G.Coventry, Lauder, A.Collier, Beveridge, Libbis.
Goals: Collingwood – G.Coventry 6, Libbis 4, Andrew 2, L.Murphy 2, F.Murphy 2, Harris, Chesswas.
Crowd: 12,000 at Glenferrie Oval

ROUND THREE May 11
COLLINGWOOD 19.20 (134)
SOUTH MELBOURNE 4.14 (38)
Best: Collingwood – G.Coventry, Rumney, Lauder, F.Murphy, Dibbs, H.Collier, A.Collier.
Goals: Collingwood – G.Coventry 11, Libbis 3, H.Collier 3, Clayden 2.
Crowd: 18,000 at Victoria Park

ROUND FOUR May 18
COLLINGWOOD 12.13 (85)
GEELONG 6.13 (49)
Best: Collingwood – S.Coventry, Dibbs, A.Collier, Wescott, L.Murphy, Beveridge.
Goals: Collingwood – L.Murphy 3, F.Murphy 2, H.Collier 2, G.Coventry 2, Makeham, Libbis, Rumney.
Crowd: 20,499 at Corio Oval

ROUND FIVE May 25
COLLINGWOOD 16.19 (115)
FITZROY 8.11 (59)
Best: Collingwood – A.Collier, Clayden, Makeham, Wescott, G.Coventry, MacLeod, Libbis.
Goals: Collingwood – G.Coventry 6, Libbis 3, L.Murphy 3, F.Murphy, Harris, Rumney, H.Collier.
Crowd: 18,000 at Victoria Park

ROUND SIX June 1
COLLINGWOOD 20.12 (132)
NORTH MELBOURNE 11.15 (81)
Best: Collingwood – G.Coventry, Lauder, H.Collier, Gibbs, L.Murphy, Beveridge, Rumney.
Goals: Collingwood – G.Coventry 8, Gibbs 5, L.Murphy 4, Makeham, Libbis, F.Murphy.
Crowd: 10,000 at Arden St Oval

ROUND SEVEN June 15
COLLINGWOOD 12.11 (83)
MELBOURNE 9.5 (59)
Best: Collingwood – Clayden, Beveridge, F.Murphy, S.Coventry, Dibbs, L.Murphy.
Goals: Collingwood – G.Coventry 4, Gibbs 2, L.Murphy 2, Makeham, H.Collier, F.Murphy, Libbis.
Crowd: 22,000 at Victoria Park

ROUND EIGHT June 22
COLLINGWOOD 7.12 (54)
ST KILDA 7.8 (50)
Best: Collingwood – Libbis, G.Coventry, A.Collier, Lauder, MacLeod, F.Murphy.
Goals: Collingwood – G.Coventry 3, F.Murphy 2, Makeham, Harris.
Crowd: 27,000 at Junction Oval

ROUND NINE June 29
COLLINGWOOD 20.19 (139)
FOOTSCRAY 14.10 (94)
Best: Collingwood – G.Coventry, S.Coventry, A.Collier, Chesswas, MacLeod, Makeham.
Goals: Collingwood – G.Coventry 8, Gibbs 3, H.Collier 3, Harris 2, Makeham, Libbis, F.Murphy, L.Murphy.
Crowd: 18,000 at Victoria Park

ROUND TEN July 6
COLLINGWOOD 15.15 (105)
CARLTON 11.10 (76)
Best: Collingwood – G.Coventry, Bowyer, Andrew, Gibbs, S.Coventry, H.Collier, Clayden.
Goals: Collingwood – G.Coventry 7, L.Murphy 2, H.Collier 2, Libbis, Ross, Clayden, Rumney.
Crowd: 33,000 at Victoria Park

ROUND ELEVEN July 13
COLLINGWOOD 13.14 (92)
ESSENDON 11.7 (73)
Best: Collingwood – G.Coventry, L.Murphy, Clayden, Ross, Andrew, Libbis, MacLeod.
Goals: Collingwood – G.Coventry 7, Andrew 2, H.Collier 2, Harris, Ross.
Crowd: 17,000 at Windy Hill

ROUND TWELVE July 20
COLLINGWOOD 16.21 (117)
RICHMOND 11.9 (75)
Best: Collingwood – A.Collier, Clayden, Ahern, G.Coventry, L.Murphy, Beveridge, Libbis.
Goals: Collingwood – G.Coventry 7, L.Murphy 4, Edmonds 3, H.Collier, Harris.
Crowd: 33,000 at Punt Road Oval

ROUND THIRTEEN July 27
COLLINGWOOD 22.10 (142)
HAWTHORN 7.14 (56)
Best: Collingwood – G.Coventry, Dibbs, Rumney, Chesswas, S.Coventry, Edmonds, Bowyer.
Goals: Collingwood – G.Coventry 16, Edmonds 2, H.Collier 2, S.Coventry 2.
Crowd: 7,000 at Victoria Park

ROUND FOURTEEN August 3
COLLINGWOOD 10.10 (70)
SOUTH MELBOURNE 6.7 (43)
Best: Collingwood – Bowyer, Muir, A.Collier, H.Collier, Gibbs, Ross, Wescott.
Goals: Collingwood – G.Coventry 4, Edmonds, Makeham, Gibbs, Ross, Harris, Clayden.
Crowd: 20,000 at the Lake Oval

ROUND FIFTEEN August 10
COLLINGWOOD 13.9 (87)
GEELONG 8.12 (60)
Best: Collingwood – A.Collier, Lauder, Rumney, H.Collier, Clayden, Edmonds, Harris.
Goals: Collingwood – G.Coventry 4, Edmonds 2, Clayden 2, H.Collier 2, L.Murphy, Makeham, Gibbs.
Crowd: 14,000 at Victoria Park

ROUND SIXTEEN August 17
COLLINGWOOD 16.15 (111)
FITZROY 8.7 (55)
Best: Collingwood – G.Coventry, Edmonds, Lauder, Bowyer, Dibbs, A.Collier, Libbis, L.Murphy.
Goals: Collingwood – G.Coventry 7, Edmonds 3, S.Coventry 2, Beveridge, Clayden, Makeham, Gibbs.
Crowd: 13,000 at Brunswick St Oval

ROUND SEVENTEEN August 24
COLLINGWOOD 21.12 (138)
NORTH MELBOURNE 8.13 (61)
Best: Collingwood – G.Coventry, Wescott, Rumney, Libbis, H.Collier, Clayden, Bowyer.
Goals: Collingwood – G.Coventry 10, Libbis 3, H.Collier 3, L.Murphy 2, Edmonds, Bowyer, F.Murphy.
Crowd: 6,000 at Victoria Park

ROUND EIGHTEEN August 31
COLLINGWOOD 14.12 (96)
MELBOURNE 5.10 (40)
Best: Collingwood – S.Coventry, Libbis, Chesswas, A.Collier, Beveridge, Edmonds, Harris.
Goals: Collingwood – Chesswas 3, Makeham 2, G.Coventry 2, Libbis 2, F.Murphy 2, Edmonds 2, H.Collier.
Crowd: 41,316 at the MCG

PREMIER'S FINALS

SECOND SEMI-FINAL September 14
COLLINGWOOD	8.13 (61)
RICHMOND	18.15 (123)

Best: Collingwood – Libbis, Clayden, Wescott, Dibbs, Harris, H.Collier.
Goals: Collingwood – G.Coventry 4, Libbis 3, Clayden.
Crowd: 51,069 at the MCG

GRAND FINAL September 28
COLLINGWOOD	6.3	7.6	9.6	11.13 (79)	
RICHMOND	2.0	3.3	5.5	7.8 (50)	

Best: Collingwood – Ahern, Clayden, S.Coventry, Dibbs, Libbis, Wescott.
Goals: Collingwood – Edmonds 5, G.Coventry 2, F.Murphy 2, H.Collier, Libbis.
Crowd: 63,336 at the MCG

GRAND FINAL LINE-UPS

COLL	B:	L.Wescott	C.Dibbs	G.Clayden
RICH	F:	J.Fincher	J.Baggott	J.Titus
COLL	HB:	A.Lauder	A.Collier	H.Rumney
RICH	HF:	R.Empey	T.O'Halloran	H.Weidner
COLL	C:	H.Chesswas	J.Beveridge	P.Bowyer
RICH	C:	A.Geddes	D.Lilburne (capt)	C.Watson
COLL	HF:	F.Murphy	Len Murphy	B.Makeham
RICH	HB:	T.Dunne	J.Murdoch	M.Sheahan
COLL	F:	H.Edmonds	G.Coventry	H.Collier
RICH	B:	F.Heifner	B.Benton	D.Harris
COLL	R:	S.Coventry (capt)	C.Ahern	B.Libbis
RICH	R:	P.Bentley	S.Ryan	M.Hunter

COLL	Coach:	Jock McHale
RICH	Coach:	Frank 'Checker' Hughes

SNAPSHOT

Win-loss record: 19-1

Highest score: 22.10 (142), round 13, v Hawthorn.

Greatest winning margin: 96 points, round 3, v South Melbourne.

Lowest score: 7.12 (54), round 8, v St Kilda.

Greatest losing margin: 62 points, second semi-final, v Richmond.

Most goals by a player in a game: 9, Gordon Coventry, round 2, v Fitzroy; round 5, v St Kilda; grand final, v Richmond.

Most consecutive wins: 18

Most consecutive losses: 1

Club awards: Best & Fairest: Albert Collier; Leading goalkicker: Gordon Coventry (124 goals).

Putting it into perspective:
Three premierships in a row took the Magpies past Fitzroy as the game's most successful team with eight flags and they joined Carlton as the only other team to have won three consecutive Grand Finals.

1929

		P	W	L	D	%	Pts
1	Collingwood (1)	18	18	0		171.7	72
2	Carlton (3)	18	15	3		136.9	60
3	Richmond (2)	18	12	5	1	121.7	50
4	St Kilda (4)	18	12	6		130.3	48
5	Melbourne	18	11	6	1	105.5	46
6	Essendon	18	9	8	1	96.0	38
7	Geelong	18	8	10		108.6	32
8	South Melb	18	7	11		84.8	28
9	Footscray	18	6	11	1	86.6	26
10	Hawthorn	18	4	14		76.9	16
11	Fitzroy	18	3	15		73.3	12
12	North Melb	18	1	17		60.2	4

(18 home and away rounds)

PLAYERS USED

COLLINGWOOD	GUERNSEY	GAMES	GOALS
Ahern, Charlie	2	3	0
Andrew, Bruce	1	4	5
Beveridge, Jack	4	19	1
Bird, Leo	13	1	0
Bowyer, Percy	3	10	2
Chesswas, Harry	9	19	4
Clayden, George	10	20	8
Collier, Albert	5	18	0
Collier, Harry	6	20	27
Coventry, Gordon	7	20	124
Coventry, Syd	8	20	4
Dibbs, Charlie	11	19	0
Edmonds, Horrie	12	9	19
Gibbs, George	14	16	13
Harris, John	15	19	9
Lauder, Albert	16	15	0
Libbis, Billy	17	19	24
MacLeod, Norm	22	19	0
Makeham, Bob	18	17	10
Muir, Bob	21	2	0
Murphy, Frank	19	13	18
Murphy, Len	20	16	24
Ross, Bob	23	4	3
Rumney, Harold	24	20	3
Veevers, Ken	25	1	0
Wescott, Leo	26	17	0

**COLLINGWOOD 14.16 (100) d
GEELONG 9.16 (70)**

FOURTH FLAG JUST THE TONIC

With their coach sick in bed, Collingwood found something special to deliver a record-breaking flag to Victoria Park. By GLENN McFARLANE

RIVAL VFL clubs could barely believe their eyes when they scanned *The Sporting Globe* a few days after Collingwood's record-breaking fourth successive premiership in October 1930. There, in black and white, was the "secret" of the Magpies' unparalleled success, the very reason behind the club's machine-like efficiency, and its utter dominance over four years and a total of 82 matches.

Just a few columns beneath the summation of the club's remarkable Grand Final victory over Geelong, a headline attracted plenty of attention—"Collingwood Premiers reveal training secret." If there had been any substance to it, it would have been the football scoop of the year. Someone, it seemed, had finally found the elixir of Collingwood's invincibility. The reality was that it turned out to be an ingenious advertisement for Forbes Phosferrine, proclaiming proudly that Collingwood had, for the second year in a row, used the "energy-tonic" to overcome tired legs, tough opposition and an early finals defeat to prevail in the only game that matters, the Grand Final.

The advertisement went even further to say: "These champions trained on this amazing energy-giving tonic—and the result—premiers again." It cited a letter written by club officials to the makers of Forbes Phosferrine a year earlier. It read: "We consider the use of this valuable tonic was one of the main factors in the success of the team in the (1929) Grand Final. After our indifferent display in the previous match, when our players showed the efforts of a strenuous season, we gratefully accepted your suggestions to use Phosferrine—as many of the committee, being old players, remember our late secretary Mr Copeland had supplied us with the tonic, with good results, some years ago."

Whether the use of Forbes Phosferrine had anything to do with Collingwood's performances in the 1929 and '30 Grand Finals is debatable. More likely it was just a good piece of advertising sense. After all, the use of the Collingwood 'Machine' in the advertisement proved one thing—the Magpies had become a part of popular culture.

As the tentacles of a global depression wrapped around communities all around Australia, this star-studded football team from working class Collingwood had assumed the role as hero for many people in what was one of the nation's hardest times. The achievements of the football club acted as an inspiration, as an encouragement and, just as important, as a diversion. In certain pockets of Victoria, the team was just as well known and revered as Don Bradman, who had slayed the English bowlers in the middle of 1930. In some quarters, they were as highly rated as the champion racehorse Phar Lap, the galloper who was taking the country by storm. The chestnut known as 'the Red Terror' would take on the best in the Melbourne Cup just a month later before conquering the world at Agua Caliente, in Mexico, just 18 months later.

Thanks to the efforts of its players, coach 'Jock' McHale and its officials, Collingwood had established itself as the best-run and most-respected sporting club in Australia. They were true sporting heroes in a time when the country was crying out for inspiration and greatness.

Almost from the time that Collingwood had carried off the 1929 premiership, plans were underway to become the first club to win four flags in a row. But the final piece in the quadrella of Grand Final victories would almost be the hardest to attain. As one military man in the crowd on Grand Final day in 1930 was overheard saying, "great danger often lies in the moments of triumph." While the Magpies had finished the home-and-away season as minor premiers for the fifth straight season (yes, another record), they had been surprisingly vulnerable at certain stages of the season, most notably in the first half of the Grand Final against Geelong. Other clubs had started to adopt similar tactics to Collingwood. The addition of a 19th man in 1930 had provided clubs with the flexibility to cover the loss of injured players. Collingwood had had some injury concerns during the season, and a new team loomed ominously as a freshly motivated challenger.

Three teams managed to beat Collingwood during the regular season—Geelong, Fitzroy and Carlton—and the momentum heading into the finals appeared to be the younger, fresher Cats. They had only managed to secure fourth spot in the final round by winning their match against Fitzroy, with Melbourne losing to lowly Hawthorn. But they had played themselves into some serious form and had no trouble accounting for Carlton in the first semi-final. Collingwood had scrambled to a three-point win over Richmond in the second semi-final to set up a clash with Geelong. The Cats were quietly confident, too, having beaten the Magpies at Victoria Park during the season in their only other clash with them back in round four. Secretly, it was said that they believed they had "the wood" on Collingwood, though they knew they had to beat them twice to win the premiership.

In the lead-up to the game, Collingwood president Harry Curtis was forced to comment publicly on the rumours sweeping Melbourne that the Magpies might be tempted to not try as hard in the match and channel all their energies into winning the Grand Final. Such an outcome would have its benefits. It would provide the VFL and the two clubs with extra match revenue. Curtis called the rumours "moonshine" and protested that such a professional club would never pass up the chance to lock in a fourth successive premiership. It was to be history in the making, and Curtis didn't want to have to rely on the double chance to make it happen. There was confidence among the supporters, too, before that final against Geelong, with the result being that "many were snapping up all the even money bets offering."

But the money that was wagered on Collingwood to win that day was gone within the first 30 minutes of play. Geelong was fresher after the week's break and seemingly more hungry, as the Magpies looked more than a little leg weary a week after ending Richmond's season for the fourth season in a row. Almost from the first bounce of the ball from umpire Bob Scott, *The Herald* said: "Geelong's pace and initiative left Collingwood standing... the Magpies were listless and tired." The Cats kicked four goals to nil in the opening term. By half-time they had stretched that margin out to 37 points.

After a typical Collingwood rally in the third term, which included four goals to one, Geelong was too good in the final term. The Cats finished it off strongly, and managed to hold on to win by 25 points. Collingwood, as the leading team at the end of the home and away season exercised its right to challenge the Cats, who advanced to that play-off as the premiership favourites. *The Sporting Globe* echoed the thoughts of just how confident the Cats were when it said: "Geelong firmly believe they will be the masters of the Magpies."

Collingwood was under more than a little duress leading into the Grand Final. 'Jock' McHale was ill with pleurisy and his doctors ruled out any chance of him attending the Grand Final. How would the Magpies operate without their long-time coach? He had not missed a game as a coach since taking over in 1912. His message to the players at half-time had invariably played a role in lifting Collingwood onto many famous victories.

Bruce Andrew, a member of the 1930 side, recalled years later the planning that McHale put into preparations that week from his bed at his Brunswick home. Andrew said: "On the Sunday, he sent for some members of his selection committee to talk over the game. Then, on the Tuesday, he sent for the secretary, then Mr Frank Wraith. He gave Mr Wraith specific instructions that the team was not to use a ball at training on the Tuesday or the Thursday nights. He said, 'I am satisfied from what I've heard that the players have had too much football and are leg weary.' Everyone was loudly critical. McHale, a sick man though he was, took full responsibility." Those doubting McHale's instructions would have plenty of ammunition at half-time.

When "the day dawned calm and fine, it was generally regarded as being in favour of Geelong." Many felt a changing of the guard was about to take place. The Cats lost Ted Baker, a former Magpie, with an injury, but Collingwood gambled on playing the injured pair of George Clayden and Len Murphy. They included Bill Aldag, playing only his fifth game, to add some extra bulk as they "made no secret of their intention of adopting vigorous tactics from the start to throw Geelong off their game."

Missing their coach, and with the weight of history against then, the Magpies went into the game as underdogs, but internally the belief was still there that they could add to their 1927, '28 and '29 pennants, even if those outside of the club were not as convinced. *The Sun News-Pictorial* concluded on the morning of the match that: "It is today or never (for Collingwood) to pull off the greatest record in league history, for it will probably be many years, if at all, before another team get as close to four premierships on end."

True to its game plan, Collingwood was aggressive at Geelong from the outset, as *The Sporting Globe* saying "the shock tactics were evident early... the Woodsmen swung into the fray fiercely. The Magpies tried to (un)settle Geelong with their vim and ruggedness." But, as hard as they tried, the Magpies could not combat the speed of their opponents. Geelong's pace in the opening half was causing Collingwood plenty of grief, as McHale listened helplessly from his sick bed.

Clayden received an official censure from the umpire when he refused to give the ball back to his opponent for "two to three minutes". This was all a part of the Collingwood delaying tactics, to try and slow the game down. It was a way in which they were trying to combat the blistering pace Geelong was showing. The Cats' first goal came soon after Clayden's penalty when Bob Troughton had a "flashing shot on the run" to give the visitors a seven-point advantage early on. It was followed soon after by another from Ted Llewellen, giving Geelong an early break.

Typically, the Magpies fought hard to stay in touch, with Len Murphy opening the club's account with a "rather lucky snap." Still, Collingwood's aggression was counting against it rather than acting as an advantage. *The Herald* suggested: "The Magpies were still inclined to play the man, while Geelong was concentrating more on the ball." But there was nothing untoward about Gordon Coventry who was playing "a clean, resourceful game" and it paid dividends when he booted Collingwood's second goal after a strong mark. Then he followed it up with another with a little help from his friends. Harry Collier and Clayden "assisted Coventry to the Magpies' third goal, to put them three points up" late in the opening term. While Geelong seemed to have a faster, more resourceful start to the game, the Magpies had somehow wrested control of the scoreboard by the quarter-time change of ends. It remained to be seen whether they could retain it.

Geelong captain Arthur 'Bull' Coghlan was winded in the opening stages of the second term after a tough clash with Aldag. That seemed to spark the Cats into action as "suddenly Geelong broke clear and a lightning attack was crowned by (Bob) Troughton with the third goal from a fine running shot." Too much aggression again hurt Collingwood. Albert Collier gave away two important free kicks, the latter allowing Bill Kuhlken to score the Cats' fourth goal. Shortly after, Llewellen extended their lead from a "long running shot." The pendulum had swung firmly in Geelong's favour and this was only accentuated when Arthur Rayson scored another goal to open up a half-time lead of 21 points.

The Sporting Globe recorded: "Geelong looked to be the winning side at half-time, their air work and pace worried their opponents who valiantly tried to stem the tide." But the task appeared to be beyond Collingwood as the players moved towards their respective changerooms. The crowd was oddly silent, still trying to come to terms with what had happened in that quarter, with Collingwood supporters despondent that the quest for four flags in a row looked forlorn. As hard at the players had tried, their opponents just seemed to have all the answers.

And the man who had lifted Collingwood at half-time breaks for almost a generation was not there. He was stuck in his Brunswick home, listening on the radio, and hoping that somehow his plan to keep the players fresh during the week would pay dividends. With McHale absent, it was left to one of his close friends, veteran administrator and former player Bob Rush, to instil something into the team and to lift them when they desperately required it. Rush was a passionate Magpie, and had been a part of the club since 1899, so he knew what buttons to push. A fine orator, and a man of great integrity, Rush was to make the speech of his life. He implored his players to lift for the sake of the club's proud traditions. Better still, he reminded them that McHale was listening in, and would know which players were doing well and which were letting the coach and the side down. Harry Collier later recalled it was one of the most "inspirational" speeches he had heard. Those words from Rush appeared to provide the perfect tonic for a team that looked flat. The roar of the players as they left the rooms told Rush, and anyone else within earshot, that this Collingwood team was determined to make the most of its shot at history.

Resuming with Fred Froude replacing the injured Len Murphy, Collingwood proceeded to produce one of the best quarters of its four-year reign. The Coventry brothers combined for the first goal of the term, with Gordon finishing off some brilliant work from Syd. Then it was Bob Makeham—by day a farmer from Woodleigh, by weekend a champion footballer—who rose to the occasion in what would prove his most important performance in black and white. Makeham "overshadowed (Reg) Hickey to smartly snap Collingwood's fifth goal." More goals followed as the game swung back in Collingwood's favour. Harry Collier cut the deficit to one point when he snapped a goal. In less than five minutes, a dramatic transformation had come over the game. All of a sudden, *The Sporting Globe* said that Geelong was "listless and ragged whereas Collingwood was tearing along in their best style."

Froude, in only his seventh game, wasted no time getting involved. He and Horrie 'Tubby' Edmonds "helped G. Coventry to Collingwood's seventh goal as drizzling started". Then some "clever play by Andrew preceded Collingwood's eighth goal, snapped by (Jack) Beveridge." But it wasn't over there. Makeham followed with another goal, thanks to a "smart snap."

Geelong had been overwhelmed, but it finally managed a behind. To that stage, Collingwood had already scored 6.4 for the third term, and was chasing more. It was said that "when G. Coventry snapped the Magpies' 10th goal, it put Geelong almost out of the race and he followed it with one more before the three-quarter time bell."

Collingwood's famed third-term burst, so evident over the four years, had once more been telling, effecting a 53-point turnaround in the space of half an hour after booting 8.6 to 0.1. They had gone into half-time 21 points down. As the Magpies spoke as a group at three-quarter time break, the MCG scoreboard showed them leading by 32 points.

The Sporting Globe summed it up when it suggested that, "Geelong's collapse was near complete." How McHale must have felt as he tuned into the third term, realising his dream of four successive premierships was almost complete. Sure, he was not there. But as he had preached, the club was always bigger than the individual. And the club had seemingly responded once more to a difficult situation. *The Sun News Pictorial* described the third quarter as "one of the finest performances ever seen in football... it was an abject lesson to every team in rising to the occasion after being apparently beaten, and by sheer grit, and magnificent teamwork, sweeping aside every obstacle in the way of finals success."

While the Collingwood supporters in the 45,022-strong crowd savoured the last half hour of the game, the Magpie players continued to play with desperation and purpose. It was said that "Collingwood, dropping its vigorous play, moved into action from the moment of resumption, it became a fast, dashing side with every man in position and backing up perfectly." It would prove the perfect finale for the 'Machine'. While the Cats scored through Troughton and Jack Williams, 'Tubby' Edmonds scored another goal for the Magpies as both teams managed three majors each for the term. The final margin ended up being 30 points in the 1930 Grand Final, meaning the Magpies had become the only team to win four successive premiership pennants.

"When the final bell sounded, the crowd warmly applauded Collingwood and the opposition players shook hands as they left the field. Syd Coventry, the Collingwood skipper, tried to seize the ball, but Scott, the umpire, was too quick for him." It was about the only time that Coventry had been denied on the day. Still, Coventry—an inspirational leader who was doubly important in the absence of McHale that day—was afforded plenty of attention at the end of the game. He was carried off from the field on the shoulders of teammates and trainers. There was near pandemonium as the players finally won their way into the rooms.

As *The Sun News-Pictorial* reported: "The crush to reach the Collingwood dressingroom after the game was tremendous. The team arrived safely, thanks to the new covered race leading from the arena, but visitors in the rooms had an uncomfortable few minutes before they could enter and offer their congratulations."

Somehow Geelong's captain Arthur Coghlan had worked his way through the crush and into the winning rooms. Above the noise, he said, "We were full out to win, but you were too solid for us." His counterpart, Syd Coventry, added, "We were up against the greatest odds a team could face at half-time, and I thank the boys for the way they rose to the occasion. It was a wonderful effort from the whole team." It was a wonderful end to four years of incredible period of success for Collingwood, like no other team in the history of the competition has ever attained.

Collingwood had plenty of outstanding individuals in that team. Gordon Coventry won the competition goal-kicking award in all four seasons. Syd Coventry, Albert Collier and Harry Collier had won Brownlow Medals (even though Harry's medal was a retrospective one that he would not received for another 59 years). But the 'Machine' was all about the team, and not individuals. Individual achievements were fine, but they were never to get in the way of team success.

Twelve of the team members played in all four flags—the Coventrys, the Colliers, Jack Beveridge, George Clayden, Harold Chesswas, Charlie Dibbs, Bill Libbis, Bob Makeham, Frank Murphy and Harold Rumney. Two others—Len Murphy and 'Harry' Lauder—played in three, while Bruce Andrew, Percy Bowyer, Horrie Edmonds, 'Leo' Wescott, Percy Rowe and 'Jiggy' Harris managed to play in two of them. Another seven players—Charlie Ahern, Bill Aldag, Fred Froude, Norm MacLeod, Charlie Milburn, Joe Poulter and Ernie Wilson—played in one of the four straight flags. That night the Magpies celebrated and planned more premierships. More than a few wags suggested that the club's streak would never end, that they would keep on winning premierships.

Far away from those celebrations at Victoria Park, rival clubs were beginning to plot the downfall of Collingwood, to bring an end to the competition's greatest streak of success. *The Sporting Globe* forecast this a few days after the 1930 Grand Final triumph, wondering, "How long their dominance will continue can only be conjectured, but some of the other clubs should be profiting by the lessons the Magpies are teaching."

Heaven knows how many bottles of Forbes Phosferrine were sold in 1931.

1930 COLLINGWOOD

PREMIER'S SEASON

COLLINGWOOD: 1930

ROUND ONE May 3
COLLINGWOOD 10.14 (74)
RICHMOND 7.18 (60)
Best: Collingwood – Andrew, Ross, L.Murphy, Gibbs, Edmonds, H.Collier, Libbis.
Goals: Collingwood – G.Coventry 3, Edmonds 2, Gibbs 2, L.Murphy, Beveridge, Libbis.
Crowd: 32,000 at Punt Road Oval

ROUND TWO May 10
COLLINGWOOD 11.12 (78)
HAWTHORN 10.10 (70)
Best: Collingwood – G.Coventry, Bowyer, Rumney, MacLeod, Ross, Clayden.
Goals: Collingwood – G.Coventry 5, Clayden 4, H.Collier, Ross.
Crowd: 19,000 at Victoria Park

ROUND THREE May 17
COLLINGWOOD 16.19 (115)
SOUTH MELBOURNE 12.12 (84)
Best: Collingwood – G.Coventry, H.Collier, Lauder, Ross, Bird, Regan, Bowyer.
Goals: Collingwood – G.Coventry 7, Bird 4, Ross 3, H.Collier, Libbis.
Crowd: 18,000 at the Lake Oval

ROUND FOUR May 24
COLLINGWOOD 10.12 (72)
GEELONG 12.18 (90)
Best: Collingwood – Regan, MacLeod, Libbis, F.Murphy, Clayden, Chesswas, Dibbs.
Goals: Collingwood – L.Murphy 2, G.Coventry 2, Clayden 2, F.Murphy, H.Collier, Ross, Bird.
Crowd: 17,000 at Victoria Park

ROUND FIVE May 31
COLLINGWOOD 9.12 (66)
FITZROY 10.11 (71)
Best: Collingwood – Bowyer, Makeham, Edmonds, Froude, Gibbs, G.Coventry.
Goals: Collingwood – G.Coventry 4, Edmonds 2, Froude 2, F.Murphy.
Crowd: 21,000 at Brunswick St Oval

ROUND SIX June 7
COLLINGWOOD 15.24 (114)
NORTH MELBOURNE 8.9 (57)
Best: Collingwood – Libbis, Makeham, G.Coventry, Andrew, Dibbs, S.Coventry, Edmonds.
Goals: Collingwood – G.Coventry 6, Edmonds 3, Libbis 2, Makeham, H.Collier, Froude, F.Murphy.
Crowd: 10,000 at Victoria Park

ROUND SEVEN June 14
COLLINGWOOD 14.13 (97)
MELBOURNE 11.13 (79)
Best: Collingwood – S.Coventry, H.Collier, F.Murphy, Froude, L.Murphy, Everett.
Goals: Collingwood – G.Coventry 3, Edmonds 2, H.Collier 2, Froude 2, Barr 2, Libbis, F.Murphy, L.Murphy.
Crowd: 28,779 at the MCG

ROUND EIGHT June 21
COLLINGWOOD 22.11 (143)
ST KILDA 14.8 (92)
Best: Collingwood – Edmonds, H.Collier, Libbis, Bowyer, Everett, A.Collier, F.Murphy.
Goals: Collingwood – Edmonds 7, G.Coventry 5, L.Murphy 3, H.Collier 3, F.Murphy 2, Makeham 2.
Crowd: 15,000 at Victoria Park

ROUND NINE June 28
COLLINGWOOD 19.10 (124)
FOOTSCRAY 5.14 (44)
Best: Collingwood – G.Coventry, A.Collier, Makeham, Gibbs, H.Collier, Kelly, Bird.
Goals: Collingwood – G.Coventry 9, H.Collier 3, F.Murphy 2, L.Murphy 2, Edmonds, Chesswas, Clayden.
Crowd: 14,000 at the Western Oval

ROUND TEN July 5
COLLINGWOOD 16.16 (112)
CARLTON 16.20 (116)
Best: Collingwood – Clayden, Rumney, H.Collier, Libbis, Chesswas, F.Murphy, S.Coventry.
Goals: Collingwood – G.Coventry 4, Libbis 3, Chesswas 3, Edmonds 2, F.Murphy 2, L.Murphy, H.Collier.
Crowd: 40,000 at Princes Park

ROUND ELEVEN July 12
COLLINGWOOD 14.14 (98)
ESSENDON 9.14 (68)
Best: Collingwood – G.Coventry, Andrew, Gibbs, Dibbs, A.Collier, H.Collier.
Goals: Collingwood – G.Coventry 7, H.Collier 3, Edmonds 2, L.Murphy, Libbis.
Crowd: 16,000 at Victoria Park

ROUND TWELVE July 19
COLLINGWOOD 25.17 (167)
FITZROY 13.16 (94)
Best: Collingwood – G.Coventry, L.Murphy, Lauder, Gibbs, MacLeod, Libbis, Edmonds.
Goals: Collingwood – G.Coventry 17, Libbis 3, Edmonds 2, Clayden, H.Collier, Chesswas.
Crowd: 14,000 at Victoria Park

ROUND THIRTEEN July 26
COLLINGWOOD 18.13 (121)
NORTH MELBOURNE 4.15 (39)
Best: Collingwood – Edmonds, G.Coventry, Bird, A.Collier, Dibbs, Bowyer, Andrew, Kelly.
Goals: Collingwood – G.Coventry 7, Edmonds 6, S.Coventry, Beveridge, Ross, F.Murphy, Makeham.
Crowd: 8,000 at Arden St Oval

ROUND FOURTEEN August 16
COLLINGWOOD 15.14 (104)
MELBOURNE 8.9 (57)
Best: Collingwood – H.Collier, F.Murphy, Edmonds, Clayden, Kelly, L.Murphy.
Goals: Collingwood – G.Coventry 5, H.Collier 5, Edmonds 2, Makeham, Beveridge, Bird.
Crowd: 15,000 at Victoria Park

ROUND FIFTEEN August 23
COLLINGWOOD 17.13 (115)
ST KILDA 14.7 (91)
Best: Collingwood – H.Collier, Lauder, G.Coventry, Andrew, S.Coventry, Libbis.
Goals: Collingwood – G.Coventry 6, H.Collier 3, Libbis 3, L.Murphy 2, Bird, Clayden, Edmonds.
Crowd: 16,000 at the Junction Oval

ROUND SIXTEEN August 30
COLLINGWOOD 16.20 (116)
FOOTSCRAY 10.17 (77)
Best: Collingwood – G.Coventry, H.Collier, Makeham, Froude, Clayden, Bird.
Goals: Collingwood – G.Coventry 6, H.Collier 4, Edmonds 2, Bird 2, F.Murphy, Libbis.
Crowd: 10,000 at Victoria Park

ROUND SEVENTEEN September 6
COLLINGWOOD 16.10 (106)
CARLTON 12.11 (83)
Best: Collingwood – Chesswas, Makeham, G.Coventry, Aldag, Libbis, H.Collier, Froude.
Goals: Collingwood – G.Coventry 6, H.Collier 3, F.Murphy 2, L.Murphy 2, Froude, Edmonds, Clayden.
Crowd: 30,000 at Victoria Park

ROUND EIGHTEEN September 13
COLLINGWOOD 17.7 (109)
ESSENDON 10.6 (66)
Best: Collingwood – Bowyer, Rumney, MacLeod, Kelly, F.Murphy, A.Collier, Makeham.
Goals: Collingwood – G.Coventry 3, H.Collier 3, Libbis 3, Makeham 2, F.Murphy 2, Edmonds 2, L.Murphy, S.Coventry.
Crowd: 14,000 at Windy Hill

PREMIER'S FINALS

SECOND SEMI-FINAL September 27

COLLINGWOOD	14.10 (94)
RICHMOND	14.7 (91)

Best: Collingwood – S.Coventry, H.Collier, Libbis, Beveridge, F.Murphy, L.Murphy, Rumney, Dibbs.
Goals: Collingwood – Libbis 4, G.Coventry 3, H.Collier 3, Barr, F.Murphy, Makeham, Edmonds.
Crowd: 40,218 at the MCG

FINAL October 4

COLLINGWOOD	9.11 (65)
GEELONG	12.19 (91)

Best: Collingwood – Lauder, Dibbs, Rumney, Beveridge, S.Coventry, G.Coventry, L.Murphy, F.Murphy, H.Collier.
Goals: Collingwood – F.Murphy 3, G.Coventry 3, Makeham, Bird, Gibbs.
Crowd: 41,495 at the MCG

GRAND FINAL October 11

COLLINGWOOD	3.2	3.7	11.13	14.16 (100)
GEELONG	2.5	6.10	6.11	9.16 (70)

Best: Collingwood – Andrew, Clayden, H.Collier, G.Coventry, Makeham, F.Murphy.
Goals: Collingwood – G.Coventry 7, Makeham 2, Beveridge, H.Collier, Edmonds, Froude, L.Murphy.
Crowd: 45,022 at the MCG

GRAND FINAL LINE-UPS

COLL	B:	A.Lauder	C.Dibbs	P.Bowyer
GEEL	F:	T.Llewellen	B.Kuhlken	B.Troughton
COLL	HB:	H.Rumney	A.Collier	G.Clayden
GEEL	HF:	A.Rayson	J.Collins	L.Hardiman
COLL	C:	B.Andrew	J.Beveridge	H.Chesswas
GEEL	C:	F.Keppel	J.Williams	J.Carney
COLL	HF:	B.Makeham	F.Murphy	B.Aldag
GEEL	HB:	A.Coghlan (capt)	R.Hickey	R.McDonald
COLL	F:	H.Edmonds	G.Coventry	H.Collier
GEEL	B:	M.Lamb	G.Todd	F.Mockridge
COLL	R:	S.Coventry (capt)	Len Murphy	B.Libbis
GEEL	R:	P.Hardiman	J.Evans	L.Metherell
COLL	Reserve:	F.Froude	**Coach:** Jock McHale	
GEEL	Reserve:	R.Lancaster	**Coach:** Arthur Coghlan	

SNAPSHOT

Win-loss record: 17-4

Highest score: 25.17 (167), round 12, v Fitzroy.

Greatest winning margin: 82 points, round 13, v North Melbourne.

Lowest score: 9.11 (65), preliminary final, v Geelong.

Greatest losing margin: 26 points, preliminary final, v Geelong.

Most goals by a player in a game: 17, Gordon Coventry, round 12, v Fitzroy.

Most consecutive wins: 9

Most consecutive losses: 2

Club awards: Best & Fairest: Harry Collier; Leading goalkicker: Gordon Coventry (118 goals).

Putting it into perspective:
The Magpies created history by becoming the first team to win four consecutive Grand Finals. In total the club had now played in 18 Grand Finals for a competition-record nine premierships. Their Grand Final appearance in 1930 was their sixth consecutive such appearance.

1930

	P	W	L	D	%	Pts
1 Collingwood (1)	18	15	3		144.3	60
2 Carlton (3)	18	15	3		141.6	60
3 Richmond (4)	18	11	7		124.7	44
4 Geelong (2)	18	11	7		118.7	44
5 Melbourne	18	11	7		104.7	44
6 Essendon	18	10	8		105.5	40
7 South Melb	18	9	9		100.0	36
8 St Kilda	18	8	10		101.3	32
9 Fitzroy	18	7	11		89.2	28
10 Hawthorn	18	6	12		77.3	24
11 Footscray	18	4	14		75.8	16
12 North Melb	18	1	17		51.8	4

(18 home and away rounds)

PLAYERS USED

COLLINGWOOD	GUERNSEY	GAMES	GOALS
Aldag, Bill	30	3	0
Andrew, Bruce	1	11	0
Barr, Elvin	2	7	3
Beveridge, Jack	5	12	4
Bird, Leo	3	15	10
Bowyer, Percy	4	18	0
Chesswas, Harry	10	18	5
Clayden, George	11	21	10
Collier, Albert	6	19	0
Collier, Harry	7	21	39
Coventry, Gordon	8	21	118
Coventry, Syd	9	21	2
Dibbs, Charlie	12	19	0
Edmonds, Horrie	13	18	39
Everett, Bert	29	4	0
Froude, Fred	28	7	7
George, Jack	14	3	0
Gibbs, George	15	11	3
Kelly, Frank	17	12	0
Lauder, Albert	18	13	0
Libbis, Billy	19	20	23
MacLeod, Norm	23	16	0
Makeham, Bob	20	21	11
Murphy, Frank	21	19	20
Murphy, Len	22	20	17
Regan, Jack	27	4	0
Ross, Bob	25	5	6
Rumney, Harold	26	20	0

**GEELONG 9.14 (68) d
RICHMOND 7.6 (48)**

CATS SHINE IN HARD TIMES

The town of Geelong was behind its footballers as they revived memories of the strong and skilful teams of yesteryear. By JOHN HARMS

IN THE late 1920s, a time of prosperity and promise, much seemed right with world. Even in the mean streets of Collingwood where life hardened the faces, people were happy. They took comfort in the mighty Collingwood football team. Their boys. With 'Jock' McHale as coach, Syd Coventry as skipper and his brother Gordon kicking goals, with the Colliers roaming Victoria Park like henchmen in a Dickens novel, with John Wren helping in whatever way he could, the loyal folk of the flat believed their footy team would dominate the League forever.

But things changed. In late 1929, shortly after the Pies had won their third successive premiership, the crash of the stock market in New York threatened to unravel the tightly woven thread of the capitalist economies, with the grimmest of social consequences. Almost immediately, jobs were lost, mortgages and rents weren't paid. As the crisis deepened many people across Australia experienced tremendous hardship, and deprivation.

Thousands were footy fans; some were footy players.

The Depression was insidious. In Geelong, which was typical of most industrial communities, 30 per cent of working people lost their jobs, and signed up for assistance through Trades Hall.

Many businesses shut their doors. Banks foreclosed on properties. Landlords evicted families who couldn't pay their rent. It had sinister consequences: often the unemployed were blamed for their lot, and welfare payments were often stigmatised.

The people of Collingwood had to battle more than ever. They worked where they could, and if they could, or left Melbourne and tried their luck 'on the wallaby', picking up work 'on the fruit' or 'on the wheat' and jumping the rattlers to Queensland. Old-timers remember John Wren's people bringing boxes of vegetables to the cobbled laneways of Carringbush.

While life was cruel for some, the mighty Magpies were premiers again in 1930.

But only just. Geelong had taken it right up to them. The Cats snuck in to the final four in the last round of the 1930 home and away season when they thrashed Fitzroy, and lowly Hawthorn upset Melbourne. Geelong went on to beat Collingwood convincingly in the final. But under the Argus system Collingwood, as minor premiers, exercised its right to challenge and overpowered Geelong the following week.

The officials at Geelong believed they needed only a new player or two to add to their list to take it up to the Magpies. The scouts went recruiting, and not just in western Victoria. They had found a couple for the 1930 season: burly Len Metherell from Subiaco and Bob Troughton from West Torrens.

The first move was to appoint a new coach for 1931. The committee gave the responsibility to Charlie Clymo, who remains a mysterious figure in the history of football. Originally from Eaglehawk, he had been brought up by an aunt and uncle who sold hay, chaff, poultry and firewood. He was recruited by St Kilda in 1907. In three seasons he played 43 games, despite spending weekdays in Bendigo where he worked as a miner.

He moved to Ballarat, coaching sides to premierships over the years. He was successful at Golden Point, the home club of gun forward Jack Collins.

To the squad of the 1930 season Geelong added the West Australian George Moloney, and Tommy Quinn from Port Adelaide. Moloney was only 175cm but he was a star for Claremont and he looked like he would hold down a key forward's position. Quinn, a strong rover from Port Adelaide, had impressed other Geelong players at the interstate carnival in 1930.

Collingwood, despised by the other clubs and their supporters, remained the team to beat. Through gritted teeth people asked: could 'the Machine' extend its period of dominance to five in a row? Neighbouring suburb Richmond, where the Depression had had a major impact on the tight-knit working-class community, had lost the 1927, '28 and '29 finals to Collingwood but had a strong side, and the Tigers had also recruited well, picking up the Strang brothers, Gordon and Doug, from Albury.

Football was always going to be extremely competitive during these tough times. Wally 'Jumbo' Sharland played for Geelong in the early '20s before becoming a respected football writer, and later a radio commentator. He recognised the difficulties facing the community generally. In *The Sporting Globe* just before the start of the 1931 season he wrote: "Unfortunately the only money many players will get this winter is their football cash. Many are out of work with no prospect of securing a job."

And that was the footballers who managed to get on the park. They weren't well-remunerated—the Coulter Law meant payments were limited to three quid a game.

But at least that was something.

As the new season opened League officials were confident football, which remained comparatively cheap for fans by comparison with other pursuits, would remain popular. And they were right. Football offered at least some hope to supporters.

In Geelong, not all citizens were happy. Some were critical that the Geelong recruits, who had been found work at Ford and other Geelong businesses, were taking the jobs of local men whose families were suffering. Critics also claimed that in travelling to Melbourne to the football, fans were spending money outside the economy of Geelong.

There was also criticism of the worldly footy fraternity. Despite the hardship, radios (still a novelty) remained popular, and there was an ongoing debate in Geelong as to whether football or live community hymn singing (which attracted around 800 people each Saturday) should be broadcast on 3GL. Eventually a plebiscite was held in 1931. Football proved more popular and a compromise was reached. Hymn-singing was broadcast on Tuesday nights.

In some cases the authorities tried to make provisions for the prevailing circumstances. In the lead-up to the season the railways reduced the cost of travelling to Melbourne from 5/- to 4/6 although, as people looked forward to the opening game against Collingwood, it was going to cost another sixpence to get to Victoria Park.

That match was a crackerjack affair. In hostile territory, Geelong went down by less than a kick. Moloney kicked seven of the Cats' 12 goals in an impressive debut. Not far away at Punt Road, Richmond beat Carlton in another close match.

Geelong accounted for easybeats St Kilda the next week. Moloney kicked 12 and was the talk of the town. And in round four the Cats beat another contender, Carlton, by a kick.

Although attendances were slightly down, the game was well and truly back.

It seemed there was more public interest in the football than in the meeting of the Australian state premiers who had come together to discuss approaches to dealing with the economic crisis. Those trying to put bread on the table were already suspicious of their leaders, whom they believed were more likely to pursue policies that kept the British bond-holders happy than look after their own. At that meeting it was made clear that Australia would not be able to raise more overseas funds until it could show it was living within its means. That message was sent to the people, many of whom just wanted to know where their next meal was coming from.

Footy at least could lift the soul, however fleetingly, and offered hope.

Clubs found ways of supporting their own. At Geelong, the beautiful and much-loved Corio Oval came to symbolise the community's attempt to help. The blanket went around at half-time, and the boys who sold the *Football Record* donated their earnings to the cause.

Yet across communities the mood was often sombre. Apart from the economic hardships, the sadnesses of the Great War never left the hearts of many grieving families. This was the Victoria as captured in George Johnson's famous novel *My Brother Jack,* but made worse by the economic circumstances. Suffering diggers were visible, some still wearing the last of their army clobber, some unable to cope with the atrocities they had seen. Limbless soldiers enjoyed free entry to the football, a tiny consolation. Apart from the soup kitchens and the organisations formed to help those out of work, Geelong also had an Unemployed Soldiers' Depot.

Tensions surfaced. A significant divide between those who had retained their jobs and those on some sort of sustenance. In Geelong the community tried to help: it established the Mother Hubbard Appeal, which attempted to centralise support for those in need.

But these were complex social issues.

That their footballers were doing well was important to Geelong people—it had been since Geelong became known as that town with the football team in the glory days of the 1880s. After a couple of close losses in the opening rounds of the 1931 season they strung together some impressive wins. Although it was a very wet winter, the Cats were at their best when they opened up the play, making full use of their strength, pace and skill. This fitted nicely with the tradition of Geelong sides.

But they could also mix it in close with the best of them. Their tough old ruckman Arthur 'Bull' Coghlan led the way. He was a natural leader, in a team which boasted a number of outstanding leaders. Balding, and looking like he'd copped his fair share on the footy field (he was suspended for the latter part of the 1925 season and all of 1926 for striking North Melbourne's Harold Johnston), Coghlan made his presence felt, blocking and shepherding, and generally looking after his rovers, the nuggetty Tommy Quinn and the left-footed skipper Ted Baker, and his quick lightweights.

One of the speedsters was Jack Carney from Colac, perhaps the smallest player of all time. Just 160cm, and 58kg, the wingman was known as 'Mickey the Mouse'. He worked beautifully with Edward 'Carji' Greeves the champion centreman. Greeves was the archetypal amateur, the lad from Geelong College. He was named after Carjillo, the Rajah of Bong, a character in a popular musical in the mid-'20s. He won the inaugural Brownlow Medal in 1924 and played in the '25 premiership. Greeves was a star. He had missed the latter part of 1930 with a knee injury and his return lifted Geelong. Breaking out of the centre, he projected long drop kicks which gave his forwards every chance.

He had plenty to kick to. Jack Collins was just 21 and had it all: he was one of those gifted athletes who could leap and run and when he was on no one could get near him. He is still regarded as one of the great centre half-forwards of all time. Collins had some talent around him. Les Hardiman, who could play back or forward, was even more famous for his ability to soar. And then there was George Moloney, who could find the goals. Jack Evans, with hands as big as frying pans, often played as the second ruckman.

The defence was built on the two key backmen, George 'Jocka' Todd at full-back, and the great Reg Hickey at centre half back. Todd was not far off 30, old for a footballer in those days. His battles with Gordon Coventry were memorable and the champion Collingwood full-forward regarded him highly. Todd had a tremendous understanding with his young back pocket player, another lad from Geelong College, Milton Lamb, who, though small, was regarded as extremely brave.

Hickey was a stalwart figure at centre half-back. A leader on and off the field, he represented the best of the Catholic and sporting traditions, and there was a sense for more than a decade that if Reg Hickey were in the Geelong team the town had little to worry about.

The flankers included the dasher Rupe McDonald and Jack Williams who ran in straight lines. Williams was often sent out with a job to do. He had the pace to play on the Richmond champion Jack Titus, a lightly framed forward, who was a fine lead and good mark, and could get away from the bigger defenders.

Geelong had a lot of talent.

Through the long winter the team gave its fans something to admire. The Cats beat each of the contenders. They thrashed Richmond at Corio, the *Advertiser* suggesting this was "the first knot in the Tiger's tail". They kicked 4.19 to Collingwood's 4.6 at home as well. Having lost just three matches, they finished top on percentage, ahead of Richmond.

It was an even year, especially for those in the middle of the table trying to secure a place in the finals. Footscray emerged as a contender, beating the Tigers in round 14, but it had no forwards. Melbourne won its share of games. St Kilda beat Collingwood in a classic at the Junction Oval when the full-forwards, Bill Mohr and Gordon Coventry, kicked 11 goals each. Haydn Bunton had arrived at Fitzroy and despite winning the 1931 Brownlow Medal, he could not lift the side beyond four wins.

The Blues won the games they needed to, and finished third, and surprisingly Collingwood, who had slipped somewhat, needed to win its last fixture to ensure fourth position. It thrashed Melbourne.

A new finals system was implemented. League delegate Percy Page and young Ken McIntyre, a Geelong lad who was in his final year of an arts degree at Melbourne University, proposed the format.

In the first week of the finals, Carlton, led by Harry 'Soapy' Vallence's 11 goals, thrashed the Pies to move to the preliminary final. The Collingwood machine had finally ground to a halt.

Geelong seemed to have the Tigers' measure. Yet, in the second semi-final, the Cats were outclassed by Richmond, who had winners all over the ground. Geelong fumbled its way through the match to lose by 33 points.

It got worse for Geelong. By quarter-time in the preliminary final all looked lost. Kicking against the wind the Cats failed to score, while the Blues piled on 7.5. But Geelong rallied and by half-time led by three points. In the second half, the match was in the balance for a long time, with the Cats playing what the *Geelong Advertiser* called "inspired football". Metherell and Coghlan led the way, and with Greeves playing "rattling good football". The Cats managed to hold Carlton who had the strong breeze in the third quarter, and were confident coming home. Despite dominating play, they registered a series of points, before sealing victory with Rayson's goal.

In the week of the Grand Final, Geelong was buzzing. Some employers let their charges work late each day so they could have Saturday morning off. The woollen mills announced they would close for Grand Final day. The annual schoolgirls athletics carnival had been scheduled that afternoon and many of the girls and their parents wanted to go to the football. Local businessman

Julius Solomon offered to set up a PA system so the radio broadcast could be heard across the oval.

That Saturday more than 3000 Geelong folk travelled by special trains to Melbourne. Many who stayed home listened to the radio broadcast across Geelong and the Western District.

Richmond was determined to make up for the Grand Final losses of previous years. It had a strong side: Titus, O'Neill and Bolger (who would go no to be part of one of the great full-back lines of all time), Judkins, Zschech and Geddes across the centre, and Jack Dyer, just 17 years old, named as the first ruckman. The Strang brothers were picked in the two key forward positions. They had arrived at the club in 1931, having enjoyed brilliant careers in Albury. Doug was a brilliant mark. The Tigers could play fast, free-flowing footy, although their tendency was to engage their opponents in a tight, brutal contest.

As the crowd roared and the game got under way, a gusty wind blew towards the Punt Road pocket, making conditions tricky; it was hard to judge the ball in flight. Many mistakes led to many scrimmages. *The Argus* described the opening quarter as "strong, vigorous and desperate".

Geelong, kicking with the breeze, started brilliantly. Les Hardiman took a big mark, went back for his kick, and punted truly to settle the Geelong nerves. Richmond closed things up and the "rough and tumble" contest became rather willing with "players bowled over like nine pins". Richmond's Bolger ("in his anxiety") threw Troughton to the ground "by the neck". Umpire Bob Scott, whom all agreed had a stellar game with the whistle, warned the Richmond defender. Soon after, Titus crunched Lamb with a late tackle which raised the ire of the Geelong crowd. Lamb had been his reliable self, saving a goal on the line, and backing up Todd as he always did.

Bill Morrow, older brother of Geelong ruckman and club stalwart Tom Morrow (who played in the '51 premiership side), had travelled to the match with his father. He was nine years old. "I remember the Richmond blokes, and their bare arms. They had huge, shiny arms," he said in 1995. "And they wouldn't leave George Moloney alone. Moloney went down a couple of times." It was a tough contest.

At the first break Geelong led by a goal.

The second term opened with another Hardiman mark and left-foot snap which sailed through. Both sides continued to make handling errors, but Richmond barged their way forward, resulting in quick goals to Gordon Strang, after a mark where he was head and shoulders above the pack, and Jack Twyford. Richmond led by eight points.

Then, reported *The Argus,* Geelong "rose to the occasion".

'Mickey the Mouse' Carney was instrumental. He brought the crowd to its feet when he received a pass from Hickey and took off, running 80 yards with his pursuer unable to make any ground on him. It was, said 'Stab Kick' of the *Advertiser,* "one of the most thrilling incidents seen on any ground this season". Once Geelong created space even independent observers said it looked the goods. Troughton ran on to a pass from Greeves and goaled. And it was Carney, yet again, setting up Moloney who snapped over his shoulder. Carney continued to open up the Richmond defence and provided Collins (who was playing with "reckless abandon") with opportunities. 'Mickey the Mouse' had turned the game. At half-time the Cats led and looked the better side.

Geelong dominated the third quarter. Goals to Metherell and Baker allowed the Cats to draw clear, but they were wasteful, and the Tigers remained in the game. Geddes battled hard on one wing, but Carney continued to make the play on the other, leading Judkins a merry dance. The Geelong defence was too strong. The half-back line was resolute, with Hickey clearing on many occasions, and when the ball did go deep into Richmond's forward line old Jocka Todd outmanoeuvred his high-marking opponents.

By the final quarter the Richmond spirit had been broken and *The Argus* correspondent was a little critical of its "failure to see the fight out". Carney remained on the same wing so ended up playing on the dangerous Geddes who had kept Richmond's fortunes alive. The Cats, who seemed to run the game out better, were in control and it finished 'tamely' with the margin at 20 points.

Carney was clearly the best man on the ground. *The Argus* lauded the "little wingman" for his "dash, his persistence and his pluck… His play was spectacular and compelling." The *Advertiser* was understandably a little more effusive, describing Carney's game as "amazing". But all reporters praised Geelong's team effort, especially the ruckmen, and the key defenders who held it all together.

Geelong was the premier.

And Charlie Clymo was the premiership coach. Yet within months he had left the club to take up a secure job in the Ballarat railway yards. His belief in physical fitness had served the 1931 team very well.

Later that night the players were greeted by 3000 people at the Geelong station. The St Augustine's Band played as the crowd made its way up the hill to the City Hall where the mayor tried to make himself heard. He was drowned out by the constant demand: "Three Cheers for Carney." The voices demanded Carney be hoisted high, and the tide of joy carried him along.

In a time of great hardship, it was one of the most memorable nights in the history of Geelong—the town and the footy club.

1931 GEELONG

PREMIER'S SEASON

GEELONG: 1931

ROUND ONE May 2
GEELONG 12.15 (87)
COLLINGWOOD 13.14 (92)
Best: Geelong – Moloney, Collins, Metherell, Evans, Coghlan, Todd, Lamb, L.Hardiman.
Goals: Geelong – Moloney 7, Rayson 2, L.Hardiman 2, Baker.
Crowd: 16,000 at Victoria Park

ROUND TWO May 9
GEELONG 20.6 (126)
ST KILDA 7.12 (54)
Best: Geelong – Moloney, Todd, Hickey, McDonald, Collins, Carney, Metherell, L.Hardiman.
Goals: Geelong – Moloney 12, Troughton 2, L.Hardiman 2, Baker, Kuhlken, Metherell, Quinn.
Crowd: 9,500 at Corio Oval

ROUND THREE May 16
GEELONG 11.17 (83)
MELBOURNE 12.15 (87)
Best: Geelong – Baker, L.Hardiman, Hickey, Todd, Collins, Metherell, Quinn, Rayson.
Goals: Geelong – L.Hardiman 3, Rayson 2, Troughton 2, Quinn, Evans, Metherell, Moloney.
Crowd: 19,767 at the MCG

ROUND FOUR May 23
GEELONG 11.14 (80)
CARLTON 11.8 (74)
Best: Geelong – Metherell, Todd, Hickey, Kuhlken, Rayson, Greeves, Collins, Evans.
Goals: Geelong – Rayson 3, Kuhlken 3, Baker 2, Moloney 2, Collins.
Crowd: 12,500 at Corio Oval

ROUND FIVE May 30
GEELONG 20.22 (142)
FITZROY 12.9 (81)
Best: Geelong – Metherell, Moloney, Hickey, McDonald, Carney, Walker, Kelly.
Goals: Geelong – Moloney 5, Quinn 5, Collins 3, Rayson 2, Troughton 2, Llewellen, Kuhlken, Baker.
Crowd: 9,000 at Corio Oval

ROUND SIX June 8
GEELONG 13.15 (93)
SOUTH MELBOURNE 6.8 (44)
Best: Geelong – Metherell, Troughton, Kelly, Carney, Hickey, Todd, L.Hardiman, Williams.
Goals: Geelong – Baker 3, Moloney 3, Metherell 2, L.Hardiman 2, Rayson, P.Hardiman, Quinn.
Crowd: 30,000 at the Lake Oval

ROUND SEVEN June 13
GEELONG 12.15 (87)
RICHMOND 8.12 (60)
Best: Geelong – Baker, Quinn, L.Hardiman, Carney, Kelly, Troughton, Todd, Lamb, Williams.
Goals: Geelong – Quinn 4, Moloney 3, L.Hardiman 2, Rayson, Troughton, Baker.
Crowd: 18,250 at Corio Oval

ROUND EIGHT June 20
GEELONG 13.11 (89)
ESSENDON 7.13 (55)
Best: Geelong – Carney, Metherell, Coghlan, Evans, Baker, McDonald, Hickey, Collins.
Goals: Geelong – L.Hardiman 4, Moloney 3, Baker 2, Rayson, Collins, Metherell, Quinn.
Crowd: 10,000 at Windy Hill

ROUND NINE July 4
GEELONG 13.9 (87)
HAWTHORN 9.7 (61)
Best: Geelong – Hickey, Todd, Lamb, P.Hardiman, Baker, Quinn, Carney, Moloney.
Goals: Geelong – Moloney 7, Rayson 2, Metherell, Kuhlken, Baker, Evans.
Crowd: 9,500 at Corio Oval

ROUND TEN July 11
GEELONG 7.10 (52)
FOOTSCRAY 3.5 (23)
Best: Geelong – Quinn, Hickey, McDonald, Coghlan, Metherell, Moloney, Walker, Kuhlken.
Goals: Geelong – Moloney 3, Quinn, Baker, Metherell, Rayson.
Crowd: 9,000 at Corio Oval

ROUND ELEVEN July 18
GEELONG 19.17 (131)
NORTH MELBOURNE 9.10 (64)
Best: Geelong – Walker, Carney, Quinn, Metherell, Moloney, L.Hardiman, Williams, Hickey.
Goals: Geelong – Moloney 5, Kuhlken 4, L.Hardiman 4, Troughton 2, Metherell 2, Baker, Rayson.
Crowd: 4,000 at Arden St Oval

ROUND TWELVE July 25
GEELONG 4.19 (43)
COLLINGWOOD 4.6 (30)
Best: Geelong – Carney, Hickey, Todd, McDonald, Troughton, Quinn, Metherell, Rayson.
Goals: Geelong – Rayson 2, Quinn, Moloney.
Crowd: 15,000 at Corio Oval

ROUND THIRTEEN August 1
GEELONG 15.10 (100)
ST KILDA 7.10 (52)
Best: Geelong – Metherell, Todd, McDonald, Hickey, Lamb, Coghlan, Carney, Moloney.
Goals: Geelong – Metherell 4, L.Hardiman 3, Kuhlken 2, Quinn 2, Baker, Moloney, Troughton, Walker.
Crowd: 16,000 at the Junction Oval

ROUND FOURTEEN August 8
GEELONG 11.11 (77)
MELBOURNE 6.9 (45)
Best: Geelong – Moloney, Evans, Metherell, Hickey, Collins, Quinn, Baker, Kelly.
Goals: Geelong – Moloney 6, Baker, Collins, L.Hardiman, Troughton, Quinn.
Crowd: 9,250 at Corio Oval

ROUND FIFTEEN August 22
GEELONG 3.10 (28)
CARLTON 5.9 (39)
Best: Geelong – Todd, Hickey, Evans, Lamb, Metherell, Carney, L.Hardiman, P.Hardiman.
Goals: Geelong – Moloney 2, Metherell.
Crowd: 18,000 at Princes Park

ROUND SIXTEEN August 29
GEELONG 9.22 (76)
FITZROY 9.8 (62)
Best: Geelong – Troughton, Todd, Lamb, McDonald, Metherell, Evans, Baker, Quinn.
Goals: Geelong – Llewellen 2, Moloney 2, Baker 2, Metherell, Collins, Quinn.
Crowd: 8,000 at Brunswick St Oval

ROUND SEVENTEEN September 5
GEELONG 16.12 (108)
SOUTH MELBOURNE 8.11 (59)
Best: Geelong – Lamb, Hickey, Todd, Carney, Troughton, Metherell, Evans, Coghlan.
Goals: Geelong – Collins 4, L.Hardiman 3, Moloney 3, Metherell 3, Baker, Evans, Rayson.
Crowd: 10,500 at Corio Oval

ROUND EIGHTEEN September 12
GEELONG 11.17 (83)
RICHMOND 8.8 (56)
Best: Geelong – Lamb, Todd, McDonald, Hickey, Collins, L.Hardiman, Moloney, Troughton.
Goals: Geelong – Rayson 3, L.Hardiman 3, Moloney 2, Collins, P.Hardiman, Quinn.
Crowd: 15,000 at Punt Road Oval

PREMIER'S FINALS

SECOND SEMI-FINAL September 26

GEELONG	10.6 (66)
RICHMOND	15.9 (99)

Best: Geelong – Troughton, Hickey, Carney, Walker, Todd, Lamb, McDonald.
Goals: Geelong – Troughton 3, Rayson 2, Evans 2, Moloney, L.Hardiman, Quinn.
Crowd: 48,353 at the MCG

PRELIMINARY FINAL October 3

GEELONG	11.17 (83)
CARLTON	11.11 (77)

Best: Geelong – Greeves, Hickey, Todd, Carney, Metherell, Coghlan, Evans, Collins.
Goals: Geelong – Moloney 4, Evans 3, Rayson, Quinn, Metherell, Coghlan.
Crowd: 36,653 at the MCG

GRAND FINAL October 10

GEELONG	2.3 5.6 8.11 9.14 (68)
RICHMOND	1.2 4.5 5.5 7.6 (48)

Best: Geelong – Hickey, Carney, Lamb, McDonald, L.Hardiman, Williams.
Goals: Geelong – Metherell 2, Baker 2, L.Hardiman 2, Troughton, Collins, Moloney.
Crowd: 60,712 at the MCG

GRAND FINAL LINE-UPS

GEEL	B:	M.Lamb	G.Todd	P.Hardiman
RICH	F:	J.Dyer	D.Strang	F.Ford
GEEL	HB:	R.McDonald	R.Hickey	J.Williams
RICH	HF:	J.Titus	G.Strang	J.Twyford
GEEL	C:	J.Carney	E.Greeves	J.Walker
RICH	C:	S.Judkins	E.Zschech	A.Geddes
GEEL	HF:	L.Hardiman	J.Collins	B.Troughton
RICH	HB:	M.Bolger	T.Dunne	B.McCormack
GEEL	F:	J.Evans	G.Moloney	T.Quinn
RICH	B:	K.O'Neill	J.Murdoch	F.Heifner
GEEL	R:	A.Coghlan	L.Metherell	E.Baker (capt)
RICH	R:	J.Bisset	B.Foster	M.Hunter (capt)
GEEL	Reserve: F.Mockridge		Coach: Charlie Clymo	
RICH	Reserve: T.O'Halloran		Coach: 'Checker' Hughes	

SNAPSHOT

Win-loss record: 17-4

Highest score: 20.22 (142), round 5, v Fitzroy.

Greatest winning margin: 72 points, round 2, v St Kilda.

Lowest score: 3.10 (28), round 15, v Carlton.

Greatest losing margin: 33 points, second semi-final, v Richmond.

Most goals by a player in a game: 12, George Moloney, round 2, v St Kilda.

Most consecutive wins: 11

Most consecutive losses: 1 (four times).

Club awards: Best & Fairest: George Todd; Leading goalkicker: George Moloney (74 goals).

Putting it into perspective:
The Cats' second premiership occurred in their second consecutive Grand Final and their third appearance overall. And strangely enough their final scores in all three Grand Finals were almost identical, 9.15, 9.16 and 9.14.

1931

		P	W	L	D	%	Pts
1	Geelong (1)	18	15	3		151.4	60
2	Richmond (2)	18	15	3		141.1	60
3	Carlton (3)	18	12	6		125.1	48
4	Collingwood (4)	18	12	6		124.0	48
5	Footscray	18	12	6		110.2	48
6	Essendon	18	10	8		99.2	40
7	South Melb	18	9	9		99.1	36
8	Melbourne	18	8	10		91.7	32
9	St Kilda	18	8	10		89.2	32
10	Fitzroy	18	4	14		86.0	16
11	Hawthorn	18	3	15		82.1	12
12	North Melb	18	0	18		50.8	0

(18 home and away rounds)

PLAYERS USED

GEELONG	GUERNSEY	GAMES	GOALS
Baker, Ted	2	20	21
Carney, Jack	12	21	0
Coghlan, Arthur	13	17	1
Coles, Clive	9	1	0
Collins, Jack	10	19	13
Evans, Jack	5	20	8
Greeves, Edward	20	4	0
Hardiman, Les	25	17	32
Hardiman, Peter	27	17	2
Hickey, Reg	18	20	0
Kelly, Max	23	8	0
Kuhlken, Bill	1	11	12
Lamb, Milton	7	20	0
Lancaster, Ralph	4	5	0
Laver, Les	29	1	0
Llewellen, Ted	8	10	3
Madden, Russell	22	2	0
McDonald, Rupe	6	21	0
Metherell, Len	3	21	21
Mockridge, Frank	17	7	0
Moloney, George	14	21	74
Quinn, Tommy	16	21	22
Rayson, Arthur	28	18	25
Sellwood, Joe	26	3	0
Stokes, Mac	9	1	0
Todd, George	19	21	0
Troughton, Bob	11	20	15
Walker, Jack	15	14	1
Williams, Jack	24	18	0

**RICHMOND 13.14 (92) d
CARLTON 12.11 (83)**

TOUGH AT THE TOP

Competition to play in the Richmond line-up was intense because the team was so good—and because players needed the money. By PAUL DAFFEY

THE STORY of Richmond legend Jack Dyer's breakthrough into the League football illustrates the way of football during the Depression. In 1931, Dyer was a 17-year-old whose spectacular performances in the Richmond reserves warranted senior selection, but he was unable to force his way into the team ahead of any of the Tigers' phalanx of big men. Jack Bisset was a 30-year-old ruckman who had returned to the Tigers after a season with Wimmera region club Nhill. According to Dyer's 1963 autobiography *Captain Blood*, Bisset feigned a hand injury so that Dyer could get his chance in the senior team. When the teenager was picked ahead of Bisset for his second game, the veteran follower said he would never help a youngster again. Dyer then lost his place to the elder player, but won back his spot before the end of the home and away rounds. Both men played in the 1931 finals.

The Depression years created what Dyer called "desperate men". League reserves teams featured several ageing players who should have retired but they kept pushing their bodies because they needed the match payments. Players without employment became brutally professional, even to the extent of trying to injure teammates who were vying for the same spot. There was no let-up in any game because players were desperate to avoid being dropped. According to the 1932 Annual Report, Richmond that season paid £255 in sustenance that season to players who were without a job. The club was a bulwark against the ravages of the Depression.

"Football was the only income for many players' families and an injury meant no money," Dyer said.

A small item in *The Age* on April 25, 1932, on the eve of the football season, must have given rise to envy throughout the VFL. In the item it was announced that the Melbourne Football Club had secured employment for seven players, meaning there were no unemployed players on its list. Many Richmond players had a "set" against the Fuchsias because of their club's amateur footballers; the Tigers disapproved of the fact that they kept out players who needed match payments. In Richmond's 1932 Annual Report, it said: "No greater service can be done than that of securing employment for players."

The report stated the club's indebtedness to vice-president H.L. Roberts for helping to place ruckman Fred 'Fritz' Heifner and rover Ray Martin in employment at the Richmond Brewery; for helping to place half-back Basil McCormack in employment with the Producers and Citizens Assurance Co.; and for lining up co-manager's positions for the Strang brothers Gordon and Doug at the Royal Hotel in Punt Road (where the Richmond Football Club was formed in 1885). But the report also said the club had been unable to place new players in employment for two years.

Richmond coach Frank 'Checker' Hughes was a man for these times. Hughes grew up in rough and tumble Richmond and played junior football for Burnley, on Richmond's fringe. As a player, he was a shrewd rover with a fierce competitive instinct. After beginning his senior career with the Tigers in 1914, aged 20, he served in the infantry forces in Word War 1, where he earned a medal for actions above and beyond the call of duty. On his return to Richmond he played in the 1920-21 premiership teams. He was the playing-coach at Tasmanian club Ulverstone for three years, 1924-26, before returning to Richmond to begin as senior coach in 1927, aged 33.

On Hughes's return to Richmond in 1927, he found a kindred spirit.

Bill Maybury was a servant of the club who had earned life membership in 1912 and became secretary in 1917. When Maybury was deposed as secretary after an election at the annual meeting in 1924, there was uproar. The man who replaced him was Percy Page. Brian Hansen, in his book *Tigerland*, described Page as a pugnacious administrator.

Checker Hughes was taken on as coach in similar circumstances. Former centreman Mel Morris was a club great when he was appointed Richmond coach before the 1926 season. The Tigers finished seventh of the 12 clubs that year.

At the end of the year, Checker Hughes replaced Morris amid great controversy. Hughes repaid the gamble by coaching the Tigers to runners-up finishes four times in five years (1927-29, 1931), one fourth (1930) and a premiership (1932).

Page and Hughes were many things—purposeful, driven, combative—and they were vigilant recruiters. A glance at a list of the players enticed to the club after Hughes's appointment as coach in 1927 reveals the building blocks of the Tigers' brilliant team of the Depression years. In 1927, Jack Baggott, Stan Judkins, Joe Murdoch and Heifner made their debuts. A year later, nine new players made their mark including Bisset and Bert Foster. In 1930 Martin Bolger, Ray Martin, Kevin O'Neill and Eric Zschech, all future household names, were introduced.

It was in 1930 that Hughes went to see 16-year-old Dyer play for St Ignatius Old Boys. Hughes was wary of the local hype surrounding Dyer, but after watching the teenager cut a swathe through the opposition in a Metropolitan Association Grand Final he approached the young tearaway and promised him that he would have the red 'V' on his jumper replaced with the white 'V' of a Victorian jumper if he signed with the Tigers.

Dyer played six games in his debut season of 1931. Then he began the 1932 season like a comet. Despite being just 18, his spectacular marking and strong work in the packs made him a standout. After round six of the 1932 season, he made good his coach's promise when he represented Victoria against Tasmania in Hobart. Dyer played 10 outstanding League games in 1932 before being struck down by a knee injury in a nondescript victory over North Melbourne at Punt Road in round 11. Although he made several attempts to return to the field, the injury kept him out for the rest of the year.

After the home and away rounds of the 1932 season, Dyer polled 12 votes (four best on grounds) to be Richmond's equal-highest vote-winner in the Brownlow Medal. Wingman Judkins, the Brownlow 1930 winner, also got 12 votes, while high-flying Gordon Strang got 10. Dyer returned to the field for the Tigers in 1933. He played until 1949, but his knee was never the same.

In 1921 Richmond won the premiership without one player who had been recruited directly from the country. Almost all of the team were recruited from clubs in the Richmond area, like Richmond Juniors, Burnley, Beverley and Balmain Church of Christ.

Richmond's 1932 premiership team showed that the Tigers, like many VFL clubs at the time, were casting a wider net. That Tigers team included country recruits like Maurie Sheahan (full-back, Ballarat), Kevin O'Neill (back pocket, Echuca), Basil McCormack (half-back, Rochester), Eric

Zschech (centre, Minyip), and Gordon and Doug Strang (centre half-forward, full-forward, East Albury).

The Strang brothers were a phenomenon, and helped to raise the Tigers just when it appeared they might be slipping, having finished fourth in 1930. Gordon was 22 years of age and Doug was 18 when they joined before the 1931 season. They were tall (both were 185cm) and angular, and they had strong hands. In the pair's debut game in the opening round in 1931, Gordon, known as 'Cocker', took 12 marks. In round two Doug kicked a club-record 14 goals (and Jack Titus kicked eight) as the Tigers scored a League record 30.19 (199) to 4.7 (31) against North Melbourne at Punt Road. Collingwood coach Jock McHale was moved at the time to say he had never seen two bush recruits like the Strang brothers.

McHale described Doug Strang as a freakish mark. In 1932 Doug kicked 29 goals in the last five matches, including seven in the second semi-final. He won Richmond's goalkicking award in his first three seasons, 1931-33, before leaving at 24 to coach Kyneton.

While the Strangs brought youth to Richmond in the early 1930s, the team featured plenty of experience. According to the 1932 Annual Report, there were no 10-year players, but 10 players had passed the five-year mark. Halfback Basil McCormack, wingman Allan Geddes, ruckman Perc Bentley and centre half-forward Tom O'Halloran had been playing senior football for eight years; versatile forward Jack 'Skinny' Titus had been there for seven years; half-backs Baggott and Murdoch had played for six years; utility Bill Benton, ruckman Bert Foster and wingman Judkins had passed the five-year mark.

While wingmen Geddes and Judkins were noted for their pace and skill, and Bert Foster was renowned for his scrupulous fairness, the rest had the hard edge of Depression footballers.

The lead-up to Richmond's 1932 season was notable for some changes. Jack Archer was replaced as president by B.V. 'Barney' Herbert, the former ruckman who had made the "Eat 'em alive" catchcry famous during the premiership years of 1920-21, and Percy Page stepped down as secretary because of ill health. Page's replacement was John Smith. Bentley was elected to replace Maurie Hunter as Richmond captain. The Tigers' quest was to end its string of seconds—four in five years—and win the premiership.

The matches against fellow top teams during the 1932 season featured several epic struggles. The Tigers lost to Carlton by one point in round three and then defeated the Blues by five points in round 14. They lost their only match against South Melbourne, in round eight at Punt Road, by two points. They lost their only match against Collingwood, in round 10 at Victoria Park, by 12 points. They drew with reigning premier Geelong at Corio Park in round six and then defeated the Cats by eight points at Punt Road in round 17.

The Tigers were rarely the subject of the major headlines. The top teams were Geelong early in the season, South Melbourne for much of the season, and then Carlton in the end. Richmond was as low as fifth mid-season and rose to second only late in the season.

Even when the Tigers defeated Carlton by five points in round 14, they failed to attract the main headline in *The Age*. The headlines and sub-headlines were, in order, 'MANY SURPRISES', 'South Melbourne and Geelong fail', 'Richmond beat Carlton with last kick'. Finally, the next week, after Richmond had scraped home by five points in a sodden struggle against Footscray, the Tigers earned the main headline: 'RICHMOND'S NARROW ESCAPE', 'South Melbourne's clear-cut win', 'Struggle for the four'.

The first match against Carlton was at Punt Road. Richmond should have been in unassailable position 15 minutes into last quarter but it had kicked eight consecutive behinds, including six that should have been goals. Finally, the Tigers broke through for a goal but Carlton then scored three quick goals to steal the lead. The Tigers mounted four attacks that were repelled by the Blues' backline. The Blues won by a point, 12.12 (84) to 10.23 (83). Champion Carlton full-forward Harry 'Soapy' Vallence kicked six goals.

In the return match at Princes Park, it was goal for goal throughout the last quarter. Richmond kicked two goals and Carlton replied with two. Scores were level. Seven minutes of struggle ensued, with both teams scoring two behinds in this period. Scores were level again. Richmond kicked a goal and Carlton replied. Players, the desperate men of the Depression, were hurling themselves after the ball. "Positions were forgotten in the grim trial of strength," said *The Age*.

Carlton forward Jack Green had a set shot in time-on but missed. The Blues were up by a point. Richmond captain Perc Bentley kicked a ball in from the southern wing towards Doug Strang deep into the forward line. "Strang, unmarked for the moment, marked in front amidst terrific excitement," said *The Age*. His goal sealed Richmond's five-point win, 13.13 (91) to 12.14 (86).

Carlton and Richmond maintained momentum from this match to take the top two positions on the ladder, with Collingwood third and South Melbourne fading to fourth. Geelong slumped to fifth.

Collingwood saw off South Melbourne by 26 points in the first semi-final.

Interest in the second semi-final was huge. A crowd of 62,326, a record for an Australian Football game, went to the MCG to see if the Blues could overturn their poor recent record against Richmond in finals.

The first quarter was a parade of skills, featuring "spectacular aerial work often bordering on the sensational", said *The Age*. The Strang brothers, Titus, O'Halloran and Carlton's Charlie Davey flew like birds. Carlton led by five points at three-quarter time. Tigers coach Checker Hughes urged his team to play in surges, to run the Blues off their feet. The Tigers cut loose. Quick goals to Maurie Hunter and Doug Strang spelt a warning. Hunter scored another goal. Doug Strang took two big marks for two goals. Hunter kicked two more. *The Age* said: "The one-sided affair went on, with Carlton throwing out distress signals all over the ground. Towards the end, Richmond slackened their pace and Carlton secured a few goals, but the match was over."

The Tigers kicked 8.5 to 2.3 in the last quarter to win by 25 points, 18.16 (124) to 14.15 (99). Their score was a record for a semi-final. According to *The Age*, the Strang brothers took 13 marks each and Davey took 11 marks for Carlton. Doug Strang kicked seven goals and Hunter six. Richmond players voted unanimously that centreman Zschech was best on ground. His performance earned him a hat from a supporter, Mick Kanis. Soapy Vallence kicked 4.5.

Carlton's poor final quarter meant that Collingwood went into the preliminary final as favourite. Popular prediction proved a poor guide. Carlton, employing "a rugged, straight-ahead style", according to *The Age*, won by 75 points, 23.10 (157) to 11.16 (82). The score was a record for a finals match. Soapy Vallence kicked 11 goals, equalling the finals record he had scored in a semi-final against Collingwood the previous year. In the 1932 semi-final, Vallence kicked his 11th early in the last quarter and then had another six shots for five behinds. His final tally was 11.9.

Both teams had concerns with chest injuries going into the Grand Final. Carlton ruckman Maurie 'Mocha' Johnson was cleared of damaged ribs. *The Argus* said Richmond's Murdoch had had his chest crushed. Murdoch was still in pain the day before the match, but he too was cleared to play. Wingman Geddes had managed to come up from a leg injury. There were no selection shocks.

The record crowd of 69,720 at the 1932 Grand Final supported the VFL's adoption of the Page-McIntyre system of finals in 1931. (Percy Page was one of two club delegates who suggested the system that made things more unpredictable for the minor premier.) Under the Challenge finals system, the minor premier had had the right of challenge. The biggest crowds under this system went to semi-finals. The enormous crowd at the 1932 Grand Final confirmed the popularity of the Page-McIntyre system as well as the popularity of football during the Depression years.

Conditions for the match were ideal. Richmond started with Skinny Titus at centre half-forward and Gordon Strang on a forward flank, where he would swap with O'Halloran on the ball. *The Age* said the match featured hard clashes and superb high marking, while elbows and fists were used at various points. Richmond half-back Baggott, who had twice won the goalkicking as a half-forward, was doing a good job of quelling Carlton match-winner Cresswell 'Mickey' Crisp. Fellow half-back McCormack had the dangerous Keith Shea covered. The Tigers led by 15 points at half-time and seven points at three-quarter time.

Early in the last quarter, Zschech wheeled out of the centre and found his captain, Perc Bentley, who kicked a goal. Powerful defence by Johnson enable Carlton to take the ball down to the other end, where Vallence kicked a goal. Soapy kicked another. The Blues were within a point. Maurie Sheahan, the Richmond full-back, raced up to the Tigers' half-back line to break up an attack. A chain of possessions took the ball forward, where O'Halloran kicked the goal.

Maurie Hunter then suffered a knee injury after what was described by *The Age* as a "fierce rush" by a Carlton opponent. Nineteenth man Jack Anderson came on. His freshness enabled him to leave tired and bruised opponents behind.

Keith Shea whipped ball towards the Carlton goal. The ball "bounced trickily" away from Baggott. Vallence seized on it, handballed to the running Horrie Bullen, who dashed through for a goal. Carlton had edged into the lead. The match was as taut as an instep. *The Age* excelled in describing the Grand Final's final minutes:

> Excitement rose to white heat, for Richmond were then throwing out danger signals... O'Neill hurled opponents to left and right as he battered his way through to open another attack.
>
> Tremendous cheering and excited screaming followed the progress of a match-turning thrust through Sheahan, Judkins, Bentley, Heifner and D. Strang, the latter marking and goaling to put Richmond two points ahead. Playing desperately, Carlton gathered all their forces for a counter offensive, and pandemonium broke loose when Clark dropped the ball in front of Vallence, and the forward, while hotly pressed by Sheahan, and being forced away from goal, cleverly tapped the ball back to Bullen, who goaled instantly. Four points ahead again, Carlton were favourites for the premiership. Gill, with one of the greatest marks of the season, held Richmond out, but the ultimate premiers were fighting doggedly, and skittling everything in their path. Judkins flashed into the picture, and G. Strang marked high, and forwarded, but at the critical moment a Carlton ruckman dropped the ball. Anderson rushed fiercely to it, knocked down

opponents, and kicked the goal, regaining for Richmond their two points lead. Kelly forwarded, but Bolger marked safely, and Kelly again turned play back.

Women became hysterical with the terrific excitement as the play swung backwards and forwards. Zschech marked coolly again at centre, and shot play out to Heifner, whose rugged determination and amazing strength were telling in the crisis. He forwarded, and the greatest roar of the day signaled a splendid mark by Titus at the goal front. Titus, on whose kick depended the fate of thousands of small bets on the outcome of the game—including a number of his own—aimed true, and the goal gave Richmond relief.

Wildly thrilling play ensued, with the crowd rocking and swaying with the mighty tension. McCormack halted a Carlton drive, Bentley held up the next, Geddes and Judkins kept play away from the danger zone, and Heifner and Baggott forwarded, where an attack swung out of bounds. Carlton fought it out magnificently, but a great mark by O'Halloran stopped them. Geddes had beaten his opponent pointless, and struck the goalpost with his shot, and Carlton were preparing for a last desperate, dying effort when the bell tolled, a great shout of exultation announcing the victory and Richmond's premiership. Players embraced one another, and were carried shoulder high from the arena. Several were kissed by delighted Richmond supporters, and there were wonderful scenes of enthusiasm.

The final score of a memorable contest was 13.13 (92) to 12.11 (83). The Tigers had won by nine points. Doug Strang had finished with four goals and Vallence five. Gordon Strang had taken 16 marks.

After the match, Richmond president Barney Herbert led the celebrations while wearing his 1921 premiership jumper with, according to *The Argus*, "various weird trimmings".

Percy Page by then had recovered from his health scare and had accepted the position as Melbourne's secretary. After Richmond's 1932 Grand Final victory, he was allowed in to the rooms on account of his long service to the Tigers in previous years. When the premiership celebrations had passed, Page asked Checker Hughes if he would like to join him at Melbourne. Hughes had no job. Page offered to put him on as a sales representative at his printing business in Queen Street.

Hughes, after ending Richmond's run of near losses with a premiership, joined Melbourne as coach before the 1933 season. In the years to come, he and Page would be considered the men most responsible for leading Melbourne into a golden age.

1932 RICHMOND

PREMIER'S SEASON

RICHMOND: 1932

ROUND ONE April 30
RICHMOND 16.20 (116)
ST KILDA 6.14 (50)
Best: Richmond – Dyer, G.Strang, Foster, Martin, Baggott, Murdoch, McCormack.
Goals: Richmond – Titus 5, Hunter 3, D.Strang 2, O'Halloran 2, Dyer 2, Bentley, Bolger.
Crowd: 25,000 at Punt Road Oval

ROUND TWO May 7
RICHMOND 15.26 (116)
MELBOURNE 7.13 (55)
Best: Richmond – Titus, G.Strang, Judkins, O'Neill, Bentley, Dyer, Baggott.
Goals: Richmond – G.Strang 7, Titus 5, Baggott, Dyer, O'Halloran.
Crowd: 13,000 at the Motordrome.

ROUND THREE May 14
RICHMOND 10.23 (83)
CARLTON 12.12 (84)
Best: Richmond – O'Neill, Judkins, Foster, Dyer, Bolger, Baggott, Zschech, Martin.
Goals: Richmond – D.Strang 3, Zschech 2, Dyer, O'Neill, G.Strang, Kolb, Titus.
Crowd: 24,500 at Punt Road Oval

ROUND FOUR May 21
RICHMOND 7.9 (51)
FOOTSCRAY 6.12 (48)
Best: Richmond – Dyer, Baggott, Foster, Geddes, Martin, Bentley, Collinson.
Goals: Richmond – Dyer 2, Martin 2, Collinson, Bentley, Titus.
Crowd: 19,000 at the Western Oval

ROUND FIVE May 28
RICHMOND 13.18 (96)
HAWTHORN 6.9 (45)
Best: Richmond – Martin, O'Neill, Dyer, Titus, Judkins, Bolger, McCormack, G.Strang.
Goals: Richmond – Titus 4, Dyer 3, McConchie 2, Martin, Heifner, O'Neill, Twyford.
Crowd: 10,000 at Punt Road Oval

ROUND SIX June 4
RICHMOND 9.15 (69)
GEELONG 9.15 (69)
Best: Richmond – Baggott, Zschech, Foster, O'Neill, D.Strang, G.Strang, Martin.
Goals: Richmond – G.Strang 2, D.Strang 2, Titus 2, Dyer, Twyford, Bentley.
Crowd: 17,000 at Corio Oval

ROUND SEVEN June 18
RICHMOND 14.16 (100)
FITZROY 8.13 (61)
Best: Richmond – Titus, Geddes, Bentley, Weidner, Bentley, Judkins, Bolger.
Goals: Richmond – Titus 5, Weidner 3, D.Strang 2, G.Strang, Dyer, Geddes, Bentley.
Crowd: 13,000 at Punt Road Oval

ROUND EIGHT June 25
RICHMOND 8.7 (55)
SOUTH MELBOURNE 8.9 (57)
Best: Richmond – Martin, Foster, O'Neill, Twyford, D.Strang, Dyer, Hunter.
Goals: Richmond – Hunter 2, Titus 2, Martin, Foster, D.Strang, Dyer.
Crowd: 35,000 at Punt Road Oval

ROUND NINE July 2
RICHMOND 11.14 (80)
ESSENDON 4.18 (42)
Best: Richmond – Hunter, G.Strang, Sheahan, Murdoch, Dyer, Judkins, Bolger.
Goals: Richmond – Hunter 3, G.Strang 3, Martin, Heifner, Titus, Dyer, D.Strang.
Crowd: 20,000 at Windy Hill

ROUND TEN July 9
RICHMOND 11.12 (78)
COLLINGWOOD 14.6 (90)
Best: Richmond – G.Strang, Martin, Benton, Bentley, Foster, Bolger, McCormack.
Goals: Richmond – G.Strang 5, D.Strang, Bentley, Foster, Dockendorff, Hunter, Benton.
Crowd: 20,000 at Victoria Park

ROUND ELEVEN July 16
RICHMOND 8.10 (58)
NORTH MELBOURNE 6.7 (43)
Best: Richmond – Heifner, Baggott, O'Halloran, Judkins, Bentley, G.Strang, Murdoch.
Goals: Richmond – G.Strang 3, Martin, Hunter, O'Halloran, Zschech, Bentley.
Crowd: 11,500 at Punt Road Oval

ROUND TWELVE July 23
RICHMOND 12.13 (85)
ST KILDA 7.12 (54)
Best: Richmond – Titus, Geddes, O'Neill, Bentley, G.Strang, Bolger, Judkins.
Goals: Richmond – Titus 5, G.Strang 2, Benton 2, D.Strang, Bentley, Martin.
Crowd: 18,000 at the Junction Oval

ROUND THIRTEEN July 30
RICHMOND 12.18 (90)
MELBOURNE 10.6 (66)
Best: Richmond – Benton, Murdoch, Judkins, Baggott, Titus, McCormack, O'Neill.
Goals: Richmond – Titus 3, Benton 3, Bentley 3, G.Strang 2, D.Strang.
Crowd: 11,000 at Punt Road Oval

ROUND FOURTEEN August 6
RICHMOND 13.13 (91)
CARLTON 12.14 (86)
Best: Richmond – Martin, Hunter, Judkins, O'Neill, D.Strang, Baggott, Sheahan.
Goals: Richmond – D.Strang 4, Baggott 2, Geddes 2, Hunter 2, Martin, Twyford, McConchie.
Crowd: 31,000 at Princes Park

ROUND FIFTEEN August 13
RICHMOND 9.11 (65)
FOOTSCRAY 8.12 (60)
Best: Richmond – Murdoch, Twyford, Baggott, G.Strang, O'Halloran, Titus, Judkins.
Goals: Richmond – D.Strang 2, O'Halloran, Hunter, Heifner, Martin, G.Strang, Geddes, Titus.
Crowd: 25,000 at Punt Road Oval

ROUND SIXTEEN August 20
RICHMOND 16.16 (112)
HAWTHORN 6.9 (45)
Best: Richmond – D.Strang, Judkins, Twyford, Murdoch, Heifner, G.Strang, Sheahan.
Goals: Richmond – D.Strang 9, G.Strang 3, Hunter 3, Titus.
Crowd: 10,000 at Glenferrie Oval

ROUND SEVENTEEN August 27
RICHMOND 13.8 (86)
GEELONG 9.20 (74)
Best: Richmond – D.Strang, Bolger, Geddes, Zschech, Judkins, Twyford, Murdoch.
Goals: Richmond – D.Strang 5, Titus 2, Martin 2, Hunter, Zschech, McConchie, Bentley.
Crowd: 26,000 at Punt Road Oval

ROUND EIGHTEEN September 3
RICHMOND 14.11 (95)
FITZROY 10.7 (67)
Best: Richmond – Judkins, Bolger, Twyford, D.Strang, Martin, McCormack, Baggott.
Goals: Richmond – D.Strang 4, Hunter 3, Martin 3, G.Strang, Bentley, McConchie, Twyford.
Crowd: 14,000 at Brunswick St Oval

GRAND FINALS VOLUME I

PREMIER'S FINALS

SECOND SEMI-FINAL September 17

RICHMOND	18.16 (124)
CARLTON	14.15 (99)

Best: Richmond – Zschech, Baggott, Murdoch, McCormack, Bolger, O'Halloran, O'Neill.
Goals: Richmond – D.Strang 7, Hunter 6, G.Strang, Anderson, Titus, O'Halloran, Martin.
Crowd: 63,326 at the MCG

GRAND FINAL October 1

RICHMOND	3.3 7.9 8.12 13.14 (92)
CARLTON	2.3 5.6 7.11 12.11 (83)

Best: Richmond – G.Strang, McCormack, O'Neill, Baggott, Titus, Bolger.
Goals: Richmond – D.Strang 4, Titus 2, Hunter, Heifner, Martin, G.Strang, Anderson, Bentley, O'Halloran.
Crowd: 69,724 at the MCG

GRAND FINAL LINE-UPS

RICH	B:	M.Bolger	M.Sheahan	K.O'Neill
CARL	F:	H.Bullen	H.Vallence	R.Cooper
RICH	HB:	J.Baggott	J.Murdoch	B.McCormack
CARL	HF:	K.Shea	A.Egan	C.Crisp
RICH	C:	S.Judkins	E.Zschech	A.Geddes
CARL	C:	J.Kelly	C.Martyn (capt)	L.Opray
RICH	HF:	J.Twyford	G.Strang	J.Titus
CARL	HB:	E.Huxtable	G.Mackie	F.Gilby
RICH	F:	F.Heifner	D.Strang	M.Hunter
CARL	B:	J.Crowe	F.Gill	C.Street
RICH	R:	P.Bentley (capt)	T.O'Halloran	R.Martin
CARL	R:	C.Davey	M.Johnson	A.Clarke
RICH	Reserve:	J.Anderson	**Coach:** Frank 'Checker' Hughes	
CARL	Reserve:	J.Young	**Coach:** Dan Minogue	

SNAPSHOT

Win-loss record: 16-3-1

Highest score: 18.16 (124), second semi-final, v Carlton.

Greatest winning margin: 67 points, round 16, v Hawthorn.

Lowest score: 7.9 (51), round 4, v Footscray.

Greatest losing margin: 12 points, round 17, v Geelong.

Most goals by a player in a game: 9, Doug Strang, round 16, v Hawthorn.

Most consecutive wins: 10

Most consecutive losses: 1 (three times).

Club awards: Best & Fairest: Jack Dyer; Leading goalkicker: Doug Strang (49 goals)

Putting it into perspective:
The Tigers' third premiership from eight Grand Final appearances cemented them as one of the strongest teams in recent seasons. Between 1927 and 1932 they had only missed one Grand Final (1930) and had played in a total of 12 finals.

1932

	P	W	L	D	%	Pts
1 Carlton (2)	18	15	3		137.8	60
2 Richmond (1)	18	14	3	1	139.2	58
3 Collingwood (3)	18	14	4		111.6	56
4 South Melb (4)	18	13	5		118.0	52
5 Geelong	18	11	6	1	139.7	46
6 Essendon	18	10	8		103.0	40
7 Footscray	18	9	9		103.5	36
8 North Melb	18	8	10		97.1	32
9 Melbourne	18	4	14		76.5	16
10 Fitzroy	18	3	15		76.2	12
11 St Kilda	18	3	15		72.0	12
12 Hawthorn	18	3	15		64.1	12

(18 home and away rounds)

PLAYERS USED

RICHMOND	GUERNSEY	GAMES	GOALS
Anderson, Jack	19	4	2
Baggott, Jack	14	19	3
Bentley, Perc	1	20	13
Benton, Bill	3	10	6
Bolger, Martin	9	18	1
Collinson, Ted	10	4	1
Dockendorff, Sid	32	1	1
Dyer, Jack	17	10	13
Foster, Bert	11	11	2
Geddes, Allan	8	14	4
Gray, Wally	26	10	1
Heifner, Fred	33	18	4
Hunter, Maurie	20	15	27
Judkins, Stan	6	20	0
Kolb, Charlie	15	3	1
Martin, Ray	27	20	16
McConchie, Jack	31	6	5
McCormack, Basil	9	20	0
Murdoch, Joe	13	19	0
O'Halloran, Tom	18	13	7
O'Neill, Kevin	16	20	2
Sheahan, Maurie	4	19	0
Stanway, Horrie	22	1	0
Strang, Doug	28	19	49
Strang, Gordon	23	19	33
Titus, Jack	12	17	41
Twyford, Jack	2	16	4
Weidner, Harry	7	3	3
Zschech, Eric	25	20	4

**SOUTH MELBOURNE 9.17 (71) d
RICHMOND 4.5 (29)**

EXCELLENCE FROM AFAR

South Melbourne's army of recruits took some time to blend, but stormed home late in the season to claim the flag in emphatic fashion. By JIM MAIN

IT HAS become part of football mythology that grocery magnate Archie Crofts initiated the "Foreign Legion" recruiting policy that helped South Melbourne annex the 1933 VFL premiership. Not so!

In fact, Crofts did not take charge of football's most ambitious recruiting drive until more than halfway through the campaign to sign Australia's most talented footballers.

South's determination to achieve the ultimate football success was initiated in 1931 under club president Jack Rohan, with Crofts at that stage a South vice-president.

South in 1931 had finished seventh under the unique leadership of brothers Paddy (coach) and Joe Scanlan (captain). However, Rohan, Crofts and the rest of the South committee decided the club needed new leadership and offered West Australian Johnny Leonard the position of captain-coach.

Leonard not only accepted, he told the club he could help sign several West Australians. The Foreign Legion policy was born and, through Leonard's personal contacts, South signed Sandgropers Brighton Diggins and Bill Faul (both from Subiaco) and Gilbert Beard (South Fremantle).

However, the recruiting drive did not end there, as South also snared Richmond ruckman Jack Bisset after it heard he was unhappy at Punt Road.

It also recruited brilliant youngster Herbie Matthews after Collingwood had shown interest in him.

Matthews, son of former South player Ernest 'Butcher' Matthews, had been sent from the family home in South Melbourne to live with his grandparents in Fairfield, deep in Collingwood's heartland. The Magpies desperately tried to lure young Matthews to Victoria Park, but he wanted to play only with South.

Along with this huge batch of 1932 newcomers, South also had an extremely promising young player in high-flying half-forward Bob Pratt, who had been recruited from Mitcham in 1930.

The only problem for South was that its trio of West Australian stars had to fulfil a three-month residential qualification to play for the Bloods and all missed the start of the season.

South, under Leonard's stewardship in 1932, finished fourth and then went down to Collingwood by 26 points in the first semi-final. That was not good enough for Rohan and Crofts and, despite claims by rival clubs that the Bloods had broken the Coulter Law (a scheme devised by VFL official Gordon Coulter to restrict match payments to three pounds a match), South expanded its recruiting drive.

Meanwhile, Richmond defeated Carlton by nine points in the 1932 Grand Final and seemed destined to be at or near the top of the ladder for years to come.

The Tigers had a good young side led by ruckman Perc Bentley and were well-coached by former player Frank 'Checker' Hughes. South aspired to be as powerful as Richmond and knew it needed to build its playing strength even further.

However, the Bloods were dealt a savage blow before the start of the 1933 season when Leonard informed the club that he had to return to Western Australia as he had been posted back to Perth by his employer, football manufacturer Ross Faulkner.

Leonard advised South that he believed ruckman Bisset was the right man to take over as captain-coach. The former Tiger not only was handed the leadership reins, he was told the club would give him the playing resources he needed for success.

Rohan, meanwhile, decided it was time to relinquish the club presidency and asked Crofts to take over because of the grocery king's financial resources.

Australia was still deep in recession following the 1929 Wall Street stock market crash, but Crofts ran a chain of highly successful grocery stores and not only was willing to recruit the players South needed for success but—just as importantly—he was able to provide them with employment.

Working for Crofts was no sinecure. He demanded a good day's work for a good day's wage, even if the employee was a champion footballer. Faul was one of Crofts' employees and, after he complained about the heavy workload affecting his football, Crofts replied in writing:

> "Dear Sir,
>
> My attention has been drawn to your request that you should be allowed the necessary time to enable you to attend football training, and I desire to remind you that, when you were appointed a Branch Manager, it was explained that your added responsibilities would make training for football very difficult. It is impracticable to allow Managers continual time off, as they are held responsible for the stock in their shops and the maintaining of a satisfactory balance.

South, through Crofts' resources, prepared for the 1933 season by signing East Perth's Jim 'Brum' O'Meara, West Torrens' Wilbur Harris and Subiaco's Johnny Bowe, along with Frank Davies and Laurie Nash from Tasmania.

The signing of Test cricketer Nash was the greatest coup of all as the talented all-rounder had been born and bred in Richmond and was the son of former Collingwood captain Bob Nash. Almost every VFL club had tried to sign Nash, but South had the inside running through a personal contact.

Nash had left Victoria to play cricket in Tasmania. In the football season he played with the City Launceston club, whose coach was former South Melbourne and St Kilda star Roy Cazaly. However, cricket at that stage came first, and after taking seven for 50 for Tasmania in a tour match against South Africa, Nash was selected to play for Australia in a Test against the Springboks at the MCG.

Cricket or football? Nash's cricket career might have been blossoming, but football beckoned after City Launceston president Hugh Cameron contacted close friend and former South captain Joe Scanlan to give him the inside running to sign the multi-talented Nash.

Scanlan was smuggled aboard the trans-Tasman steamer *Nairana* and returned to Melbourne with Nash's signature. The Bloods found Nash employment with the Melbourne Sports Depot and even arranged accommodation for their new star and wife Irene.

The jigsaw might have been complete, but South's brazen recruiting flurry in an era of extreme austerity raised calls to investigate whether South had breached the Coulter Law. *The Sporting Globe* even published an editorial asking how South could sign so many interstate stars "when payments were fixed by the law and theoretically no club could offer a greater financial lure than three pounds a week".

No charges were laid against South and the Red and Whites opened the season with a new image. *The Sporting Globe's* Hec De Lacy suggested that because South had so many West Australians on its list, the club should be nicknamed the Swans. The club has been known as the Swans ever since.

The opening round of the 1933 season saw South scheduled to play Carlton at Princes Park, no easy task seeing that the Blues had been pipped by Richmond in the previous year's grand Final. Although Faul had yet to fulfil his residential requirements, Nash was scheduled to make his VFL debut and fans flocked to Princes Park to see the Test cricketer in action on the football field.

Nash, wearing No.25, lined up at centre half-back in front of almost 38,000 fans, but had a quiet game in Carlton's four-point victory. South dominated most of the play, but Pratt's inaccuracy, with 5.7, cost it the game.

South might have defeated Footscray by 26 points at the Lake Oval the following week, but when Collingwood defeated the Bloods/Swans by 14 points at Victoria Park in round three, the signs were ominous for the hugely ambitious South administration.

Although South temporarily recovered, a 23-point defeat by Geelong at the Corio Oval in round seven meant it had only a 4-3 start to the season—hardly the form of a premiership contender. Even worse, Richmond defeated South by five points at the Lake Oval in round eight and Fitzroy the next week defeated the Bloods by 19 points at Brunswick Street. It left South with a 4-5 win-loss ratio, and football writers wondered whether the Red and Whites would even make the finals.

The match against Richmond was highly controversial as South led until the Tigers rallied in the final term to snatch a 12-point lead. With only minutes to play, South attacked and half-forward Peter Reville kicked a behind. Then, as Tiger defender Maurie Sheahan wasted time in taking the kick-out, umpire Jack McMurray snr blew his whistle and awarded Pratt a free kick. The resulting goal left South just short of victory, but fans debated McMurray's decision for weeks and fans ached for a South-Richmond return match in the finals as the two clubs were not drawn to play each other over the rest of the home and away series.

On the other hand, Richmond was flying, with just one loss—to Footscray by 16 points at the Western Oval in round three. The Tigers were on track for back-to-back premierships and, halfway through the season, it appeared either Geelong or Carlton would challenge them for the flag.

Suddenly, however, the huge influx of South newcomers gelled and the Bloods went through the rest of the home and away season undefeated to clinch second position behind Richmond. South even passed its biggest test in round 14 when it defeated Collingwood by six points at the Lake Oval for its first victory over the Magpies in 10 years.

Under the Page-McIntyre final four system, third-placed Carlton played fourth-placed Geelong in the first semi-final, with South scheduled to play Richmond in the second semi-final the following week.

After Geelong defeated Carlton by 13 points, public attention turned to the South-Richmond clash, with most pundits expecting the Tigers to march straight into the Grand Final. South, however, triumphed by 18 points after trailing by 35 points at half-time.

It was a remarkable turnaround, especially as the Tigers still led by 28 points at the final change. Bisset, in a final effort to turn his side's fortunes around, made several telling positional moves. He shifted Jack Austin to full-back to replace the injured (hip) Ron Hillis, pushed Pratt to centre half-forward and placed Ossie Bertram, another West Torrens recruit, at full-forward.

South erased Richmond's lead within 15 minutes and then cruised to victory to enter its first Grand Final since defeating Collingwood in 1918.

The *Football Record*, in reviewing the second semi-final, said: "The final burst of the Southern lads will not soon be forgotten by those who saw it. From an apparently hopeless position they put in such a magnificent succession of paralysing thrusts that the over-confident Tigers were taken completely by surprise. It is just possible that with a victory in sight Richmond relaxed a little. If that is so, South were not long in taking every advantage of their opponents' lapses. And few will deny that they thoroughly deserved the victory."

The rest of the media mocked Richmond for its fade-out and *The Sun News Pictorial* ran a cartoon of a South player kicking a tiger out of his way, with the caption: "South mistook the fearsome tiger for a domestic cat and booted it to oblivion with abandon." There also was a cartoon of Pratt and Peter Reville dancing in victory.

Although Richmond defeated Geelong by nine points in a tough, brutal preliminary final, the Tigers were unconvincing as the Cats wasted countless opportunities in front of goal to score 14 behinds to Richmond's five.

South's only worry going into the Grand Final against Richmond on September 30 was whether classy full-back Hillis could overcome his hip injury. Hillis and Collingwood's Jack Regan were rated the finest full-backs in the competition.

Hillis eventually was ruled out. Jock McKenzie was moved into the side in a back pocket and Hec McKay was named at full-back. Richmond, on the other hand, made four changes: Maurie Hunter and Jack McConchie were injured,

Doug Strang was suspended and Jack Twyford, who had played two games with South in 1929, was dropped. Into the side came champion winger Stan Judkins, along with Horrie Farmer, Bert Foster and Jack Stenhouse.

South, however, also was without brilliant speedster Austin Robertson, who had elected earlier in the season to tour the United States for a series of foot races against 1932 Olympic sprint gold medallist Eddie Tolan. Robertson, in the lead-up to the Grand Final, wrote from San Francisco to his old club, saying: "Tell the boys I will be with them in spirit."

Former captain-coach Leonard told the club he would listen on radio in Perth to the broadcast of the big match. He also wrote to the club: "There will be no one playing harder than me for South on Saturday, and they will win." Leonard also urged the West Australian contingent to "keep up the prestige of the 'Gropers".

South finally was acknowledged publicly as the Swans and a cartoon by Alex Gurney (creator of the famous *Wally and the Major* comic strip) in *The Herald* depicted a swan nestling in a bed of footballs, with the caption reading: "South are hatching a few plots against Richmond."

The weather bureau predicted a cool but fine Grand Final day, with a light south-easterly wind and an outside chance of late showers. The morning newspapers ran previews of the big match, but the main headlines centred around Germany setting up labour camps to boost employment.

Apart from who would win the premiership, there also was enormous public interest in whether Pratt would kick three goals to overtake Collingwood's Gordon 'Nuts' Coventry as the season's leading goalkicker, with Coventry finishing his season on 108 and Pratt going into the Grand Final on 106.

The big match started at 2.45pm following a curtain-raiser between Kew and Abbotsford for the League Sub-District Second Grade premiership. *The Sporting Globe* (the "pink-'un") ran a goal-by-goal report of the big Swans-Tigers clash, telling readers that although Richmond was the first team on to the MCG, South received "a warmer reception".

An Australian record crowd of 75,754 attended the big match and saw Richmond kick with the wind to the Jolimont (large scoreboard) end for the first quarter. However, South controlled the early play through the bullocking work of centre half-forward Diggins. *The Sporting Globe* reported: "The speed and crisp foot-passing of the Red and Whites had Richmond defending desperately."

South missed three early chances to goal, with one 50m place kick by Reville touched on the line. Finally, Diggins broke through for the first goal of the match. Pratt immediately followed up with another and Richmond was on the back foot. A third goal, by Len Thomas, gave South a 21-point lead at the first break.

It looked bleak for Richmond, especially with Len Thomas dominant in the centre and Reville and Pratt on top up forward. Richmond reacted to South's early dominance by switching Jack Baggott from the forward line to defence, but South was in full flight early in the second quarter and stretched its lead to 27 points when Reville goaled with a drop kick.

The Tigers eventually broke through when good ruck work by Bentley gave Farmer a clear run at goal. And, to lift Tiger spirits even further, South suffered a terrible blow when dashing half-back Hugh McLaughlin injured a knee and was carried from the ground, replaced by 19th man Gilbert Beard.

McLaughlin's injury temporarily unsettled South and Gordon Strang (brother of the suspended Doug) kicked the Tigers' second goal just minutes later. However, the Swans eventually resettled and goals by Terry Brain and Pratt gave them a 28-point lead at the main break.

Pratt's second goal, late in the quarter, drew him level with Coventry on the season's goalkicking list and, with South holding such a big lead, interest centred on whether Pratt could kick another goal. *The Sporting Globe* noted: "The Swans had the 1933 premiership in their sights."

Richmond, despite straining every sinew in an effort to overhaul South, continually ran into a one-man roadblock. South centre half-back Laurie Nash was almost impassable, taking mark after mark with his superb reading of the play.

On the other hand, South kept swarming over the ball like busy red and white bullants over the entire third quarter and was rewarded with goals to Diggins and Brain. The match was as good as over with South leading by 39 points at the final change. But would Pratt kick that elusive third goal?

With South fans already licking their lips in anticipation of premiership success, they rose as one when Pratt marked just 25m from goal. But, inexplicably, his shot failed to make the distance.

Although Ray Martin kicked an early goal for Richmond, the result seemed inevitable. Finally, Pratt swooped on the ball 20m from goal and kicked accurately for his third of the match and his 109th for the season.

South fans not only celebrated Pratt topping the VFL goalkicking, but also the certainty that the Swans would win the 1933 premiership. Amazingly, Pratt finished the match with 3.9, plus four shots going out of bounds.

South won by 42 points and, at the first toll of the bell, Swan fans jumped the MCG fence to mob their heroes, who were carried from the ground shoulder-high.

All newspaper reports indicated that Nash clearly was best on ground and he said immediately after the match: "I knew we would be premiers. I formed that impression after we defeated the Tigers in the second semi-final. I did not think the Tigers could go and defeat Geelong and South in turn—it was too much for them."

The Sporting Globe credited Nash with 29 kicks and 13 marks, while Thomas racked up 32 possessions and 10 marks in the centre.

Nash was so brilliant that Richmond president and former Tiger player Bernie 'Barney' Herbert said he "cried tears of blood out there seeing Nash in the wrong colours" when he learned that the South champion had been born and bred in Richmond. Herbert added: "I would like to hand my little hat to one of the finest footballers I have seen in years, Laurie Nash. That's not pleasant to say from a club point of view, but from a sporting point of view I have nothing but admiration for a good, clean little footballer."

Pratt revealed years after the Grand Final that he had been nursing a knee injury for several weeks and even told club secretary Dick Mullaly the day before the Grand Final that he was no certain starter. Mullaly told Pratt: "If we win tomorrow, every player who takes the field will get a big bonus."

Pratt said after the Grand Final that it was amazing how the word "bonus" helped cure his knee problem.

Richmond held its Grand Final "wake" at the Port Phillip Club Hotel in the heart of Melbourne and the players later were driven to several picture theatres around Richmond before attending a club dance at the Punt Road Oval. Each Tiger player was presented with an ashtray embossed with the club logo.

South celebrated long and hard its first premiership for 15 years, starting with a reception at the South Melbourne Town Hall. South captain-coach Bisset told an enthusiastic crowd of 5000 waiting outside the town hall that every player had done his part. He said he did not like to individualise, but said he could not help himself in declaring that Nash had been the match-winner.

South continued its celebrations at the Queens Bridge Hotel, just outside the city, and then went to the Tivoli Theatre where they were introduced to patrons at the revue interval. From there, the team cheekily hopped aboard a charabanc for a tour of… Richmond!

The Swans held a smoke night on the Thursday after the Grand Final, with Crofts telling players, officials, patrons and fans that the 1933 premiership was only the start of a golden run. Although South made each Grand Final from 1934-36, it lost all three and had to wait until 2005 when, as the Sydney Swans, it next won a premiership.

1933 SOUTH MELBOURNE

PREMIER'S SEASON

SOUTH MELBOURNE: 1933

ROUND ONE April 29
SOUTH MELBOURNE 11.17 (83)
CARLTON 12.15 (87)
Best: South Melbourne – Nash, Pratt, Bisset, Thomas, Reville, Clarke, Diggins.
Goals: South Melbourne – Pratt 5, Nash 2, Reville, Brain, Robertson, Bertram.
Crowd: 37,000 at Princes Park

ROUND TWO May 6
SOUTH MELBOURNE 18.17 (125)
FOOTSCRAY 14.15 (99)
Best: South Melbourne – Pratt, Matthews, Pettiona, McKay, Clarke, Faul, Nash, Reville.
Goals: South Melbourne – Pratt 7, Pettiona 3, Reville 2, Thomas 2, Bertram, Beard, Mietzcke, Robertson.
Crowd: 29,000 at the Lake Oval

ROUND THREE May 13
SOUTH MELBOURNE 9.3 (57)
COLLINGWOOD 10.11 (71)
Best: South Melbourne – Pratt, Nash, Bertram, Matthews, Wade, Clarke, McKay, Thomas.
Goals: South Melbourne – Pratt 5, Thomas 2, Reville, Fahey.
Crowd: 10,000 at Victoria Park

ROUND FOUR May 20
SOUTH MELBOURNE 11.14 (80)
ST KILDA 10.16 (76)
Best: South Melbourne – Pratt, Thomas, Faul, Fahey, Hillis, Bisset, Clarke, Beard.
Goals: South Melbourne – Pratt 6, Reville 3, Matthews, Bertram.
Crowd: 20,000 at the Lake Oval

ROUND FIVE May 27
SOUTH MELBOURNE 17.15 (117)
ESSENDON 12.11 (83)
Best: South Melbourne – Bertram, Wade, Faul, Thomas, Reville, Pratt, Matthews, Nash.
Goals: South Melbourne – Bertram 5, Pratt 5, Fahey 2, Hillis, Thomas, Reville, O'Meara, Brain.
Crowd: 18,000 at Windy Hill

ROUND SIX June 3
SOUTH MELBOURNE 10.13 (73)
HAWTHORN 9.6 (60)
Best: South Melbourne – Clarke, Faul, Faul, Hillis, Beard, Bertram, Matthews, Bowe.
Goals: South Melbourne – Bertram 4, Pratt 3, Reville, Bisset, O'Meara.
Crowd: 13,000 at the Lake Oval

ROUND SEVEN June 10
SOUTH MELBOURNE 13.15 (93)
GEELONG 17.14 (116)
Best: South Melbourne – Pratt, Faul, Bisset, Clarke, Brain, O'Meara, Nash, Harris.
Goals: South Melbourne – Pratt 9, Reville 2, O'Meara, Brain.
Crowd: 14,000 at Corio Oval

ROUND EIGHT June 10
SOUTH MELBOURNE 15.13 (103)
RICHMOND 16.12 (108)
Best: South Melbourne – Clarke, Bertram, Brain, Reville, Pratt, McLaughlin, Faul.
Goals: South Melbourne – Pratt 5, Reville 3, Brain 3, O'Meara, Mietzcke, Fahey, Clarke.
Crowd: 30,000 at the Lake Oval

ROUND NINE June 24
SOUTH MELBOURNE 11.12 (78)
FITZROY 15.7 (97)
Best: South Melbourne – Pratt, Nash, Thomas, Reville, Thomas, Clarke, McLaughlin.
Goals: South Melbourne – Pratt 7, Reville 2, Brain, Davies.
Crowd: 20,000 at Brunswick St Oval

ROUND TEN July 1
SOUTH MELBOURNE 13.10 (88)
MELBOURNE 12.9 (81)
Best: South Melbourne – Brain, Bertram, Pratt, Bowe, Kelleher, Bisset, Davies, Austin.
Goals: South Melbourne – Pratt 6, Bertram 3, Reville 2, Brain, Davies.
Crowd: 10,000 at the Lake Oval

ROUND ELEVEN July 8
SOUTH MELBOURNE 15.13 (103)
NORTH MELBOURNE 13.12 (90)
Best: South Melbourne – Pratt, Clarke, McLaughlin, Austin, Gilmour, Brain, Reville.
Goals: South Melbourne – Pratt 10, Brain 3, Reville, Welch.
Crowd: 15,000 at Arden St Oval

ROUND TWELVE July 15
SOUTH MELBOURNE 15.13 (103)
CARLTON 9.6 (60)
Best: South Melbourne – Pratt, Hillis, Bisset, Brain, Gilmour, Austin, Matthews, Clarke.
Goals: South Melbourne – Pratt 11, Reville, Brain, Diggins, Austin.
Crowd: 32,000 at the Lake Oval

ROUND THIRTEEN July 22
SOUTH MELBOURNE 19.15 (129)
FOOTSCRAY 8.11 (59)
Best: South Melbourne – O'Meara, Hillis, Bowe, Welch, Faul, McKay, Pratt, McKenzie.
Goals: South Melbourne – Pratt 6, O'Meara 5, Welch 2, Brain 2, Diggins, Beard, Austin, Reville.
Crowd: 27,000 at the Western Oval

ROUND FOURTEEN July 29
SOUTH MELBOURNE 13.11 (89)
COLLINGWOOD 12.11 (83)
Best: South Melbourne – Nash, Beard, Diggins, Reville, Pratt, Matthews, Bowe, Faul.
Goals: South Melbourne – Pratt 5, Brain 3, O'Meara, Diggins, Reville, Austin, Bisset.
Crowd: 24,000 at the Lake Oval

ROUND FIFTEEN August 5
SOUTH MELBOURNE 13.15 (93)
ST KILDA 8.19 (67)
Best: South Melbourne – Beard, Bertram, Gilmour, Thomas, McKenzie, Nash, McKay.
Goals: South Melbourne – Bertram 5, Beard 4, Nash 3, Reville.
Crowd: 20,000 at the Junction Oval

ROUND SIXTEEN August 19
SOUTH MELBOURNE 11.16 (82)
ESSENDON 6.4 (40)
Best: South Melbourne – Clarke, Thomas, Pratt, Nash, Austin, Beard, Reville, O'Meara.
Goals: South Melbourne – Pratt 5, Reville 3, Brain 2, O'Meara.
Crowd: 13,000 at the Lake Oval

ROUND SEVENTEEN August 26
SOUTH MELBOURNE 17.11 (113)
HAWTHORN 8.12 (60)
Best: South Melbourne – Nash, Hillis, McLaughlin, McKenzie, Bisset, Matthews, Bertram.
Goals: South Melbourne – Nash 6, O'Meara 2, Bertram 2, Reville 2, Matthews 2, Brain, Diggins, Davies.
Crowd: 12,500 at Glenferrie Oval

ROUND EIGHTEEN September 2
SOUTH MELBOURNE 23.17 (155)
GEELONG 6.10 (46)
Best: South Melbourne – Reville, Pratt, Bowe, Faul, Thomas, Diggins, Bertram, Clarke.
Goals: South Melbourne – Pratt 7, Reville 7, Bertram 5, Brain 2, Matthews 2.
Crowd: 30,000 at the Lake Oval

PREMIER'S FINALS

SECOND SEMI-FINAL September 16

SOUTH MELBOURNE	14.11 (95)
RICHMOND	11.11 (77)

Best: South Melbourne – McLaughlin, Clarke, Austin, Brain, Faul, McKay, Bowe, Bertram.
Goals: South Melbourne – Pratt 4, Reville 3, O'Meara 2, Brain 2, Clarke, Bertram, Diggins.
Crowd: 49,303 at the MCG

GRAND FINAL September 30

SOUTH MELBOURNE	3.5	6.7	8.12	9.17 (71)
RICHMOND	0.2	2.3	3.3	4.5 (29)

Best: South Melbourne – Nash, Diggins, Austin, Clarke, Bowe, Bisset.
Goals: South Melbourne – Pratt 3, Diggins 2, Brain 2, Reville, Thomas.
Crowd: 75,754 at the MCG

GRAND FINAL LINE-UPS

STH M	B:	J.McKenzie	H.McKay	J.Austin
RICH	F:	J.Dyer	J.Titus	B.Foster
STH M	HB:	F.Faul	L.Nash	H.McLaughlin
RICH	HF:	H.Farmer	T.O'Halloran	J.Baggott
STH M	C:	H.Clarke	L.Thomas	J.Bowe
RICH	C:	S.Judkins	E.Zschech	A.Geddes
STH M	HF:	J.O'Meara	B.Diggins	P.Reville
RICH	HB:	J.Stenhouse	J.Murdoch	B.McCormack
STH M	F:	H.Matthews	B.Pratt	O.Bertram
RICH	B:	M.Bolger	M.Sheahan	K.O'Neill
STH M	R:	J.Bisset (capt)	D.Kelleher	T.Brain
RICH	R:	P.Bentley (capt)	G.Strang	R.Martin
STH M	Reserve: B.Beard		**Coach:** Jack Bisset	
RICH	Reserve: J.Anderson		**Coach:** Billy Schmidt	

SNAPSHOT

Win-loss record: 15-5

Highest score: 23.17 (155), round 18, v Geelong.

Greatest winning margin: 109 points, round 18, v Geelong.

Lowest score: 9.3 (57), round 3, v Collingwood.

Greatest losing margin: 23 points, round 7, v Geelong.

Most goals by a player in a game: 11, Bob Pratt, round 12, v Carlton.

Most consecutive wins: 11

Most consecutive losses: 3

Club awards: Best & Fairest: Harry Clarke; Leading goalkicker: Bob Pratt (109 goals).

Putting it into perspective:
South Melbourne's seventh Grand Final appearance resulted in its third premiership and first since 1918. In the Swans' 15-year premiership drought they played in just seven finals including just one between 1924-1932.

1933

		P	W	L	D	%	Pts
1	Richmond (2)	18	15	3		141.1	60
2	South Melb (1)	18	13	5		127.5	52
3	Carlton (4)	18	13	5		114.4	52
4	Geelong (3)	18	12	6		130.4	48
5	Fitzroy	18	11	6	1	105.6	46
6	Collingwood	18	11	7		112.9	44
7	Footscray	18	11	7		97.7	44
8	North Melb	18	7	10	1	85.2	30
9	St Kilda	18	6	12		80.9	24
10	Melbourne	18	3	15		82.0	12
11	Hawthorn	18	3	15		73.7	12
12	Essendon	18	2	16		77.1	8

(18 home and away rounds)

PLAYERS USED

SOUTH MELBOURNE	GUERNSEY	GAMES	GOALS
Austin, Jack	3	11	3
Backway, Fred	31	1	0
Beard, Bert	34	14	6
Bertram, Ossie	10	15	28
Bisset, Jack	1	19	2
Bowe, Johnny	18	17	0
Brain, Terry	5	17	26
Clarke, Harry	6	19	2
Davies, Frank	19	7	3
Diggins, Brighton	17	13	7
Fahey, Jock	24	6	4
Faul, Bill	14	20	0
Gilmour, Alan	22	8	0
Harris, Wilbur	20	3	0
Hearn, Maurie	33	3	0
Hillis, Ron	4	19	1
Kelleher, Dinny	29	7	0
Matthews, J. Herbie	2	16	5
McKay, Hec	9	20	0
McKenzie, Jock	30	9	0
McLaughlin, Hugh	8	16	0
Mietzcke, Art	7	5	2
Nash, Laurie	25	18	11
O'Meara, Jim	11	18	15
Pettiona, Cecil	15	7	3
Pratt, Bob	23	18	109
Reville, Peter	21	20	39
Robertson, Austin	16	2	2
Thomas, Len	12	19	6
Wade, Jack	28	5	0
Welch, Alan	27	8	3

**RICHMOND 19.14 (128) d
SOUTH MELBOURNE 12.17 (89)**

TIGERS FIND FINE BALANCE

The Richmond defenders' teamwork overwhelmed the prolific Swans attack. By PAUL DAFFEY

THE 1934 VFL season ranked among the best in Australian Football at the time, and it still stacks up as a classic season now. It was a season in which goals rained down like confetti—a season of exhilarating high scores in which almost every team had a star full-forward. Eight players kicked more than 50 goals in 1934. South Melbourne full-forward Bob Pratt kicked 150, while Collingwood veteran Gordon Coventry kicked 105, including his 1000th career goal. Richmond's Jack Titus kicked 80. Even lowly Hawthorn had a player who kicked 80 goals. It was Jack Green, the former Carlton player. A decade previously, he would have held the League record with 80 goals.

On the other hand, it was a season in which defence mattered more than most. Richmond's team had one of the most famous full-back lines of all time. Kevin O'Neill, Maurie Sheahan and Martin Bolger played in that formation for 90 games from 1930 to '36. Between the three of them they had a winning mix of steadiness and adventure. When playing South Melbourne, they worked as a unit to bump and fluster Pratt off his game. It was Collingwood's practice, however, to leave Jack Regan one out on the Southern flyer. Regan was known as the 'Prince of Full-Backs'. The Magpies hierarchy trusted him to be able to curb Pratt while others concentrated on matters further upfield, like Pratt's teammate Laurie Nash.

In the decade to 1934, according to Russell Holmesby in *More Than a Game*, two stipulations helped full-forwards. In 1925 a rule was introduced in which a player who had kicked or forced the ball out of bounds would be penalised. This meant that play was more concentrated in the middle part of the ground—what we now call the corridor. Key position players became more important, and most attacking moves went through the full-forward. The second factor was the shape of footballs. In 1930 they were standardised so that they had to be 58cm around the belly. This made them longer and skinnier than they had been. They were easier to mark and kick. Forwards found they offered more accuracy.

Forwards in 1934 also found they excited more attention. They were more in the news. Photos of Pratt's towering marks astonished newspaper readers. Cigarettes cards of footballers tapped into fans' desire to connect with the stars. Holmesby draws a parallel between the rising stardom of full-forwards in state competitions around Australia in the 1930s and the rise of the Hollywood star factory. Fans were fascinated by the pin-ups. All around those pin-ups basked in their glow.

South Melbourne's attack was so potent in 1934 that its aggregate points tally for the home and away rounds was 2187, a tally that eclipsed Collingwood's record from 1930 of 1931 points. And yet the Bloods finished only third on the ladder. Carlton had the next highest points tally (1986) and yet the Blues finished only fifth on the ladder. Collingwood (1915), Geelong (1834) and Melbourne (1623) finished with points tallies that roughly equated to their positions on the ladder. Richmond, on the other hand, had only the sixth highest aggregate, (1618—a whopping 569 points fewer than South), and yet it finished on top.

Of course Pratt was the main pin-up among the full-forwards in 1934. After being recruited from Mitcham in Melbourne's outer eastern suburbs, he settled into the life of a star spearhead in 1932 when he kicked 71 goals. The next year he kicked 109. But it was in 1934, aged 21 (he turned 22 just before the finals), that he leapt into the heavens. In the opening two rounds he kicked eight goals against Collingwood and 10 against Carlton. In round three, against Essendon at the Lake Oval, he kicked eight goals in the opening 12 minutes of the last quarter and ended up with 15 for the match. He passed his century early in the return match against Carlton in round 13. In the third quarter of that match, he kicked eight goals.

And so it went on. He broke Gordon Coventry's record of 124 goals, set in 1929. He kicked 138 for the 18 home and away games (average 7.7 a game). But in the finals, against the best teams, his output slowed. He kicked four, six and two goals. The last match was the Grand Final against Richmond. The defenders, as the newspapers liked to say, were vigorous in their tasks.

It's an irony that some of the Richmond defenders who had such a good record of curbing Bob Pratt feature as Pratt's stepladders in the most famous image of him taking a mark. In *The Age* on Monday, September 10, 1934, there was a photo of Pratt taken from side-on, at enough of an angle to be able to see the No. 10 on his guernsey. Pratt reaches for the sky while sending an unnamed Richmond player craning towards the turf, with Martin Bolger trying to regain his balance at the back of the pack. Richmond won that game and kept Pratt to three goals, but it's the image of Pratt's mighty leap that endures.

Pratt's partner in attack was Laurie Nash. In 1934 Nash played the first eight games at centre half-back (Pratt had 61 goals by then), before the recruitment of Lindsay 'Bluey' Richards released him to go to centre half-forward. In the first match in which Pratt and Nash shared duties in attack, in round nine against North Melbourne at Arden Street, South kicked 10.8 to nil in the first quarter. Pratt ended up with eight goals and Nash seven. In the five weeks from round 11 to round 15, South recorded five consecutives scores of more than 20 goals. Its average winning margin in this time was 10 goals. Pratt kicked 51 goals in those five games, while Nash kicked 27.

In the middle of this splurge, Victoria played South Australia in a state match at the MCG. Pratt missed the match through injury. Nash started at centre half-forward before being switched to the goalsquare. Without Pratt to share the billing, Nash gave full vent to his considerable talents. He kicked 18.2.

Richmond, for all its defensive strengths, had several attacking weapons itself. Jack 'Skinny' Titus was a veteran in his ninth season. His wiry frame tempted coaches to use him out from goal but it was his natural way to lead out from the goalsquare, where his pace, agility and strong hands made him a perfect target. Titus, in the way of many in Richmond's team in this era, had plenty of cheek. His main method in putting his opponent off his game was to spit on his opponent's boots. In 1934 his 80 goals surpassed Doug Strang's club record of 68 goals, set just two years earlier.

The resting ruckman played in a forward pocket. In 1934, this was either Perc Bentley, the captain-coach, or Jack Dyer, the follower who, even at just 20 years of age, was considered the best big man in the game. When Titus led out, Bentley or Dyer would drop back into the goalsquare.

The centre half-forward position was shared mainly between Doug Strang, a freakish flyer, Tom O'Halloran, a veteran flyer in his 10th season, and Dave Baxter, who was in his first year. Baxter, recruited from Serviceton on the South Australian border, was just one of two rookies who established themselves in Richmond's 1934 team; the other was Dick Harris, a fiery rover who was recruited from Warrnambool.

Jack Dyer later described Harris as the toughest little player he had seen. In 1934 he kicked 51 goals, a vaulting figure for a rover playing out of a forward pocket in his first season. Harris's roving partner was Ray Martin, who was also handy around goal. In 1934 Martin finished equal third in the Brownlow Medal. (Dick Reynolds of Essendon won.) Richmond in 1934 was not a plundering team like South Melbourne, but it had more avenues to goal.

In defence, the three men across the full-back line were known as 'the Three Musketeers'. Martin Bolger was a steady back pocket, skilful and determined, who used his strength in tight tussles. He went on to win the club best and fairest in 1936.

Kevin O'Neill played in the other back pocket. He was more of a dasher who backed his judgement, and was able to use his body to outmanoeuvre taller opponents. O'Neill was the Tigers' best player in their loss to South Melbourne in the 1933 Grand Final. He was also a regular Victorian representative.

Maurie Sheahan was a man of strength and dependability, in the vein of the best full-backs through the ages. *The Sporting Globe* said of him: "Maurie carries a lot of condition and relies on his judgement to spoil the aerialists opposed to him. In the off-season he tries to keep his weight down by playing cricket with a Burnley team."

The Three Musketeers received great help from the two tough and talented half-back flankers, Jack Baggott and Basil McCormack, who dropped back to lend a hand.

Richmond finished on top of the ladder after the 1934 home and away rounds with a record of 15-3, ahead of Geelong (14-3-1), South Melbourne (14-4) and Collingwood (13-4-1). Richmond's losses were to Collingwood (round three), Geelong (round nine, in the only game played between the teams) and Melbourne (round 12).

Significantly, the Tigers had had least points kicked against them (1334). Geelong was not far behind, with 1355. South Melbourne was third on the table with 1560 points—more than 200 points more than its two main rivals. And yet the Swans were favoured by many, in part because of their firepower, but also because of their defeat of Richmond in the Grand Final the previous season.

The 1933 season was a source of great anger at Tigerland. The Tigers finished on top of the ladder, two games clear of South Melbourne, and looked to be confirming those rankings when it led by six goals at half-time of the second semi-final. Then the Swans overran the Tigers to win by three goals.

The preliminary final was against Geelong in mud and slush at the MCG. Richmond won a bruising affair by nine points, but the effort took its toll. In the Grand Final, the Tigers were flat. South Melbourne cantered home by 42 points, 9.17 (71) to 4.5 (29), despite the fact that the Richmond defenders had held Bob Pratt to three goals.

The Richmond committee believed its team had cost the club a certain premiership by going to sleep in the third quarter of the semi-final, when it had the use of a breeze. The blame was sheeted home to coach Bill Schmidt, who was sacked despite leading the Tigers to the Grand Final in his one season in charge.

Schmidt's replacement for the 1934 season was Perc Bentley, a 27-year-old ruckman who had served as Richmond captain the previous two seasons. In 1933 Bentley was also captain of Victoria. Although he was aggressive and robust on the field, he was modest and popular off it.

Richmond's first match against South Melbourne in 1934 was at the Lake Oval in round six. The Tigers set up a wall at half-back to stop supply to Pratt, while the full-back line harried him throughout. The Tigers won by 44 points. Pratt kicked four. *The Age* reported that South "wilted before a terrific battering from a powerful Richmond combination". "It could be seen from the outset that the lighter Southerners would be unable to stand up to the ultra-vigorous work of the weighty, hefty visitors," it said.

Geelong was much the better team in the second half during its 22-point victory over Richmond in round nine at Corio.

The Tigers' return match against South Melbourne was in round 17. On the day that Geelong defeated Essendon by 116 points, Richmond held out against the Swans to win by six points before an enormous crowd of 42,000. Jack Titus kicked 4.3 for Richmond; Pratt kicked 3.4, and made his leap into folklore.

The next week Geelong slipped up against South Melbourne at the Lake Oval. It was a result that ended the Cats' winning streak at 11, and pushed them down to second. Richmond defeated Hawthorn to take top spot.

The Swans might have been bundled out of the finals straight away if not for Collingwood's atrocious kicking. The Magpies kicked 10 behinds—and no goals—in the third quarter, while the Swans kicked 2.2. Scores were level at the final change. Pratt kicked a goal with the last kick of the match to give the Swans a three-point win, 11.12 (78) to 9.21 (75).

In its preview of the second semi-final between Richmond and Geelong, *The Richmond, Hawthorn, Camberwell Chronicle* responded to a reader's question on how many "six-footers" there would be in the Richmond line-up. There would be six: Perc Bentley, Dave Baxter, Bert Foster, Tom O'Halloran, Jack Dyer and Gordon Strang, while Joe Murdoch and Maurie Sheahan were "just under". Another six-footer, Doug Strang, would miss the match because of the knee injury he suffered against South Melbourne in round 17.

The match was played in sodden conditions, so much so that Richmond coach Perc Bentley instructed his team to wear sleeves in the second half. The Tigers emerged from the main break looking "a flock of rosellas", reported *The Richmond, Hawthorn, Camberwell Chronicle*, because the players had been forced to put on training jumpers under their sleeveless black and yellow guernseys.

Richmond kicked 14 goals to two in the second half to score by 84 points, 19.20 (134) to 7.8 (50). Skinny Titus kicked five goals, Dick Harris kicked four and Perc Bentley kicked three. There were eight goalkickers in all. The Tigers' score was the highest for a semi-final. They were through to their seventh Grand Final in eight years.

Geelong was still stunned when South Melbourne climbed over it in the preliminary final. The Swans won by an even 10 goals, 15.18 (108) to 7.6 (48). Pratt kicked six while Laurie Nash and rover Ossie Bertram both kicked four. Follower Peter Reville was the only other goalkicker, with one. The Grand Final would provide a contrast in attacking styles. Richmond would try to share the goals while South would channel through the big two.

Richmond's line-up for the 1934 Grand Final featured only three changes to the team that contested the 1933 Grand Final. The inclusions were Dave Baxter, Dick Harris and Horrie 'Tubby' Edmonds, the former Collingwood forward who had kicked five goals against Richmond in the 1929 Grand Final. Doug Strang, who had missed the 1933 Grand Final through suspension, was ruled out of the 1934 decider because of his knee injury.

South Melbourne had injury clouds over Laurie Nash, follower Brighton Diggins and rover Terry Brain, but all were cleared to play. Ron Hillis, the highly regarded full-back, had missed the preliminary final through injury, but was shocked when he missed out selection for the Grand Final. Hillis had won a best and fairest from full-back, in 1930, and had played for Victoria. Jack Austin was named in his stead.

According to *Bloodstained Angels* by Mark Branagan and Mike Lefebvre, Bob Pratt dropped a bombshell before the match when he informed South president Archie Crofts that he had been offered £100—the equivalent of roughly two seasons of match payments—to play dead. Crofts told him not to tell his teammates.

1934 RICHMOND

In its preview, *The Richmond, Hawthorn, Camberwell Chronicle* gave an insight into the Tigers' approach to big games when it quoted an unnamed senior VFL official who, during the course of his duties, would go into both teams' rooms before a match: "The Tigers are always happy and noisy and the officials fraternise with them, while in other dressingrooms the seriousness of the occasion causes almost a silence."

The *Chronicle* reported that Dan Minogue, Richmond's premiership coach in 1920-21 and now the Carlton coach, had tipped the Tigers to win because of their defence.

A crowd of 65,335—10,000 down on the previous year's attendance—filed into the MCG on a day of perfect sunshine. Richmond captain-coach Perc Bentley and South Melbourne captain-coach Jack Bisset, great friends when they played in the ruck together at Richmond, lined up against each other for the first bounce. Richmond centreman Eric Zschech opened the scoring with a long, drop-kick goal. Dick Harris and Joe Murdoch both snapped goals. The Tigers had kicked the first three goals through varied routes.

The Sporting Globe noted: "Classic marking duels between Nash and the high-marking Gordon Strang stirred the crowd. Nash broke away for two goals in the first quarter but Strang won most rounds of their long battle."

Bob Pratt unshackled himself early in the second quarter to take a screamer in the goalsquare that, according to *The Sporting Globe*, had "every spectator applauding wildly". His goal brought his season's tally to 149. At the other end, Skinny Titus kicked four for the quarter, through a combination of skill, courage, sure hands and, on one occasion, dead-eye accuracy from the boundary line. Jack Austin was getting a bath. By this stage, Pratt was so fed up with being harassed by Richmond defenders that he was screaming at teamamtes upfield to give him a hand. The *Globe* said: "Pratt was forced to fight the grimmest encounter of his career. By terrific energy and tenacity the Tiger defenders Sheahan, Bolger, O'Neill and Baggott pinned the champion down to one goal in the first half."

The Tigers led by 27 points at the main break.

South Melbourne was expected to rally in the third quarter but the fanatical Richmond players refused to let them. Pratt was "skilfully crowded and buffeted when he went for the ball", the *Globe* said. "In the third quarter Richmond surprised the critics by achieving control in the air against a first-rate marking side. Then the masterly play of Allan Geddes and Stan Judkins on wings gave the Tigers the call across the centre. They went in remorselessly for the kill and slammed on six goals. Never before in five seasons had the dashing South side with its array of champions faced a 10-goal deficit at the last change—16.11 to 6.11."

Nash by this stage had kicked 2.4. In the last quarter he slammed on four goals in a brilliant cameo before, finally, Pratt was able to escape the clutches of the Richmond defenders. He took a big mark just out from goal. "Harried, bustled and jolted, Bob Pratt had spent nearly three quarters of the game in total eclipse. Towards the end he marked over his forceful opponents and kicked his second goal for the day," the *Globe* said.

His tally of 150 goals from 21 games came at an average of 7.1 per game.

With Richmond's victory assured, South Melbourne vice-captain Peter Reville began to vent his frustration. According to the evidence of umpire Scott at the subsequent tribunal hearing, Reville ran 10 yards and hit Richmond's Bert Taylor between the temple and the ear. Boundary umpire Lancaster saw Reville go into a pack, drive his knee into one player and then strike another, Kevin O'Neill, whose nose was broken. Martin Bolger held Reville on the ground by the throat while boundary umpire Fitt told him to play fair. A goal umpire said he saw Reville "connect with several players with fists and elbows". Umpire Scott reported that Reville abused him in a threatening manner for the final 10 minutes.

Reville was suspended for the following season. Kevin O'Neill was suspended for four matches for striking Reville.

The game ended with Richmond the clear victor by 39 points, 19.14 (128) to 12.17 (89). The Tigers' score was a Grand Final record, nudging out Melbourne's 17.17 (119) in 1926. Titus finished with six goals in a best-on-ground performance. Tom O'Halloran and Dick Harris kicked three each. Nash kicked six goals and Pratt two for the Swans.

Richmond fully deserved its victory. It had beaten every team during the season, including South Melbourne three times. Despite criticism over its forward line's firepower, it had stuck to Perc Bentley's plan and encouraged various routes to goal—and it had kicked 19 goals in each of its finals. Its defence had stood firm. Given the team's balance, Richmond people believed it to be the club's greatest team.

The Sporting Globe summed up the Tigers' victory: "They matched them in pace, beat them in the air, and foiled all their attacks with one of the most rugged defences seen in the League in the last 25 years."

In Richmond's Annual Report, the club noted: "South Melbourne fielded a team that represented the very best available from their extensive resources."

You can still see the Tigers officials smirking now.

1934 RICHMOND

PREMIER'S SEASON

RICHMOND: 1934

ROUND ONE May 5
RICHMOND 18.14 (122)
MELBOURNE 12.9 (81)
Best: Richmond – Titus, Judkins, D.Strang, Bolger, Sheahan, Murdoch, O'Neill.
Goals: Richmond – Titus 8, McConchie 2, Martin 2, Baxter 2, Harris 2, G.Strang, Foster.
Crowd: 17,000 at Punt Road Oval

ROUND TWO May 12
RICHMOND 13.9 (87)
ST KILDA 12.11 (83)
Best: Richmond – D.Strang, McCormack, Geddes, Bentley, Baxter, Harris, Martin.
Goals: Richmond – D.Strang 4, Harris 3, Martin 2, Titus 2, Bentley, Baxter.
Crowd: 24,000 at the Junction Oval

ROUND THREE May 19
RICHMOND 14.20 (104)
CARLTON 9.13 (67)
Best: Richmond – Geddes, Murdoch, McCormack, Titus, Martin, Judkins, Sheahan.
Goals: Richmond – Titus 5, Harris 3, G.Strang 2, Martin, Zschech, Bentley, Foster.
Crowd: 37,000 at Punt Road Oval

ROUND FOUR May 26
RICHMOND 9.9 (63)
COLLINGWOOD 13.13 (91)
Best: Richmond – Bolger, Dyer, McCormack, Baxter, G.Strang, Murdoch, Zschech.
Goals: Richmond – G.Strang 3, Baxter 3, Bentley, Harris, Martin.
Crowd: 26,000 at Victoria Park

ROUND FIVE June 4
RICHMOND 15.12 (102)
ESSENDON 12.8 (80)
Best: Richmond – Titus, Sheahan, Baxter, G.Strang, Garvie, Jordan, Martin, O'Neill.
Goals: Richmond – Titus 6, Martin 3, G.Strang 2, Jordan, Harris, Guinane, Bentley.
Crowd: 24,500 at Punt Road Oval

ROUND SIX June 9
RICHMOND 16.12 (108)
SOUTH MELBOURNE 9.10 (64)
Best: Richmond – Harris, O'Neill, Saunders, Dyer, Foster, Murdoch, Titus, Bolger.
Goals: Richmond – Titus 6, Harris 5, G.Strang 2, Dyer, Bentley, Baxter.
Crowd: 32,000 at the Lake Oval

ROUND SEVEN June 23
RICHMOND 16.14 (110)
HAWTHORN 11.15 (81)
Best: Richmond – Geddes, Titus, McConchie, O'Neill, Bolger, Martin, G.Strang.
Goals: Richmond – Titus 6, G.Strang 2, O'Halloran 2, Baxter 2, Martin, Harris, Dyer, Zschech.
Crowd: 10,000 at Punt Road Oval

ROUND EIGHT June 30
RICHMOND 9.10 (64)
FOOTSCRAY 6.12 (48)
Best: Richmond – Murdoch, Martin, Judkins, McCormack, Geddes, Murdoch, Heifner.
Goals: Richmond – Titus 4, Harris 2, Heifner, Zschech, Martin.
Crowd: 14,000 at Punt Road Oval

ROUND NINE July 7
RICHMOND 4.9 (33)
GEELONG 7.13 (55)
Best: Richmond – O'Neill, Bolger, Foster, McCormack, Judkins, Harris, G.Strang.
Goals: Richmond – Harris 3, McCormack.
Crowd: 16,500 at Corio Oval

ROUND TEN July 14
RICHMOND 10.16 (76)
FITZROY 9.9 (63)
Best: Richmond – Martin, G.Strang, Geddes, Titus, Bentley, Dyer, Edmonds, O'Neill.
Goals: Richmond – Titus 3, Martin 2, Dyer 2, Edmonds, Harris, Symonds.
Crowd: 17,500 at Punt Road Oval

ROUND ELEVEN July 21
RICHMOND 15.9 (99)
NORTH MELBOURNE 11.12 (78)
Best: Richmond – Harris, Murdoch, Heifner, G.Strang, Titus, Foster, Martin, Saunders.
Goals: Richmond – Titus 6, Harris 5, G.Strang 2, Bentley, Baxter.
Crowd: 6,000 at Arden St Oval

ROUND TWELVE July 28
RICHMOND 14.11 (95)
MELBOURNE 13.23 (101)
Best: Richmond – Judkins, Dyer, Martin, Sheahan, Harris, Titus, Murdoch, Zschech.
Goals: Richmond – Bentley 4, Titus 3, Harris 3, G.Strang 2, Dyer, Baxter.
Crowd: 13,805 at the MCG

ROUND THIRTEEN August 4
RICHMOND 7.25 (67)
ST KILDA 5.8 (38)
Best: Richmond – O'Halloran, Titus, Martin, O'Neill, Murdoch, G.Strang, Sheahan.
Goals: Richmond – Titus 3, Edmonds, Harris, Bentley, Baxter.
Crowd: 16,000 at Punt Road Oval

ROUND FOURTEEN August 18
RICHMOND 16.13 (109)
CARLTON 14.12 (96)
Best: Richmond – Harris, Dyer, Geddes, Martin, McCormack, Foster, Titus, D.Strang.
Goals: Richmond – Harris 5, Titus 4, D.Strang 2, Bentley 2, Judkins, Geddes, Dyer.
Crowd: 30,000 at Princes Park

ROUND FIFTEEN August 25
RICHMOND 12.14 (86)
COLLINGWOOD 11.9 (75)
Best: Richmond – D.Strang, Foster, Guinane, Judkins, Baggott, Harris, Titus, Murdoch.
Goals: Richmond – Titus 4, Harris 3, Murdoch 3, Martin, Edmonds.
Crowd: 26,500 at Punt Road Oval

ROUND SIXTEEN September 1
RICHMOND 15.23 (113)
ESSENDON 13.12 (90)
Best: Richmond – Dyer, O'Halloran, D.Strang, Baxter, G.Strang, McCormack, Bolger.
Goals: Richmond – Baxter 3, Titus 3, D.Strang 2, Harris 2, Geddes, Jordon, Edmonds, Dyer, O'Halloran.
Crowd: 10,000 at Windy Hill

ROUND SEVENTEEN September 8
RICHMOND 14.14 (98)
SOUTH MELBOURNE 13.14 (92)
Best: Richmond – McCormack, Foster, Martin, Titus, Baggott, Stenhouse, Sheahan.
Goals: Richmond – Titus 4, Martin 3, Sheahan 2, Edmonds 2, Foster, Baxter, Harris.
Crowd: 40,000 at Punt Road Oval

ROUND EIGHTEEN September 15
RICHMOND 11.16 (82)
HAWTHORN 7.9 (51)
Best: Richmond – Foster, Geddes, McCormack, Bentley, Edmonds, O'Halloran, Harris.
Goals: Richmond – Edmonds 2, Harris 2, O'Halloran 2, Titus 2, Foster, Baxter, Martin.
Crowd: 4,000 at Glenferrie Oval

PREMIER'S FINALS

SECOND SEMI-FINAL September 29
RICHMOND	19.20 (134)
GEELONG	7.8 (50)

Best: Richmond – Martin, Titus, Baggott, Judkins, Bentley, O'Halloran, McCormack, Foster.
Goals: Richmond – Titus 5, Harris 4, Bentley 3, O'Halloran 2, Martin 2, Murdoch, Dyer, Baxter.
Crowd: 35,934 at the MCG

GRAND FINAL October 13
RICHMOND	4.4 10.8 16.11 19.14 (128)
SOUTH MELBOURNE	4.3 6.5 6.11 12.17 (89)

Best: Richmond – Titus, Bolger, Baggott, McCormack, G.Strang, Martin.
Goals: Richmond – Titus 6, O'Halloran 3, Harris 3, Bentley 2, Martin 2, Baxter, Murdoch, Zschech.
Crowd: 65,335

GRAND FINAL LINE-UPS

RICH	B:	M.Bolger	M.Sheahan	K.O'Neill
STH M	F:	B.Diggins	B.Pratt	O.Bertram
RICH	HB:	J.Baggott	G.Strang	B.McCormack
STH M	HF:	P.Reville	L.Nash	J.O'Meara
RICH	C:	S.Judkins	E.Zschech	A.Geddes
STH M	C:	H.Clarke	L.Thomas	H.Matthews
RICH	HF:	T.O'Halloran	D.Baxter	J.Murdoch
STH M	HB:	B.Faul	L.Richards	H.McLaughlin
RICH	F:	B.Foster	J.Titus	D.Harris
STH M	B:	H.McKay	J.Austin	J.McKenzie
RICH	R:	P.Bentley (capt)	J.Dyer	R.Martin
STH M	R:	J.Bisset (capt)	D.Kelleher	T.Brain
RICH	Reserve: H.Edmonds		Coach: Perc Bentley	
STH M	Reserve: W.Harris		Coach: Jack Bisset	

SNAPSHOT

Win-loss record: 17-3

Highest score: 19.20 (134), second semi-final, v Geelong.

Greatest winning margin: 84 points, second semi-final, v Geelong.

Lowest score: 4.9 (33), round 9, v Geelong.

Greatest losing margin: 28 points, round 4, v Collingwood.

Most goals by a player in a game: 8, Jack Titus, round 1, v Melbourne.

Most consecutive wins: 8

Most consecutive losses: 1 (three times).

Club awards: Best & Fairest: Ray Martin; Leading goalkicker: Jack Titus (80 goals)

Putting it into perspective:
Richmond continued a successful era, playing in its fourth consecutive Grand Final and seventh in eight years since 1927. It was the club's fourth premiership, their second in three seasons and their first under new coach Perc Bentley.

1934

	P	W	L	D	%	Pts
1 Richmond (1)	18	15	3		121.3	60
2 Geelong (3)	18	14	3	1	135.4	58
3 South Melb (2)	18	14	4		140.2	56
4 Collingwood (4)	18	13	4	1	121.9	54
5 Carlton	18	12	6		116.3	48
6 Melbourne	18	9	9		97.2	36
7 St Kilda	18	9	9		95.8	36
8 Fitzroy	18	7	11		95.7	28
9 Footscray	18	6	12		85.0	24
10 Essendon	18	5	13		83.5	20
11 Hawthorn	18	3	15		67.8	12
12 North Melb	18	0	18		66.4	0

(18 home and away rounds)

PLAYERS USED

RICHMOND	GUERNSEY	GAMES	GOALS
Baggott, Jack	14	6	0
Baxter, Dave	2	16	19
Bentley, Perc	1	18	18
Bolger, Martin	9	19	0
Chirgwin, Dick	29	1	0
Dyer, Jack	17	16	8
Edmonds, Horrie	7	17	9
Foster, Bert	11	19	4
Garvie, Bill	10	4	0
Geddes, Allan	8	17	2
Guinane, Danny	22	6	1
Harris, Dick	20	20	51
Heifner, Fred	33	15	1
Jordon, Clarrie	32	6	2
Judkins, Stan	6	19	1
Martin, Ray	27	19	22
McConchie, Jack	31	4	2
McCormack, Basil	9	16	1
Murdoch, Joe	13	20	5
O'Halloran, Tom	18	11	10
O'Neill, Kevin	16	19	0
Saunders, Richie	30	6	0
Sheahan, Maurie	4	19	2
Stenhouse, Jack	26	6	0
Strang, Doug	28	5	8
Strang, Gordon	23	18	16
Symons, Jack	19	3	1
Titus, Jack	12	20	80
Zschech, Eric	25	20	4

**COLLINGWOOD 11.12 (78) d
SOUTH MELBOURNE 7.16 (58)**

TRIP INTO THE UNKNOWN

Although some questioned the Magpies' sojourn up north, it was a tram trip in Melbourne that had the bigger impact on success. By GLENN McFARLANE

FORMER Carlton champion Horrie Clover had a warning for Collingwood and South Melbourne as the two teams prepared to embark on a two-week mid-season trip through the northern states of Australia in 1935. The message from Clover was simple: trying to further the cause of Australian football, as important as that belief might be, could cost both sides winning a premiership.

Clover, writing in *The Sporting Globe,* was emphatic when he forecast the difficulties that such a trip during the state representative break could have on the Magpies and the Bloods as the season intensified. He stated: "Can a League club, making an extended mid-season trip to other states, return to hard competitive football in Melbourne with their prospects of winning the premiership unimpaired? My experience is that the long-distance travelling, irregular training, different diet and climatic conditions can easily result in a lack of form." Clover added that while he held no fears about players treating the trip as a holiday, he questioned whether the "hard grounds" up north would ruin the teams' shot at the premiership.

Clover was by no means the only critic of the decision to travel to Brisbane, Newcastle and Sydney from July 21 to August 6, to play three "friendly" matches and to help educate the rugby states on Australian Football. However, Clover, a veteran of 147 games with the Blues from 1920-31, and a respected football voice, was clearly the most vocal. Putting a show on for the northern neighbours was a noble act, he pointed out, but it was hardly conducive to winning a flag.

Clover, and his ghostwriter, had clearly forgotten about what happened in 1927 when the Magpies had taken their team across the Nullarbor to Perth. It would become one of the most famous tours in the club's history, credited by many of those fortunate enough to be on it as the catalyst for Collingwood's four successive premierships from 1927-1930. By travelling north in 1935, Collingwood was hoping to engender that spirit of '27. Just as it was in 1927, Collingwood had a first-year captain and was trying to rebuild for more glories. Back then, it had been Syd Coventry, who would become the club's most successful captain in terms of premierships won. But Coventry had retired at the end of the 1934 season, having finally succumbed to an offer to coach Footscray. Plucky little rover Harry Collier seemed to be the logical replacement.

Collier was considerably smaller in stature to Coventry (about 9cm), but just as tough. He was an exceptional footballer and a natural successor. Fittingly, his brother, Albert, was chosen as his deputy, and the pair set about providing inspiration and protection for a core of young Collingwood players coming through the ranks as coach Jock McHale sought to remodel 'the Machine' that had dominated football just a handful of years earlier. To help consolidate Collier's new role, and the Magpies' desire to once more reach great heights, Collingwood agreed that an interstate trip—long used by the club to foster team spirit—could be the recipe to engender the camaraderie that had produced such stunning results in 1927.

The interstate opportunity also provided the club with the chance to play a series of matches against the team considered its greatest threat to the 1935 title, South Melbourne. Prior to its departure, Collingwood had played South Melbourne twice for a 1-1 result. It had defeated the Southerners at Victoria Park by only two points in the opening round. But the second meeting in round 12 confused matters when South won convincingly by 53 points, a result that justified their premiership favouritism, and highlighted to McHale that a lot of work was still required before the inevitable meeting in September.

In that second game, South Melbourne's most important player, champion goalkicker Bob Pratt, had kicked 10 goals, the same number as Collingwood managed. Pratt, who had kicked a VFL record of 150 goals a year earlier, loomed as the man who stood between the Magpies and their 10th VFL premiership. He had won the league goalkicking awards in 1933 and '34, and was well on the way to making it a hat-trick in '35.

McHale was pleased that the "friendly" matches would allow him and his team to cast a critical eye on South before the finals. Although few took these matches too seriously and they were largely offensive, the Magpies managed to win two of the three contested. They won the first match in Brisbane by 32 points and scored narrowly by three points in Newcastle.

However, the result was reversed when the teams reached Sydney, with South Melbourne delighting the crowd of 11,600, winning by four goals. The only downside for the Bloods that day was an ankle injury suffered by Pratt, who was "crippled by the hard ground." The venture cost both clubs £1000 each, minus a grant of £100 from the Australian National Football Council, but was hailed as an overwhelming success. The Sydney match was marred by a "hurricane force" wind, but the locals marvelled at the execution of the torpedo punt, which *The Argus* said was "not employed to any extent in Sydney".

On their return to Melbourne, and with Clover searching for signs of weakness, it was Collingwood who initially adapted better. In their return game, the Magpies convincingly beat Geelong at home, while the Bloods were upset by Carlton. That meant there was only half a game between the two teams at the end of round 15. But that was South's last stumble of the home-and-season. It closed out the regular season with four successive wins. Collingwood won three of their four remaining games, but drew the other with Melbourne—the club's second draw of the season to sit alongside the round-two draw against Fitzroy. Still, both clubs had erased doubts that their mid-year trip would be a negative, with South finishing on top, and Collingwood a game behind in second. Carlton was just half a game away in third spot.

South Melbourne looked ominous in brushing past Collingwood by 21 points in the semi-final, with Pratt kicking six goals, to advance to the Grand Final. But those in the Magpies' camp were not worried with the proceedings. Some figured the number of young players in Collingwood's team would need some more seasoning in finals football before they would be ready. A number of club insiders, including president Harry Curtis, were convinced the Grand Final would be a very different story.

First, though, Collingwood had to overcome Richmond, who had accounted for Carlton in the first week of the finals. At half-time, it was no certainty. The previous year's premier had clung to a three-point margin at the long break, but it was never going to be enough. The Magpies swept over the top of the Tigers in the second half to win by 28 points and set up a seventh clash in 1935 with South Melbourne. But this was the one that really mattered and, fittingly, it would come 39 years to the day of the two clubs' meeting in the 1896 VFA Grand Final, Collingwood's first triumph. Fans hoped it was an omen.

Still, the pundits favoured South Melbourne, given its superior performance in the finals and the semi-final margin. So, too, did most of the partial observers. Even a few players were cocky about the outcome, with Austin Robertson saying before the game: "You can't name the odds on South Melbourne." *The Herald* concluded that the minor premier had too many good players and "on paper, the result seems certain". Clearly, South Melbourne had more individual brilliance than Collingwood, but McHale always had a greater belief in team above individuals.

So much of South's game revolved around Pratt, and that was something that even Harry Collier feared. No shrinking violet when it came to confidence, Collier knew Collingwood would have to be at its top to beat South Melbourne with Pratt in the team. Years later he would recall that when he was on his way to training on the Thursday night before the last training session ahead of the Grand Final, he was thinking to himself: "If Pratt wasn't in the side, we'd knock them off, for sure." Collier was confident that Collingwood would make a real game of it, but he was worried about the influence Pratt could have on the outcome.

Yet, unbeknown to Collier, one of football's most remarkable off-field accidents had changed the focus of the game and had delivered Collingwood a decided advantage. Just a few hours earlier, the man Collier had been musing about had been alighting from a busy tram along busy, congested High Street, Prahran. It was about 2pm and as he disembarked, Pratt stepped in front of a truck loaded with bricks, and was knocked down. He was immediately taken home and examined by the club's doctor who diagnosed a sprained right ankle, a lacerated right leg, an injured left foot and a badly bruised finger. South Melbourne's secretary R. T. Mullaly tried to sugarcoat the damage when he said that night: "Pratt had a wonderful escape. He is not too bad and he will probably be able to have a try out on Saturday."

But the escape was all Collingwood's. The Magpies would have the good fortune of tackling South Melbourne without its best player. News of the Pratt injury was one of the biggest football sensations of the decade and all sorts of wild and unsubstantiated rumours began to sweep Melbourne. Two of the most common conspiracy theories centred on whether the accident was connected to football betting, or whether it had been arranged by a Collingwood supporter intent on making sure the Magpies won the premiership. Neither was true. Years later, Pratt himself would mention that there had been speculation swirling around the city that notorious Melbourne gangster 'Squizzy' Taylor had somehow been involved. He wasn't. Taylor had been dead for eight years, the victim of a shootout with 'Snowy' Cutmore back in 1927.

Truth is sometimes stranger than fiction. The man who accidentally ran Pratt down was actually a South Melbourne supporter, Mr C.T. Peters, who was so distraught with what had occurred that he went around to the champion goalkicker's house that night to give him a packet of cigarettes as his apology. There were mixed feelings in the Collingwood camp. Some were happy that their greatest threat was not playing. Others wanted to have a crack at South with Pratt in the team. Collingwood secretary Frank Wraith summed it up when he said: "He is a dangerous opponent on the field, but we have a soft spot for players like Pratt."

Pratt spent Grand Final eve in the heart of Melbourne undergoing "diathermy treatment", or deep tissue heat treatment. Although his specialist said Pratt was improving hour by hour, he conceded that he "did not hold out much hope of him playing in the Grand Final". Pratt was named in the team, but no one seriously believed he would play.

Although the Magpies could not consider four players due to injury—Len Murphy, Jack Knight, George Carter and Jack Power—it had a near perfect blend of experience and youth. The remnants of the Machine meant that the likes of the Collier brothers, Gordon Coventry, Harold Rumney, Charlie Dibbs and Percy Bowyer were still there, but there were rising stars in Jack Regan, Phonse Kyne, Alby Pannam and Marcus Whelan, to name a few. On averages, South was taller, heavier and almost a year older than the Magpies. But Collingwood had five players with more than 150 games of experience; South had none.

As expected, the match started with some tough clashes. It was, according to *The Sporting Globe,* a "gruelling" initiation, "replete with hard knocks, doubtful and otherwise, and all were on tiptoe, not knowing when the next outbreak would occur." Herb Matthews had come into the team for South Melbourne and he started in the centre, while Laurie Nash took charge at centre-half-forward and Roy Moore had the onerous task of acting as full-forward in the place of Pratt.

Kyne "missed an easy shot" in the first minute of the match, putting the opening score on the board. However, it was South Melbourne who began the match full of running, exerting plenty of pressure on the Magpies. The Bloods kicked the opening goal when Moore "pulled down a spectacular mark" and made no mistake from close in with a "long skimming drop kick. Then Nash, "picking up smartly, snapped through (their) second goal."

South led by two goals late in the term due to its "nippiness" and strength in the middle of the ground. But inaccuracy was a real issue. "Six scoring shots had netted the Southerners only two goals and this inaccuracy was likely to prove costly against the experienced Magpies," said *The Argus.*

The Magpies seemed to take a long time to settle into the game, and it wasn't until late in the first quarter that "at last Harry Collier set Collingwood moving with something like their real precision." The skipper's efforts were rewarded when "Pannam was given a free kick 30 yards out on the boundary line, (and) he kicked the side's first goal." This was immediately followed by another goal to South when "(Frank) Davies tried a long shot from the boundary line and the ball was just carried the distance to roll through for South's third goal." The margin was out to 15 points at quarter-time, but it could have been much greater, with *The Sporting Globe* saying: "They (South) were pacier and by far the most polished and accomplished side."

Ominously, South Melbourne commenced the attacking in the opening minutes of the second term. Again, it dominated possession, but failed to capitalise on its chances. The door was left ajar, and some fine work from Kyne at centre half-forward finally "brought about Collingwood's revival". Kyne had a hand in Gordon Coventry's first goal, which was snapped "over his head", bringing the Magpies supporters to their feet. Coventry kicked another soon after, while the Southerners managed to add a further goal from Davies.

Collingwood regained the lead again for the first time since that first minute of the match when Coventry goaled again after "three parts of the session had expired". Then came five minutes of "hectic" play "during which players were bowled over in all directions and fists flew freely in the crunches. South foolishly fell into the trap of playing the man and its game fell away."

The game was momentarily held up while two boundary umpires ran across the ground to speak to three players who had a minute earlier swung blows at each other after a Collingwood player had been tossed over the back of a South player. *The Sporting Globe* wrote: "Never more at home when the game is hard, Collingwood was seen to be at a far better advantage than their opponents, while South appeared rattled."

The success of the Magpies had been due to their "intelligent use of the breeze" in the second quarter, even though it had diminished in its intensity. Collingwood relied heavily on accurate goalkicking and long, direct kicking rather than unnecessary short passing. By half-time, the Magpies had opened up a lead of 10 points, thanks especially to Kyne's dominance.

Collingwood got the perfect start against the wind in the third term when Leo Morgan was able to weave his way through a pack and drive the ball long to Coventry. The Magpie veteran "marked his kick and punted (the) seventh goal". South Melbourne rallied briefly with a goal to Dinny Kelleher, "from a superb kick", and another to Moore put them right back in the contest. The Swans trailed by only four points. The game was on in earnest and it "showed what the Southerners could do when they minded to make the goal their objective and were not diverted to the close, rugged play into which Collingwood now and then led them."

However, just when the pressure was mounting, Collingwood responded with a timely goal, and once more the team was "acting like a machine". When the bell rang for three-quarter time the Magpies led by two goals. McHale desperately tried to urge his players onto another premiership. South Melbourne captain Jack Bisset, injured in the opening term, and again in the third quarter, was assisted off the ground by trainers and taken to hospital; his game and his season over. South would have to try and do it without him.

In the early stages of the last quarter of the season, it seemed as if South Melbourne was making inroads on Collingwood's lead. Then, realising the urgency of the situation, Harry Collier, stepped forward to change the course of the contest. *The Sporting Globe* described it: "A free to Collier about 40 yards out proved disastrous for South. Coolly taking aim, the captain made the most of his opportunity and raised his side's ninth goal, and virtually sealed South's doom." Still, the margin was only 19 points with plenty of football left.

South's seventh goal came just a few minutes later when "(Terry) Brain's pass found (Roy) McEachen (who had replaced Bisset) unguarded in front." He kicked a goal as a matter of course and South fought grimly with renewed effort. They gave "the Collingwood backs a few torrid moments, but it was impossible to rattle the Magpies. They weathered the storm, even when Dibbs, who had been defending grandly, was carried off with serious concussion."

Collingwood maintained that intensity and by mid-quarter South was a "spent force". The Bloods were simply unable to penetrate the tight Magpie defence and the absence of Pratt was being sorely felt. At the other end, South was also unable to stop several moves into Collingwood's attack. The issue was put beyond doubt when McHale's men slotted through two late goals. First, "little (Keith) Stackpole", who had replaced Dibbs on the field, kicked a goal, while Pannam ensured "all interest had gone from the game" when he extended the margin to a comfortable 20 points.

The Herald observed: "The Magpies were a far more versatile team, adapting themselves to all emergencies, winning in the heavy clashes and taking the straight route to goal whenever possible. South foolishly tried to show Collingwood a few points about hard bumping, but they came off second best, and declined into a ragged and uncertain team."

The final bell was met with raucous celebrations. The crowd went wild as first-year captain Collier was jubilantly carried from the field. The first to congratulate Collingwood officially was the VFL president, Dr W.C.

McClelland, who summed it up by saying: "You were able to prove most emphatically in the minds of the football public that you were the better team." Collingwood president Harry Curtis went further, saying: "To me, this is the greatest premiership the club has won yet. We had a young team to be remodelled for this and other premierships in the future, and our plans have so far been successful."

By way of contrast to the wild celebrations, trainers were trying to revive Dibbs in the corner of the victorious room. *The Herald* observed: "Stretched out on the table where he lay from the time he was carried from the field, Dibbs was unaware of the celebrations or the reasons for them." He was one of the last to leave the rooms after the revellers had moved on, and was sent home in a taxi with his wife. But while Dibbs, who had played his 216th and last game with Collingwood, was about to have an early night, due to the concussion suffered in the last term, the celebrations back at Victoria Park— and elsewhere—were riotous.

That night a piano was wheeled onto the ground and there were countless renditions of *Good Old Collingwood Forever* as well as other tunes of the day, extending well into the early hours of the morning. It continued into the next day. The players were delighted with both the victory, and the £5 bonus that had been presented to them by wealthy businessman Jim Ryan.

After Sunday night's celebrations, Harry Collier and Harold Rumney and their wives—plus Collier's twin brothers—were squeezed into the captain's car as they left Victoria Park. Inexplicably, Collier lost control of the car and crashed into the front gate of Archbishop Daniel Mannix's house. He scampered away quickly, leaving behind the front bumper bar. Both players would be forced to apologise to Mannix, who famously said he could "mend his own fences" and the incident faded into Collingwood folklore.

Curtis, in his review of the 1935 season, said he believed the trip to the northern states was a crucial part of the club's success. He had told that to South Melbourne as they commiserated in their rooms shortly after the Grand Final. The president said: "We feel inwardly that the success was brought about by South Melbourne helping us make the trip to Queensland and New South Wales during the season and cementing friendships which led to the determination to win the premiership."

So much for Clover's dire warnings; the trip had sown the seeds of a premiership, with possibly more to come. After all, as Collingwood barrackers acknowledged, Clover *was* a Carlton player.

1935 COLLINGWOOD

PREMIER'S SEASON

COLLINGWOOD: 1935

ROUND ONE April 27
COLLINGWOOD   15.18 (108)
SOUTH MELBOURNE   15.16 (106)
Best: Collingwood – Riley, Froude, Bowyer, H.Collier, Kyne, Regan, Fraser, Morgan.
Goals: Collingwood – Riley 5, Kyne 3, G.Coventry 3, Doherty, Bowyer, H.Collier, Whelan.
Crowd: 30,000 at Victoria Park

ROUND TWO May 6
COLLINGWOOD   14.9 (93)
FITZROY   14.9 (93)
Best: Collingwood – Regan, A.Collier, Dibbs, Carmody, Woods, Froude, Whelan, H.Collier.
Goals: Collingwood – G.Coventry 4, Riley 3, Ryan 2, Kyne 2, Doherty 2, Bowyer.
Crowd: 36,000 at Brunswick St Oval

ROUND THREE May 11
COLLINGWOOD   21.17 (143)
ESSENDON   12.11 (83)
Best: Collingwood – A.Pannam, Riley, Carmody, Rumney, Bowyer, Kyne, Dibbs, Regan.
Goals: Collingwood – A.Pannam 7, Riley 5, Doherty 4, G.Coventry 2, Bowyer, H.Collier, Woods.
Crowd: 18,000 at Victoria Park

ROUND FOUR May 18
COLLINGWOOD   17.13 (115)
GEELONG   14.17 (101)
Best: Collingwood – G.Coventry, Froude, Whelan, Bowyer, A.Collier, Doherty, H.Collier.
Goals: Collingwood – G.Coventry 7, A.Pannam 3, Riley 2, Doherty 2, A.Collier, Kyne, Bowyer.
Crowd: 13,000 at Corio Oval

ROUND FIVE May 25
COLLINGWOOD   13.20 (98)
MELBOURNE   9.15 (69)
Best: Collingwood – Regan, Kyne, Dibbs, Froude, Carter, A.Collier, Riley, Whelan.
Goals: Collingwood – G.Coventry 4, Riley 3, Carter 3, H.Collier 2, Doherty.
Crowd: 16,057 at the MCG

ROUND SIX June 1
COLLINGWOOD   23.11 (149)
FOOTSCRAY   14.14 (98)
Best: Collingwood – G.Coventry, Doherty, Woods, Morgan, A.Collier, Carmody, Bowyer.
Goals: Collingwood – G.Coventry 9, Doherty 7, Kyne 2, A.Pannam 2, Riley 2, L.Murphy.
Crowd: 17,500 at Victoria Park

ROUND SEVEN June 8
COLLINGWOOD   19.16 (130)
ST KILDA   16.15 (111)
Best: Collingwood – A.Pannam, Rumney, Dibbs, Froude, Carmody, G.Coventry, H.Collier.
Goals: Collingwood – A.Pannam 7, G.Coventry 5, H.Collier 3, Doherty 2, Kyne, Carter.
Crowd: 17,000 at the Junction Oval

ROUND EIGHT June 15
COLLINGWOOD   16.30 (126)
NORTH MELBOURNE   6.10 (46)
Best: Collingwood – Woods, Froude, Bowyer, Dibbs, A.Pannam, H.Collier, Kyne, Regan.
Goals: Collingwood – A.Pannam 4, H.Collier 3, G.Coventry 2, Carter 2, Ross 2, L.Murphy, Riley, Kyne.
Crowd: 8,000 at Victoria Park

ROUND NINE June 22
COLLINGWOOD   8.10 (58)
CARLTON   13.9 (87)
Best: Collingwood – A.Pannam, L.Murphy, Carter, Ross, Kyne, Rumney, Knight.
Goals: Collingwood – A.Pannam 4, G.Coventry 2, Riley, Doherty.
Crowd: 17,000 at Princes Park

ROUND TEN June 29
COLLINGWOOD   13.4 (82)
RICHMOND   11.14 (80)
Best: Collingwood – Knight, Riley, Rumney, H.Collier, Carmody, A.Pannam, Bowyer.
Goals: Collingwood – Knight 5, Carmody 3, Doherty 2, A.Pannam, Kyne, G.Coventry.
Crowd: 25,000 at Punt Road Oval

ROUND ELEVEN July 6
COLLINGWOOD   17.20 (122)
HAWTHORN   12.3 (75)
Best: Collingwood – Whelan, Power, Bowyer, Fraser, Doherty, H.Collier, L.Murphy.
Goals: Collingwood – G.Coventry 4, Doherty 4, A.Pannam 3, Riley 2, Kyne, Woods, L.Murphy, H.Collier.
Crowd: 8,000 at Victoria Park

ROUND TWELVE July 13
COLLINGWOOD   10.11 (71)
SOUTH MELBOURNE   18.16 (124)
Best: Collingwood – Regan, Woods, H.Collier, A.Pannam, A.Collier, Carnody, Bowyer.
Goals: Collingwood – A.Pannam 4, G.Coventry 3, Kyne 2, Doherty.
Crowd: 31,000 at the Lake Oval

ROUND THIRTEEN July 20
COLLINGWOOD   14.21 (105)
FITZROY   12.10 (82)
Best: Collingwood – H.Collier, Whelan, Riley, Stackpole, Dibbs, Woods, Regan.
Goals: Collingwood – Riley 4, G.Coventry 3, Carter 3, Knight 2, A.Pannam 2.
Crowd: 18,000 at Victoria Park

ROUND FOURTEEN August 17
COLLINGWOOD   16.17 (113)
ESSENDON   16.10 (106)
Best: Collingwood – G.Coventry, Kyne, Morgan, H.Collier, A.Pannam, Riley, Whelan.
Goals: Collingwood – G.Coventry 8, A.Pannam 3, Riley 3, Kyne 2.
Crowd: 11,000 at Windy Hill

ROUND FIFTEEN August 10
COLLINGWOOD   22.13 (145)
GEELONG   16.15 (111)
Best: Collingwood – G.Coventry, Bowyer, Riley, A.Collier, Froude, H.Collier, Regan.
Goals: Collingwood – G.Coventry 9, Riley 4, Bowyer 3, Doherty 2, Fraser, H.Collier, L.Murphy, Whelan.
Crowd: 9,000 at Victoria Park

ROUND SIXTEEN August 24
COLLINGWOOD   11.13 (79)
MELBOURNE   10.19 (79)
Best: Collingwood – Dibbs, L.Murphy, Carmody, H.Collier, Kyne, A.Collier, Fyfe.
Goals: Collingwood – G.Coventry 3, Knight 2, Kyne 2, H.Collier 2, Carmody, Morgan.
Crowd: 10,500 at Victoria Park

ROUND SEVENTEEN August 31
COLLINGWOOD   12.14 (86)
FOOTSCRAY   6.17 (53)
Best: Collingwood – Dibbs, G.Coventry, Froude, Morgan, Riley, Regan, Bowyer.
Goals: Collingwood – G.Coventry 5, Riley 2, Todd 2, Ross, Fricker, Kyne.
Crowd: 7,500 at the Western Oval

ROUND EIGHTEEN September 7
COLLINGWOOD   9.18 (72)
ST KILDA   7.15 (57)
Best: Collingwood – Whelan, A.Collier, Regan, Fraser, H.Collier, Rumney, Ross.
Goals: Collingwood – G.Coventry 3, Knight, Doherty, L.Murphy, Todd, H.Collier, A.Pannam.
Crowd: 16,000 at Victoria Park

GRAND FINALS VOLUME I

PREMIER'S FINALS

SECOND SEMI-FINAL September 21

COLLINGWOOD	11.17 (83)
SOUTH MELBOURNE	15.14 (104)

Best: Collingwood – Rumney, A.Collier, H.Collier, Bowyer, Fraser, Regan, Kyne.
Goals: Collingwood – G.Coventry 3, Todd 3, H.Collier 2, A.Collier, Kyne, Knight.
Crowd: 53,766 at the MCG

PRELIMINARY FINAL September 28

COLLINGWOOD	14.10 (94)
RICHMOND	9.12 (66)

Best: Collingwood – Regan, Bowyer, A.Collier, Dibbs, Kyne, Riley, Doherty, Whelan.
Goals: Collingwood – G.Coventry 4, A.Pannam 3, Kyne 2, Bowyer 2, Knight, H.Collier, Riley.
Crowd: 46,191 at the MCG

GRAND FINAL October 5

COLLINGWOOD	1.3 6.6 8.10 11.12 (78)
SOUTH MELBOURNE	3.6 4.8 6.10 7.16 (58)

Best: Collingwood – H.Collier, Regan, A.Collier, Kyne, Froude, Rumney, Whelan.
Goals: Collingwood – G.Coventry 4, Kyne 2, A.Pannam 2, H.Collier, A.Collier, Stackpole.
Crowd: 54,154

GRAND FINAL LINE-UPS

COLL	B:	J.Ross	C.Dibbs	H.Rumney
STH M	F:	D.Kelleher	R.Moore	F.Davies
COLL	HB:	B.Woods	J.Regan	F.Froude
STH M	HF:	A.Robertson	L.Nash	J.O'Meara
COLL	C:	J.Carmody	M.Whelan	L.Morgan
STH M	C:	H.Clarke	H.Matthews	J.Reid
COLL	HF:	L.Riley	P.Kyne	V.Doherty
STH M	HB:	B.Faul	L.Richards	J.McKenzie
COLL	F:	K.Fraser	G.Coventry	A.Pannam
STH M	B:	J.Austin	R.Hillis	R.Humphries
COLL	R:	A.Collier	P.Bowyer	H.Collier (capt)
STH M	R:	J.Bisset (capt)	B.Diggins	T.Brain
COLL	Reserve:	K.Stackpole	**Coach:** Jock McHale	
STH M	Reserve:	R.McEachern	**Coach:** Jack Bisset	

SNAPSHOT

Win-loss record: 16-3-2

Highest score: 23.11 (149), round 6, v Footscray.

Greatest winning margin: 80 points, round 8, v North Melbourne.

Lowest score: 8.10 (58), round 9, v Carlton.

Greatest losing margin: 53 points, round 12, v South Melbourne.

Most goals by a player in a game: 9, Gordon Coventry, round 6, v Footscray; round 15, v Geelong.

Most consecutive wins: 6

Most consecutive losses: 1

Club awards: Best & Fairest: Albert Collier; Leading goalkicker: Gordon Coventry (88 goals).

Putting it into perspective:

Collingwood's 10th premiership continued its dominance of the competition. The Magpies were now the most successful team in the competition, three flags ahead of Fitzroy in second place, and had played in a record 19 Grand Finals.

1935

		P	W	L	D	%	Pts
1	South Melb (2)	18	16	2		137.6	64
2	**Collingwood (1)**	18	14	2	2	121.4	60
3	Carlton (4)	18	14	3	1	141.6	58
4	Richmond (3)	18	12	6		117.4	48
5	St Kilda	18	11	7		110.6	44
6	Melbourne	18	8	9	1	101.2	34
7	Fitzroy	18	8	9	1	90.2	34
8	Essendon	18	7	11		89.6	28
9	Geelong	18	6	11	1	96.3	26
10	Hawthorn	18	5	13		80.9	20
11	Footscray	18	2	14	2	73.5	12
12	North Melb	18	1	17		65.1	4

(18 home and away rounds)

PLAYERS USED

COLLINGWOOD	GUERNSEY	GAMES	GOALS
Albiston, Harold	1	1	0
Boag, Tommy	3	1	0
Bowyer, Percy	4	19	9
Boyall, Marcus	1	1	0
Carmody, Jack	5	19	4
Carter, George	6	9	9
Collier, Albert	7	18	3
Collier, Harry	8	20	19
Coventry, Gordon	9	21	88
Dibbs, Charlie	10	20	0
Doherty, Vin	11	17	30
Fraser, Keith	14	17	1
Fricker, Pat	12	4	1
Froude, Fred	13	19	0
Fyfe, Alec	2	4	0
Gibson, Reg	15	6	0
Gray, Eddie	16	1	0
Kanngieser, George	16	1	0
Knight, Jack	15	14	12
Kyne, Phonse	17	18	24
Morgan, Leo	18	16	1
Murphy, Len	19	19	5
Pannam, Alby	15	15	46
Power, Jack	3	3	0
Regan, Jack	25	18	0
Riley, Lou	23	19	38
Ross, Jack	24	16	3
Rumney, Harold	22	16	0
Ryan, Alan	26	4	2
Stackpole, Keith	27	3	1
Todd, Ron	35	4	6
Whelan, Marcus	28	16	2
Woods, Bervin	29	20	2

**COLLINGWOOD 11.23 (89) d
SOUTH MELBOURNE 10.18 (78)**

A WISH THAT CAME TRUE

Several sets of brothers have made mighty contributions to Collingwood. In 1936 it was the Colliers. By GLENN McFARLANE

A FEW minutes were spared for Collingwood captain Harry Collier after the traditional players' meeting at Victoria Park on the Thursday night before the 1936 Grand Final against South Melbourne. It was Collier's 29th birthday and his teammates were offering their best wishes. Someone cried out from the back of the group: "What do you want for your birthday, Harry?" Collier flashed his trademark cheeky smile, saying the only thing that he desired was another premiership. Nothing else mattered.

Granted, Collier's birthday wish was never going to be an easy assignment. Collingwood was, once again, one of the leading teams of the 1936 season, winning its first nine games to set up its season, and even knocking off its greatest challenger, South Melbourne, in the second semi-final to advance to the club's 20th premiership play-off. However, many football pundits and all those without a predilection for the black and white thought South Melbourne might be better primed in the deciding match. After all, South had won the minor premiership, with a game to spare from the Magpies, and many believed they had simply "lacked match practice" in the semi-final.

And this time South Melbourne had their greatest weapon, champion forward Bob Pratt. The memory of his shock absence from the Grand Final 12 months earlier was still fresh in the minds of Bloods supporters and gave them cause for optimism. Some of them had no doubt Pratt's presence would make all the difference when it came to the deciding match, saying: "We were robbed last year by Pratt's absence, but we'll win this one, for sure."

Collingwood had also been weakened by absences that ranked as the worst and most ill-timed in the club's history. Earlier in the season, Harry Collier's extraordinarily important brother and vice-captain, Albert Collier, had been rubbed out for eight matches and his absence in the round-10 match against South Melbourne was one of the key reasons for the club's 11-point loss. At least he would be eligible to play in the finals.

Two other Collingwood players were not so lucky. First, one of the game's fairest players, champion goal-kicker Gordon Coventry, faced the wrath of the tribunal on a charge of striking in the 16-point win over Richmond at Punt Road in round 13. Incredibly, he was handed an eight-match suspension that resonated throughout the football world, and created a wave of protest in Collingwood. Richmond full-back Joe Murdoch, knowing Coventry had boils on the nape of his neck, gave the area constant attention, to the point where it enraged the normally unflappable sharpshooter, prompting him into a rare case of retaliation.

Coventry fought back when his natural instinct would normally have been to turn the other cheek. He threw a punch, and copped the massive penalty, his impeccable record seemingly counting for nothing. The eight-game penalty would cost Coventry the chance to play in a sixth premiership, and put in jeopardy Collingwood's chance of actually making it happen. There were protests—official and otherwise—and Coventry announced a premature retirement. He would later reverse his decision after being convinced he could not end with a suspension, and return to seek one last shot at a flag the following year.

Len Murphy was missing, too, on Grand Final day 1936, for a second successive season. In 1935, he had hurt his shoulder in the early stages of the preliminary final win over Richmond. But it was a suspension that cost him in 1936, thanks to a yet another eight-match penalty, after clashing heavily with South Melbourne's Brighton Diggins in the second semi-final.

With key players missing, and with South Melbourne tipped to gain its revenge from the previous year's loss, Collingwood entered the Grand Final with most of the football pundits believing it was the underdog. This was despite the fact the Magpies had produced a stunning six goal to two final quarter to hold out South by 13 points a fortnight earlier. *The Sporting Globe* predicted: "Although they narrowly defeated the Southerners in the semi-final, it is very doubtful on current form and circumstances whether the Woodsmen will be able to repeat the feat in the vital Grand Final. Indeed, indications point the other way." Some said the game came down to a choice between "Collingwood's tenacious teamwork and South's electric bursts".

Still, those close to Collingwood knew that famous, almost intangible spirit was still brimming. The belief had never wavered and the leadership of the old hands at Victoria Park, especially from the Collier brothers, and their wily old coach 'Jock' McHale, acted as a lesson and an inspiration for the younger core of players. All were determined not to let the club down.

Aside from the Colliers, and a handful of others, most of the Collingwood team consisted of relatively young and moderately experienced players. The Magpies had no player over 30 (Harry Collier was the oldest), while South Melbourne would field three players over 30. The youngest Magpie was Ron Todd, less than 20 days short of his 20th birthday, a Magpie fan since birth, who carried one of the toughest roles entering the Grand Final. Todd had to carry the load in attack in the absence of Coventry. The Grand Final was only his 16th game. The teenager who was born in the suburb, whose Mum was best friends with Dick Lee's wife, and who had worn "Uncle Dick's" No.13 on his black and white jumper as a kid, would have an important role to play. Todd, wearing No.20, knew the importance of his role in helping to bring about a Magpies' premiership that he experienced as a supporter in the 1920s, and now he wanted to experience one as a player.

The thing about this Collingwood team was that it was not overawed by South Melbourne, despite the fact that the Bloods' team was collectively a year-and-a-half older on average. Most of the young Magpies were local products, almost weaned on the stories of the club's great successes. Only three "country" players were in the side that took their place on the MCG that day: Marcus Whelan, from Bacchus Marsh; Jack Knight, from Bendigo; and Bervin Woods, from Mortlake before joining Brunswick. There were a few other "outsiders", with James Crowe from Carlton and Lou Riley from Melbourne.

The team wanted to fulfil the birthday wish that Harry Collier had yearned for a few days earlier. No one wanted to let him down. No one wanted to deny one of the club's favourite sons what would be a sixth individual premiership. Collier summed up the feelings of his players on the eve of the match, saying: "Our chaps are fairly jumping out of our skins with fitness; and they are in great heart. I think we will be in front at the end of the game."

A crowd of 74,091—almost 20,000 more than the previous year's play-off—crammed into the Melbourne Cricket Ground on Grand Final day 1936, clambering for every vantage point, jostling for position and desperate to find the best spots. The crush led to several accidents and falls from the various stands, some of which caused serious injury. In fact, 72 people were treated by the ambulance operators during the afternoon, with three cases requiring admittance to hospital. Pity poor Andrew Kelly, 28, from Clifton Hill, who missed the match after falling out of a stand. Or Alfred Williams, 60, from Collingwood, also a casualty in the crush, suffering a broken leg and ending up in hospital.

Still, there were plenty of people who did get to enjoy their afternoon. Three trucks from Orbost, including one that was carrying 26 people, arrived in Melbourne on the morning of the match. They had travelled "230 miles" to watch a game of football. Well, it wasn't just any old game. People had come from far and wide to see the most important match of the season. The Governor, Lord Huntingfield, was one of them. He was introduced to both teams before the ball was bounced.

Each team was hoping for an omen in its favour. South Melbourne won the toss for the colour of the shorts to be worn, choosing white. Their rationale was simple. All three teams to have won finals that season had worn away 'knicks'. Collingwood coach Jock McHale wasn't worried about that, saying the black shorts "will do us". McHale said it was "even better" that Collingwood had been drawn to have the Melbourne dressingrooms, which he felt were the club's "lucky" rooms at the MCG. But McHale had more than luck on his side. He believed he had the strategy to beat South Melbourne. Part of that was to play Jack Ross at centre half-back on Laurie Nash. Ross was giving away 6cm and 13kg, but would play the game of his life. Nash was still dangerous for most of the game, but Ross negated his impact. And McHale used Keith Fraser, a big man at 183cm, on the South Melbourne resting rovers. It worked, too.

Collingwood was the first team to emerge from the rooms "some minutes before the start". The players were eager to get out there. They watched from the boundary line as the Footscray seconds disposed of Melbourne. South Melbourne followed a few minutes later, its appearance generating a roar of support marginally better than that afforded the Magpies. It was agreed that South "seemed to be the choice of the unbiased public".

Jack Bisset, captain-coach of the Bloods, who had declared after the 1935 Grand Final that he was "tired of football", had refocused his attention towards beating Collingwood this time around. He won the toss and had no hesitation choosing the Richmond end, to where a moderate breeze was blowing. But South Melbourne's aggressive football in the opening term counted against them rather than helped them. This handed the Magpies the first chance to play the ball rather than engage in physical contests, while the Bloods appeared to be more intent on going for the man.

One observer said: "South, the heavier side, definitely employed shock tactics at the outset... the Magpies did not seem to retaliate." Instead, Collingwood used this to its advantage, and was able to steal an early break by kicking the first two goals of the match. The first came within the opening minute. *The Sporting Globe* described it: "A free to (Percy) Bowyer was the opening incident, followed by a free to (Leo) Morgan. A driving kick (went) to Knight, who marked cleverly and Collingwood were a goal ahead." Knight's mark was a spectacular one, "over four players", and the goal was a fitting reward. Soon after, South Melbourne full-back Ron Hillis was penalised for fouling Todd "two yards from the line and an easy second goal appeared for the Magpies." It was precisely the sort of start that McHale had hoped for.

As the first quarter wore on, South Melbourne's forays into the forward line became more frequent. Nash, whose father had captained Collingwood a generation earlier, kicked South Melbourne's first goal of the game, a fine snap orchestrated by good work up the field from Austin Robertson. Robertson, a one-time world sprint champion, showed a glimpse of his exceptional pace a few minutes later when he produced "champagne football" with a fine running goal to level the scores.

Alby Pannam, in his fourth season, and chasing back-to-back flags as his father Charlie had attained in 1902-03, was making an enormous impact on the game. Carrying a famous black and white name, the cheeky forward-rover booted the club's third goal from a "left foot shot". The Magpies had hit the lead again, thanks to the clever play of Pannam and the blistering work from centreman Marcus Whelan. But the Bloods kept coming, with Roy Moore kicking their third goal after a passage of play that involved Herb Matthews and Nash "without Collingwood touching the ball".

The Magpies clung to a two-point lead at the first change, but the difference could have been greater. One report suggested: "Collingwood were the more effective team, and their open system contrasted with the flurried movement of South, who lacked sense of position in attack and understanding in other parts of the field."

Still, the contest remained a close one, and South Melbourne attacked from the outset in the second term. In the first minute of resuming, the Bloods pulled the lead back off the Magpies. Umpire Blackburn, according to *The Sporting Globe*, "allowed Moore to mark and goal for South, although Nash had been fouled further out". Soon after Maurie Johnson "snapped full points with a marvellous left foot snap from the boundary" to increase their lead. It was said that South Melbourne had been "improving in their cohesive play and clapping on more pace." For a time, Collingwood was simply trying to keep up.

Pannam bobbed up when he was required to reply with a much-needed goal for the Magpies, "helped by Morgan and Todd" after a South Melbourne kick-out went astray. It came after a series of wasted opportunities from Collingwood, which had too many players missing relatively easy chances at goal. Todd was the chief offender, with nerves wracking his poise, and by midway through the term, he had kicked 1.5 in a frustrating display. Finally Todd found his range again, kicking his second major, and Collingwood's fifth, when he marked a ball from Morgan, largely thanks to the fine work from up the field of Albert Collier.

Pannam, "proving a difficult customer to guard, pushed Collingwood's lead out to 15 points when he posted the club's sixth goal after intercepting a kick-in from Hillis." South was increasingly becoming "rattled". This was further highlighted when Todd ran around his opponent and snapped another goal. Aside from that opening burst at the start of the term, Collingwood had "done most of the attacking for the quarter, and they would have had a winning lead if their forwards had been more accurate." The score-line was clearly in Collingwood's favour at half-time—it was 7.16 (58) to South's 5.7 (37).

But McHale was stressing the point to his players at the long break that it was not enough. He knew the talent and firepower of South would cause his team concern at some stage. It was simply a matter of when. Still, the prospects of a fightback were made all the more difficult when Todd slotted through the opening goal of the third term to stretch the margin out to 27 points. It was suggested that "South could not cope with the scientific football" that McHale's team was playing at that stage.

Then South's "turning point" came. Owen Evans managed to force his way through a pack and scored the Bloods' first goal for the quarter with a "big running drop (kick). The success seemed to put more heart into South, and they tore into the fray with renewed vigour." This was followed by two more goals, to Moore and Pratt, for the term as the Bloods whittled back Collingwood's lead. The margin was only seven points at the last change. It could have even been less, as South was deep in attack when the three-quarter time bell sounded. This set the scene for a dramatic and desperate final half-hour.

With the pain of the previous year still burning, South Melbourne cut the difference to one point after just a few minutes of play in the premiership-deciding quarter. It came from Johnson, and the Bloods appeared to be finishing fast over the tiring and less experienced Magpies. Gamely, the Collingwood defenders stopped several more South Melbourne sorties in attack. The Bloods kept coming, but the Magpie backmen kept repelling.

It was somehow fitting that, when the game was absolutely in the balance, Pannam once more produced some magic. He kicked a beautiful left-foot snap goal in the middle stages of the term to give the Magpies a bit of breathing space. Better still, he followed it up with another, his fifth goal, to all but lock in the premiership. He was best afield, and proved "as elusive and slippery as an eel... (he) ran in and out of packs with the smoothness and certainty of water." Pannam had combined perfectly with Todd, who had overcome his early jitters in front of goal to finish the game with four goals. Coventry sat helplessly in the stands, but Todd's performance gave real hope for the future.

At the other end of the ground, brilliant full-back Jack Regan restricted Pratt, keeping him to only three goals. It meant Pratt had kicked only six goals in his three games against Collingwood for the season—the same as he had kicked in the semi-final against Collingwood a year earlier. The efforts of Jack Ross to restrict Nash also proved crucial for the Magpies.

When the final bell sounded, with the ball in Albert Collier's hands, Collingwood had won by 11 points, after what had been a tight, tense afternoon. It was a struggle, but it had still provided some grand highlights, particularly from Collingwood.

If Collingwood's older brigade had played a massive role in the previous year's Grand Final win, in terms of best players, in the 1936 play-off there was a distinct changing of the guard. Pannam was best afield. Others of the new breed to impress were Whelan, Kyne and Todd; all would play roles in the club's chase for more success in the coming years.

But Fitzroy's Brownlow Medal winner Denis 'Dinny' Ryan, writing in *The Argus,* claimed the greatest strength of the Magpies was the fact that it was always difficult to limit the club's best players to just a handful. He wrote: "Each seemed to realise he was only one of a team, and to keep that fact in mind rather than to seek momentary glory for himself alone. That is as it should be. And I think that is the supreme lesson that Collingwood, best disciplined of all the clubs, and deservedly premiers 1936, has to offer the rest of the League teams."

Jack Worrall, in *The Australasian,* wrote: "Men must be made of iron to stand the modern method in a Grand Final. The high marking was capital, the handling and cleverness of Collingwood's small men something out of the common, the team work excellent, and the knowledge and judgement supreme. The game was won by team work and brains, and every man pulled his weight—not so the losing team."

There were some joyous scenes at the conclusion of the match. *The Herald* reported: "While the final bell was still ringing, supporters were crowded round the entrance to the Collingwood dressingroom for a chance to congratulate members of the team. The combined effort of several officials was not sufficient to prevent hundreds of spectators forcing their way inside (the rooms)." Witnesses could have been forgiven for thinking this was the club's first pennant, given the fervour with which it was celebrated. It was Collingwood's 11th VFL premiership, and the sixth pennant in 10 seasons.

President Harry Curtis, who was also celebrating his 43rd birthday that afternoon, addressed the players in the rooms after the game. He said: "The traditional fighting spirit of Collingwood carried the club through to its brilliant win today—the spirit enabled you (the players) to go out and defeat a strong side in South Melbourne, in spite of the fact that the latter had an average height advantage of two inches and was more than a stone heavier compared with our size."

Size clearly didn't necessarily equate with success. There were handshakes galore, and plenty of backslapping. The biggest cheer came when Curtis finished his victory recitation by announcing that "a supporter of the club" who preferred to remain anonymous, but whom everyone knew, had donated 100 pounds to be divided between the members of the team. There was also the promise of 25 pounds each to coach McHale and Harry Collier.

For Collier, the gift from legendary club benefactor John Wren was a bonus. His birthday wish from a few days earlier had been confined solely to winning another premiership. It had nothing to do with money as any extra form of motivation. Harry just wanted a sixth premiership, as did his younger and equally important brother Albert. And they got it. Their mother threw a party at the family home in Northcote that night "to celebrate her son's birthday and the premiership". It wasn't as riotous as the celebrations 12 months earlier, but the players and officials had a great night. And when another birthday cake was presented to him that night, Harry Collier did not hesitate. He dared to dream of more wishes, more flags, and more glories.

1936 COLLINGWOOD

PREMIER'S SEASON

COLLINGWOOD: 1936

ROUND ONE May 2
COLLINGWOOD 15.14 (104)
HAWTHORN 12.11 (83)
Best: Collingwood – Kyne, H.Collier, Woods, Doherty, Regan, Fraser, Bowyer, Froude.
Goals: Collingwood – Kyne 5, Doherty 4, G.Coventry 3, A.Pannam 2, Todd.
Crowd: 14,000 at Glenferrie Oval

ROUND TWO May 9
COLLINGWOOD 16.12 (108)
RICHMOND 10.12 (72)
Best: Collingwood – G.Coventry, L.Murphy, Whelan, H.Collier, Morgan, Knight, Regan.
Goals: Collingwood – G.Coventry 8, H.Collier 3, Knight 2, Kyne, A.Pannam, Doherty.
Crowd: 26,500 at Victoria Park

ROUND THREE May 16
COLLINGWOOD 25.14 (164)
FITZROY 12.12 (84)
Best: Collingwood – A.Pannam, G.Coventry, Regan, Woods, H.Collier, A.Collier, Kyne.
Goals: Collingwood – G.Coventry 8, A.Pannam 7, Stackpole 3, H.Collier 3, Doherty, L.Murphy, Morgan, Whelan.
Crowd: 20,000 at Brunswick St Oval

ROUND FOUR May 23
COLLINGWOOD 20.17 (137)
ESSENDON 13.10 (88)
Best: Collingwood – Regan, Bowyer, G.Coventry, Kyne, Fraser, A.Collier, H.Collier.
Goals: Collingwood – G.Coventry 6, Kyne 4, Doherty 3, H.Collier 3, Dowling 2, A.Pannam, Carter.
Crowd: 11,000 at Victoria Park

ROUND FIVE May 30
COLLINGWOOD 16.17 (113)
ST KILDA 9.14 (68)
Best: Collingwood – Doherty, Knight, Ross, Bowyer, Kyne, Regan, G.Coventry, Whelan.
Goals: Collingwood – G.Coventry 6, Doherty 5, Kyne 2, Riley, H.Collier, Morgan.
Crowd: 28,000 at Victoria Park

ROUND SIX June 6
COLLINGWOOD 12.16 (88)
CARLTON 11.16 (82)
Best: Collingwood – Kyne, Froude, Morgan, Woods, A.Pannam, L.Murphy, Doherty.
Goals: Collingwood – A.Pannam 3, Knight 2, Doherty 2, G.Coventry 2, Bowyer, Riley, Kyne.
Crowd: 46,000 at Princes Park

ROUND SEVEN June 13
COLLINGWOOD 14.5 (89)
MELBOURNE 9.13 (67)
Best: Collingwood – Carmody, Regan, Bowyer, Whelan, Todd, Knight, A.Pannam.
Goals: Collingwood – G.Coventry 4, Knight 2, Kyne 2, A.Pannam 2, Doherty 2, H.Collier, Morgan.
Crowd: 11,250 at Victoria Park

ROUND EIGHT June 20
COLLINGWOOD 16.10 (106)
FOOTSCRAY 11.13 (79)
Best: Collingwood – A.Collier, Kyne, Doherty, Regan, Dowling, A.Pannam, Whelan.
Goals: Collingwood – Doherty 4, G.Coventry 4, Dowling 3, Knight 2, A.Pannam, Woods, H.Collier.
Crowd: 11,500 at the Western Oval

ROUND NINE June 27
COLLINGWOOD 17.19 (121)
NORTH MELBOURNE 8.7 (55)
Best: Collingwood – Whelan, Fraser, G.Coventry, L.Murphy, Doherty, A.Collier, H.Collier.
Goals: Collingwood – G.Coventry 5, Doherty 3, Bowyer 2, H.Collier 2, Dowling, Kyne, Knight, A.Pannam, Stackpole.
Crowd: 11,500 at Victoria Park

ROUND TEN July 11
COLLINGWOOD 12.19 (91)
SOUTH MELBOURNE 14.18 (102)
Best: Collingwood – Ross, Froude, H.Collier, Kyne, A.Pannam, Stackpole, Whelan.
Goals: Collingwood – A.Pannam 3, Kyne 3, G.Coventry 3, H.Collier 2, Doherty.
Crowd: 25,800 at Victoria Park

ROUND ELEVEN July 18
COLLINGWOOD 11.9 (75)
GEELONG 13.15 (93)
Best: Collingwood – Whelan, Bowyer, Todd, A.Pannam, Kyne, Carmody, Ross.
Goals: Collingwood – Kyne 3, A.Pannam 2, Todd 2, Gibson, Fraser, Boyall, G.Coventry.
Crowd: 10,000 at Corio Oval

ROUND TWELVE July 25
COLLINGWOOD 14.18 (102)
HAWTHORN 6.12 (48)
Best: Collingwood – Fraser, Stackpole, Fricker, H.Collier, G.Coventry, Morgan.
Goals: Collingwood – G.Coventry 5, Bowyer 2, A.Pannam 2, Kyne, Jones, Fricker, H.Collier, Doherty.
Crowd: 7,000 at Victoria Park

ROUND THIRTEEN August 1
COLLINGWOOD 14.12 (96)
RICHMOND 11.14 (80)
Best: Collingwood – Knight, Crowe, Regan, Woods, G.Coventry, Carmody, A.Pannam.
Goals: Collingwood – G.Coventry 5, A.Pannam 2, Carmody 2, Carter 2, H.Collier 2, Doherty.
Crowd: 26,000 at Punt Road Oval

ROUND FOURTEEN August 8
COLLINGWOOD 13.12 (90)
FITZROY 11.8 (74)
Best: Collingwood – Todd, Morgan, Dowling, A.Pannam, Carter, H.Collier, Knight.
Goals: Collingwood – Todd 5, Carter 4, A.Pannam 2, Stackpole, Riley.
Crowd: 16,400 at Victoria Park

ROUND FIFTEEN August 15
COLLINGWOOD 14.16 (100)
ESSENDON 8.10 (58)
Best: Collingwood – A.Pannam, Regan, Crowe, Stackpole, Fraser, L.Murphy, Fricker.
Goals: Collingwood – A.Pannam 5, Stackpole 3, Kyne 3, Whelan, Todd, Carter.
Crowd: 9,000 at Windy Hill

ROUND SIXTEEN August 22
COLLINGWOOD 14.13 (97)
ST KILDA 11.11 (77)
Best: Collingwood – Woods, L.Murphy, Carmody, Ross, Kyne, Todd, A.Collier.
Goals: Collingwood – Todd 4, Kyne 3, Stackpole 3, Doherty, Bowyer, H.Collier, A.Pannam.
Crowd: 14,300 at the Junction Oval

ROUND SEVENTEEN August 29
COLLINGWOOD 13.11 (89)
CARLTON 13.12 (90)
Best: Collingwood – A.Collier, Stackpole, Carmody, Bowyer, Knight, Whelan, Kyne.
Goals: Collingwood – H.Collier 3, Knight 2, Whelan 2, Kyne 2, A.Pannam 2, Todd, A.Collier.
Crowd: 30,100 at Victoria Park

ROUND EIGHTEEN September 5
COLLINGWOOD 11.18 (84)
MELBOURNE 9.13 (67)
Best: Collingwood – A.Pannam, Froude, Regan, Stackpole, Woods, Crowe, L.Murphy.
Goals: Collingwood – Knight 3, L.Murphy 3, Doherty 2, Kyne, H.Collier, A.Pannam.
Crowd: 21,648 at the MCG

PREMIER'S FINALS

SECOND SEMI-FINAL September 19
COLLINGWOOD	12.18 (90)
SOUTH MELBOURNE	10.17 (77)

Best: Collingwood – Whelan, A.Pannam, Morgan, H.Collier, Woods, Froude, Bowyer.
Goals: Collingwood – Kyne 3, Knight 3, A.Pannam 2, Doherty 2, Riley, Stackpole.
Crowd: 55,573 at the MCG

GRAND FINAL October 3
COLLINGWOOD	3.6	7.16	8.19	11.23	(89)
SOUTH MELBOURNE	3.4	5.7	8.12	10.18	(78)

Best: Collingwood – A.Pannam, Whelan, Kyne, Carmody, Todd, Fraser.
Goals: Collingwood – A.Pannam 5, Todd 4, Knight, Kyne.
Crowd: 74,091 at the MCG

GRAND FINAL LINE-UPS

COLL	B:	J.Crowe	J.Regan	B.Woods
STH M	F:	M.Johnson	B.Pratt	R.Moore
COLL	HB:	J.Ross	K.Fraser	F.Froude
STH M	HF:	O.Evans	L.Nash	S.Dineen
COLL	C:	J.Carmody	M.Whelan	L.Morgan
STH M	C:	H.Matthews	L.Thomas	J.Reid
COLL	HF:	L.Riley	P.Kyne	V.Doherty
STH M	HB:	B.Faul	J.Graham	J.Cleary
COLL	F:	J.Knight	R.Todd	A.Pannam
STH M	B:	L.Richards	R.Hillis	J.Austin
COLL	R:	A.Collier	P.Bowyer	H.Collier (capt)
STH M	R:	J.Bisset (capt)	D.Kelleher	A.Robertson
COLL	Reserve: K.Stackpole		**Coach:** Jock McHale	
STH M	Reserve: C.Pettiona		**Coach:** Jack Bisset	

SNAPSHOT

Win-loss record: 17-3

Highest score: 25.14 (164), round 3, v Fitzroy.

Greatest winning margin: 80 points, round 3, v Fitzroy.

Lowest score: 11.9 (75), round 11, v Geelong.

Greatest losing margin: 18 points, round 11, v Geelong.

Most goals by a player in a game: 8, Gordon Coventry, round 2, v Richmond; round 3, v Fitzroy.

Most consecutive wins: 9

Most consecutive losses: 2

Club awards: Best & Fairest: Jack Regan; Leading goalkicker: Gordon Coventry (60 goals).

Putting it into perspective:
Back-to-back premierships once again for the Magpies; their 20th Grand Final appearance resulted in their 11th flag and stamped the club as the team of the decade. Since 1927 they had played in six Grand Finals for six flags.

1936

		P	W	L	D	%	Pts
1	South Melb (2)	18	16	2		118.5	64
2	Collingwood (1)	18	15	3		135.6	60
3	Carlton (4)	18	12	6		124.8	48
4	Melbourne (3)	18	12	6		118.8	48
5	Geelong	18	11	7		125.8	44
6	Richmond	18	10	8		107.9	40
7	St Kilda	18	9	9		96.1	36
8	Essendon	18	6	12		85.1	24
9	Hawthorn	18	6	12		80.9	24
10	Footscray	18	5	13		86.5	20
11	North Melb	18	4	14		75.9	16
12	Fitzroy	18	2	16		68.9	8

(18 home and away rounds)

PLAYERS USED

COLLINGWOOD	GUERNSEY	GAMES	GOALS
Bowyer, Percy	3	20	6
Boyall, Marcus	24	3	1
Carmody, Jack	4	18	2
Carter, George	5	7	8
Collier, Albert	2	14	1
Collier, Harry	1	20	24
Coventry, Gordon	6	13	60
Crowe, Jim	34	13	0
Doherty, Vin	7	20	33
Dowling, Ron	23	10	6
Fraser, Keith	9	18	1
Fricker, Pat	25	8	1
Froude, Fred	8	16	0
Gibson, Reg	10	2	1
Jones, Harry	28	2	1
Knight, Jack	12	15	18
Kyne, Phonse	12	19	36
McCann, Ron	35	1	0
Morgan, Leo	13	12	3
Murphy, Len	14	18	4
Pannam, Alby	21	19	45
Regan, Jack	16	19	0
Riley, Lou	17	6	4
Ross, Jack	18	18	0
Ryan, Alan	33	5	0
Stackpole, Keith	19	15	12
Todd, Ron	20	12	18
Whelan, Marcus	21	19	4
Woods, Bervin	22	18	1

**GEELONG 18.14 (122) d
COLLINGWOOD 12.18 (90)**

AS IT SHOULD BE PLAYED

The skills, the spirit, the magic of this match will be talked about as long as footy makes fans' hearts soar. By JOHN HARMS

FOR MANY years, the 1937 Grand Final between Geelong and Collingwood was considered the greatest game of Australian football of all time. It was remembered as an epic contest which helped lift the reputation of the code—from a game played by rough-and-tumble oafs compelled by their base passions to do whatever it took to win, to a grand and glorious expression of pure endeavour which could elevate the soul. This match entered the public memory not as an expression of thuggery and corruption, but as footy-art, where the grace and beauty of the play, and the pure spirit of the contest that it conjured, seemed to highlight that, even in Australia, people yearned for the transcendent.

For a moment those who had never understood what the fuss was about did. On the genoa couches of the leafy suburbs, the sober classes were invited to see in football those things which they sought in opera and the plays of Shakespeare. It took football to alter the direction of their gaze which so often had been back, cringingly, towards the old country. And the football was a tram-ride down the road at the cricket ground. It was theirs. Local. Somehow in their image.

That it was between Geelong and Collingwood was not inconsequential.

Formed in 1859, Geelong was the second oldest football club. It was the established club of a rural city hell-bent on showing that it was no poor cousin to Melbourne. Geelong had dominated football in the early years of the VFA, winning seven of nine premierships between 1878 and 1886. Football was a key part of its identity.

Melburnians joked about 'Sleepy Hollow'. But the locals were proud of their city and its achievements. As the good folk of Geelong prepared to celebrate their centenary in 1938, they comforted themselves in the knowledge that they were a people who believed in progress: in science and technology, in mechanised industry, in transport and communication, all of which served their growing economy. They had built silos and factories, and wharves to export their goods; they had built churches and schools; they had developed a culture of entertainment and the arts. And they loved their football team, the success of which, they believed, was the strongest indication of what a fine people they were.

Collingwood, the feared reigning premier of 1935 and 1936, was the club of the slum suburb; the club of the battlers who had done it harder than most through the Depression years. Collingwood had no grammar school, nor did its finest head off to Oxford. Its principal benefactor, John Wren, had started life as a punter and a bookie. Collingwood had its own way.

The Collingwood Football Club took great pride in its history. In less than half a century it had enjoyed phenomenal success, the key to which was a culture built on loyalty, solidarity, and determination.

At Collingwood the sense of historical continuity was profound. Jock McHale had been coach since 1912. He was highly successful, and much-loved. His team included Gordon 'Nuts' Coventry who had been kicking goals for the Magpies since 1920. Coventry was only the second full-forward at Collingwood since 1907, Dick Lee having held down the position before him. The tough Collier brothers, Harry and Albert, still dominated at Victoria Park. And Harold Rumney was back from a season in the VFA as captain-coach of Northcote.

Geelong had Reg Hickey, regarded universally as the most influential man in the club's history. Having grown up on a farm in Cressy, Hickey first played with Geelong in 1926, quickly establishing himself at centre half-back, and later at full-back. He was the rock on which the Geelong defence was built; reliable, inspiring confidence in those around him. Strong and athletic, he could hold his position in marking contests, but was never dour. He would often dash clear from defence to set up Geelong attacks with his trademark drop kicks.

He was a natural leader, on and off the field. Bob Davis (whom Hickey coached to the 1951 and '52 premierships) once said: "[At Geelong] there were none higher or more respected. He was a very moral man, and this shone through in everything he did."

Hickey, who was from the same family as Father John Brosnan (parish priest, Pentridge Prison chaplain, champion of working-class politics, and fanatical Geelong supporter), was an elder statesman wherever he was involved. He had coached Geelong in 1932 before the committee unburdened the young man of the responsibility by appointing Arthur Coghlan for two years and then Percy Parratt for 1935. In 1936 former Collingwood full-back Charlie Dibbs was made non-playing coach. No doubt he brought some of the Magpies' approach with him. But Dibbs had been injured with what was termed 'serious spinal concussion' in the 1935 Grand Final and ongoing effects of the injury surfaced. He was forced to resign after seven matches. Hickey took over as captain-coach again and almost led an improving Geelong side towards the 1936 finals. They finished fifth, one game out of the four.

Soon after the 1936 season, the Geelong premiership team of 1886 held a 50-year reunion. It was a memorable time. There was always a sense in Geelong that football was important, and Hickey, who had a feeling for people and what mattered to them, knew that only too well. He believed he had a team that could contend for a premiership the next season.

Hickey wanted his team to be as prepared for the new season as it could possibly be. He always placed a strong emphasis on fitness, or as it was sometimes called in those days 'wind'. Defender Tom Arklay claimed the coach was a 'fitness fanatic'. The squad included tremendous pace. Local Chilwell boy Jack Grant, who played on a half-back flank, went on to win the Stawell Gift in 1938. Other fast and skilful players included centreman Fred Hawking, the classy and skilful wingman Angie Muller and second rover Jack Metherell from Western Australia.

In those years Geelong was often drawn to play Collingwood in the first round of the season. In 1937 Geelong travelled to Victoria Park where the players stood and watched as Collingwood unfurled its premiership flag. It was what being a Collingwood person was all about. Lou Richards, whose uncle Alby Pannam played for the Pies, was a Collingwood man through and through. In *Boots and All* he wrote:

> I was born into a Magpie family, and reared in the Magpie nest, kicking tin cans and paper footballs around the streets of Collingwood and Abbotsford... maybe this helped to breed the type of footballer for which Collingwood is typically famous... to get a kick was an art in itself because it was no holds barred.

Richards may well have been there as a 14-year-old to watch his Magpies beat Geelong by a couple of goals. On the same day Melbourne, a likely improver, beat Richmond easily.

The Cats lost in round three at Windy Hill and their mediocre start to the season continued when they were beaten by Richmond at Punt Road in round six. From that moment on they strung together a series of wins against the weaker clubs and in round 12 at Corio Oval handled Collingwood without much trouble.

In those days about a third of the people of Geelong went to the footy. One of them was seven-year-old Geoffrey Blainey, now an eminent Australian historian. He remembered the beautiful drop kicking especially of 'old Reg Hickey'.

The players all looked old to a young boy.

Blainey recalled:

> Many players in those Days had no teeth, and that gave them an old man appearance as they grinned through their gums. Geelong had a ruckman named George Dougherty, and we saw him one summer day at Barwon Heads fishing from the rocks. He looked quite young away from the football ground, and we stared at him in puzzlement: 'Are you George Dougherty?' He gave us some fish he had caught. No fish ever tasted as sweet.

Visiting teams found it near-impossible to win at Corio Oval. Some Collingwood blokes said it was because of the onion weed sown in to the turf. It was very slippery when it was wet and there was a view that only Geelong players knew how to stand up on it.

Geelong extended its unbeaten run to 12 matches by the end of the home and away season. It thrashed Richmond in round 17 at Corio Oval, holding the Tigers to just a handful of behinds after half-time. Meanwhile Collingwood faltered, losing to Melbourne in a high-scoring match at home (which cost it second place on the ladder), and also to Carlton, which was desperately trying to make it in to the final four. Carlton eventually missed out.

And so the four finished Geelong, Melbourne, Collingwood and Richmond.

Collingwood won the first semi-final against Richmond and Geelong was too strong for Melbourne. The Demons were expected to bounce back in the preliminary final. But Collingwood played magnificently, finding the form of its premiership years, to beat them by 10 goals.

The footy community was divided over who was the rightful favourite in the Grand Final. Some looked to the combative style of the Pies; their toughness and finals experience. Others reckoned the pace of Geelong would be too hard for the Pies to contain, as it had been in the round 12 match when Geelong's speedsters found space on Corio. Both had a run to protect: Collingwood was playing for its third flag in a row; Geelong its 14th win.

On paper, Collingwood, though older, had the better-credentialled side, which included the gifted young Ron Todd, in just his third season. Todd, with his high-marking, had added spice to the Pies' forward line, while at the other end of the ground Jack Regan was the meanest of marking full-backs.

Reg Hickey and the Geelong match committee had picked a side with an array of ruckmen and key position players, which, had it not been for the pace of the flankers, looked a little top-heavy. No doubt he understood there was physical work to be done in the clinches.

The Saturday of the Grand Final was sunny and clear; a perfect day for football. And this no doubt encouraged those who had hoped to attend. They came from everywhere. Thousands made their way on the trains from Geelong to Spencer Street and on to the MCG.

By the final quarter of the seconds (actually the preliminary final and a willing affair between Collingwood and Carlton) it was clear a big crowd was in.

Jack Hardiman, a cousin of Les and Peter Hardiman, was relieved to make it to the MCG. A resident of Sydney, he had ridden his push-bike down the Hume Highway for the match. He joined the throng of men and women, crammed in to the stadium, some of whom sat on the turf between the fence and the boundary line, and in one pocket actually on to the playing arena.

It was a wonderful sight: a record crowd of 88,540.

As the players took their positions you could still hear arguments for the merit of both sides. They really were evenly matched. Geelong's hopes were with its classy centre-line: Slack, Hawking and Muller, and in its terrier on-baller Tommy Quinn from Port Adelaide, who had helped the Cats to the 1931 flag. Quinn had become a key leader. They also needed the spring-heeled Les Hardiman to dominate up forward and looked for some of the other marking forwards—Abbott, Dougherty and Evans—to get on the end of a couple. In defence, Hickey went to Coventry ('my old mate', as he called him), and Joe Sellwood was given the toughest task: to keep Ron Todd quiet.

Ruckman Alby 'Leeter' Collier readied himself for battle, his brother Harry at his side. Both had hair parted near the middle and plastered to their heads in the California-Poppy style of the 1930s. Both, like well-named down-pit miners, looked old before their time. Geelong's two-pronged ruck attack was made up of Peter Hardiman and Jack Evans, who may have learnt something of ruck play from Roy Cazaly as a young fella at Minyip. At their feet was Quinn.

Quinn was quick to win the footy and move it on to Pixie Coles who put the first goal on the board. But the Pies retaliated. Todd was on fire, making space, flying for marks, and generally giving Sellwood a bath. After a mark and goal, he again got away, passing to Coventry for another. The Cats looked nervous and unsure. Harry Collier won the footy and again the Pies went forward for yet another goal. When the Cats attacked Regan outpointed Hardiman who was not being helped by Geelong's poor kicking. The Cats looked anxious. 'We were walking on air,' Tommy Arklay remembered.

In no time the score was six goals to one and the crowd was disappointed. In those days a young Manning Clark barracked for Geelong (he switched to Carlton after the war). The emerging historian and writer sat in the stand with his father, and brother Russell. "This is disgraceful," Russell yelled. "I've had enough."

In his disappointment Russell, studying to be an Anglican clergyman, stormed off. 'Come off it,' his companions admonished him, just as the Cats put a score on the board, before Quinn, who was having a fierce battle with the Collingwood rovers, got clear and found big Evans for a goal on quarter-time.

As the players changed ends, Hickey knew the situation was grim. Regan and Todd, at opposite ends of the ground, were completely on top. Popular mythology will tell you that Hickey 'turned his team around *at three-quarter time*, putting the backs into the forward line, and the forwards into the back line'. That is not true.

Hickey made major changes *at quarter-time*. He moved Les Hardiman to centre half-back on Todd (Hickey later said Hardiman wasn't thrilled with the idea), he moved Dougherty to full-forward and Sellwood to the forward pocket. He gave a number of his players a run in the ruck, including Gordon Abbott who had previously lined up at centre half-forward. When Jack Evans came off the ball he also spent time at full-forward where it was hoped he'd pull down a mark or two.

In those days players were encouraged to maintain their positions, so the key moves had to work. At the start of the second quarter Collingwood attacked again, but missed with a series of shots before Phonse Kyne marked and goaled for the Pies to lead by 27 points. At that point, the Cats seemed to settle, and the pattern of play changed. In the perfect conditions the game had been played at a cracking pace, which was starting to work to the favour of Geelong. Les Hardiman spoiled Todd consistently, while Hickey remained solid, and the Cats' little men, led by Quinn, mopped up well, running the football out of the busy Collingwood forward line and finding teammates up the ground. The Cats poured on the pressure. The 'tenacious hands of Jack Evans ripped the ball away from Regan' for a fine mark and goal, followed by goals to Coles, Metherell (doing well in a pocket and on the ball), and Coles again. Sellwood goaled and the Cats were within a kick at half-time.

The third quarter was an absolute beauty, with the football being swept from end to end. When Evans marked (the most spectacular grab of the day) and kicked truly the Cats had hit the front. Fans roared for both sides. Jack Grant, the flash, won possession and tore through the middle of the ground, before passing to Hawking, to Quinn, and on to Coles who eluded four opponents before running in to an open goal.

Collingwood tired. Fred Froude did all he could to stem the tide, and Regan battled on, but the Cats looked to have the running. Albert 'Leeter' Collier demanded the boys stick at it. His brother marked and, on three quarter-time, set the ball for his place kick. Harry could restore the lead for the Magpies. His shot just missed. The crowd sighed, and took a breath. The scores were level.

All at the ground were talking about the wonderful skills: the long kicking and high marking, the running and bouncing, the clashes in close.

Spectators sensed they were being treated to a classic sporting contest. And so did the footballers themselves. The game had been played in such good spirit that as they resumed their positions after 'lemons' the players (to a man, folklore says) shook the hands of their opponents.

Geelong had the pace, but, as all of the newspaper reports of the day suggested, it was a matter of which side had the stamina. Again big Leeter Collier tried to lead the way, but the first Collingwood attack was met by the safe marking hands of Geelong's captain-coach. Hickey's pass found Dougherty, on to Slack, who passed to Metherell, who twisted and turned, and with the aid of a crunching shepherd from Abbott, got away, and registered Geelong's 13th goal.

Then Abbott marked and goaled and the Cats were right on top. Les Hardiman, whom Hickey was to later describe as being the best player on the ground that day, was thrashing Todd in a magnificent display at centre half-back. In the famous photo, which shows that athleticism and spectacular leaping is by no means the preserve of recent generations, Hardiman and Todd fly high over Gordon Coventry.

Coventry, on his 36th birthday, did not have one of his better games, although he was not without his chances: he missed a number of opportunities in the second quarter.

Further goals to Wills and Abbott had the Cats well clear and the game reached that point where the dispirited opponent plods in the face of the rampant victor. The Cats nipped here and there, intercepting the tired Collingwood passes, and managed two more goals which allowed their fans throughout the stadium to celebrate.

It had been a thrilling contest with Geelong winning by 32 points. It was a match to be remembered and celebrated, and that is exactly what happened.

In *Boots and All,* published in 1963, Lou Richards wrote a chapter titled 'They still talk of 1937', and, in the years that followed, newspapers, magazines and journals returned to the game. Those articles talk of the pace, the skills (especially the kicking and marking), and the intensity of the contest played in the right spirit.

What followed the match also contributed to the mythology that surrounds the game. Commentators—Ivor Warne-Smith, who had won a premiership and Brownlow Medal while at Melbourne, in *The Argus*; Hec de Lacy of *The Sporting Globe*; the correspondents in the *Geelong Advertiser*—wrote of the match in glowing terms. Plays were heroic. The skills were phenomenal. The ball moved from end to end. The crowd was smitten by the quality of the football. This was civilisation at its high-point!

And that is how the players remembered it: as a match of substance.

Reg Hickey exemplified the attitude that prevailed on the day:

> "I was on my old mate Gordon Coventry who was playing his last game," he recalled. "I've always had a tremendous regard for the Magpies. Players like Nuts, the Colliers and Jack Regan were among my closest mates. Sure they played it hard and they didn't like losing, but they never squealed, and as far as I was concerned, we were always the best of mates after the toughest game. Collingwood's formula for success—its determination, team work and club spirit—are things I have always tried to copy."

That sort of respect among players must also have contributed to the nature of the contest.

Geelong had won, and after receiving the Collingwood officials in the dressingrooms, they thought about returning home. Just as they had been in 1931, the players were met by a throng at the train station, and to that was added the din of car horns. The St Augustine's Band was there to lead the procession up the hill to the City Hall again.

But this time it was Reg Hickey they wanted. "Speech, speech, speech," they cried.

He was their favourite son; a leader in the community.

And he would go on to have a distinguished coaching career and a powerful influence on many around him.

1937 GEELONG

PREMIER'S SEASON

GEELONG: 1937

ROUND ONE April 24
GEELONG 13.12 (90)
COLLINGWOOD 15.16 (106)
Best: Geelong – Hickey, Grant, Mahon, P.Hardiman, Sellwood, Hawking, Metherell.
Goals: Geelong – Metherell 4, Sellwood 3, Quinn 2, Evans 2, Tuckey, Muller.
Crowd: 21,000 at Victoria Park

ROUND TWO May 1
GEELONG 8.12 (60)
CARLTON 6.13 (49)
Best: Geelong – Quinn, L.Hardiman, Hore, Everett, P.Hardiman, Abbott.
Goals: Geelong – Sellwood 2, Metherell 2, Wills 2, Mahon, Evans.
Crowd: 13,600 at Corio Oval

ROUND THREE May 8
GEELONG 14.20 (104)
ESSENDON 18.13 (121)
Best: Geelong – Arklay, P.Hardiman, Metherell, Grant, Everett, Hickey, Sellwood.
Goals: Geelong – Metherell 3, Everett 3, Grant 2, Dougherty 2, L.Hardiman 2, Hore, Wills.
Crowd: 11,000 at Windy Hill

ROUND FOUR May 15
GEELONG 12.20 (92)
SOUTH MELBOURNE 7.11 (53)
Best: Geelong – Sellwood, Hickey, Quinn, Mahon, L.Hardiman, Wills, Abbott.
Goals: Geelong – Sellwood 5, Metherell 2, Wills 2, Quinn, Evans, Dougherty.
Crowd: 11,500 at Corio Oval

ROUND FIVE May 22
GEELONG 21.23 (149)
HAWTHORN 7.11 (53)
Best: Geelong – Quinn, Evans, Hawking, Abbott, Glenister, Metherell, Slack.
Goals: Geelong – Evans 4, Metherell 4, Wills 3, Dougherty 3, Glenister 3, Quinn 2, Abbott, Sellwood.
Crowd: 7,300 at Corio Oval

ROUND SIX May 29
GEELONG 12.6 (78)
RICHMOND 15.19 (109)
Best: Geelong – Abbott, Muller, Arklay, Everett, Glenister, P.Hardiman, Johnson.
Goals: Geelong – Metherell 3, Glenister 3, L.Hardiman 2, Dougherty 2, Abbott, Wills.
Crowd: 17,000 at Punt Road Oval

ROUND SEVEN June 5
GEELONG 16.19 (115)
FITZROY 10.10 (70)
Best: Geelong – L.Hardiman, Hickey, Grant, Johnson, Dougherty, Sellwood.
Goals: Geelong – L.Hardiman 5, Evans 3, Dougherty 3, Helmer 2, Glenister 2, Wills.
Crowd: 8,000 at Corio Oval

ROUND EIGHT June 12
GEELONG 16.13 (109)
ST KILDA 11.15 (81)
Best: Geelong – L.Hardiman, Quinn, Everett, Metherell, Hickey, Hawking.
Goals: Geelong – Metherell 5, Glenister 4, Coles 3, L.Hardiman 2, Dougherty 2.
Crowd: 12,600 at Corio Oval

ROUND NINE June 19
GEELONG 15.14 (104)
MELBOURNE 9.17 (71)
Best: Geelong – Quinn, Sellwood, Hore, Miller, Arklay, Coles, L.Hardiman.
Goals: Geelong – Coles 4, Metherell 3, L.Hardiman 3, Quinn, Glenister, Evans, Helmer, Dougherty.
Crowd: 29,376 at the MCG

ROUND TEN June 26
GEELONG 18.16 (124)
NORTH MELBOURNE 4.14 (38)
Best: Geelong – L.Hardiman, Evans, Quinn, P.Hardiman, Helmer, Everett, Hickey.
Goals: Geelong – L.Hardiman 8, Coles 3, Quinn 2, Hawking 2, Glenister, Evans, Metherell.
Crowd: 9,000 at Corio Oval

ROUND ELEVEN July 3
GEELONG 13.15 (93)
FOOTSCRAY 11.8 (74)
Best: Geelong – Arklay, Muller, Grant, Hawking, L.Hardiman, Sellwood, Glenister.
Goals: Geelong – Glenister 3, L.Hardiman 3, Metherell 3, Dougherty 2, Evans 2.
Crowd: 5,500 at the Western Oval

ROUND TWELVE July 10
GEELONG 13.16 (94)
COLLINGWOOD 10.11 (71)
Best: Geelong – Metherell, P.Hardiman, Coles, Quinn, Arklay, Hickey, Everett.
Goals: Geelong – Metherell 6, Helmer 2, Coles 2, L.Hardiman, Dougherty, Glenister.
Crowd: 16,000 at Corio Oval

ROUND THIRTEEN July 17
GEELONG 13.14 (92)
CARLTON 9.13 (67)
Best: Geelong – Quinn, L.Hardiman, Hickey, Slack, Evans, Abbott, Hore, Sellwood.
Goals: Geelong – L.Hardiman 3, Metherell 2, Quinn 2, P.Hardiman, Glenister, Wills, Coles, Dougherty, Abbott.
Crowd: 15,000 at Princes Park

ROUND FOURTEEN July 24
GEELONG 13.22 (100)
ESSENDON 9.12 (66)
Best: Geelong – Sellwood, Helmer, Quinn, Metherell, Hickey, Abbott, L.Hardiman.
Goals: Geelong – Metherell 4, L.Hardiman 3, Quinn 2, Coles 2, Evans, Dougherty.
Crowd: 8,000 at Corio Oval

ROUND FIFTEEN July 31
GEELONG 16.11 (107)
SOUTH MELBOURNE 13.10 (88)
Best: Geelong – Hawking, Dougherty, L.Hardiman, Glenister, Hickey, Mahon.
Goals: Geelong – L.Hardiman 4, Glenister 4, Evans 3, Metherell 3, Quinn, Coles.
Crowd: 12,000 at the Lake Oval

ROUND SIXTEEN August 14
GEELONG 17.12 (114)
HAWTHORN 13.11 (91)
Best: Geelong – Dougherty, Wills, Everett, Quinn, Evans, Abbott, Metherell, Coles.
Goals: Geelong – Dougherty 5, Metherell 4, Quinn 3, Coles 3, Evans, Foley.
Crowd: 6,000 at Glenferrie Oval

ROUND SEVENTEEN August 21
GEELONG 14.6 (90)
RICHMOND 8.11 (59)
Best: Geelong – Metherell, Evans, Sellwood, Dougherty, Abbott, Muller, Quinn.
Goals: Geelong – Metherell 6, Dougherty 4, L.Hardiman 3, Abbott.
Crowd: 11,500 at Corio Oval

ROUND EIGHTEEN August 28
GEELONG 16.13 (109)
FITZROY 12.9 (81)
Best: Geelong – Dougherty, Dyer, Hawking, Everett, Hickey, Metherell, L.Hardiman.
Goals: Geelong – Dougherty 6, Metherell 4, Abbott 2, L.Hardiman, Glenister, Coles, Wills.
Crowd: 10,000 at Brunswick St Oval

PREMIER'S FINALS

SECOND SEMI-FINAL September 11
GEELONG 19.11 (125)
MELBOURNE 16.17 (113)
Best: Geelong – Quinn, Muller, Metherell, Glenister, Evans, Dougherty, Arklay.
Goals: Geelong – Metherell 8, Dougherty 4, Quinn 2, L.Hardiman 2, Evans, Glenister, Abbott.
Crowd: 47,730 at the MCG

GRAND FINAL September 25
GEELONG 3.3 8.5 12.8 18.14 (122)
COLLINGWOOD 6.3 8.10 11.14 12.18 (90)
Best: Geelong – Muller, Quinn, L.Hardiman, P.Hardiman, Metherell.
Goals: Geelong – Evans 6, Metherell 4, Coles 4, Abbott 2, Sellwood, Wills.
Crowd: 88,540 at the MCG

GRAND FINAL LINE-UPS

GEEL	B:	A.Everett	R.Hickey (capt)	B.Hore
COLL	F:	P.Kyne	G.Coventry	A.Pannam
GEEL	HB:	J.Grant	J.Sellwood	T.Arklay
COLL	HF:	D.Fothergill	R.Todd	V.Doherty
GEEL	C:	L.Slack	F.Hawking	A.Muller
COLL	C:	J.Carmody	M.Whelan	R.Dowling
GEEL	HF:	J.Wills	G.Abbott	C.Coles
COLL	HB:	F.Froude	M.Boyall	J.Ross
GEEL	F:	G.Dougherty	L.Hardiman	J.Metherell
COLL	B:	H.Rumney	J.Regan	B.Woods
GEEL	R:	P.Hardiman	J.Evans	T.Quinn
COLL	R:	A.Collier	P.Bowyer	H.Collier (capt)
GEEL	Reserve: G.Mahon		Coach: Reg Hickey	
COLL	Reserve: Len Murphy		Coach: Jock McHale	

SNAPSHOT

Win-loss record: 17-3

Highest score: 21.23 (149), round 5, v Hawthorn.

Greatest winning margin: 96 points, round 5, v Hawthorn.

Lowest score: 8.12 (60), round 2, v Carlton.

Greatest losing margin: 31 points, round 6, v Richmond.

Most goals by a player in a game: 8, Les Hardiman, round 10, v North Melbourne; Jack Metherell, second semi-final, v Melbourne.

Most consecutive wins: 14

Most consecutive losses: 1 (three times).

Club awards: Best & Fairest: Tommy Quinn; Leading goalkicker: Jack Metherell (71 goals).

Putting it into perspective:
The Cats won their third premiership from four Grand Final appearances. It was their third Grand Final clash with Collingwood and their second flag since 1930. In their two finals they kicked a total of 37 goals, including their highest finals score.

1937

	P	W	L	D	%	Pts
1 Geelong (1)	18	15	3		135.3	60
2 Melbourne (3)	18	15	3		131.2	60
3 Collingwood (2)	18	13	5		129.0	52
4 Richmond (4)	18	11	6	1	108.0	46
5 Carlton	18	11	7		110.9	44
6 St Kilda	18	10	8		101.3	40
7 Fitzroy	18	7	11		93.1	28
8 Hawthorn	18	7	11		84.4	28
9 South Melb	18	6	11	1	89.9	26
10 Essendon	18	5	13		90.6	20
11 Footscray	18	4	14		81.8	16
12 North Melb	18	3	15		64.2	12

(18 home and away rounds)

PLAYERS USED

GEELONG	GUERNSEY	GAMES	GOALS
Abbott, Gordon	7	12	9
Arklay, Tom	8	20	0
Coles, Clive	13	16	24
Dean, Leo	1	3	0
Dougherty, George	6	19	38
Dyer, Bill	2	2	0
Evans, Jack	5	19	27
Everett, Allan	10	18	3
Foley, Ashley	24	2	1
Glenister, Norm	23	16	25
Grant, Jack	14	17	2
Hardiman, Les	25	19	42
Hardiman, Peter	27	16	1
Hawking, Fred	17	19	2
Helmer, Clyde	29	8	5
Hickey, Reg	18	19	0
Hore, Bernie	9	19	1
Howard, Stan	3	3	0
Johnson, Frank	11	2	0
Mahon, Geoff	15	13	1
Metherell, Jack	22	19	71
Miller, Bernie	31	6	0
Mullane, Stan	35	6	0
Muller, Angie	28	17	1
Quinn, Tommy	16	20	5
Sellwood, Joe	21	20	12
Slack, Laurie	4	16	0
Tucker, Neil	20	3	1
Wills, Jim	26	16	13

CARLTON 15.10 (100) d
COLLINGWOOD 13.7 (85)

EAGER BLUES END DROUGHT

First-year coach Brighton Diggins, described by a former teammate as a man on whom the gods smiled, led Carlton out of its long stint of premiership darkness. By HOWARD KOTTON and TONY DE BOLFO

THE late Jim Francis had fond memories of the 1938 Grand Final when he was interviewed in 2002 for the Carlton Football Club's archives. Francis played at centre half-back in a defence that he remembers for being settled. It read: McIntyre, Gill and Park across the full-back line; Anderson, Francis and Chitty across the half-back line.

"It was a record crowd—96,000-plus—and they broke the gate down," Francis said. "They got a big telegraph post, broke the gate down and sat around the white line. We had to jump over the people to get on to the Melbourne ground before we could play the game.

"I can't remember much about the match, but I know I got into a bit of trouble afterwards. I had to face the committee because I didn't go to the Brunswick Town Hall after the Grand Final... my wife Shirl was in St Andrew's Hospital with Jimmy (Francis's son), who had been born a few days before the Grand Final. When I told them that it was 'case dismissed'."

In casting his eye over the team sheet for the 1938 Grand Final, Francis's mind took him back to those happy days.

"Gee whiz, that's bringing back some memories... haven't seen that for a while," he said on seeing the 19 names. "There's Rod McLean," he said of Brock McLean's grandfather. "'Madcap' we used to call him—all he wanted to do was fight.

"And there's Bob Chitty... they used to say, 'How tough's Chitty?' and I'd say, 'You can hit him with an axe, but you'll only blunt the bloody axe'. That was just about right. He [Chitty] would go pretty close to being the toughest player I ever saw, I reckon... although Rod McLean was pretty tough."

Carlton's 15-point Grand Final triumph over Collingwood in the 1938 Grand Final—15.10 (100) to 13.7 (85)—brought an end to the Blues' longest premiership drought—23 seasons since coach Norman 'Hackenschmidt' Clark had completed the September double in 1914-15. In the interim, the Blues had played in finals more often than not, and lost Grand Finals in 1916 (Fitzroy), 1921 and 1932 (both to Richmond).

The leader of the 1938 team was captain-coach Brighton Diggins, who had been a member of the acclaimed "foreign legion" at South Melbourne during the early and mid-1930s. Diggins played at centre half-forward for the Swans during their Grand Final victory in 1933.

Diggins returned to his native Western Australia after falling out with South Melbourne in 1937. The following year South begrudgingly granted him permission to hold talks with Carlton and its newly appointed president Ken Luke. Ultimately, Diggins was appointed as captain-coach to replace Percy Rowe in what would prove a masterstroke.

And yet Diggins might never have led the Blues to the Grand Final. Early into his tenure at Princes Park, he told *The Herald* that he had been offered a job on a trading ship in Northern Australia, but he had knocked it back.

"I gave the offer serious consideration but felt that, having only just taken over the leadership at Carlton, I was obliged to carry on—if only for one season. If the same opportunity comes along after that, I may decide to drop out of football," he told *The Herald*.

On his arrival at Princes Park Diggins demanded greater vigour, beginning on the track. The Carlton hierarchy employed renowned physical educator Herbert Trueman to conduct a series of "physical culture" sessions.

Trueman boasted links with Melbourne University. As *The Herald* reported: "He is an expert in physical culture, and designed the exercises given to Carlton players to strengthen and develop the muscles of the neck, arms, legs and thighs."

By the time Diggins and Trueman had begun to make their mark, Carlton's senior playing core had lost players. Keith Shea had gone Subiaco in the WAFL. Clen Denning (who famously booted six goals with his first six kicks in the VFL) had left for neighbouring Fitzroy and Edward 'Ansell' Clarke, the feisty former Carlton captain and club best and fairest, had taken up duties as senior coach at St Kilda.

Crucially, Harry 'Soapy' Vallence, the 32-year-old full-forward, resolved to continue his career with the Blues despite serious overtures from VFA outfit Williamstown, while Harry Hollingshead, who had gone bush, was persuaded by Diggins to return to Carlton and share ruck responsibilities.

Don McIntyre won Carlton's best and fairest as a defender in 1937. In 2008, when he was interviewed for the Carlton archives, he was the last surviving member of the victorious 1938 team. He said Diggins was "a big fellow with a good personality and very charming smile".

"He was one of the luckiest fellows who ever played. He came from South Melbourne, and captained and coached the premiership team in his first year of '38," McIntyre said.

But for McIntyre, too, this was a case of right place, right time. "As far as I was concerned it was unexpected to get there [to Carlton] and to play as many games as I did... I had a charmed life, no doubt about it," he said.

Daniel Gordon McIntyre was born in Geelong on March 5, 1913, and as a young boy he followed Geelong with great enthusiasm. But after pursuing a career as a schoolteacher in the 1930s, he was posted to Pakenham and it became clear that if he were to play League football, it wouldn't be with his beloved Cats. He was in Pakenham in 1933 and 1934.

Pakenham's president was an avid Carlton supporter, so it was not surprising that a couple of Carlton talent scouts turned up at the old Pakenham ground to entice young McIntyre to move to the 'Big Smoke'. As McIntyre said: "They came up to watch a game and interview me, and that was it. The next thing was an invitation to join them and start training.

"In those days there was zoning and the question of clearances was a bit tricky and caused a fair bit of discussion, but I stepped out of Geelong without any trouble. I got the clearance when it was submitted."

McIntyre joined Carlton in 1935 and made his debut in the drawn round-seven match against Footscray at the Western Oval, wearing the No.2 guernsey later made famous by John Nicholls and Greg Williams.

McIntyre, who went on to play 100 games with the Blues, conceded that Carlton's facilities were hardly palatial in the late 1930s.

"The Heatley Stand was relatively new and the facilities were just fair," he said. "The training room was basically a bare room with a few lockers, tables and what have you, and the bathing facilities were just so-so.

"I well remember being set back the first time I went into the shower room. There was one enormous bath which took either four or five in, and quite often you'd be in there with four or five others because there weren't enough showers to go around. So Carlton's facilities at that time, when compared with today's facilities, were equivalent to a third-rate country club more than anything else."

What made the club, according to McIntyre, was the people. "I was very impressed from day one with the management of Carlton," he said. "They were a remarkably impressive lot of blokes.

"There was Dave Crone, who was in his last year as president then, followed by Ken Luke, who everyone knows was such an outstanding man to be in charge of whatever he undertook; Harry Bell, who was also the assistant librarian at the State Parliamentary Library; Bill Bryson the treasurer; and Horrie Clover, who was still around serving on the committee having recently retired… the whole lot of them were very impressive for someone of my age anyhow.

"The outstanding character really in the public eye, who was at the last stage of his career, was Harry Vallence. He was a remarkable bloke, Harry. He had a very good personality and got on with people very easily indeed, whether on Sunday social occasions down at Mornington or at other social places around. He had a very good singing voice and after a drink or two he could easily be talked into entertaining the people who were there."

Vallence kicked five goals in Carlton's opening-round victory over Hawthorn at Glenferrie, while McIntyre, Frank Gill and Jim Park formed a formidable full-back line.

Another key plank of the backline was Chitty. The tough defender had made a promising start to his VFL career after joining the club from Cudgewa, in the Upper Murray region. Chitty played eight games in his debut season in 1937 and was a regular member of the team by 1938.

The Carltonites squandered many an opportunity against Richmond in the second round at Princes Park, but got up by a point. *The Argus*'s Percy Taylor wrote: "It demonstrated the ability to fight back—a characteristic that has not been ever to the fore in recent years."

Richmond officials considered a protest over the result, arguing that a behind awarded to Carlton during the third quarter was incorrect, but the result stood.

Having thrashed Fitzroy by 51 points at home in round four, Carlton confronted Collingwood at that most unsavoury of football bastions, Victoria Park. The Blues began slowly, trailing by 39 points at half-time, but booted nine goals to three in the third quarter to emerge with a valiant 16-point win.

In the battle of the full-forwards, Ron Todd booted 11 and Vallence eight. Importantly, the Blues boasted a better spread of goalkickers, with Albert 'Mick' Price bobbing up with four goals and Ron 'Socks' Cooper three, including the one to put Carlton ahead late in the contest.

There was a sensational postscript when Blues rover Jack Carney had to be whisked to hospital with a lacerated lip after an incident following the siren. Collingwood captain Harry Collier was later found guilty over the infraction. He was suspended for 14 matches.

The Victoria Park encounter must have taken its toll given that the Blues lowered their colours for the first time in the season, to Melbourne by five points in round six. Vallence kicked seven goals in that match and followed up with another bag of five in the 39-point rout of St Kilda in round seven. The win over the Saints came at a price when Diggins was forced from the fray with a rib complaint.

Ruckman and forward McLean was unavailable for almost two months after breaking his foot in a work-related accident, but key forward Ken Baxter of Werribee—the only man to be a member of Carlton's 1938, 1945 and 1947 premiership teams—proved a most worthy replacement.

After playing a key role in the 27-point win over the Bulldogs in Round 8 of the 1938 season, Baxter was dubbed "the best find of the League football season" by *The Herald's* Harry Marshall.

"Superb marking backed a sound sense of position," Marshall wrote. "He (Baxter) has a great pair of hands, and a rare determination in going for the ball. The packs do not worry him, and he approaches a mark with an attitude of, 'This ball's mine.' Baxter is the type of player who should develop. He has certainly solved the Carlton centre half-forward problem of many seasons' standing."

The victory over Footscray was the second of a six-game winning streak. After the Bulldogs, the Blues defeated North Melbourne (by 50 points at Arden Street), South Melbourne (by 36 points at the Lake Oval), Geelong (by six points at Princes Park) and Hawthorn (by 21 points at Princes Park).

Carlton's form fluctuated between rounds 13 and 17, with three losses from five games. The first loss was a 41-point defeat at the hands of Richmond at Punt Road on an afternoon in which the Tigers' gun forwards Jack Titus and Dick Harris contributed 11 goals.

Carlton centreman Cresswell 'Mickey' Crisp, who had captained Victoria to victory over Western Australia at the MCG the previous Saturday, booted six goals during the six-point victory over Essendon at Princes Park in round 14.

Vallence booted 11 of his team's 19 goals in the 50-point hiding of Fitzroy at Brunswick Street in round 15.

The much anticipated return leg with the Magpies at Princes Park was also Vallence's 200th senior appearance. The great full-forward earlier in the season had received congratulatory letters and telegrams (including one from St Kilda full-forward Wilbur "Bill" Mohr) acknowledging his 700th career goal.

In this match, Vallence's Collingwood counterpart Ron Todd booted seven goals while the Carlton forwards displayed frustrating inaccuracy. Vallence kicked three goals. The 20-point loss took the gloss off his milestone.

In the penultimate home and away contest, Diggins's men again lowered their colours, this time to Melbourne. A victory against St Kilda in the final game was welcome but the aftermath was mired in controversy when Socks Cooper was rubbed out for four matches after being found guilty of striking St Kilda's Doug Rayment. His suspension cost him a place in the Grand Final team.

This was a bitter pill for Cooper, who had featured in all 18 matches during the season.

Carlton advanced to the 1938 Grand Final after accounting for Geelong by 32 points in the second semi-final, with Baxter booting eight. Five goals to three in the second quarter set up the victory. Collingwood then defeated Geelong in the preliminary final to set up a Grand Final between the competition's two greatest rivals.

The Age correspondent captured the moment: "For 23 long years Carlton have been striving desperately to win a League premiership and they can be expected to take more than ordinary physical risks tomorrow to spreadeagle Collingwood—the one side now barring the path to the pennant," he wrote.

Carlton legend Horrie Clover, in penning his preview for *The Herald*, was in no doubt about the result. "Carlton are so fit and confident after heading the League ladder, and played so well to win their semi-final, that I expect them to defeat Collingwood in their League final tomorrow," he wrote. "In my 19 years' association with League football, I have not seen the Dark Blues train more impressively than the 1938 team has this week."

The Grand Final attracted a crowd of 96,486, with many spectators camped in the area between the boundary line and the pickets, as Jim Francis had recalled.

'Forward' wrote in *The Age*: "Just on 10,000 persons jumped the fence and sat four to six deep in the arena. Hundreds of persons fainted in the packed 'outer' crowd, and a few were taken to hospital when the fence collapsed on one spot, severely gashing the hands of people who fell beneath the weight of hundreds pressing forward.

"Just before the great game opened the ground authorities shut the gates to prevent further accidents. This led to an angry outburst by hundreds who arrived late, and scores attempted to storm their way into the Melbourne Cricket Club reserve.

"One gatekeeper was severely buffeted but held the crowd back 'til a number of police constables arrived. Later, other members of the outer crowd jumped the fence leading to the MCC area, and the police were again called into action."

At the same time, the correspondent heaped praise on the faithful.

"On the whole, however, the crowd behaved splendidly, the thousands on the arena who encroached over the boundary line sitting as tightly packed as possible to enable boundary play to proceed," he wrote.

"It was an extraordinary sight and one that dictated that in time to come those ancient wooden grandstands must inevitably give way to an extension of the magnificent £100,000 concrete grandstand completed last season. Accommodation for a crowd of 120,000 is badly needed."

The decision to grant the 1956 Olympic Games to Melbourne precipitated the construction of more concrete grandstands and indeed by 1970, the next time Carlton and Collingwood clashed in a Grand Final, the MCG could—although it was a tight squeeze—accommodate those 120,000 people.

McIntyre's recollections also reflect the mayhem: "The older southern stand stretched around to Bay 14 or 15 at the time, and then there was quite a lot of standing room. In this particular game, the Grand Final against Collingwood, the ground was closed at half-past one because it was chock-a-block full.

"There were 97,000 there and the pressure of the people standing in the area at the sou'-west corner where the opening was for the groundsmen and the like to go on, broke the fence. And quite a number—hundreds or thousands or so—were distributed around the outer side between the boundary line and the fence. The crowd was so thick that when you got in through the members area there it was almost like playing a quarter or two before you even got to the dressingroom to get in."

Whereas Baxter was the difference with his eight goals in the second semi-final, his role in the Grand Final was to quell the influence of Collingwood's playmaking full-back Jack Regan. He kicked three goals despite playing a negative role.

Carlton half-back Jack Hale, who was forced from the fray in the second semi-final by a bad knock to the head, played a pivotal role in the Grand Final by nullifying the Magpie champion Des Fothergill.

The 1938 Grand Final was the last hurrah for Vallence and indeed for fullback Jim Park. The latter would be killed in action while serving with the armed forces in New Guinea in 1943. Baxter's third goal assured the Blues of victory.

McIntyre said: "My memory of the game itself is pretty dim in the main. I've thought about it on a number of occasions and the only impression I have is that there was nothing close or exciting about it, as it was around about the two to three-goal margin most of the time and that's the way it was in the end. On recollection it wasn't a very high standard game at all."

Carlton led at every change to win by 15 points.

And what of the festivities?

"A bit tame," he said. "I didn't drink in those days, so that was one thing. I know they had a couple of entertainers doing the usual things of singing and telling stories... and Harry Vallence was the only one worth listening to when he and a couple of other players got up to sing a song or two.

"By and large it didn't impress me too much, but of course when you're a non-drinker in that sort of atmosphere it colours the outlook a little bit—and also, you're a bit weary after having played the game and going on towards midnight after that."

Which probably is why McIntyre can probably relate the following tale of Brighton Diggins on Grand Final night: "I remember at the premiership dinner in the old Hotel Argus in Elizabeth Street we were all seated and ready to start eating and there was no Brighton around.

"After about 10 minutes we saw him coming to the door and holding up both hands full of notes... he'd been collecting whatever he could from his betting, at double-figure odds, before the season ever started.

"He was very, very lucky that bloke."

Diggins was the Carlton captain-coach for two more years, for finishes of fifth both seasons. He was limited to only four games in 1940 because of injury, and retired as captain and coach after the season. He had played 65 games for South Melbourne and 31 for Carlton, and had played a large hand in premierships for both clubs.

1938 CARLTON

PREMIER'S SEASON

CARLTON: 1938

ROUND ONE April 23
CARLTON 14.8 (92)
HAWTHORN 11.10 (76)
Best: Carlton – Chitty, Vallence, M.Crisp, Gill, McInnes, Carney, Price, Diggins.
Goals: Carlton – Price 5, Vallence 5, Hollingshead 2, M.Crisp, Cooper.
Crowd: 18,000 at Glenferrie Oval

ROUND TWO April 30
CARLTON 12.23 (95)
RICHMOND 14.10 (94)
Best: Carlton – Gill, Green, Diggins, Anderson, Vallence, Hale, Huxtable.
Goals: Carlton – Vallence 3, Price 3, Cooper 2, Shields 2, M.Crisp, Hollingshead.
Crowd: 32,000 at Princes Park

ROUND THREE May 7
CARLTON 15.12 (102)
ESSENDON 14.17 (101)
Best: Carlton – M.Crisp, Hollingshead, Baxter, Francis, Chitty, Wrout, Hale.
Goals: Carlton – Hollingshead 5, Price 3, Schmidt 2, Vallence 2, M.Crisp, Wrout, Huxtable.
Crowd: 17,000 at Windy Hill

ROUND FOUR May 14
CARLTON 17.19 (121)
FITZROY 10.10 (70)
Best: Carlton – Baxter, M.Crisp, Cooper, Chitty, Park, Hale, Diggins, Vallence.
Goals: Carlton – Cooper 5, Price 3, Vallence 3, Baxter 2, Anderson, M.Crisp, Carney, McElroy.
Crowd: 16,000 at Princes Park

ROUND FIVE May 21
CARLTON 19.16 (130)
COLLINGWOOD 17.12 (114)
Best: Carlton – Vallence, Hale, Price, M.Crisp, Diggins, Gill, McIntyre, Cooper.
Goals: Carlton – Vallence 8, Price 4, Cooper 3, Hale 2, G.Crisp, Baxter.
Crowd: 38,000 at Victoria Park

ROUND SIX May 28
CARLTON 14.18 (102)
MELBOURNE 16.11 (107)
Best: Carlton – Vallence, G.Crisp, Huxtable, Baxter, Cooper, Hale, Park.
Goals: Carlton – Vallence 7, Cooper 3, Baxter 3, McElroy.
Crowd: 20,000 at Princes Park

ROUND SEVEN June 4
CARLTON 12.18 (90)
ST KILDA 6.15 (51)
Best: Carlton – M.Crisp, Vallence, Fox, Gill, Park, Diggins, Hale, McIntyre.
Goals: Carlton – Vallence 5, Ayers 3, Hale 2, Cooper, Diggins.
Crowd: 24,000 at the Junction Oval

ROUND EIGHT June 13
CARLTON 15.20 (110)
FOOTSCRAY 12.11 (83)
Best: Carlton – Carney, Park, Francis, Vallence, M.Crisp, Baxter, Gill.
Goals: Carlton – Baxter 4, Vallence 4, Cooper 2, Hale 2, McElroy, Park, Price.
Crowd: 43,000 at Princes Park

ROUND NINE June 18
CARLTON 16.25 (121)
NORTH MELBOURNE 11.5 (71)
Best: Carlton – Vallence, Hale, McInnes, McLean, Schmidt, M.Crisp, Hale.
Goals: Carlton – Vallence 7, Price 3, Hollingshead 2, Baxter 2, Hale, McInnes.
Crowd: 13,000 at Arden St Oval

ROUND TEN June 25
CARLTON 16.13 (109)
SOUTH MELBOURNE 11.7 (73)
Best: Carlton – McLean, McElroy, Francis, Baxter, G.Crisp, M.Crisp, Butler.
Goals: Carlton – Butler 3, Vallence 3, G.Crisp 2, M.Crisp 2, Baxter 2, Schmidt 2, Cooper, Hollingshead.
Crowd: 14,000 at the Lake Oval

ROUND ELEVEN July 2
CARLTON 12.16 (88)
GEELONG 12.10 (82)
Best: Carlton – Vallence, Carney, Chitty, Francis, Anderson, Hale, Baxter.
Goals: Carlton – Vallence 6, Baxter 3, McLean, Cooper, McElroy.
Crowd: 19,500 at Princes Park

ROUND TWELVE July 9
CARLTON 12.12 (84)
HAWTHORN 8.15 (63)
Best: Carlton – Chitty, McLean, Hollingshead, M.Crisp, Diggins, Vallence, Baxter.
Goals: Carlton – Vallence 3, Butler 2, M.Crisp 2, McInnes 2, Cooper, Schmidt, Hollingshead.
Crowd: 14,000 at Princes Park

ROUND THIRTEEN July 23
CARLTON 12.19 (91)
RICHMOND 20.12 (132)
Best: Carlton – M.Crisp, Gill, Diggins, Cooper, McLean, Park, Hale, Anderson.
Goals: Carlton – M.Crisp 6, Fox 3, Anderson 2, Diggins.
Crowd: 28,000 at Punt Road Oval

ROUND FOURTEEN July 30
CARLTON 11.16 (82)
ESSENDON 10.16 (76)
Best: Carlton – Hale, Park, M.Crisp, Shields, G.Crisp, Chitty, Diggins, Savage.
Goals: Carlton – Anderson 2, Savage 2, Vallence 2, Cooper 2, Hale, Diggins, Green.
Crowd: 18,000 at Princes Park

ROUND FIFTEEN August 6
CARLTON 19.12 (126)
FITZROY 11.10 (76)
Best: Carlton – Vallence, Anderson, M.Crisp, Gill, McInnes, Francis, Hale, G.Crisp.
Goals: Carlton – Vallence 11, Price 3, Hollingshead 2, Cooper 2, Anderson.
Crowd: 17,000 at Brunswick St Oval

ROUND SIXTEEN August 13
CARLTON 14.17 (101)
COLLINGWOOD 19.7 (121)
Best: Carlton – M.Crisp, Hollingshead, Gill, Diggins, Vallence, Francis, Green.
Goals: Carlton – Price 4, Vallence 3, Cooper 2, McLean, Anderson, Savage, Hollingshead, M.Crisp.
Crowd: 37,000 at Princes Park

ROUND SEVENTEEN August 20
CARLTON 11.13 (79)
MELBOURNE 14.12 (96)
Best: Carlton – McLean, Vallence, Diggins, McInnes, Hale, Price, Cooper
Goals: Carlton – Vallence 3, Cooper 2, Hollingshead 2, M.Crisp, Hale, Baxter, Price.
Crowd: 25,241 at the MCG

ROUND EIGHTEEN August 27
CARLTON 15.14 (104)
ST KILDA 13.10 (88)
Best: Carlton – Huxtable, Park, Carney, Wrout, Diggins, Francis, Hollingshead.
Goals: Carlton – Wrout 5, Vallence 3, Hale 2, Cooper 2, Hollingshead, Watkins, McLean.
Crowd: 16,000 at Princes Park

PREMIER'S FINALS

SECOND SEMI-FINAL September 10
CARLTON 16.17 (113)
GEELONG 10.21 (81)
Best: Carlton – Carney, Francis, M.Crisp, Wrout, Baxter, Price, Hale, Diggins.
Goals: Carlton – Baxter 8, Price 3, Vallence 2, Wrout, Schmidt, Hollingshead.
Crowd: 65,332 at the MCG

GRAND FINAL September 24
CARLTON 3.2 7.6 11.9 15.10 (100)
COLLINGWOOD 3.1 4.4 8.5 13.7 (85)
Best: Carlton – Hale, Wrout, M.Crisp, Diggins, Green, Gill, Park, Anderson, Francis.
Goals: Carlton – Wrout 4, Baxter 3, Hale 2, Schmidt 2, M.Crisp, Price, Vallence, Green.
Crowd: 96,486 at the MCG

GRAND FINAL LINE-UPS

CARL	B:	D.McIntyre	F.Gill	J.Park
COLL	F:	J.Knight	R.Todd	A.Pannam
CARL	HB:	F.Anderson	J.Francis	B.Chitty
COLL	HF:	P.Kyne	G.Hocking	V.Doherty
CARL	C:	J.Carney	M.Crisp	B.Green
COLL	C:	R.Dowling	M.Whelan	L.Morgan
CARL	HF:	P.Schmidt	J.Wrout	H.Vallence
COLL	HB:	J.Ross	M.Boyall	F.Froude
CARL	F:	R.McLean	K.Baxter	M.Price
COLL	B:	D.Balfour	J.Regan	B.Woods
CARL	R:	B.Diggins (capt)	H.Hollingshead	J.Hale
COLL	R:	A.Collier (capt)	A.Williams	D.Fothergill
CARL	Reserve:	C.McInnes	**Coach:** Brighton Diggins	
COLL	Reserve:	J.Carmody	**Coach:** Jock McHale	

SNAPSHOT

Win-loss record: 16-4

Highest score: 19.16 (130), round 5, v Collingwood.

Greatest winning margin: 51 points, round 4, v Fitzroy.

Lowest score: 11.13 (79), round 17, v Melbourne.

Greatest losing margin: 41 points, round 13, v Richmond.

Most goals by a player in a game: 11, Harry Vallence, round 15, v Fitzroy.

Most consecutive wins: 6

Most consecutive losses: 2

Club awards: Best & Fairest: Mickey Crisp; Leading goalkicker: Harry Vallence (81 goals).

Putting it into perspective:
The Blues' sixth premiership from 12 Grand Finals broke a 23-year flag drought. It was their first win since 1915 and their second Grand Final win over Collingwood. Their final score of 15.10 (100) was a new club highest score in a Grand Final.

1938

		P	W	L	D	%	Pts
1	Carlton (1)	18	14	4		116.1	56
2	Geelong (3)	18	13	5		129.2	52
3	Footscray (4)	18	13	5		124.3	52
4	Collingwood (2)	18	12	6		117.6	48
5	Melbourne	18	11	7		106.0	44
6	Richmond	18	10	8		111.8	40
7	Essendon	18	9	9		102.3	36
8	St Kilda	18	9	9		91.8	36
9	North Melb	18	6	12		74.7	24
10	Fitzroy	18	5	13		88.6	20
11	Hawthorn	18	4	14		82.4	16
12	South Melb	18	2	16		71.8	8

(18 home and away rounds)

PLAYERS USED

CARLTON	GUERNSEY	GAMES	GOALS
Anderson, Frank	1	20	7
Ayers, Fred	3	4	3
Baxter, Ken	4	14	29
Butler, Bert	29	7	5
Carney, Jack	7	19	1
Chitty, Bob	6	15	0
Collard, George	31	8	3
Cooper, Ron	19	18	30
Crisp, Gordon	8	7	3
Crisp, Mickey	12	19	17
Fox, Kevin	27	7	3
Francis, Jim	10	20	0
Gill, Frank	21	18	0
Green, Bob	32	20	2
Hale, Jack	11	19	13
Hollingshead, Harry	17	13	19
Huxtable, Eric	9	10	1
McElroy, Jack	15	10	4
McInnes, Charlie	31	12	3
McIntyre, Don	2	20	0
McLean, Rod	14	13	3
Park, Jim	26	19	1
Price, Mick	30	17	34
Sanger, Arthur	16	1	0
Savage, Ron	24	3	3
Schmidt, Paul	23	10	8
Shields, Arch	25	3	2
Vallence, Harry	22	19	81
Watkins, Les	18	1	1
Wrout, Jack	28	5	11

BIOGRAPHIES

Rohan Connolly has been covering AFL football since 1983, starting on *The Sun News-Pictorial* before moving to *The Age* in 1987. He has been a regular part of 3AW's football coverage since 1996. He has worked extensively in pay-TV, and has contributed to a wide range of football books. A five-time Australian Football Media Association award-winner for news, feature writing and columns, he remains a passionate football fan with a particular penchant for Essendon, having been a regular on the Windy Hill terraces from the age of five.

Paul Daffey is a Melbourne journalist and author who has worked on newspapers around the world but whose writing tends to be on local events in Victoria, usually but not always of a sporting nature. His books include *Local Rites: A Year in Grass Roots Football in Victoria and Beyond* and *Beyond the Big Sticks: Country Football Around Australia*. He is a contributor to and (with John Harms) co-editor of *The Footy Almanac: The AFL Season One Game at a Time*. He has appeared regularly on radio on SEN and the ABC.

Tony De Bolfo followed his father and grandfather to the Garton Street end of Princes Park in 1972 after being handed his first season's ticket by the Blues' then secretary, the 1947 Brownlow medallist Bert Deacon. Tony was a sportswriter at *Inside Football*, *The Australian* and the *Herald Sun*. He has also penned the biographies of Carlton champions Stephen Kernahan, Stephen Silvagni and Anthony Koutoufides. Since his 2007 appointment by Carlton's late president Richard Pratt as Visy advisor to the football club, Tony has examined the football club's rich history in his research for *Out Of The Blue* and now assists as its in-house journalist and historian.

Chris Donald is the author of *Fitzroy: For the love of the jumper*, *Haydn Bunton: Best and fairest*, and *Kevin Murray: Heart of the Lion* (all Pennon Publishing). He has edited Mark Opolion's *A Decade of Pride* (Pennon) and Tim Hall's *Giant Killers* (Ark House Press). He has a Master of Creative Media degree from RMIT University and a Diploma of Arts (Professional Writing and Editing) from the University of Ballarat. He is a university English teacher in China. Before he left Australia, Chris was a contributor to *Inside Football* and *The Weekly Times*.

John Harms is a writer, publisher and broadcaster. His books include *Loose Men Everywhere*, *Memoirs of a Mug Punter* and *The Pearl: Steve Renouf's story*. Each year he contributes to and collates (along with Paul Daffey) a volume of football writing, *The Footy Almanac*. His website www.footyalmanac.com.au is a community of enthusiastic sportswriters and readers, which has emerged out of those collections. He has numerous spots on ABC radio around the country, and can be seen on ABC TV's *Offsiders*.

Howard Kotton is an experienced sports writer and sub-editor based in Melbourne. He started his journalistic career at the *Australian Jewish News* in 1977 and worked in suburban and country newspapers before joining the Herald and Weekly Times in 1982. He was deputy sports editor at the *West Australian* in 1989-90. Since returning to Melbourne, he has assumed roles in various forms of media, including TV (Channel Seven), radio (SEN 1116 and Radio Sport National) and afl.com.au. He has worked as a writer and sub-editor for the Slattery Media Group since January 2008. He has had a deep passion for Carlton since his birth in Brunswick in 1959.

Barry Levinson has been a sports journalist for 14 years. He is currently a news producer at Network Ten and has previously worked as a reporter for afl.com.au and as producer of 3AW's football coverage. He has also hosted and produced programs for SEN 1116 and worked as a tennis commentator for Australian Open Radio. A staunch Fitzroy fan during his childhood, Barry switched to Melbourne in 2001 and is desperate to witness a Demons premiership.

Michael Lovett is one of the country's most experienced football writers and is in his 37th year in journalism. He has worked on a variety of newspapers and magazines—starting at the *Ballarat Courier* in 1974. Since then he has reported on major sport, specialising in football and cricket, for *The Sporting Globe* (1976-82) and *The Herald* (1982-89). He was appointed editor of *Basketball Week* (1990-93), became editor of *Inside Football* (1993-96) and was editor of the *AFL Record* between 1997-2008 before becoming production editor. He has edited the *AFL Season Guide* every year since 1997. His father, grandfather and uncle were all journalists.

Jim Main started his career in journalism more than 40 years ago after studying law at the University of Melbourne. He has worked on *The Herald*, *The Australian* and on Fleet Street with the *Daily Express*. He has covered sports, including Olympic and Commonwealth games around the world. The author of more than 60 books, he is a winner of the Sir William Walkley Award and, while working in London, the *Daily Express's* Lord Beaverbrook Award. He was inducted into the Melbourne Cricket Club Media Hall of Fame in 2003.

Glenn McFarlane grew up on stories of how his grandfather, Charlie Dibbs, played in five premierships with Collingwood during the 1920s and '30s, as a member of the famous Machine side. He attended his first Grand Final as a kid in the drawn game of 1977. Incredibly, the first Grand Final his three children—Lachlan, Elise and Charlotte—attended was the 2010 drawn game. A sports journalist with the *Herald Sun* and *Sunday Herald Sun* for 20 years, Glenn has been lucky enough to attend every Grand Final since 1981. He has also written a number of books on football, including *The Official Collingwood Illustrated Encyclopedia* and *The Machine: The inside story of football's greatest team*.

Adam McNicol grew up in Manangatang in Victoria's Mallee region. Since graduating from RMIT University, he has worked as a journalist for WIN Television in Mildura and Ballarat, along with Channel 10 in Melbourne, and has written extensively about bush footy for *The Age*. In 2009 he wrote *The Danihers*, a biography of the four brothers—Terry, Neale, Anthony and Chris—who played for Essendon. In 2010 Adam co-authored *All Bets Are Off*, the autobiography of former Melbourne forward David Schwarz. His latest book, *Manangatang*, was released in April 2011. He works for AFL Media at Etihad Stadium in Melbourne.

Robert Pascoe is Dean Laureate and Professor of History at Victoria University, Melbourne. In 1995 he produced *The Winter Game*, one of the first national histories of the Australian game. His current project is a social history of life and football in colonial Victoria, under the working title *Tribal Melbourne*, co-authored with Dr Mark Pennings (QUT).

Emma Quayle fell in love with football watching Essendon play at Windy Hill. She joined *The Age* sports department in 1991. Her first book, *The Draft: Inside the AFL's search for talent*, was published in 2008, and she collaborated with former Essendon player Adam Ramanauskas on his book, *Nine Lives: Football, cancer and getting on with life*, in 2010. Emma won the AFL Players Association's journalism award in 2009, and was judged the AFL Media Association's most outstanding feature writer in 2010.

Geoff Slattery has covered the AFL game as a reporter, writer, and publisher since 1977 and is the chief executive of the Slattery Media Group.

BIBLIOGRAPHY

NEWSPAPERS AND PERIODICALS
Sport
Table Talk
The Age
The Argus
The Australasian
The Bulletin
The Football Record
The Geelong Advertiser
The Mercury and Weekly Courier
The Richmond Guardian
The Richmond, Hawthorn, Camberwell Chronicle
The Sporting Globe
The South Melbourne Record
The Stawell News And Pleasant Creek Chronicle
The Sun News-Pictorial
The Winner
Victorian Football Follower

ANNUAL REPORTS
Fitzroy 1922
Richmond 1920, 1921, 1932, 1934
South Melbourne 1909, 1918, 1933

BOOKS AND PERIODICALS
Graeme and Brant Atkinson, *The Complete Book of AFL Finals*, The Five Mile Press, 2009

Graeme Atkinson and Michael Hanlon, *3AW Book of Footy Records*, Matchbooks, 1989

Rhett Bartlett, *Richmond FC: The Tigers: A century of League football*, Geoff Slattery Publishing, 2007

Geoffrey Blainey, *A Game of Our Own* (revised edition), Black Inc, 2003

Geoffrey Blainey, "Football the Way It Was" in Ross Fitzgerald and Ken Spillman, *The Greatest Game*, Heinemann, 1988.

Mark Branagan and Mike Lefebvre, *Bloodstained Angels: The rise and fall of the Foreign Legion*, Mark Branagan and Mike Lefebvre, 1995

C.M.H. Clark *A History of Australia*, Vols V and VI, Melbourne University Press, 1981, 1987.

Chris Donald, *Fitzroy: For the love of the jumper: 100 players who made the Lions roar*, Pennon Publishing, 2002

Jack Dyer with Brian Hansen, *Captain Blood*, Stanley Paul (London), 1965

Jules Feldmann and Russell Holmesby, *The Point of It All*, Playright Publishing, 1992

Marc Fiddian, *The Other Side of Smith Street: Fitzroy v Collingwood down the years*, Raccoon Trail Books, 2007

Marc Fiddian, *The Swan Lake Spectacular: How South Melbourne won the 1933 VFL Premiership*, Galaxy, 2004

Brian Hansen, *Tigerland: The history of the Richmond Football Club from 1885*, Richmond Former Players and Officals Association, 1989

Brian Hansen, *The Blue Boys: The history of the Carlton Football Club since 1864*, Brian Hansen Publications, 2002

Brian Hansen, *The Magpies: The official centenary history of the CFC 1892-1992*, Brian Hansen with Senis Carla Nom, 1992

Rob Hess and Bob Stewart (editors), *More Than a Game: An unauthorised history of Australian rules football*, Melbourne University Press, 1998

Paul Hogan, *Tigers of Old: A complete history of every player to represent The Richmond Football Club between 1908 and 1996*, Richmond Football Club, 1996

Russell Holmesby and Jim Main (editors), *The Encyclopedia of AFL Footballers: Every AFL/VFL player since 1897*, BAS Publishing, ninth edition, 2011

Michael Lovett (editor), *AFL Record Season Guide, 2011*, The Slattery Media Group, 2011

Jim Main, *Fallen: The ultimate heroes: Footballers who never returned from the War*, Crown Content, 2002

Jim Main, *Fitzroy: Merging into the future: The history of the Fitzroy Football Club, incorporating the Brisbane Bears and Brisbane Lions*, BAS Publishing, 2007

Jim Main, *In the Blood: Celebrating the red and white 1874-2009*, BAS Publishing, 2009

John Murray (editor), *We Are Geelong: The story of the Geelong Football Club*, The Slattery Media Group, 2009

Michael Maplestone, *Flying Higher: History of the Essendon Football Club 1872-1996*, Essendon Football Club, 1996

Michael Maplestone, *Those Magnificent Men 1897-1987*, Essendon Football Club, 1988

Simon Matthews, *Champions of Essendon: Ranking the 60 greatest Bombers of all time*, Hardie Grant Books, 2002

Janet McCalman, *Struggletown: Public and private life in Richmond 1900-1965*, Melbourne University Press, 1984

Glenn McFarlane and Richard Stremski, *The Premiership's a Cakewalk*, Spicers Papers, 1998

Glenn McFarlane and Michael Roberts, *The Machine: The inside story of football's greatest team*, Collingwood Football Club, 2005

Adam Muyt, *Maroon and Blue: Recollections and Tales of the Fitzroy Football Club*, Vulgar Press, 2006

Robert Pascoe, *The Winter Game: The complete history of Australian football*, Text Publishing 1995

Lou Richards, *Boots and All*, Stanley Paul (London), 1963.

Michael Roberts, *A Century of the Best: The stories of Collingwood's favourite sons : The official publication to mark 100 years of the Collingwood Football Club*, Collingwood Football Club, 1991

Michael Roberts and Glenn McFarlane, *Collingwood at Victoria Park*, Lothian, 1999

Michael Roberts and Glenn McFarlane, *The Official Collingwood Illustrated Encyclopedia*, Geoff Slattery Publishing and Lothian, 2004

Leonie Sandercock and Ian Turner, *Up Where Cazaly? The great Australian game*, Granada Publishing, 1981

Russell Stephens, *The Road To Kardinia*, Playright Publishing, Sydney, 1996.

Richard Stremski, *Kill For Collingwood*, Allen and Unwin, 1986

Mike Sutherland, Rod Nicholson and Stewart Murrihy, *The First One Hundred Seasons: Fitzroy Football Club, 1883-1983*, Fitzroy Football Club, 1983

Ian Turner "Work and Play in Victorian Victoria", *Victorian Historical Journal*, Vol. 49, No. 1, February 1978

Various authors, *An Illustrated History of the Essendon Football Club*, Geoff Slattery Publishing, 2007

Various authors, *100 Years of Australian Football 1987-1996*, Penguin Books, 1996

James Weston (editor), *The Australian Game of Football Since 1858*, Geoff Slattery Publishing, 2008